MARINE SALVAGE

Marine Salvage

THE UNFORGIVING BUSINESS OF NO CURE, NO PAY

Joseph N. Gores

Preface by Willard Bascom

DOUBLEDAY & COMPANY, INC.
Garden City, New York
1971

LIBRARY OF CONGRESS CATALOG CARD NUMBER 70-139025
COPYRIGHT © 1971 BY OCEAN SCIENCE AND ENGINEERING INC.
ALL RIGHTS RESERVED
PRINTED IN THE UNITED STATES OF AMERICA

*This book is respectfully dedicated to
them that go
down to ships in the sea
and especially to such great salvage men as*
FREDERICK YOUNG   ROBERT H. DAVIS
JOHN IRON   EDWARD ELLSBERG
and the incomparable
ERNEST F. COX

CONTENTS

ACKNOWLEDGMENTS — xv
AUTHOR'S NOTE — xvii
PREFACE   *Willard Bascom* — xix

Prelude
THE BELL OF DOOM — 1

CHAPTER ONE
MEN BELOW — 3
    Naked Divers · Air from the Surface · Problems of Pressure · Augustus Siebe · Hard-Hat Diving Suit

CHAPTER TWO
LLOYD'S OF LONDON — 11
    Early History · Policy Writing · John Julius Angerstein · Lloyd's "Standard Form" · Modern Lloyd's · The Bell of Doom · Evolution of Admiralty Salvage Law · Lloyd's "No Cure, No Pay" Salvage Contract

I. FULL FATHOM FIVE

CHAPTER THREE
DIVERS DOWN — 21
    Beginnings: *Mary Rose* and *Royal George* · Augustus Siebe's "Close" Suit · The Squeeze · Blow-ups · The Bends: Paul Bert and John Haldane · Loss of the *General Grant* ·

CONTENTS

Salvage of the *Hamilla Mitchell*'s Treasure · *Grosser Kurfurst*—Revolutionary Salvage Method

CHAPTER FOUR
DEEP-WATER TREASURES   33

Angel Erostrabe · Alexander Lambert · Recovering the *Orinoco*'s Treasure · The *Empress of Ireland*'s Safe · The Riddle of the *Tubantia* · Forty-three Tons of Gold · Incredible Salvage Task: The *Laurentic* · Sand More Valuable than Gold

CHAPTER FIVE
THE IRON DUKE   48

Early Armored Diving Suits · Davis Observation Chamber · Neufeldt and Kuhnke's Iron Duke · The Search for the *Egypt* · Loss of the *Artiglio* · The *Egypt*'s Bullion Room · Recovering *Niagara*'s Gold from Seventy-three Fathoms

CHAPTER SIX
FIFTY FATHOMS AND BEYOND   62

Problems of Compressed Air · Oxy-Helium Diving · Exotic Gas Mixtures · Tragedy in the Sealab Program · John Light and the *Lusitania* · Beginnings of Airplane Salvage · Search for the *Yoke Peter* · An Airplane Under Ice

CHAPTER SEVEN
PALOMARES AND AFTER   80

Bomber-Tanker Crash over Palomares · Offshore Salvage Fleet · First Test for Submersibles · Francisco Simo Orts Points the Way · First Contact with Robert · Robert Gets Away · Successful Recovery · OSE Does It Right off Los Angeles

CONTENTS ix

II. SHE GOES ALONE

CHAPTER EIGHT
EARLY SUBMERSIBLES 101

>Record Dive to *F-4* · Submarine Dynamics · The Long History of Submersibles · *Gymnote,* First Modern Submarine · Free Escape from Sunken Submarines · *K-13*: First Use of Compressed Air

CHAPTER NINE
"SUBMARINE SUNK HERE" 114

>Loss of *S-51* · Tragedy Aboard the *S-4* · Raising the *S-4* · Difficulties of Submarine Salvage · *Poseidon* Proves Value of Escape Lung · *Squalus* and the McCann Rescue Chamber · Raising *Squalus*

CHAPTER TEN
OPERATION SUBSMASH 130

>Fatal Delay Aboard *Thetis* · Exposure Kills *Truculent* Survivors · Secret Device Aboard *U-307* · *Affray* Is Missing · Shelford's Blue Line · Disappearance of *Thresher* · Shocking Facts Exposed · *Scorpion* Is Overdue · The Navy Is at Fault?

III. ADRIFT

CHAPTER ELEVEN
MARY CELESTE AND AFTER 151

>A Famous Derelict · Loss of the *Oler* with All Hands · The *Arab* and the *Protection* on Lake Michigan · A Clever Towing Job · Some Exploits of John Iron · Fires Aboard

CHAPTER TWELVE
ABANDONED BY CREWS 164

>Difficulties of Salvage Towing · The *Kearny*'s Remarkable Repairs · Saving the *Porcupine* · Fire Aboard the *Strathallan* · Opposition by *Pozarica*'s Captain · Attempt to Save USS *Masaryk*

CHAPTER THIRTEEN
LEICESTER AND JOSEPHINE 177

>The Disappearing SAMs · *Leicester* Caught by a Hurricane · Race for the *Leicester* · *Josephine* Takes Her in Tow · Another Hurricane: Bermuda · Salvage of the *Leicester* and the *Josephine* · Saving Half of the *Bridgewater* · The Chilling Odyssey of the *Aygaz*

x   CONTENTS

IV. THE SHALLOW SEAS

CHAPTER FOURTEEN
FROM *THETIS* TO *LEONARDO*   193

    The Diving Bell and the *Thetis* · Early Shallow-Water Salvage Attempts · Some Bizarre Diving Stories · Beginnings of Underwater Demolition · Forming the Salvage Section · Exploits of Frederick W. Young · Compressed Air for the *Leonardo*

CHAPTER FIFTEEN
COX OF SCAPA FLOW   209

    A Fleet Is Scuttled · An Obsession Is Born · Ernest Cox Buys a Navy—on the Bottom · The First Destroyer · First Attempt on the *Hindenburg* · *Von Moltke* · The *Von Moltke* Tow—Upside Down · The Unstable *Seydlitz* · New Tricks to Raise the *Kaiser* · Second *Hindenburg* Attempt · Foul Air on the *Von der Tann* · First Fatality: *Prinz-Regent Luitpold*

CHAPTER SIXTEEN
SEAL AND BLOW   231

    Divers' Tales · U. S. Navy's Weakness in Salvage · Unconventional Methods at Massawa · Wartime Salvage in the Pacific · Japan's "Unsinkable" *Nachi* · Seven Million Cans of Salmon

V. SAFE HARBOR

CHAPTER SEVENTEEN
CAISSONS, COMPRESSORS, AND PUMPS   247

    Harbor Clearance in Crimea · The Forgotten *Maine* · Removing the *Vindictive* · John Iron's Remarkable Efforts · *St. Paul* Foreshadows the *Normandie*

CHAPTER EIGHTEEN
ELLSBERG AT MASSAWA   260

    Sabotage at Massawa · Improvising on the Italian Dry Dock · The Scuttled *Liebenfels* · The Second Dry Dock · Awful Botch: Raising the *Gera* · A Mine Aboard the *Brenta* · Gasoline Storage Tanks for Pontoons

CONTENTS xi

CHAPTER NINETEEN
IN BOMB ALLEY 276
    Trouble with the *Spahi* · Three Sunken Dry Docks at Oran · General Delivery to the Rescue · Lubricating with Sea Water · A Saga: The *Max Barendt* · Opening Tripoli Harbor · The *Valiant* Saga · Clearing Mines at Piraeus

CHAPTER TWENTY
IN WAR AND PEACE 291
    Lionel Crabb Learns About Mines · Cherbourg, 1944 · Fire on the *Normandie* · Controlled Pumping · Pearl Harbor · The Trincomalee Dry Dock · San Francisco's Anti-Torpedo Nets · Unusual Salvage Assignment: Bikini Atoll, 1946 · Pontoons, Water Ballast, Air, and Beach Gear on AFDM-2 · The *Shiga*: Salvaged Jetliner Flies Again

VI. ON THE BEACH

CHAPTER TWENTY-ONE
EARLY STRANDINGS 311
    The Irresistible *Grosvenor* · *La Lutine* and the Bell of Doom · The U. S. Life-Saving Service · Tragic Operation on the *City of New York* · A Cargo of Rails: The *Abercorn* · A Fatal Error in Judgment: The *Mimi*

CHAPTER TWENTY-TWO
THE ADMIRALTY SALVAGE SECTION 322
    A Complex Operation: *Silurias* · Salvage Against the Odds: *Ulidia* · Live Torpedoes: Young Saves UC-5 · Wheeler's Five Vessels in Ten Days · A Dubious Exchange: H-3 for the *Milwaukee* · Seven Destroyers on the Rocks · The *Philip*'s Durable Cargo

CHAPTER TWENTY-THREE
MOSTLY PEACEFUL 334
    Liverpool and Glasgow Salvage Association · John Iron, Dover Harbor Master · USS *Thomas Stone* · An Unconventional Attempt: The *Leopard* · The *Zeeland* Flies a Kite

CONTENTS

CHAPTER TWENTY-FOUR
SUPERTANKERS   344

An Early Supertanker · The *African Queen* Goes Aground · Salvage by a Motley Crew · *Mare Nostrum* Towed on a Bubble of Air · Loss of the *Torrey Canyon* · Salvage Attempts Fail as Beaches Are Polluted · Destructive Results of Oil Spill · New Anti-Pollution Ideas

VII. GOODIES AND GOBBLERS

CHAPTER TWENTY-FIVE
MEDITERRANEAN BEGINNINGS   363

Marine Archaeology a Recent Science · Early Mediterranean Finds · Early History of SCUBA Diving · The Aqualung Is Tested · Archaeological SCUBA Diving Begins in the Med · Cousteau at Grand Congloue · The Incomparable Peter Throckmorton

CHAPTER TWENTY-SIX
PIECES OF EIGHT   380

Effects of the Sea on Wooden Wrecks · William Phips: An Early Treasure Hunter · Indispensable Tool: The Air Lift · The Americas' Top Marine Archaeologist · Marx's First Find: The *Monitor* · The Wreck at Punta Matancero · Gentle Blackmail by Pablo Bush Romero · Central Archaeological Find of the Americas

CHAPTER TWENTY-SEVEN
GOLD, *CENOTES*, AND SUNKEN CITIES   399

World's Leading Treasure Seeker · Real Eight's "Secret Weapon": The Prop-Wash · Unfair Texas Confiscation · Notable Successes of Alex Storm · The *Cenote* at Chichén Itzá · Sunken Cities in the Mediterranean · Père A. Poidebard, Strategic Archaeologist · The Exploration of Port Royal

CHAPTER TWENTY-EIGHT
FROM *VASA* TO THE *ASSOCIATION*   417

European Sunken Cities · Vigo Bay's Stubborn Treasure · *Vasa* · New Methods of Preservation · The Galleon of Tobermory Bay: Incredible Boondoggle · Looting vs. Archaeology: The *Santa María* · An Exciting Find: The *Association*

CHAPTER TWENTY-NINE
ISLAND TREASURES 433

   An Anchor from the *Bounty* · The Wreck of the *Batavia* ·
   The Search for the *Batavia* · The Great Basses · The
   Port au Prince · An Ingenious Japanese Operation

VIII. TOMORROW . . .

CHAPTER THIRTY
FISH-MEN AND SUBMERSIBLES 449

   World-Record SCUBA Dive on Compressed Air · Breathing Liquids · The Italian "Chariots" · British X-Craft ·
   The New Experimental Submersibles · Use of Submersibles for Salvage Limited · Raising the *Emerald Straits*

CHAPTER THIRTY-ONE
SOLVING THE PROBLEMS 466

   Polyurethane Foam · Abortive Salvage Attempts on the *Andrea Doria* · Polystyrene Granules Used on *Martin S* ·
   The Problems of Deepwater Salvage · OSE: Solving the Problems · Men Stay at the Surface · The Alcoa-OSE *Seaprobe* System · Applications

APPENDIX I
LLOYD'S STANDARD FORM OF SALVAGE AGREEMENT 483

APPENDIX II
THE LEGALITIES OF SALVAGE 491

   Definition of Civil Salvage Service · Subjects of Salvage ·
   Danger · Voluntariness · Success · Salvage Awards ·
   The Salvors · Remedies for Non-Payment of Salvage Awards

BIBLIOGRAPHY 499

   Books · Periodicals · Newspapers · Miscellaneous Publications

INDEX 513

ACKNOWLEDGMENTS

Time Magazine, that great anonymous Viewpoint, recently pointed out that stealing from one book is plagiarism, while stealing from many is research.

I have done a great deal of research in preparing this volume.

The recipients of my attentions appear in the Bibliography; while I cannot thank them personally, at least I can list them alphabetically. My accuracy is theirs; my errors are my own.

There are several people, however, to whom my gratitude is much more personal.

Willard Bascom, President of Ocean Science and Engineering, first conceived the book, because the subject fascinated him and he didn't have time to write it himself. Technical advice aside, Willard gave me a totally free hand in what I said and how I said it.

My wife, Susan, typed. Typed and listened and typed and read and typed. And when my spirits flagged, put in the sword with the *élan* of a matador earning an ear—and so the book was finished.

James Dawson, founding director of Ocean Industry Insurers Ltd., was untiring in assembling and airmailing from London vast amounts of material concerning Lloyd's and European salvage. Without his enthusiastic support, there would have been no book.

Fellow writer Jack Leavitt was generous with his immense library (before which even the Library of Congress must slightly blanch), providing a great many volumes of elsewhere unobtainable material.

Harold H. Stubbs, formerly a Navy master diver and now with OSE, was unstinting of his time in vetting certain sections of the book, and of his memory in recalling anecdotes about intriguing salvage jobs on which he had worked.

Will Bernardin, Treasurer of OSE, disrupted his frantic schedule to send Herb Retsky into the wilderness of the Navy Department and the National Archives to obtain many of the rare photos in this book.

ACKNOWLEDGMENTS

F. Worth Hobbs, Vice-President of Ocean Search, Inc., was wonderfully patient and generous of his time in eleventh-hour work on the manuscript.

Bob Marx kindly donated his unique pictures of the underwater excavations at the sunken city of Port Royal, as well as his unparalleled knowledge concerning the technicalities of archaeological salvage.

Dean and Shirley Dickensheet bravely brought their expertise and unerring eye to the unappetizing task of proofreading the immense manuscript.

Larry Ashmead and Judith M. Glushanok of Doubleday were enthusiastic far beyond the dictates of their editorial positions, and I owe them a great debt of gratitude.

Finally, I must thank John "Gaff" Gaffney, Editor of *Dive Magazine*; Captain Alec G. Winton and his long-suffering crew of the *Oceaneer*; Lillian S. Gagos, who kept the OSE Xerox at white heat; Don Bline and Priscilla Salter of Westinghouse Corporation; Fred Anderson, Project Engineer at EG&G International; Wilko Neehus of N. V. Bureau Wijsmuller, Holland; G. Lykke Jensen of Karl Krøyer Company, Denmark; Don Sorte, President of International Hydrodynamics, Vancouver, B.C.; the Director of Public Relations, Royal Navy; the U. S. Bureau of Ships, National Archives; the U. S. Naval Photographic Center; and most especially Mendel L. Peterson of the Smithsonian Institution, who gave me dope about archaeological salvage I never would have found anywhere else.

JNG
San Francisco
September 1970

AUTHOR'S NOTE

I have tried to avoid scientific, engineering, and nautical terms wherever possible, because they bore the average reader and because I don't understand many of them anyway. A few, however, have crept in and, I hope, have been adequately explained in the text or the footnotes. Those listed below pop up often enough to justify being here foregathered for easy reference.

WIND FORCE AS REGISTERED ON BEAUFORT'S SCALE:

BEAUFORT'S SCALE	SEAMEN'S DESCRIPTION	WIND VELOCITY
Force 0	Calm	under 1 knot
Force 1	Light air	1– 3 knots
Force 2	Light breeze	4– 6 knots
Force 3	Gentle breeze	7–10 knots
Force 4	Moderate breeze	11–16 knots
Force 5	Fresh breeze	17–21 knots
Force 6	Strong breeze	22–27 knots
Force 7	Moderate gale	28–33 knots
Force 8	Gale	34–40 knots
Force 9	Strong gale	41–47 knots
Force 10	Whole (full) gale	48–55 knots
Force 11	Storm	56–63 knots
Force 12	Hurricane	64 knots and up

- 1 knot (nautical mile)=6080.2 feet (1.15 statute miles) or 1 minute of arc at the Equator.
- 1 fathom=6 feet.
- 1 atmosphere of pressure=14.7 pounds per square inch (air pressure at sea level).

Plimsoll line(s) or mark(s)=load-line mark(s) on the side of a merchant vessel to indicate the depth to which she may be immersed under various conditions. (A ship fully loaded is often referred to as being "down to her marks".)

It will be noted that sometimes money is listed in dollars, at other times in English pounds; this is because the source material listed them this way. Since the value of pounds relative to that of dollars has changed three times in this century alone (from about $5 to $2.80 to $2.40 per £1), and since the buying power of both currencies has altered drastically during the centuries this book covers, I felt that any attempt at conversion would end in a hopeless muddle.

Finally, certain knowledgeable readers will find certain of the stories herein recounted differing in detail from the versions with which they are familiar. When a writer consults up to a dozen sources for a single salvage anecdote, all he can do is sort of average out the differences, selecting what seems most probable and rejecting what seems most fanciful.

JNG

PREFACE

This book is about the history and present status of the unforgiving business of marine salvage. The salvage game is a tough one. The playing surface is rough—uncomfortable, windy, and miserable. Beneath it, the cold depths are opaque and forbidding. The objects of salvage were not designed to be retrieved, so they are most unco-operative.

Generally, the damaged areas of sunken and grounded ships are down and out of sight, so the risk is unestimable. Often, local conditions seem to create a lee, where the sea is unusually calm; then the sand will move in to form a tombolo, and the ship's back will be broken. The salvage ships and equipment that would be most useful are invariably far away in another ocean; and in the statistically good-weather season, when the salvor wants to work, the weather contrives to be the worst in twenty years.

It is hard for the salvor to believe that whatever gods there may be, overseeing the perversity of inanimate objects and natural forces, are not conspiring against him. Those difficulties are bad enough, but it is the rules of the game that hurt the most: No cure, no pay! That's the marine version of "winner take all." It means that if the salvor is not entirely successful, he collects nothing; the sea wins. There are no payments for heroic efforts, for risk of life and equipment, or for half-salvaging a ship. No cure, no pay is the relentless rule; the salvor takes all the risk.

Obviously, a risky and difficult business such as this must be populated by a remarkable collection of men. Some are financial masochists; some are adventurers who cannot stand routine; some are engineers who are challenged by the nearly impossible. A few seem normal. All are courageous and love the sea.

There are no reliable figures on the subject, but I suspect that most marine salvage companies are unsuccessful. Many have been organized to go after specific wrecks, with high hopes but poor engineering and even worse financial control. There are numerous individual wrecks on which a dozen companies have gone bankrupt. And some salvage companies, after several successes in a row, have become overconfident and pushed their luck on a job that turned out to be beyond their capability. The shipowners and insurers shed a few crocodile tears over their demise—and next time deal with an optimistic new entrant into the business.

In fact, Lloyd's itself—the great marine-insurance risk arena—does not seem to be too happy a place to play. Probably half the insurers there have lost money over the past five years, since it's often cheaper to build a new ship than to bother about salvaging and repairing an old one. And, since the owner would rather have a new one, he does not encourage anyone to make a salvage attempt. In any case, once the salvor is well into a no-cure, no-pay job, it is very hard for him to quit and lose all that has been invested so far; so he continues on in hopes of minimizing losses. Many a "successful" salvage has been completed by a company that wished it had never begun.

So what attracts people to salvage? They have to risk their own money, and ships, and lives to try to move great weights against the opposition of large natural forces. Probably the new entrants into the business are not capable of realistically calculating the odds against them —salvage jobs invariably look easier than they really are. Second, salvage work is likely to attract romanticists who see themselves as "conquerors" of the sea—snatching valuables from the oblivion of the depths as thousands cheer. Third, some people, including me, have set their lives on an oceanic course and are determined to do whatever can be done to create wealth from the opportunities in the marine business. We hope to reduce the odds against us by means of modern engineering and taut management; we hope the romantic flavor will be reflected in good public relations; and we are challenged by the difficulties that each job presents —principally the one of making money, which is the criterion for a corporation effort.

This book is intended as a contribution to general knowledge of the sea by summarizing the history of marine salvage in an easily readable form. It is mainly a collection of accounts and anecdotes of a thousand salvage jobs. Some of the solutions were very ingenious; some were very risky; all required a lot of hard work by someone. There are examples of tragedy and comedy, of bad luck and good fortune, of failure and success. At any rate, most of the salvage techniques that have ever been used are described here in non-technical terms.

It is not meant to be a how-to-do-it book, or a really detailed description of any one job—indeed, much of that data is never recorded. However, anyone with a seagoing background who knows the main physical principles of how ships and winches and divers operate, will have little difficulty in estimating the approximate horsepowers and pressures and cable sizes that were used. Hopefully, the daring risks taken so often by the hundreds of heroes of this book are presented well enough so that the reader's blood pressure goes up a bit and he sweats vicariously with the salvor as a ship or a diver's life hangs in the balance.

I have been involved in many kinds of ocean work since 1945, including shoreline engineering jobs; deep-ocean exploration; scientific projects; fishing, dredging, and mining schemes; deep-water drilling and oil production; shipbuilding . . . Somehow, without making a conscious effort to do so, I have repeatedly found myself in contact with salvage people.

First, there were the men of the amphibious Navy. Their business is putting boats and ships on the beach and getting them off again—sometimes in high surf and under enemy fire. It was not unusual to roll boats over in the breakers, to get them hard aground on sand bars, or to broach them on steep beaches so that a few waves would demolish them. Many of these boats were salvaged by other small craft, which would dash in between the biggest waves to attach a line and try to tow the beached boat off. The first low tide on a beach after a large amphibious landing operation reveals a maze of sunken craft amid deep gouges in the sand made by salvage attempts. Sometimes, in practice operations, wheeled lifting units called jeheemies were used; these would straddle a small boat, pick it up, and set it straight in water that would float it.

Then I became involved in two strandings involving large freighters. In 1948 the *Ioannis Kulukundis* went aground near Point Arguello, California, in a heavy fog and big breakers. The circumstances were such that I was the only one who could get to it for several days, using amphibious trucks called dukevs, which easily run in and out through surf that stops any other kind of boat. Among those we transported out to the ship were Tony Martinolich and Ernie Judd, two of the top Pacific coast salvage experts. From them I learned a lot about what to look for in the way of structural failures and what might be done to refloat a ship so grounded—although that ship was abandoned without a salvage attempt. As a gesture of good will, I took the Greek crew with its luggage ashore—and got the University of California in trouble with the customs and immigration authorities.

A year later the *Kenkoku Maru* went onto a rocky beach near Fort Bragg, California. She was empty of cargo and went up at high tide, tearing out her bottom. The Smith-Rice Company took a no-cure, no-pay contract to get her off, and I was there as the lowly unpaid assistant whom old Mr. Rice used to make a few tide and displacement calculations. I really didn't think he'd succeed, but with several tugs, a lot of ground tackle, and some big waves to bounce her a bit, he brought her off on the last high tide—and towed her to San Francisco on her inner double bottom and a lot of compressed air. He cured, but narrowly.

In 1950, while working on the problem of finding and salvaging antiship mines in harbors, I learned to dive with both hard-hat and shallow-water gear, and soon afterward was given an early-model Aqualung and shoved overboard by my friend Captain Doug Fane, leader of the Pacific Underwater Demolition Teams. Captain Jacques-Yves Cousteau became a friend about 1955, a few years after I had led the first diving expedition around the Pacific, using what were then called "the Cousteaus" to dive on wrecked ships (without hope of salvage) in Bikini, Eniwetok, Tonga, Samoa, and other remote islands.

Sometime during the twenty-five years of working with Navy people, I got to know Admiral Momsen (of lung fame) and Captain Harold Saunders (the Navy's famed hydrodynamicist who was the engineering officer on several submarine salvage jobs), Captains Bill Searle and Eugene Mitchell (chiefs of Navy Salvage), and diving officers Herman Kuntz and Harold Stubbs. The Navy's Deep Submergence and special submarine research people contributed Captain Bill Nicholson, Dr. John Craven, Howard Talkington, Dr. Bill McLain, and many others to the collection.

On other occasions I encountered Peter Keeble working with Sammy Collins hunting for diamonds under the sea off South West Africa; Dick Anderson working on various wrecks off California; Bob Marx salvaging gold from Spanish galleons along the coast of Florida and Mexico; John Light diving to confirm his theory of the *Lusitania*'s sinking; Bruno Valati filming various salvage operations; Peter Throckmorton and George Bass, who do archaeological salvage on very ancient ships.

Captain David Noble, the famous surveyor of London's offshore oil rigs, and Dr. Tony Denton, his right-hand man (no rig gets insured without their OK), as well as Jim Dawson, Lloyd's leading oceanographic-ship and submarine underwriter, are members of the club.

These are all truly remarkable men, many of whom are mad in their own ways, but still having all the wonderful gutsy qualities that one associates with the diving and salvage business. Their stories, as well as those of the great salvage men that came before them, are too good to remain untold. So this book was conceived and organized to recount the romantic and exciting aspects of this risky and difficult business. It examines the past, inspects the present, estimates the future. What more can you ask?

—WILLARD BASCOM

Methought I saw a thousand fearful wrecks;
Ten thousand men that fishes gnaw'd upon;
Wedges of gold, great anchors, heaps of pearl,
Inestimable stones, unvalued jewels,
All scattered in the bottom of the sea.
                                WILLIAM SHAKESPEARE
                        Richard III, Act I, scene iv

MARINE SALVAGE

PRELUDE

The Bell of Doom

"Individually we are underwriters.
Collectively we are Lloyd's."

CHAPTER ONE

Men Below

Mark Twain, the great American humorist, had but one "permanent ambition" as a boy: to be a steamboat pilot on the Mississippi River. To this end he was apprenticed to a pilot who, as part of his training, asked him for the name of the first point on the river above New Orleans.

"I was gratified to be able to answer promptly," Twain wrote of the incident later. "I said I didn't know."

A man involved in a marine salvage job—almost *any* marine salvage job—usually starts out in the same position as Twain: he won't know how to accomplish his task. But he will figure something out. The story of salvage really is no more than a history of the remarkably varied ways that man, ever since he began dropping things into the ocean, has figured out to get them back again.

The item in question might be a cargo of bootleg whiskey off an old rumrunner sunk during Prohibition, or a downed satellite from the deep waters of the mid-Atlantic. The salvor can be a one-man operator lifting brass fittings off a wrecked yacht, or a whole government putting

$65 million into a desperate search for a lost hydrogen bomb. But in both operations the enemy is the same: the sea. And for both, the difference between success and failure is the ingenuity of individual men.

This book is the story of these men, and of their triumphs over the awesomely impersonal antagonism of the sea. Sometimes, it is the story of their defeats. We will not dwell on the smash of waves, the scream of gales, the unutterable silence of depths where there are tons of pressure per square inch; for this is a story of men, not of oceans. But in the background always will be the sea, the enemy. It is an essential element of the drama.

There are only three kinds of marine salvage: strandings, sinkings, and towings. But these can encompass dragging a tanker off a sandbank at high tide, scooping a fistful of Spanish gold from beneath the coral of four centuries, or bringing up the gas-bloated bodies from a sunken passenger liner. Ships, cargoes, submarine cables, mines, dumped atomic wastes, submariners entombed alive hundreds of feet down—they all entail ocean salvage, and they can range from black tragedy to high comedy.

NAKED DIVERS

If we define diving as the art of descending under water and staying there for a period of time, however short, then marine salvage probably began with the first man who entered the ocean deliberately. Since his reason could not have been thirst, it might have been an attempt to recover something—or someone—that had fallen in. The average adult gets a pain in the ears from diving into the deep end of the swimming pool; to him, sixty seconds seems an eternity under water. But to a Greek sponge diver or a Polynesian shell diver, four minutes is possible, five not unheard of; and dives of a hundred feet unassisted by any external air supply are common. Nature has, after all, furnished many precedents for the naked diver's methods. Whales, seals, cormorants, even mosquito larvae all dive in the same way: they take a big breath at the surface and hold it until they come back up.

There is a Sumerian legend concerning Gilgamesh, who dived beneath the waves trying to find a seaweed that would give him eternal life. Since Gilgamesh is no longer with us, he apparently failed in his quest. Even before his people flourished in southern Babylon, however, the Mesopotamians may have had divers; their middens have yielded carved mother-of-pearl ornaments dating from 4500 B.C. Similar ornaments from the VIth dynasty (3200 B.C.) have been found at Thebes.

But the earliest divers for whom we can adduce "hard" evidence are the Cretans (circa 3000 B.C.): pottery and carvings recovered from excavations at Knossos depict fish and crustaceans in a natural habitat that could have been described only by divers who had observed it. Their equipment probably was a faceplate of thin, polished horn or tortoise shell that had been given a waterproof join with the face by wrappings of gum- or resin-treated cloth.

Homer uses a diver simile in the *Iliad* (circa 800 B.C.) to describe the crash of Hector's chariot during the seige of Troy.

> He, diver-like, from his exalted stand
> Behind the steeds, pitched headlong and expired. . .

And Herodotus, in 460 B.C., mentions a Greek diver named Scyllias, who was hired by Xerxes to remove treasure from Persian vessels shipwrecked off Mount Pelion. Scyllias decided to go over to the Greeks, and forestalled pursuit by cutting the mooring lines of the Persian vessels and then swimming some ten miles under water without surfacing.

"My own opinion," Herodotus remarks sagely, "is that he made the passage in a boat."

This contention seems to have considerable merit.

Aristotle's *Natural History* (circa 350 B.C.) is so accurate in describing fish that he must have been a diver himself or have been supplied with specimens by divers; indeed, the "imperial purple" used in the garments of Grecian royalty came from a genus of shellfish. Sponges, filled with water and carried on long marches, served both Greek and Roman soldiers as primitive canteens.

The siege of Tyre (335 B.C.) was won by Alexander when he used divers to destroy the boom defenses of the harbor; according to Thucydides, the Greeks did the same thing at the siege of Syracuse in 415 B.C. During the same period, the islanders of Rhodes, in the Aegean, off the southwest coast of Turkey, set up scales of recompense for salvors reflecting the difficulty of the profession. According to Livy, the divers received half of what they recovered from twenty-four feet of water, a third from twelve feet, and a tenth from anything under three feet. Plutarch's *Lives* (35 B.C.) mentions that Antony, conned into a fishing contest before Cleopatra, hired a Levantine diver to sneak a prize-winning fish onto his hook. But Cleo got wind of it, and hired a different diver to hang a large dried and salted kipper on Antony's line instead.

Military men, meanwhile, had seized on Scyllias' idea of cutting an enemy's mooring lines. Naval divers used the trick at the sieges of Byzantium (A.D. 196), Les Andelys (1203) and Mayence (1793). When Richard the Lion-Hearted besieged Ptolemais (modern Acre) in 1191, Seljuk Turk divers carried messages in and out of the city under the sea walls. And during the Turkish siege of Malta (1565), there were bloody knife battles between Moslem and Christian divers in the harbor. As late as the siege of Cádiz in 1805, Spanish warships carried naked divers for this purpose.

Not that diving was limited to the Mediterranean basin; evidence indicates that there were divers along virtually every warm-water coast on earth. Cave paintings in northern Australia's desolate Arnhem Land show aboriginal divers with spears and fish on primitive stringers; and in the Bahamas, the Lucayans were incredibly adept divers and spear fishermen. Greedy Spanish overlords wiped out the entire race by working them to death diving for pearls. The Polynesians in the South Pacific and the Amas of Japan still follow traditional diving methods. The Ama women divers at Mikimoto, wearing only shorts and goggles, make 145-foot dives a dozen times a day. And fourteenth-century European travelers to the Persian Gulf describe pearl divers using masks and nose clips of tortoise shell.

AIR FROM THE SURFACE

But it was neither naked divers nor the demands of warfare that changed diving from a foolhardy adventure into a tool of the salvage industry. It was man's growing knowledge of applied physics. The diver, obviously, has only two ways of getting air: he can take it down with him, or he can receive it from the surface through a pipe or hose. Aristotle mentions that Greek divers carried containers (goatskins?) filled with air; but man soon began attempting a continuous air supply from the surface.

As usual, he was anticipated. The whip-tailed larva of *Eristalis tenax*, a grub about the size of a date pit, lives in carcasses that have putrefied to the point of liquidity. *Eristalis* has a stumpy tail; but drop him into six inches of water and his tail extends to reach the surface. There, a flange-like tip floats open, like a tiny lily pad. Inside the transparent outer sheath are a pair of air tubes through which *Eristalis* draws in oxygen and excretes carbon dioxide.

Man's initial efforts to supply himself with surface air were not nearly so successful. A certain Flavius Vegetius, writing a minor Roman treatise on warfare in A.D. 375, makes the first mention of a diving suit and indeed gives us a picture of his design. The diver has a leather bag tied around his head, which makes him look a bit like a subsurface Ku-Klux-Klanner; but the peak of this cap is a tube that reaches up to the surface, where the upper end is kept afloat by a bladder of air. In one hand our hero carries a halberd; in the other he clutches a tired-looking fish. Perhaps it is a seeing-eye fish, since the leather bag has no eyeholes in it. A diver actually descending in such a getup would smother within a few minutes.

Leonardo da Vinci sketched, about 1500, several hypothetical breathing devices in his notebooks; one variant was a full diving suit that thoughtfully made provision for the function that had led the Romans to dub their divers "urinators." Niccolo Fontana (1551) suggested a "suit" that resembled a gigantic hourglass, in which the diver stood with his head in a large glass ball; and in 1609 yet another Italian, Bonajuto Lorini, brought it right back to the place where Vegetius had left it nearly thirteen centuries before: he "invented" a diving mask with a leather breathing pipe to the surface.

The French took their turn next. Le Sieur Freminet's *machine hydrostatergatique*, tested in 1774, furnished a copper helmet and a small air reservoir; the pipes between were "water-cooled"—which was supposed to "regenerate" the air. It didn't. Ten years later, Forfait worked out a sandwich-board arrangement which the diver wore fore and aft; springs over the shoulders kept the boards apart. The unfortunate wretch who wore it was to keep flexing his right leg, which had a cord tied around the big toe, to operate the bellows and thus cause him to rise or descend. It didn't work either.

The German Frederic Drieberg made his big splash in 1808. He put a watertight bag containing a double bellows on the diver's back and a remarkably decorative crown on his head. Otherwise he left the poor man stark naked. A series of radius rods and pivots attached the bellows to the back of the crown. To work the bellows—and thus to breathe—the diver had to keep nodding his head, like a man stricken by palsy, as he advanced through the depths.

PROBLEMS OF PRESSURE

None of these inventors, obviously, had been under the sea; it seems doubtful that many of them even bothered to visit a beach and watch the waves roll in. True, a Scotsman named Charles Spaulding drowned in one of his own infernal devices in 1783, but the history is brightened with few such diverting occurrences. Usually they sent someone else down to perish, never even guessing that the central problem was not air to breathe, but water pressure, which had to be equalized.

Any boy trying to recover golf balls from a water hazard with a length of garden hose has discovered very rapidly how hard it is to drag down air at atmospheric pressure into lungs subjected to water pressure. Man's body is designed to withstand the 14.7 pounds per square inch (psi) pressure exerted by air at sea level, not the extra weight of the water. Every thirty-three feet in depth adds another "atmosphere" (14.7 psi) of pressure (climbing 14,100-foot Pike's Peak would *decrease* air pressure by only about half this amount), so the diver must have some breathing medium containing oxygen compressed to the same pressure as the water around him if he hopes to survive.

Thus the many early divers who disappeared into the ocean depths did not really suffocate. They were pulped into a shapeless mass by water pressure that at a modest 133 feet adds some sixty tons to the weight the body bears at sea level.

The first inventor to grapple with this problem was William Forder of England, in 1802. His suit had a copper casing over the head and torso, with leather sleeves and breeches covering the rest of the body. Though Forder supplied air from a surface bellows through an air hose like many before him, he also fed the air into the suit itself in an attempt to equalize the pressure. He failed, but only because his bellows had been designed to fan a hearth fire, not supply a diver with air.

AUGUSTUS SIEBE

A mere seventeen years later, in 1819, Augustus Siebe of England designed his "open" diving suit, which delivered a constant surface-air supply under pressure from a force pump. The suit itself had a helmet attached to a waterproof jacket, which was open at the waist to allow the diver's exhalations to escape. Siebe's suit was most effective in the preliminary attempts to salvage HMS *Royal George* from the mud of Spithead Harbor floor, where the 104-gun, three-decker "ship-of-the-line" had lain since sinking in 1782 with nine hundred men aboard. The main problem Siebe's diver faced, of course, was that of bending over too far so that his jacket would fill with water.

HARD-HAT DIVING SUIT

In 1837, Siebe modified his design in three ways: he enclosed the diver's entire body (except the hands) in a watertight suit; he added weighted boots to the feet; and he put an escape valve in the helmet so the diver's spent breath could escape.

With these modifications, Siebe in one stroke invented the hard-hat diving suit and completed its evolution. Today's suit is the same in every essential respect: a single garment fitting the diver from neck to foot, made of sheet rubber sandwiched between two layers of twill. There is no sewing; instead, all seams are glued and pressed with hand rollers to eliminate air bubbles. Over the shoulders fits the corselet of the helmet, with studs around the edge, over which the outer of the suit's two collars is fastened. A segmented ring on the corselet takes a corresponding ring on the helmet, which is locked down by a quarter turn. On the wrists are cuffs of vulcanized rubber, fitted over the suit's cuffs to make a watertight joint. The boots, fastened around the ankles with hemp lanyards, are either leather with wood-and-lead soles, or brass with renewable leather uppers. Forty-five pounds of lead weights complete the body covering.

The helmet generally is of tinned copper, hand-beaten into shape with wooden mallets, with brass neck ring brazed in, ducts for the entrance of the air hose, and windows fitted with brass protective screens. The one directly in front of the diver's face is left clear for better vision, even though this can be dangerous.

In September 1926 a diver named John Lee was working on a routine salvage operation on the sunken steamship *Glencona*, which was blocking the channel in Morecambe Bay, England. Lee was down to check the placement of explosives when he lost his footing on the slanted deck. He fell overboard. The glass "eye" of his helmet struck a metal projection and was smashed.

Not only was his air rushing out, which meant he might drown, but the fall also subjected him to a tremendous "squeeze" from the water pressure. The hard-hat diver is very much like an automobile tire, suspended in a balance between two opposing forces of equal magnitude— in a diver's case, water pressure and air pressure. Lee, falling toward the point where his air pressure would be less than the water pressure, was in danger of having the blood forced from his extremities and lower body into his chest cavity in one enormous hemorrhage.

He was quick-witted enough to get his hands over the opening, lacerating them badly but slowing the air outflow sufficiently to keep breathing. At the bottom he gave the emergency pull on his lines, and was hauled up unconscious. After a few days in the hospital, he was able to return to the job.

Diving helmets are of many different types, with bolts, locks, or flanges to hold them on, but all have several features in common. All modern helmets have an interior phone for communication with the surface, and both air-intake and air-outlet fittings are equipped with non-return valves and hand-adjustable seating springs for control of relative buoyancy and as insurance against a squeeze or a blowup.

The air hose (air pipe, air line) comes in lengths up to sixty feet and is designed to withstand heavy internal pressures without bursting. It has an outer layer of rubber, then canvas, then rubber with tinned-steel wire embedded in it, then canvas, and then a final, inner layer of rubber.

There is also a life line, for raising and lowering the diver, and a telephone rope of plaited hemp with a core of heavily insulated phone wires capable of withstanding an 850-pound pull without interruption of electrical continuity. The phone provides a much surer, swifter, and broader communication between diver and surface tender than the old hand signals could.

Divers, by the way, often feel that their tenders are slack in their rather life-and-death job; but it is only rarely that a diver does anything about it. One was Tom Loutitt, perhaps the most famous of early British salvage divers; he was such a wild man that his employers invariably referred to him (with a shake of the head) as "that old devil."

Tom was aboard the salvage steamer *Hyaena* and decided that his tender needed to be taught a lesson. Loutitt probably was right, as this gentleman had taken to knotting the life line around his wrist instead of carefully tending it as the manual prescribed, and then settling dreamily on the gunnel of the ship to stare into space.

Tom chose his time well. He was down in eight fathoms one day when, without warning, he gave a tremendous heave on the life line. This yanked the hapless tender right off the ship and into the water, since he was unable to free his wrist. Tom didn't stop there, however. He hauled lustily on the line, hand over hand, until he had dragged his victim to the bottom, some fifty feet below the surface.

There he belabored him mightily around the head and ears before releasing him. The tender floundered to the surface, where he lay gasping on top of the water and coughing until dragged aboard the *Hyaena*.

Without the genius of Augustus Siebe in developing the hard-hat diving suit, marine salvage could not have developed as it did; yet even with the necessary equipment, man still must be highly motivated to challenge the immeasurable energy and power of the sea. Most of this motivation has been supplied by a unique organization that began as a London coffeehouse during the 1690s, and by a piece of paper: a salvage agreement signed between that organization and an obscure salvor in the Dardanelles some two hundred years later.

CHAPTER TWO

Lloyd's of London

~~~~~~

The phrase "insure it with Lloyd's" has become known to almost everyone, like some unnervingly successful advertising slogan. The irony is that no one, ever, anywhere, has at any time insured anything with Lloyd's. It is not an insurance company at all, but rather an international market of insurance—and the world's foremost center of shipping intelligence. One insures "at" Lloyd's, not "with" Lloyd's, for its Underwriting Members are individuals who compete with one another and who carry their own profits and losses.

The closest analogy for Lloyd's is the New York Stock Exchange, which is a market place for shares, just as Lloyd's is a market place for insurance. Members of the Stock Exchange must be licensed to practice there; and Lloyd's underwriters must have met strict standards, financial and otherwise, before they are admitted to the society. They also must place all their received premiums in a Trust Fund, from which they can draw only ascertained profits, and they must contribute to a Central

Guarantee Fund, which makes a Lloyd's policy almost unassailable. Each underwriter's liability includes his private estate, and none of them can deal directly with the public; they deal instead with the 220 Corporation-approved brokers who are there to protect the customers' interests.

Part of the strength of Lloyd's is its combination of the latest computerized operational techniques with an almost ferocious regard for tradition. Over two million insurance policies are issued there annually, but because it began life as a London coffeehouse during the reign of James II, its staff members wear livery and are known as "waiters"; the Casualty Sheets, which are posted daily, still are hand written; and entries in the Casualty Book, listing the names of ocean vessels that have been lost, are still made with a quill pen. Even the underwriters do business not in offices, but in "stalls" that hark back to the high-backed private booths of the coffeehouse.

EARLY HISTORY

Edward Lloyd first appears on public record during 1689. His establishment was in Tower Street near the Thames, so his customers were shipowners and masters, bankers, and merchants whose orientation was maritime. As early as 1696 Lloyd was furnishing quills, ink, and paper to his customers, and was producing a small newssheet called *Lloyd's News*. This handwritten listing of the news from various ships, pinned to the coffeehouse wall, was discontinued after he misreported some doings in the House of Lords; but his customers started *Lloyd's List* in 1734, a nautical newssheet that still is printed and is today London's oldest continuous daily newspaper.

Lloyd moved his coffeehouse to Lombard Street, and a third move was made to Pope's Head Alley after his death in 1713. By that time, all pretense that it was anything but a private club had been abandoned; the customers controlled the premises so completely that those not interested in shipping or marine insurance were denied entry.

Men seeking such insurance, of course, always could find several risk-minded gentlemen gathered there—which was greatly preferable to seeking them singly elsewhere. These risk takers were known as "underwriters" because they wrote their signatures and the shares of the venture they were accepting "one under the other" on the policy of insurance. The "gentlemen of the coffee house" also held frequent ship auctions, called "sales by candle" because of the unique way they were conducted. A pin was inserted into a candle, which was lighted to begin the bidding. Bidding continued while the flame burned down; the winning offer was the last one made before the pin fell out.

The British Government gave Lloyd's an inadvertent boost in 1720 by granting monopolistic charters of insurance to the London and the

Royal Exchange Assurance Corporations. No other company, said the charters, could write insurance. Lloyd's underwriters, however, were not a company but a mere "society" of competing individuals who in some strange way shared a very marked common loyalty, so they were exempt from this prohibition. And because neither the London nor the Royal Exchange had much interest in the highly speculative marine risks, Lloyd's flourished.

POLICY WRITING

During those years was evolved the ritual of policy writing that still is observed today; the only change is that a broker now represents the customer. Once the broker has received a request for coverage, he makes out a "slip"—a folded sheet of paper on which the details of the proposed risk are written. In the Underwriting Room he seeks agreement with an underwriter who specializes in this sort of coverage. When a premium is agreed upon, the underwriter puts on the slip the amount of the risk he is accepting—called "writing a line"—and scrawls his initials, known as a "lead." The broker gets other underwriters to follow this "lead" until the total risk is covered.

Today, because ships, planes, factories, and construction projects worth millions often are being insured, the underwriter (known as a "name" in this context) usually is committing a syndicate of underwriters, not merely himself. His initials—sole evidence of agreement until the actual policy is issued—are binding upon him and his syndicate. Currently there are three hundred such groups, ranging in size from a few individuals to a few hundred.

JOHN JULIUS ANGERSTEIN

Under the urging of the "Father of Lloyd's," John Julius Angerstein, a Committee of Customers was appointed in 1771 to search for new premises; the move was made in 1774 to the Royal Exchange. Angerstein's personal prestige was so great that a policy bearing his lead was known as a "Julius." His committee evolved into today's Committee of Members, which controls the operations of Lloyd's and also directs the activities of the fifteen hundred Lloyd's Agents who represent the corporation (but not the individual underwriters) around the world. The Committee is elected by ballot for a four-year term, with a year's retirement mandatory before a Member is again eligible.

War with France came in 1793, and Lloyd's underwriters found themselves backing Britain's naval might by insuring it: one of them, Robert Sheddon, paid out £190,000 on shipping losses during a two-year period of the war. By 1815 Lloyd's was the single most dominant influence in British naval operations; and in a time when no government made provision for war victims, Lloyd's underwriters were subscribing a "Patriotic Fund" for this purpose that still exists.

Joseph Marryat, a Member of Parliament as well as a Member of Lloyd's, induced the others to sign a trust deed vesting their corporate funds in a Committee of Treasury, which led to the Lloyd's Act of 1871. This act of incorporation imposed further controls on individual subscribers, but let the society act as a corporate entity.

LLOYD'S "STANDARD FORM"

Tradition is so strong at Lloyd's that its marine insurance form has roots in a Florentine policy of 1523 and wording from a common printed form evolved in the seventeenth century. This Standard Form was "revised and confirmed" in 1779, and the only changes since have been clauses added separately to meet the special requirements of each class of insurance. Because every clause and phrase of the Standard Form has been judicially interpreted at one time or another, its cumbersome language is itself a bulwark against litigation.

MODERN LLOYD'S

Since 1957, Lloyd's home has been a vast modern building on London's Lime Street. The Underwriters Room is about the size of an American football field, with some forty-four thousand square feet of floor space besides extensive second-floor galleries for non-marine insurance. The energetic Cuthbert Heath began accepting risks for burglary and loss of profits, and jewelers' block policies in the 1890s; fire, compensation, and motor insurance followed. Lloyd's wrote the first aviation policy in 1911—only eight years after the Wright Brothers' premier flight.

Today three-fourths of Lloyd's business is foreign (with over half of that in North America), so it now admits foreign Underwriting Members. They must, however, deposit three times the $36,000 minimum required of British Members, and must show assets of $240,000. In March 1969 another change was instituted: Underwriting Members now are able to hold their Security Deposits (pledged against claims) in British equity shares, instead of keeping a minimum 50 per cent in British Government bonds. These deposits, totaling some $150 million, still are held available should underwriting losses ever exceed premium income; but since premiums brought in over $1 billion last year, the contingency seems rather remote.

Perhaps the most radical change in Lloyd's recent history occurred in January 1970, when it began admitting British women—mainly wives and widows of Members—as Inactive Members. They must be British citizens, permanent residents of the United Kingdom, and show $180,000 in assets.

Lloyd's reputation received its greatest international boost in 1906, following the San Francisco earthquake and fire, which killed 452 and destroyed $350 million worth of property. While American insurance companies folded right and left, Lloyd's immediately paid off dollar for dollar on every policy it carried. Today Lloyd's will accept any legitimate risk, except long-term life insurance, ranging from commercial nuclear power plants to gambling that rain won't fall on a given day (rain gauge furnished with such policies).

THE BELL OF DOOM

In the coffeehouse days, a boy called a "kidney" would make announcements from a pulpit or rostrum; his modern counterpart is the Caller, a functionary who broadcasts the names of brokers who are wanted for some particular piece of business. Since there are 220 brokers and six thousand underwriters, such a communication system obviously is necessary. The Caller also rings the *Lutine* bell, which hangs above the rostrum—one ring for good news, two for bad—before making important announcements concerning maritime affairs. In the days of sail, the *Lutine* bell was called the Bell of Doom, for its news usually was bad. Wooden ships often sank within minutes, and the first word of trouble was, generally speaking, also the last. The *Lutine* herself sank in Holland's Zuider Zee in 1799 with £1,175,000 aboard, little of which ever has been recovered. The bell, along with the rudder and rudder chain, was found in 1859; the rudder became a table, which also belongs to Lloyd's.

The bell is seldom rung now, but on May 27, 1941, in the dark early days of World War II, it heralded news that Germany's massive "unsinkable" battleship, the *Bismarck*, had been sunk by British warships. Just three days before, the *Bismarck* had sent to the bottom Britain's battleship, the *Hood*; and her depredations along the convoy route from America had raised insurance rates on Allied shipping to an unprecedented $25 for each $100 of insured value.

The leading War Risk underwriter was quoting this rate to a broker on an American ship about to leave New York, when the *Bismarck* news was announced. As a tremendous cheer thundered through the Underwriters Room, the War Risk man turned back to the broker.

"Right," he said. "I now will quote ten dollars per hundred. How's that?"

The impact of this unique society on the development of marine salvage has been incalculable. It is obvious that anytime an underwriter or a syndicate pays off on a major marine loss, all practicable attempts to recoup something from the disaster will be made. A fact to give would-be treasure hunters pause is that *no* ship insured at Lloyd's (which writes more marine insurance than all the world's insurance companies combined) has gone down carrying large amounts of gold, silver, jewels, or specie without recovery being attempted. Many of history's most intricate and fascinating salvage operations have been undertaken on Lloyd's initiative; the boldest, perhaps, is the nearly incredible deep-water *Egypt* operation from 1929 to 1934.[1]

Lloyd's underwriters established the Salvage Association of London (as American underwriters later established the U. S. Salvage Association) to represent underwriters and owners at wreck sites, and to make such technical inspections and evaluations as are necessary to determine whether salvage should be undertaken. Lloyd's also offered a good deal of support to groups such as the Liverpool and Glasgow Salvage Association, which existed solely for the purpose of aiding distressed ships. Such concerns maintained complete salvage units (both staff and fleet) in year-round readiness for immediate operation in any sort of weather.

The greatest spur to the profession of salvor, however, has without doubt been Lloyd's Standard Form of Salvage Agreement. In order to understand the Form's[2] influence, it is necessary to look briefly at the evolution of admiralty law as regards salvage; for virtually every maritime nation bases its own marine law on British Admiralty statutes.

EVOLUTION OF ADMIRALTY SALVAGE LAW

Until A.D. 1275, all shipwrecked goods in Great Britain, whether at sea or cast up on the shore, were considered Wreck[3] and belonged to the Crown. Edward I's Statute of Westminster, however, restricted the rights of the Crown to *unclaimed* wrecks only.

The first law relating directly to salvage came in 1353, during the reign of Edward III. This granted to the Admiralty the Crown's rights of jurisdiction over unclaimed wrecks on the high seas, while simultaneously establishing the principle that wrecks washed ashore came under local jurisdiction.

In the following centuries, admiralty courts gradually evolved the practice of making salvage awards to men who tried to prevent disaster (salvage in the modern sense) rather than encourage it. That ferocious things were going on along Britain's coastlines can be seen by the fact that George II, in 1753, made it a felony to put out false lights that would lure ships onto the rocks, and also made it a felony to beat, wound, or obstruct people trying to escape from foundering vessels.

"Many wicked enormities," George remarked in considerable understatement, "have been committed to the disgrace of the nation."

Even as late as 1809, George III had to legislate against boatmen who had been cutting ships' cables in harbors, bays, and rivers so they could recover and sell the anchors as well as systematically loot any ships that went ashore as a result of being cast adrift.

It was not until the Merchant Shipping Act of 1894 that all salvage jurisdiction was consolidated in admiralty courts; yet Lloyd's already had formulated its first Salvage Agreement (assuming just such consolidation) some four years before.

LLOYD'S "NO CURE, NO PAY" SALVAGE CONTRACT

Enunciated in 1890 between a salvor in the Dardanelles and the Committee of Lloyd's, the Agreement stipulated that the salvor would accept whatever remuneration the Committee decided upon, and made payment contingent upon the *preservation of some part of the property in peril*. This "no cure, no pay" feature of the Lloyd's Form is essential to any salvage agreement.[4] To protect the salvor, the amount of payment was made subject to the decision of an arbitrator (if one was appointed). The first so-called Standard Form was issued by Lloyd's in 1892, and underwent only minor revision until 1926. In that year a revolutionary clause was added, allowing for appeal from the arbitrator's decision. The only way that this Appeal Arbitrator's decision can be challenged, however, is on a point of law. In such a case, it goes into admiralty court or, if the point is involved enough, to the House of Lords.

Few such appeals are made. Today, all arbitrators are lawyers, most of them with twenty years' or more experience, while at least two must have commanded their own ships at sea.

As for the Agreement itself, countless legal decisions have made its basic outline practically unassailable. As Lord Wright remarked in a decision involving the Form: "Its validity is not and could not be contested." The courts theoretically can challenge the Standard Form, of course, but seldom do; thus, properly executed, it in practice excludes the concerned parties from recourse to admiralty court.

Today a Lloyd's Standard Form will be accepted as valid even if signed after the salvage service has been rendered. It can be written out in longhand on an ordinary sheet of paper, and some jurists hold that a wireless message from the endangered vessel's owner, written out and recorded by the wireless operators, would serve as a legal Lloyd's Standard Form.

Thus Lloyd's continues to exert a unique influence on the world's maritime affairs. Despite the fact that half of her premium income now derives from non-marine insurance, and despite her growing involvement in the complex, expanding world of nuclear power and developing nations, Lloyd's soul is nautical. As recently as 1969 one of her members, James Dawson, formed a syndicate called Ocean Industries Insurers to specialize in the insurance problems of oceanographic-engineering and scientific-research firms.

And Lloyd's proudest possession is still the logbook of HMS *Euryalus*, Nelson's signal frigate at the Battle of Trafalgar. A famous phrase in the entry for October 21, 1805, sums up not only the men of the British fleet that day, but also, in a curious way, the history of Lloyd's.

"England," wrote Nelson, "expects that every man will do his duty."

It is not by accident that Lloyd's coat of arms carries a single word as its motto.

Fidentia. Which means trust.

[1] See pages 50–57.
[2] See APPENDIX I for the full text of this document.
[3] See the definition in APPENDIX II.
[4] See APPENDIX II for a discussion of payment in cases in which no salvage is effected.

I

Full Fathom Five

Full fathom five thy father lies;
Of his bones are coral made;
Those are pearls that were his eyes . . .
WILLIAM SHAKESPEARE
The Tempest, I, ii

CHAPTER THREE

Divers Down

In his brief, stormy existence, man has exhibited a remarkably perverse ability to keep dropping things—such as ships—into progressively less accessible reaches of the world's great oceans. To a pre-Christ Rhodian salvor, sticking an arm underwater to pick something up off the bottom meant a 10 per cent reward. In 1611, which is probably when Shakespeare wrote *The Tempest*, such redoubtable seafarers as the British still viewed "full fathom five" as deep water.

Salvors in his day, such as they were, worked from the surface, if at all. Two ships that sank in the same harbor nearly 250 years apart, in fact, show the almost total ignorance that prevailed concerning salvage problems and methods.

BEGINNINGS: MARY ROSE AND ROYAL GEORGE

HMS *Mary Rose* was a 60-gun British man-of-war under command of Sir George Carew. She was lying at Spithead in Portsmouth Harbor with other elements of the British fleet; since it was the summer of 1545, Henry VIII was as usual at war with both the French and the Scots, and a sharp engagement with the French Navy was expected as soon as wind and weather would allow the 105-ship British flotilla out of harbor. On June 18, however, well in advance of the engagement, *Mary Rose* suddenly heeled over and sank. Only a handful of the seven hundred aboard her survived.

Noble heads were shaken at court over this un-navylike conduct; not only had the *Mary Rose* gone down before a shot was fired, she had gone down while at anchor in calm waters. Since Carew wisely had drowned with his vessel, recriminations were muted, and certain nobles, such as the Duke of Suffolk, decided to raise the sunken warship. A matter of six short weeks, he announced breezily. He would get ". . . two of the greatest hulks that may be gotten, . . five of the greatest cables that may be had, ten great hawsers, . . five pullies bound with iron," and "sixty English mariners." The hulks would be floated at the surface above the vessel, one on either side; a cat's cradle of cables would be somehow gotten around the vessel; and she would be dragged to the surface.

That "somehow" was the downfall of Suffolk's plan, even though he claimed the ship would be afloat again by the Fifth or the Sixth of August. That it wasn't, is confirmed by the fact that salvors going down after the *Royal George*, which sank on August 29, 1782, also at Spithead in Portsmouth Harbor, came across the collapsed and rotted remains of the *Mary Rose*. They even brought up one or two of her cannon.

The *Royal George* also was a man-of-war (108 guns), commanded by Lord Hawke, which in a holiday spirit had been loaded up with thirteen hundred men, women, and children. A small leak being discovered below the waterline, the ship was heeled over for repairs by simply carting all her cannon to the side away from the leak. As she was in this position, a group of remarkable idiots aboard a lighter began discharging their cargo of rum—on the heavy side of the vessel! Over she went, and down. With her went all but three hundred of those aboard.

Since she was upright in only sixty-five feet of water, with her spars sticking out of the water, she was an instant hazard to navigation. Raising her was proposed, and a certain Mr. Tracey came up with a plan. Though 237 years had passed since *Mary Rose*, his plan was distressingly familiar. Get two large hulks, he said, float them on either side of the vessel, make a cat's cradle of cables . . .

He did, at least, mention the possibility of using the tide to help them.

It was not until 1839 that anything constructive was done about the *Royal George*. A dashing colonel of the Royal Sappers and Miners, named Pasley, was told to remove the hulk. Pasley did just that, using a heady mixture of his "mad, married, or Methodist" sappers with wildly unstable iron cylinders of gunpowder that varied in weight from sixty pounds to as much as a ton. He decided to detonate the gunpowder by means of wires leading from voltaic batteries at the surface; since he knew nothing about underwater work, he called for diving suits in which to send down his men. He got three. One he rejected out of hand; the second he tried, nearly drowning his diver; the third he used.

AUGUSTUS SIEBE'S "CLOSE" SUIT

This was the "close" diving suit designed by Augustus Siebe two years before, a modification of his "open" suit of 1819. In August 1840 the first dive from the salvage vessel *Firebrand* was made on the *Royal George*. More followed. The vessel soon was disposed of, and some ten tons of copper, as well as eighteen hundred feet of timber, were salvaged.

The operation on the *Royal George*, however, had another distinction besides that of introducing the triple arts of diving, demolition, and salvage under water. It featured the beginning of a bogus tradition that Hollywood has doggedly espoused through scores of soggy epics in studio water tanks: the tradition of sea-floor battles between hard-hat divers.

Such fights almost never occur in real life, since the two-hundred-pound suits are just too cumbersome for that sort of nonsense. Two of the divers on the *Royal George*, however, had a grand subterranean brawl. Since regular divers had refused to work on the wreck (sixty-five feet, they said, was too deep!), Pasley was using Army noncoms at the magnificent salary of twenty-five cents a day. Two of the lads, Girvan and Jones, each claimed to have spotted a certain cannon first. Gestures led to blows. Jones, a much smaller man, soon broke away and tried to escape up the shot rope (called the bull rope at that time), but Girvan seized his legs to drag him back.

Panicked, Jones kicked backward—and his weighted iron boot went right through the other man's faceplate. Luckily for both of them, at that instant the tenders yanked them to the surface, having become alarmed at the extreme agitation of their life lines. Neither man was hurt, and in future they dived as a team.

Oddly enough, bull-voiced, cocky little Jones, Corporal of Engineers, became the iron man of the salvage operation. Nobody knew anything about the dangers of pressure, but Jones must have had an incredible ability to withstand it. He once was down on the wreck for five hours straight with no apparent ill effects.

"Whatever success has attended our operations," said Pasley, "is chiefly attributable to the exertions of Corporal Jones."

The *Royal George*, of course, was far from a deep-water operation. It lay in only sixty-five feet of water, while the average depth of the world's oceans is 12,600 feet (2100 fathoms). This is *five times* the average height of the world's continents *above* sea level; indeed, Mount Everest, at 29,028 feet the world's highest peak, would fit in the Marianas Trench off the Philippines with more than a mile and a quarter to spare. Salt water covers 140 million square miles, occupies 324 million cubic miles in volume, and accounts for fifteen times as much of the earth's surface as does the land above sea level. No, the *Royal George* was not deep-water stuff.

Still, it was a handsome start. Siebe's suit made diving a profession, rather than hare-brained madness. The U. S. Navy established a diving school at Newport, Rhode Island, as far back as 1882, when a retired chief gunner's mate named Jacob Anderson began holding two-week, twenty-man courses; but the only work the brass could dream up for the divers was recovery of practice torpedoes from the Newport Firing Range.

By 1906, two British divers (G. C. C. Damant and A. Catto) had set a world's record with 210 feet. In November 1914, the U. S. Navy's remarkable warrant gunner George Stillson, working with Navy Assistant Surgeon George French, broke this with a 274-foot dive.[1]

Until Sealab III, the greatest operational open sea dive was made in 1950 by Pete Prickett of the U. S. Navy's Experimental Diving Unit (EDU), who reached five hundred feet off the Galápagos Islands. This was while breathing an oxygen-helium mixture, as was the six hundred-foot "bounce" dive (descending very rapidly to the record depth from a shallower depth, and returning immediately) by the Royal Navy's George Wookey in October 1956. This could hardly count as an operational dive, and Wookey came up badly "bent" from nitrogen bubbles in the blood. Both of these dives, by the way, were well beyond the collapse depth of World War II submarines.

The point that must be made about all these dives, however, is that they were test dives, not work dives carried out under salvage conditions. Some of the most intriguing hard-hat dives were made in the early days, when the real dangers faced by divers were still mysterious, misunderstood, or not even known.

Fiction to the contrary, a man beneath the sea has little to fear from giant squid or even hungry sharks. Danger to hard-hat salvage diver or weekend SCUBA enthusiast alike comes from the fact that he is operating in a hostile environment. We have evolved from our salt-sea beginnings into air breathers whose bodies are structured for existing in a sea-level atmosphere. To stray very far from that 14.7-pounds-per-square-inch pressure means formidable problems. For the diver, every thirty-three feet in depth adds another atmosphere of pressure—thus doubling the weight of water the body is sustaining.

To exist under water, therefore, the diver must have a constant source of air or other oxygen-fortified breathing medium at a pressure equal to that of the water around him. The blood does the rest, circulating this air equally throughout the body. Since water (like air) exerts its pressure in all directions at once, it supports bodies immersed in it from all directions at once. Thus the body, which has no air spaces except the lungs, parts of the stomach, and sections of the lower intestine, does not distort as long as it is subjected to equal water pressure over its entire surface; and this simple fact makes deep diving in a non-rigid rubber suit possible.

THE SQUEEZE

If, however, part of the body is under pressure while the rest is not, the liquid in the unprotected part will attempt to rush into the protected, and if the pressure is great enough, will burst it like a ripe seed pod. Hence, in the early days of hard-hat diving, a "squeeze"— the pressure of the air coming into the diver's rigid, protecting helmet being less than the surrounding water pressure. Cases exist of divers who have lost their air being rammed right up into their helmets in a sort of jelly, leaving only a mass of mangled flesh and crushed bones in their flexible rubber suit.

Peter Keeble, in a few blunt, savage sentences, tells of bringing up a diver in Alexandria Harbor during World War II after an accident that subjected him to a squeeze.

"His helmet broke the surface. Another heave and the suit came into sight, dangling emptily on the air hose. The arms hung lifeless, the rubber cuffs empty but for a trickle of water dripping from them. The water was deeply tinged with crimson."

In a moment's carelessness, the tender had released the diver's life line and air hose at the same moment that the diver had released his hold on the diving stage. He had fallen a mere forty feet—but it had been enough.

"We pulled the limp suit over the bulwarks into the diving boat," Keeble went on. "Somebody, with a shaking hand, reached to unscrew the front glass of the helmet—and released a warm, sickening flood. Most of the diver had been forced into the copper dome of his helmet."

BLOW-UPS

The invention of the non-return valve just about eliminated the danger of the classic squeeze; but too little pressure was not the only danger faced by early divers in relation to their air supply. Too much air can also kill or cripple a man under water. This is the "blow-up"—when the air in the suit exceeds in pressure the water outside, and the suit inflates like a balloon and the diver's arms and legs fly out straight, like giant sausages. He cannot even get at his air outlet valve, since it is on his helmet and he cannot bend an arm enough to reach it. So he will pop up to the surface. If he comes up under his own salvage ship, he probably will be dashed to pieces against it. Or his suit will split or explode, and he will drop like a stone, weighted as he is with two hundred pounds of copper, iron, and lead, to drown.

THE BENDS: PAUL BERT AND JOHN HALDANE

Even if he is rescued, and cannot either be sent directly to the bottom again or popped into a decompression chamber (a boiler-shaped steel cylinder with compressed-air lines feeding it and gauges to measure the interior air pressure), he is in danger of another disease, known as "the bends." By far the most common hazard faced by divers, they also can be the most dangerous.

The bends—or caisson disease or compressed-air sickness—have been known since antiquity. In mild form they are merely a stiffness of the joints such as elbows or knees; severe cases curl the man up in agony —hence, bends—or, if the spine is affected, leave him paralyzed for life. The French physiologist Paul Bert (1833–86), was the first man to isolate bubbles of nitrogen in the blood as the cause of the bends. He found that of the three major gases in the air (oxygen 21%, nitrogen, 78%, carbon dioxide 1% minus traces of the rare gases), only nitrogen accumulates rapidly in the blood of a diver under pressure. Oxygen is absorbed by the tissues; carbon dioxide is exhaled.

Nitrogen, however, goes into solution in the blood. If a diver comes up with proper decompression stops, the nitrogen comes out of solution and is exhaled. If decompression is too rapid, the nitrogen bubbles up in the blood the way a carbonated beverage froths up in the bottle when the removal of the cap releases the pressure that has held it in solution. The nitrogen bubbles lodge in the spinal cord, the joints, or the muscles, causing pain or paralysis; and only immediate recompression can help.

Bert recommended a gradual, uniform decompression; it helped, but was not totally effective. Then, in 1905, physiologist John Scott Haldane (the mountain-climbing Scotsman who first won fame by telling miners to carry mice with them to test the purity of the air below ground) came up with "stage" decompression. He had found that down to thirty-five fathoms, the total pressure could be safely halved at any given time. Tables were worked out whereby divers come halfway up, pause for a measured time, halve that distance, pause for a shorter decompression period, and come to the surface when further decompression is no longer necessary. The Haldane tables are now obsolete, but his concept is not.

All of which makes a diver's life sound grim and dangerous. Dangerous it is; grim it is not. Divers' humor is masculine and rough; they have fun with their job and take a great pride in it which excludes outsiders.

One such incident was during World War II, aboard a Navy salvage vessel that had an assistant engineer whose handsome good looks had earned him the nickname of "Hollywood." Hollywood was an egotistical sort who, when something went amiss with the ship's screws, insisted on being suited up and sent below to examine the trouble. He claimed to have had diving experience, and intimated that anyway, as an engineer and a gentleman by act of Congress, he was better qualified for such a technical job.

So he was sent below. He did not realize that the diver who dressed him for the descent had very carefully hitched one of his shoulder straps up tighter than the other. Once under water, the compressed air being fed to the helmet makes it tend to rise from the shoulders; these straps hold it down.

"Hey! I can't see!" exclaimed Hollywood once he was under water. "My helmet is on crooked!"

His superior knew nothing of diving; the helmet had seemed to be on straight when Hollywood had gone over the side, so Hollywood's stock slid to zero with the engineer at that moment. But his troubles were not over. While he was down, the waiting divers carefully nailed his shoes to the deck in front of the diving stool. He had been divested of his cumbersome equipment, and just had thrust his feet into the shoes, when the Captain appeared. Eager for glory, Hollywood leaped to his feet, made a smart pace forward, and snapped a salute.

"Captain—" he began.

And physics intervened. While Hollywood had moved forward, his shoes had not. He crashed face down on the steel deck in front of his shocked and horrified commander.

"This man has the bends!" cried the senior officer. "Get him into the recompression chamber at once!"

Eager hands lifted the fallen warrior to rush him into the chamber; it is possible, even, that certain of the hands chanced to cover his mouth *en route*. In any event, he raised no objections as he was hustled into the steel cylinder.

Neither did he ever don a diving suit again.

It is not just outsiders who find themselves the butt of divers' humor. Diving Officers—those who direct diving operations from the surface—seldom don hard-hat suits and "go below." One of the minor mysteries of the deep is that when they do, they usually come up sopping.

Divers explain it this way: It is the end of a hard day's diving. All the gear is being secured, and the working divers are looking forward to some rest—when the Diving Officer's familiar cry rings out: "All right, wait a minute, you guys. I wanna make a dive."

Being clean in mind and body, divers explain, strong in will and courage, and *never, never* temperamental, they are always delighted to rerig all the diving gear so that the Diving Officer can indulge himself in a happy frolic beneath the waves. The only things out of the ordinary might be a few muttered remarks under the breath, and perhaps a few well-shielded thrusts to the armpits and crotch of the suit that soon will be donned by the Diving Officer.

Upon returning from his dive, very wet, the Diving Officer is perplexed.

"Better check this suit, men. It seems to be taking in water through the armpits and crotch."

Yes, one of the mysteries of the deep.

Deep-water attempts to salvage a vessel itself, intact, are fairly rare. They entail tremendous planning by marine engineers or salvage experts, and detailed, intricate work by the divers down on the wreck; for each salvage job, after all, is completely different and presents a complex pattern of variables that are unique to that particular job. Besides the riddle of restoring buoyancy to the vessel itself, there are the problems of complex tides and currents; and, in northern latitudes particularly, the weather. Many salvage operations have been carried out in the lulls between an almost endless series of storms.

The professionals are very aware of these factors, and of the difficulties of depth, water pressure, and the weight of wood and metal that must be raised; the amateurs are not. Some truly remarkable suggestions have been made over the years.

One man told the British Admiralty that they should freeze the water in the vessel they wished to raise. Since ice floats, the ice in the ship would rise to the surface and carry the ship with it. Simple, no? No.

After the sinking of the *Lusitania* in 1915, an American offered the use of a submarine he had designed himself. This sub would fire a series of torpedoes *through* the ship, right through it from side to side; and each torpedo would carry with it a steel cable. These would be lifting cables, see? You just hook winches on each end at the surface and . . . The *Lusitania* weighs thirty-five thousand tons and is lying in *three hundred feet of water?* Oh . . .

Another: Bolt two large steel planes, like a submarine's diving rudders, at an angle on either side of a sunken vessel's prow. Then two or three tugs fasten towing cables "through the nose" of the ship, get up steam, and go tearing away. With a small enough vessel in shallow water, this actually would work: guided by the rudders, the ship would plane right up to the surface.

But not the 35,000-ton *Lusitania.* Not for her or any ship her size to be thus hustled into the nearest port like a water skier behind a launch. It makes one rather queasy to contemplate the *Andrea Doria*, say, skipping into New York Harbor at several hundred knots.

The deep-water salvor's job is simplified if all he wants is something off the sunken vessel, such as cargo or treasure. He then can do whatever is necessary to the ship itself. Explosives can also be used if the ship is to be salvaged not for its intrinsic value or for its cargo, but merely to clear it aside because it is a danger to navigation.

LOSS OF THE GENERAL GRANT

Whatever the reason that the salvors are there, the problems they face are immense and the failures are frequent. Some of the most intriguing attempts have been resounding failures. The *General Grant* was a wooden clipper ship that went down on the night of May 13, 1866. Accounts differ as to how much gold the 1200-ton vessel took with her—estimates range between $3 million and $12 million on today's market—but she carried eighty-three passengers and twenty-one crewmen, wool, general cargo, and nine tons of spelter (a zinc ore mined in Australia).

The *Grant*, en route from Australia to England, somehow lost her bearings so thoroughly while trying for Cape Horn that she ended up in the Auckland Islands, some three hundred miles south of New Zealand. Here she rammed head-on into the jagged cliffs of Disappointment Island during a heavy storm. The towering breakers carried the wreckage into a scooped-out cavern in the cliffs, from which only about a dozen of the people aboard escaped. Captain William Loughlin elected to go down with his ship and did just that, bizarrely waving a handkerchief at the survivors while he and his craft disappeared.

Until December 1867 they subsisted on seals, goats, and pigs. Finally the whaling ship *Amherst* arrived, brought by a plea for help that one of the men had scratched on a carved miniature boat he had thrown into the sea a year and a half before.

An Australian syndicate made the first attempt to salvage the *Grant's* gold, unsuccessfully, in 1885. Over the years many consortiums and individuals followed, all enjoying an equal lack of success. Finally, New Zealand declared that the wreck belonged to the state, and began leasing salvage rights. Some would-be salvors claimed that the spelter was not zinc ore at all, but rather was gold (nine *tons* of gold?) disguised to mislead either pirates or customs officials. Color is lent to this contention by two facts: in 1968 the current leaseholder recovered (he says) $3.5 million from the wreck, yet he is planning another effort; and spelter was not mined in Australia *until twenty-two years after the vessel had been wrecked.*

The *General Grant* always has been accessible, apart from the tremendous surf smashing into its rocky cairn; it was just a matter of time until someone tough enough, persistent enough, and lucky enough came along to make a successful attempt. Sometimes, however, a salvage job will look impossible in light of existing technology, will be declared impossible by all the experts—and then will be successfully carried out.

SALVAGE OF THE *HAMILLA MITCHELL'S* TREASURE

In 1868 a wooden sailing vessel named the *Hamilla Mitchell* went down on the infamous Leuconna Reef, near Shanghai, in the South China Sea. Besides her general cargo she was carrying £50,000 in specie. The Lloyd's underwriters concerned promptly paid off on the owners' claim and then sent the Shanghai Lloyd's Agent to survey the site.

Impossible he reported. The *Hamilla Mitchell* was lying on a submerged reef some twenty fathoms below the surface—a most formidable depth for that day, when decompression was unknown.

But in London a certain Captain Lodge decided he wanted to gamble on getting that £50,000 in gold. He got salvage rights from the underwriters, then hired R. Ridyard and W. Penk, two of Siebe, Gorman and Company's crack divers. When the three men arrived in Shanghai with their equipment, Lodge chartered the *Maggie*, a small pilot cutter he thought would work as a salvage vessel.

At Leuconna Reef, they found that the actual diving had to be done from a small whaler, because the waters around the reef were too dangerous for the larger vessel. When Penk and Ridyard began diving, they found the situation worse than even the Lloyd's Agent's report had indicated. The after third of the *Hamilla Mitchell*—that part of it containing the strong room—had been hanging out unsupported in open water, and in a storm after the sinking, had broken off and rolled down a subterranean slope to 160 feet.

The divers took turns at the bottom, constantly risking the bends; but finally Ridyard broke into the strong room. The wooden chests containing the gold had been destroyed by wood-boring worms, so he wandered through every boy's dream of Treasure Island. Gold coins lay about in great stacks: he walked on gold; he could hear the rasp and slither of gold beneath his heavy iron boots as he stepped. In four loads, he sent the contents of sixty-four chests to the surface. Finally, exhausted, he returned to the whaler, where he waited while his partner climbed the craggy side of Leuconna Island to a fresh-water spring.

While drawing the water, Penk looked about to the horizon, as all seamen do; and he saw, approaching the side of the island that had been hidden from them while they were on the wreck, scores of Chinese junks. He fled down the island to the whaler, which was pulled immediately to the *Maggie*. Lodge slipped his anchor and made all possible sail as they tried to pull away from the island.

All of them knew that the junks were manned by Chinese pirates, trying to creep up unseen to kill them and hijack the gold. But despite their warning, the wind was so light that the junks kept gaining. The big sweep oars were broken out, and all of them, including Lodge and the exhausted Ridyard, worked like galley slaves in their attempt to outstrip the pursuers. At the last possible moment, their sails caught a breeze and they began to pull away. The junks continued after them until dark, however; finally, under cover of night, Lodge slipped his pursuers and brought the *Maggie* safely into Shanghai.

There they counted their take, and found that they had recovered £40,000 of the total treasure aboard the vessel. Later they returned to the *Hamilla Mitchell* and recovered the other £10,000 worth of specie.

GROSSER KURFURST— REVOLUTIONARY SALVAGE METHOD

Another early salvage operation, the attempt to raise the German warship *Grosser Kurfurst*, is made intriguing by the method contemplated for raising the heavily armored vessel. The *Kurfurst* had gone down near Dover in 1880, after a collision with another German ship, the *König Wilhelm*. The armor-plated *Kurfurst* had sunk in twenty fathoms of water—upside down, with the keel uppermost. She was right in the channel fairway under a strong tidal run, but the London Wrecking Company thought they could raise her because she was holed in only one place, on the port quarter below her armor plating.

The salvors proposed to cover this rupture with an iron patch. Riveted around the rim of the patch was a hollow channel iron, into which was packed a high-pressure rubber hose like a fireman's water hose. Once the patch was in place, the hose would be pumped full of water under tremendous pressure to increase its diameter. This would in turn form a watertight seal with the irregular surface of the hull plating around the hole.

Along each side of the keel would be a heavy wire cable fastened at bow and stern with heavy chains. Every ten feet along the length of each cable would be stays, brought up around the sides of the ship from the portholes. Flexible pontoons would be sunk, attached to the stays, and pumped full of air. These would furnish a thousand tons of lift; not, as was usual in such an operation at that time, to raise the vessel, but merely to keep her from rolling over once she was brought to the surface.

What made the proposed operation unique is that they planned to do the actual lifting by pumping the overturned hull full of compressed air. Thus, like a giant diving bell, she would raise herself to the surface. There she would be turned upright by some method the salvors never got around to explaining.

Today, compressed air is considered the salvor's most potent tool and is used on virtually all salvage operations. But the *Grosser Kurfurst* operation was being planned in 1880. The raising of the small (in comparison to the *Kurfurst*) British submarine *K-13* was still thirty-seven years away. That would be the first successful raising of a sunken vessel with compressed air. The first use of it to raise a ship of the *Kurfurst's* size wouldn't be until 1921, with the raising of the *Leonardo da Vinci*. If the completely practicable plan to raise the *Kurfurst* had been put into operation, compressed air as a salvage technique probably would have become a standard method many years before it did.

But the *Grosser Kurfurst* was never raised. The most chronic difficulty to plague all private salvage concerns halted operations: the London Wrecking Company ran out of money. They ran out so thoroughly, in fact, that the firm went bankrupt. As was proved by the *Normandie* operation in 1942, salvage attempts can easily cost millions of dollars. And, in the case of a no-cure, no-pay operation such as the *Kurfurst*, the salvor often discovers halfway through that his capital is gone.

And so salvors continued to rely on the old methods for nearly another half century, until the fifteen-year proceedings at Scapa Flow—an engineering feat perhaps equal to the building of the Egyptian pyramids—dramatically and forever altered marine salvage methods all over the world. Chapter Fifteen covers this truly remarkable operation.

---

[1] See the operation on the U.S. submarine *F-4*, pp. 101-4.

CHAPTER FOUR

Deep-Water Treasures

〜〜〜〜〜〜〜〜〜〜〜〜〜〜〜〜〜〜〜〜〜〜〜〜〜〜〜〜

If a salvor's primary aim is recovering something aboard the sunken vessel, his methods are radically different from those used in raising the ship itself. To recover cargo, his divers may have only to remove the hatch covers and direct the lowering of the cargo slings from the vessel above. To recover treasure, however, both diver and salvage master make careful plans and study the layout or blueprints of the sunken vessel, for the strongbox always will be in a protected, semi-inaccessible place. And the salvors know that the act of sinking, or subsequent waves, tides, or currents, may have battered the hull to such an extent that plans are meaningless.

Sometimes it is the salvor himself who batters the hull.

ÁNGEL EROSTRABE

In 1891 the steamship *Skyro* was bound from Cartagena to London when, off Cape Finisterre, on the west coast of Spain, she struck the

Mexiddo Reef in heavy fog. Her bottom ripped, the *Skyro* went down within twenty minutes, coming to rest on the bottom at thirty fathoms. In her belly she carried £12,000 in silver bars.

For four long years she lay untouched, while the Lloyd's underwriters paid off on the silver and . . . brooded. No salvage firm of the day had attempted operations in thirty fathoms, and no diver had worked at that depth. But in 1894 a British salvor named J. K. Moffat signed a salvage contract with them, and then hired the famous Spanish diver Angel Erostrabe to make the attempt.

He failed.

The next year Moffat brought him back again with better equipment. This time Erostrabe succeeded in reaching the deck of the *Skyro* 171 feet below the surface. Then began one of the greatest feats of single-handed salvage diving ever accomplished. The weather was terrible, the position nakedly exposed to wild waves, strong currents, and howling winds; and Erostrabe had to dive alone, since no other man known was able to reach that depth.

The strong room, he knew, was down three decks. This meant he had to carefully blast a hole down through the ship's body with dynamite and gelignite. When he reached the deck above the strong room, he set his charges with immense care and delicacy; and yet, when he reached the room, he found the ceiling collapsed to within eighteen inches of the steel floor. Being a stubborn man, Erostrabe began painstakingly blowing away the walls and the floor of the strong room itself.

It took him two years. Finally, however, he had recovered fifty-nine bars, worth £10,000. During the operation he literally blew the *Skyro* to pieces, so that when he was finished only the vessel's boilers and engines stood higher than himself above the sea floor. His share of the recovery was £500—and he had been permanently impaired by the bends, never again able to engage in deep diving.

ALEXANDER LAMBERT

Another of the great early hard-hat divers, Alexander Lambert, replaced Erostrabe as the strongest, most daring diver known. He was a huge man, built like Mr. America and utterly fearless. Once, while coppering the bottom of a coaling hulk in an Indian Ocean port, he became the center of attention for a five-foot shark. The gray predator's repeated passes interfered with his work, so Lambert finally held up his left hand, ungloved, as bait. The shark came for it. Lambert jerked his hand aside and stabbed the passing fish several times in the belly with his heavy-bladed diver's knife. Then he grabbed its tail, slung a couple of turns of the shot rope about it, and signaled his tenders to haul away. They brought it up still alive and flapping.

Unfortunately, even the great Lambert was not indestructible. He was working on the *Alphonso XII*, a steamer that had sunk in twenty-nine fathoms of water off Point Gando on Grand Canary Island. With her had gone £100,000 worth of gold 25-peseta pieces bound for Cuba. Lambert had been hired, along with his partner Tester, for the recovery attempt.

Finding the treasure room below three decks and, like Erostrabe before him, feeling it impossible to work his way down the tortuous passages to it, Lambert determined to blast his way in. He did, using explosive tonite,[1] and finally pried up the trap door of the treasure room with a crowbar. A cable was lowered, and he got a rope around the first of the treasure chests to which he could fasten the cable hook. Up it went, with £10,000 worth of coins. On subsequent dives he managed to send up £60,000 more. His share was £3500, besides his £40 per month salary.

Tester had to recover the other £20,000 alone, however. On his last dive, Lambert had been paralyzed for life.

RECOVERING THE *ORINOCO*'S TREASURE

Sometimes, brains are more important than blasting in the recovery of treasure from a sunken vessel. One such case was the *Orinoco*, a 1500-ton steamer, two hundred feet long, which sank in twenty-one fathoms of water a few hours out of Puerto Bello, Venezuela. On a dark night in the late 1890s, she had collided with an abandoned derelict that was without lights. The *Orinoco* carried to the bottom something like a hundred tons of silver ingots.

The underwriter, a New York gentleman named Cook, paid off on the silver; and then, quite naturally, began casting about for a way of recovering the silver he had purchased. First he tried a local hard-hat diver from Puerto Bello. But that worthy, after working several weeks from a small boat, was able only to "pin-point" the wreck's location: it lay, he announced grandly, in a five-mile stretch of coastline and within one mile of shore.

Cook hired Captain Hiram Perkins, his two-masted schooner *Fleetwing*, and a pair of American divers named Jack Marvin and Ben Allen. He told them that the silver was in the aftermost of the *Orinoco*'s three holds, in a steel compartment that ran the width of the vessel against the engine-room bulkhead and down in the bilges. The compartment was locked and sealed on top.

In Puerto Bello, Perkins took aboard a patent metal-detector: a length of two-inch pipe with contact pieces here and there on its exterior. From its upper end ran an electrical wire that led up to a zinc plate, a meter with a bell, and some dry-cell batteries on the deck of the *Fleetwing*. If a contact piece touched metal, the bell was supposed to ring. Then the divers were to rush down and check whatever the detector indicated. For six fruitless days they swept the probable area of the wreck, with never a tinkle of their bell. Then, on the first run of the sixth day, the metal detector ...

Snagged.

Snagged on something unusually high off the bottom. Even though the bell hadn't rung, Perkins anchored fore and aft and took soundings. Eighteen fathoms. Close enough to twenty-one fathoms for him to send Jack Marvin down the metal-detector line for a look. The water was so clear that, standing on a deck listing 30 degrees to port, Marvin could read the sunken vessel's name: *Orinoco*. The metal-detector had detected, albeit in a way not envisioned by its designer.

Marvin returned to the *Fleetwing*, and Allen went down to fasten a heavy mooring line to the hulk's bow. While he was down, a sudden heavy storm blew up, ripping *Fleetwing* from her light mooring lines, dragging her weather anchor, so she swung away from the wreck and would have been driven off if Allen's newly fastened mooring had not held. The diver himself, however, was swung so wildly about that he ended up fouled in the cordage and wire shrouds of the *Orinoco*. Marvin went down his air line to free him, and then the *Fleetwing* ran for Puerto Bello.

When the weather cleared they returned, and the divers began ripping rotted tarpaulins off the after hatch covers. Next came the waterlogged wooden coamings themselves, ripped off with wire ropes let down by the *Fleetwing*'s deck winches.

Aha! Inside the after hold itself. But ...

But it was full of coffee. Tons of coffee beans, swollen with water and long since burst from their burlap bags.

Back to Puerto Bello. This time Perkins rented a large air compressor to work a creation of his own. This was a long, straight section of six-inch pipe, with a one-inch nozzle at the lower end operated by a control valve. On the upper end of the pipe was a 45-degree elbow, with a half-length of pipe attached to that. An air hose led from the compressor to the nozzle.

When the compressor started, the diver with the contraption opened the control valve. The air was pumped down the hose, then into and up the pipe, through the elbow, and out the half-length of pipe. This created a very strong suction at the nozzle—which thus sucked up coffee beans, water, bits of burlap, and squirted the whole lot over the side of the *Orinoco*.

The device took a month to clear the way down to the strong room. When they broke the seal, they found the room stacked with eight thousand silver bars weighing twenty-five pounds each. All they had to send them up in was an iron coal bucket. Somehow, in ten working days, they recovered sixty-six tons of silver, despite weather so rough that it often took half an hour just to get the bucket in place.

Once, the laden bucket began swinging so wildly in the crowded hold that it slammed Ben Allen up against the bulkhead. This partially crushed his helmet, but worse, it smashed in the glass facepiece. To keep his air from rushing out, Allen slapped a piece of burlap over the hole and held it there with one hand, while with the other he climbed on top of the specie locker. Between swings of the berserk bucket, he got to an iron bulkhead ladder, climbed to the deck, and gave the distress signal before he collapsed.

They hauled him up, pumped the water out of his lungs, and again headed for Puerto Bello. To the hospital? No. To rent the helmet of the local diver who had been unsuccessful in the first attempts at the treasure, so they could go back and finish the removal of the silver.

Another early deep-water salvage job on which human ingenuity was at least as important as equipment was the *Empress of Ireland* salvage attempt. The *Empress* was *en route* to Europe in May 29, 1914, when she was rammed by the Danish freighter *Storstad* just off the mouth of Canada's St. Lawrence River. She went down almost immediately, carrying to their deaths the staggering total of 1024 passengers and crewmen.

Her owner, the Canadian Pacific Steamship Company, hired a Canadian salvage firm to bring up the quarter million dollars she had carried, the mail she had been transporting to England, and most especially the bodies of the passengers. Though the ship was lying on her side in thirty fathoms of water, swept by the icy currents of the St. Lawrence tideway, the salvage work was quick and efficient. Up came the silver, the mail, and drowned passengers by the hundreds—many of them rendered unrecognizable by the feeding of voracious crabs. The great depth, the cold, and the terrific currents also took their toll of divers: dozens of cases of the bends were suffered, and one man was killed when he fell off the bow of the sunken steamer and was jammed up into his helmet in a classic squeeze.

THE *EMPRESS OF IRELAND*'S SAFE

With the last recoverable body on the way up, the salvors should have been able to leave. But a new problem had arisen. Relatives by the hundreds began filing claims—supported by legal documents and sworn affidavits—for jewels and monies that the dead passengers were supposed to have left in the purser's safe. These claims rose to such an alarming total that the insurance underwriters decided they had to recover the safe and bring it back to port—unopened, undamaged, and completely intact.

So their salvage master, a clever old gent named William Wallace Witherspoon, was told to bring his crew back. Witherspoon lived up to his title. With the ship on its side, and the purser's cabin on the bottom side, he knew he could not get the safe out of the cabin through the now-vertical superstructure hatches as he normally would have done. But on the uppermost side of the *Empress* was a side loading port. That was it.

Witherspoon's divers got into the purser's room without too much difficulty, but then the fun began. They had to get that huge, heavy safe off the bulkhead to which it was bolted. They had to do it in pitch blackness, in icy cold, and they had to do it without explosives—any damage sustained by it or its contents would negate the whole reason for the recovery.

Part of the group finally got it loose using heavy, clumsy wrenches, while others were smashing away all the furniture with crowbars and sledge hammers. A third crew of divers was blowing the cargo-port door off its hinges with a light dynamite charge.

Finally all was ready. A hawser was run down from the salvage ship, was snaked through the corridors to the purser's room, and was fastened to the safe. Inch by inch the monster was dragged out of the room by the salvage vessel's winches: up corridors, around right-angle turns, through doorways, always in cold and darkness, until it finally lay beneath the open port.

The divers rerigged it for hoisting, and, above, Witherspoon gave the order. The steam winches began chattering, and the safe was dragged free and began its perilous ascent. Just as it broke water, the line began slipping. As the safe swung free of the water, the sling was only inches from the top. It held. As the safe touched deck, waiting representatives of the Canadian Government swarmed over it, sealing it immediately. It was transferred, under heavy guard, to another vessel for removal to Montreal. There, under the eye of hundreds of claimants' legal representatives, it was opened.

The purser's safe contained money and gems worth less than 5 per cent of the amount claimed by the heirs and legatees.

Since the *Empress of Ireland* has reminded us of the venality of man, mention should be made of the *Tubantia* affair. It poses a riddle (even today) and presents an irony, and also shows how a simple salvage operation can become the focus of upheavals political, legal, and monetary.

THE RIDDLE OF THE *TUBANTIA*

The *Tubantia* was a Dutch liner, 14,400 tons displacement, that left Amsterdam for Buenos Aires in March 1916 carrying 360 passengers and crewmen and seven hundred tons of general cargo. At 2:00 A.M., only a few hours from Amsterdam, she was struck by a torpedo. Within three hours she had sunk some thirty miles from the Dutch coast and in twenty fathoms of water. No lives were lost.

Almost before the lifeboats were in the water, Germany was stridently (perhaps hopefully?) proclaiming that its U-boats had not been involved in the sinking of the neutral Dutch vessel; more than likely, the Kaiser's military minions sniffed, it had been the British. Perfidious Albion, to use Napoleon's colorful phrase, strenuously denied the charge. By odd circumstance, the problem was easily resolved. In exploding, the torpedo had scattered fragments in several of the lifeboats —boats that were then used to bring the passengers safely off the *Tubantia*.

The fragments definitely were from a German torpedo.

In apparently real surprise, the Germans suggested that it obviously had been one of their spare torpedoes that just happened to have been drifting around loose at the surface. And the careless *Tubantia* had run it down. Happened all the time.

Sorry, said the court of inquiry. Several crewmen already had testified to seeing the white wake of the torpedo as it streaked toward their ship.

Sorry, said a group of Duch divers who went down to examine the hulk. The *Tubantia* was holed right amidships—a difficult spot with which to hit a torpedo one is running down—and *six feet below the waterline.*

Sorry, said Germany in February 1922, when the vessel's owners put in a claim for compensation with the International Committee of Inquiry at The Hague. Sorry, and ouch. Germany had to pay £800,000 damages for the *Tubantia*'s sinking. She paid promptly, but with the air of someone who feels a terrible error has been made.

And then a curious thing happened. The ship had been down six years; her cargo of general merchandise (and possibly three hundred big Dutch cheeses) was obviously worthless by that time. Yet barely a month after the vessel's owners had received their compensation, in April 1922, and thus officially relinquished ownership of the *Tubantia*, a well-equipped salvage flotilla set out. It was run by three Frenchmen, the brothers Estier (Francois, Henri, and Adolphe), and an Englishman named Sippe.

Their vessel, the *Tempête*, located the *Tubantia* in May and was positioned over her until driven off by the November storms. With the good weather of April 1923 they returned and once more began blasting a hole fourteen by ten feet in the No. 4 hold—which had held only the three hundred Dutch cheeses. They worked steadily on the 541-foot, side-lying vessel until July 9, despite heavy tides, fogs, and formidable seas.

On July 9 a second curious thing happened. Another salvage vessel, the *Semper Paratus*, arrived on the scene; descended, vulture-like, might be a better image. The Italian brothers in charge, Count Charles and Lieutenant James Landi, made one of the most flagrant attempts at claim jumping in the history of ocean salvage. They dropped anchor right beside the *Tempête*; they began sweeping operations over the wreck; they sent high-speed cutters dashing about through the Estiers' buoys, dragging a grapnel to foul their moorings and cut their lines; and they did all this while divers from the French ship were down, terribly endangering the lives of the men on the botton.

Finally, they sent their own divers down the *Tempête*'s shot lines and right into that weirdly enticing No. 4 hold. This was too much. Off steamed the *Tempête*, direct to admiralty court for an injunction against the Italians. With enforcement of the court order, the *Semper Paratus* departed forever.

Unfortunately, Sippe and his French confreres had spent all of their money—£40,000, to be exact. They also packed it in. For eight more years the *Tubantia* rusted away, her three hundred Dutch cheeses presumably losing value with each passing year.

But then in 1931 the third curious thing happened. A British salvage vessel from Sunderland, the *Reclaimer*, turned up over that touchingly irresistible Dutch liner. The object of their affections? The *Tubantia*'s No. 4 hold. The Britons, perhaps undercapitalized in that depression year, lasted only one season. And when they returned, they sent a wire to some unnamed backers that somehow became public and that at first glance seemed to clear up the mystery of the *Tubantia*'s fatal allure.

FAILED TO FIND BULLION IN THE WRECK OF THE DUTCH LINER TUBANTIA.

Of course. Gold! Gold always could explain everything.

But wait a minute. What gold? There is absolutely no official record anywhere that the *Tubantia* was carrying gold. Her owners obviously knew nothing of it, nor did her crew.

Rumor, however, supplies a possible answer (rumor that the three well-equipped salvage expeditions suggest might have some factual foundation). Aboard the *Tubantia*, it was whispered, had been £2 million in smuggled gold. Smuggled how? Smuggled where?

In the No. 4 hold. Packed into three hundred round Dutch cheeses.

That leaves the most intriguing question of all: *whose* gold? Some government's, obviously, since few individuals in that day—or this— would have that sort of bullion available.

Which government?

Which government insisted stridently, almost desperately, that it had not been involved in the sinking? Which government came up with alternate ideas, as if trying to convince *herself* that she could not have made such a monumental error? Which government had strong friends in Argentina, friends who needed a great deal of gold to capitalize their organized attempts to keep the United States from entering the war on behalf of Britain?

And therein lies the irony. If there ever was any gold, it was German gold. Lost by the action of a German submarine. Not only did they lose their bullion, they had to pay £800,000 for the privilege!

There is no doubt which government owned the greatest cache of gold ever to be lost in an ocean sinking; nor is there any doubt of the existence of the gold, either. It was aboard HMS *Laurentic*, forty-three *tons* of it, worth at that time £5 million. The attempts to salvage it were the work of one man: Commander Guybon C. C. Damant, the same Damant who, in 1906, had set the world's diving record of 210 feet.

FORTY-THREE TONS OF GOLD

The *Laurentic* was a converted White Star liner, a 15,000-ton vessel fast enough to outrun submarines, that had been converted into an armed naval cruiser. In January 1917 she was carrying 3211 gold ingots from Liverpool to Halifax, Nova Scotia, to pay for the wheat, cotton, steel, and powder that Britain needed for the war against the Kaiser. She took the route around Northern Ireland to avoid German U-boats along the usual shipping routes. And the ploy worked: the *Laurentic* was not spotted by any German submarine.

Instead, she struck a mine one of them had laid off the mouth of Lough Swilly. This was just out of the Irish Sea into the fortunately shallow Atlantic, and the *Laurentic* sank immediately, taking 354 of her 745-man complement with her. Whatever comfort Britain could take was in the comparative shallowness of the sea—twenty-two fathoms— because the gold had gone down with her and had to be recovered. Frenzied by the need of that bullion to bolster a faltering British pound against devaluation, the Admiralty ordered Damant to begin salvage operations immediately, despite the fact that it was wartime and winter.

Damant was no stranger to either peril or improvisation in dealing with underwater problems. In 1907, when in charge of divers trying to recover *Torpedo Boat* 99 from 150 feet of water in the English Channel, off Torquay, he had improvised desperately trying to save the life of one of his divers. Walter Trapnell had gotten both life line and air hose snagged on the wreck and could not get back to the surface. Another diver, Sydney Leverett, tried to help him; but he did not have enough air hose to even get down to the trapped man.

There was no more air hose aboard Damant's "diving boat," and they did not even have a rowboat to send ashore. There was, however, spare hose on the archaic hand pump supplying air to Trapnell. Damant stripped it off, spliced it into Leverett's hose, and then tapped *both* divers into one pump. The tenders worked madly to keep enough air flowing down for both men, while Leverett feverishly tried to free his trapped partner.

He finally did, but Trapnell, after nearly six hours at that depth in the icy water, died anyway. Damant's improvisation, however, had worked brilliantly. He had been twenty-six years old at the time.

It was this man who now arrived at the *Laurentic* site in a converted mooring lighter, the *Volunteer*, under orders to treat the assignment as a military exercise rather than a salvage operation. He found the vessel on her port bilge at a 60-degree angle, with her decks a mere sixty feet below the surface. This actually was unfortunate, because the unsheltered site of the wreck was exposed not only to the full sweep of any northern or western gale, but also to the high waves raised by the southerlies. Divers on the deck of the *Laurentic* were swept ruthlessly about by the great horizontal surges of the surface waves. The huge blocks at the end of the lifeboat falls were swinging free from their davits, such a danger to the divers that they had to be cut loose one by one before entrance to the ship could be attempted.

Added to all this and to the terrific tides and currents was the constant menace of German submarines. One of the divers was down on the wreck for just a few moments when he was jerked right off the ship by a tremendous pull on his lines. In a few moments he was being dragged through the water exactly like a hooked fish on the end of a line.

Before passing out, he was able to close down his outlet valve enough so that his suit filled with air and he planed up to the surface. Just as he arrived there, he was jerked bodily from the water, again like a hooked fish, was swung through the air, and crashed down with a great clank on the ship's deck.

A submarine had been moving in on the salvors when a crewman had spotted the periscope. Damant, fearful of risking all his men by pausing to bring up the diver, had cut the heavy ground tackle that moored him to the wreck, and run for it. As they had run, they had brought in the diver, dragging him through the water, reeling him in like a hooked fish.

They returned to the *Laurentic*, and found the entry port by which the gold originally had been loaded. They blew out the door with a charge of guncotton, but found their way still blocked by a heavy, latticed, iron gate. That was blown away also, and the heavy packing crates filling the port were shifted. Not all of them had to be, however: many casks and cases were buoyant enough from air trapped inside to come rumbling up out of the passageway with such verve that they sent the divers scrambling.

On the fourteenth day of diving, E. C. Miller got down to the strong room and smashed open its steel door with a sledge and chisel. He sank right down into the room and fetched up against the stacks of bullion boxes, each a foot square and six inches deep, each weighing 140 pounds.

It looked at that point like a salvage operation removed from conventionality only by the huge mass of gold involved: the strong room was intact, after all, and the gold accessible. Despite the fact that his bottom time was over, Miller manhandled one of the heavy boxes up the corridors to the entry port and out onto the deck, where it could be picked up by a line from above. During his sixty-minute dive the next day, he got three more boxes. Wonderful. In those two days, they recovered £32,000.

Then came the tremendous midwinter gales and snow squalls. The salvors had to run for shelter from a northerly gale that blew for a solid week. When Damant returned, still working against the clock, he found that his conventional operation suddenly had turned into a nightmare. The entry port, which had been sixty-two feet below the surface, suddenly was 103! Under the battering of the storm, the *Laurentic* had folded up like an accordion. Damant himself went down to seek out the passageway up which Miller had brought the gold; but he found it squeezed down to a mere eighteen inches between buckled steel plates.

Nothing for it but successive small charges of guncotton to gradually force those crumpled sheets of steel apart so the strong room could be reached again. But when Miller, after weeks of work, entered the strong room, joy was short-lived. He dropped right across the room to the opposite wall—which now was right down at the bottom, 120 feet deep. Worse, the room was completely empty! Miller examined it inch by inch, by touch alone, in the blackness of the ship's interior. The plating had given way with the twisting of the ship, had torn open, and had spilled the gold into the enormous, frightful tangle of wreckage in the *Laurentic*'s port bilge.

INCREDIBLE SALVAGE TASK: THE *LAURENTIC*

Now what? Damant decided he had only one way to go: he had to cut his way down vertically, plate by plate, beam by beam, from a point on the upper deck that they would estimate as being above the gold's new resting place. And such a cut could only be done by explosives, because between the salvors and the gold lay *three hundred tons* of crumpled, twisted steel!

They ran into trouble immediately. Since the steel plates were lying free in the water, with no strain upon them, they did not break with the explosions. Instead, they merely vibrated, flapped up and down in the water like flags in the wind. This meant a line had to be run down from the salvage ship's boom and clamped to the free edge; tension then could be given to the plate by winching down a bit. With the plate now strained hard out, a diver would crawl in under it to place a charge of guncotton at the hinge—the place where it was held by other wreckage.

A diver named Blachford was down in this position when a flawed shackle parted. The plate promptly dropped on his back.

His tenders did not know what was wrong, but Blachford suddenly called over the telephone, "Give me all the air you can!"

They did. This lessened the terrible weight pressing down on his body, but introduced a new factor: how much air could the suit take without exploding? Though Damant did not know what was wrong, he finally had the flow of air lessened despite Blachford's pleas. It would do no good to kill the man by exploding his suit.

Meanwhile, a diver named Clear already was on his way down, tracing the trapped man by his ascending air bubbles. He had a spare wire sling held by a marlin lanyard to his wrist, so he put the wire bridle over the plate's free end, clamped it down, and gave the order to haul away. The plate rose, but so did Balchford, free, but suddenly in danger from the blow-up, which had him spread-eagled helplessly. Clear bled the excess air from the suit for him, and Blachford was safe, unharmed by his ordeal.

After two months of diving made extremely hazardous by the underwater shocks from German mines being exploded by British mine sweepers in the vicinity, they began finding the occasional loose ingot again. When September weather forced a halt for the year, they had returned £800,000 worth of gold to the British Treasury.

Meanwhile, in April, the United States had entered the war. England's fears of devaluation had vanished, and with them the crushing urgency for the *Laurentic*'s gold. The Admiralty ordered operations halted for the duration of the war. In the spring of 1919, Damant returned in the new salvage vessel *Racer*, to find their work area threatened by the immense superstructures that in a happier time had carried the

Laurentic's first- and second-class cabins. The salvors' burrowing had undermined these great structures, which now were inclining toward one another from either side of the hole gaping between them.

Work went forward, however, and soon another £470,000 worth of ingots had been recovered—when suddenly the source dried up. There seemed to be no more, even though £3.7 million still was somewhere in the wreck. Then Damant realized that the bulk of the bullion had gone, not out through the ruptured bulkhead as they had believed, but through the strong-room floor instead—to bury itself somewhere in the vast jumble of the ship's hold.

Then came the winter of 1920, another year of disaster for his plans. That season's storms neatly dropped the two massive superstructures into their work area in the center of the ship, filling it with a tremendous amount of trash, rubbish, and twisted metal. Even worse, the storms had deposited great loads of sand, stone, and gravel in the hole, and this formed a nearly cement-hard conglomerate with iron bedsteads running through it to serve as reinforcing rods.

So for two years, 1920 and 1921, their labors were restricted to efforts at clearing their worksite. Explosives were of no use; nor were suction pumps any good: the conglomerate was too hard to be sucked away. Grabs were tried, then clamshell dredging buckets. Worthless. All of them worthless.

SAND MORE VALUABLE THAN GOLD

Finally Damant hit upon high-pressure water hoses to break up the mass, which then was hand-packed into bags by the divers and carted off. Meanwhile, storms, tides, and currents kept steadily washing new sand and gravel back into the vessel.

Occasional ingots of gold helped spur the men on, and Damant managed to involve them in a competition: how much sand could a man dig out in a thirty-minute dive under standard conditions? Scores were kept, and the work went forward keenly.

"Human nature being what it is," said Damant, "there was a tendency for some men to spend their whole half hour in poking about for odd bars. It is odd to find oneself cursing X for bringing up untold gold and blessing Y for producing a sack of dirty sand and stones."

Bless he did, however, and in the spring of 1922 his men returned to find that the sea could give as well as take away. All over the work area, gold ingots were sticking up from a sand swept clean by winter storms. On the first day, nineteen ingots were recovered. Another time it was ninety of them, nestled in the wreckage of the boxes that once had held them. Between April and August they recovered a staggering £1.5 million worth; and a tenth of that was found in one incredible day.

Such caches did not come easily, however; they had to be uncovered by the expedient of uncovering the *Laurentic*'s steel shell, compartment by compartment, and then each ingot had to be dug out by hand. This meant working upside down in narrow places, for the ship's plating had been pushed into giant ripples and wrinkles—with the heavy ingots lying, of course, at the lowest point in the crease of the ripple. Blow-ups were a constant danger, for the diver's air gradually would work up to his feet, making them lighter than his helmet despite their iron boots.

One diver, Light, stayed too long in a head-down position and found himself suddenly, upside down, bobbing forty feet from the bottom like a balloon on a string. He had popped out of the crease in a blow-up; but, because he had tied off his air line to a piece of wreckage before starting work, he had gone up only to the end of his forty-foot slack.

Blachford went to his aid, but unfortunately Damant told him to cut the lanyard holding the air line to the wreckage before climbing up Light's life line to turn the man right side up. As soon as the lanyard was cut, Light shot for the surface again, his excessive buoyancy dragging Blachford with him. They both were rescued and immediately recompressed, Light in the chamber and Blachford by being sent down again. Neither was injured.

By October they had dug 895 ingots from the crumpled plates of the *Laurentic*'s hull. Some of the bars had been twisted into a "U"; others had been squeezed out like toothpaste or had rivetheads or pebbles buried deeply in them. The divers had become so proficient at digging that their fingers could distinguish by touch alone among gold, a rock, a chunk of brass, or a shard of porcelain ware. Even experienced divers joining the crew took about six months to develop this uncanny ability to "feel" gold.

In 1923 another £2 million was raised, leaving only 154 of the original 3211 ingots—worth £240,000—still unfound. The entire inner shell of the *Laurentic*, however, had been exposed and searched. Where was the missing bullion? Obviously, it had slipped away through rents in the hull of the ship. Nothing for it but to keep on looking.

In 1924, Damant calmly sent down a string of explosive charges, with which he cut up a two thousand-square-foot area of the *Laurentic*'s final layer, exposing the bare sand beneath. And another 129 ingots. That season ended the diving operations, with a record of recovery unequaled in the history of ocean salvage.

Of 3211 ingots lost in 1917 with the *Laurentic*, only 25 were still missing. Damant's crew had made a 99.2 per cent recovery at a cost of only 2.5 per cent of total value recovered. Under the worst possible conditions for diving, a large ocean liner had been cut literally to pieces from top to bottom in over five thousand salvage dives, made without loss of life or even serious injury. The ship's company got a bonus of two shillings sixpence for every £100 recovered, but individual divers received nothing beyond the general bonus no matter what exceptional finds they might have made.

Except for one man. He sent up, single-handed, £45,000 worth of ingots in a single day. For him there was a very special reward indeed.

The ship's company voted to give him a carton of cigarettes!

---

[1] An explosive consisting of guncotton and a nitrate or a nitro compound.

CHAPTER FIVE

The Iron Duke

As early as 1715, nearly fifty years before Freminet's *machine hydrostatergatique*, with its "water-cooled" pipes to regenerate the air, an Englishman named John Lethbridge had made primitive attempts to overcome pressure with the invention of the first armored diving suit. These rigid or semi-rigid suits are supposed to be strong enough by their structure alone to shield the wearer from water pressure, allowing the diver to breathe air at atmospheric pressure and avoid tedious decompression.

EARLY ARMORED DIVING SUITS

Lethbridge's design was not successful, of course. For one thing, his "shell" of wainscot (six feet high, two and one half feet in diameter at the head and eighteen inches at the feet) left the arms uncovered. And air was to be fed into it from a surface bellows that obviously was not powerful enough to get air down to any depth at all. Finally, the diver was virtually immobilized, hanging face down in his not-very-waterproof barrel.

Perhaps it was about one of Lethbridge's creations that a quite intelligent student of the diving suit, Desaguliers, was speaking in 1728 when he described a test he had seen. Since the diver's arms and legs were exposed, he pointed out, his circulation would be stopped. As for the test itself . . .

"These Armor-Machines are quite useless. The Diver, having bled at the Nose, Mouth, and Eyes, died soon after the Trial."

Yes, I suppose he did.

While rubber-suit design was stumbling out of its morass of ignorance to eventual success in 1839 with Siebe's close-suit design, the armored-suit boys took a bit longer to come up with a workable model—almost a hundred years, in fact—even though an English gent named W. H. Taylor came up with the first articulated armored suit a year before Siebe's success. Unfortunately, the "workable" joints had nothing over them to keep out pressure except a layer of canvas, and he made the old mistake of leaving the diver's hands and feet uncovered. Since the poor man was to be breathing atmospheric air during the dive, he would have come up from any appreciable depth with only stumps for extremities.

In 1856, an American, L. D. Philips, oddly anticipated the features of the few successful armored-suit designs there have been—all in the twentieth century. It was all there: hands and feet covered, work done by metal nippers operated by the diver through a waterproof stuffing box, and ball-and-socket joints—an excellent answer to the problems of pressure. Unfortunately, there was a good deal else besides. The diver was supposed to propel his very weighty self about by a pitiful little hand-turned screw propeller in front of his navel, and his buoyancy was to be provided by a basketball-sized balloon in a net atop his helmet. It would not have provided enough lift for the naked diver himself, let alone the several hundred pounds of tin in which he was to be encased.

Armored-suit patents had reached blizzard proportions by the 1890s, none of them in the smallest degree workable, because their inventors, to a man, were abysmally ignorant of even the knowledge then currently available concerning actual undersea conditions. By 1904, an Italian named Restucci, however, had come up with an idea that, while terribly complicated, was scientifically sound. He proposed to supply atmospheric air to the suit and the diver, with air under high compression for the joints. Unfortunately, this very intriguing design was never built.

In 1912, what surely must be the most *appealing* of armored suits was proposed by two Italians, Leone Durand and Melchiorre Bembina. The suit was fitted with four spherical wheels (made out of oak) so it could be towed along the bottom. Thus, inspired by Henry Ford, the diver could be trundled along with his nose in the mud (as in Lethbridge's design, he rode face down), his chassis actually provided with headlights and a steering wheel of sorts. Bravely equipped, apparently, with everything but bucket seats and four on the floor, our intrepid salvor could roll down whatever underseas highways he might be fortunate enough to find.

The suit was never constructed.

DAVIS OBSERVATION CHAMBER

That same year, however, 1912, Robert H. Davis patented his Davis Observation Chamber. The armored-suit boys didn't know it yet, but the redoubtable Davis actually had made them obsolete before they even came up with a workable design. The armored suit—usually called the iron duke or iron man—should, after all, fulfill two theoretical functions.

First, it should contain air at atmospheric pressure but be able by design strength alone to resist great pressures. And second, it should allow the wearer to move about and work rather freely, no matter what the depth.

The Davis Observation Chamber fulfilled the first requirement magnificently. It was just a mummy-case-like steel cylinder with five glass observation eyes around the somewhat bulbous head. The diver could stand (or half-sit on a small stool) in relative comfort. He breathed atmospheric air and could converse with surface tenders through his telephone. In case of trouble, he had several hours' air supply in bottles, as well as a rebreather with a CO_2 absorbent to stretch his air.

No iron duke ever has fulfilled the first function any better than the observation chamber, and no iron duke has ever fulfilled the second function at all.

The firm of Neufeldt and Kuhnke of Kiel, however, made the first commercially usable iron duke in 1923. It was a large metal shell in two sections that were bolted together at the waist. The air supply was self-contained in cylinders that the diver operated himself, and he had room inside to remove his arms from the articulated metal claws with which he actually did outside work. There was sufficient air for six hours, and the suit was tested down to five hundred feet. The joints were ball-and-socket, with ball bearings and strip rubber waterproofing. Around the suit was a ballast tank for positive or negative buoyancy.

It weighed 850 pounds.

It is ironical that the salvage operation that made the Neufeldt and Kuhnke iron duke famous also made painfully obvious that the observation chamber did the suit's job as well or better. This was on the salvage of the SS *Egypt*, a P & O Line steamship of 7941 gross tons displacement, which was en route from London to Bombay under command of Andrew Collyer.

On May 20, 1922, in dense fog off the Armen lighthouse, Finistère, France, she was rammed on the portside by the French freighter *Seine*. The *Seine*, though only of 1383 gross tons displacement, had been built for ice breaking and had sharply pointed, reinforced bows, which sliced the *Egypt* so thoroughly that the P & O ship went down within twenty minutes. Eighty-six of the 335 passengers and crewmen aboard drowned. She came to rest in sixty-six fathoms of water—just short of the numbing depth of four hundred feet.

As she went down, the *Egypt* sent out a wireless message: SOS SOS SOS POSITION 48° 10′ N. 5° 30′ W. EGYPT.

That message was important, because aboard the *Egypt* were 1089 gold ingots, thirty-seven boxes of British gold sovereigns (three and one half tons, 164,979 pieces), and 1229 silver ingots—eight tons of gold in all and forty-three tons of silver. The whole was valued at and insured at Lloyd's of London for £1,058,879. The underwriters paid off within ten days—and in the process illustrated very well why Lloyd's carries such an unparalleled reputation for integrity. When they learned that some £20,000 worth of cargo inadvertently had been omitted from the insurance coverage, they paid off on that, too.

Despite the tremendous depth, the Salvage Association entered into a contract of salvage with two Englishmen: a consulting engineer named C. P. Sandberg and an electrical engineer named James Swinburne. They had a patented observation chamber, much like the Davis design—it eventually would be instrumental in the *Egypt* operation—and engineers' approaches to the problems they faced.

THE SEARCH FOR THE EGYPT

The first problem was nearly insuperable: where was the *Egypt*? In 1923 they hired a Swedish firm, Gothenburg Towage and Salvage Company, to find out. The company's Captain Hedback, in command of the *Fritjof*, spent an enervating season tramping the seas some twenty-five miles southwest of the island of Ushant. His peregrinations netted a new probable (in his eyes) site for the *Egypt*: 48°6′ N. Lat., 5°29′ W. Long. He dubbed it Hedback's Point and went home in disgust.

Sandberg and Swinburne next contracted with a French firm. They lasted two seasons before packing it in, with results even less positive than Hedback's. After spending 1925 and 1926 on the site, they hadn't even come up with any possible co-ordinates for the *Egypt*'s position.

Three times lucky, perhaps? In 1928, the two engineers made an arrangement of recovery with an Italian firm: the Society for Maritime

Recovery, which called itself SORIMA for short. It was formed, bankrolled, and directed by Commander Giovanni Quaglia, who brought to his task the highest qualifications a salvor can have: guts, determination, deep-water experience, a good salvage vessel (the *Artiglio*), three master divers (Alberto Gianni, Aristide Franceschi, and Alberto Bargellini), and a superb salvage crew.

Quaglia proposed to use a Neufeldt and Kuhnke iron duke on the *Egypt*—provided he could first find the ship. His deep-water experience with the iron duke was impressive. From one deep-lying wreck, the men of the *Artiglio* had raised 450 tons of copper and 250 tons of zinc; from another, off the Italian Riviera, seven hundred amphorae. The steamer *Washington*, sunk in Rapallo Bay at fifty-three fathoms by a German submarine during World War I, had given up some seven thousand tons of scrap metal and railroad equipment to his determined crew. Quaglia claimed to have used immense electromagnets for that job, magnets so powerful they could drag a locomotive boiler to the surface.

And in the first winter season after they had begun the search for the *Egypt*, SORIMA turned defeat on the *Elizabethville* to victory: They had lifted the captain's safe off the vessel, which lay in forty fathoms near Belle Isle, because it was supposed to be stuffed with diamonds. But it was stuffed only with papers. However, the salvors brought eight tons of Congo elephant tusks up from the ship and paid for their expenses.

This was the company now engaged on a no-cure, no-pay attempt to salvage the *Egypt*'s treasure. They began work in 1929, with a variety of sites to explore. First was that radioed by the *Egypt* on the night she had gone down. Then there was the different position espoused by the *Seine*, which had sunk her; there was Hedback's Point; there were the positions at which British torpedo boats had picked up mail sacks off the *Egypt*, and finally there was the position triangulated by the Ushant and Pointe du Raz radio stations. Both had picked up the *Egypt*'s transmissions that night. None of the positions agreed with any of the others.

Artiglio and her auxiliary, the *Rostro*, began at Hedback's Point. They buoyed off an area, six by ten miles, that included *all* the suggested positions, and then used Hedback's as a focal point. The ships worked abeam of each other as trawlers: off the stern they trailed a loop of steel wire cable somewhat over a mile long and weighted under each ship; thus it would drag along the ocean floor as the ships moved slowly forward on their parallel courses.

SORIMA's salvors began getting hard strikes immediately—too many of them; each had to be examined by a diver in an iron duke to eliminate it as a possibility. They quickly learned that the bottom was strewn at that point with rock pinnacles some thirty to forty feet high, on which the sweep wire continually snagged. The wire frequently frayed and often broke; by the time the bad weather drove them elsewhere, the frustrated salvors had tried everything, including an Italian friar with a divining rod and an electromagnet that was supposed to locate large subaqueous masses of metal but never did.

During the winter, as his men were aboard the *Elizabethville* finding ivory, Quaglia was working on a new sweep. This was weighted at each end of its mile length with four tons of lead, as the other had been; but at hundred-yard intervals it was supported by surface buoys. The eighteen evenly spaced buoys, he hoped, would hold the sweeping part of the cable some twenty-five feet above the bottom so it would only snag on something high—such as the top hamper of a steamer, for instance.

Near the end of August 1930, after a frustrating summer, Quaglia's new sweep snagged something less than a mile from Hedback's Point. On the twenty-ninth, Bargellini went down in an iron duke and found a ship lying essentially intact and on an even keel on the bottom, preserved by its depth from battering by the waves.

First step, identification. Not as easy as it sounds, in inky depths on a ship that, if the right one, already had been there for over eight years. They used explosives to blow free a three-ton crane from the wreck; it was the same type as one the *Egypt* was known to have carried, but that was not good enough for Quaglia. He therefore decided to retrieve the captain's safe from a small wooden cabin atop the superstructure. Grappling hooks were used to tear off the cabin roof, and a lobster-claw bucket, directed by a diver in an iron duke, reached inside to clutch the safe. Yes. It was the *Egypt*.

But that was the end of that year's work on the site: the weather had turned too nasty. They felt themselves lucky to get four days of consecutive time over the wreck even at the best of times; in the winter it was impossible.

LOSS OF THE *ARTIGLIO*

To help finance the *Egypt* venture, and to keep his crew busy and together during the winter, Quaglia contracted with the French Government to demolish several wrecks in shallower and more sheltered water. One of these was the American munitions ship *Florence*, which had been sunk off Quiberon by a German time bomb in 1917. Lying as she was off Belle Isle in only sixty feet of water, she presented a clear and present danger to navigation; the French wanted her cut down below the draft of even the largest vessels.

This meant blasting, a rather touchy operation since the ship had gone down carrying several hundred tons of munitions. True, they hadn't gone off when the time bomb had exploded, but still . . .

When their first two timid charges blew small holes in the side of the *Florence*, the *Artiglio* was a full two miles distant. A bit shamefaced, the men worked from October to December on the ship, bit by bit blowing it to pieces with charges getting larger and larger while the *Artiglio* strayed closer and closer.

Their final charge was laid on December 7, 1930, with the salvage vessel only a hundred yards away. When the explosives went off, so did those hundred of tons of munitions that had lain in waiting for thirteen years. A tremendous waterspout two hundred yards high came down on top of the *Artiglio* and sank it instantly: only seven of her nineteen crewmen survived; and among those drowned were the three master divers. In one instant, SORIMA's team of precision salvors were wiped out.

With bitter determination, Quaglia determined to rebuild it all—his ship, his crew, his diving team. The outfitting of his replacement vessel, *Artiglio II*, was done with such urgency that by May 1931 it was moored over the sunken *Egypt*, as its predecessor would have been. The new crew had been built around the nucleus of the old, and the only surviving diver, Raffaelli, now headed up a team of three newcomers.

Artiglio II was at that time the world's best-equipped deep-water salvage vessel, with heavy-duty cranes and a variety of grabs: parrot beaks, dredging types that could lift several tons, narrow grabs for getting into a narrow strong room, circular grabs (which closed like the fingers of clasped hands), and even ingenious vacuum grabs for inaccessible places.

Quaglia needed permanent mooring for his vessel now. He got it with six 5-ton concrete blocks laid in a circle six hundred yards in diameter around the *Egypt*. Secured to each anchor was a working buoy, to which the *Artiglio II* was moored with wire hawsers. Then he drilled his crew in the mooring procedure until they could do it in twenty minutes flat. In all but the wildest blows, the ship would let go all but the windward buoy, and would ride it out facing the waves and announcing its presence at three-minute intervals with its warning siren.

All the salvage ship's mechanical grab equipment and heavy-duty cranes were needed, because the bullion room was three decks down, and divers in their cumbersome iron dukes could not hope to reach it through the passageways and down flights of stairs. And the dukes were too big to be dropped down the *Egypt*'s narrow loading shaft.

This left blasting: blowing the ship away piecemeal and plucking away the pieces with the cranes until they were right down to the plating over the 28 by 4½ by 8 foot strong room, which ran athwartship for half the *Egypt*'s width. Into this mighty hole in the superstructure and steel hull, as it grew, would be lowered a diver in an iron duke to direct the placing of the charges by the unseeing men four hundred feet above, and to direct the lowering of the various grabs and lifts that would be expected to remove the debris, steel plates, and wreckage of the successive small blasts.

Master diver Raffaelli was most often down; soon, realizing that the iron duke could be used only as an observation chamber, nothing more, he abandoned it in favor of the Sandberg and Swinburne steel shell. It made an ideal observation post for directing the activities of the men overhead, exactly as an artillery observer directs the gunners in the placement of their shells.

The "shells" that Raffaelli was directing were explosive charges in tubes (eight feet long, four inches in diameter) that were attached to spars that, up on the *Artiglio II*, had been fastened together into frames the exact size and shape of the piece of steel deck plating to be blown away. At one end of each tube was an opening for a detonator that would be fired from the salvage ship. Sometimes the proper laying of a frame might take as long as four hours. When it was correctly positioned, Raffaelli would order it lowered away, then would himself be hoisted up to deck. The firing circuit would be completed, the switch closed, and the charge fired.

All this immense care had to be taken because they had to keep from excessively jarring the hulk of the *Egypt*. With fifty tons of bullion resting on the floor of the strong room, there was a very real danger of dropping it right through the steel plates supporting it and into the hold, from which it might never be recovered.

Once the charge had been detonated, the diver in his chamber would be lowered again to direct the giant grab in its task of lifting away the ruptured plates with its sharp steel jaws. If a plate was still attached, they would winch down to bring the weight of the *Artiglio II* against it until it tore loose; then they would drop it over the side of the *Egypt* and go on.

By the end of August 1931, the hole in the *Egypt* was big enough to drop a tract home through. By the end of September, the boat deck, promenade deck, and upper deck had been torn out for a hundred feet: the hole was fifty-five feet wide and thirty-three feet deep. After each blast, cabin furniture, bedding, and cabin fittings would rain into the work area, and each bit had to be laboriously lifted out by grabs. When the weather drove them away at the end of November, they had reached the main deck—but not the strong room under it. After three years, Quaglia had spent a half million dollars and had not salvaged a *sou*— and the whole maritime world was laughing. Everyone had said it was impossible to salvage anything from four hundred feet down.

Soon the laughter became louder. In May 1932, the *Artiglio II* returned with faster hoisting winches and a special grab, called the orange peel, which could enter a yard-wide opening, could be closed to scoop up whatever was beneath it, and then could be raised ten feet where, automatically, a second, larger, clam-shell grab would close completely around it to form a tight receptacle. So they wouldn't drop coins, said Quaglia.

While the scoffers enjoyed themselves, the salvors were setting their delicately measured explosive charges, for right under those main deck plates lay the bullion room, its bulkheads still intact even though bulged inward by their blasting.

THE *EGYPT*'S BULLION ROOM

Or was it the bullion room? The orange-peel grab worked superbly, but for days, and then weeks, all it brought up was detritus: cartridges, rifles, shotguns, miscellaneous baggage . . . Had they, by some hideous mistake, blasted their way down to the baggage room rather than the strong room? True, they had begun getting sodden bundles of five-, ten-, and hundred-*rupee* notes that the *Egypt* had been taking to Hyderabad; but these could not be called treasure: the whole issue had long since been replaced. Were the scoffers right, after all?

No. On June 22, 1932, they brought up—gold! Two sovereigns, worth ten dollars, would not help much to pay off Quaglia's massive debts, but still . . .

On the next lift, up came two gold ingots.

When the weather suspended operations temporarily just three days later, the *Artiglio II* crossed the channel to England with a staggering £80,000 worth of bullion. They landed in triumph at Plymouth—only to have their gold immediately confiscated by a British sheriff. The French salvage company that had not been able to even *find* the *Egypt* had not been idle after all: it had gotten out a secret writ of attachment against Quaglia, claiming prior salvage rights to the *Egypt* and claiming a share of the gold. When the suit came before an English magistrate on October 26, however, it was dismissed as "without merit," and the judge strongly intimated that "scavenger" was a better term than "salvor" for the Frenchmen's profession.

Meanwhile, *Artiglio II* had returned to the wreck. A new method had to be found for keeping the diver in his observation chamber within directing distance of the grabs, now that they were working in the bullion room itself. This was solved by shackling the observation shell directly to the grab's cable with a ten-foot wire; thus the diver went wherever the grab went.

When weather drove them off for the year on November 3, the storms had been so incessant that in five months they had been over the wreck only five times, for a total of 188 hours of diver bottom time. Yet they had recovered 865 of the 1089 gold ingots, 83,300 of the 164,979 gold coins, and six tons of the silver. The working seasons of 1933 and 1934 were spent in recovering most of the rest of the treasure.

To get the final gold coins from the nearly stripped treasure room, Quaglia brought in an ingenious vacuum grab. It was a cylinder-shaped tank with an opening in the bottom sealed by a glass sheath. From this sheath, inside the tank, ran a short, curved pipe. Once the grab was in position, the sheath would be broken by a surface-fired bayonet-striker (electric detonators are often used in such grabs today). Of course, as the glass broke, there would be a tremendous rush of water to fill the interior vacuum. It would rush up the pipe, carrying with it any coins in the vicinity—and would neatly drop them to the bottom of the tank outside the entrance pipe. The grab would be lifted and emptied, and a new glass diaphragm would be fitted.

The *Egypt* operation was halted in 1934, after six years and a million dollars. Indirectly, twelve lives had gone into it. SORIMA received 50 per cent of the treasure's current value, Sandberg and Swinburne got 12½ per cent, and the Lloyd's underwriters received 37½ per cent.

Robert H. Davis conducted tests (which were repeated by the British Admiralty after World War II) on the iron dukes that confirmed the experiences of the divers on the *Egypt*: observation chambers do the job much more cheaply, and just as well. While hard-hat divers can work in currents up to two knots, a duke is good for just one knot. And if enough weight is added to overcome the currents, the duke sinks to the bottom and mires hopelessly in the mud. And on a wreck there is great difficulty in maintaining position so the hand grips can be manipulated—the hand grips don't work well anyway, because the diver has no sense of touch. So today the iron duke is just a historical curiosity.

Before we abandon him to his place in history, however, we must touch upon the iron duke invented by three divers who shall remain mercifully anonymous. They were all *habitués* of a certain British waterfront pub, and in their public-house deliberations had decided that an effective armored suit could be made in the form and design of a lobster's armored shell. "Scientific testing" was done by carrying scores of tender baby lobsters down with them on deep dives—to see if the little fellows would collapse with the untoward pressure.

None of them did, so our heroes moved forward, actually constructing a copper submarine armor that reproduced faithfully the overlapping plates of a lobster's shell. One of them was "canned" in the copper suit and down he went to test it, while a breathless group of diving enthusiasts waited to cheer his success.

After just a few minutes of bottom time, however, his tender felt extreme agitation of the life line. There was no phone, so he quickly had the heavy, cumbersome suit winched up. But the moment the diver's helmet cleared the water they could hear him, even through the heavy metal, groaning, shouting, and screaming. The more they worked to get him aboard, the louder he yelled; his face, they could see through the glass eye in front, was contorted with agony.

With great solicitude they set him on the deck. But the moment he was clear of the lifting derrick, he seized up a handy boathook and with one enraged sweep knocked his unfortunate attendant right overboard. Nor was that all. As they tried to approach, he kept cursing and swinging, until someone crept up behind and lassoed him like a little dogie on the range, jerking his arms against his sides and immobilizing him. Only then could they finally unscrew his helmet and get his tale of woe.

Tale, indeed.

On the way down all had been serene and lovely; it had worked perfectly, in fact, until he arrived at the bottom and tested the suit's flexibility by *bending over*. As he straightened up again, a portion of the suit suddenly collapsed with the pressure. Two of the metal shells, shaped like the horny overlapping shells of a lobster's flexible tail, closed down on a portion of the diver's anatomy.

Also, alas, the tail.

Every movement he made, every cruel jerk on the line by the tender, caused a tighter, more agonizing grip. And lessening water pressure as he was brought up made the suit's weight hang more heavily upon him—and upon his trapped posterior. Small wonder he had attacked the unwittingly sadistic tender! Small wonder, also, that the lobster-shell armored suit has not taken its place in the arsenal of salvage weaponry.

The observation chamber, however, is of great use even in today's relentlessly advancing technology. In 1940, it figured prominently in the record-shattering attempts at salvage on the mail steamer *Niagara*. This 13,000-ton vessel was en route from South Africa to British Columbia when, on June 19, she struck a German mine some thirty miles from Whangarei Harbor, New Zealand. In little more than an hour, she had found bottom at seventy-three fathoms.

RECOVERING NIAGARA'S GOLD FROM SEVENTY-THREE FATHOMS

Aboard the *Niagara* was £2.5 million in sterling. On December 9, six months after the sinking, salvage operations were begun by J. P. Williams of Melbourne and James Herd of Brisbane. To the task they brought the *Claymore*, an old former coasting vessel newly equipped with Davis Observation Chamber, grabs, explosives, sweep wires, and other salvage equipment. Enemy mines were so numerous in the area that naval mine sweepers had to move ahead of the *Claymore* to clear a path for it.

The only available calculation of the *Niagara*'s location was a bearing taken by the third officer nine minutes before she struck; the salvors reviewed all possible data—the fact that she had floated nearly an hour and a half after the blast, under a strong wind and in a two-knot current—and established an area of prime possibility that covered some nine square miles. To aid in the sweep operations they had a launch, the *Waitemata*, which was carrying echo-sounding equipment.

Sweeping was done by the *Claymore* and a third vessel, the *Betsy*, with a 1¼-inch trawl wire that was kept down on the bottom by two otter boards angled fanwise from the sterns of the two vessels. Starting from a given point in the center of the search area, they moved out from it in spreading concentric circles at three knots, each sweep clearing a lane five hundred feet wide. Because the sea bottom was smooth and sandy, without mounds, gullies, or rock outcroppings, the rather primitive sonar equipment aboard the *Waitemata* was of considerable use.

As seems necessary for salvage operations, the weather was foul; so foul, indeed, that the motor launch *Rosie* was smashed against the stern of the *Claymore* and sunk. Often, the fleet had to run for shelter in Whangarei Harbor. The greatest dangers, however, came from the enemy mines—known as "sea eggs" to salvors—which had been strewn with a prodigal hand in the shipping lanes by the only Nazi raider in the entire Pacific, the *Orion*.

On one occasion, chief diver J. Johnstone had been down in an observation chamber on an experimental descent. When he returned to the *Claymore*, they raised their anchors to continue their sweeping operations. One anchor, however, brought up first a mass of sea growth and then . . . a mine. Two of the mine's five deadly lead horns (breaking off any of the horns releases the acid that detonates this type of mine) were fouled in the anchor chain.

The *Claymore* hove to with the mine lying so close that it was scraping agonizingly against the steel plates of the hull. Williams lowered the anchor away again, ever so gently, and then sent a hard-hat diver down to buoy the mine off on one of the vessel's permanent moorings. Once that was done, the ship slipped her cable so as to stand away for a mine sweeper. When it arrived, Williams removed everyone from the *Claymore* except himself, diver Johnstone, and the diver's attendants.

Johnstone went down the anchor chain again and shackled a light sweep wire to the mine. Then he freed it from the chain. It popped up toward the surface until stopped by the sweep wire a bare two feet below the *Claymore*'s keel. In the process, Johnstone's life line had gotten twisted *around the horns of the mine;* he was dragged to the surface with it and found himself desperately hanging on two of the horns, between the mine and the ship with his helmet grinding against the *Claymore*'s hull.

Williams, meanwhile, unaware of Johnstone's plight, had sent word to the mine sweeper to winch in the light wire that Johnstone had attached; the idea being, of course, to drag the mine away from the *Claymore*. The wire parted, however, and the mine—still carrying Johnstone—swirled back almost against the salvage vessel again. In all, it took Johnstone another seven hours to free himself and get back aboard while Williams maneuvered the ship away from the mine so they could sink it with machine-gun fire.

After nine more weeks of tedious sweeping operations, a large object fouled the sweep wire on February 2, 1941. Johnstone went down in the Davis Observation Chamber for a look, finding bottom at 432 feet. He swept over the object, saw a ship's davits, then a porthole, finally the vessel's side. It was the *Niagara*. His news was met with excitement topside.

"To celebrate the successful conclusion of the first phase of the treasure hunt," he remarked later, "the cook was promoted to 'chef,' and each member of the crew had two eggs for his tea."

High carouse, indeed.

The *Niagara* lay at a 70-degree angle, making the task of blasting down through debris and several decks to the strong room a delicate and difficult task. As with the *Egypt*, an overly heavy charge might have blown the gold right out of the strong room and into some inaccessible corner of the wreck. Blasting, directed by Johnstone from his observation shell, commenced on April 21; the first blast sent up pieces of the deckhouse and a wounded shark. The second ruptured the fuel tanks. This was frustrating, as it ruined visibility over the wreck for days with a thick blanket of oil. Despite this setback, however, the hole in the ship's side was forty feet by twenty feet within a month, and on June 1 a diver in a shell—as the observation chambers are often called—entered the wreck for the first time.

It was not until October that they reached the door of the bullion room itself. The chamber was tiny, 9½ feet by 6½ by 8, and the door somehow had to be removed without disturbing the treasure room or the gold inside it. The charge was laid with such accuracy and care, however, that when detonated it merely blew the door off its hinges—so gently that it stood for a moment before falling softly backward into the strong room.

On October 13 the first box of gold was brought out in the ragged jaws of the grab: it contained two bars worth £8000 each. The work soon became so standardized that the grab could make a round trip, coming up with gold—or, if they were unlucky, debris—every twenty minutes. During a nine-hour period on November 11, for instance, the grab made twenty-eight lifts, with forty-five boxes worth £350,000. On the twenty-second, over a hundred boxes were recovered.

The operation lasted a bit over a year, recovering all but £55,000 worth of the treasure that had foundered with the *Niagara*. Rumors suggest that this remaining sum was later recovered by the shadowy, tight-lipped, fascinating salvor Risdon Beazley, of England, but no official word has ever been released. In any event, the depth of 432 feet set a record for recovery from the ocean floor.

It was a record, however, that would not long stand.

CHAPTER SIX

Fifty Fathoms and Beyond

While the armored diving suit was being developed (and was being rendered obsolete by the parallel development of the submersible observation chamber), much more pertinent experimentation was going on in the refinement of hard-hat diving. Remarkably little of this work was directed at the suit itself: this has remained, in all essentials, the same outfit that Siebe invented in 1837. The overriding concern has instead been what the diver can breathe when he gets down where compressed air no longer serves. It is not an easy problem, for this sort of diving adds new dangers to the diver's completely adequate array of bends, blow-ups, and squeezes.

PROBLEMS OF COMPRESSED AIR

Paul Bert, the French physiologist of the 1870s, not only isolated nitrogen as the cause of the bends; his experiments with pure oxygen gave Robert H. Davis the idea of using this gas to wash excess nitrogen from the blood for shorter decompression times. It was Bert, also, who found that oxygen under high pressure is poisonous to man, even though uncompressed oxygen can be breathed for prolonged periods without harmful effect.

"Pressure," Bert said, "acts on living beings not as a direct physical agent, but as a chemical agent changing the proportions of oxygen contained in the blood, and causing asphyxia when there is not enough of it, or toxic symptoms where there is too much."

As early as 1928, when Davis began experimenting with his new Submersible Decompression Chamber, it had become apparent that compressed air was unsatisfactory for deep diving. J. S. Haldane's rule that pressure could be safely halved during ascent was found non-operable at depths beyond fifty fathoms (ten atmospheres of pressure). The oxygen built up in the blood stream, slowed circulation, and thus retarded the discharge of nitrogen and other gases from the lungs and circulatory system. This meant that decompression times for that depth and beyond were so long that the danger of oxygen poisoning appeared.

Another problem at pressures greater than ten atmospheres is carbon dioxide; 1 per cent of this gas in the blood stream at ten atmospheres equals ten per cent at the surface. Though CO_2 is the natural stimulant that causes breathing, it can easily build up to dangerous concentrations under pressure, since the diver constantly produces it himself by the sugar oxidation necessary to maintain body heat.

It was in hopes of minimizing these effects while allowing divers to go deeper and stay longer that Davis invented his Submersible Decompression Chamber (SDC). The SDC was a steel cylinder lowered to sixty feet with a diver and a tender inside, and pressurized for the depth at which the diver would be working. He could leave and enter the chamber through the open bottom (air pressure, of course, would keep the water out), have his helmet removed by the tender following his dive, and could be given pure oxygen to speed his decompression. The whole chamber could be slung aboard the vessel as soon as he entered it, thus eliminating long decompression stops under water.

Even the SDC, however, could not overcome the drawbacks inherent in compressed air; yet pure oxygen, while negating the possibility of the bends, could not safely be used at pressures above one atmosphere—a mere thirty-three feet of water.

Some new mixture obviously had to be found.

Oddly enough, it was astronomers who allowed divers to break through the three-hundred-foot diving limit set by compressed air. While observing an eclipse of the sun through a spectroscope in the 1800s, Frenchman Jules Janssen isolated sodium yellow bands. Joseph Norman Lockyer, an amateur stargazer in Britain, subsequently began trying to identify the yellow bands as hydrogen.

They weren't. They were something else, he found; something new and unknown: helium. Like hydrogen, helium occurs as only 1/250,000 of the weight of gases constituting sea-level atmosphere. But because they are the lightest gases known, helium and hydrogen *are* the atmosphere at altitudes above five hundred miles.

OXY-HELIUM DIVING

It was an American scientist and associate of Thomas A. Edison, Elihu Thomson, who isolated those properties of helium that make it desirable as a mixer for divers' oxygen: It is chemically inert, has a density only one-seventh that of nitrogen, and is virtually isoluble. Nor is it nearly as volatile as hydrogen, which requires such careful handling to avoid a murderous explosion.

There was just one little drawback. Helium was so rare that it cost $2500 per cubic foot. Then hugh quantities of it were discovered in a natural-gas well in Texas, and the price fell sharply.

Work in helium-oxygen mixtures was begun in 1924, using animals as subjects, at the Mines Experiment Station in Pittsburgh, Pennsylvania. By 1927, work was begun on human subjects by the newly established Navy Experimental Diving Unit (EDU) in Washington, D.C. Their facility at the Washington Navy Yard had what was at that time the world's most advanced hyperbaric test facility. During the 1930s, laborious tests were conducted to work out relative proportions of the gases for various depths, to develop helium-oxygen diving equipment, and to establish accurate decompression tables.

The problems were many. First, a great deal of helium and oxygen were needed, since a seventy-five-cubic-foot cylinder of the mixture would be used by the diver every two minutes. This meant that a recirculating rebreather had to be developed, so that the helium would be reused; this required that the carbon dioxide in the diver's exhalations be filtered out through an absorbent in a canister at the back of his helmet. Solving this problem meant that a seventy-five-cubic-foot cylinder would furnish enough mix for over two hours instead of two minutes.

Second, the mixture had to be absolutely correct. If the diver got too much helium, his decompression period would be dangerously long. Too much oxygen, on the other hand, would induce nervous symptoms, nausea, dizziness, choking, impaired judgment, blackouts, and convulsions similar to epileptic fits. Acute oxygen poisoning can cause death. The trick was to balance the mix so the diver was always getting oxygen at a pressure no less than atmospheric, but no greater than he would get while breathing *pure* oxygen at a thirty-three-foot depth.

Finally, the deeper the diver, the greater the percentage of carbon dioxide that had to be eliminated. In very deep dives the absorbent canister had to be efficient enough to virtually eliminate this gas. The absorbent used in American deep-diving suits was a flaky material called shell-natron, which became highly caustic if touched by water. Thus any leak at all, however minute, in either the canister or the rebreathing system, meant the diver's face would be blistered, his lungs seared, and in extreme cases, his eyeballs scorched. Since then, other "scrubbers," such as lythium hydroxide and Beralyme crystals, have also been used.

The first real test outside laboratory conditions for the American oxy-helium mixture came in 1938, when the submarine *Squalus* (see Chapter Nine) went down in 260 feet of water with thirty-three live survivors trapped aboard. Oxy-helium was used by the divers for five months on all phases of the deep-water salvage operation, with excellent results. Salvors were enthusiastic the world over; it seemed that there would be no limit to the depths at which divers could, in time, work.

Thus, in the years before World War II, routine diving beyond 250 feet was the exclusive province of the Americans. The Royal Navy was keen on diving, but had no ready access to helium. They did, however, develop the art of compressed-air diving to a fine degree, and applied what was learned to salvage techniques.

As it did in so many fields, the war finally spurred further research in deep-diving techniques. Injector-type deep-diving rubber suits were developed for use in conjunction with the Davis SDC; absorbent canisters and injectors became more efficient, with the whole unit replacing the diver's back weights to reduce poundage. Amplified telephones such as the Siebe, Gorman and Company thermionic system were developed. These are miniature loud-speakers in the helmet itself that serve as both transmitter and receiver, with volume controlled from the surface; but a diver working in a helium atmosphere still sounds like a hyperthyroid Donald Duck. In September 1970, Westinghouse sponsored a series of competitive tests in the field of helium voice unscramblers that showed there is still a long way to go. The difficulty, of course, is that the human voice is designed to work in an atmosphere of a certain density. Because helium has less mass, hence less density, than air, distortion is an inevitable result.

Following the war, in 1946, the Admiralty's Experimental Diving Unit was formed under command of William O. Shelford—who would gain fame five years later while searching for the sunken British submarine *Affray* (see Chapter Ten). His tests led to a world-record dive on August 28, 1948, from HMS *Reclaim* by Petty Officer W. Bollard in Loch Eyne, Scotland; he reached ninety fathoms (540 feet) on an oxy-helium mixture—forty feet beyond the maximum depth for which the Neufeldt and Kuhnke iron duke had been designed!

Two years later, in 1950, came EDU diver Pete Prickett's five-hundred-foot open-sea dive, and in 1956, the Royal Navy's George Wookey made his six-hundred-foot bounce dive in Olsofjord, Norway. Both divers were using oxy-helium mixtures.

EXOTIC GAS MIXTURES

Meanwhile, some rather startling experimentation was going on in the use of other exotic breathing mixtures. Swedish engineer Arne Zetterström made a soft-dress dive to 528 feet in 1945 on an oxygen-hydrogen mixture. Zetterström was killed during the *ascent*, by incredible stupidity on the part of certain of his tenders[1]; but this does not negate the validity of his experiments. Indeed, certain physiologists believe that man might some day be able to breathe water through surgically introduced devices in the body, because water is essentially hydrogen and oxygen. If man can breathe this mixture in the form of compressed gases, why not in its liquid state as well?[2] Indeed, biochemist Robert E. Davies of Oxford advises divers to flood their lungs with water if they run out of air while on a dive—literally, to pull off their mouth-pieces and breathe water rather than breathe their own exhaled CO_2. A man with water in his lungs, gotten to a respirator fast enough, might be pumped out and made to work again; but an overdose of carbon dioxide is always fatal. No other scientist has gone as far verbally as Dr. Davies; but it was thinking along these lines that led to the liquid-breathing experiments discussed in Chapter Thirty.

In 1961, Hannes Keller, a 27-year-old Swiss mathematics teacher, and Kenneth MacLeish, science editor of *Life Magazine*, broke Zetterström's record, on Lake Maggiore, Switzerland. Breathing an exotic mixture of nine gases worked out by Keller, they reached the astounding depth (in rubber SCUBA suits!) of 725 feet—the equivalent of 685 feet in salt water.

In December of the following year, Keller and Peter Small, a cofounder of the British Sub-Aqua Club, got down to the even more remarkable depth of a thousand feet in an airtight chamber designed by Keller. He left the bottom hatch briefly, breathing from an air hose, to plant American and Swiss flags; but in re-entering, his flipper caught in the hatch. This broke the seal, so both men lost consciousness on the way up. When the capsule reached 240 feet, SCUBA diver Dick Anderson, who is today America's top photo-journalist dealing with ocean-related subjects, dived down with a young Englishman named Christopher Whittaker. They closed the chamber's two external bleed valves but could see no gas escaping from the bottom hatch.

On their return to the surface, they were told to descend again to the chamber, which was now at two hundred feet. It was still impossible to pressurize the chamber. Anderson this time found the tip of Keller's flipper caught in the hatch. By pushing up against the hatch with his head and shoulders, he raised it enough so he could push the flipper aside with the blade of a diving knife. There still was not a perfect seal, however; as he worked on it, he directed Whittaker to go up and tell the tenders to haul in the chamber immediately.

Whittaker departed. Minutes passed without anything happening. Anderson realized his "no decompression time" was almost past, so he had to surface.

Whittaker, whom he thought had returned to the support ship, *Eureka*, had disappeared. He was never seen again. Small died of a probable gas embolism. Keller survived. The coroner's investigating committee later remarked that "Hannes Keller owes his life to the unusual ability and courage of this one man . . . Richard Anderson."

Then came the loss of the nuclear submarine *Thresher* (See Chapter Ten) in April 1963. The U. S. Navy's Deep Submergence Systems Project (DSSP), which resulted from this disaster, went to work on a whole array of shiny new concepts—a nuclear research submarine, vehicles and systems for deepwater submarine location and rescuing, deepwater ship salvage, deepwater small-object recovery. All these bear upon marine salvage techniques, and they might be expected to have a profound effect upon the art.

This is not the place, or the book, to consider the political and monetary problems that have dogged DSSP; but one project, the Sealab Man-in-the-Sea program, has had some effect on deep-diving techniques and thus indirectly on marine salvage.

The Navy's Sealab grew out of an old idea (it was predicted in the seventeenth century by Bishop John Wilkins) that was actually first attempted in a modest way off the Mediterranean island of Pomègues by Jacques-Yves Cousteau. His research group kept men in an artificial environment forty feet down for a week during September 1962. The cylinder was seventeen feet long by eight feet high, and was called Continental Shelf Station Number One (CONSHELF ONE).

Cousteau's second successful experiment, CONSHELF TWO, was carried out in the Red Sea, using a submarine hangar, tool shed, and five-room headquarters/billet thirty-six feet down, where five men lived for a month. They acted as Control Center for a second habitat, *Deep Cabin*, where two men lived at a ninety-foot depth on a helium-oxygen mixture for a week. They were able to range from ninety feet down to 330 (they actually exceeded instructions and went to 365 feet, but for a long time were afraid to admit to Cousteau what they had done) without any depth drunkenness.

TRAGEDY IN THE SEALAB PROGRAM

The U. S. Navy had been watching the CONSHELF experiments while conducting (unfortunately on a low-priority basis) its own deep-diving experiments. Borrowing some Cousteau techniques, the Navy instituted Sealab I around a cigar-shaped habitat (made from two floats welded together end on) forty feet long and ten feet in diameter. Sealab I was a qualified success, keeping four men at a depth of 193 feet near Bermuda for twelve days, starting on July 20, 1964. The men were breathing a helium-oxygen mixture (in the curious alphabet-scrambling complex of an industrial age, this has become a "heliox" mixture) and suffered no ill effects.

So Sealab II was undertaken: a larger cylinder (fifty-seven feet long, twelve in diameter, with a midships conning tower) divided into four compartments, in which three 10-man teams on a fifteen-day rotating basis were to spend forty-five days at a depth of 205 feet. The first team of divers entered the habitat on August 28, 1967, near Scripps Marine Canyon, near La Jolla, California. The twenty-eight men spent a total of 450 man-days on the bottom, with four hundred man-hours of work outside the capsule. The experiment went fairly well.

Meanwhile, however, DSSP had taken over the program. With *Thresher* still ringing in its ears, the Navy was pushing, and pushing hard, for successes by her aquanauts to equal those of NASA's astronauts. There was a tremendous infusion of money—and an operationally unnecessary "hurry-up" atmosphere. Publicity handouts were numerous, and work schedules tight in an attempt to get Sealab III on the bottom in record time to still critics of the program. The "Yellow Submarine" was built at a cost of $4 million; it was not strikingly different from the Sealab II habitat, except that two new rooms, each eight by twelve feet, had been added. It looked rather like a railroad tank car without wheels.

What *was* new was the depth: *610 feet!* That was quite a jump from 205 feet, but Captain William N. Nicholson, the new, DSSP-installed head of the project, said they hoped to reach a depth of 850 feet within three years, and "1500 to 2000 feet" within five.

Then came the setbacks. First major slippage was caused by selection of the wrong metals for the diving-chamber complex (which was aggravated by a nationwide steel strike). Further delay was caused by problems in the support ship *Elk River*. During training exercises, a faulty hatch came open, causing extensive damage to the personnel-transfer capsule. But by February 1969, the habitat was in position 610 feet down near San Clemente Island, some sixty miles from San Diego, California.

The day before the project was to be launched, the Yellow Submarine sprang a helium leak; several of them, in fact, around the ports where the power and communication lines entered from the *Elk River*.[3] On February 15, a team of divers was sent down to repair the leaks, but found it impossible from outside the habitat. They retreated to their descent capsule complaining of being bitterly cold.

"We felt we wouldn't have the capability of raising Sealab if those leaks weren't sealed," later admitted Captain George F. Bond, whose pioneering in helium-oxygen techniques had made Sealab possible, but who had been replaced as program head when DSSP took over. "If it flooded down there, it would have cost $4 million, and delayed the program another three years."

Besides, the press was waiting with pencils poised to report Sealab's wonders to the world, and DSSP wanted to accommodate them.

At 4:58 A.M. on February 16, only about six hours after their return from the first dive, two of the aquanauts again left the descent capsule to try to enter the habitat. They had been without sleep for twenty hours, so the Navy had issued them amphetamine tablets to keep them awake. The men were Team Leader Robert Barth, acknowledged as one of the world's best skin divers, and civilian aquanaut Barry L. Cannon, whose rating nearly equaled Barth's.

As they tried to open the habitat doors, Cannon went into a jackknife position and was obviously in trouble. By the time Barth had gotten him back into the capsule and up to the medics aboard *Elk River*, forty-one minutes had elapsed. Cannon was dead before they reached the surface.

The Navy first feared that the beautifully conditioned thirty-three-year-old diver had suffered a heart attack, then switched blame to a fouled or faulty umbilical cord back to the transfer capsule. There seemed to be at least a possibility also that Cannon's body had been unable to physically tolerate the severe body heat loss that comes from breathing a helium mixture in water only sixteen degrees above freezing.

The San Diego County Coroner's autopsy, however, showed that the diver had succumbed to carbon dioxide poisoning. This centered attention on the equipment, and testimony at the Court of Inquiry brought out the fact that, by a tragic oversight, the Beralyme-crystal CO_2 scrubber had not been inserted into one of the heliox breathing rigs used in the dive. The assumption that it was Cannon's rig is inescapable; any diver using a rebreather at twenty atmospheres of pressure without this scrubber would *have* to die. He would be asphyxiated by the carbon dioxide being fed into his breathing system by his own exhalations.

Bond, with a mixture of sorrow, confusion, and anger, testified, "To my knowledge, never before has our program had anything like the number of sheer equipment failures seen in Sealab III."

Other men, speaking off the record, had reported that many of the parts used in the accelerated Sealab program under DSSP have not met the specifications necessary for a (Naval Ship Systems Command) certification of seaworthiness. Such claims are highly suspect. Cannon died not from equipment *failure*, but because a vital piece of equipment was *missing*. Safety-checking procedures failed; but it must be remembered that divers, like parachutists, are ultimately and traditionally responsible for the condition of their own gear.

Sealab is at least temporarily moribund, but a great deal about deep diving was learned from it. And at least one salvage operation, the fascinating free-lance attempt carried out by John Light on the 32,000-ton Cunard liner *Lusitania*, claims to have borrowed Sealab techniques.

JOHN LIGHT AND THE *LUSITANIA*

The 790-foot *Lusitania* was once the most famous ship in the world, even though few today remember her name. She was spanking new, and fast—her top speed of twenty-five knots would outstrip any existing submarine of her day. Unfortunately, she was not fast enough to outrun a torpedo. On May 7, 1915, she was en route from New York to Liverpool when she was struck by a torpedo fired from the German submarine U-20. The ship sank within eighteen minutes, going down in 310 feet of water in St. George's Channel some twelve miles off the southeast coast of Ireland. She carried 1198 of her 1959 passengers and crewmen with her.

As rescue vessels scooped up the relatively few survivors and the bodies of the dead, including ninety-four children, public indignation ran high. Some 124 American nationals had died, among them Charles Frohman, the David Merrick of his day, and the millionaire financier Alfred Vanderbilt. A major reason for America's entering the war nearly two years later was the sinking of the *Lusitania* and other unarmed civilian vessels like her.

Rumors of six million dollars' worth of gold aboard the ship immediately began circulating, as they always seem to do in such situations, and the promoters began coming out of the woodwork. Most entertaining of these was a certain Benjamin Franklin Leavitt, who made a very good thing for a number of years from inducing the share-buying public to support the Leavitt Lusitania Salvage Company, Inc.

Leavitt's first task was to "prove" that he could reach the *Lusitania* at her 310-foot depth. Our doughty salvor/promoter sank himself beneath the waters of mighty Lake Michigan in a semi-armored compressed-air diving suit, and when he reappeared, modestly admitted that he had attained the depth of 361 feet.

This was promptly recognized as a world's record.

Recognized, that is, by non-divers. Even in 1920, divers knew that if Leavitt actually had reached that depth and returned in the period of time he was down, he would have come up twisted into a pretzel by the bends.

But few share-buyers are deep-sea divers. "She has in her strong room $5 million in gold," Leavitt blithely announced. "This is a moderate estimate in view of the fact that many millionaires were among the passengers. There is also a $5 million cargo in copper, brass and tin . . ."

Leavitt estimated that returns would be twenty to one, and intimated that this was only the beginning. He knew, he said, of twelve other wrecks his company eventually would salve, containing among them $127 million in gold and silver.

Leavitt once had brought 350 tons of copper ore up from a Civil War wreck in Lake Michigan, the *Pewaubic*, and with the copper had saved a woman's square-toed shoe. This he kept on his desk in New York to hand with great ceremony to whatever reporter happened to be interviewing him.

"After we'd had it here awhile," he would remark sadly, "a piece of her foot fell out of it."

By August 1922 Leavitt had raised some $95,000 in shares, without raising anything at all from the *Lusitania*. He hadn't even been near her. He tried unsuccessfully to pay Charles S. Rickards, the captain of his salvage vessel, the *Blakeley*, with $10,000 worth of stock in the Leavitt Lusitania Salvage Company, Inc. When this wise old sea dog declined, Leavitt briskly departed for environs unknown.

Before he did, however, he was challenged by a certain Count Charles Landi of the Aye Ready Salvage Company, whom we last met trying to claim-jump the brothers Estier on the *Tubantia* in 1923. Landi actually was a salvor, having skillfully towed a number of torpedoed-but-still-floating vessels during World War I. *His* diving suit, he said, would get him not only to the *Lusitania*'s 310 feet, not only to Leavitt's measly 361 feet, but to a truly princely 500 *feet!* On compressed air, of course.

Meanwhile, Landi offered as credentials the fact that he had raised HMS *King Alfred*, 14,000 gross tons displacement, from Belfast Lough (he actually had *towed* the 4000-ton *Alfred* for a few miles after it had been torpedoed). On getting down to the sunken *Alfred* in his marvelous suit, Landi said, he had found a phonograph on which was a half-played record of *Rule Britannia*, just as it had been when the fatal torpeodo had struck.

There on the sea bottom he had cranked up the phonograph, the count said tremulously, stood at attention in his diving suit, and had played the rest of *Rule Britannia*.

Anyone who could do that obviously would find the *Lusitania* mere child's play. Not only would he salvage her gold, he would *raise the entire ship to the surface!*

"I expect to have her afloat in the Atlantic," he announced with simple grandeur, "for the traffic rush next spring."

Meanwhile, back at the *Lusitania*, nobody even *found* the hulk until 1935. In that year, a primitive echo-sounding device fixed her position well enough so that a British diver, Jim Jarrat, could claim to have gotten down to the wreck and to have walked about on it. Following World War II, another British salvage firm succeeded in getting pictures of the hulk with an underwater camera. But until Light started operations from the Little Irish town of Kinsale in March 1968, no attempts had been made to salvage anything from the vessel. As for the rumors of gold, the *Lusitania*'s cargo manifest showed a total value of only $750,000; and gold would have been flowing west across the Atlantic to safekeeping in America, not the other way around.

The British War Risks Commission (nominal owner of the vessel) was so unimpressed by the rumors of gold that in 1966 it sold John Light the entire hulk, plus its cargo, for £1000. Included in the manifest were 200,000 pounds of sheet brass and 111,762 pounds of copper. It is this possibly salvageable metal, not non-existent gold, that had motivated the free-lance salvage consortium to begin operations.

"This is a financial undertaking, pure and simple," Light explained at the time. "I'm interested only in salvage."

In his first year of operation, Light personally dived thirty-seven times to the wreck, and his crew made at least one hundred working dives. They intended first to raise the *Lusitania*'s four 14½-ton manganese propellers (utilizing flexible pontoons that were to have been fixed under the screws and inflated), and then the copper and brass—which alone might be worth nearly eight hundred thousand dollars in today's scrap market.

What makes the operation worth noting is that Light, who spent three years as a U. S. Navy diver, claims to have borrowed a technique from the Sealab experiments. Into the hull of his 368-ton, 151-foot salvage ship, the *Kinsarra*, he built a twenty-three-by-seventeen-foot living compartment for his four-man diving teams. The men ate and slept there, constantly breathing the oxy-helium mixture compressed to 110 psi (about 15 atmospheres of pressure) that they used during their dives. This meant they needed no decompression and in their skintight, heated rubber suits could work a full six-hour day on the bottom. They passed directly from the chamber into the sea through an air lock, and their work was monitored by underwater television cameras.

Unfortunately, in December 1969, Light at least temporarily suspended operations due to financial problems.

Robert H. Davis once claimed that sixty-six fathoms would always be the practical limit of the working dive, but such experiments will keep the individual diver in moderately deepwater salvage operations indefinitely. The mandatory 24- to 48-hour "stand-off" (thumb-rule of staying out of the water for a predetermined time after deep dives) for men working beyond four hundred feet makes operating costs heavy; but 450-foot working dives are now common in both Navy and civilian salvage operations.

Salvage from depths in excess of twelve thousand feet already is being seriously considered, as we shall see in the Future section of this book, by many oceanographic engineers. They are developing new technologies that depend not on divers, but on deep-diving submersibles and surface-controlled robots. An interesting fact about these new deepwater salvage methods is their ready application to the salvaging of aircraft as well as ships.

A ship goes down for one essential reason: it loses buoyancy. Whether human error has flooded or capsized it, or the finger of God has poked a hole in it, it sinks because its air spaces are filled and it no longer is displacing its weight in water. But when an airplane crashes, there is an immediate and terrible urgency to find out why; poor design, allowing unforeseen metal stresses to develop, a prime cause of crashes, means other planes will crash if subjected to the same stresses.

The problem is complicated by the fact that the plane usually disintegrates upon contact with the water, if it has not broken up in the air. So the marine salvor ends up searching not for a three-hundred-foot ship, but for a three-foot section of wing or tail, or for a small metal box containing a flight recorder. Hence the proliferation of techniques keyed to small-object location and recovery.

BEGINNINGS OF AIRPLANE SALVAGE

Perhaps the first underwater salvage job involving a downed aircraft was during the early years of World War II, when Jacques-Yves Cousteau was still perfecting his SCUBA gear in Nazi-occupied France. The pilot of a new, twin-engine naval plane had been deluded by a mirage into making a full-speed landing on the wind-roughed surface of the water. Fishermen had picked up his body, and Cousteau's Undersea Research Group was sent down to find and photograph the plane so a critique of the accident could be prepared.

No one knew just where the plane rested, since it had skipped across the surface of the water like a thrown flat stone, but the divers were led to it by silvery bubbles of gasoline rising from the wing tanks. They found the craft upright on the bottom at 120 feet, its propellers gone and the engine cowlings split by the impact of the water.

The copilot was still seated in the ruptured cockpit, his eyes open, his face calm and wise, his parachute mushroomed out behind him. The third crewman, the engineer, was nearly a hundred feet away, resting on his back in the bottom vegetation with one leg folded under him. His right arm was extended, and his forefinger was pointing straight up as if it were a torch lighting the way back to the surface. His chute, opened by the impact with the water, was laid out beneath him as carefully as if it had been prepared for repacking in a rigging plant.

The divers got their pictures, then attached lines to the chutes and brought both bodies to the surface.

Hollywood notwithstanding, the recovery of an intact airplane from the sea is very rare. Most airplanes shatter—literally—on contact with the surface. Because water is incompressible, a hydraulic ram effect is produced by an object striking it at sufficient velocity. In such a case, the impact can exceed that of striking the ground at the same speed.

Probably the first raising of a sunken aircraft occurred in 1943, involving a then-new British dive bomber called the Beaufort, and the U. S. Navy's first submarine rescue ship, the *Chanticleer*. The *Chanticleer* was on training maneuvers in the Indian Ocean west of Australia when a Beaufort taking a practice run at the vessel nosed over and knifed into the sea at the end of its dive. It was the fourth such dive bomber to go down in this manner, and the *Chanticleer* was ordered to attempt recovery of the plane, since the first three had crashed on land and had burned so completely that no study of the wreckage had been possible.

Master diver Joseph S. Karneke conceived the idea of being towed along on the diving stage a hundred feet down in his hard-hat suit, so he could scan the bottom for wreckage. There was the danger of fouling his lines in the ship's propellers, of falling off the stage and being killed by a squeeze, or of being swept into the bottom before they could bring him up; but within fifteen minutes he saw, in the clear tropical water, the remains of the Beaufort scattered along the sandy bottom some thirty feet below.

He went down the line of their marker buoy, bringing a recovery wire with him on a loose shackle fixed to his own life line, and landed some hundred yards from the wrecked plane. It was hidden from view by a low sand mound: when he arrived, he found over a dozen huge, man-eating white sharks ahead of him, drawn by the scent of blood from the dead crewmen. The panicked Karneke crouched under the upright tail section and reported to his tender.

"If the sharks aren't bothering you, why not go ahead and hook the line to the tail section?" came the casually unfeeling reply.

Karneke did, fastening the hook of the recovery wire around the fuselage forward of the rudder, and then retreated to the sand mound. When he looked back, the sharks were diving like aircraft on the dead crewmen, clouding the water around the plane with strips and flakes of human flesh. Karneke was hauled up to his decompression stop at thirty feet, but then to his horror saw that the wrecked plane was being dragged over for lifting to the ship.

Karneke began yelling to them to stop, since the sharks had come along to keep tearing at the two bodies still aboard. The salvors stopped, all right—when the Beaufort was at the same depth as the cowering Karneke. The sharks, in their attack pattern, came so close that they kept brushing against him and threatening to knock him right off the diving stage. He rolled into a tight ball, his hands crossed under his arms and his head lowered to his drawn-up knees, afraid even to put out a hand to grasp a stay or a cable.

Finally the crewmen raised the Beaufort to the surface; the sharks streaked off to attack the two bodies that had been thrown free in the crash; and Karneke got back to the *Chanticleer* without further incident. The salvaged tail section showed that an elevator-control cable had been designed in such a way that it rubbed against the surrounding metal surfaces, wore thin, and with the pull-up of the cable as the plane came out of its dive, snapped and sent the bomber out of control.

SEARCH FOR THE YOKE PETER

It was not until the era of the big jet passenger planes, following World War II, however, that the development of deepwater small-object recovery really began. On January 10, 1954, a BOAC Comet (the world's first commercial jetliner) took off from Rome with thirty-five people aboard. While flying over the Mediterranean island of Elba at twenty-six thousand feet, the Comet, called *Yoke Peter*, exploded "with a dull report" and broke up in midair. Admiral Lord Louis Mountbatten, NATO Commander in Chief for the Mediterranean Fleet, was instructed to find and raise the remains for examination by the Department of Transport and Power. Mountbatten brought in five Royal Navy ships, five Italian drag ships, and British divers from the commercial salvage firm of Risdon Beazley. Commander C. G. Fosberg of the Royal Navy was put in command of salvage operations.

Some fifteen bodies had been recovered at the surface, along with minor wreckage and those pitiful personal remnants that make an air crash so poignant: a tattered valise, sodden letters, a pajama top, a woman's high-heeled shoe. It was obvious that the bodies and the debris could have been miles from the actual sunken wreckage; so the first task facing Fosberg's salvage officers, V. Campbell and a commercial salvor named J. B. Pollard, was to determine where the plane lay. They started with the position reports given by eyewitnesses and by other aircraft. Despite the fact that only three of their fifteen informants actually had seen the Comet strike the water, all the positions tallied to a marked degree.

Just determining what those positions were was a remarkable feat, because Cape Calagazta, a point near the suspected crash area, contained large outcroppings of magnetic iron ore, which rendered compass plotting impossible.

Commander Lombardi, harbor master of Portoferraio, overcame this problem by turning his sextant on its side and taking positions from four different angles to establish where each witness had been standing at the time of the crash. He then plotted three more angles for each, fixing the direction in which the aircraft had been falling.

Captain C. N. Parry of HMS *Wrangler*, one of the British anti-submarine frigates dispatched to probe with asdic (the British-developed equivalent of sonar) once the target area had been defined, felt they should seek eyewitnesses on a small island to the west of Elba called Pianosa. He found only a deaf, aged warder, who had seen "the sea on fire." The warder's six-year-old granddaughter, who had been with him at the time, confirmed the position he had indicated—which in turn confirmed the co-ordinates gleaned from the other sightings: a small triangle some seven miles south of Elba.

The frigates were brought in to begin wire-sweep operations and to make an asdic pattern over the search area. They got over a dozen hard contacts or "hits"—but they had no means of classifying them.

Then an Elba dragger, the *Favilla*, recovered the first bits of wreckage. She found some aluminum and a passenger's zipper bag; but again, she had no way of knowing *where* in her sweep of the bottom she had picked them up. Soon, scattered bits and pieces of detritus began showing up all over the search area.

Finally the Admiralty salvage vessel *Sea Salvor* was brought in, along with a boom-defense ship usually used in anti-submarine work, HMS *Barhill*. The depth at the point where they were searching varied from 400 to 480 feet. *Sea Salvor* had a four-ton grab with ten-foot jaws for delicately lifting any pieces of wreckage discovered without crushing them too badly, and two Galeazzi Submarine Observation Chambers for her three master divers (Bray, Galpin, and Docherty). With *Sea Salvor* was HMS *Wakeful*, on which had been installed three underwater TV cameras; they had been built in nine days for this operation by Bertrand Horlock and Donald Coleman. The cameras were pressurized for fifteen hundred feet, and had powerful flood lamps and remote controls so that surface tenders could change focus, aperture, and even the lens itself. The camera was also equipped with a large fin to steady it for towing at speeds up to four knots. This proved impractical, however, due to bottom turbulence, which limited visibility so drastically that even drifting moved the camera too fast.

This left one alternative: mooring over each contact found by the frigates in their asdic search, lowering the camera, and examining whatever was on the bottom.

Although it was the Mediterranean, supposed home of balmy breezes and warm seas, it was also January: gale-force winds often veered through a full 180 degrees in the course of a single day, and marker buoys would be blown as much as half a mile off station. The job of the *Barhill* was to lay a six-point mooring (utilizing five-ton anchors and 2¼-inch cable) around each contact so the *Wakeful* could lower its TV cameras and check out the site. On one contact they had to adjust the moorings eighty times.

The initial contacts were disappointing: sunken dan buoys, World War II mine-laying equipment, a World War I wreck, ancient Roman amphorae, and then, finally, a real shocker: onto the monitoring screen suddenly came the face of a woman—a woman on the sea floor sixty-five fathoms below, her face moving as if alive, her lips mouthing soundless words, her eyes staring in mute appeal.

Then they caught on: the camera was panning across a four-foot nude female statue from an ancient galley that had broken open and spilled its cargo out across the bottom. The glare of their own floodlights on the slow surge of deep-water turbulence had caused a wavery or shimmery effect that had lent the stone face its momentary illusion of life.

A month after the crash, the screen was just as abruptly filled with the torn and twisted wreckage of the Comet. A tail plane and vertical fin could be seen, and then a deep furrow in the seabed as if a heavy truck had been driven across a muddy field.

This first major contact was made at a depth of 430 feet, and was dubbed GEORGE. In all, GEORGE yielded fifteen chunks of *Yoke Peter*, including the plane's cockpit and the nosewheel from its tricycle landing gear. Then came word that *Yoke Yoke*, another Comet, had exploded and burst apart after leaving Rome Airport. Altitude: twenty-six thousand feet.

All Comets were grounded. Salvage efforts were redoubled.

As pieces were spotted and identified by the TV camera, the divers were sent down in their observation chambers to direct the lowering and working of the four-ton grab that actually brought up the wreckage. By April 9, when the *Sea Salvor* finally departed, she had recovered the Comet's pressure dome, most of its fuselage plating and cabin furniture, wing spars, all four engines, and the entire fore section—which had contained the flight controls deemed vital in determining the cause of the crash.

They weren't, as it turned out. They told nothing.

Eventually, from a four-square-mile target area, more than 70 per cent of the aircraft was recovered either by the *Sea Salvor* or the trawlers that continued to operate after her departure. But it was a full eight months after *Yoke Peter*'s loss that the section that finally told them the reason for the crashes was brought up.

Across the top of the cabin between the forward wing spars were two glass ports that housed the direction-finding aerials for the plane's radar. In the corner of one of these windows was a reinforcing plate; and in the plate was a one-fourth-inch-long crack. The crack had been stopped by a one-sixteenth-inch hole at its end—a common practice in repairing such minute fissures to bring the area back up to design specifications. Examination of this piece showed that design specifications had not allowed for enough in-flight stress; it was from this tiny crack that the separation of fuselage pieces radiated. These hairline cracks had caused the crash: air had roared into them with such velocity that it had peeled the metal fuselage back, thus exploding the Comet with its own depressurization.

A few years later, similar techniques were used by the British Government to locate and raise the main fuselage of a Viscount airliner that had crashed in 252 feet of water off the Tuskar Lighthouse, in the Irish Sea. The divers used a Davis Submersible Decompression Chamber (SDC) that time, surveying the wreckage with closed-circuit TV cameras aboard their chamber. Television, an electronic device developed during the 1930s but ignored because no practical use could be envisioned for it, had gone under water to become the newest tool in an expanding technology of ocean salvage.

AN AIRPLANE UNDER ICE

Another aircraft-salvage job that deserves mention here was one carried out by master diver Harold H. Stubbs and other members of the U. S. Navy's Norfolk, Virginia, Salvage Team in December 1964 at an Air Force base in Newfoundland. What made the job unique was not the depth at which the salvors had to work—the plane, a KC-97 tanker, had gone off the end of a runway and had settled in twenty fathoms of lake water—it was the conditions under which the work was done.

The ten-man team had to dive through holes chopped in ice three feet thick, in water temperatures so low that condensation in the air lines of their usual hard-hat rigs quickly froze solid. Even if complete blockage of the lines did not result, the air supply was drastically reduced and the divers found themselves struck in the face by ice flakes with each breath they drew.

They used SCUBA rigs instead and one-fourth-inch wet suits, and individual divers could stand only fifteen minutes bottom time on each dive. Constructive work beyond that time was impossible.

They found the aircraft on the bottom with the cockpit folded under; it was decided to cut her in half with underwater torches and raise the tail section first. To do this, an air line was run down from the surface to an open hatch on the fuselage. A diver would take down a string of ten small lifting balloons (each capable of lifting two hundred pounds) and would apply the first balloon to the airline. When it was full, it would tear out of his hand and rise into the interior of the plane, dragging the next balloon into position for filling. Two hundred of these small balloons were packed into the tail section in this way.

Next, a manila line was run under the ice from the beach to a wire choker placed around the tail. Then the line went through a block and up through a hole in the ice so that divers at the surface could heave it taut. This brought the choker up around the fuselage and into position. To this choker were fixed several larger lifting balloons.

As Stubbs and the others had hoped, inflating these large balloons raised the tail section off the bottom and brought it up against the bottom of the surface ice hard enough to break through. When the line was pulled taut from shore, the balloons submerged again—and continued to break the ice so the section could be dragged out. The same procedure was successfully followed with the fore section of the aircraft.

It took the salvage team, working in almost total darkness amid twisted, jagged pieces of wreckage, four weeks to recover 94 per cent of the aircraft—which provided the investigating board with sufficient wreckage to determine the cause of the crash.

The KC-97 at Newfoundland was salvaged through the ingenuity of individual men such as Harold Stubbs working under adverse conditions with rather primitive equipment. In 1966, near a remote Spanish coastal village called Palomares, another U. S. Air Force tanker—a KC-135—was involved in a mid-air collision that would forever alter the techniques of deepwater aircraft location and recovery.

---

[1] While his winchmen stopped him for a decompression stop, others at the bow of the ship continued hauling, bringing him up before he could make a switch-over from hydrogen-oxygen to nitrogen-oxygen for the reduced depth. He smothered.

[2] The problem is the difference in density between air (.0024) and water (.5), and in viscosity. The diaphragm simply is not strong enough to breathe a liquid for very long.

[3] Helium is almost impossible to contain, because its molecules are so small. They will pass through a seal capable of holding other gases like, as Willard Bascom puts it, "ants through chicken wire."

CHAPTER SEVEN

Palomares and After

The most expensive salvage operation in history began on Monday, January 17, 1966, and ended less than three months later on Thursday, April 7. The deep-water phase of the co-ordinated land-sea-air operation involved eighteen naval vessels; the over-all search involved thirty-eight hundred men and cost the United States $84 million. It was both an operational triumph and a public-relations fiasco: triumph, because the U. S. Navy succeeded in an almost impossible assignment; fiasco, because the U. S. Government was evasive and indecisive in telling the world just what the searchers were doing. Yet the recovery of the nuclear device from a submarine slope 2850 feet below the surface of the Mediterranean, off Palomares, Spain, was one of the great, decisive moments in the history of American salvage.

The blunt truth of Palomares is that the Navy, working with a vast array of mechanical and electronic devices so experimental that many of them had not even been field-tested before this operation, *did find and recover* the bomb the Air Force had lost. And there was no other salvage force in the world that could have done so.

BOMBER-TANKER CRASH OVER PALOMARES

It all began routinely on Monday, January 17. A B-52 from the SAC 68th Bomber Wing, of Goldsborough, North Carolina, part of the Strategic Air Command's round-the-clock defensive alert, rendezvoused in the Mediterranean off the southeast coast of Spain with a KC-135 jet tanker, which was to refuel it. Pumping began at 10:11 A.M. from the tanker's huge, winged-pipe refueling boom, which had coupled with the B-52's intake cone. The aircraft were 150 feet apart, moving at 365 knots; 30,500 feet below was Palomares, a twelve-hundred-soul village on the Costa del Sol, which is noted for its tomatoes, onions, string beans, melons, and citrus groves.

Suddenly one of the B-52's eight engines burst into flame. The pilot cut the fuel and activated the built-in extinguisher.

"Fire! Retract the boom!" cried an observer aboard the KC-135.

Too late. The engine exploded, shooting flames toward the intake cone with its hundreds of gallons of highly inflammable fuel. Burning sections of the B-52's wing began falling off.

10:22 A.M. One mile from the coast and Palomares. The order was given to jettison armaments. At the same moment, the B-52 exploded and the flames shot out to engulf the KC-135. Those crewmen still alive began bailing out as the giant bomber began scattering great chunks of burning wreckage on Palomares. Both planes struck the ground, blew up, and disintegrated over a fifteen-square-mile area of field, beach, and sea. The wreckage burned for five hours.

The people of Palomares had fled into their homes, dragging what livestock they could with them, and by some miracle no one was injured in any way by the debris raining down on the village. Seven crewmen died.

Five miles from the coast was the sixty-six-foot fishing smack *Manuela Orts Simo*, owned and captained by forty-six-year-old Francisco Simo Orts. A candy-striped parachute landed in the water eighty yards from the boat, carrying a five-foot, light-blue object. A few seconds later, a big gray parachute also splashed down, carrying something that looked like a man, but was larger and metallic. As he went to the rescue of the three surviving B-52 crewmen who had landed safely in the water, Simo noted his position with an eye sharpened by seventeen years of fishing that same coast in every type of weather.

Soon rescue and spotter planes were crisscrossing the sky while dozens of fishing boats, motor launches, yachts, cargo vessels—even tankers—were searching the ocean for survivors or debris. By the next morning a hundred airmen, technicians, crash experts, and scientists had arrived from Torregón; by that night their number had reached three hundred, a tent city was springing up, and fields were being declared "restricted zones," for unknown reasons.

Geiger counters were appearing in the hands of the searchers, but it was not until Thursday, January 20, that the Air Force issued a tight-lipped communiqué admitting what the B-52 had been carrying.

"The SAC bomber which was engaged in a refueling operation off the coast of Spain and suffered an accident with a KC-135 was carrying unarmed nuclear armaments. Radiological surveys have established that there is no danger to public health or safety . . ."

The official dispatches continued to deny that more than one bomb had been involved, even though three of them had been recovered on land within eighteen hours of the crash. They were twenty-five megatons each, each with an explosive capacity equaling 25 million tons of TNT—1250 times more powerful than the Hiroshima bomb. If any of them had exploded on contact with the ground, it would have wiped out everything within an eight-mile radius of flashpoint—killing, in that area, some fifty thousand people—and would have set fire to all combustible material within a fifty-mile radius. Poisonous, radioactive fall-out would have rained down on thousands of square miles.

Nuclear weapons are constructed so that it is extremely difficult to detonate one accidentally. Palomares was the thirteenth publicly known accident to an American plane carrying nuclear devices; in none of them had there been a nuclear explosion. Those at Palomares were hydrogen, or fusion, bombs, called thermonuclear because an explosion of their hydrogen nuclei would have to be triggered by the explosion of an atom bomb. This, in turn, had to be triggered by its shell of ordinary TNT, which in *its* turn had to be triggered by several detonators set off simultaneously by a battery-activated electric charge. All the detonators had to go off at exactly the same instant or the TNT would explode unevenly, and the implosion designed to set off the nuclear chain reaction would instead merely scatter the nuclear material rather than "squeeze" it.

So there was no nuclear explosion at Palomares. But six hundred men (by the twenty-first) moving shoulder to shoulder across the landscape with Geiger counters and other electronic equipment suggested that *something* was wrong—and made the American attempts at secrecy almost surrealistic.

REPORTER: Is there any risk of radiation, or are you merely taking precautions?

INFORMATION OFFICER: No comment.

REPORTER: Where can we get that information, Colonel?

INFORMATION OFFICER: From me. (A pause.) I have no comment

to make about anything, and I cannot comment on why I have to say "no comment."

OFFSHORE SALVAGE FLEET

While twenty questions went forward ashore, an impressive armada was building up at sea as a result of a high-level panic session in Washington two days after the planes had collided. This had been called under a National Contingency Plan previously established by the Joint Chiefs of Staff for such emergencies. The plan had two elements:

1. The recovery of any ordnance or hardware lost in the ocean beyond the low-tide mark was the Navy's responsibility, no matter which service had lost the hardware.

2. The service that had custody of the equipment at the time of the loss had to pay the costs of recovery.

That meant that the lost bomb was the Navy's baby, but that the Air Force would have to pay for getting it back.

As soon as Rear Admiral Roy Swanson had a valid, clear-cut request from the Air Force for action, he christened the project SALVOPS MED and initiated action. This involved a two-prong operation: the actual salvage force at the scene in Spain (Task Force 65), and a Technical Advisory Group (TAG) in Washington.

The TAG's personnel list shifted constantly, but some men were permanent. Swanson himself, of course; Commander Bill Searle, Superintendent of Salvage for the Navy; Assistant Secretary of the Navy (Research and Development) Captain Ed Snyder; and such knowledgeable military men and civilians as Sam Applegarth, Frank Andrews, Chester A. "Bucky" Buchanan, and Ed Wardwell.

Meanwhile, at Palomares, the fleet tug *Kiowa* had arrived on the eighteenth; by the twenty-first, two mine sweepers, the *Sagacity* and the *Pinnacle*, had begun sweeping with electronic mine-detection gear and were sending their divers into the sixty-foot shallows. Two more mine sweepers, the *Skill* and the *Nimble*, soon joined them. By January 23, Rear Admiral William S. Guest, Deputy Commander of the Naval Striking and Support Forces, Southern Europe, had been placed in charge of the marine salvage operation. Under him, in command of Task Force 65, was Vice Admiral William E. Ellis. The force, besides the *Kiowa* and the four mine sweepers, by then consisted of the destroyer USS *MacDonough*, the landing ship *Fort Snelling*, the submarine rescue vessel *Petrel* (ideal for this operation because of its sophisticated sonar detection gear and its diving/search operation facilities), and the oiler USS *Nespelen*.

Guest was given a free hand in obtaining the latest military and civilian hardware; Admiral Swanson knew that the time to get all conceivably necessary men and hardware on site was immediately, before his superiors had a chance to start brooding about it. The many accounts of the Palomares operation that have appeared all stress the apparently wasteful prodigality the Navy showed in getting men and machines to the site; but the only place the salvors themselves have ever felt they overprocured was in the case of divers. They had SCUBA divers, hard-hat divers, compressed-air rigs, mixed-gas rigs . . . too many divers.

But there was a reason for this. In the early days, the job was seen essentially as an Explosive Ordnance Disposal (EOD) problem: in simple words, a job much like mine clearance. In the case of Palomares, this would mean literally hundreds of divers to personally examine several square miles of ocean bottom, essentially by groping in the mud with their fingers.

Guest's first acquisition was the Westinghouse Ocean Bottom Scanning Sonar (OBSS)—a torpedo-shaped "fish" with outsized fins that was designed to be towed some thirty feet above the sea bottom at a one-knot speed, scanning 260 feet on either side with side-looking sonar.

Guest ordered the latest deep-sea television unit from the Naval Ordnance Test Station at Pasadena, California. It consisted of three telescope-shaped cameras that could be lowered by cable from a surface ship to transmit pictures onto the monitor screen overhead, and could stand the pressure of two thousand feet.

Honeywell Corporation supplied its Sea Scanner, an eight-foot metal cylinder containing electronic echo-ranging gear that projected a narrow, high-frequency sound beam (searchlight sonar) from the surface to the bottom, scanning ahead and down and also sweeping from side to side. It automatically indicated distance, direction, and depth of any object spotted.

Ashore, the Naval Oceanographic Office was establishing navigation reference points, since the most difficult part of any small-object search is to know exactly where you are when you make contact with your target. If that target is, say, three hundred fathoms below you, almost total accuracy is required if you are to return and retrieve it after a passing electronic sensor has pointed it out. Upon learning that this supposed precision electronic placing system was allowing errors up to 250 yards on existing charts, Guest decided instead on the British Decca Navigational System. This utilizes a master and two slave stations, with the position-indicating receivers on the ships themselves. It gave accuracy to within ten feet.

Guest's salvage crew was as expert as his equipment was complex. Captain Ray Pitts was Searle's personal representative on the site; Jon Lindbergh was on hand as a civilian adviser after Searle's telegram had chased him through the bush of East Africa, where he had been on safari, and from Nairobi, Kenya, to New York, where it finally caught up with him. Captain Horace C. "Cliff" Page and Commander Roy Springer of the Office of Naval Research were in command of operations; a 130-man Navy diving team was headed by Lieutenant Commander DeWitt "Red" Moody, a bomb-disposal and SCUBA-gear expert, and hard-hat master diver Harold Stubbs. Commander J. B. Mooney, who had piloted the *Trieste* when it discovered the remains of the *Thresher* (see Chapter Ten) in August 1964, was his chief adviser. Ocean Systems, Inc., was the prime civilian contractor, with supervision of all civilians on the job, no matter what company nominally employed them. The fleet crews totaled twenty-two hundred men.

Only one problem remained in the minds of civilian observers: what was Guest supposed to be looking for? Navy public-relations types remained tight-lipped, but within days it was an open secret that a *fourth* bomb had been lost, had not been recovered ashore despite fantastically intensive searching, and hence was believed to have gone into the ocean.

On January 26, the oceanographic survey vessel *Dutton* arrived to chart the bottom of the 120-square-mile search area. Every tiniest scrap of wreckage was to be found and recovered, as well as the bomb itself. On the twenty-sixth also, Guest read, for the first time, the report filed by Francisco Simo concerning the parachutes he had seen go into the sea near his boat. The fisherman claimed that he could lead investigators directly to the spot again, even though he had taken only visual sights at the time. Men went out on Simo's trawler to mark the area, but at that time there was no reason to give his report any special attention. Literally hundreds of such reports had been received, virtually all of which the salvors knew would prove inaccurate; and also, the Navy knew the only way to undertake such a massive job was steadily, logically, and progressively. This method had worked on the *Thresher* search and would work again on the *Scorpion* (see Chapter Ten). It is the basic creed of mine-hunting: give credence numbers to the possible sites on the basis of available data, and look in the High Probability Areas first. In doing so, try to combine sophisticated searching techniques with old-fashioned seamanship.

Guest's orders concerning all debris from the B-52, including the bomb, were threefold: 1) search and locate; 2) verify and mark the wreckage with buoys; 3) make the actual recovery. But finding that bomb presented almost insurmountable difficulties. The underwater terrain was extremely rough, with great canyons cutting through rocky seabed down to depths of four thousand feet and more. Silt and mud covered the hard rocks in places; when stirred up by divers or subs, it reduced the visibility. Several "contacts" at five hundred feet or deeper had been made, but there was absolutely no way of raising the material contacted—or even of knowing what it was. A contact is an anomolous signal from the sensing gear; it may be an old wreck, a rock, or the object being sought. Guest called for more hardware: deep-water recovery hardware.

The Navy responded. En route to Palomares, Guest was told, were the bathyscaphe *Trieste II*, and an underwater Deep Jeep—a small, fat, cigar-shaped vehicle the size of a compact car, which was suspended by a cable and cruised about by its own power while plying underwater spotlights and television cameras. Its big drawback was that it was not equipped to pick anything up.

FIRST TEST FOR SUBMERSIBLES

On January 28, Secretary of Defense Robert MacNamara asked the Woods Hole Oceanographic Institute and Reynolds Aluminum Corporation for the use of their experimental submersibles, the *Alvin* and the *Aluminaut*.

Alvin was twenty-two feet long, weighed thirteen tons, and could stay down at a depth of six thousand feet for twenty-four hours. It had a two-man crew and a fifteen-mile range at a four-knot top speed. Its guidance equipment included magnetic compass, fathometer, sonar telephone, scanning sonar, and closed-circuit TV. It also had a telescopic grappling claw, which, unfortunately, was not ready and had to be shipped after the submersible itself.

Reynolds' *Aluminaut* was larger—fifty-one feet long and weighing eighty-one tons. Its design specifications were for a fifteen-thousand-foot depth, but it had been tested only to sixty-five hundred. It had an operational crew of two (six maximum) and a 3.8-knot cruising speed. Its equipment included underwater phones; a fathometer; a continuous-transmission, frequency-modulated scanning sonar; underwater lighting equipment; a directable TV camera; and a gyro-compass. Like *Alvin*, it had recovery equipment—a pair of nine-foot mechanical arms, which, also the *Alvin's*, were not ready for use.

Aluminaut had to be shipped by sea aboard the USS *Plymouth Rock*, a landing ship, dock (LSD) that would be mother ship to all the submersibles because of its large, docklike well, which could be flooded to become a launching and recovery area for the small underwater craft. *Alvin* was small enough to be flown, in two sections, to Spain; but as they prepared to take off from Otis Air Force Base in Massachusetts, an enormous blizzard grounded all planes.

The Department of Defense therefore ordered to the scene the Perry *Cubmarine*, a submersible owned by Ocean Systems, Inc. This had only a six-hundred-foot maximum depth, a six-hour down time, and a two-knot speed. Its essential equipment was more spartan than either *Alvin*'s or *Aluminaut*'s, consisting only of sonar telephone, gyro-compass, and fathometer. But it had many advantages over a diver for searching the sea floor visually, and it could release marker buoys above objects spotted. It also was much less expensive to operate than the other subs; and Guest was following Swanson's lead in securing every available piece of submersible hardware for Palomares.

By February 9, when the *Aluminaut* arrived, Guest was ensconced aboard his new flagship, the guided-missile cruiser USS *Boston*. Around him lay a curtain of eleven warships and a tremendous radar and sonar net to keep off any foreign powers, especially a Russian spy-ship-cum-trawler that was moving in and was under twenty-four-hour surveillance. Over a hundred sea-floor contacts awaited the arrival of the submersibles to examine and retrieve them. Two were conceivably pieces of the missing bomb—if it had broken up on contact with the ocean. This seemed unlikely, since sea-water samples being taken every eight hours showed no hint of radioactive contamination.

Francisco Simo Orts, meanwhile, was again asked to lead investigators to the spot where he claimed the parachutes had gone down. He did it perfectly. Simo Orts knew his ocean.

Meanwhile, the Navy, using a computer on sophisticated mathematical calculations involving the known land sites of the three recovered bombs, tried to establish the point of actual collision in the air. This resulted, finally, in a triangle some twenty miles long and ten miles along the base, which was considered the primary Zone of High Probability for the site of the errant bomb.

But, then, why couldn't anybody find it?

On February 10, everything was ready for the initial dunking of *Aluminaut* and *Alvin*. Everything, that is, except the natural forces, which are ineluctably opposed to ocean salvage operations. A sudden sixty-mile-an-hour mistral blew out of the Sierra Lisbona. This cut visibility to one yard, tore *Alvin* loose from his moorings, and threatened to capsize and perhaps sink him. All operations were halted for several days.

On the fifteenth, both submersibles were finally ready for work. They were to examine those two intriguing contacts—each some two thousand feet down—which might just possibly be pieces of the bomb. They were wing fragments from the B-52, it developed, but by then the subs had another, more embarrassing mission. The Air Force had sent another B-52 up to the same altitude, position, and course as the one that had crashed, and this B-52 had dropped a dummy nuclear bomb so they could watch it land and thus get a good idea of how the real bomb might have acted.

The Air Force had lost its dummy bomb, too.

The storm ended, and the entire flotilla went into action for the first time. The search area was divided by depth.

Down to 130 feet: frogmen in a shoulder-to-shoulder search.

Down to 200 feet: Sea Scanners and oxy-helium divers.

Down to 400 feet: hard-hat divers, mine sweepers, OBSS side-looking sonar, and the *Cubmarine* (hastily equipped with a robot grappling arm).

Beyond 400 feet: OBSS, underwater TV, *Alvin*, and *Aluminaut*.

Meanwhile, more highly specialized ships were arriving every hour, crammed with the most complex array of locating equipment ever assembled. The oceanographic research vessel *Mizar* carried UTE (Underwater Tracking Equipment), side-looking sonar, and underwater TV and still cameras—all mounted on underwater sleds known as "fish sleds" so they could be towed around the search area. To pull the sleds, the *Mizar* had three miles of 30,000-pound-test armored signal cable on special winches. She was thus equipped to locate the bomb and then direct the submersibles to it.

Another new ship was the USS *Luiseno*, a 1675-ton fleet tug equipped with decompression chamber, towing winch, and heavy-duty lifting winch, which soon proved useful in raising a ten-ton wing section that had been discovered by the frogmen.

A third key vessel was the USS *Hoist*, a 1900-ton salvage vessel equipped with two hoisting booms capable of lugging ten tons and twenty tons respectively to the surface. This ship would be used exclusively for recovery of debris from the wrecked airplane.

The final new type of vessel on the scene was the *Privateer*, a 250-ton support and tracking vessel owned by Reynolds Aluminum. It had the latest radar, loran, and radio gear, as well as an echo sounder with a precision depth recorder that gave an enlarged presentation of the signal from the bottom. Her sonar telephones were sensitive enough to keep in touch with *Aluminaut* over distances as great as twelve thousand yards.

While this bewildering array of ships was arriving, the four mine sweepers were being relieved by four new ones: *Ability*, *Rival*, *Salute*, and *Multiple*. Each one was fitted out with interrogators for the Decca Navigational System. These sent a steady stream of position demands to the master station ashore, which was located near an old Moorish fort on the bluffs overlooking the sea.

Seven weeks after the crash, on March 1, the U. S. Government finally got around to admitting publicly that there had been more than one H-bomb involved in the crash, and that one of these had been (ahem) "lost." The man made happiest by this burst of candor was the poor, bedeviled Information Officer, finally freed from such "press briefings" as the following:

"If you think we have found what you think we are looking for . . ." (long pause) "Well, think what you like! But don't think it's the truth!"

In announcing the loss of the bombs, Washington opened the whole can of worms. It admitted that two of the three bombs recovered ashore had split their casings, exploded their TNT, and spewed radioactive fissionable material about. It was enriched U-235 and plutonium 239, which had a . . . hum, well, actually, an effective radioactive life of, er, 24,400 years. Oh, nothing to worry about, of course. It just meant that 265 acres of farmland had to be carefully stripped of its topsoil, which then had to be packed into five thousand 55-gallon oil drums, shipped to the United States, and interred in a nuclear graveyard.

By March 3, two hundred underwater contacts had been recorded. *Alvin* had made fifty dives, and it and *Aluminaut* had brought up many pieces of wreckage with their robot grappling arms. They also had attached lifting cables so surface vessels could use their powerful winches on the heavier pieces.

FRANCISCO SIMO ORTS POINTS THE WAY

Francisco Simo, meanwhile, kept patiently taking investigators out to *his* site, and watching them write down the positions on their charts[1] and go away. He was indicating an area where the water was over two thousand feet deep, and only *Alvin* or *Aluminaut* could operate at that depth. Even so, Guest was coming around to a belief that Simo was one of those rare men who are truly accurate observers.

At the moment, Guest had troubles other than Spanish fishermen. The Russian spy ship/trawler kept moving closer to the search area, until it finally was only three miles away. What the Americans would have done had she actually steamed into the armada of salvage vessels was never tested; one day, for no discernible reason, she pulled up anchor and left.

On March 8, U. S. Ambassador to Spain Angier Biddle Duke took an icy plunge into the ocean off Palomares to show the world that the water was not contaminated with radioactivity. The world's reaction is not recorded.

By March 9, 358 contacts had been made. Over a hundred of them were still to be investigated, but 175 pieces of the plane—from ten ounces to ten tons each—had been recovered. Even the tail plates of the bomb had been brought up by *Aluminaut*, and Guest had begun to fear that the bomb itself, parachute still probably attached, might have been dragged out to sea by the strong tidal currents. He decided to designate the 27.33 square miles around Simo's area as a second, lesser Zone of High Probability.

With this official benediction ringing in its metal ears, *Alvin* went to Simo's area on Tuesday, March 15, to make a test dive with some new equipment. Pilots Valentine Wilson and Marvin McCamis thought they could test it more thoroughly out there in the deep water.

FIRST CONTACT WITH ROBERT

They reached the sea floor an hour after their 9:20-A.M. entry. It was an area of great valleys and steep slopes, so they cruised about with all scanners scanning, all sonars pinging, and all eyes peering at the television or out the windows. At 11:50 A.M. they were going up a very steep slope; when they got up to 2550 feet, with visibility only eight feet, a section of parachute came into view. For a few minutes they hovered over a twenty-foot-wide gully, intently looking by the illumination of their powerful undersea lamps.

Then came the electrifying message through the sonar telephone aboard the support ship *Rival:* "INSTRUMENT PANEL! INSTRUMENT PANEL!"

That was the code designation for the missing H-bomb. Working from Simo's position, *Alvin* had taken just eighty minutes to locate it—after the Navy had spent fifty-eight days (at $1 million a day) looking in the wrong part of the ocean.

The most immediate danger was that *Alvin*, in attempting to photograph the parachute-shrouded object for certain identification, might knock it off the slope and into an adjoining crevice—which was too narrow for even that small sub to follow. There was also the danger of detonating the bomb's TNT with a sudden bump or jolt.

Alvin took pictures for four hours, then was ordered to cut lights and motors, and to stand by in submarine sentry duty until the *Aluminaut* could come down and relieve it.

This took over an hour; when they met, it was the first subsurface rendezvous of submersibles in history. *Aluminaut* did more than relieve the smaller sub, however: it also brought with it a sonar transponder—an electronic device that was to be attached to the bomb or its parachute. The important feature of this homing device is that a sonar signal from a searching ship triggers it, and it sends out its own signal on a different frequency. This makes it possible to identify and home on a transponder.

Attaching the transponder to the parachute took three hours; *Aluminaut* had to stay there another twenty-one hours while the photographs were being developed to confirm that it was the bomb. It was. Guest designated it CONTACT 261, called the bomb ROBERT, and named the parachute DOUGLAS (the names of his two sons).

The submersibles now began taking turns trying to hook lifting lines into the parachute shrouds. Robert refused to co-operate, burying himself deeper in the mud and also sliding an inch at a time toward the edge of that adjoining unplumbed crevice. By March 19, Guest had decided it wasn't going to work. He ordered the submersibles' crews to try to hook an anchor into the parachute or its shrouds instead, so they could drag Robert into a shallower and safer position before trying to raise him.

That same afternoon a thirty-five-knot gale blew up, preventing all work by the submersibles. It was not until March 23 that *Alvin* could rush back to the bomb's location. The salvors' great fear was that the storm had disturbed deep-water tidal currents enough to shift the bomb, bury it, or maybe dump it over the edge of the crevice.

But Robert was waiting for them patiently. From the salvage ship's boom, they lowered the rescue rig—a three-inch nylon line and an anchor—and *Alvin* began trying to hook the shrouds of the chute. It was a long process, because each try stirred up enough silt so that a half-hour wait was necessary. Then the bomb suddenly moved, and slid three feet down the slope toward the crevice.

Alvin left hurriedly. *Aluminaut* came down. The work went on—unsuccessfully.

Guest and his advisers feared that the submersibles might never get the anchor hooked into the shrouds, so they decided to try the newly developed CURV. This remotely controlled search and salvage machine, brain child of Howard Talkington of NOTS, is officially designated as the Cable-Controlled Underwater Research Vehicle. CURV looked very much like a helicopter landing gear with a lot of things hanging off it—a one-ton frame structure made of fifteen-foot lengths of pipe. Mounted on it were four ballast tubes (for depth control), three electric propulsion motors, mercury-vapor lamps pressurized for deep diving, sonar, and optical and television cameras. CURV had three outstanding liabilities: it was in Long Beach, California; its detachable claw (with which they had hoped to grasp Robert) could not open wide enough to seize the bomb; and it was pressurized for only two thousand feet.

CURV could be "modified" for twenty-eight hundred feet, Guest said, and the claw could be used to grasp the parachute and shrouds rather than the bomb itself, then could be detached and left hanging there on the parachute with a buoyed line attached. This line could be winched up, and Robert could be dragged to safer, shallower water.

The modified CURV arrived on March 25; the same night, *Alvin* made another attempt to hook the anchor into the parachute shrouds, came down right on top of the bomb, and was nearly engulfed by the obstreperous parachute known as Douglas. In backing off, *Alvin* accidentally dragged the anchor into the nylon folds and neatly hooked them.

Immediately, *Hoist* was brought in to drag the warhead up the 70-degree slope to a safer resting place. Robert and Douglas together weighed less than two thousand pounds; the three-inch nylon lifting line had a test strength of over ten thousand. But when Robert was thirty feet above the bottom . . . the line parted! It had been sawed through by a rough edge of one of the anchor flukes.

ROBERT GETS AWAY

The crew of the *Alvin* watched in absolute horror as Robert (still lovingly enfolded by Douglas) plunged down the slope like a good broken-field runner, leap-frogged the gully, side-stepped the crevice, and disappeared into a flurry of mud on the other side.

Aluminaut went down immediately, as *Alvin*'s batteries were exhausted, and tracked the transponder's signals to a depth of 2850 feet. The bomb now rested on a slippery 35-degree slope above a hole forty-two hundred feet deep. Its position was precarious.

CURV, which hadn't even been in the water yet, had to be hastily modified for this new depth. Then surface storms stopped operations for several days. *Alvin* finally got back down on April 1, but by then the bomb had disappeared!

Its transponder was still working, however; they realized that Robert had been buried by sliding mud. For several days, CURV, *Alvin*, and *Aluminaut* groped unsuccessfully in the mud with their remote-control claws. Finally, on the fifth, CURV's cameras showed that Douglas had been uncovered by a kindly current and was flapping lazily above the mud. CURV homed in with its high-resolution sonar, and from two feet away snapped shut its claw in the billowing silk. The claw was ejected, and its buoy automatically headed for the surface, dragging the recovery line with it.

Now *Alvin* returned, hoping to get into place a five-eighth-inch braided nylon line with a breaking strength of 10,800 pounds. It made several unsuccessful runs; then its crew reported that Robert was moving downward again. In thirty hours it slid some three hundred feet west-southwest. Desperate now, Wilson and McCamis aboard the submersible ran in closer than ever in an attempt to hook their line. Instead they ran head-on into the parachute. They were enveloped, held fast on the bottom; and they had only four hours left on their batteries.

"*Alvin* to Control. *Alvin* to Control. We are entangled with Robert and completely covered."

Their message was for information only; there was nothing at all that those at the surface could do to help them. They switched off their interior lights to conserve juice while they began their delicate maneuvering. Finally, fortunately, the sub pulled free.

They resurfaced, recharged, and by 10:00 A.M. the next day were back on the bottom, despite twenty-two-knot surface winds and five-foot seas. Before rough weather halted operations entirely, they succeeded in getting their line hooked into the top of the parachute.

Shortly after 1:00 A.M. on the seventh, CURV went down. At 3:15 A.M., the robot also fouled the parachute, just as *Alvin* had done. But this time there was no human intelligence to guide it free. The two lines on the parachute began getting more and more taut, for now they carried CURV's extra ton as well—and the bomb was still on the move. At 7:00 A.M., Guest made his decision.

"We have to take the weapon now," he told the crew, "before it is too late."

He had decided to draw everything up at once: bomb, CURV, and parachute, depending primarily on the recovery line just attached by CURV, but also determined to pick up part of the strain with CURV's electrical cable.

"Commence lifting!" he ordered.

SUCCESSFUL RECOVERY

The bomb came up at a rate of twenty-seven feet per minute; at 8:19 A.M. there was a harrowing crisis when CURV suddenly disentangled itself and swung free. The men at the controls somehow dragged it completely clear without snagging or breaking the lift lines. When Robert was a hundred feet below the surface, the lift was halted so that Moody and his SCUBA divers could swim down and strap several wires about the round metal belly.

At 8:45 A.M. the ten-foot silvery bomb came from the sea. The lift had taken one hour and forty-five minutes; the nuclear warhead had been on the bottom seventy-nine days, twenty-two hours, and twenty-three minutes. Checking with radiation-detection meters showed there had been no radioactive leakage. Several electric plugs were disconnected to defuse the TNT detonating charge, and at 10:14 A.M. Guest uttered the words terminating Robert's odyssey.

"The bomb has fallen safe," he announced.

The next day, newsmen aboard the *Albany* were allowed to view and photograph Robert in his place of honor on the *Petrel*'s fantail. This was to forestall Russian suggestions that it really hadn't been recovered. One of the reporters asked Guest what of value remained below.

"Anyone who wants to pick up anything on the bottom can sure as hell have it," he replied. "It's not worth anything."

The Palomares salvage operation was finished—the most extensive and most costly in history. The most advanced technological methods in the world were used to ensure its success. It must have been frustrating to the men who had found the bomb and raised it: their work was denigrated in the press, and to some extent neutralized by rather frenzied government bureaucratic hysteria. Despite its "bad press" in many news media, Palomares was a salvage triumph. And the techniques worked out there were not only instrumental in the later *Scorpion* operation; they radically advanced the state of the salvage art.

Two years after Palomares, on January 21, 1968, it happened again. Another SAC B-52 carrying four nuclear bombs was on routine patrol when a fire broke out in the cabin. The crippled plane headed for the closest haven, Thule Air Force Base, Greenland, but the seven-man crew had to abandon it short of their destination. The copilot was killed, and the plane crashed on the ice covering North Star Bay, some seven miles short of the air base.

Denmark, which owns Greenland, has a long-standing interdiction of U.S. overflights of their territory with nuclear-device-bearing planes. But the Danish Government recognized the emergency nature of the situation, and no international incident developed. Instead, a tight security lid was clamped down over the incident.

Certain details have emerged, however. Low-level alpha radiation was recorded on the foot gear of the searchers who first reached the site. This led to fears that the bombs may have broken up on contact with the ice; and it seemed at least possible that the giant burning plane might have melted right through the seven-foot ice and sunk into the bay.

Bill Searle, as head of Navy Salvage, again was alerted to the possibility that he might have to go out looking for dunked nuclear hardware. He called in the Navy's prime civilian contractor, Ocean Systems, and began planning two possible salvage approaches.

First was the possibility of diving through the ice, which definitely was within the state of the art at the time. Divers would wear heated wet suits; North Star Bay averaged only about seventy-two feet in depth, and nowhere was deeper than 132 feet. Again, well within technical reach of the salvors. If the plane *had* burned through, and the bombs *had* sunk intact to the sea floor, time was a factor, and this method was indicated.

But searchers ashore, meanwhile, had found important new evidence on the floe, and the Air Force had gotten positively chatty about their finds.

"Serial numbers on weapon fragments found on the ice at the site of the crash," their release stated, "correspond with Strategic Air Command records of numbers on various components of the four weapons."

1. Today's hard-hat diving suit is essentially the same as that invented by Augustus Siebe in 1837. A single rubber-and-twill garment, a tinned copper helmet that locks onto the suit's segmented corselet ring, and lead-soled shoes. PHOTO CREDIT: *Wide World Photos*

2. The new surface-demand suit the Royal Navy uses for depths down to 600 feet. It owes much of its design to SCUBA gear. The rubber suit and helmet allow much greater diver maneuverability. PHOTO CREDIT: *Royal Navy*

3. A reconstruction of Edward Lloyd's coffeehouse (1689), birthplace of Lloyd's of London. Note shipping news chalked on the blackboard — forerunner of the newssheet *Lloyd's News*. Notice of a "sale by candle" is posted on the wall behind the "pulpit." PHOTO CREDIT: *Lloyd's of London*

4. The *Titanic* slip. A broker makes out a "slip" containing the details of the proposed coverage. Underwriters put on the slip (and initial) the amount of the risk they are accepting, which is known as "writing a line." Amounts are in British pounds. PHOTO CREDIT: *Lloyd's of London*

5. The Underwriters Room in the new (1957) Lloyd's of London building is the size of an American football field, with 44,000 square feet of floor space. Underwriters in the second-floor galleries specialize in non-marine insurance risks. PHOTO CREDIT: *Lloyd's of London*

6. The SDC (Submersible Decompression Chamber) was invented by Robert H. Davis in 1928. Here, a Royal Navy SDC is winched back aboard HMS *Reclaim* following sea-bottom tests in 1965. Cylinders contain oxy-helium breathing mixture used by the divers.
PHOTO CREDIT: *Royal Navy*

7. A Royal Navy diver re-enters the SDC after a 600-foot descent off Toulon, France. Inner air pressure prevents water from entering the chamber's open bottom. Diver commences decompression while the chamber is being returned to the surface. PHOTO CREDIT: *Royal Navy*

8. The Yellow Submarine: The U. S. Navy's habitat for Sealab III being winched from the water of San Francisco Bay following its first "wet test." Later, diver Barry Cannon lost his life during disastrous deepwater (610 feet) tests off San Clemente Island in February 1969. PHOTO CREDIT: U.S. Navy

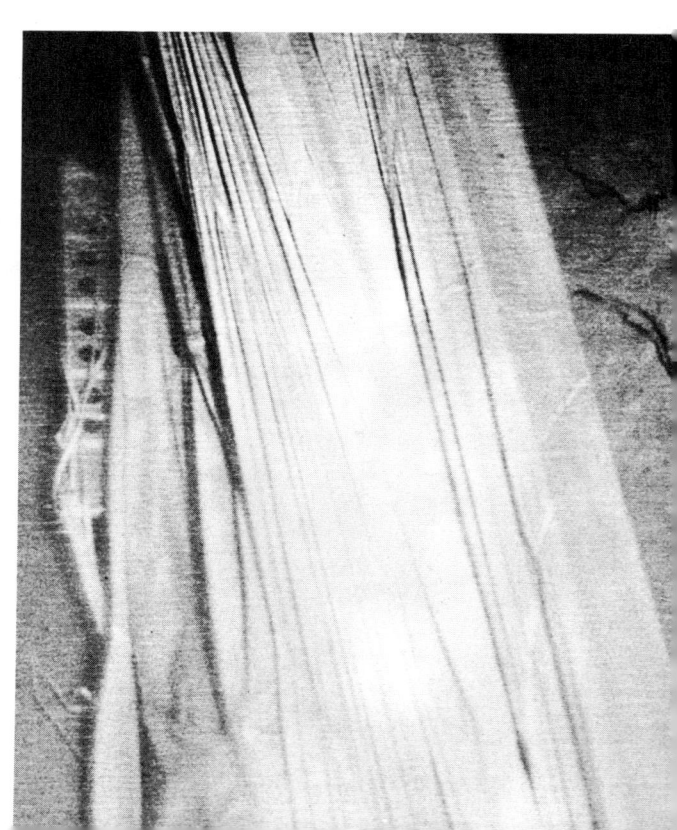

9. "INSTRUMENT PANEL! INSTRUMENT PANEL!" These words on the sonar telephone from submersible Alvin on the seafloor at 2550 feet, off Palomares, Spain, marked the discovery of the nuclear device lost there in the crash of a B-52 bomber in January 1966. The bomb's holed metal bomb-rack bracket can be seen at left, under the bomb's parachute. PHOTO CREDIT: U.S. Navy

10. U. S. Navy submarine *S-51*, lost with 34 crewmen on September 25, 1925, is towed triumphantly into New York Harbor nearly a year later. The vessel, with only the American flag flying from its conning tower visible, is supported by the pontoons used in raising it. PHOTO CREDIT: *U. S. Bureau of Ships*

11. On the first attempt to raise *S-51*, she slipped her lifting cables and shrugged off her pontoons to slide back to the bottom 132 feet below. One of the out-of-control pontoons, similar to the one shown, burst from the surface like an errant rocket. PHOTO CREDIT: *Wide World Photos*

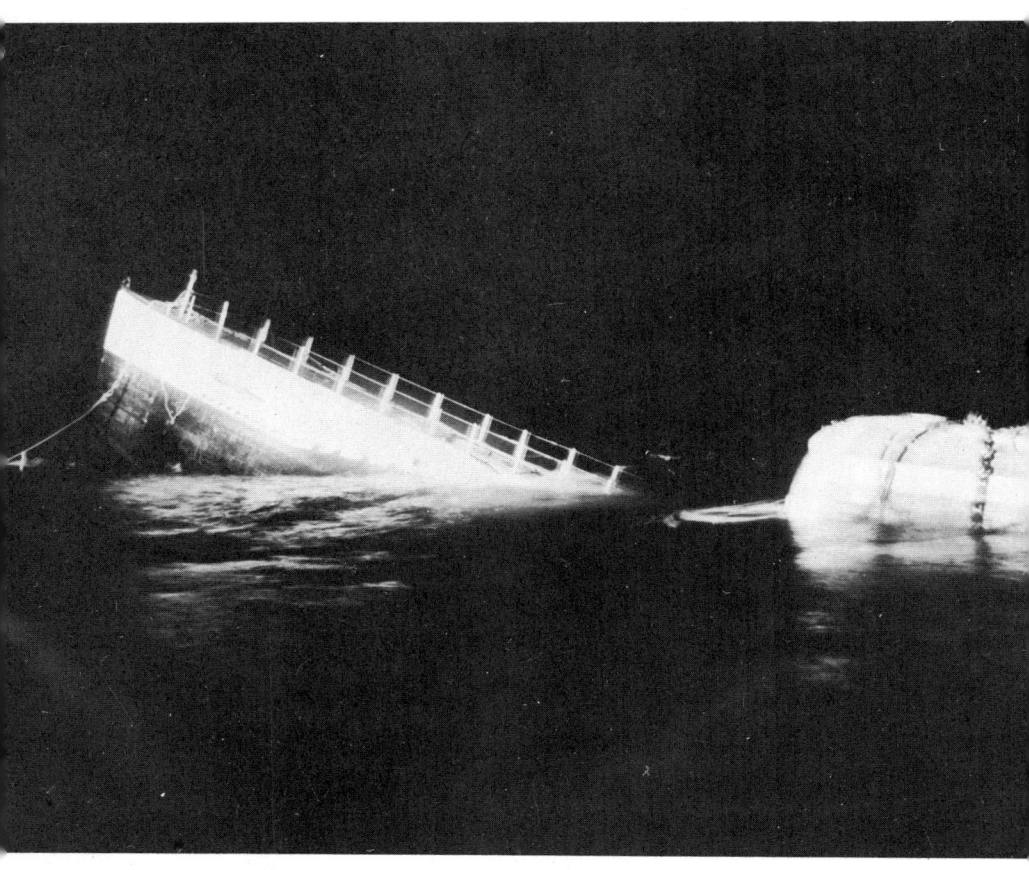

12. U. S. Navy submarine *S-4* breaks the surface with the aid of pontoons on December 12, 1928, after being deliberately sunk in 60 feet of water under control conditions. The tests failed because the stern (due to an unforeseen engine-room leak) remained firmly stuck in the mud. PHOTO CREDIT: *Wide World Photos*

This changed the whole picture. Six hundred containers of ice, snow, and other residue were painfully collected and carefully sealed, and stored against the summer thaw, when they could be shipped back to the United States by MSTS ships for disposal. That could not be the end of it, however. The breakup of the bombs meant, inevitably, that radioactive material had spilled out of the bomb cases, had been caught in the ice where it had eluded the searchers, and would drop to the bottom of the bay once the ice had melted.

The Air Force knew there was virtually no danger of the radioactive debris affecting marine life in the area—the water would act as an effective shield against that—but there was danger of some of it being washed ashore. Picked up barehanded by an unsuspecting person, it could cause a fatal dose of radiation poisoning.

That meant a subsurface search of the cold black waters of North Star Bay by the Navy once the ice had cleared. Searle now had to plan his operation against the appearance of the "window"—the two-month summer, when the ice would melt sufficiently to make the bay accessible to surface craft. The salvage ships would have to pass through Baffin Bay, part of which remains frozen year round, but the *Mizar*, most probable vessel for the attempt, had a hull reinforced against ice.

As it developed, *Mizar* was not needed. Instead, the Navy leased Electric Boat's *Star III*, a spanking-new experimental deep submersible (see Chapter Thirty), for the underwater work. The Danes were very co-operative, furnishing scientists and the 54-foot survey ship *Aglantha*. *Star III* spent ten days in repeated dives; what she found, if anything, has never been released. Radiological monitoring of the area continued for a year, and the Danes said their scientists would be making "ecological surveys" of the bay for some time.

It seems unlikely, however, that the U. S. Government would have closed the investigation if anything of potential value or potential danger were left around for some other nation's salvors to pick up.

One other deepwater airplane-recovery operation ought to be mentioned here. Although nuclear armaments were not involved, many of the same search, locate, and recovery problems were; and the salvors solved them in somewhat different ways.

OSE DOES IT RIGHT OFF LOS ANGELES

Until January 1969, Los Angeles had never had a major airliner crash. Then, within three days of each other, a Scandinavian Airlines 707 and a United Airlines 727 crashed in the sea off L.A. International Airport. The SAS plane undershot the airstrip as it was coming in, presumably as the result of a missetting of the altimeter.

Most of it remained afloat, and most of the crew and passengers escaped into life rafts; however, the tail section, aft of the wing, broke off and sank immediately, taking with it fifteen persons.

Ocean Science and Engineering, Inc., immediately contacted SAS regarding the salvage of the lost tail and began work the following day on a no-cure, no-pay contract. The company's ship *Oceaneer*, captained by Alec Winton, was hastily equipped with autotape precise-position indicator, EG&G side-looking sonar, and an underwater television camera. In the first two days, the search was complicated by dozens of small craft out "looking"—mainly for floating souvenirs. On the third day, the ship reported by radiotelephone that it had new and important information and would come into Marina del Rey at noon.

The excitement in the voices made it clear that the search had produced results, so Willard Bascom, OSE's president, who is always looking for an excuse to go to sea, and Jack Mardesich, the company's chief field engineer, met the ship at the pier. The news was this: two excellent sonar contacts two thousand feet apart were almost certainly parts of the aircraft; both had been plainly marked with white buoys. One site was still sending up bits of flotsam (the ship had brought in a handbag and some shoes), so *Oceaneer* had left its small boat tied to the buoy with two men to maintain OSE's claim to the find.

Oceaneer, with Bascom and Mardesich aboard, returned to the buoy and picked up two shivering men and some more flotsam just at dusk. Clearly, the main part of the tail with the bodies and flight recorder had been found (although with the pilots alive the latter was not needed), but OSE had not settled the value of the "cure" payment with SAS. So it was decided that *Oceaneer* would cruise in the area that night until a price could be put on salvaging the tail. The sea was dark and stormy, with gusty showers and wind over twenty knots, so the crew was astonished to see day-fishing boats and pleasure craft heading out to sea at 9:00 P.M.

The ship's radio was turned on, and *Oceaneer* learned that a second plane was down. This was fantastic: a specifically equipped salvage ship operating within a few miles of a crash at sea! In a few days, a search and salvage contract had been worked out with Jacobson Brothers (owner of the J-Star search television equipment) and United Airlines (owner of the aircraft). *Oceaneer* was now working a paying job. SAS was forgotten in the intense night-and-day search for the new wreck.

About a week later, Lockheed's submarine *Deep Quest* arrived to "search" for the SAS plane. It dived alongside one of the OSE buoys and announced loudly that it had "found" the tail section after only fifteen minutes of looking. Later the plane's wheels were found at the second buoy. Lockheed continued to make headlines with its sub while both SAS and UAL writhed; the last thing an airline wants is to have its name associated with a crash in daily press releases.

Both crashes at once became the subject of intense scrutiny by the National Transportation Safety Board, for, as Tom Saunders, their chief investigator, said, "The constantly increasing demand for safer aircraft and improved operating procedures requires that we probe every crash to determine its cause."

The Navy at Palomares had been rather tardy in listening to the testimony of the fisherman Francisco Simo, but Carl Christensen, whom United Airlines had assigned to the recovery project, and the NTSB men, began by seeking out and interviewing every shore witness they could find. The plane had gone down at night, in broken clouds with rain and lashing winds; the Coast Guard had a tentative position marked, but it was a guess—and not a very good one. These men therefore carefully re-examined the Los Angeles Airport radar plot of the plane's take-off direction, and then worked out the maximum and minimum turning radii, which would bound the wreck's position.

Oceaneer started its search with the side-looking sonar fish at the Coast Guard's plotted location. From there, the vessel worked in ever-widening circles until fourteen square miles had been covered. The EG&G Oceanographic Recorder made a permanent, continuous, graphic record with a helical electrode of the things "seen" by the sonar fish below; these included many curious lumps and bumps known *not* to be wreckage from the 727 jetliner, as well as a fascinating profile of Los Angeles' main sewer pipe.

At 3:00 P.M. on February 1—less than two weeks after the plane had gone down, only a week since OSE had begun searching—the smooth bottom record was flecked with marks in an oval pattern some two thousand feet long.

Fred Anderson, Project Engineer from EG&G, who was watching the record of the side-looking sonar and interpreting its record, saw the wreck first and relayed the information to Captain Winton.

Now the Jacobson Brothers "J-Star" was brought into play. J-Star is an underwater television camera complete with its own lights which can be pointed and focused from the surface. It is steady (instead of swinging or rotating, like many systems), because it is suspended between four light wires leading to anchors at compass points. By adjusting the lengths of opposite wires, the position of the camera can be delicately adjusted to examine and study bottom details.

The J-Star was immediately lowered to make a preliminary inspection. It found and returned to the surface a twisted piece of metal that confirmed the identity of the wreck nearly a thousand feet below. Three position buoys were set out for mooring the *Oceaneer*, and then a careful map was made of the fragments. J-Star was sent down again to examine the wreckage piece by piece and plot the relative position of each of the major fragments. The airline was most vitally concerned with the location of the engines, the flight recorder, and the pilot's voice recorder.

Once the position chart had been completed, the actual salvage work began. The engines were first, and were brought up by the ingenious device of attaching a hydraulically powered claw below the J-Star. The television eye would tell the salvors in the *Oceaneer* above just when they should close the claw. Three engines, each about four feet in diameter and fifteen feet long (five thousand pounds), were brought to the surface in a single day from 960 feet of water, a new record for deepwater salvage. The tail section came next, and much of the balance was trawled up with nets.

Before the end of the month—only six weeks after the 727 had crashed—the experts were organizing and assembling the pieces, searching for the cause of the crash.

Tom Saunders of NTSB, deeply impressed, passed on his "congratulations to the men and companies who successfully salvaged this aircraft from deep water."

---

[1] The Navy men went to the length of secretly moving the vessel while Simo was below at lunch, then asking him on his return to deck if he was *sure* this was the site. Simo invariably responded, "You have moved the boat. The site is *over there*."

II

She Goes Alone

> None of the world's oceans can be denied to her, even though she goes alone . . .
>
> REAR ADMIRAL L. R. DASPIT
> at the launching of the
> nuclear submarine *Thresher*.

CHAPTER EIGHT

Early Submersibles

Raising sunken submarines holds a unique position in the lore of marine salvage. If it is tried at all, it begins with an attempt to locate and make contact with the missing vessel immediately, and ends with saving, or failing to save, those crewmen who might still be alive aboard the sunken sub. Following this, there *may* be a separate, conventional operation to raise the submarine itself.

Even here, the motive usually is unique to submarines: they are raised either to recover the bodies, or to find out why they sank in the first place. When the American *F-4* went down off Hawaii, on March 25, 1915, for example, the Navy ordered her raised even though the hulk was considered worthless and the great depth at which she lay, 304 feet, precluded any possibility of saving the crew. This was forced by a public outcry almost exactly like that which was to greet the loss of the nuclear submarine *Thresher* forty-eight years later.[1]

RECORD DIVE TO F-4

It took salvage master Julius Furer, a U. S. Navy officer, some time just to find the *F-4*, which was lying two miles east of the entrance to Pearl Harbor. Bubbles of oil and air finally led him to the site, so Furer sent Chief Gunner's Mate Agraz, a part American Indian diver, down to see if he could spot the wreck. Agraz got down to 215 feet—*five feet deeper than Damant's world record of a few years before*—but still could see neither the *F-4* nor the bottom.

Tugs soon snared the submarine—but there was no lifting equipment available. This meant that Furer faced some formidable problems in carrying out Rear Admiral Moore's salvage order, even apart from the depth of nearly fifty-one fathoms. First of all, tide lifts were the usual method of raising sunken craft in 1915. Lifting-lighters at the surface would be "watered" and then fastened in this partially submerged condition to the sunken vessel at low tide. The rising water, and the simultaneous pumping out of the lighter, would bring the ship off the bottom so it could be towed landward until it grounded again. The lines would be shortened at the next low tide, the process would be repeated, and so the vessel eventually would be beached.

The tides at Honolulu are only eighteen inches.

With 304 feet to go, Furer hurriedly decided on a mechanical lift. *F-4*, after all, was of a modest 260-ton displacement; she could feasibly be winched dead-weight to the surface. Put the winches on the lifting-lighters, and . . .

There were no lighters in Honolulu.

The inventive Furer borrowed a pair of 104-foot garbage scows. They were bottom dumpers, so the wells, or mud-pockets, in their centers could be used for the lowering of the lifting cables from the winches.

In Honolulu, however, there were no winches.

The salvors improvised again: they used sugar-mill shafting for the drums around which the lifting cables could be bent. With power for these winches and compressed air for the hard-hat divers furnished by the salvage ship's generators . . .

But there was no salvage ship, either.

This time it was an old dredge that was pressed into service. Their equipment problems settled, the salvors next had to get the lifting cables under the submarine. They used the conventional "sweeping" method for this: trailing enormous loops of cable off the stern of their salvage ship and slipping them, one by one, under the hull of the sub. Four such cables would suffice; the trick was to place them correctly, so that the *F-4* would not break in half of her own weight once she was off the bottom.

Normally, divers would go down to visually check the placement of the cables: but in 1915, remember, the world's deep-diving record had unofficially been broken by their own Gunner's Mate Agraz in getting to just 215 feet. This was nearly a hundred feet short of the F-4, but Furer, like all salvage men the world over, was stubborn. He needed divers: he was going to have divers.

On April 12, he got them. Men, diving gear, and a decompression chamber arrived from the New York Navy Yard Diving School aboard the USS *Maryland*. In charge of the four-man team was George Stillson, holder of the 274-foot world depth record. Just two days later, diver Frank Crilley made it all the way down to the sunken sub. He reported her lying upright, unholed, with her rudder set as if she had been in a turn when she had gone down. He also found that the two 7-ton slings already in place had to be shifted. Crilley's only ill effects from the record-shattering dive were a temporary case of the bends and a mild dose of pneumonia.

Then the lift began. The sugar-drum winches got F-4 a dozen feet off the bottom—and a cable broke. They tried to rerig it, but a gale blew up, which snapped the rest of them. This dumped the sub back on the bottom, stern first, so she buried her tail in the mud. The salvors eased the cable strain by putting a fifteen-fathom shot of anchor chain in the center of each sling, but it took them twenty-one days to resweep the new cables.

This lift was so successful that they were able to ground F-4 in a mere fifty feet of water just outside Pearl Harbor. Then another storm blew the improvised salvage fleet into shelter; when they returned, they found that the sub's hull had collapsed under one of the lifting cables.

If anything went wrong this time, they would be dumping the hulk right in the middle of Pearl Harbor; so they decided to try something different for the final effort. Furer casually invented the method that was later to become the standard means of raising sunken submarines: submersible pontoons. No such animal existed, so he ordered four of them, each thirty-two feet long and twelve feet in diameter, made of steel, from the Mare Island Naval Ship Yard at Vallejo, California. The pontoons would exert a combined lifting capacity of 420 tons. They would need it, Furer knew, since the sub was now filling rapidly with mud. The watertight compartments of the pontoons were flooded, the lifting cables were threaded through their hawse holes, and they were submerged down to the wreck. On August 29, 1915, they were "blown"—the water inside them was forced out with compressed air—and within two hours F-4 popped to the surface.

Subsequent examination showed that sixteen of the twenty-two crewmen had sought refuge aft, but that their watertight compartment door had collapsed and they had drowned. It was found that acid leaking from the storage-battery jars somehow had gotten through the sheet lead protecting the main-ballast-tank bulkhead, so that water could seep through the corroded tank bulkhead into the battery compartment. This destroyed the trim of the *F-4* at a critical moment in a dive. Down she had gone.

A mechanical lift was also used on the British *L-55*, sunk in the Baltic Sea by enemy warships during World War I. It lay forgotten until 1926, when a fishing trawler happened to bring up a piece of her deck cannon. This sent the fledgling Communist government of Russia flapping into action. In April 1928, they managed to bring her to the surface from the soft bottom on which she was resting at 104 feet.

The singular fact about the *L-55* operation is that this British sub was repaired and renovated by the Communists and commissioned into the Soviet Navy. There it served for many years.

SUBMARINE DYNAMICS

All bodies, including subs, float or sink in water according to their displacement: that is, their buoyancy depends on whether they weigh more or less than the water they replace. Anything that will sink at all will sink until it hits bottom. Increasing the weight will sink it statically; it is also possible to make an object dive, or submerge dynamically.

Modern submarines use both methods simultaneously to submerge. Ballast tanks are flooded until the vessel is nearly awash; at the same time, she moves forward with her diving planes (horizontal rudders) at a slight downward inclination. Adjustments of these diving planes also keep her at an assigned subsurface cruising depth once she is submerged. Injury or malfunction of the rudders can spell disaster.

During World War I the British submarine *AE-2* was cruising fifty feet down when her diving rudders jammed. Her captain, Commander Stoker, was able to get her to the surface, but she broke water a bare hundred yards from several enemy torpedo boats. Stoker could only order the forward ballast tanks flooded and the motors driven FULL AHEAD. *AE-2* safely submerged again.

But then they couldn't make her stop going down, not until Stoker blew all ballast and ordered FULL ASTERN for all motors. Up she went again, backward; and the German anti-sub boats attacked as her stern broke water.

Ballast tanks flooded. FULL AHEAD. Down went *AE-2* again, nose first, now at such a steep angle that men were standing on bulkheads between compartments rather than on decks. Nothing for it but FULL ASTERN again, ballast tanks blown, and back up to the surface.

That time the German torpedo boats got her.

Until the all-important problem of depth-keeping was solved, submarines were little more than a nautical curiosity—even though the idea of a ship that could sail under the sea was first suggested by William Bourne of England in 1578. Early subs, trimmed to sink statically, just kept going until they hit bottom or imploded. The trouble was that their engines (God help them, the earliest ones were *hand* propelled!) were not powerful enough to control the cruising depth.

Watch a goldfish hover in his bowl, with only an occasional languid wave of his tail; fish have solved the depth-keeping problem by a swim bladder, or air sac, in their bodies. This is a thin, opaque membrane that can be filled with either air or oxygen. In most ocean fish it is a closed system, with a gland called a red body to derive oxygen as needed from the fish's blood stream, and a second organ in the wall of the bladder itself to absorb oxygen that has become excess.

The submarine's trim tanks, which can be blown with compressed air or flooded with sea water to hold it at cruising depth, are very similar in function to the swim bladder; but man took a long time to figure this out. The first undersea boats were probably those recorded by the Swedish historian Olaf Magnus in 1505: sealskin underwater kayaks the Greenlanders had devised for piratical expeditions. The submarines would approach ships under water and bore holes in the wooden bottoms.

THE LONG HISTORY OF SUBMERSIBLES

Russian Cossacks in the mid-1600s used similar cowhide submersibles against Turkish ships in the Sublime Porte, supplying the forty-man crew of rowers with air through breathing reeds.

Yes, rowers. The first real submarine, built in 1620[2] by a Dutchman, Cornelius van Drebbel, also used oars. The craft was made of wood covered with greased leather, and then was strengthened with iron bands. In a test before England's James I it actually "submerged" a dozen feet or so, and was used for some ten years to furnish a novelty ride between Greenwich and Westminster on the Thames.

Another "man-powered" submarine was that "invented" by a certain John Day of Yarmouth, England, who in 1774 bummed £340 from an unknown backer to convert a fifty-ton sloop, the *Maria*, into a submersible. He was going down to three hundred feet for twenty-four hours, he said, but meanwhile he planned a "test dive" to 130 feet. He was sealed into his red-painted craft with a candle, some biscuits, and a bottle of drinking water on a pleasant afternoon in June. All that ever came back up were a few bursts of air bubbles.

One Dr. Falck, an acquaintance, opined that Day had frozen to death.

Oars lasted in the inventors' abortive designs until 1776, when an American named David Bushnell, in a patriotic froth over the Revolutionary War, dreamed up a small, wooden, egg-shaped submersible called the *Turtle*. Bushnell's *Turtle* was propelled by primitive, hand-operated screw propellers, one mounted horizontally for lateral movement, the second mounted vertically for submergence once the ballast tank had been flooded.

The poor devil who operated the *Turtle* was expected to be in perpetual motion: he had to work the propellers; steer (the handle of the tiller fit under one arm); work the water pump and air valve with his feet; be his own lookout through the conning-tower portholes; and, in the white heat of action, screw a magazine containing 150 pounds of powder and a clockwork detonator into the side of an enemy vessel.

The *Turtle*, in the hands of a certain Connecticut sergeant named Ezra Lee, actually launched an attack against the British warship HMS *Eagle*. Lee arrived under the stern of the vessel in the dead of night and at dead slack tide—conditions perfect—and began screwing his explosives into the hull.

Poor Ezra had one rather major problem, however. The *Eagle* had recently been copper-sheathed against *teredos*.[3] Daylight caught the determined Lee still cranking away, bumping along, covering the vessel from bow to stern and back to bow, feverishly searching for an unsheathed area of hull. He didn't find it.

Nobody on the *Eagle* ever knew they had been under attack.

During the Civil War, American interest in submarines was spurred by the Confederate Davids, small hand-propelled subs given the biblical appellation because their purpose was to maul Northern blockade ships many times their size. The *David of Hunley* actually blew up the Union frigate *Housatonic* in 1864—the first successful submarine attack in history —but the Union Goliath sank right on top of her and destroyed both ship and crew.

At about the same time, Europeans were advancing to iron-hulled and power-driven designs. "Power-driven" is a relative term: the *Porpoise*, built in 1886 by J. F. Waddington of England, was thirty-seven feet long and seven and a half feet in diameter, and had a motor that was driven by electric accumulators. And what did they accumulate? *Seven* horsepower. Waddington somehow got four knots submerged speed from fewer horsepower than are developed by the hydraulic lifting device that raises a Cadillac's automatic window.

A really quite brilliant inventor of submersibles was Wilhelm Bauer, a corporal in the Bavarian Light Horse Artillery. His first undersea boat, a porpoise-shaped vessel of iron, was launched at Kiel in 1849. This *Brandtaucher*, or *Fire-Diver*, broke the Danish blockade of Kiel in December 1850 when the Danes fled at sight of the strange craft; but *Fire-Diver* deserves a place in this history because it necessitated the first free escape from a submarine (that is, without an escape lung or similar device). By a series of mishaps, Bauer and his crew ended up sixty feet deep with the nose of their craft buried in the mud and the stern of it nearly stove in. Bauer finally talked his two companions into flooding the craft so inner pressure would equalize with exterior water pressure, thus allowing them to escape.

Each man went up in his individual air bubble like, Bauer said, a champagne cork. They all survived without injury.

In 1855 Bauer launched a second, more successful craft, *Le Diable-Marin*—the *Sea-Devil*. Neither the Russians nor the British would buy the *Sea-Devil* for use against the other in the Crimean War—the purpose that Bauer had envisioned when he built it. He therefore made a series of 134 test dives with an eleven-man crew, to depths of 150 feet, during the months of May–October 1856, recording scientific data in an excellent manner and even attempting underwater photographs through the windows. *Sea-Devil* finally sank, fortunately without loss of life, and Bauer withdrew from the submarine-inventing game. He had realized that underwater craft would not really be practicable until someone created sufficiently powerful engines to drive them.

Unfortunately for the U. S. Navy, an American inventor named Oliver Halstead never attained such an insight—at least not before he had sold a submarine monstrosity called the *Intelligent Whale* to the Navy during the 1870s. The *Whale* managed, at various times, to drown thirty-nine men during its Brooklyn Navy Yard tests. Happily, Halstead was shot to death by his mistress' husband before he could make further alterations in the *Whale* which the Navy might have been tempted to test.

GYMNOTE, FIRST MODERN SUBMARINE

Gymnote, the first modern submarine, was designed by Dupuy de Lôme and built in 1888 for the French Navy. It had a sixty-foot cigar-shaped hull of rolled sheet steel, submerged by vertical screws in conjunction with diving rudders, and had an action radius of 125 miles. Its electric motors furnished five knots submerged, and seven at the surface.

As more subs were built, more were lost; and searching for a lost submarine creates an atmosphere of stark drama unknown to any other salvage operation. When a conventional ship is sunk, those aboard her either remain at the surface or they drown; but submarine crewmen can be trapped, still alive, in their sunken vessel. This gives a terrible urgency to such search operations; yet, relatively few crews have been saved.

If the craft goes down in waters deeper than its designed capabilities, then the pressure will crush the ship and crew alike. Submarine hulls, like any other structures deriving part of their strength from their shape, have their collapse point. In shallower water, where the sub settles intact on the bottom, the crew sometimes can close off the waterproof doors between their compartment and that which is flooded. Then, once they have used up their oxygen, they will have the dubious pleasure of suffocating rather than of drowning or being crushed to death.

The greatest difficulty that would-be rescuers face is finding the lost submarine in the first place. Conditions should have been ideal for locating the S-4, which sank in 1927 after colliding with a Coast Guard cutter. The cutter took position readings three minutes after the crash; the site was buoyed immediately; it was less than a mile from trained shore observers who witnessed the accident; and it was lying in a relatively modest 110 feet of water.

The rescuers spent twelve hours just trying to *find* it.

And even if the position is known exactly, things can go tragically awry. In 1904 the French *Farfadet* submerged during a trial run with some of her hatches still open. Water entered so explosively that three men were fired right out of the conning tower[4] by suddenly compressed air blowing out a bulkhead.

Fourteen other crewmen were still alive in another compartment when *Farfadet* settled on the bottom; since her exact position was marked, salvors worked swiftly. A floating crane was brought up while divers were getting cables through the lifting eyes on the sub's superstructure. The cables were spun onto the crane's drums, and a mechanical dead-weight lift was begun.

Farfadet came up smoothly and swiftly. As her hull broke water, the salvors prepared to open the hatch. That was when the crane broke. The vessel plunged once more to the bottom, and there it stayed, since no other lifting device was available.

Signals were exchanged with the trapped men until they suffocated.

Farfadet was not the only sub lost because someone forgot to close down the hatches. The British *K-13* sank during her trial run in 1917 because the engine-room ventilators were left open; the Russian *Dolphin* went down when the wash of a passing steamer flooded her open hatches; and the British *M-2* opened her hatches too soon while returning to the surface following a dive.

But even more subs have been lost through collision with surface vessels. These always occur through neglect, or because of the submarine's blind period during surfacing, when the periscope is lowered but visual sights cannot yet be taken. The British have been especially unlucky: *A-1* in 1904, *A-4* in 1905, *C-11* in 1909 (after being rammed by the steamer *Eddystone*). Three years later the *B-2* (run down by the steamer *America*), and in 1915 the *E-4* and *E-41* after they collided. *H-42* was rammed by one of her own destroyers off Gibraltar in 1922, and the *M-1* went down in 1925 after being struck by the Swedish steamer *Vidar*. *H-47* was rammed by another sub two years later, and in 1931 the *Poseidon* went down in the China Sea after the Chinese steamer *Yuta* struck her in heavy fog.

FREE ESCAPE FROM SUNKEN SUBMARINES

One of these collisions featured a seemingly miraculous escape which, upon examination, proved to depend upon one man's ingenuity and guts. The submarines E-4 and E-41 collided during maneuvers in the Irish Sea in July 1915. Both went down, E-4 so abruptly that her entire crew drowned, E-41 slowly enough for her entire crew to escape through the conning-tower hatch—except for one man. A chief petty officer named Brown was in the engine room when the crash came; he managed to slam shut the watertight door in the bulkhead while the sub was settling in sixty feet of water.

Brown had no submarine escape gear—none had yet been adopted by any of the world's navies—but he knew that his only hope lay in trying for the surface. This meant somehow opening a hatch cover that had approximately six tons of water pressing it down.

The sailor opened a valve and began flooding his sanctuary with sea water. As the level rose, he knew, it would compress the air trapped in the engine room; when the pressure inside equaled the water pressure outside, he hoped to shove open the hatch and be carried out with the escaping air. Unfortunately, the rising water short-circuited the electric current in the sub, so Brown began getting severe shocks from any metal he touched, and the wet batteries began giving off choking chlorine gas.

Desperate, he tried to shove open the hatch cover too soon: some air escaped, and the cover slammed down, crushing the fingers of one hand. With his uninjured hand he opened all the additional valves he could in order to speed up the flooding process. The water rose until Brown, standing on the engines with his head jammed against the top of the compartment, had only his face above water. He gave a mighty heave and the hatch cover flew open to drop back against the deck. The rush of air carried him to the surface, where he was picked up. He survived.

The submarine is a weapon of war: just how deadly a weapon, was demonstrated by World War I, the first global conflict in the modern sense. Experimentation and development intensified, so that, a few years after the war, one British submarine, the M-2, even carried a midget seaplane in a converted gun housing for reconnaissance work.

German U-boats (U for *untersee*) started the highly effective submarine blockade of Britain in 1915; indeed, the Germans' unrestricted use of subs against merchant vessels and unarmed passenger liners such as the *Lusitania* led the United States to enter the war, in April 1917.

The British tried to overcome the menace with patrol boats, mine fields, and cable nets strung across harbor mouths. The nets were buoyed at the surface so a snagged submarine would agitate the markers, just as a netted fish will agitate the floats on a commercial fisherman's net, and the Admiralty's Salvage Section could drop depth charges to destroy it.

Sometimes they would find German subs that had gone down because of mechanical failure; with no means of escape, the sailors often would have shot themselves to escape slow suffocation, or even have battered their own brains out against the interior of the iron pressure hull.

Certain submarines, such as the *U-44* under Captain Paul Wagenfur, were equipped with special apparatus that allowed them to lay large mine fields while submerged. Wagenfur succeeded in completely closing Waterford Harbor at one time; but then the German Naval High Command issued an order for subs to "destroy without trace" any Allied shipping they could.

On July 31, 1917, *U-44* disabled the unarmed freighter *Belgian Prince* in St. George's Channel. While the *Prince* was scuttled, Wagenfur had the crew brought back to his sub and stripped of life belts, their outer clothing, and all their personal papers. Wagenfur lined them up on the sub's deck and then submerged, leaving the helpless sailors to drown in accord with the High Command's order.

Three of the seamen, however, were wearing life belts under their shirts, and survived. The resultant furious search for *U-44* drove Wagenfur back to mine-laying around Waterford, and on the night of August 4, his submerged vessel unwittingly strayed into a British mine field. When one of his released mines struck a British one, both exploded, ripping off the stern of the sub. Everyone drowned except one man, who lived long enough to identify it as the infamous *U-44* for the fishermen who picked him up.

Two days later, the Admiralty ordered Commander G. Davis of the Salvage Section to recover the submarine for study by British experts. Davis and his men, dragging with grapnels, found the hulk at ninety feet. It lay directly athwart the strong prevailing currents, but the local tides were nearly twenty feet; Davis determined to let them work for him.

After nine days of sweeping, his salvage fleet had their lifting cables in position under the sub. Then a month of gales halted operations. On September 10, they returned with a very large, flat barge whose hull was segmented into watertight compartments. The barge was flooded so that it rode five feet deeper than usual, and was fastened to the lifting cables at low tide. As the tide rose, the barge was pumped out: *U-44* ended up twenty-five feet off the bottom and was towed a mile toward shore before she grounded. After a similar operation the next day, she was only three miles from Waterford.

Then another storm struck, nearly wiping out the operation and the salvage fleet as well. When it abated, the salvors gingerly reset their cables and shoreward progress went on, tide after tide, for the next twenty days. The gamble paid off.

British intelligence had wanted Wagenfur's secret papers, orders, and code books as much as the Admiralty had wanted the sub itself. When another German sub was sunk some forty miles off the northeast coast of England in the war's waning days, intelligence decided they wanted the same things from her.

Despite the hazards of working at 190 feet, Commodore Frederick Young of the Salvage Section sent his men down to seek those all-important secret documents. Operating by a sense of touch alone in the icy blackness, his divers felt out the conning-tower hatch, by which they planned entry. They found it was being held partially open by some obstruction: the obstruction proved to be a human arm.

Clutched in the dead fingers were the papers they sought.

The captain, apparently realizing that his vessel was doomed, must have rushed to the open hatch to throw out his secret orders, only to be caught by an inrush of water. The water not only must have slammed down the hatch cover on his arm, but also would have caused death within seconds; and his trapped hand would have instinctively clutched the papers in a grip of steel. There they had remained until the British divers found them.

K-13: FIRST USE OF COMPRESSED AIR

Another of Young's exploits was raising the K-13, a big (334 feet long), radical British submarine which had diesel engines, electric motors, and a steam turbine, and a hefty 2600-ton submerged displacement (this includes the weight of water in the flooded ballast tanks—for the K-13, 800 tons). The K-13's most unusual feature, however, was ten-ton drop keels fore and aft: slip-weights that could be jettisoned in time of crisis to give the craft immediate positive buoyancy.

On January 29, 1917, K-13 was undergoing final acceptance trials at Gareloch, a seven-mile-long branch of the Firth of Clyde in southwest Scotland, before joining the fleet. Commander Godfrey Herbert ordered a fifteen-minute dynamic dive—and someone left open the outsized ventilators for the steam turbines. K-13 went down like a stone, flooded aft and with thirty-two of her eighty men drowned.

Herbert blew all ballast as he ordered the drop keels let go. The fore keel jettisoned correctly; the after remained in place. K-13 buried four yards of her stern in the mud some sixty feet from the surface. That left forty-eight survivors in the forepart of the vessel who, even if the watertight bulkheads held, would soon suffocate. Indeed, by morning the air was so foul that Herbert and Commander F. H. M. Goodhart, aboard as an observer, determined on a bold plan.

The two officers entered the conning tower, which was fitted with an upper and a lower hatch and hence was a crude air lock. Air was fed in through the high-pressure pipe normally used to blow the sub's whistle.

When the air compressed to the same pressure as the water outside, they hoped to exit from the upper hatch—which was forward—as Brown had done from the *E-41* two years before. Complicating their task was a flooded wooden wheelhouse over the conning tower, in which the single exit hatch was aft.

The conning-tower hatch blew open unexpectedly, sweeping both men up into the wheelhouse. Herbert was carried right out of the after hatch in that mighty burst of air and straight to the surface, barely wet. He popped out so close to Young's newly arrived *Ranger* that a diver just descending the ladder reached out and plucked him bodily from the water as he appeared.

"Where's Goodhart?" demanded the stunned Herbert.

Goodhart was dead: he had been hurled straight up against the wheelhouse ceiling.

Herbert, Young, and Commander Kay of the *Thrush* immediately sent divers down. Working in mud to their armpits, the divers reported that the mud and the flooded compartments made K-13 too heavy for a mechanical lift. Young decided to raise just the prow, cut a hole in it, and release the trapped men. Kay rigged a submarine lamp in front of the sub's periscope to flash the plan in Morse to the men within.

By that evening, the thirtieth, they had connected with the sub's air system, and in the morning began pumping untainted air inside as well as blowing the forward ballast tanks. It was after dark on the thirty-first before lifting cables around the prow brought the nose of the sub out of the water. Surface arc lamps were set up for the welders.

First they cut an eighteen-inch hole through the K-13's outer hull, then started on the pressure hull. When they finally did get through the inner skin, air trapped inside burst out and snuffed the torch.

"Get us some matches down here!" yelled one of the welders.

Before anyone in the *Ranger* could move, a hand came through the cut from the *inside*, holding a box of wooden matches.

"Here you are," said a cheery voice.

The forty-six men climbed to safety after being trapped fifty-seven hours. As the last one cleared the sub, the bollards that held the lifting cables tore out, and the prow of K-13 went down again.

Later, Young's divers sealed the compartments one by one and pumped the hull full of compressed air. Sand pumps blew away the sticky bottom silt holding the stern; K-13 was raised and cleaned up, and joined the fleet only six weeks behind schedule.

She was recommissioned, however, under a new number.

American submarines never "fired a shot in anger" during World War I, and the British, at first, were not much better. When they did get under way, however, their submariners could only be described as cheeky in the way they handled their craft.

She Goes Alone

During the Allied landings at Gallipoli in April 1915, Captain Martin E. Nasmith carried out some operations with HMS submarine *E-11* that would make a modern commander's hair turn gray. To enter the enemy-controlled Sea of Marmara, for example, he commandeered a dhow (an Arab sailing vessel, lateen-rigged), fastened it to his conning tower, and used it as a disguise against enemy observers. Chasing a Turkish vessel into the harbor of Rodosto (now Tekirdag), he ended up in water so shallow that he couldn't even get his periscope under. Undaunted, he fired a torpedo to sink the ship at the quay to which it had fled. Shortly thereafter, he engaged in a running gun battle with a squadron of Turkish cavalry ashore.

Nasmith also proved himself an inventive salvor. He refused to abandon torpedoes that had missed their targets; torpedoes, after all, were hard to come by between the Dardanelles and the Bosporus. So, going against contemporary practice, he set his torpedoes to float, rather than sink, at the end of a run.

E-11 would overtake the torpedo from behind, and Nasmith would send a man into the water to remove the detonator. This accomplished, he would flood *E-11*'s after ballast tanks, thus causing her nose to rise out of the water and expose the fore torpedo tubes. The sailor in the water would drag the torpedo over to the sub tail-on, and wrestle it into the mouth of the tube. Nasmith would close the outer tube hatch, blow the tube with compressed air, then open the inner hatch, bring the torpedo in, and replace the detonator for future use.

Small wonder that Britannia ruled the waves in those days!

---

[1] See pages 140–43.

[2] It is interesting to note that this is the same year the *Mayflower* sailed for America. Subs have been around for a long time.

[3] The common term for these unique and destructive little invertebrates is "shipworm," yet *Teredo navalis* (and the smaller but similar *Bankia*) are not worms at all, but burrowing pelecypods—mollusks. In effect, degenerate clams. *Teredos* reach a length of two feet; their shells are two ½-inch plates that they use as boring tools to scoop out chambers in the wood for their bodies. They do not eat wood; but in burrowing they cause damage at least equal to that of wood-eating termites on land.

[4] It might be well to point out here that a sub's conning tower is merely the place where the controls are located. Virtually any modern military vessel has a conning tower.

CHAPTER NINE

"Submarine Sunk Here"

~~~~~~

The first of the wars "to end all wars" was over; the world turned eagerly—if briefly—to peace. Hollywood discovered the submarine, and sweaty-faced extras began to find themselves trapped in mock-up hulls on studio lots, waiting for the clank of rescuers' boots on the ersatz steel overhead. But the S-5 affair, for sheer melodrama, equaled anything in an imaginative screen writer's scenario. The submarine was on routine submerged patrol off the eastern seaboard when it tried to surface; the after ballast tanks blew, but the forward ones did not. S-5 promptly nosed over, and in this undignified position proceeded to the surface.

This left the crew—with no escape gear of any sort—in a submarine swinging bow down in the open sea like a giant pendulum, its stern sticking out slightly but not far enough to attract the attention of any passing ships. Radio equipment was useless, since radio beams do not pierce water. Facing suffocation, the crew sent the submarine's telephone buoy to the surface, and through the long dark and daylight hours forlornly rang for help in the empty ocean.

Enter the troop ship *General Goethals,* en route to Panama. It passed so close to the disabled sub that one of the crewmen claimed he heard a telephone ringing. A telephone? In the open sea? But then others heard it, too. Finally, even the captain heard it. He ordered all engines stopped and sent off half a dozen men to investigate.

On the S-5, the crew had been ringing their phone for thirty-five hours without response—surely a record in the history of Mr. Bell's invention—and without real hope of any. But then the receiver was picked up. The *General Goethals* had arrived in the proverbial nick of time.

This, however, did little to lessen their plight. Their air would be exhausted in two hours, and the *Goethals,* apart from slinging a couple of hawsers around the stern of the sub to keep it from sinking completely, could only begin transmitting SOS signals.

No one answered. Within radius of their wireless, no ship was monitoring their transmission band.

Enter now, on the mainland, a schoolboy named Moore who was a ham radio operator before the term existed. Fooling around with a homemade crystal set, he was electrified by a genuine distress signal crackling out of his receiver. He began busily transmitting, a nearby naval depot heard him, and two destroyers were dispatched to the coordinates he had passed on.

The rescue ships arrived to find that the engineers on the *Goethals* had rigged a makeshift cutting torch and had succeeded in cutting an opening through the sub's twin hulls large enough for fresh air to be pumped in. Rivet-cutters were used to remove one of the plates, and the twenty-eight men scrambled to safety after forty hours in their vertical prison.

It is an anomaly of public opinion that during wartime, when "missing, presumed sunk," is the stark epitaph of scores of submarine crews, there is little agitation for safety devices aboard subs. H. A. Fleuss of Siebe, Gorman and Company had developed a self-contained diving unit (forerunner of today's SCUBA gear) in 1878; modifications by Robert H. Davis of the same firm produced, by 1914, the Davis Submarine Escape Lung. It consisted of a face mask, a breathing bag, a cylinder of oxygen, and a cylinder of caustic potash to absorb the carbon dioxide exhaled by the wearer. Given to a submarine crewman, today's improved Davis Submarine Escape Apparatus has a theoretical escape capability down to six hundred feet.

Yet none of the world's navies furnished their submarine crews with them until forced to do so; and it was not until peacetime tragedy, which called down upon them the wraths of congresses and parliaments, that it was done.

In October 1923, the American O-5 sank in forty feet of water near the Panama Canal. All but three of the crewmen got clear at the surface as it started down. One man, Charles Butler, was trapped by water rushing into the engine room, and another, Lawrence Brown, was asleep in the torpedo room. Brown would have drowned had not Henry Breault run forward to wake him and been able to slam shut the bulkhead door just before the inrushing water arrived.

Butler breathed in an air pocket until he got the escape hatch open. He was blown to the surface with such force by the escaping air that he was thrown completely from the water like a leaping marlin, after only eight minutes aboard the flooded sub.

The other two men had to wait three hours before divers got lifting cables slung around the O-5, and nine more before the craft was brought to the surface. Then the cables broke, dropping her back to the bottom, so they had another sixteen hours before they finally were saved.

LOSS OF S-51

No one died aboard the O-5, but public opinion had been alerted to the dangers of the "silent service." And then on the evening of September 25, 1925, real tragedy struck. S-51, a medium-sized craft of 993 tons submerged displacement, was surface-cruising toward Boston with her normal complement of thirty-seven officers and men. Fifteen miles east of Block Island, with the right-of-way and displaying the proper lights, she was rammed on the portside by the steamer *City of Rome*. Passengers on the liner could see the despairing face of the captain on the sub's bridge below them.

"For God's sake!" he cried, "throw us a line!"

No one did. The *City of Rome* did not even slow down.

The S-51, battery compartment slashed open, heeled to starboard and went down in 132 feet of water. Only nine men, those closest to the conning tower, made it out; and only three of these were alive in the icy Atlantic waters when the *City of Rome* finally decided to stop and send back boats. Several more hours passed before she radioed news of the disaster.

Divers aboard the Navy salvage ship *Falcon* were rushed to the scene in hopes of saving those who had gone down with the sub. They located the site by bubbles of air and oil still coming to the surface; but upon descending, they found the S-51 flooded.

There was no one to save, and they knew why she had gone down; but public demand that the crewmen be brought up and given decent burial made the Navy decide to raise the submarine. The job was given to Captain Ernest King and Commander Edward Ellsberg of the Naval Salvage Department. The plan was simple: eight submersible pontoons would be sunk in pairs on either side of S-51, connected by a cradle of heavy lifting chains under the sub, and then blown with compressed air for a lifting force of 640 tons. The additional necessary buoyancy would come from sealing and blowing the S-51's four undamaged main compartments.

A simple plan. It took nearly a year of continuous, hazardous, back-breaking work to carry out.

First, the site was extremely exposed and prey to innumerable North Atlantic storms; the water was icy; the sub's interior totally black, dangerously cramped, and unnervingly equipped with dead bodies. Of equal importance, the *Falcon* was so crowded that morale was affected; divers had only an hour of bottom time at twenty-two fathoms; and men experienced in work at that depth were so scarce that they all were overworked, hence plagued by injury and illness.

In port, construction of the pontoons was begun; at the site, divers began closing off the engine room by sealing bulkhead doors, hatches, and valves on pipes and exhausts. Working by a sense of touch alone, they fought drifting debris and continually fouled their air lines on protruding pipes and valves; the hatch was blocked by a body so firmly wedged that they could not move it. The main air-induction valve refused to close, so finally a great section of the superstructure had to be removed so they could get at it from outside.

"It took five days and twenty dives," Ellsberg remarked later, "to close a valve that should have closed in five seconds."

To seal the control room, the salvors first had to close the bulkhead door between it and the ruptured battery room. They rehearsed aboard another sub, S-50, but still the divers got stuck in the doorway and one was nearly killed. The gun-access trunk, a small air lock leading to the deck directly in front of the conning tower, was blocked by two dead bodies. Finally they were successful, and went on to the two remaining compartments.

The pontoons were ready by the end of October. They weighed forty tons each (thirty-two feet long, fourteen feet in diameter) and were as usual sectioned into three compartments, which could be watered or blown independently. Once positioned over the hulk, the pontoons would be flooded and sunk into place. The problem was to lower them close to the wreck but not close enough to foul it, keeping them from going out of control, dropping, and crushing the sub like an empty tin can in the process. This meant shackling them to guidelines with manila hawsers, and lowering them slowly on an even keel.

Things went wrong on the very first pontoon. Waves kept breaking into an open valve; the forward end filled, the after end came up abruptly, and down it went like a stubby, forty-ton battering ram, so fast that the guidelines running through bitts on the side of the *Falcon* started smoking. Luckily for the entire operation, it missed the S-51.

Raising it meant clearing away a vast jumble of lines, chains, hawsers, cables, and wires, including a guide that had to be cast loose from a shackle pin. It stuck. For *two weeks* the divers strove to cut it free, using an underwater oxygen torch producing a "cool" flame that was maddeningly slow.

"If I could take off my helmet," one frustrated diver shouted up through his telephone, "and get my teeth on that wire, I could *chew* it in half faster than this damned torch . . ."

Finally, all the pontoons were in place so that the salvors could begin running the chain cables for the lifting cradle under the sub from one side to the other. In earlier operations, these had been placed by "sweeping" from the surface; on the S-51, the salvors planned to tunnel through the mud from one side to the other with water pumped down by means of pressure hoses from the *Falcon*.

Since it was a new technique, they didn't know what to expect. On the first attempt, a startled yelp came up from the diver.

"Turn off the water! I'm fifty feet from the sub and I don't know where the hose is!"

They had made no provision for back pressure; since a man under water has much less leverage than, say, a fireman handling a similar hose on a city street, the pressure had jet-propelled him backward. Experimentation showed that the divers could handle only forty pounds of pressure. The first tunnel took five weeks, and once caved in on a diver to trap him in a viscid black tomb of mud. Over the phone came his labored breathing: the tenders feared he was being crushed to death.

In reality, he calmly had worked the still flowing nozzle down so it was pointed toward his feet; the water hose washed his way right out of the cave-in. He stood up, turned around, and went back into the tunnel to continue his work. Divers must not only be adequate craftsmen and engineers, of great physical strength and even greater bravery; they must also be of a certain phlegmatic temperament. They must not have too vivid an imagination, for they must see danger and even horror as merely routine.

Meanwhile, Ellsberg had been experimenting with a vented hose nozzle. This featured an outlet that directed a lesser stream of water backward to balance the main stream being directed forward, thus theoretically taking up most of the back pressure.

On the first trial, they cautiously gave the diver thirty pounds of pressure—ten less than he handled with the regular nozzle. He called for more, so they upped it to fifty. More, he said. Seventy. More. A hundred. When he asked for more, they gave him one-fifty, the pump's capacity. Still he wanted more, so they tightened down the safety valve and upped it to two hundred.

The pump blew a cylinder head.

The salvors were delighted to make a new, heavier head of boiler plate and send the diver down again. The first tunnel had taken five weeks; the other three were completed in a single afternoon.

Their final task on the bottom was the fitting of special hatch covers. Those on a submarine are designed to keep water pressure out, not air pressure in; they kept blowing open when air was pumped into the compartments. Finally covers weighing seven hundred pounds each were constructed, and a small derrick was built on the sub's superstructure just to lower them into place.

On June 22, 1926—nine months after S-51 had gone down—they started the lift. Compressed air was flowing down nicely when a savage gale blew up, so savage that the entire salvage fleet determined to run for shelter. Before they could, a huge mass of bubbles spread under the *Falcon's* quarter, and just as they got the vessel moved aside, the prow of the S-51 came roaring into view, festooned with the four bow-lifting pontoons.

S-51 had come up, wrong end to and at just the wrong time. When the stern bobbed up also, two of its pontoons sprang high into the air like playful dolphins as their cable slipped off the stern. S-51 slid right out of her cradle, in a welter of flying chains, lines, and cables, back to the bottom.

The storm blew itself out, the salvors returned, and by July 5, had everything back in place. S-51 surfaced correctly and was towed into the New York naval dry dock. There the hatches were opened and a medical work detail, protected from the poisonous gases of the rotting bodies by gas masks, entered to bring forth the eighteen dead crewmen.

The loss of all but three men from the S-51 caused a brief flurry of public demand for submarine escape devices, and easy promises by the Navy to furnish them. But time passed, headlines changed, and appropriations were cut. The pressures for reform eased off . . .

TRAGEDY ABOARD THE S-4

But just over two years later, in December 1927, the S-4 was lost. The sinkings were remarkably parallel. Like the S-51, S-4 was a double-hulled submarine, 231 feet long, eight hundred tons surface displacement, a crew of about forty, and with two diesel engines for surface cruising and two electric motors (operating from storage batteries) for power while submerged. The Navy had over fifty of these "S" boats.

In midafternoon of December 17, she was surfacing after a test run just three quarters of a mile from Cape Cod; her periscopes were half housed, so she could not see the Coast Guard cutter *Paulding* coming off the starboard bow. *Paulding* struck the sub just forward of the conning tower, as the *City of Rome* had struck the *S-51*; and like the *S-51*, the submarine rolled heavily, her battery room ripped open, and sank.

There the parallel ends. The *Paulding* stopped instantly, lowered lifeboats, dropped a marker buoy, took cross bearings on shore features, and radioed for aid. A man named Gracie ran out from shore in a surfboat to begin sweeping with a grapnel where the sub's vestigial oil slick remained. He was still four hours in hooking the sub. For seven hours he hung on, while the *Falcon*, the *S-4*'s sub tender *Bushnell*, and the *Wright*, towing four of the pontoons used on the *S-51*, steamed frantically for the site from their respective ports.

Minutes before the *Bushnell* arrived with marker buoys, Gracie's grapnel slipped off; he spent another eight hours in hooking the *S-4* again. By that time it was eleven A.M. on the eighteenth, and a dozen ships were there.

On the *S-4*, meanwhile, six men in the torpedo room just forward of the flooded battery room had been able to slam and dog down their bulkhead door as the sub started down. In the control room just aft of the punctured battery room, the watertight door also was dogged down to safely seal off the sub's three after compartments. Ballast had been ordered blown, but since the forward ballast lines had been sliced open by the crash, this merely wasted precious air.

As long as the crew had possession of the control room, they had a chance of raising at least the stern. But then a ventilator duct burst, and a curtain caught in it from the other side to prevent their closing down the valve. They were driven aft again, to the engine room. There the thirty-four men waited, 110 feet down, with no chance of helping themselves, inadequately clothed for a temperature two degrees above freezing. Forward waited the other six men.

At the surface, the weather was terrible and getting worse, but the salvage master, Captain Ernest King, ordered the *Falcon* to anchor to windward, veer cable down to the buoyed line, then hold position by hawsers run over to flanking mine sweepers. They had to wait until 2:00 P.M.—22 hours after the collision—before hard-hat diver Tom Eadie could slide hand over hand down the grappling line to the sub's conning tower. He tramped the length of the hull, tapping on hatch covers; only the six men in the torpedo room responded.

King and Saunders, Captain of the *Falcon*, conferred with Admiral Brumby on the terrible decision they had to make. Should they attempt a link-up of their compressed-air hoses with the sub's interior—to send in air for the survivors to breathe—or should they link up with the main ballast tanks in an attempt to bring the sub to the surface before the trapped men ran out of air?

The factors were complex. First, only one compartment seemed to be holed (they had no way of knowing that the control room, though undamaged, was flooded). Next, the ballast tanks and lines seemed to be intact (again, Eadie had been unable to see the ruptured forward ballast line). Finally, they had received no response from the crewmen trapped aft (it seems likely they already had smothered).

The salvors decided to blow the ballast tanks.

A diver named Carr made the connection, and for an hour compressed air rushed down to the stricken sub. When it began boiling back to the surface in a froth of bubbles, they knew S-4 was not going to rise. They had made the wrong decision.

Although it was 8:00 P.M. of a wild, black, howling night, diver Fred Michaels requested permission to try connecting an air line to the torpedo room in hopes of saving the six men there. The *Falcon* was pitching so badly that Michaels missed the S-4 completely and landed waist deep in the ooze alongside. A full dozen men had to heave on his safety line to pull him free. His tenders set him down again, on the sub this time—but right in the midst of the battery room's twisted superstructure wreckage. Then again the sea showed her teeth in random but tragic malevolence.

The *Falcon* dipped in a wave trough, giving slack to his lines. A loop of his air line went over one side of the submarine, a wave crest raised the *Falcon*, and the loop was pulled up tight under some protruding wreckage. The next trough dropped a loop of his life line over the *other* side of the sub; the next wave drew it taut under wreckage on that side. The whole thing took perhaps a dozen seconds.

Each wave drew the loops tighter, dragging him to a crouch, to his knees, and finally flat on his stomach with his faceplate jammed against the steel deck. He could not move; soon he was unconscious.

On the *Falcon* the tenders had no idea of what was wrong; but Tom Eadie, though he already had been down beyond prescribed safety limits, went to Michaels' aid. He landed safely on the S-4 and was led to Michaels by the trapped diver's thousand-watt submarine lamp. Using a hack saw, he took over two hours just to free the air line. As he started on the life line, his own suit caught on a ragged metal projection and was ripped open.

Eadie should have returned to the surface immediately; one slip on the slick steel plates, so his head got lower than the rip, and the air would flow from his suit and he would be killed. Eadie kept sawing away, without even telling his tenders of his predicament. He freed Michaels and brought the unconscious man to the surface. Later he was awarded the Medal of Honor for his bravery.

But the delay was just long enough to preclude any more dives.

For two days of vicious storms, they could not go back down. Communication of sorts was maintained by messages tapped in Morse on the sub's hull and picked up by microphones aboard the salvage ship.

Finally the six trapped sailors sent a message that their air was nearly gone and, on the night of the nineteenth, made a despairing query.

"Is there any hope?"

The helpless salvors sent the only message they could: "Everything possible is being done."

Waiting was all that was possible. At 6:15 on the morning of the twentieth, after sixty-three hours on the bottom, the doomed men sent their final communication.

"We understand," they tapped. "All is well."

The following afternoon the savage gale abated and the divers went down immediately. They could not find the sub. For hours they searched frantically, always within fifty feet of her but unable to see more than three feet as they floundered about in the mud. Finally a grapnel hooked the S-4, and divers went down the line to fit an air hose to a listening tube on the sub's prow.

For several hours they alternated: pumping, venting, pushing in fresh air, sucking out foul from the torpedo room. It was a sort of giant mouth-to-mouth resuscitation attempt with the sub, but it was much too late. Atmospheric air contains .003 per cent of carbon dioxide; .2 per cent doubles the human respiration rate. The air pumped from the S-4's torpedo room tested out at a full 7 per cent.

RAISING THE S-4

The crew was gone; that left the sub herself. The procedure used on the S-51, they decided, should be repeated: seal up the four undamaged compartments, tunnel under the hull for the passage of lifting chains to which pontoons would be attached, then blow the pontoons and the sealed compartments to bring her to the surface. It took only three months—as opposed to nearly a year for the S-51—but some of the problems they solved were equally difficult.

First was the "fog" of silt raised from the muddy bottom. This sediment was so thick that a diver could hold a thousand-watt lamp against his faceplate, directed toward his eyes, and *could not tell whether the lamp was lighted or not!*

A worse problem was the intense cold, which made the air passing down through their lines almost too cold to breathe. Air warmed before it was sent down deposited moisture that soon froze solid, sealing off the hoses.

The solution was found in the fact that compressing air generates heat. Temperatures in compression tanks can reach 100 degrees Fahrenheit, so the salvors took the hot air from the storage tanks and passed it through chambers cooled by sea-water coils, which condensed the moisture in the air. Then the air went to another heating chamber and down the air hoses. It reached the diver at just the right temperature for breathing but freed of excess moisture, which might freeze.

Another problem was sealing the upper conning-tower hatch. No matter what they tried, it kept blowing open when they pumped compressed air into the control room. Finally they put two steel bars across the cover and set a metal cylinder around it. Into this they piled five thousand pounds of lead, over which they poured four hundred pounds of cement. This still had to be topped with another half ton of lead before the hatch held.

During January and February all the compartments were sealed, the tunnels dug and lifting chains positioned, and the pontoons sunk into place. On March 17, the compressors were started, and in a few hours the wooden-cased metal pontoons brought the sub up in a smooth rush. The tugs and salvage vessels fixed additional cables for the tow to Boston, but then a heavy gale blew up. Pontoons began whipping about, as the official Navy report stated, "like toy balloons with short strings, trying to break away in a strong breeze." King brought the crippled sub successfully to port by sending two ships to windward, thus breaking up the force of the waves and shielding the convoy from the battering winds.

During the three-month operation, one full month was lost because of weather too stormy for divers to go down. A total of 564 salvage dives were made.

DIFFICULTIES OF SUBMARINE SALVAGE

The deaths aboard the S-4, especially the poignant, lingering end of the six men trapped in the torpedo room, made plain the need for some sort of submarine safety features. The Navy, badly wanting some good publicity, conceived the idea of turning S-4 into a submarine test ship equipped with all the latest safety devices. Once they were installed, she would be resunk under control conditions and then her imaginary crew would be "rescued"—thus proving how effective the Navy miraculously had become in saving trapped submariners.

S-4 was dropped into sixty feet of water with her ballast tanks flooded, and the highly experienced crew aboard the *Falcon* was told to go and raise her. In they rushed, as the submarine's little position buoys popped automatically to the surface, and down went the divers.

They found S-4 resting on the bottom with only a slight list to starboard, and quickly began running ropes through the four lifting eyes that had been installed for the test. These ropes would be used to draw down cables, which in turn would draw down the heavy lifting chains.

But by dark of the first day, they had reeved only one chain.

The next day, in an unexpected gale, the divers were able to shackle up the three other lifting chains—but that was all.

On the third day (the "crew" had now been down some sixty hours and would have been getting pretty ragged around the edges), they flooded the pontoons, took them down into position over the sub, and fastened them to the lifting chains. By eight o'clock that night the *Falcon's* compressors were pumping away, blowing the pontoons and the sub's ballast tanks. Powerful lamps were focused on the surface where S-4 would pop into view.

She didn't pop.

The engineers went into a frenzy of slide-rule sliding, and then the remaining compartments in the pontoons were unwatered—furnishing much more lift than even the most pessimistic calculations had indicated necessary. Finally, there was a great surge of boiling water, and into view hove the prow of the S-4.

But only the prow. The stern remained firmly on the bottom. The hypothetical crew suffocated that night, so when the divers swarmed over the submarine the next morning it all seemed a bit of an exercise in futility. They found that somehow the engine room had sprung a *real* leak and had flooded while the sub had been on the bottom. Their calculations had not included this possibility.

Thus do salvors get gray before their time. And Navy brass. The Navy hurriedly adopted the Momsen Escape Lung, a variant of the Davis patent, and gave the go-ahead to development of an escape chamber.

The trouble with agitation for submarine safety features is that it comes from an uninformed public, who have little knowledge of the sea and even less of submarines. Thus, three rather vital factors are usually overlooked in the cries for instant reform.

First, marine designers would have no difficulty in constructing a submarine that would be safe for the crewmen in almost any conceivable conditions; but such a submarine would be so cumbersome that it would have no military utility—which means no utility whatsoever, since submarines are a tool of war.

Second, submarine officers and men usually object to complex safety features. They know that their wartime safety depends on the speed and efficiency of their craft; and most peacetime sinkings are the result of either mechanical failure or human error. Safety devices installed on certain British subs have been destroyed by the crews themselves once the vessel cleared port.

The third factor is that most feasible submarine safety devices have long since been explored by marine engineers. Drop-keels, such as those on the *K-13*, proved only an embarrassment; and lifting eyes lost whatever dubious utility they may have possessed, once submarine displacement tonnage got beyond the capacity of portable cranes. It is often physically impossible to get bulky lifting gear to the scene quickly, so the basic necessity was giving submarine crews their own escape means independent of any surface efforts being made on their behalf.

The British Royal Navy had long been experimenting with individual escape lungs for each crewman, as well as escape chambers built right into the sub itself. As was shown in the *E-41* escape, even escape chambers are not always necessary, since air will be trapped in the upper portion of even a damaged watertight compartment if the damage is modest in scope and fairly low on the hull.

POSEIDON PROVES VALUE OF ESCAPE LUNG

The sinking of the British *Poseidon* on June 9, 1931, however, proved the value of the Davis Submarine Escape Lung. The *Poseidon* was a new, fast submarine with nearly eighteen knots surface speed; surface-cruising during maneuvers in the South China Sea, she was run down in heavy fog by the Chinese steamer *Yuta*.

Cleft open just forward of the conning tower, she heeled over and went down in two minutes. Thirty-one men got free; of the other twenty-one, all but eight were drowned instantly. In the torpedo room, Chief Petty Officer Patrick Willis was able to get the bulkhead door slammed shut and dogged down, even though, as the sub settled nose first on the bottom at 120 feet, the frame sprang enough to let in a continuing stream of water. Then the batteries shorted out, killing the lights and leaving only flashlights to work with.

Willis told the others they would flood the compartment and then escape using their Davis lungs. Before opening the valves, Willis strung a length of cable across the chamber for them to stand on as the water rose. After two hours it was five feet below the hatchway, but the air was so hot and foul that two men succumbed and drowned. Finally Willis had Lovock and Holt try to raise the cover. It wouldn't move. Fifteen minutes later, it gave a few inches. On their third attempt, it opened and the two men were swept up into the ocean.

The hatch slammed shut behind them, so the others had to wait another hour, until the water reached their necks. A mighty heave sent the cover flopping open against the deck, and out went the other four after three and one-fourth hours on the bottom.

One man died from hitting his head against the edge of the hatchway; another panicked during the ascent and held his breath. Air expanding rapidly in his lungs as the pressure lessened, ruptured them, so he died of a massive air embolism. The others survived.

The U. S. Navy had already begun issuing to its submarine crews the Momsen lung, and had authorized the construction of an escape bell, or chamber, designed by Commander Allen R. McCann. But there was no call for the chamber until 1939, when the *Squalus* went down.

SQUALUS AND THE McCANN RESCUE CHAMBER

Squalus (SQUAY-luss) was a 1450-ton submarine, 310 feet long, which had been commissioned on March 4, 1939, at a cost of $4,300,000. At 8:30 A.M. on May 23, less than twelve weeks after her launching, she was making a shallow test dive near the Isle of Shoals off the New Hampshire coast as part of her shakedown run. Aboard were fifty-nine men, including three civilian observers.

The gauges on the control panel showed all valves closed, but actually an air-induction valve was still open—the sub was so new that the lubricating oil had not yet worked through her entire system. Designed to feed large amounts of air into the vessel at the surface, the valve let in huge gushes of water with tremendous force. The four after compartments were flooded immediately, and the twenty-six men in them were drowned within seconds.

"Blow all ballast!" shouted Lieutenant Oliver Naquin, captain of the vessel.

Too late. The *Squalus* was already on her way to the bottom, stern first, in 260 feet of water. She came to rest upright, angled up 11 degrees toward the bow; by then, the thirty-three survivors had slammed shut and dogged down the after bulkhead door of the control room, sealing off the unflooded forward compartments. Both lights and emergency circuits had shorted out. In the dark, Naquin ordered his men to wrap themselves in blankets and mattresses against the cold, and to conserve air by moving as little as possible. He then released the bow marker buoy, which carried to the surface a telephone and a plate reading SUBMARINE SQUALUS SUNK HERE, TELEPHONE INSIDE BOW BUOY.

When the *Squalus* did not report at 9:30 A.M. as scheduled, her sister ship, the *Sculpin*, went searching. She spotted the buoy, but as her crew was talking with Naquin a wave drove the *Scuplin* to leeward, parting the phone line.

Commander Charles B. Momsen, inventor of the Navy's escape lung and head of the Experimental Diving Unit, arrived aboard the *Falcon*; he sent down diver Martin Sibitsky who, because of the 260-foot depth, was breathing a helium-oxygen mixture instead of compressed air. Hearing him walking on the deck overhead, the crewmen began tapping messages on the hull, which were picked up by the *Sculpin*. Naquin had already decided against using the Momsen lungs except in a final emergency, since help was at hand and his men were not highly trained in the use of the escape gear.

Morning brought perfect diving weather. Sibitsky went down the line on the grappling iron that had been used to locate the sub, and secured to the torpedo-room hatch cover the interior haul-down cable of the McCann Rescue Chamber that the *Falcon* carried.

Commander McCann had designed the chamber in 1927 after the S-4 sinking: a nine-ton, pear-shaped chamber (small end down) that was ten feet high, with a maximum diameter of seven feet, nine inches, and a base diameter of five feet. The bottom of this base was designed to fit over a submarine escape hatch, and had a rubber washer to make a watertight joint between the bottom of the chamber and the machined flange around the escape hatch.

Inside the chamber was a winch to work the haul-down cable that Sibitsky had attached to the hatch cover. The winch would bring the compartment down tight on the hatch against its own positive buoyancy, the water would be pumped from the base of the chamber, and the hatch would be opened, allowing the men to transfer from the sub into the chamber. Then the hatch would be closed and the chamber would rise, paying out cable, with its payload of men; the extended cable then would be a guide to bring the chamber back with absolute accuracy for future loads.

Two divers, Badders and Mihalowski, rode the McCann Rescue Chamber to the *Squalus*, where they attached their watertight seal, pumped out the water, and opened the hatch. Seven crewmen were carried to the surface in twenty-one minutes; three more successful trips followed, the final one taking until nearly midnight because the rescue bell jammed on its hauling cable 150 feet from the surface for several hours.[1]

RAISING *SQUALUS*

Squalus was new (she had made only nineteen dives) and also undamaged; the Navy was determined to raise her. The salvors, commanded by Rear Admiral Cyrus Cole and captained by R. S. Edwards, decided against a single lift. They would use her own fuel and ballast tanks and pontoons to get her to 160 feet, carry her shoreward until she grounded, repeat the process to a depth of one hundred feet, and then make the final lift to the surface.

Several factors dictated their method. The air-induction valve that had sunk her could not be closed at the 240-foot depth, so the after four sections could not be completely blown for the lift. Fifteen feet of her stern was sunk in the mud. And because of the great depth, divers with compressed air had a bottom time of only twenty minutes; the helium and oxygen would be used wherever possible, but supplies of the exotic gas mixture were limited.

Method determined, they began blowing out the tunnels under the hull for the lifting chains. A new technique was tried here: The diver stood on the sub's deck and used a lance, a hollow, self-propelling pipe bent to the hull's curvature, which squirted out water under pressure. Once the lance had gone completely around the sub, it was left there as a sleeve for the guide wires and then the heavy lifting chains. Their only real trouble occurred on June 10, when two divers blew up one after the other and came bobbing spread-eagled to the surface. Later another diver, using compressed air, suffered an attack of nitrogen narcosis and tried to cut his own air line because he kept tripping over it. But none of them was permanently injured, and on June 21, the tunneling was completed. The heavy chains of the lifting cradle were hauled down.

Pontooning was begun on July 4. The pontoons were big—32 feet long and over 13 feet in diameter, with a weight of 80 tons and a blown buoyancy of 60 tons. Two were placed at 80 feet, two at 180, and one at 200, over the stern; two more, at 85 and 140 feet, went over the bow. The sub would thus be raised 80 feet and towed shoreward until she grounded.

The first "blow and tow" operation was scheduled for July 13. Trailing down to the *Squalus* from the *Falcon's* compressors was 13,600 feet of air hose—"spaghetti" to the divers. They wanted to bring the stern up to 160 feet first, so in sequence they blew the Number 3 Main Ballast Tank, the 180-foot pontoons, the 200-foot pontoon, the Number 1 Oil Tank, and finally the numbers 3, 4, and 5 fuel tanks. At 3:00 P.M., with a roar and geysers of water, the stern tore loose from the mud. The two stern 80-foot pontoons flopped out on top of the ocean and came to rest.

That left the nose buried in the mud, and the salvors gingerly began trying to coax it up to 160 feet and an even keel with the stern. What they feared, of course, was the bow getting out of control and shooting straight up to the surface. The upper bow pontoon was blown, then the Number 1 Main Ballast Tank. The slide rules said, "Rise!" but the *Squalus'* bow didn't. So they blew Number 2 Main Ballast.

There was a tremendous, thirty-foot geyser, followed by the upper bow pontoon—and, in a moment, the second pontoon, which was supposed to be down at sixty feet. Then up came the bow, out of control, snorting air and spouting like a whale. She rose some twenty feet from the water at a 60-degree angle, and then *Squalus* slid neatly backward out of her cradle of lifting chains as if she were going down a launching ramp.

"Close those valves on the pontoons!" yelled Edwards at the pontoon detail standing by in surfboats.

The gutsy sailors leaped aboard the bucking pontoons and rode them like rodeo champs, often being carried completely underwater as the pontoons gyrated and rolled, always in danger of being crushed between them as they smashed together.

No one was killed, but it was a disaster. The submarine was back on the bottom at 240 feet; the pontoons, air fittings broken and lifting cables snarled, were lying across one another at odd angles on the surface;

and two and one-half miles of air line had to be disconnected, untangled, and reconnected.

It took until July 18, before the dejected divers could even get back down to the *Squalus*; they found chaos. She still was upright, but she was strewn with cables and hawsers and had five hundred feet of towing line wrapped around her conning tower. It took thirteen days just to find one pontoon, which perversely had gone back down with the sub, and six more days to lift it. The lifting-chain tunnels could not be started until August 6, and the second lift could not be scheduled until the twelfth.

The lift that day was perfect, bringing *Squalus* up to 160 feet, at which depth she was grounded after a tow shoreward by the tug *Wandank*. A lift and five-mile tow on the seventeenth left her resting on the bottom at ninety-six feet. There two divers removed the air-induction plates and cap, and screwed down the valve that had originally sunk her.

The final lift attempt, on August 28, was an incredible botch. The bow came up at such a list that it spilled its air and went down again. They then raised the stern first, which came obediently to the surface; but then the bow wouldn't rise again. Finally they had to let the stern back down.

A storm interrupted, preventing further attempts until September 13. It was a dead-calm day, and after several false starts they brought both ends of the sub to the surface at the same time. Getting the *Squalus* up the tortuous Piscataqua River to the navy yard included an eight-minute grounding that necessitated raising pressure inside the sub another ten pounds per square inch to get her off the sandbank.

In dry dock, the twenty-five bodies aboard were removed (one man was missing, which has never been completely explained); none of the dead men had even had a chance to open the boxes containing their escape lungs. The Navy spent $1,400,000 in refitting, and in 1940 the *Squalus* was recommissioned as the *Sailfish*, just in time to serve with our submarine fleet during World War II.

---

[1] Navy salvage crews regularly make dummy runs with the chamber on submarines deliberately bottomed. From the sub hatch, a rescue buoy on a wire is released. The rescue team must find the buoy and transfer its wire to the reel of a winch inside a McCann Rescue Bell which is then winched down to the sub's escape hatch—exactly as was done on the *Squalus*.

Since sub crews have the best food in the Navy, the "rescuers" usually ask that sandwiches be brought aboard the bell for them by the "escaping" submarine crewmen.

"Some of the old burly chiefs on the subs would have such choice replies to our requests for sandwiches, 'Tell them to go to hell,'" recalls master diver Harold Stubbs. "This would necessitate our leaving a few gallons of water in the lower hatch to be dumped into the sub when the escape hatch was opened. Usually on the next run we were treated to steak sandwiches and they in turn would have a dry boat. This is what is known as communication."

CHAPTER TEN

Operation Subsmash

~~~~~~~~~~~~~~~~~~~~~~~~~~~~~

The British submarine *Thetis* went down on June 1, 1939, three months to the day after she was commissioned, and three months to the day before the Nazis invaded Poland to start World War II. Soon public concern for single crews would be lost in the greater concern for whole fleets, whole nations, our civilization itself; but on that summer day individual tragedies were still important.

FATAL DELAY ABOARD *THETIS*

For years Robert H. Davis, of Siebe, Gorman and Company, had been urging *speed* in submarine escape operations. Having the crew wait for outside assistance, he said, was usually a mistake. The *Thetis* demonstrated this dramatically. It was a relatively small sub—1095 tons displacement, 265 feet long—but its normal complement had been swelled to ninety-nine by shipyard workers aboard for the shakedown cruise.

No one has ever discovered just why she went down when she did, abruptly and without warning; but most of the men aboard managed to crowd into a compartment furnished with a Davis Escape Chamber. The Davis Escape Chamber is a cylinder built right into the hull of the submarine, with a port at the bottom and an air-release valve in the hatch cover at the top. The man enters, floods the chamber until the interior pressure equals water pressure outside the sub, and then, with the release valve, lets out the trapped, compressed air. The chamber fills with water. Breathing through his Davis Escape Lung, he merely opens the hatch and rises toward the surface. Those remaining shut the hatch and open the port to drain the chamber, and it is ready for the next man.

Once in the compartment, however, the men of the *Thetis* delayed, hoping for external rescue. None was forthcoming, so they finally prepared to use the escape chamber. Two men were put into it and rose to the surface; two more successfully followed. Meanwhile, the air was fouling badly, affecting their judgment.

Then, because of the large number still waiting, four men were crowded in. Unable to get out, they were hauled back into the compartment—which so unnerved the others that none of them would try again.

They waited patiently until they smothered.

Submarine escape has three distinct phases: the pre-escape period, between the sinking and the crew's exit; the escape itself; and the time the escaped man is at the surface waiting to be picked up. The *Thetis* disaster emphasized the great danger of delay during the pre-escape period—waiting for outside aid that may never materialize.

During the escape itself, the crewman must avoid striking his head on the submarine's superstructure. Unconscious, he probably would drown during the ascent. A worse danger, oddly, is holding one's breath. At, say, three hundred feet, the human lungs hold ten times the air that they do at the surface. Unless a man breathes out during the ascent, rapidly-expanding compressed air ruptures the lungs and enters the blood stream to cause air embolisms.

The British *Umpire* was sunk during World War II in one of those anonymous, almost unnoticed tragedies that seem the submarine's wartime fate. It was a black night in the North Sea, and the *Umpire* was surface-cruising with a large Allied convoy moving toward England.

Suddenly her navigational gear went out. The Captain, on the conning tower with two lookouts, just had time to shout "Full astern together!" before one of the convoy's trawlers struck the submarine near the starboard bow.

The two vessels were locked in their kiss of death for thirty seconds; when they parted, *Umpire* heeled to port and went down. The Captain and the lookouts were the only ones left at the surface, and the lookouts sank before help arrived.

Meanwhile, below, *Umpire* came to rest at eighty feet with a 30-degree list to starboard. The four men in the control room had gotten their compartment closed off, and had determined, though they were without escape lungs, to go out through the conning-tower hatch. All four reached the surface, but two had held their breath during the ascent and died later of ruptured lungs.

Aft in an engine room that was slowly but steadily flooding because the bulkhead door would not close completely, twenty more men prepared to escape by use of an escape trunk. This is another invention of the remarkable Robert H. Davis: a small telescoping or removable cylindrical trunk that is fastened below the hatch in emergencies. The compartment then is flooded so the bottom end of the trunk is submerged. A man ducks under water to come up inside it, opens the air vent in the escape hatch above his head, and allows the air in the trunk—but of course not the air in the rest of the compartment—to escape. His trunk is now full of water, so he can open the hatch and exit. The rest of the men can follow him one after the other by ducking into the trunk.

Only seventeen of those in the *Umpire*'s engine room had escape lungs, so the three unequipped men were sent up first, clinging to the legs of others. Two of those without lungs did not reach the surface, for they struck their heads in exiting and, apparently unconscious, let go of their companions. A seaman named Killan (later awarded the British Empire Medal) then went up the trunk to make sure it was clear, returned to the engine room, and sent the others out one by one. He was last to leave.

An interesting aside is that the watertight bulkhead door could be shut manually only when the sub was on an even keel; and the hooked ladder of the escape trunk was worse than worthless, because it lay diagonally across the trunk's interior rather than hanging vertically. The Admiralty designers never had considered that a submarine might sink in some other position than a rigidly upright one.

Even if a submarine crewman makes his escape to the surface, he still faces cold, exposure, rough seas, strong tides, shock. He usually has undergone several hours of great physical stress already, has been breathing polluted air, and, if emerging from 180 feet down or more, may get the bends from the highly compressed air of a partially flooded compartment.

EXPOSURE KILLS *TRUCULENT* SURVIVORS

The 450-ton British submarine *Truculent* had eighty men aboard when, at 7:05 P.M. on January 12, 1950, she was struck by the Swedish motor ship *Divina* in mid-channel of the Thames estuary seventeen miles northwest of Margate. Seventy-nine crewmen were aboard; the captain was hurled clear by the impact, since he was on the conning-tower bridge when the collision occurred. He and four others who escaped from the conning tower were picked up by the Dutch steamer *Aldijk*, which, along with HMS destroyer *Cowdray* and the *Divina*, was trying to pick up survivors.

The submarine settled upright in sixty-five feet of water, with the damaged sections shut off from the sub's after watertight compartments by swift action of the crew. Escape operations were begun just thirty-five minutes after the crash, under the direction of First Lieutenant Hindes. The men queued up for their turn at the escape hatch in a holiday mood, laughing and joking as if they were waiting for a cinema. Most of them escaped before the air fouled so badly that those left were overcome. In all, nearly forty men successfully made their way to the surface, some using Davis escape apparatus and others by free escape.

Because of the weather conditions on that bitterly cold, totally black night, only fifteen of them were saved. The rest sank quietly beneath the waves during the dark and freezing night.

Unfortunately, no one knew this at the time. Although ships crisscrossed the surrounding area in search of survivors, the main thrust of the salvage operation was directed at the *Truculent* herself; so few survivors had been found that it was assumed the rest of the crew was still below in the iron hulk, awaiting rescue.

Lionel Crabb, famous for his frogman exploits during the war (see Chapter Twenty), knew that hard-hat divers could reach the submarine only during slack water, while SCUBA divers might be able to operate even during the tide rush. He and Jimmy Hodges, another SCUBA-diving enthusiast, hurried to Sheerness and at dawn were on the pier, where a fast motor launch was being held for them and their equipment.

They found the launch jammed with reporters and cameramen who said they had been promised space on the first boat out. The newsmen refused to move. After learning that Crabb and Hodges were the only hope the men feared trapped in the sub might have, they still refused to move. Finally dockyard officials had to be summoned to clear the boat for the divers.

Precious time had been lost. Crabb and Hodges dressed during the trip out; because of the three-knot tide, they could not fasten the launch's line to the submarine's marker buoy, for fear of tearing it loose. They had to snag the *Truculent* with their anchor before they could go down, which took several passes; boatloads of sight-seers refused to give them the free passage they needed.

Crabb and Hodges went hand over hand down the anchor cable, but the tide was so powerful they could not reach the *Truculent*. They waited thirty minutes for a 1½-knot slackening, then tried again. This time they made it to the hull; the water was so murky that their powerful sodium diving lamps furnished only one foot of visibility.

There was no response to their tapping above each compartment, and when they tried to enter the after escape hatch they found the twill escape sleeve hopelessly fouled. This alone told them that the *Truculent* was a dead ship. They returned to the surface.

The search for survivors was abandoned on January 16.

Later the *Truculent* was salvaged in a ten-week operation by a mechanical lift using power-operated cranes and heavy deck purchases. Two specially designed lifting vessels provided a powered lift of six hundred tons each over their stern gantries, and the submarine was lightened an additional 150 tons by the injection of compressed air into her side ballast tanks. The nine-inch[1] wire sling brought her to the surface at low-water spring tides just four hours after the lift was begun.

The *Truculent* sank in peacetime, when human life seems very important. But World War II had ended just five years before; and it had been a war, even more than World War I, that had subordinated the fate of individuals to the fate of nations. Then submarine salvage had not centered around the saving of crews, for human life was cheaper than matériel, and much cheaper than ideas.

Peter Keeble was operating a Royal Navy salvage unit out of Alexandria when he was ordered to the submarine base at Beirut, Lebanon. Here he was told that the German *U-307* had been sunk in the eastern Mediterranean and that one of the British destroyers had gotten an excellent position fix.

SECRET DEVICE ABOARD *U-307*

Aboard *U-307*, according to survivors, was a new, top-secret infrared tracking device. German subs equipped with it could lie just awash at night—thus presenting a "cluttered" or negative radar echo—could scan the surface for Allied shipping, and could attack in darkness. The British wanted desperately to get the device from the *U-307* for study. It was football-shaped, Keeble was told, and fixed to a bulkhead in the control room, with an attached explosive charge and a self-destruct mechanism which would have to be dismantled.

For a week Keeble practiced blindfolded in a full-size plywood mock-up of the *U-307*'s control room, until he could find his way about without thought or hesitation. Then he and an Admiralty expert named Walters left on the *Prince Salvor* for the destroyer's co-ordinates, where, guarded by an anti-submarine escort and Spitfires overhead, they went into a box search. This meant methodically covering the ocean in parallel courses a quarter mile apart to scan the bottom with a fathometer. At dawn on their second day they had a contact at forty fathoms of the right size and shape for the submarine, and on their fourth pass snagged it with sweep wires. After mooring, they sent a diver down to confirm that they were indeed over the U-307.

Keeble went down the next morning. He entered the conning tower and darkness; on the ladder, his boot struck something resilient. He stamped on it. No movement. Trying to edge around it, he ended up astride it, and realized belatedly that he was straddling the bloated body of a German officer who had gotten wedged in the narrow opening.

Being unable to get by any other way, Keeble blindly began sawing with his heavy diver's knife. Finally the obstruction sagged, then fell away in two pieces, and he went on down into the control room.

Once there, already beyond the safety limit of bottom time for 240 feet of water, he oriented himself from the periscope housing and worked forward along the starboard side, clumsy and slow-moving from the growing overcharge of nitrogen in his blood. Beyond a chart table with papers and heavy metal parallel rule still in place, he found the football-shaped device fastened to the bulkhead. He began unscrewing it, but dropped his screwdriver. With a pliers and wrench he finally got it free from everything but the conduit pipes.

Just then something tapped Keeble on the back of his helmet. Hallucinating a bit from the nitrogen, he reached back and seized . . . a hand! It was another dead German, summoned by the water currents Keeble's movements had generated. The diver sluggishly pushed away the corpse, and continued.

But the conduit piping would not come free from the box. He tried to loosen it with his wrench; he dropped the wrench. Next he tried his knife. The blade broke. No other tools: but then he remembered the heavy parallel rule on the table. Keeble wedged it behind the device, heaved backward, and had the precious infrared sensor free in his hands.

He sent it up in a weighted bag, returned to the diving stage at ninety feet, and went straight to the surface. After recompression and gradual decompression in a chamber, he went to Walters' room; the expert was happily dismantling the top-secret device for examination.

"What puzzles me," he remarked, "is how you managed to short-circuit the demolition charge without touching it off. The contacts were closed, but—"

"The demolition charge!" yelped Keeble in dismay. "Christ! I forgot all about it!"

From the sinking of the *Housatonic* by the *David of Hunley* in January 1894, no American submarine sank an enemy vessel in battle until December 16, 1941, when the USS *Swordfish* sent the SS *Atsutsan Maru* of the Imperial Japanese Fleet to the bottom. American subs made up for lost time during World War II; they sank eleven hundred Japanese surface craft in the Pacific theater alone.

One of the most phenomenally successful of American submarines, USS *Tang*, also figured in a tense, harrowing, and only somewhat successful submarine escape operation. The *Tang* was three hundred feet long, carrying eighty-eight men and twenty-four torpedoes. Operating out of Pearl Harbor, she sank seventeen Japanese ships in four patrols. In September 1944, she departed on her fifth and final mission.

Arriving at the Taiwan Strait between China and Formosa, Commander Richard H. O'Kane decided to lie in wait; the Battle of Leyte Gulf was beginning, and the strait seemed ideal for the movement of Japanese ships. O'Kane was right. He sank two freighters, then spotted a column of three tankers and two transports, and in ten brilliant minutes sank them all. One ship, trying to ram him, hit the other disabled vessels instead—at the same moment that four of the *Tang*'s torpedoes struck the mass of wreckage.

O'Kane sank or crippled six more ships the next day, using nine torpedoes for the job, but then was spotted by a Japanese destroyer, and fired his last torpedo at it. Instead of going toward the target, the torpedo described a tight circle, came back, and blew open three of the *Tang*'s compartments.

O'Kane, in the conning tower, was blown free from the sub along with eight other men. A tenth, Lieutenant Lawrence Savadkin, joined them five minutes later, having breathed small pockets of air in the several compartments he coolly passed through on his way to the conning-tower hatch.

The other seventy-nine men were not so lucky. Forty-nine of them had died when the torpedo struck; the other thirty were still alive 180 feet down in the compartments forward of the flooded sections of the sub.

For two hours they waited while the Japanese, not realizing that the sub had been sunk by her own torpedo, plastered the area around the *Tang* with depth charges. While waiting, the men burned their secret papers in the prescribed drill, but this turned out to have been a poor idea. It not only consumed a good deal of their oxygen; it also raised the carbon dioxide content and fouled the sub's air with smoke. When they gathered about the escape lock in the forward torpedo room with their DSEA gear (Davis Submarine Escape Apparatus), an electrical fire broke out in the forward battery compartment, which blistered paint, started rubber door gaskets burning, and filled the already fouled air with more deadly smoke.

Only thirteen men escaped from the sub; the other seventeen passed out, sank, and drowned in the partially flooded compartment. Five of the thirteen who escaped did not reach the surface; three more were too weak to keep afloat, and sank. The other five were picked up by the Japanese.

Six of the fifteen captured men died from prison-camp treatment; so only nine of the *Tang's* original crew, including Commander O'Kane, ultimately survived the sinking.

The rapid development during World War II of sonar—or, as the British call it, asdic²—has been most significant to deepwater-salvage location methods. Sonar—(So)und (Na)vigation and (R)anging—depends upon the fact that sound travels in water with a finite, measurable velocity. Thus, the length of time required for a signal sent out from a ship to bounce back as a "reflection" from some object—the seabed, a shoal of fish, a submarine—can be converted into space measurement, and distance from the sending ship can be judged. A fathometer automates the entire operation at the vessel's bridge, so water depth can be read on a dial or recorded by a stylus on a roll of paper.

But in hunting for a lost submarine or a sunken vessel, conventional sonar has its limitations. Searching a sandy bottom, which presents a smooth profile, for a "bump" or protrusion, as the *Prince Salvor* did in its search for the *U-307*, is fine; but a craggy or rockstrewn bottom, with "lots of garbage," as the salvage men say, drastically limits sonar's usefulness. The search for the British submarine *Affray* marked the beginnings of a new locating technique made necessary by this limitation.

AFFRAY IS MISSING

The *Affray* was 286 feet long, had an 1800-ton displacement, and carried a crew of seventy-five officers and men. On a training cruise off Portsmouth, England, *Affray* did not report in by radio at 9:00 A.M. on April 17, 1951, as scheduled. By eleven o'clock, the emergency operation known as SUBSMASH was in motion: all normal naval operations in the area ceased, and over forty vessels from the British, American, French, and Danish military and merchant fleets were engaged in active search for either traces or survivors of the *Affray*.

At 1:00 A.M. on the eighteenth, two subs reported hearing coded sonar signals from the *Affray*; surface vessels working an asdic pattern in the area confirmed the presence of a wreck. Newspapers brayed that the *Affray* had been located thirty miles from the Isle of Wight and that the crew would be rescued momentarily.

Divers went down and found the drowned, barnacle-clad hulk of a World War II submarine.

By dark of the nineteenth, visual ranging for survivors or distress signals was abandoned; the crew had been down beyond their known air supply. Now began exhaustive examination of the bottom with subsurface detection devices. Some fifteen hundred square miles had to be covered: an area strewn with the wrecks of two wars, and with rocks, tide rips, great shoals of fish—all of which can cause false echoes on a sonar sounder. And since *Affray* was a dead ship, the searchers had no screws or motors to aid them.

That meant a physical investigation of every sounding echo that might conceivably be the sub. Involved in the search were a flotilla of anti-submarine frigates with highly sensitive sonar sounders, two survey ships similarly equipped, and the *Reclaim*, the British salvage vessel from which had been set the world's hard-hat record of 540 feet by divers using an oxygen-helium mixture. Between April and June they charted some 150 contacts or "hits" that could have been the *Affray*, and sent divers down to thirty-four wrecks, and thirty other contacts that proved to be rocks.

The tremendous tide rip gave divers only twelve minutes of bottom time spanning dead slack tide: otherwise they would be swept helplessly away. Currents were so swift that *Reclaim*, trying to stay over the wreck being examined, regularly snapped 4½-inch mooring cables like laundry string. One man found a Liberty ship from World War II resting upright and apparently undamaged on the bottom; in its holds were trucks, jeeps, and hundreds of auto tires. Another diver, getting afoul of a derrick on another wreck, was jerked free by tides so vicious that his telephone connection was ripped right off. He shot to the surface in a flurry of bubbles, a hole five-eighths inch in diameter gaping in his helmet; but because he went up feet first, his overinflated suit acted as a miniature diving bell and he didn't even get wet.

SHELFORD'S BLUE LINE

While this fleet commanded by Captain R. S. Foster-Brown was logging 23,800 miles in its crisscross search, a team headed by Captain William O. Shelford was sorting out hundreds of signals from the search ships of the original SUBSMASH. He finally came up with Shelford's Blue Line: his estimate of the *Affray*'s probable course since her last radio contact on the morning of April 16.

The famous SCUBA diver, frogman, and underwater demolition expert Commander Lionel Crabb showed up.[3] He had been convinced by Rosse Stamp of the Admiralty Research Laboratory that an underwater television camera was just the thing for the search, even though none was yet in existence in England. The U. S. Navy had used one down to thirty fathoms during the Bikini atom bomb tests in 1947, to examine the devastation wrought by the bomb; and what the Americans could do, Stamp and Crabb reasoned, they could do.

"Underwater television?" Shelford is quoted as saying. "Right, Crabbie, you lay that on, and I'll lay on the dancing girls."

Stamp knew nothing about TV, but he borrowed a Marconi TV camera from the BBC and went to work. For three weeks, he and his four-man team labored day and night, trying to design a watertight container incorporating tremendously powerful lamps and controls that could be worked from the surface.

"A marvelous bit of knitting," Stamp called his finished Rube Goldberg device. It was mainly held together by vast amounts of Bostick, an ordinary English household glue.

But it worked. Crabb, with a seasick Stamp at his elbow, ran the camera himself aboard the *Reclaim* so that if it failed, only he would be to blame. Shelford was delighted: it gave better definition in the depths than the human eye, and could be used in tides that would prohibit not only divers but observers in a shell. To convince the Portsmouth Command and the Admiralty of the wonders of underwater TV, Shelford ensconced a number of high brass in a comfortable room with a monitoring screen. The screen showed a diver working on the ocean floor 150 feet below, and the Admiral was given a telephone connected directly with him.

"Hullo, diver. Do you hear me?"

"Loud and clear, sir."

Delighted, the Admiral said, "Diver, please write something on your blackboard."

The diver chalked diligently away for a few moments, his back to the camera, then whirled and held aloft his board for the TV's all-seeing eye to scan.

Chalked on it was: WHAT ABOUT A RISE IN PAY FOR DIVERS?

The TV was approved, if not the pay raise. When a sonar contact was made with a wreck on June 15, in 276 feet of water, and a diver in an observation chamber confirmed that it was a new (as opposed to overgrown) submarine hulk, the TV camera was there to be trundled over the side. At 210 feet a radar aerial appeared on the screen. The camera panned slowly, across a superstructure, across a conning tower . . . on which appeared the word AFFRAY in bold black letters. The fifty-seven-day search for the missing sub was finished.

The hulk lay nearly forty miles west of the position the "experts" had plotted: but it lay right on Shelford's Blue Line, the *more probable course of the Affray* he had scrawled with a grease pencil on a chartroom plastic overlay one day in disgust at the positions the others had favored. Unfortunately, the hulk also lay right in the midst of vicious tides and currents.

Reclaim, following Admiralty directives to discover why *Affray* had sunk, dumped eight-ton clumps of concrete in a square around the sub, then moored herself to them by a combination of buoys, three-ton bower anchors, and 4½-inch steel cables. Most of the preliminary work was done with the TV camera, which sometimes meant jockeying the ship for hours just to reposition the crude device a mere six inches. The first diver down reported that the snort (or snorkel), a slender, 35-foot tube abaft the conning tower, was snapped off and lying over the side of the vessel. After four dives, a recovery wire was hooked around this tube, and it was brought gingerly to the surface.

To the men aboard the *Reclaim*, their task seemed finished. The snort is an air-intake pipe that allows a submarine to "breathe" and to recharge her batteries while cruising submerged to periscope depth. If it had snapped off short just where it entered the sub, one hundred gallons of water a second would have deluged the vessel's interior; as she went down, this intake would have been doubled by increasing pressure. That it had done so seemed obvious to the divers, for they could see fish swimming in and out of the sub through the remaining stub of the snort.

Certain Admiralty men, however, abruptly began suggesting that it hadn't been the snort at all that had sunk the *Affray*, but rather an explosion in the battery room. This could easily have been confirmed by checking nearby valves (they would all have been blown outward if such an explosion had occurred), but the divers were expressly forbidden to check them.

It is obvious that a battery explosion (for which no slightest shred of evidence has ever been advanced) would have been no one's fault; whereas a snapped-off snort would indicate either faulty design or inadequate matériel maintenance. Either could be directly attributable to certain individuals in the Admiralty. It appears significant that in the fall of 1951 all diving on the *Affray* was abruptly abandoned and that in January 1952 the buoys marking the sub's exact position were removed.

No further work has ever been done on the *Affray*.

If the *Affray* suggested the lengths to which some British bureaucrats would go in protecting themselves from public censure, the affair of the U.S. nuclear submarine *Thresher* put a great deal of public pressure on the U. S. Navy.

DISAPPEARANCE OF *THRESHER*

At the time she went down, the United States had some thirty nuclear subs, but none with *Thresher*'s capabilities. She was 278 feet long, had a 3700-ton displacement, was nuclear powered, and had cost $45 million to build. On Wednesday, April 10, 1963, she was on a shakedown cruise 220 miles east of Boston after minor structural modifications at the Portsmouth, New Hampshire, shipyard. The submarine rescue ship *Skylark* hovered overhead while *Thresher's* 129 men (sixteen officers, ninety-six enlisted men, seventeen civilians) took her down to a probable one thousand feet. She reported minor difficulties aft at 9:30 A.M., and reported that she was assuming an up angle—that is, she was returning to the surface. Then, over the *Skylark's* underwater sound system, came the sound of *Thresher* blowing her ballast tanks. Four minutes later came a garbled transmission ending in the words "test depth."

Thresher was never heard from again.

To the surface languidly drifted two slight oil slicks, some bits of cork and plastic, and a dozen gloves. She had disappeared in 8400 feet of water; a five-man naval board of inquiry was set up to begin solemn and futile deliberations, while the bathyscaphe *Trieste* was trundled aboard an LSD (landing ship, dock) in San Diego for the trip east through the Panama Canal. *Trieste* (equipped with underwater lamps, sonar, and Edgerton and underwater TV cameras), was considered the ideal search vehicle, since *Thresher* was down in depths where the pressure was two tons per square inch.[4]

The Navy experts knew the range of possibilities that existed, the "scenarios," as the projections of various eventualities are known, but many involved in the search were remarkably naïve. They expected to find a beautifully intact submarine lying upright on the ocean floor. This ignored the fact that beyond the sub's estimated collapse depth of two thousand feet, it probably would have imploded, scattering debris across a large area of sea bottom.

On site, there was a great deal of activity, with scores of ships rushing about. Some trailed special sonars; others had TV cameras to drag about. Magnetometers tried to detect the magnetic-field changes that large masses of metal cause; electrodes probed for self-potential electrical currents, which dissimilar masses of metal set up in sea water; and Geiger counters snooped for possible radiation from the vessel's reactor. Near-collisions occurred by the dozens, for no one had thought to grid off the target area and work it systematically from one section to the next.

"The plot of their search tracks," remarked a civilian observer with considerable awe, "looked like a plate of spaghetti dropped on the floor."

In the first week of June, someone triumphantly announced that pictures of the *Thresher* had been taken with an Edgerton camera. This ingenious device resembles a pair of capped pipes about three feet long and half a foot in diameter. Inside one is an electronic flash with an eight-second recycling unit, inside the other, a Leica f/2.8 50mm lens and a hundred-foot reel of 35mm film. This is fed onto a take-up spool by a surface operator, who can interrupt a constant A.C. circuit with a push button and thus take eight hundred pictures, at eight-second intervals, per reel. The one drawback is that he shoots blind, since he has no directional control.

A spokesman for Lamont Geophysical Laboratory, which operated the research vessel *Conrad*, had decided that a sequence taken by the *Conrad* showed bits of the *Thresher*. These, he said, were blades of the horizontal rudders; *there*, he said, was a fragment of the hull; and *that*, he said, was a section of the conning tower.

The *Trieste* was readied for descent. Navy Secretary Fred Korth remarked that the photos showed "a rent in the hull." A ranking officer said there had been an implosion.

The *Conrad* affair itself, however, was more like an explosion. It had been photographing not the *Thresher*, but its own undersea rig: the camera had been snapping pictures of its lowering cable like a gut-shot hyena snapping at its own entrails.

By the last week of June, the Court of Inquiry was ready to report its findings, after the testimony of 120 witnesses filled seventeen hundred pages in twelve volumes. Certain news media charged that the findings added up to nothing at all, but they contained everything that had been discovered. Considering the depth at which *Thresher* had been lost, it was remarkable that the remains were located at all. The court felt it probable that a pipe in the *Thresher*'s salt-water system had ruptured during the deep dive, just as its sister ship's had done on sea trials.

"The enormous pressure of sea water surrounding the submarine subjected her interior to a violent spray of water and progressive flooding. *Thresher* slowed and began to sink. Within moments she had exceeded her collapse depth and totally flooded. She came to rest on the ocean floor 8400 feet below the surface."

From the nature of the submarine's remains, it seems highly unlikely that she was actually flooded when she reached collapse depth; the debris that was discovered and photographed suggests that she imploded. Violently. Like a raw egg crushed in a weight lifter's fist. And she did not "come to rest" on the ocean floor. She rained down pieces of metal, shards of bone, and pulped human flesh over hundreds of square yards.

In early July the *Trieste* went out for the first time, and in mid-September she brought back from her eighth dive the single pitiful relic ever raised from *Thresher*: a fifty-seven-inch section of twisted brass pipe. She also took pictures of a compartment hatch bearing the number 593, which had been the *Thresher*'s official designation, and of a two-ton air bottle that had struck the bottom with such velocity (probably in excess of one hundred miles an hour) that half its four-yard length was buried in the sediment. Lieutenant Commander Donald L. Keach, one of *Trieste*'s pilots, reported that the area looked like a vast junk yard.

Navy Secretary Korth accepted the evidence and quickly tried to close the file.

SHOCKING FACTS EXPOSED

Congress, however, still under terrific public pressure, held hearings in its Joint Committee on Atomic Energy, at which a disturbing picture began to emerge. The Portsmouth shipyard had found that a full 14 per cent of the silver-brazed joints holding the *Thresher's* sea-water pipes together had substandard bonds. The shipyard told the Navy, which did nothing; so, without telling the Navy, the yard quit checking.

In March 1964 Vice Admiral Hyman G. Rickover, father of the nuclear submarine, was called upon to testify. Never a man to mince words, he raised the point that the Navy report had skimmed over by saying blandly, *Thresher slowed and began to sink.* Rickover asked why. Why were there so many deviations from design specifications in the ballast tanks and ballast-pumping system? And would "the inadequate ballast-tank blowing system" have been able to unwater the tanks at *any* depth?

Not likely, it developed.

During the *eight years* that they had been part of our Navy, no nuclear sub's emergency deballasting system had *ever* been tested at maximum depth. After the loss of the *Thresher*, a hurried dockside experiment was made with another sub. *Even at the surface*, the buoyancy tanks could not be blown by the emergency system: ice had formed too thickly in the high-pressure lines for the air to get through.

Navy Secretary Korth was caught in a cleft stick, and fought grimly (and unsuccessfully) to keep the findings of the Congressional Atomic Energy Committee from being made public. Considering the Navy's difficulty in getting and keeping submarine crews, there is some merit on his side of the dispute. Bad publicity, he explained, "could have an extremely detrimental effect" on the Navy's submarine recruiting program.

In May 1964 a high-level task force called Deep-Submergence Systems Review Group talked the Navy into initiating a $300-million deep-ocean rescue and search program. One of the five projects was to be submarine location and rescue. Central to this program would be the DSRV—the Deep-Submergence Rescue Vehicle. This would be a thirty-ton, three-man, fifty-foot submarine vessel designed to mate with a disabled sub on the ocean floor (down to thirty-five hundred feet) by an escape hatch through which the trapped crewmen, twenty-four at a time, could enter the rescue vehicle. The DSRV was intended to be able to hover over and be attached to a wreck (even one listed at a steep angle), in spite of currents and waves. It would be equipped with optical and electronic sensors, hydrophones with a directional-listening feature, sector-scan sonar, vertical-obstacle sonar, altitude-and-depth sonar, doppler sonar, and side-looking sonar that could reach out eight hundred feet on either side of the craft.

To date, the DSRV is not yet operational.

In retrospect, the *Thresher* tragedy produced some good as well as evil. The Navy learned that it wasn't as clever as it thought it was in the matter of silver-brazed pipe joints, and as a result, made a great many changes in the construction and maintenance of nuclear submarines. Pipes are now tested electronically not only for current condition, but to forecast future metal fatigue; and the subs have been redesigned to drastically reduce the number of systems (including pipes and valves) that are submitted to sea pressure.

SCORPION IS OVERDUE

Then at 8:00 P.M. on May 21, 1968, a submarine called *Scorpion* sent a routine message from 250 miles south of the Azores. "Position 35:07 north, 41:42 west, speed 18 knots, course 290."

Scorpion was due into Norfolk, Virginia, at 1:00 P.M. on the twenty-seventh. Between, lay twenty-five hundred miles of open sea, very deep water almost all the way, with the poorly charted Mid-Atlantic Ridge the dominant feature; but the trip, like the radio message, was considered routine.

She was never heard from again.

Like the *Thresher*, *Scorpion* was nuclear powered: 3075-ton displacement, 252 feet long, a crew of ninety-nine officers and men. Because she maintained the radio silence that is standard for nuclear subs on deepwater missions, it was not until the twenty-seventh that the Navy knew anything was wrong. At 7:00 P.M. the *Scorpion* was announced as "overdue"; but fifty-five ships and thirty-five aircraft already were searching. They tracked fifty miles on either side of her proposed route, listened for radio and sonar signals, watched for debris and oil, and hoped: hoped that the sub had gone down in water shallower than her (classified) collapse depth, since her crew had food, water, and air-purifying equipment good for seventy days on the bottom.

SUB-MISS became SUB-SUNK when it was obvious she was not coming in. The relatively shallow Atlantic shelf was searched first, for if she was down in this area intact and with crewmen still alive, the Navy could attempt rescue, which would be impossible in deeper water. The second intensive search area was the tops of known seamounts in the extended track area; one of them, it was reasoned, might rise closer to the surface than the charts showed, and the *Scorpion* might be resting on top of it. The track itself was surface-searched in case she was lying on the surface with her electrical systems knocked out by something—perhaps even a collision with a whale.

Days went by, increasing tensions with false sightings. A 250-foot submarine hulk was found off Virginia; but it was from World War II. *Scorpion*'s code name, Brandywine, was heard on a radio transmission, but a quick check showed that eight vessels legitimately bore the name Brandywine. After nine days, the Navy declared that the submarine was "presumed lost," and the search was redesignated as SUB-LOST.

The vast armada of life-saving forces was pulled off, leaving only the oceanographic survey ship *Bowditch*, and the *Mizar*, which had been so instrumental in the Palomares nuclear bomb and *Thresher* search operations. *Mizar*'s "sled" (a framework of heavy steel pipes to support and protect the instrumentation) was dragged behind on twenty thousand feet of coaxial cable at a one-knot speed some twenty to thirty feet off the bottom. On the sled was a magnetometer, an Edgerton camera with two Edgerton strobe units to provide illumination for its 120-degree fisheye lens, and a side-looking and downward-looking sonar.

Back in Washington, meanwhile, damning "facts" began to emerge. *Scorpion*'s hull had hairline cracks. The hydraulic fittings around her periscope housing leaked. There were further leaks around her propeller shaft. Her navigational gear had possible malfunctions.

The press had a field day, which made it apparent that none of the reporters had ever served aboard a submarine. HY-80 steel, for instance, the steel used in nuclear submarines, *always* develops hairline cracks. It is a property of the steel. They are easily buffed away without damage to the hull. *All* periscope housings leak; the oil and water constantly drizzling down on the crewmen is one reason subs originally were nicknamed "pig boats." Leakage around a sub's propeller shaft is not only common, *it is designed into* the sub. Each watch must check to see that "the trickle" around the shaft is visible. The sea water is used as a lubricant to keep the rapidly spinning shaft from seizing up. And the subsequent Court of Inquiry could elicit no sworn testimony concerning any navigational-gear malfunctions.

So much for damning facts.

On November 10, 1968, official word was passed that the *Scorpion* had been found by the most massive search in the history of naval operations, involving six thousand men and four hundred ships and planes. A few days previously, on October 30, the *Mizar* had sent a wire to Naval Operations.

"OBJECTS IDENTIFIED AS PORTIONS OF THE HULL OF THE SUBMARINE USS SCORPION HAVE BEEN LOCATED ABOUT 400 MILES SOUTHWEST OF THE AZORES IN MORE THAN 10,000 FEET OF WATER."

In other words, a mere 150 miles from her last radioed position. How had the Navy found her? The late columnist Drew Pearson, in a piece that elsewhere displayed his total misunderstanding of the forces operating upon a submarine approaching collapse depth, claimed that the Russians found *Scorpion* and politely told the Navy where it had gone down; but excellent detective work by the Navy seems a more probable answer.[5] Anchored around the United States on the continental shelf are hydrophones and other detection gear, placed there at depths from six hundred feet all the way out to the edge of the sixteen thousand-foot Atlantic Basin, as an early-warning system against attack by missile-launching Russian nuclear subs.

None of them had recorded the passage of the *Scorpion*; but one of the sonar arrays near the Azores recorded a sound that might have been the sub breaking up. Into play then had to come the underwater TV cameras, the Edgerton cameras, the magnetometers, the sonar sensors. Added were the newly developed metal pods like miniature torpedoes which, trolled above the ocean floor, could reach out a thousand feet on either side with side-looking sonar.

Thus the bits and pieces that were left of the *Scorpion* were found and photographed. Nowhere near the site were there any underwater mounts or ridges, so the Court of Inquiry that sat for the *Scorpion* affair from June 1968 to January 1969 suggested four other possible causes for the sinking.

THE NAVY IS AT FAULT?

First, control failure. The sub's diving mechanism may have locked in a dive position while *Scorpion* was running fast and deep, so she reached collapse depth before the crew could make the necessary mechanical corrections to bring her up again.

Second, flooding from a pipe failure similar to that aboard the *Thresher* five years before.

Third, a torpedo malfunction. Pictures taken of the wreckage rule out the possibility that a fired torpedo had, like the torpedo from the *Tang*, homed back on the hull of the *Scorpion* herself; but there is a chance that a torpedo inside the sub itself may have malfunctioned and exploded. This too, however, seems highly unlikely, as it is doubtful that she even carried any.

Finally, in one of the cases above, crewmen might have panicked and begun pulling the wrong levers or pushing the wrong buttons. This also is questionable in view of the high degree of training maintained by the crews, as well as their tested psychological stability.

Which is the correct one will probably never be known.

That leaves one very pressing question: What happens in the future when a similar sub sinks (as it surely will) in water shallower than her collapse depth? What options do her crewmen have?

Down to six hundred feet, they could eject for free ascent and have reasonable hope of reaching the surface. But even then it is doubtful that anyone would be there to pick them up; for nuclear subs carry only a few flares, which first must be fired to the surface, and a pair of three-foot orange radio buoys that broadcast SOS SUB SUNK for *six hours only.*

Beyond six hundred feet, they could discharge oil to make a surface slick. They could also pound on the hull. Sensitive modern sonar sensors probably could pick up the noise from ten miles away.

What about the DSRV, the Navy's miniature submersible, designed specifically to rescue crews of sunken nuclear subs? It simply does not yet exist in any operational way.[6] And if it did, it *still* would have to find the sub before it could rescue the crew.

Which leaves . . . the McCann Rescue Chamber. Yes, the same chamber used in 1939 to rescue the crewmen of the *Squalus.* It is supposedly good for thirteen hundred feet; but from there down to the submarine's collapse depth . . .

"We all recognize that if a submarine is lost in deep water, there is nothing that can be done about it."

Speaking is Captain W. M. Nicholson,[7] head of the Deep Submergence Systems Project, admitting that we are operating an entire fleet of nuclear subs at depths where recovery of the crew is impossible if anything goes wrong. After twenty-one accidental sinkings of American submarines since 1900, with a loss of 431 lives, many outside the Navy are clamoring that submarine rescue techniques must be radically updated, but much of this is emotional. The same clamorer accepts without a shudder the crash of a giant jet liner that kills all aboard, and merely shrugs off the yearly carnage on the nation's highways. The cries for reform do not come from the crewmen who serve on these submarines.

One of the heaviest attacks centers on a proposed radio beacon which would be housed in the sub's hull and would *automatically* be released if the sub dropped down to a certain depth. There it would begin automatically transmitting to whatever electronic ears might be listening. Proponents of the device, recognizing that an accidental release of the beacon could lead enemy attack forces to the sub's position in time of war, say it could be removed before the sub went to a battle station.

But it is at least conceivable that U.S. submarines already have occasional clandestine tasks assigned to them; and it is no secret that U.S. and Russian subs track each other to launch simulated attacks. An accidentally released radio beacon in such circumstances would at best be a terrible embarrassment.

The Navy could festoon her nuclear submarines with enough devices to assure perfect safety—and in so doing would render the vessels useless.

The inescapable fact remains that the submarine is a weapon, an instrument of war; and that crewing on one of them is potentially a most hazardous occupation.

[1] On large lifting cables, this figure refers to circumference, not diameter.

[2] (A)llied (S)ubmarine (D)etection (I)nvestigation (C)ommittee.

[3] It is possible that Crabb, supposedly drowned on April 19, 1956, during a secret espionage mission in Portsmouth Harbor against the Soviet cruiser *Ordzhonikidze*, actually was kidnapped by Russian SCUBA divers and shanghaied into the Russian Navy, in which he may still serve.

[4] In 1960, Jacques Piccard, and Lt. Don Walsh, USN, took the *Trieste* to the record depth of 35,800 feet (6.78 miles) in the Challenger Deep, southwest of Guam. Pressure at bottom: 7.54 tons psi.

[5] The most the Russians could have done was hear the implosion on one of their hydrophones.

[6] The probability exists that DSRV will be operational when this book is published.

[7] Following the loss of the *Scorpion*.

III

Adrift

> White on my wasted path
> Wave after wave in wrath
> Frets 'gainst his fellow, warring where to send me.
> Flung forward, heaved aside,
> Witless and dazed I bide
> The mercy of the comber that shall end me.
>
> RUDYARD KIPLING
> *The Derelict*

CHAPTER ELEVEN

Mary Celeste and After

Perhaps the most famous ship ever salvaged, at least among people who collect tales of "things that go 'bump!' in the night," is the *Mary Celeste*. The disappearance of her crew has been attributed at various times to sea monsters, dematerialization, a selective natural force (very fashionable today in explaining disappearances of ships or planes in the "Bermuda triangle"), and even an early flying saucer. As luminous a celebrity as A. Conan Doyle produced a fictional explanation ("J. Habakuk Jephson's Statement") in 1884, with the *Mary Celeste* thinly disguised as the *Marie Celeste*.

Only the flat-earth people seem to have refrained from expatiating upon the fate of the *Celeste's* captain and crew.

A FAMOUS DERELICT

On December 4, 1872, a derelict vessel was spotted some six hundred miles from the coast of Portugal by a British brigantine, *Dei Gratia*.

When she drew close enough to be identified as the *Mary Celeste*, the brigantine's Captain Morehouse was also able to see that she was under short canvas with two sheets missing, and that her lower foretopsail was slack. The ship was running smoothly under a brisk north wind, however.

Morehouse found the vessel completely deserted, with the wheel swinging idly. A piece of the rail had been removed so that the lifeboat could be swung out. It, like the crew, was missing; so were the chronometer, sextant, navigation books, and ship's papers—all except the log book.

The last entry in the log was for November 24, 1872—ten days before the *Dei Gratia* found her. It merely recorded that the *Celeste* was then "about 110 miles due west of the island of Santa Maria in the Azores."

Routine. And when Morehouse examined the ship, he *could find nothing at all wrong with it*. She was not leaking; and if she had been, her pumps were intact and undamaged. There were no signs of a fight or struggle. The crewmen's sea chests containing all their clothing and personal articles were still stowed forward. Even the cargo of seventeen hundred casks of commercial alcohol was intact in the dim and dingy hold, with the exception of a single cask which had been opened.

Questions that immediately exercise the collector of mysteries are obvious. Where did the crew of the *Mary Celeste* go? *Why* did they go? Did they go willingly? If not, what *force* removed them?

Captain Morehouse was not a collector of mysteries. He was a seaman, by all accounts a good one. He had found a derelict vessel; therefore she was a salvage prize. He put a riding crew aboard with directions to follow him to Gibraltar, which he reached on December 13. The *Celeste* arrived a day later. All was done according to the admiralty laws of salvage.[1]

But the *Celeste*, contrary to usual practice, was immediately impounded, and an admiralty court of inquiry into the affair was opened with unusual haste. Solly Flood, Her Majesty's Advocate General, who was also Attorney General for Gibraltar, was a man of choleric temperament and apparently inflamed imagination: he promptly charged that Morehouse and the crew of the *Dei Gratia* were guilty of piracy and multiple murder.

The basis for Master Flood's charge looks rather thin from this far off in time: the two vessels had been anchored near each other in New York Harbor, and their skippers had taken supper together on the night before the *Celeste*'s departure. When the old sea dogs who made up the admiralty court seemed singularly untaken with the sinister connotations of all this, Flood thundered that there was more, much more.

On the starboard rail, he charged, was a cut. A cut such as *might be made by a cutlass!* Not only that, on the deck below the sliced rail was a brownish spot *which could easily be blood!*

Captain Morehouse declining to collapse on the floor babbling of his guilt, and his crew refraining from a spate of mass confessions, Flood decided on a new tack. It hadn't been the master and men of the *Dei Gratia* after all. It had been the crew of the *Celeste* herself.

"My own theory," he bellowed at the court, "is that the crew got into the alcohol and in a fury of drunkenness murdered the master, his wife and child, and the chief mate."

Indeed? But what of the *intact* cargo of alcohol (apart from a single opened cask)? What, also, of the fact that the alcohol was totally undrinkable? And finally, what had become of the crew after their bestial excesses? Had they, like the gingham dog and the calico cat, eaten one another up?

When it finally handed down its judgment in March 1873, the admiralty court did establish a precedent of sorts: it refused to offer an opinion as to what had happened aboard the *Mary Celeste*. The court cleared Morehouse categorically of piracy and murder, however, and in fact directed that he be given a salvage award equal to one-fifth the value of the *Celeste* and her cargo: £1700 for division among himself, his crew, and his vessel's owners.

The legend of the *Mary Celeste* still is compelling today, so compelling that the contemporary explanation advanced by the ship's owner, James Winchester, has been ignored. We all like a good mystery, and Winchester's interpretation—in all probability the right one—removes that element from the story entirely.

The *Celeste*'s cargo, remember, was crude alcohol—which, according to Winchester, neither the *Celeste* nor her skipper had ever carried before. One property of crude alcohol is that, heated and agitated, it gives off ignitable vapors. Warm weather and ocean storms would provide the heat and agitation. If a crewman had gone below into the unlighted hold to open one of the barrels and check on the condition of its contents—usual practice on merchant vessels—and had gotten his open light too close, there would have been a small flash and a harmless but impressive explosion.

The skipper, with wife and child aboard, could easily have thought that the cargo of alcohol was volatile and was about to explode. In such a frame of mind, he would have ordered all hands to the boat. An unexpected breeze would complete the tragedy: the ship, still under sail, would pull away from the small open boat, leaving it four hundred miles from land and easy prey to the first passing storm.

If this explanation contains too many "ifs" for the reader, three points should be considered: the ship was hastily abandoned; she was abandoned in the ship's yawl; and the abandonment (witness the removal of the navigational instruments and the ship's papers) took place in an orderly fashion. Winchester's theory meets the requirements; no other rational one does.

The *Celeste* sank from public sight in 1873, but she did not sink physically until nine years later. In 1884 an old con man named Gilman C. Parker became the owner; he loaded her with a few hundred dollars' worth of junk, insured the aging hulk for $27,000, enlisted a crew of like-minded lads, and set sail for the Caribbean. There, well sheltered from prying eyes in Haiti's Gulf of Gonaïve, they ran the vessel up on the jagged coral reef of the Rochelois Bank, removed what there was of value, soaked her in kerosene, and fired her.

They then returned to Boston to wait for the insurance money to roll in. Instead, federal marshals arrived to hale Parker and his pals into federal court on a barratry charge. A hung jury set them free, but Parker died in poverty a few months later.

Some connoisseurs of the *Celeste* affair claim to see in Parker's death a continuing curse on the vessel; but of course we already have shown that no dark powers were involved in the disappearance of her crew.

Haven't we? I say . . .

Romantic stories like that of the *Celeste* can be woven around very few of the deepwater-salvage tows that are performed each year, for they are usually dirty, slogging jobs of incessant tension, incessant work, storms, heaving seas, and heaving men. Salvage tows are undertaken for only one reason: the salvage reward. Without this, it would be much easier to merely save the people from a disabled vessel and abandon the hulk to a *Flying Dutchman* sort of existence until the inevitable storm would sink it or reef rip its guts out.

Sometimes a vessel will be abandoned by its would-be salvors even though the crew is still aboard. Today, in an age of tremendously powerful seagoing tugs, wireless, helicopters, and spotter planes, such abandonment of a tow and its crew is rare; but in the days of sail it happened with a certain chilling regularity.

LOSS OF THE OLER WITH ALL HANDS

The *Wesley M. Oler* was a one-thousand-ton, four-masted schooner loaded with guano en route from Orchilla Island, off the Venezuela coast, to New York, when she was struck by hurricane-force winds in November 1902. Their fury stripped the vessel's sails before the crew could even get aloft to shorten them. And the tremendous accompanying seas opened up scores of seams. The *Oler* limped into Nassau on November 7, under two close-reefed sails and a jib, her crew bleary-eyed from long days turn and turn about at the hand-operated pumps which had kept her afloat.

Ignoring a recommendation for extensive overhauling, the captain made only a few desultory repairs. With the ship still in questionable condition, the New York owners engaged the *Underwriter*, a three hundred-ton salvage vessel operating in Caribbean waters, to bring the *Oler* back to New York.

Underwriter left Jamaica with her tow on November 30; on December 2, they were caught by squalls and heavy rolling seas from the southeast. By the afternoon of the fourth, the *Oler*, all sails furled, was once again under Force 12 winds. At 2:00 A.M. on the fifth, the towline parted and the *Oler* disappeared into blackness.

Until dawn the *Underwriter* hung about; but as soon as she had light to see by, she tucked her tail between her legs and ran for Hatteras. There she swung north toward Hampton Roads, Virginia. If she made any pretense of searching for the *Oler*, it was a slight one.

The crippled vessel, swept continually by heavy seas, was driven into the bight between Hatteras Shoals and Cape Lookout, and went ashore on the south side of the Hatteras Inlet bar. There she was spotted, about a mile offshore, hull under, but masts still standing. A surfboat put out from Durant's Station in search of boats or wreckage-clinging castaways. They found only bodies. Most of them were still in sleeping clothes; seamen accustomed to the pitching and rolling of their vessel, they probably had not even known that the towline had parted.

Towing a vessel in deep water and heavy seas is *always* dangerous; but the dramatic incident generally occurs only when the tow runs into trouble. To the layman it is amazing how often this happens; but all seamen know the old salvage law that states, roughly, *whatever can go wrong, will*.

THE ARAB AND THE PROTECTION ON LAKE MICHIGAN

Certainly just about everything that could go wrong, did, when the schooner *Arab* ran into heavy weather in the fall of 1883 on Lake Michigan. Michigan is no Atlantic Ocean, but it is nearly 24,000 square miles of water—fifth in size, after the Caspian Sea, among the world's closed bodies of water.

The *Arab* was pounded hard on a rocky shore and seemed in such danger of breaking up that the crewmen lashed themselves to the rigging. The vessel held, however, and within a few days help arrived in the form of the *Protection*, a salvage steamer from Chicago. She sent down a diver to patch the opened seams and rock-stoved hull with oakum and straw where possible, and with large canvas patches where necessary. These were sent down rolled, with narrow wooden battens across the tops so they could be nailed in place, unrolled over the holes like window shades, and then nailed down all around.

One large rent was still blocked with the rock that had caused it; the diver stuffed a canvas mattress filled with oakum into the hole with his heavy boots. Inside, they made a box patch (like a miniature cofferdam) which fit over the hole and was covered with tightly nailed-down canvas. To keep the box from shifting, they put beam shorings between it and the deck above.

Then the *Protection* dragged her off the rocks stern first. She rode low in the water as the tow to the western shore began, but the two pumps they had put aboard were easily able to manage.

At four the next morning, before the eight salvors aboard the *Protection* could slack off their five-hundred-foot towline or even lose way, the *Arab* rolled over and sank instantly by the head. Ten feet of her port quarter remained above the surface, on which nine of the schooner's crewmen were crowded. The tenth had been trapped below decks and drowned when the box patch had let go.

Meanwhile, the slack towline had fouled the *Protection*'s propeller, so the salvage vessel was also disabled. As they worked to free it, the wind perversely rose to gale proportions.

By 11:00 A.M. things were looking desperate for the wallowing salvage ship; then the steamer *H. C. Akeley* appeared, threw her a line, and started to tow her toward the Manitou Islands. But as the wind kept increasing, the poorly laden *Akeley* started rolling. Soon her cargo broke loose. Something had to give, and at seven o'clock that evening it did: the *Akeley*'s steering gear broke. Then her engine stopped. She broached to while her crew desperately tried to raise her auxiliary sails; but the canvas was immediately torn away by the howling gale.

Both ships drifted until six the next evening, the *Akeley*'s lifeboats and smokestack meanwhile being carried off. But a ray of hope appeared: the *Protection*'s sleepless crew finally got the fouled screws cleared. They thought.

They cast off the towline and headed for shore, intending to coal up and return to tow in the *Akeley*. But ten minutes later the still-trailing ends of the *Arab*'s towline refouled the propeller, and they were drifting again. It took them until nine the next morning to come up to the town of Saugatuck, Michigan, where they dropped anchor and began blowing distress blasts on their whistle.

The nearest available aid was at St. Joseph's Life-Saving Station, which meant beach apparatus had to be transported sixty miles by rail, then ferried across the Kalamazoo River on the tug *Ganges*. The salvors went down the beach until they were opposite the *Protection*, but it proved too far out for their beach mortar to reach with a line.

At 6:00 P.M., yet another intense blizzard blew up, and at nine the *Protection*'s anchors started dragging. There was a round of good-byes and handshaking on the vessel; the men felt they would be killed when she piled up. Meanwhile, those ashore saw that the *Protection* would be blown in on the *other* side of the river, so they had to manhandle all their equipment aboard another tug—the *Graham*, this time—and ferry it back.

They set up on the beach, lit fires, and waited. But the helpless vessel fetched up on a sand bar two hundred yards out, where she was pounded heavily on the bottom before being finally driven, half-full of water, into the slack water beyond. The stern went hard aground, the head swung about, and the rescuers were able to fire a line aboard with their Lyle gun so that the stranded sailors could be transported ashore by breeches buoy.

The *Akeley* was towed into port and repaired when the storm had ceased; the *Protection* was a total loss. The *Arab*, which had started the whole sorry affair, had sunk long before.

A CLEVER TOWING JOB

One of the cleverest salvage operations involving a tow was that carried out by the steamship *Memnon* on the German tanker *Burgomeister Peterson* in the mid-Atlantic in 1896. The *Peterson* had lost her rudder and sternpost and thus was uncontrollable, capable only of running ahead without being able to guide herself.

The *Memnon*'s captain saw instantly that he had no hope of towing a rudderless ship in that tremendous gale and mountainous seas, but he had an idea, which he communicated to the German captain by wireless. This entailed running the *Memnon* up as close as he dared to windward of the *Peterson* and allowing a buoy with a line attached to drift over. This acted as a pilot for a heavy hawser, which was fastened to the portside of the crippled vessel's stern. A second hawser was sent over to be snubbed around the bitts on the starboard side.

Then he crossed the hawsers in making them fast to the bow of the *Memnon*: port to starboard and vice versa. Thus, in effect, the *Peterson* towed the *Memnon* as it might a massive, stablizing sea anchor; the crossed hawsers even gave the *Memnon* a rudimentary ability to steer the rudderless vessel from behind and bring it safely into port.

Many years later, in March 1932, the *H. F. de Bardeleben* similarly lost her rudder in the Atlantic, but among the many ships that tried to aid the American oil tanker there was none with a creative captain like the one on the *Memnon*. All the *Bardeleben* could do was run blindly on, with her crew hoping the gale would blow itself out before a continent got in their way. Newspaper feature writers dubbed her "the ship that cannot stop"; a lull in the blow finally allowed a rescue ship to bring away the crew, and the crippled vessel, with her engines stopped, quickly swung broadside to the heavy seas and foundered.

Since the First World War was in reality much less a global conflict than the second, and since huge, powerful, ocean-going tugs were not yet in existence, the number of notable salvage jobs involving tows during this period was much smaller. There were, however, two towing operations worth relating, both carried out by Captain John Iron, Harbor Master of Dover, England. By all accounts John Iron was a most remarkable man, with a driving determination, will, and courage to fit his name.

SOME EXPLOITS OF JOHN IRON

The *Terror*, with twin 15-inch guns, was one of the largest monitors[2] in the British fleet. She was torpedoed by a German U-boat off the Belgian coast, and was beached about half a mile outside Dunkirk Harbor. The torpedo had blown open her hull forward so thoroughly that only a third of it remained intact.

Such ships were in desperate demand at the time, so Iron was sent over from Dover to see how many weeks it would take to salvage the vessel, if indeed anything could be done about it at all.

That was on a Thursday. Iron-willed Iron reported by telephone that he would have her back to Dover on Sunday. The report met with a skepticism that bordered on derision—for in those days no one had yet dreamed up the idea of floating a ship with her belly ripped open on a "bubble" of compressed air.

Iron set his chief carpenter and crew to work strengthening with heavy timber balks the *Terror*'s lower deck, bulkheads, and what was left of the hull. By Sunday, despite a German air raid, he had the *Terror* as ready for sea as she was likely to get. Then he merely dragged her into the water.

And she floated. Oh, it was very low in the water that she floated, seeing that she was using the underside of her lower deck as a substitute hull; but at least some of her was above water. Iron's tugs took over, gently, slowly, coaxingly, for the forty-seven miles of bumpy English Channel that had to be crossed.

The *Terror* was in Dover before midnight.

Iron, however, did more than tow things across the Channel. When people "over there" refused a risky job that Iron thought needed doing, he went over and did it himself.

In January 1918 the steamer *Sussex*, carrying a rather prosaic load of meat, struck a mine in the Ruytingen, Holland, mine fields. As such "sea-eggs" are wont to do, the mine blew a large, coarse hole in the side of the ship. Iron, riding one of his Dover tugs over, arrived to find the craft's entire crew, including engineers, officers, and the captain himself, waist-deep in water in the stokehold.

They were feeding coal into the furnaces by hand so that their ship would not die and go down.

Iron coaxed four French tugs out of Dunkirk to help the Dover tug, and among them they managed to get the *Sussex* out of the mine field. Overtaken by dark, they let the vessel go gently ashore off Gravelines, with the idea of continuing the tow into Dunkirk the next day.

But dawn reawakened Gallic fears of German U-boats. The French tugs refused to stir, despite Iron's pleas, threats, curses, and cajolery; and he had no authority to order them out.

Iron did have authority to order out the Dover tug. He used it. Somehow this small lone vessel, aided in whatever ways possible by the crew of the *Sussex*, brought the damaged freighter off the beach at Gravelines and safely into Dunkirk Roads before dark.

FIRES ABOARD

One of the sea's great anomalies is that little is more feared on ocean-going vessels than shipboard fires. They are extremely difficult to extinguish, even though limitless supplies of water are all about, especially if they are in a hold.

The *Congress* was a 7985-ton passenger steamer en route to Seattle, Washington, from San Francisco on September 14, 1916, when a fire broke out in the after hold. At first the crew attempted to subdue the flames without alarming the 423 passengers aboard; but finally the captain admitted that the flames were out of control and sent out urgent distress signals.

Meanwhile, the crew herded life-jacketed passengers to their lifeboat stations, and the vessel was evacuated without injury or incident. Black smoke pouring from the *Congress* helped guide rescue vessels to the spot; despite icy weather, the survivors they picked up had removed their coats and were sweating from the intense heat. When the tug *Salvor* tried to get a towline aboard the burning ship, all it did was blister its own paint.

So the *Congress* was left to burn herself out, the plates of her hull glowing red hot. She smoked and fumed for days, meanwhile taking on a decided list, before salvage crews finally could tow her to Seattle. Only her steel hull and her superstructure, both seared and scorched, were left.

Shipyard crews began refurbishing her; when the renovation was completed, it had cost $2 million—exactly what the ship had cost to build in the first place.

The *Congress* was then leased by the China Mail Steamship Company, was rechristened *Nanking*, and was put into the Orient service. Soon very odd rumors concerning her began circulating along the western seaboard. It was said that she was being used to smuggle opium into the States and to carry girls shanghaied into white slavery back to China.

On several occasions these rumors led to the ship's being tied up in San Francisco under million-dollar court orders, until eventually the China Mail Company went bankrupt. The ship reverted to her original owners and was returned to the coastal passenger service as the *Emma Alexander*.

She was retired in the late thirties; but then World War II erupted and there was a terrible shortage of shipping. The tired old *Congress/Nanking/Emma Alexander* was impressed into service once again, this time as a British military transport named, for no discernible reason, *Empire Woodlarks*. She survived the war, was sold, resold ... The fire-gutted *Congress*, if she is still extant, probably has passed through so many hands that whoever owns her has no idea of her origin.

Under salvage law, all effective salvors receive awards proportionate to the services they have rendered.[3] This is fine in a simple one-ship operation such as the burning *Congress*. But some jobs get so incredibly complicated that award arbitrators are left scratching their heads for years to come. Such was the affair, early in this century, of the *Pacifique* and the *Antilla*.

It all began simply enough. In early October 1916, the steam yacht *Pacifique* was disabled by an engine breakdown some two hundred miles east of the Virginia capes. Her people had no wireless and were almost out of food when the freighter *Antilla*, loaded down with a cargo of sugar and hardwood, appeared on the scene. She quickly took the *Pacifique* in tow and turned her blunt nose toward Norfolk, Virginia.

On October 7, fire broke out in the *Antilla's* holds. They were 120 miles east of Norfolk at that time, buried in dense fog. Soon two steamers, the *Morro Castle* and the *Somerset*, arrived to give aid. In the confusion, the tow was lost and *Pacifique* drifted off into the fog. When the Coast Guard cutter *Onondaga* arrived on the morning of the eighth, she found the *Antilla's* bridge and officers' staterooms ablaze, with the fire wreaking great havoc in the sugar and hardwood below decks.

Probably because of the thick bank of fog, there was a calm sea with almost no wind, so the *Onondaga* was able to nose up to the *Antilla's* portside and snuffle enough water on her to put out the tophamper blaze. Little could be done with the fires in the hold except battening down the hatches for the tow to the Virginia capes. Just before a proper tug arrived from Norfolk, the *Pacifique* came drifting forlornly out of the fog. The Coast Guardsmen repaired her damaged boilers and gave the people aboard some food, and she elected to tag along behind the tow.

The Navy tug *Sonoma*, when she arrived, began pumping water into the *Antilla*'s holds and bunkers—so much water that by the time they arrived at Cape Charles, at noon of the ninth, the freighter had taken on a heavy list. So they had to seal all the hatches, ports, and ventilators to feed as little oxygen to the flames as possible, and then run like the devil for Hampton Roads. They made it, and there the *Albertross* and the *Resolute* put out the fire.

So the *Somerset*, *Morro Castle*, *Albertross*, *Resolute*, *Onondaga*, and *Sonoma* all had valid salvage claims against the *Antilla*. But the *Antilla* had a valid claim against the *Pacifique*. So, however, did the *Onondaga*. But not really. Because *Onondaga* and *Sonoma* were government vessels carrying out their duty (*voluntariness* is an essential part of salvage in the legal sense), their claims, even if advanced, probably would not have been valid. But of course, in some cases . . .

One is dogged by the recurrent suspicion that somewhere a group of very old and very tired lawyers still shuffles reams of age-yellowed documents, trying . . . trying so very hard . . .

To find out who did how much of what for whom.

Sometimes a fire aboard a vessel will call for radical measures which to the lay observer look like madness. But it is an inflexible rule of salvage that a captain faced with fire or water should choose water. It is better to sink a ship than to let a fire consume it.

The *War Knight* and the *O. B. Jennings* were part of a large Allied convoy moving through the English Channel on the black night of March 24, 1918, without lights in hopes of foiling possible U-boats. Both ships were tankers; the *Jennings* was down to her Plimsoll line with a cargo of naphtha. In the dark, she unintentionally cut across the bows of the *Knight*, and the latter ship struck her a staggering blow forward.

The naphtha exploded in an enormous fireball, which wiped out all but a few men in the *War Knight*'s crew. The survivors leaped into the water to escape the flames, but the burning naphtha rained down to kill all but two of them. Oddly enough, most of the *Jennings*' crewmen were aft when the ships collided, and were able to get to their boats through the circle of flames.

Then a daring British destroyer raced right into the burning mass around the ships, and one of her sailors leaped aboard the *War Knight* to take aboard the pilot wire for a heavy steel towing hawser.

More by will power than by engine power, they dragged the flaming tanker out of the searing heat . . . only to have her strike a mine. In a bid for future salvage, the destroyer towed the listing ship into shallow water and sank her on the sandy bottom with gunfire. Divers going down on the wreck later reported that salvage was not possible.

Meanwhile, the *Jennings* also had been taken in tow and was brought into Sandown Bay. But the fire refused to go out; for ten days she sat there smoking and fuming, until a rather brilliant salvage officer ordered a torpedo boat to fire on the ship and sink her.

His gamble paid off. Divers went down, connected up surface pumps with the undamaged after tanks, and pumped eight thousand tons of sorely needed naphtha from the sunken vessel. Then the holes in her hull were patched, she was sealed, pumped out, and refloated. Permanent repairs were carried out, and soon the *Jennings* joined another convoy for the United States to pick up war matériel.

A hundred miles from New York, she took a submarine torpedo amidships, which sent her down permanently.

There is some sort of special madness that seems to seize certain men of the sea when they are trying to save their own vessels. They take risks that it seems safe to assume none of the same men would take ashore to save a building.

One of the most amazing examples of this, also involving a fire aboard a ship with an inflammable cargo, was the steamship *Cardium*, out of Australia. The vessel was laden with benzine and benzoline when, in the Indian Ocean off Australia's west coast, an engine-room fire shot flames fifty feet into the air. At any moment, when they reached the highly volatile cargo, the vessel would be blown completely to pieces.

Captain W. E. Jones and *his entire crew* refused to leave the burning and apparently doomed ship. For two days and two nights without any sleep whatsoever they fought to save the *Cardium*, not even eating, trying with whatever meager fire-fighting equipment they had at hand to control the blaze. During that fifty-two-hour period in which they conquered the flames, the captain's hair turned gray.

But to what purpose?

The ship, of course, was without power, and was drifting helplessly toward the rocky Australian coast. A steamer tried to take them in tow; it found the task impossible because it could not maneuver that close to shore. Her captain urged Jones and his men to leave the *Cardium*. They refused. The steamer departed.

Meanwhile, Sparks had gotten the wireless working on emergency power and was sending out SOS signals. Another steamer responded, looked over their situation, and sent a message to Jones.

"Better abandon ship."

"Refuse to abandon," Jones returned. "The darkest hour is before the dawn. *Cheer up!*"

His unshakable confidence must have been infectious. The ship somehow got a towline aboard the *Cardium*, and both ship and cargo were brought safely into port.

The Lloyd's underwriters who had insured the vessel awarded the captain and crew £900 for their work in saving their own patently doomed ship—something very rare indeed in salvage rewards. And Captain W. E. Jones was awarded that coveted and seldom-given decoration for great personal valor, the Lloyd's Silver Medal.

[1] See APPENDIX II, "The Legalities of Salvage."
[2] These armored warships, with a very low freeboard and guns mounted on revolving turrets, were used either for coastal defense or as picket ships. The name comes from the first of such vessels, the Union ironclad *Monitor*, which met the Confederate *Merrimack* at Hampton Roads, Virginia, in 1862 (see Chapter Twenty-six).
[3] See Appendix II.

CHAPTER TWELVE

Abandoned by Crews

Salvage towing is an art that requires a great deal of patience and experience—and the right equipment. Not every old tramp steamer that happens by a crippled ship can haul her into port for a fat salvage reward.

The first major difficulty with a regular, non-salvage vessel assisting another in the open sea is that both vessels are large and cumbersome, like fat people dancing at a church social. Just getting a towline fixed is a major achievement. The stricken vessel will be dead in the water, and therefore will be riding broadside to the weather, rolling badly. This means that the rescuing vessel must pass to windward, steering a parallel course and, as she passes, somehow get a light line across to the damaged craft. This is usually accomplished with a heavy stick, rocket, or Lyle gun—depending on what equipment the rescuer has aboard, and how close he can safely get to the disabled vessel.

If he misses, he must make another pass. This, too, sounds simple, but it requires three or four miles for a large ship merely to turn around. Thus, the value of the comparatively small and highly maneuverable tug becomes apparent. A tug can move in close, get its small line to the stricken ship, bend a heavier one on its end, and eventually send over the four-to-nine-inch towing cable.

Tugs exist for towing. Their cables have an eye riven into the end, by which they can easily be made fast to the bitts of the ship being towed. The other end is fastened to a constant-tension steam winch on the tug, which helps prevent the sudden jerks, from unexpected rolls of the vessels, that are the usual cause for breakage of towing gear.

DIFFICULTIES OF SALVAGE TOWING

But when a ship gets into trouble on the open sea, there is seldom a tug about; so other ships do their best until one arrives. Often their best is not very good.

The *Powhatan* was a U. S. Army transport that was disabled five hundred miles east of Boston in the North Atlantic during freezing weather and vicious blizzards in January 1920. Aboard the 10,000-ton vessel were five hundred people and $2.5 million in cargo. Her distress signals first brought another transport, the *Northern Star*, and then the Navy destroyers *Leary* and *Sharkey*.

They all sort of swam around in a circle looking at her until the British salvage steamer *Lady Laurier* arrived. She was not a proper tug, but was at least able to hold *Powhatan* in position until, on the twenty-second, the cutter *Ossipee* arrived with boats to transfer the ship's passengers and baggage to the *Northern Star*.

Then *Lady Laurier* began her tow toward Halifax, Nova Scotia. *Powhatan* refused to steer properly, yawing wildly from side to side behind the salvage tug; so another ship that had joined the convoy, *Acushnet*, fastened onto the stern of the towed vessel to help hold her on course. The *Ossipee*, meanwhile, fastened onto the bow of the *Lady Laurier* to give added power, as two switching engines in tandem will pull a long string of freight cars.

Almost immediately, the *Acushnet*'s 10-inch towrope broke. She quickly replaced it, but as quickly, the *Ossipee*'s 12-inch rope snapped. Before they could fix that, *Acushnet*'s went again.

The tow had started on the twenty-second; it was the twenty-fourth before the *Ossipee*, maneuvering gingerly in the enormous seas, managed to reset her line to the *Lady Laurier*. Once it was in place, she swung back ahead of the salvage vessel to start towing again.

The rope broke. Immediately the *Laurier*'s rope broke. *Powhatan* was left with only the *Acushnet*'s hawser still fast. Her crew began the day-long job of heaving aboard the broken lines, chains, and hawsers, only to lose the *Acushnet*'s line in the ensuing confusion. *Powhatan* was once more adrift.

Then came a new snowstorm, blown down upon them by a terrific northeast gale. *Powhatan* disappeared into the scud.

It took them two days to find her again.

Finally, a second salvage steamer arrived, the aptly named *American Relief*. When the gale died down a bit, she got a line aboard the crippled ship's port bow; the *Ossipee* got one aboard the starboard quarter; the *Lady Laurier* got one aboard the starboard bow; and they managed to bring the *Powhatan* into Halifax on the twenty-seventh.

Powhatan was child's play compared to the towing operation done on the steamer *Stiklestad* some five years later. This ship went out of control on October 3, 1925, when her screw bearings seized up. She reported her mid-Atlantic position, and all ships on the great arc of ocean between Rotterdam and Newfoundland were asked to watch out for her and offer assistance if possible.

The salvage steamer *Reindeer*, meanwhile, set out from St. John's, Newfoundland, to aid her—not once, but several times. *Reindeer* was driven back in repeatedly by savage storms, the last of which mauled her so severely that she had to retreat into dry dock. Scratch *Reindeer*.

It was thus seventeen days after *Stiklestad* had begun drifting that the first help arrived. For two days, the steamer *Dampfern* tried to get a line aboard her. Not successful. Exit *Dampfern*.

The next day *Geraldine Mary* arrived, full of high hopes. *One week later*, she got a pilot line aboard the crippled ship; the attempts had been continual, day and night. When she tried to tow, she couldn't move the 6000-ton *Stiklestad*. On October 29, she broke her towline. She could not even stand by, since she was running out of coal.

The *Geraldine Mary* had put £24,000 into the salvage attempt in direct losses and expenses. Because she played no role in *Stiklestad*'s ultimate safety, her salvage award was very modest: £1800. It is in such cases that the teeth hidden deep in "no-cure, no-pay" salvage contracts are bared.

Meanwhile the *Stiklestad* was no closer to safety than before, and provisions were running low. The *Vittoria* took several days, in the incessant storms which did not abate for a moment, just trying to put some food aboard.

On November 3, a full thirty-one days after the *Stiklestad*'s propellers had become inoperable, the salvage steamer *American Relief*, the same one instrumental in saving the *Powhatan* five years before, managed to get a towline aboard the ship. After three days of towing, however, the hawser parted. *Stiklestad* was adrift again. Three more days passed before the tow could be re-established.

On the same day, November 9, the L. Smit and Company tug *Zwart Zee* arrived from Rotterdam and towed the helpless ship to the Azores for repairs, some fifty days after she had begun drifting. *Stiklestad* soon was repaired and back in business.

Just two months later, the *Zwart Zee* solved another complex salvage problem, which, while not equaling the *Stiklestad* tow in time, certainly equaled it in frustration.

In February 1926 the 6576-ton steamship *Manchester Producer* broke her sternpost in mid-Atlantic. Since it is this arm that holds the rudder in place, the *Producer* was helpless. Unable to steer, she drifted. Aboard was a cargo of live cattle and general foodstuffs.

The steamer *Montrose* was the first to come to *Producer*'s aid, could not help, and passed word that the *Producer* was attempting to make the Azores. The German steamer *Hanover* was next, coming alongside and getting ropes and hawsers fastened to the stern of the crippled vessel.

"They snapped like cotton," said Captain Mitchell of the *Producer*.

Then the *Menominee* showed up, a much larger, more powerful craft than the earlier rescuers, equipped with five-inch wire hawsers to use in the towing attempt.

"Went off like a cannon shot," remarked Captain Mitchell.

The *Menominee*'s crew was not to be done down by any five-inch cables. They tried to tow with their anchor chain.

The taciturn Mitchell: "Snapped like a carrot."

Menominee went her frustrated way. So, in due course, did the *Mongolian Prince* and the *London Commerce*.

Smit and Company's *Zwart Zee*, dispatched specially to aid the stricken steamer, arrived at this juncture. She got a line aboard and towed the vessel to the Azores. Facilities for the needed repairs being lacking there, she went on, taking the *Producer* all the way back to its home port of Manchester, England. This tow of over two thousand miles was one of the longest ever undertaken up to that time.

Tows carried out in the teeth of those sly and always implacable enemies, wind and wave, are harrowing enough, but wartime adds an extra dimension of danger to the job. Then it is not a salvage reward but stark human necessity, the desperate gamble to save men or matériel, that motivates the salvors.

America did not formally declare war on the Axis powers until December 8, 1941, following the Japanese attack on Pearl Harbor; but American naval and civilian ships were deeply involved in the movement of war matériel to Britain under the lend-lease agreements long before that. And the German submarines were busy, feeling no need to differentiate between British and American vessels, when both were carrying or protecting the goods of war.

THE *KEARNY'S* REMARKABLE REPAIRS

On October 17, 1941, while on convoy-defense duty in the North Atlantic, the U.S. destroyer *Kearny* was struck on the starboard side by a German torpedo. Eleven men were killed instantly in the forward boiler room; except for some steel decking on the portside and a few starboard plates, the ship was cut completely through. The deck above the boiler room was gone, along with a good section of the starboard hull. Fortunately, the bulkhead between the boiler and forward engine rooms held, so the ship did not flood aft of that.

The crew ran wire cables across the break, tightened them with turnbuckles, used wooden wedges and oakum to calk ruptured bulkheads, and then turned the *Kearny's* battered nose toward Iceland.

There, divers from the repair ship *Vulcan* measured the rupture, and artificers built a huge timber caisson, padded with oakum and canvas, which was large enough to fit all the way around the damaged area. This was weighted with iron ballast, sent down to the divers, lined up, then jammed up against the hull and winched up tight.

The caisson was pumped out so divers could repair any leaks that showed up. Then workmen went down inside the ship to burn away the ragged edges of torn plates. Carpenters spanned the hole with heavy timbers inside and out, then bolted them together right through the hull. Two-inch planking was laid over this and fastened down with spike guns. Heavy waterproof canvas went over everything.

The caisson was flooded; the patch held. With a portable pump in the compartment to take care of incidental leakage, the *Kearny* made it to the Boston Naval Ship Yard under her own power.

Within five months she was back in action.

It was in North African waters, however, during the dark days of 1942 and 1943, when the slogan was *too little, too late*, that some of the most incredible jobs were carried out. Some were successful; others were failures. But it is certain that Rommel being turned back into the desert, and the subsequent destruction of his Afrika Korps, would have been impossible without the work of the American and British salvage officers of the North African ports.

SAVING THE *PORCUPINE*

HMS destroyer *Porcupine* was struck by a torpedo from a German submarine on December 10, 1942. Commander Edward Ellsberg,[1] in charge of salvage and harbor clearance in North Africa, received word in Oran that the ship was disabled and sinking.

He gave orders for a dozen men in his salvage unit to load their few portable pumps into an Army truck and head for Arzeu, the harbor they would take the destroyer into if they could save it at all. Meanwhile Ellsberg and engineer Jock Brown commandeered a British MTB (motor torpedo boat) to get them out to the *Porcupine*.

They found the vessel due north of Cape Carbon, down so far in the stern that the fantail was awash, listing so far to starboard that the water reached the deck amidships. Yet the *Porcupine* had been struck on the portside: waves washed freely in and out of a twenty-foot space in the 1900-ton vessel where the engine room had once been. The heel to starboard was because the port engine had dropped right through the hole and sunk, ruining the vessel's trim.

A tow was under way, just barely under way; though she was four or five hours from port and might sink before she got there, they could tow at only three knots. Just a few wrinkled steel deck plates held the ship together amidships, and the two sections worked like an accordion with each wave that passed beneath.

Ellsberg and Brown went below with the *Porcupine*'s engineer to assess the damage. It was essential to see where the water was leaking into those portions of the ship that still were sound; quick computations suggested that it would go down within two hours unless the flow was countered. Examination showed that pressure was forcing water up through the manholes covering the access trunks to the flooded shaft alleys, even though the manholes were all closed and dogged down.

They discovered there was a portable electric-driven centrifugal pump that the ship's engineer was using up forward to keep his fireboxes from flooding! If they flooded, he assured them seriously, his firebrick would be soaked and his boiler insulation ruined. Ellsberg dryly pointed out that the engines wouldn't run anyway, and that dry firebrick probably would not remain dry if the *Porcupine* sank before they reached port.

The pump was shifted, and within ten minutes two hundred gallons of water a minute was being sent over the side from the stern section —enough to keep well ahead of the leaks.

Nothing could be done about the gaping hole amidships, however, except reduce the towing speed from three to two knots. The deck was totally ruptured to port, and the crack was slowly inching its way through the starboard plating as the bow and stern sections worked.

They finally reached the lee of Cape Carbon, where the tow could be speeded up to a princely three knots again; but then they had to shorten their tow so they could be maneuvered into Arzeu Harbor. This meant casting off the anchor-chain towline from the *Porcupine* (which of course, without power, had no way to winch it in herself) so a shorter towline could be fixed.

But the shackle on the bitter end of their chain was rusted solid. They tried oil on it, kerosene, sledge hammers, even cold chisels—but the lockpin was frozen stiff. Finally they laboriously sawed it in half with a hack saw.

With the short tow hooked up, they went through the opened anti-submarine nets and into the harbor. Here the overland salvage party from Oran brought up the gasoline-driven four-inch and six-inch portable pumps and began pumping out one thousand gallons a minute. As the water lowered in the stern, divers calked with oakum the leaking air port that had been letting in most of the water, as well as the hatch covers to the shaft alleys.

The stern continued to rise, and most of the starboard list disappeared, with oil being pumped from starboard to port fuel tanks to aid in the process. The *Porcupine* was saved.

Just eleven days later, on December 21, the British troopship *Strathallan*, a 25,000-ton ex-P & O liner with six thousand soldiers aboard, was torpedoed sixty miles due north of Oran.

The only word received by Ellsberg and his fifty-man crew on the salvage vessel *King Salvor* was that she had been hit in the port engine room and was sinking. They rushed out immediately, using the four hours it would take to reach the stricken vessel in the backbreaking work of lugging up from the hold all their heavy salvage pumps, along with several hundred fathoms of suction and discharge hose. This left them utterly spent.

FIRE ABOARD THE *STRATHALLAN*

Then they were passed by several destroyers returning from the *Strathallan* loaded with the soldiers taken off the hulk, and one of them sent a blinker message:

ALL TROOPS OFF. STRATHALLAN HEAVILY ON FIRE AND COMPLETELY ABANDONED BY CREW AS TOTAL LOSS.

Fire! And they had spent three hours preparing for water!

King Salvor had hose and steam-pumping equipment for a dozen fire lines; but what they needed was men. Men for the hoses, turn and turn about. But the crew had deserted the *Strathallan*, and *King Salvor* could muster a bare thirty fire fighters—since twenty men had to stay aboard to handle her and the pumps. And meanwhile, the exhausted men who might soon be fighting fire had to hump back down into the hold all the pumping equipment they had just finished bringing up.

When they reached the burning troopship at 4:30 P.M., they found her with a bare 10-degree port list, a bit down by the stern; but obviously she was not and never had been in danger of sinking from the torpedo damage itself. A tremendous fire front extended for two-thirds of her length when they arrived, but the great number of scramble nets, and the fact that all the lifeboats were gone, showed that the vessel could not even have been very seriously afire when she had been abandoned. Someone had panicked.

Three ships—the destroyer HMS *Laforey* and the armed trawlers *Restive* and *Active*—had hung about until the *King Salvor*'s arrival so the *Strathallan* could be officially declared derelict and abandoned. But Ellsberg was a salvor; he hadn't come to declare a still-floating ship derelict.

He flashed *Laforey* to stand by for any possible assistance, then made a circle of the burning ship to try to find the best place to board her. They found a crewman still aboard; the skipper had abandoned so hastily he had not even checked to see that all his men were safe. They got him off, then Jock Brown, the engineer who had accompanied Ellsberg out to the *Porcupine*, made a tremendous running leap from the *Salvor*'s highest point to the *Strathallan*'s lowest. He made fast their lines.

As Ellsberg boarded the burning ship, there was a sudden wave of gunfire from the boat deck overhead. Anti-aircraft guns, left loaded and on full automatic fire by their crews, were being heated to the point where their shells were firing, recocking the weapons after each round. Ignoring them, the exhausted salvors split up into twelve 2-man crews, four crews to each of the vessel's three decks, working without smoke masks or protective asbestos clothing. None of them had gloves. Within minutes they were scorched, burned, blistered, constantly being bombarded with hot shrapnel from the anti-aircraft guns' ricochets. But no man quit.

Ellsberg had gotten the *Restive* and the *Active* into position so that one towed while the other pushed. Unfortunately, this started an updraft which sent sparks and burning embers down onto the *Salvor*, so the crew left aboard had to add the dousing of scores of small deck fires to their other chores.

One tremendous danger they faced was from five tons of powder and TNT stored in the magazine aft, which the flames threatened soon to reach. Ellsberg noticed a fire monitor on a steel tower abaft the bridge, went up, and directed its heavy fountain of water on the ship's stern to cool the munitions below any possible flash point.

The ship would take eighteen hours to tow into port, where they could get proper foam-making equipment to smother the fire, so their job was to put out the fire in the superstructure and confine it below. But Ellsberg knew his men could not stand up to the task unrelieved for eighteen hours, so he blinkered the *Laforey*, requesting forty men for fire-fighting duty. They soon arrived under command of a lieutenant and a sublieutenant, equipped with asbestos suits, smoke masks, tin hats, smoke goggles, and even a rescue breathing apparatus with a corpsman.

Ellsberg then went over to the *Laforey* in search of someone who might be familiar with the burning ship's physical layout; such knowledge, he reasoned, would be of great value in planning their strategy.

On the bridge of the destroyer he found the *Strathallan's* Captain; that worthy had not even bothered to join those trying to save his ship. He calmly told Ellsberg that the fire had started *many hours after* the torpedo had struck! When they first had been hit, he had begun to evacuate the troops in the dark. But when the ship did not seem to be sinking, he had decided to wait until dawn. During that time, water from the torpedo damage had leaked into the fire rooms. None of the officers aboard were bright enough, not even the engineers, to put out the fires in the boilers before the water reached them. When it had, they had burst, setting the boiler room ablaze.

There had still been no danger at that time, but the Captain had decided the ship was a total loss and had evacuated his entire crew.

While Ellsberg was talking to the Captain a blinker message came from the *Strathallan*. CONSIDER IT TOO DANGEROUS TO REMAIN, the message read. REQUEST PERMISSION TO RETURN LAFOREY.

Over Ellsberg's objections, the forty-man work crew came back to the destroyer. When he had gotten his party aboard *Strathallan*, the lieutenant had set them to work throwing all the ammunition overboard, even though the fire monitor had assured them there was no danger of its going up. Before they had completed this task, he had sent word to the *Laforey* that it was too dangerous to remain. Ellsberg's dogged crew had never been relieved!

Knowing the vessel was now doomed, Ellsberg instructed Lieutenant Harding, captain of the *King Salvor*, to withdraw his men. Harding refused. He still wanted to try to save the ship; the men on the hoses, reeling from exhaustion, also refused. Only when Ellsberg, as Harding's commanding officer, gave him a direct order, was he able to clear *Strathallan* of the men from the *Salvor*.

The huge troopship finally went down. As her port list gradually increased, the row of battle ports in the vessel's lower hull dipped under water. In abandoning the ship, her officers had not even bothered to close them down—a prime rule for warships in a battle zone. Water rushed through the open ports, and the troopship rolled over and went down.

Shocked as Ellsberg was by the conduct of the captain of the *Strathallan*, he had little time to brood about it. On January 1, 1943, only ten days after that frustrating loss, another giant troopship, the 22,000-ton *Empress of Australia*, was struck by another transport while traveling in a large, blacked-out convoy. The word he received was that she was flooding rapidly, listing badly, and that her engine power would soon go out, leaving her a dead ship. Aboard her were some four thousand to five thousand troops.

He arrived on the scene to find the one-time passenger ship with a very bad starboard list accentuated by the soldiers crowding her decks. They had refused to remain below, and their presence above the ship's center of gravity added to its already considerable instability.

Aft of her third stack was a huge, V-shaped gash in her starboard quarter, reaching from below the waterline right up to her upper deck. She had no power and was drifting broadside to a stiff northwest wind.

Just as Ellsberg got aboard, she flopped from that terrific starboard list to an equally terrific port list, putting above water most of the gash through which she was flooding.

He immediately ordered her to let go her anchors before she hit Oran's seaward breakwater, and then instructed the ship's chief engineer to flood every portside compartment, including the port double bottoms, storerooms, and shaft alley—which, being so low in the vessel, would give a disproportionate amount of stability. They found the shaft alley already flooded; it was this that had rolled the ship to port just as Ellsberg arrived. The port list kept enough of the gash above water that, even with the limited amount of steam they could keep up in the boilers, they were able to run the pumps and keep ahead of the leaks.

The ship was towed through the anti-sub nets of the Mers-el-Kebir military harbor near Oran, where she could begin discharging her troops. While this was going on, divers already were at work putting a wood patch over the flooding part of the gash; on this was built a watertight cofferdam so a heavy concrete patch could be poured until it was filled right up to the main deck. The vessel was pumped out (restoring stability), and the machinery was cleaned up enough to take her back to England for permanent repairs.

OPPOSITION BY *POZARICA*'S CAPTAIN

Another of Ellsberg's hurry-up towing jobs that same month, January 1943, was the anti-aircraft cruiser *Pozarica*, which had taken a German torpedo right in the stern. As the explosion had blown away a good part of her fantail and all of her rudder, as well as bending her propeller shaft, the Captain had abandoned her with his four hundred-man crew.

Ellsberg met them on the quay at Bougie; he had no salvage equipment whatsoever in that port, but he still asked the Captain for thirty or forty of his men to have a try at saving the vessel. To Ellsberg's astonishment, the Captain said the ship was obviously a total loss, so why bother? Enraged, Ellsberg called for volunteers, asking a

Scots lieutenant of Royal Engineers for a loan of two or three squads of men. The lieutenant already had gotten a small, flat barge in hopes of a salvage attempt, and on it had humped the only pumping equipment available at Bougie, two gasoline-driven fire pumps.

As they were talking, the *Pozarica*'s Captain came over and began trying to talk them out of the salvage attempt, but his enlisted engineer ratings, as well as his junior engineer lieutenant, offered their services to Ellsberg.

They set out on a British torpedo boat with their fire pumps, a dozen soldiers, the *Pozarica* volunteers, and Ellsberg's trusted salvage chief, U. S. Navy Lieutenant George Ankers. They found the *Pozarica* in sad shape. She had a terrific list to port, and her stern was fourteen feet under the water, which reached her midships superstructure and had submerged the housing of her after gun. The forefoot and most of her keel were completely out of water.

They boarded by way of the scramble nets on her starboard side, then heaved up from their torpedo boat the two antiquated fire pumps. Ellsberg, Ankers, and the *Pozarica*'s assistant engineer found that it was the after bulkhead of the after engine room that was holding back the sea; but water was squirting through the propeller-shaft housing and already had reached the lower engine-room gratings. By running to port, it was gradually increasing the list. The diesel-driven generator on the starboard side was still out of water, Ellsberg saw, but would soon be inundated.

He had the diesel started immediately, to give them lights by which to work; but the pumps they had brought were too large to fit through the doors leading down to the engine room. Nor did they have pickup hoses long enough to bring the water from the vital engine room all the way up to the decks so it could be pumped over the side.

Then he noticed that a British destroyer, the *L-o6*, was drifting a short distance away. Her fore-section had been blown away by a torpedo, but she was in no danger of sinking, and her crew was still aboard. From the *Porcupine*, he knew that British destroyers carried a compact, portable, electrically driven centrifugal pump; they borrowed the *L-o6*'s. There was not much hose with it, but it was better than nothing.

When they got the five-hundred-pound pump back aboard the *Poazrica*, however, they had no way of getting it down to the engine room; it would fit through the bulkhead doors, but there was no tackle for lowering it. And between it and the engine room were three separate sets of vertical bulkhead ladders. If they didn't get it down before the generator in the engine room flooded, they would have no power with which to operate it.

The soldiers, eight of them, began edging along a companionway toward the head of the first ladder when the enormous George Ankers, knowing they would never be in time, brushed the four on one end aside, seized the pump alone, yelled at the others to get going, and lugged it over to the ladder. He went down a few rungs, told them to lower it onto his shoulders and to hang onto the top end of it, picking up whatever weight they could.

Then, supporting nearly the entire five hundred pounds alone, Ankers went down the three flights of ladders to the engine room. Without pause he began coupling up the suction hose. Ellsberg, meanwhile, coupled up the discharge hose, and the engineer lieutenant coupled up the electric cable to the almost flooded generator.

The pump flickered, caught, began banging away. But their discharge hose merely reached the passageway above them, which it began flooding. This was almost worse than before, since it was adding weight high up on the vessel, robbing it of further stability and adding to the port list.

Ellsberg had the Royal Engineers move one of their fire pumps to the companionway and drop its suction pump into the miniature lake being formed by the lower pump's discharge. This second pump relayed the water up to the main deck and over the side.

For three days and two nights they pumped without pause, straightening the list, putting the bow back in the water, and bringing the deckhouse clear of the sea. When the British salvage ship *Salvestor* arrived from Algiers, it was able to tow the *Pozarica* into Bougie. There, salvage divers cut enough mangled steel plates from the destroyer's stern so the ship could be towed to Algiers, where it was docked and permanent repairs were made.

Lieutenant George Ankers was recommended for the Navy Cross. The *Pozarica*'s Captain was recommended for a court-martial.

Another inventive salvor operating in North African waters was Peter Keeble, the South African who had gotten the secret infrared sensing device from the sunken German submarine U-307 (see Chapter Ten).

ATTEMPT TO SAVE USS MASARYK

One of his more harrowing operations, carried out from Alexandria in 1943, was the attempt to save the Liberty ship USS *Thomas Masaryk*. She had been passing through the Strait of Sicily in convoy when a torpedo dropped from a Nazi torpedo bomber struck her No. 3 hold. The ship began settling by the head while her crew and even the convoy hastily abandoned her: the No. 3 hold was packed with drums of acetone—a highly inflammable aircraft dope.

Keeble and his men set out in their salvage tug *Captive*, which they had recently raised from the floor of Tobruk Harbor (see Chapter

Nineteen), without any fire-fighting gear but with the hope that they might be able to tow in the *Masaryk* before it sank.

They found the ship rolling on the oily swell, sending up clouds of steam and glowing red hot around the burning hold. She was afloat on her bulkheads, Keeble saw, and probably would keep afloat that way. But she would also keep on burning. The only way to stop the fire would have been to flood the holds, but in her condition this would have sunk her.

They laid the *Captive* bow by bow with the towering Liberty, and after several tries got grapnels over the bulwarks. Keeble led a boarding party up the lines.

On deck, the boarders had to keep running; if they stood still, the steel plates would scorch their feet right through their shoes. Somehow the six dancing men got the towlines aboard and belayed to the heavy forward bollards and the heel of the foremast. But when the tow began, the *Masaryk* moved very erratically, arcing from side to side because she had a port rudder of some 10 degrees. And the party aboard could not get back to straighten out the rudder because the red-hot section of deck over the No. 3 hold lay between.

At that moment, their decision was made for them. The No. 2 hold blew, shooting hatch covers and flames high into the air. The six men went overboard. The *Captive*'s launch picked them up, and after they had been fortified with rum, redeposited them on the *Masaryk*'s stern. There they uncoupled the ship's power steering and worked her by hand to bring the rudder once more amidships.

When they entered Menelao Bay—which had the protection and shelving beach Keeble envisioned for the salvage operation—the *Captive* speeded up, running right for the shore. Then he cast loose and cut away parallel to the shore, letting the big Liberty ship run prow on into the sand. Armed launches put shells into her at the waterline until she flooded down.

This put out the fires. When the ship had cooled, they unloaded the undamaged part of the cargo, repaired the shell holes and torpedo damage, and within a few weeks had dragged her off the sand and into Alexandria to await her turn at the overworked dry docks.

---

[1] The same Commander Ellsberg who was so instrumental in raising the submarine S-51, back in 1925; he had re-entered active duty as soon as the war started, although in his fifties.

CHAPTER THIRTEEN

Leicester and *Josephine*

Two vessels created by the needs of the Second World War came together during six weeks in the fall of 1948, just three years after the end of war, for a tow operation unique in the annals of salvage. The first was a Liberty ship, one of some two hundred that were called SAMs because all of them had apparently been named after Uncle Sam. She was 420 feet long, twin-decked, with a 7600-ton displacement and a 10,000-ton capacity, a crude and ugly vessel suited ideally to her job as a war freighter.

THE DISAPPEARING SAMs

Even before the war ended, the SAMs were dubbed the "Disappearing SAMs" by sailors the world over because of their rather disquieting ability to get lost. To just disappear in the open sea.

This particular SAM had, following the war, been purchased by a British shipping firm and renamed the *Leicester*.

The second vessel was a tug. Not a usual tug, however: an ocean-rescue tug, a deep-sea vessel built to bring torpedoed ships from the North Atlantic convoys back to port. Such tugs were big—two hundred feet long, 1000 tons displacement—and rugged enough to withstand severe storms. They could haul a 15,000-ton dead weight at eight to ten knots for fifteen hundred miles without running out of fuel or overworking their big, 3200-horse diesel power plants.

This particular tug was the *Foundation Josephine*, built in 1940; during the year and a half she had been owned by Foundation Maritime of Canada she had rescued twenty-one ships. With her in the operation would be *Foundation Lillian*, a miniaturized version of the *Josephine*, with half her tonnage and half her power, but with the same function to perform: deepwater rescues and tows.

The *Leicester* left England with a forty-five-man crew on September 4, 1948, under command of Captain Hamish Lawson. She was "light" —that is, without cargo, hence "in ballast," and had the distinction of being the first ship since the time of the great three- and four-masted grain clippers to be equipped with shifting boards. Shifting boards were merely a solid fence of boards running along a vessel's midline from stem to stern; because grain acted very much like a liquid, they were used on the clipper ships, so often heeled down by the wind, to prevent a disastrous shift in cargo which might capsize the vessel.

The *Leicester* was fitted out with shifting boards because the SAM-type Liberties, unlike almost any other modern freighter, carry their fifteen hundred tons of ballast between decks rather than in their empty lower holds. It had been suggested in Admiralty Court that sudden shifts in this ballast above the center line, causing the ship to capsize, might explain the disappearances of so many "Disappearing SAMs."

No one knew the formula for determining the scantlings of shifting boards any more, so the *Leicester's* were redesigned. Vertical steel stanchions (in reality, H-beams) were welded along the ship's midline between decks—that is, the top end welded to the bottom of the top deck and the lower end welded to the top of the lower deck. Between the stanchions was placed a row of three-inch-thick horizontal fir planks. The ballast was dredged from the Thames and tended to settle very hard and firm once it was in place.

The *Leicester* left England on September 4, 1948; on the sixth, when Lawson tested the ballast, it was set so hard his heel barely dented it. The shifting boards he could see above the ballast were firmly in place. On the ninth, midway between Ireland and Newfoundland, *Leicester* rode out a Force 8 storm without difficulty.

The *Leicester's* radio went out on the thirteenth, just as she reached the Grand Banks; on the afternoon of the fourteenth, Sparks got the radio working long enough to find out that a hurricane, moving at

25 knots, was some four hundred miles southwest of them. Their paths, Lawson estimated, would cross in ten hours. When his radio went out again, he decided to swing due south in hopes of getting behind the storm.

LEICESTER CAUGHT BY A HURRICANE

Unknown to him, however, the continental high over the United States had pushed the hurricane farther east: *Leicester* unwittingly had turned right into its new course. By midafternoon on the fourteenth, Lawson had to reduce speed; and to the south he saw the ominous blue-black arch against the horizon known as a hurricane bar. He swung south by east, still trying to get behind the storm, and at 9:45 P.M. swung her due east.

And found he was running dead into the wind. They were in for it.

By eleven o'clock it was Force 10, with the ship steering badly at a mere five knots. Heavy seas swept across the foredeck. By 11:15 she was nearly out of control, even with two men on the wheel; they were in the right front quadrant of the hurricane, rolling from side to side down to 32 degrees.

The eye passed over them at midnight, with the winds temporarily down to Force 8. But as often happens in the eye, a tremendous chop built up. A huge waterspout rose up and struck the *Leicester*, shaking her from end to end.

A second struck, on the starboard flank. She heeled over to 40 degrees and hung there for a full sixty seconds.

Lawson could feel a long, muted rumbling beneath his feet, shifting boards or not. The ship rolled back slightly to a 30-degree port list . . . and stayed there.

The ballast had shifted.

He ordered oil pumped from the port to the starboard tanks in a feverish hope of offsetting the shifted weight; if they could ride out the next four or five hours they still had a chance of making it.

An enormous sea engulfed the vessel.

Lawson, caught out on the exposed bridge, was plucked right away from the ship by that great hand of water, then was slammed back some thirty feet aft of where he had started. As he clung there, dazed, the *Leicester* rolled so far to starboard that the needle went right off the face of the clinometer. When she came back she went through vertical to a 50-degree port list—*and stayed there.*

At two o'clock on the morning of the fifteenth, Lawson ordered the power cut in the boilers. Her screws were out of the water most of the time, she was rolling down to as much as 70 degrees port list, three men (including Sparks) had been washed overboard, and he was afraid of a boiler explosion because the pumps were sucking more air than water.

The day crawled by with men trying to get out an SOS on their emergency transmitter, and with the water rising to four feet in the engine room. The fireboxes flooded. They tried to make and launch rafts, but the flimsy craft were smashed to pieces by the waves. The port boats were gone, with their davits and falls actually under water; when the men tried to launch a starboard boat at 6:30 that evening, it caught on the bilge keel, flipped, and dumped its contents into the sea.

At nine o'clock that night, the Cockney cook gave a sudden shout. "Lights!" he yelled. "There's lights out there!"

It was another Liberty ship, the *Cecil N. Bean*, driven off the normal shipping lanes by the hurricane. The men of the *Leicester* put into the air everything they had in the way of flares and rockets, afraid the *Bean* would not see their dead, lightless ship.

"Those fellows sure weren't taking any chances on being missed!" the *Bean's* watch officer remarked later.

The *Bean* launched two boats: one was smashed against her own side, the other reached the *Leicester* only to have a wave rip her rudder right from its pintles. Seaman Mire on the *Leicester* jerked a rudder from one of their lifeboats, tied a life line around his waist, and jumped overboard with it. He swam to the boat, was hauled in, and helped save ten others who followed him over the side.

Another ship showed up then, drawn by the pyrotechnic display: the Argentinian refrigeration ship *Tropero*, three hundred miles off course due to the storm. She also put two boats down, and the rest of the *Leicester's* crew went into the water. Lawson was last of all, with the ship's papers in a waterproof pouch. Two men were lost.

At 3:45 A.M., the *Leicester* was left abandoned and derelict.

In Foundation Maritime's home office at Halifax, Nova Scotia, Salvage Officer Robert Featherstone heard the transmissions of the *Bean* and the *Tropero* concerning the *Leicester* at 9:00 A.M. on the sixteenth. Since the ship had been legally abandoned by her crew, he knew that Foundation Maritime could not even get a "no-cure, no-pay" contract from her owners; the *Leicester* was now officially the property of the underwriters.

But he could go after her purely on speculation, even though she probably had foundered. If they *could* find her, and bring her into port, they would be able to make a salvage claim equal to at least half her current value. Featherstone had been in salvage work for thirty years; he believed in his hunches implicitly.

And he had a hunch about the *Leicester*. At 10:15 A.M. he gave Captain John Cowley of *Foundation Josephine* orders to go after her.

The *Josephine* was under way at 10:38. Cowley and his crew were professionals, and their profession was salvage. *Foundation Lillian* had been sent out to aid another vessel on the fifteenth; she would join the search as soon as she could.

Cowley had several things against him: *Leicester* had been left in a sinking condition and listing down to 70 degrees. Her position had been given as about 40° 27′ north and 55° 10′ west, but she had been drifting for thirty hours: long enough to be 140 miles away from that approximation.

Going *for* him were his powerful radar—he could search three thousand square miles of ocean every twelve hours—and the fact that the *Lillian* was able to co-operate in his rectangular search pattern for the rather unfortunate reason that the ship she had planned to save had sunk before her arrival. *Lillian's* search had to be visual, however, as she did not have the *Josephine's* sophisticated radar eyes.

By the morning of the nineteenth, they had covered nine thousand square miles and had found an oil slick and floating wreckage at the *Leicester's* most likely position. Certainly the winds and seas had been heavy enough to swamp a ship heeled over to that impossible angle.

At noon, Featherstone reluctantly called them off.

RACE FOR THE *LEICESTER*

At noon on the twenty-first, two days later, the French steamer *Gien* reported the *Leicester* at 37° 07′ north and 52° 14′ west, drifting northeast. *Gien* had gone right on, trying to duck a new hurricane that was brewing in the Caribbean.

It would take his tugs three days to reach that position, Featherstone knew, since by then *Josephine* was tied up in an attempt to save an old Greek tramp steamer, and *Lillian* needed stores, supplies, and fuel. Three days. *Leicester* would drift one hundred to two hundred miles during that time, but . . . *in which direction?* Northeast, as the Frenchman had said? Featherstone knew the North Atlantic as he did his hand, and in that area he thought she would be drifting *south*east.

It was important that he know this, because *Zwart Zee*, L. Smit and Company's huge ocean-going tug, had cleared New York at 7:00 P.M. on the twenty-first, also to look for the *Leicester* on spec. She had nineteen knots top speed and a three-hour start on the *Lillian*, which left Halifax at 10:00 P.M. *Zwart Zee* would reach her estimate of the crippled ship's position within sixty hours; it would take the fourteen-knot *Lillian* seventy hours to reach whatever position Featherstone chose. That made it a race not just of time, but of wits.

The drift estimate for the *Leicester* would be vital. Featherstone chose southeast. He didn't know what *Zwart Zee* chose. Both tugs would be on radio silence from then on, and transmissions to them from their respective home offices would be in code.

The hurricane had lain off Florida for forty hours, mauling the coastal areas of the state.

The tugs reached their search areas on the evening of the twenty-fourth, the same night that the *Josephine* returned to the hunt. Unfortunately, in order to reach Featherstone's estimate of the *Leicester's* position, her course would take her right across the path of the hurricane moving out from Florida.

Featherstone scrupulously informed Cowley of that fact; *Josephine* should, he said in a coded message to the tug, avoid the hurricane. But he was sure, he added, that Cowley was aware that a competing tug, with excellent radar equipment lacking on the *Lillian*, was also working the area. He knew his man. Cowley battened down the hatches and plowed straight ahead into the rapidly mounting seas.

At 6:00 P.M., the steamship *Albisola* reported seeing the *Leicester* at 3600 north, 4930 west. She was 115 miles *southeast* of the *Gien's* sighting. And only ninety miles from the *Lillian*. Featherstone had been right.

Four hours later, the *Josephine* ran into the hurricane. Cowley's only acknowledgment of the storm tossing his boat about was to reduce to three-fourths speed. She rode it out. By noon of the twenty-fifth she was back up to sixteen knots and four hundred miles from the *Albisola*'s sighting.

Zwart Zee was running with all possible speed toward the same spot. *Lillian* had reached it and had found . . . nothing.

At 1:00 P.M. on the twenty-sixth, the *James McHenry* reported the hulk drifting at 3222 north and 4836 west. Again, southeast. This time *Lillian* was a bare forty miles away.

Two hours later a sailor on the tug's masthead yelped, "I sees her, b'ys!"

"Is she alone?" bellowed the mate.

"Lonely as an old maid in wintertime!"

They could hardly believe that the *Leicester* was still afloat: she was heeled so far over she seemed to be lying on her side. Waves were breaking above the edge of her boat deck, and as the salvors approached they could look right down her funnel. In this unbelievable condition she had drifted six hundred miles in ten days while passing through three heavy storms.

Featherstone, apprised of contact, wired, "IMPERATIVE YOU GET MEN ABOARD NOW TO AVOID CHANCES OF RIVAL TUG HOOKING UP IN NIGHT."

The boarders ran their dory in close and then, as the vessel rolled upward, leaped for it from the dory's lee rail. A miss meant more than a dunking: the water was alive with sharks so aggressive they snapped at the rowers' oars. The man going aboard then had to run right up the steeply slanting deck and catch hold of a hatch coaming so he would not be dumped off on the down-roll.

Shortly after midnight, the *Josephine* arrived; *Zwart Zee* had dropped off upon receiving word of *Lillian*'s success. That left the two Foundation tugs with only the little problem of dragging the derelict vessel eight hundred miles to Bermuda, the closest safe port. Their boarding party determined that the shifting boards had let go for the entire length of the hold, secured the accommodation doors along the port alleyway to keep her from shipping any more water when her lee rail would dip under, and then turned to securing the towline.

JOSEPHINE TAKES HER IN TOW

They had to get two-inch steel towing cable, which weighed five pounds a running foot, aboard from the *Josephine*; since the *Leicester*, without power, had no winches to bring the cable aboard, they had to do it the hard way, with a snatchblock[1] and an oxyacetylene torch.

They secured the port anchor with wire reeved through a link of her chain and made fast to a forward bitt. Then they cut the chain with a torch above the link stopping off the anchor. They now had a free end of chain. A light heaving line was tossed from the *Josephine*'s stern up to the *Leicester*'s pitching bow. With this they hauled aboard a manila mooring line to fasten the ships together. A second heaving line brought aboard a large bight of three-inch manila, which was dropped into the snatchblock they had already made fast to the deck with heavy cable. On the *Josephine*, one end of the manila was run through her electric capstan; the other was fastened to the hundred-pound U-shackle on the end of the towing cable.

The capstan was started, dragging the U-shackle and of course the towing cable over to the *Leicester*. The men there removed the manila and threaded the U-shackle through the link at the free end of the anchor chain.

Strain was put on the towing cable, which slowly dragged out three hundred feet of the *Leicester*'s anchor chain from the chain locker. Control was maintained by running the chain over the gypsy end of the crippled ship's winch, on which the brake could be hand-operated. Once enough chain was out, steel rope was reeved through several links of the chain and around the forward bitts. They also inserted a devil's-claw in one link of the chain. These kept too much strain from falling on the winch's brake, and with it gave the chain a three-point anchorage to take the strain from the *Leicester*'s 10,000-ton dead weight. The chain provided more spring than the cable alone, thus reducing the chance of sudden jerks creating intolerable stress loads which might capsize the heeled freighter.

The tow started shortly before noon on September 27. The *Leicester* sheered hideously to port, her rudder being jammed hard over. Often she was nearly broadside to the *Josephine*; if she went over, they knew, they had to cut loose immediately or the Liberty ship would drag the *Josephine* down with her. During the entire eight-hundred-mile tow, a crew was stationed at the tug's taffrail with a lighted oxyacetylene torch to make the cut if needed.

In Halifax, Managing Director Edward Woollcombe was working to get three things from the owners/underwriters: (1) a Lloyd's Open Form Salvage Contract, (2) a financial commitment from the owners before the vessel reached "a safe port," and (3) their agreement that a "safe port" in Bermuda would be one of Foundation Maritime's own choice.

The third was necessary because the entrance to St. George's Harbor, the only really safe port in Bermuda, was 250 feet wide and twenty-seven feet deep. In her condition, the *Leicester* drew twenty-six feet, and with her terrible sheer could be expected to perhaps try to run up the channel sideways. So Woollcombe wanted the ship put into Murray's Anchorage, which had a thirty-eight-foot channel six hundred feet wide. It also had one little drawback: it was not really a harbor at all, but rather was a nearly open roadstead at Bermuda's northern tip; its only protection was the coral reefs that fringed it.

Woollcombe was eventually successful.

Josephine brought the *Leicester* into Murray's Anchorage on the morning of October 3, despite losing one thousand gallons of lubricating oil from her port engine when a casting broke (they had no spare, so they hand-tooled a new one aboard ship). Featherstone had flown to Bermuda, and had three tugs to help bring the ship in through the channel. He also had stevedore gangs standing by to begin shifting ballast as soon as possible. It took two hours to negotiate the two-mile channel, with *Leicester* dragging coral most of the way in. She was made fast to a battleship mooring buoy.

Investigators found that the weight of the ballast had sagged the lower deck three inches. When the rolling of the vessel in the hurricane put intolerable pressure on the H-beams, they merely broke loose at the bottom and let the whole row of boards swing up for the ballast to pass underneath.

The *Lillian* pulled out for the eastern Atlantic to pick up a stricken ship; *Josephine* remained. That should have been the end of the *Leicester*'s odyssey—but it wasn't.

Featherstone felt that by the seventh, the *Leicester* would have been righted enough so she could be taken around to St. George's Harbor.

On the fifth, yet another hurricane struck, this time at Cuba, with 132-mile-per-hour winds that sank forty-nine vessels in Cuban waters. On the sixth, the list was down to twenty-six degrees. That afternoon the wind picked up. That night, though the hurricane had run up to smash seven hundred homes in Miami and was scheduled to miss Bermuda by two hundred miles, they battened down the hatches on both vessels, closed off ports and doors, and doubled moorings between the tug and her charge—which now was listing a mere twenty degrees.

ANOTHER HURRICANE: BERMUDA

That night, the hurricane made a hard 40-degree turn and headed straight for Bermuda. No recorded Caribbean hurricane had ever done that before, but that didn't help the salvage crew any. They had nowhere to run; "Might as well stay where we are at," one of the crewmen said.

The hurricane hit them with eighty-mile-an-hour winds in the late afternoon. The ships rode it out well, double-moored as they were. The eye passed at 6:45 P.M., and the worst seemed over.

At 7:00 P.M. the second quadrant of the storm hit. Winds of 122 m.p.h. were recorded, before *every single anemometer* in Bermuda was blown away. The rain shredded everything organic that it hit, leaving pockmarks in human flesh for days afterward. The twenty-by-ten-foot steel mooring drum was jammed between the ships as the winds drove them past it. *Josephine's* mooring bitts were bent inward, toward one another, like tipsy mushrooms; the mooring cable, before snapping when the bitts let go, sawed through thirty feet of half-inch steel deck plating like a wire cheese cutter through soft butter.

The *Josephine* was free, running with the storm. Cowley had the 3200-horse diesels at full speed and could not even swing his ship so she would face the wind. She struck coral at 7:45; the wind began to slack off at 10:00 P.M. Within a few minutes they could walk ashore; they were on a small island only a half mile from the mooring.

Leicester was found the next morning four hundred yards from the tug. Lying beside her were the three 30-ton concrete mooring anchors. She lay at a 30-degree list in water so shallow that ten more feet would be needed just to float her. Two holds were holed, some fuel tanks were pierced, and her rudder was gone.

SALVAGE OF THE *LEICESTER* AND THE *JOSEPHINE*

Both seemed to be dead ships, but at ten o'clock the next morning Featherstone had crews at work stevedoring, and he had borrowed a floating derrick from the Admiralty. He intended to bring both vessels off.

Ports were cut in the *Leicester*'s flanks so the ballast could be shoveled directly out of her, while divers began fitting soft "pudding" patches over her holed bottom. A leased tug began positioning ground tackle: an eight-ton anchor fifteen hundred feet off her bow, another twenty-one hundred feet off her stern. A system of heavy wire cables, steel blocks, and winches (ground tackle), Featherstone hoped, would serve to bring the Liberty ship off the rocks.

At high water on the eleventh, with seven hundred tons of ballast removed, they tried with all the power they had. She wouldn't stir. On the twelfth, a self-propelled bucket dredge buried its steel spuds (pillars) in the bottom and added its strength to the pull with a line fastened to *Leicester*'s bow. This moved her fifteen feet. She was moving toward deep water by the morning of the nineteenth, and by ten-thirty was at anchor in St. George's Harbor. It had taken the floating derrick, the dredge, two tugs, and two sets of ground tackle; but Featherstone had gotten her off.

Next was *Josephine*. Everything movable was carted out of her, and divers sealed off whatever compartments they could, as well as tanks, service tanks, and shaft tunnel. Two 8-inch pumps were put aboard to dry her out, and compressed-air hoses were run in. The tremendous hole the coral had knocked in her engine room was sealed.

A storm held them up, but on the twenty-second came the supreme effort. Compressed air banged into her, and the tug began hauling. *Josephine* grated a hundred feet seaward across the reef to jam between the coral heads. Featherstone, enraged, ordered the ship jerked first one way and then the other, fishtailing her to smash coral heads. She did. She also stove in a number of plates. But just after noon she was in deep water.

Nearly all the way in deep water. The compressed air worked for the seven-mile tow to the Hamilton Naval Dockyard, but when they brought her up against a quay her decks were awash; only a second tug fastened to her starboard side had kept her afloat.

She took six months to repair.

Leicester was taken out for New York on October 24, by the tug *Kevin Moran*. En route, another hurricane hit her; she started sinking on the morning of the twenty-ninth. The *Moran*'s captain ran with his tow for Newport News, Virginia. He brought her safely into port at 3:10 P.M. on October 31.

Leicester was repaired, eventually sold, and is still hauling freight somewhere in the world.

SAVING HALF OF THE BRIDGEWATER

The *Leicester* operation, apart from the deepwater detective work in locating her, was unique because of the vessel's incredible list; the search for the Australian tanker *Bridgewater* by the Adelaide Steamship Company tug *Yuna* in 1962 was unique because they were seeking only half a ship.

The *Bridgewater* was carrying a cargo of crude oil when she broke in two during heavy weather some 230 miles northwest of Fremantle, Australia. Her crew was rescued by the tanker *Elios* on January 30, and the next day *Yuna* set out on her odd quest. At 3:00 P.M. on February 2, she spotted *Bridgewater*'s bow section. It ended just abaft the midship accommodation and bridge, and rode down so far aft that the forefoot was out of the water.

The bow did not interest *Yuna*, who merely noted its position and moved on. The valuable machinery and any possibly undamaged oil tanks would be in the after section.

At seven o'clock the next morning they spotted it some forty miles from the position at which the ship first had broken in half. It was down at the head with draughts of forty-two feet forward and twenty-four aft. The generators were still running. A seven-man boat party got aboard and prepared the section for the tow to Fremantle, while the *Yuna*'s third engineer shut down the overheating generator and tightened down the stern gland to prevent further leakage into the engine room.

The tow went well until the evening of February 4, when Force 8 winds made them heave to, nose to the gale; at midnight on the sixth the towline parted. The *Yuna* returned to Fremantle, replenished stores and replaced broken towing gear, and went back out on the ninth.

They spotted their tow the next day, but could not start taking her in until the following morning. Until the seventeenth, they averaged seventy miles a day; then nasty weather and adverse currents actually drove them back twenty-one miles. It was not until the twentieth that they brought the section into Fremantle Harbor. There, 7840 tons of crude oil were salvaged from her undamaged tanks, and the derelict was sold for scrap.

Despite brilliant and determined long-distance tows like the *Leicester*, and offbeat ones like the *Bridgewater*, deepwater towing belongs essentially to the Dutch. The Wijsmuller Company of IJmuiden, Holland, for instance, was begun in 1906, and at the founder's death in 1923 had the world's largest fleet (twenty-one) of deepwater tugs. Today, after a temporary decline arrested after World War II, Wijsmuller hauls an incredible array of ships and equipment over one hundred thousand nautical miles a year (many of the tows are ten thousand miles or more) with a twelve-tug fleet. They have hauled aircraft carriers, suction dredgers, offshore-oil drilling platforms, drilling barges, LSTs, floating dry docks and sheerlegs, dredges, floating cranes—even a whale factory ship.

Most of these are contract tows, but Wijsmuller and L. Smit and Company, Rotterdam, often carry out extremely complex salvage tows. Many of them seem to occur just a few miles from their head offices.

On December 4, 1954, the steamship *Falcon* was caught in Force 11 winds sixty-eight miles from IJmuiden Harbor. She began taking water into her engine room, and two Wijsmuller tugs, the *Noord-Holland* and the *Cycloop*, went out. They found her at nine o'clock the next morning riding low in the water, listing to port, and shipping heavy seas. A half-inch crack ran down the starboard side amidships.

The crew had been taken off by a trawler, the *Klaas Wijker*, but a salvage engineer and a sailor from the *Cycloop* made it aboard the derelict and, despite twelve-foot waves and a broken pilot line, finally got a 4½-inch towing cable aboard and secured. Both the engine room and the stokehold were flooded; the crack had lengthened from her hull and deck plating right over her cross bunker, and the two sections worked with the waves passing beneath. The men plugged the crack with rope and canvas, then began the tow.

By the next morning, the *Falcon* was down at the head and there was twenty-six feet of water in her No. 1 hold. There was also ten feet of water in the engine room. When they were a few miles from IJmuiden, a course change heeled the *Falcon* sharply to starboard, dunking the crack totally under water and flooding her so severely that the riding crew had to be taken off. Captain De Koe of the *Cycloop* led five men back aboard, however, to ride her into IJmuiden Harbor. There she was run up onto a soft mud bank for temporary repairs before being towed to Amsterdam on December 11, for unloading and repair in dry dock.

Another tow close to home was the salvage of the Spanish tanker *Diane* on April 17, 1967. The vessel was only a few hours out of Rotterdam when she collided with another ship; part of her cargo of crude oil promptly caught fire and exploded.

Tugs and salvage steamers from several companies, as well as Dutch Government ships, rushed to the scene. Ten tugs in all tried to lend assistance by pumping water aboard the flaming ship. Four terrific explosions had blown great jagged pieces of deck plating out on either side of her like distended fish gills. The decks above the fire were red hot; it was only fortunate that the after tanks were full of water instead of oil.

The flames were finally controlled when one tug, the *Nestor*, poked its nose right into the gaping forepart of the vessel and sprayed foam on the source of the fire, the No. 2 Central Tank. After several hours the hull began to cool, and the enormous black clouds of smoke thinned.

At this point her Spanish captain calmly announced that he and the few crewmen he had aboard would make their way to safety without further assistance. And he did it, accompanied, to be sure, by ten tugs and a sister tanker; but he limped into Verlome Ship Yard under his own power at a booming 1½ knots.

Another Wijsmuller tug, the *Utrecht*, was on a contract tow in February 1964 that suddenly became a salvage tow. She was bringing two tipper barges, *NHW-66* and *NHW-73*, from Malta to Lisbon with a riding crew aboard each barge. On the morning of February 1, gale-force winds blew up and *NHW-66* began taking water. The riding crew immediately set up mobile salvage pumps, while the *Utrecht* swung into the wind and slowed to a crawl.

By the next morning, despite the work of the crew and the pumps, the barge had begun to settle. Waves were sweeping her foredeck. She kept going down by the head until by midday only the stern of the 171-foot craft was visible, poking up out of the water at a 50-degree angle. The bow was thirty-six feet down.

The crew declined to leave her, and the *Utrecht* successfully brought the crippled barge into Bône on the third. There a floating crane got a line on the bow to lift it to the surface while pumps emptied her out. It was found that all fourteen bottom doors had broken their retaining bolts to flop open and let in the sea. Divers closed them all; repairs were made so the barge could be delivered to its consignee on February 20.

THE CHILLING ODYSSEY OF THE AYGAZ

The Mediterranean also was the site, a few years later, of a rather chilling salvage tow on the tanker *Aygaz*. The Turkish vessel was caught by heavy winds and towering seas on March 24, 1969, southwest of the Greek coastal islands along the Peloponnesus Peninsula. The freighter was light, being en route to Italy for a cargo of crude. She was sighted by an Italian vessel, and reported to the Greek coastal authorities as being in trouble, shortly before the waves capsized her. She was not seen again until the twenty-sixth, when the Danish freighter *Lion Cif* spotted her overturned hulk. Naturally there was no sign of her nineteen crewmen, so the *Cif*, the weather having moderated, got lines aboard and took her in tow as a salvage prize. She brought the *Aygaz* into the harbor at Plyos, Greece, the next day.

In the harbor, anguished cries and banging on the inside of the hull were heard for the first time. Greek Navy frogmen tried to enter the ship from underneath—through the normally topside passageways—but could not find their way to the trapped men. Finally they climbed atop the overturned hull and cut through the iron plates near the rudder with torches.

From the hole they dragged four dead bodies and one man still alive, Mohamed Ozen, the ship's second engineer. The five Turkish crewmen had been trapped in the engine room when the vessel overturned; they had tried to attract attention ever since, while one after another had died in the slowly fouling air.

---

[1] This is a pulley mounted between a pair of iron sheets, one of which is hinged. The hinged side can be lifted, and a bight, or loop of rope or cable, can be dropped around the pulley, after which the hinged iron sheet is closed back down.

13. A heartbreaking moment: the bow of submarine *Squalus* comes up out of control, snorting air and spouting like a whale, on July 13, 1939. She rose 20 feet from the water at a 60-degree angle, then slid neatly backward out of her cradle of lifting chains.

PHOTO CREDITS: Captions No. 13 and No. 14, James Jones, Boston Post, from *Wide World Photos*

14. Seagulls circle the 1450-ton *Squalus* as she comes up for good two months later. Compressed air, bleeding down to atmospheric pressure, boils around the vessel. The rescue of 33 of her 59 trapped crewmen was the first successful use of the McCann Escape Bell.

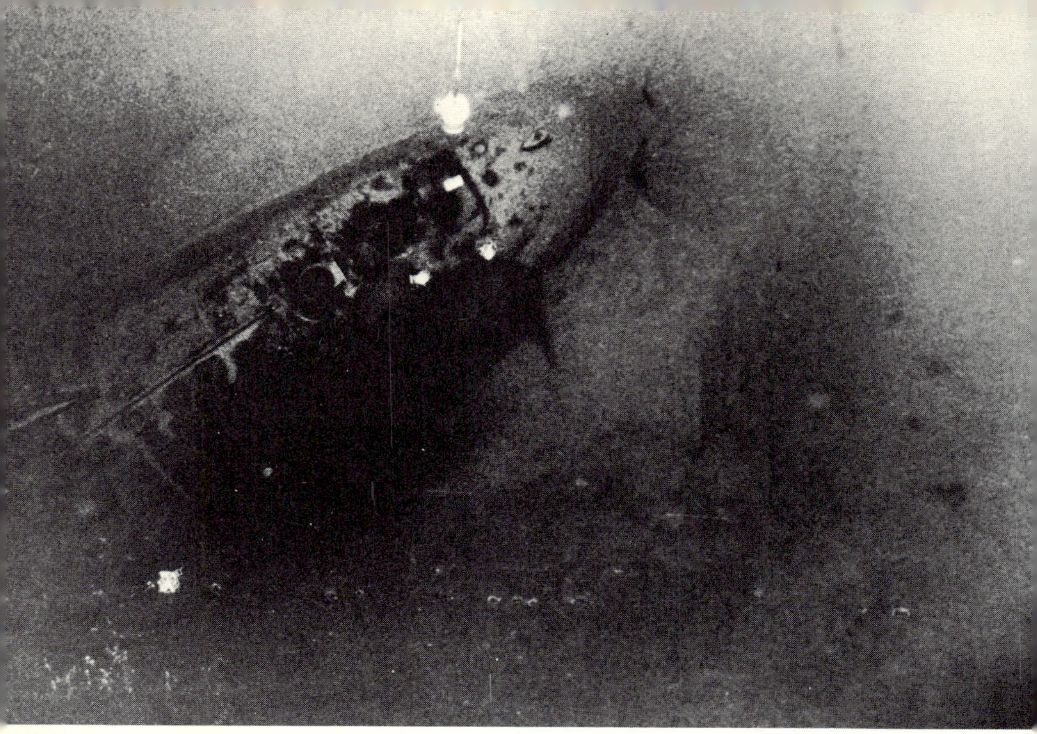

15. The bow of the nuclear submarine *Scorpion*, lost in May 1968 and found six months later. This dramatic photo was taken at *10,000 feet* on the sea floor 400 miles southwest of the Azores. Intact hull proves the sub flooded before reaching its collapse depth. PHOTO CREDIT: *U. S. Navy*

16. One of the most remarkable underwater photos ever taken: close-up of the sunken *Scorpion* in 10,000 feet of water. Note messenger-buoy storage hatch with coils of mooring line in it. Obviously damaged snorkel pipe at right suggests possible cause of the sinking. PHOTO CREDIT: *U. S. Navy*

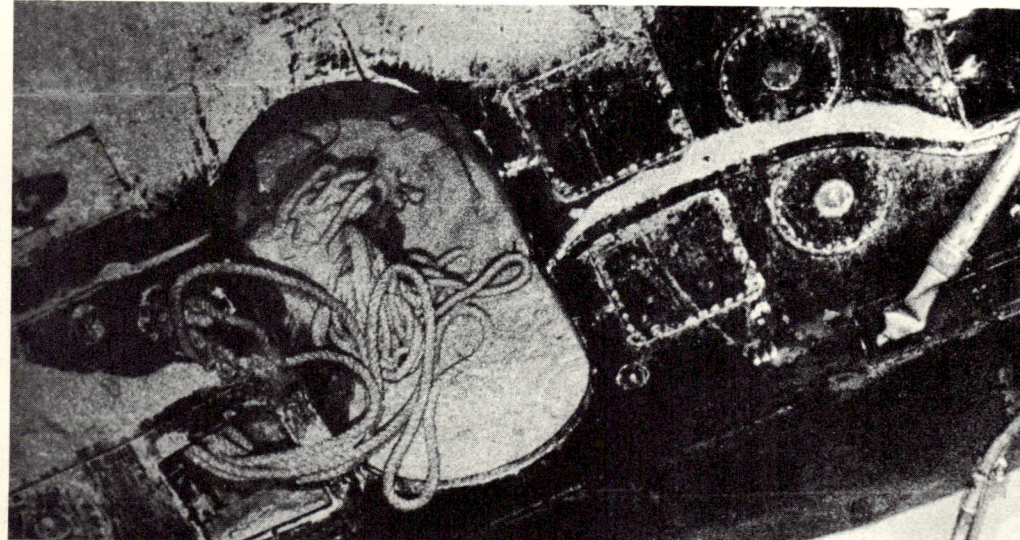

17. The stricken *Falcon* wallows helplessly in monstrous seas in December 1954, after her engine room flooded. Note wave smashing over the deck of rescuing Wijsmuller tug in foreground, one of those that saved the *Falcon* with a daring tow to IJmuiden harbor. PHOTO CREDIT: *N. V. Bureau Wijsmuller*

18. Salvors play water on the fiercely burning Spanish oil tanker *Diane*, following a mid-ocean collision and explosions in April 1967. Ice forming on salvors, equipment, and salvage tug are all part of this tough, dangerous profession. The *Diane* was saved. PHOTO CREDIT: *Cees van der Meulen*

19. SCUBA gear and plastic explosives have greatly sophisticated the techniques of underwater demolition developed by British divers before World War I. Here, members of the Royal Navy's Far East Clearance Team set charges against coral heads in a training exercise. PHOTO CREDIT: *Royal Navy*

20. A 1916 photo inside a cofferdam built on the *Western Star* with 430,000 feet of timber and 73 tons of steel rod used for interior struts and bracing. Workmen stand on deck of salved ship. The operation resembled that on the *Umegaka Maru* three years earlier. PHOTO CREDIT: *United Press International*

21. Water under great pressure spurts from forward hawse holes, while air inside the vessel, bleeding down, sends out great bursts of spray amidships. The row of heavily braced air locks on ship's hull reached the surface when the ship was at the bottom. PHOTO CREDIT: *Wide World Photos*

22. This method of raising a ship upside down with compressed air was first used by Ernest Cox on the scuttled German Imperial Fleet at Scapa Flow, which Cox bought and spent a decade raising. This is the *Grosser Kurfurst*, raised in 1938 at Scapa Flow by Cox's successors. PHOTO CREDIT: *Wide World Photos*

23. The 25,000-ton *Bayern*, in tow to Rosyth and the shipbreakers across 280 miles of open sea in 1935. Note house built on bottom of upside-down vessel. Metal Industries bought out Cox in 1931 and continued with his men and methods until World War II stopped operations. PHOTO CREDIT: *Wide World Photos*

24. HMS *Breconshire*, sunk by German aircraft at Malta in 1942 and raised by the Admiralty's Boom Defense Unit in 1949. The photo shows the bewildering multitude of compressed-air lines needed to raise the 9600-ton vessel once divers had sealed her. PHOTO CREDIT: *Royal Navy*

IV

The Shallow Seas

Cox of Scapa wrought, in his chosen work, more than any other man had ever achieved before him.
He is one of the few, the very few, of whom such an epitaph may fairly be written.

GERALD BOWMAN
The Man Who Bought a Navy

CHAPTER FOURTEEN

From *Thetis* to *Leonardo*

~~~~~~

In 1620 Sir Francis Bacon described a certain primitive, three-legged container he had seen.

"A hollow vessel made of metal," he wrote, "was let down equally to the surface of the water, and thus carried with it to the bottom of the sea the whole of the air which it contained."

On the bottom, of course, a diver could put his head inside and breathe the air therein contained. The diving bell was not new even then. It probably was invented by Bonajuto Lorini in 1531, for use in a Renaissance attempt at finding Caligula's pleasure galleys in the Lake of Nemi.

The idea of the diving bell is simplicity itself: very much like putting a water glass, open end down, in the dishwater, and trapping air inside. The main difficulty with the early ones was the extremely limited air supply they could carry to the bottom with them. Dr. Denis Papin, the famous French physicist, in 1689 suggested as a remedy the use of a force pump or bellows to maintain constant pressure within the bell. The following year Dr. Edmund Halley, the British astronomer after whom Halley's Comet was named, came up with the forerunner of successful modern diving bells, a complex arrangement of leather hoses and two lead-bottomed air buckets that were alternately lowered to the bell.

Halley's diving bell worked—but it weighed too much. Louis Dalmas, in 1764, went to the other extreme by proposing a bell made of leather, which would be held open only by the air pressure inside. It might actually have worked also, but no one was dumb enough to test the thing.

John Smeaton, the British engineer who constructed the famous Eddystone Lighthouse (its even more famous fictional keeper had a widely celebrated affair with a mermaid), invented the first practicable diving bell in 1784. This was a boxlike affair with a force pump mounted on the bell itself, the roof of which remained out of the water. This Smeaton Bell, in modification, is still used today, along with the caisson, or air-lock bell. They are practicable on subsurface construction projects, but have long been obsolete on marine salvage jobs as such.

Logical outgrowths of the diving bell are such things as the Beebe Bathysphere, a steel ball with windows and air-purifying equipment, which William Beebe took down to two thousand feet near Bermuda in 1932; the McCann Rescue Chamber[1]; the Davis SDC[2]; and by extension the descent capsule[3] used by the Sealab man-in-the-sea program.

THE DIVING BELL AND THE *THETIS*

But the diving bell has been of little use in actual salvage operations. Apart from the tremendous recovery of Spanish gold by Sir William Phips in 1687[4] (and many question whether he even used it), only one major salvage operation owed its success to the diving bell. This was the recovery of the treasure from HMS *Thetis*, a three-hundred-man, 46-gun frigate, in 1831 and 1832. The *Thetis* affair is also unique in that Admiral Sir Thomas Baker was given all the credit for it without ever visiting the site.

Thetis left Rio de Janeiro for England on December 4, 1830, carrying $810,000 in specie. Two nights later she smashed head-on into the cliffs near Cape Frio in southeast Brazil at ten knots under full sail. Most of her seams started, and her rigging came down. A few of the men leaped onto the cliff face and scrambled to safety; the rest stayed with the ship as it was carried away by the swift current and sunk in a cove a third of a mile away.

Admiral Baker declared the gold unsalvageable because of the high cliffs, deep water, swift currents, and frequent local storms; but Captain Thomas Dickinson of the sloop *Lightning* disagreed. Dickinson seems to have been the Hyman Rickover of his day: a brilliant engineer, with a far-ranging mind, who made his superiors uncomfortable. Baker finally gave grudging approval to a salvage attempt.

In 1831 the workable diving suit of Augustus Siebe still was six years away; Dickinson's choice of methods spanned naked divers and a diving bell. Since it was easier to construct a bell than a diver, he made one from the iron water tank of another vessel, HMS *Warspite*, and used a conventional Truscott's pump as a force pump to keep a constant air pressure in the inverted tank. To make the pump hoses strong enough to withstand water pressure, Dickinson first had them beaten flat with a broad-faced hammer to close the texture as much as possible, then coated them with tar, parceled them with tar-soaked canvas, and finally sewed them up in three-strand spun yarn. They worked.

He reached Cape Frio on January 24, 1831. It is actually an island three miles long and one broad, separated from the mainland by a four-hundred-foot strait. The hull of the *Thetis*, he found, had slipped off the rocks into water ranging between thirty-five and seventy feet.

Since the cove where it lay was very narrow, Dickinson first tried to string the diving bell on ropes stretched between the cliffs. He soon saw, however, that the strong winds would make the ropes vibrate, tip the bell, and spill its air, so he opted for a derrick.

This presented two new problems: First, where would he put it? And second, what would he make it out of?

He solved the first by blasting away thirteen feet of the peak from the northeast cliff, thus getting a fairly level platform eighty by sixty feet. Smaller platforms were constructed at four other appropriate places for the guying and mooring of the derrick.

Because of the spot he had been forced to choose, his derrick would have to be an incredible 158 feet long and extremely strong. The only material at hand for the construction was the mast and spars of the *Thetis* herself, washed conveniently ashore on several miles of coastline. He ended up using twenty-two different sections of timber, all lashed together with dowels and bolts, and drew the joints tight with thirty-four metal hoops. In addition, each joint was wrapped with four-inch rope. The derrick was still too flexible, which meant countless additional guys to keep it in position.

Fully mounted with all its gear, it weighed forty tons.

While this was going on, Dickinson tried a band of Carib Indian divers brought around by a Spanish ship captain. Their chief virtue seemed to be the consumption of great amounts of olive oil supposedly spat out to clear the water.

"Or," Dickinson noted drily, "to be swallowed, as circumstance or appetite demanded. Their efforts were contemptible, and not worth my stock of salad oil."

Dickinson's efforts with his diving bell certainly were not contemptible. Even divers using a small bell slung from the stern of the *Lightning's* launch soon sent up a chalked message from eight fathoms on their tally board: BE CAREFUL IN LOWERING BELL TO THE FOOT, FOR WE ARE OVER SOME DOLLARS.

Then the big bell, slung from its derrick, was tried—with nearly disastrous results. It was driven violently against the rocks, tipped, filled, and nearly drowned the two divers within, a pair of volunteers named Dewar and Heans.

"Never mind, mate," Heans told his waterlogged partner as they popped to the surface, "we haven't done with the damned thing yet."

They certainly hadn't. By the end of May, Dickinson was able to send back to the Treasury a tidy $130,000.

Then a disastrous storm struck, smashing their derrick. Refusing to give up, Dickinson returned to his original idea of a smaller bell depending from ropes strung across the cove from cliff to cliff. It worked, although they were so continually beaten against the rocks that five bells were worn out during the operation. Somehow, no divers were killed.

By March 1832 Dickinson had raised $600,000 of the $810,000 in specie, and also had raised the hackles of Admiral Baker. This worthy felt himself threatened by the altogether too successful "impossible" operation, so he summarily replaced Dickinson with the Honorable J. F. F. de Roos, commander of HMS *Algerine*. Dickinson was scrupulously fair in handing over command; he left on the bottom a large amount of treasure already located so that De Roos would not have the unhappy task of working with no gold to raise. De Roos brought up another $161,500, which meant fifteen-sixteenths of the treasure was recovered.

Upon his return to England, the amazed Dickinson discovered that Baker had claimed credit for conception and direction of the salvage operation, with Dickinson merely following the Admiral's orders. While sharing in the *Thetis'* £17,000 salvage award, Dickinson received no credit whatsoever. He appealed to the Privy Council, being a rather hard-nosed gentleman, getting the reward increased to £29,000 and seeing his name given prominent mention.

Certain of Lloyd's underwriters, erroneously taking Baker's account of the matter as correct, made censorious remarks about Dickinson for "impertinence" in appealing to the Privy Council. He replied with a spirited public letter that referred to them bitingly as "the gentlemen of the coffee house." Dickinson's later published account, showing detailed engineering knowledge, proved beyond any doubt that he was the architect of the unique operation.

EARLY SHALLOW-WATER SALVAGE ATTEMPTS

While Augustus Siebe certainly invented the diving suit that became and has remained the standard for hard-hat diving rigs, he did not invent the only one that worked. It's just that the others didn't work very well. Buck Taylor of Boston invented a suit in 1841—only four years after the Siebe closed suit was tested. It was made of India rubber, cloth, ribs and hoops of copper bands, and a copper-and-brass helmet. There was an eyebolt in the top of the helmet for raising and lowering, and an exhaust valve of sorts with a spiral seating spring. It was tested in some twenty feet of water successfully: that is, the diver was not quite asphyxiated, and the water leaking in did not quite reach his armpits.

Taylor's attempt inspired Abel Blake, of Stamford, Connecticut, to design a suit of his own. He decided on the scientific approach: his partners were a blacksmith (helmet—sheet metal), a harness maker (lead-soled shoes—leather uppers), and a sailmaker (diving suit—canvas supersaturated in linseed oil). They even made an air pump out of sheet metal, complete with valves and leather plungers.

Where did Blake come in? He was the crazy fool who wore it.

They were going to make their fortune raising coal off sunken colliers in the shallow waters around Stamford. Other people worked from the surface, laboriously picking out their winter's fuel supply with long-handled tongs. Blake's boys, with their suit, put a diver and a conveyor belt down into the hold of the collier under consideration. This Model T among conveyors had sheet-metal scoops, held together by old harness straps, which ran along a pair of wooden runners. The whole was assembled with carriage bolts, haywire, and spikes. Two manually operated cranks at the upper end made the belt go around.

The other partners got out of diving after a season or two; Blake, fascinated with it, eventually killed himself in a subsurface accident. Taylor patented and produced his suit for a number of years, but it soon gave way to the commercially viable Siebe design.

Well before the twentieth century, therefore, shallow-water salvage operations were flourishing. A few of the divers, such as the great Angel Erostrabe and Alexander Lambert, specialized in the deep, dangerous jobs where the bends lurked for the unwary or the weak; most of them, however, stayed in the shallow water, where the wrecks were numerous and easy to reach.

And where, occasionally, some grisly things could be seen.

SOME BIZARRE DIVING STORIES

Shortly after the Crimean War (1853-56), a salvage diver was down near a collapsed bridge by the ruins of Fort Paul, Sebastopol. On the bottom he found an entire battery of field artillery, which had been on the bridge when it had fallen in: skeleton horses and men entangled in heaps on the harbor floor. One skeletal soldier still was aboard his skeleton horse, each held together by rags of uniform or leather harness straps; the rider's foot was still in the stirrup.

Perhaps more frightening was the experience of a diver sent down to recover the body of a young eastern European nobleman who had been executed and thrown into the harbor. The widowed mother of the youth had pleaded with the diving master on a nearby commercial salvage project to recover her son's body for decent interment.

The diver began searching on his hands and knees because visibility was limited to only a few feet, but finally happened to look up. Seemingly advancing on him was the corpse of an aged man. His white hair floated about his head, his body moved up and down and half-turned from side to side in a rolling, circular motion. The arms waved straight out from the shoulders.

The diver turned to flee, cumbersome and slow in his heavy suit and ponderous helmet—and found himself surrounded on all sides by dancing, waving figures. Only after his frantic emergency signals had brought him to the surface did he realize what had happened. The body of each executed conspirator had been shackled by the ankle to heavy weights and thrown into the water. They had danced and floated in an upright position at the end of their fetters, activated by the currents of the diver's own motions.

In a similar incident during World War I, a British Admiralty Salvage Section diver found a dead man sitting in an armchair on the poop of a vessel in twelve fathoms of water. The corpse looked as if he had fallen asleep. Above him, the ship's ensign fluttered slowly in the currents at half-mast. The diver hoisted it to the top of the pole before proceeding with his assignment.

"I did not care to go about my work under a flag at half-mast," he explained later.

Another diver, checking a small sunken cruiser, came across the body of a marine standing at attention against a bulkhead, his rifle —with fixed bayonet—still clutched firmly in one hand.

Such bizarre occurrences in shallow-water salvage operations are, however, fortunately rare. Divers before World War I were mostly colorful professionals slowly learning new techniques in underwater work.

One man was hired, following a punting regatta on the Thames, to find a lady's engagement ring, which was, she said, of great monetary value and of greater sentimental value. By weird chance, the diver actually found it. Another was hired by an Indian cricket player named Rangi—really the Maharaja of Nawanagar—to recover a gold cigarette case dropped overboard from a Thames excursion vessel. He, too, was successful.

In 1893, W. S. Johnson made a small-object salvage recovery that must rank as the all-time prize winner. A man had been fishing off the Yorkshire Coast in sixty feet of water when he lost his watch and chain overboard. The watch was an heirloom of his wife's; he assured Johnson he knew right where he had lost it, and pleaded with the diver to search for it.

Johnson suited up and went down. Fifteen minutes later he was back at the surface with the watch and an unfortunate starfish that had become attached to it. The diver poured the watch full of olive oil and it continued to run without difficulty.

A few years later, in an English seaport, an exceptionally astute police officer called in hard-hat divers after a woman had been beaten to death with the proverbial blunt instrument. The policeman thought the instrument had been a bottle, and from the position of the body had an idea that the murderer might have thrown it off the pier to get rid of it. He sent divers down to look.

They found only fragments, but they gathered up enough of these so the detective, using a block of clay as a base, pieced them together. On the bottom of the bottle he found not only the maker's name, but a number that identified for the bottler the consignment and the public house to which it had gone.

Through a checking of dates, and a series of interrogations, the detective narrowed it down to one possible purchaser, who promptly confessed to the murder.

BEGINNINGS OF UNDERWATER DEMOLITION

Another skill that the pre-World War I divers were learning was underwater demolition, which had come a long way from the kegs of gunpowder and voltaic batteries of the *Royal George*. They learned, for one thing, which factors were important in blasting a wrecked vessel: whether the ship was wood or steel, the weather conditions, the distance of the wreck from a safe harbor, the type of wrecking equipment available, and the use intended for the salvaged material. Charges could vary from a single stick of dynamite to several tons of gelignite detonated through an electric cable from a hand exploder or a dynamo on the salvage vessel.

To disperse a wooden vessel, they found, a single charge (varying in size with the size of the ship) would suffice. The water acted as a conductor for the shock, and the whole thing would burst outward.

In blowing up a steel vessel, the price of scrap metal would determine their tactics; if the steel was to be sold, the ship would be "rough-cut" into small sections. The cuts would be made with strings of explosives packed in rubber-cloth bags and placed in sailcloth containers. These "strings" would be placed around the hull and over the deck of the section to be removed, and then all detonated at once.

And the salvors had to learn when not to use explosives at all.

In 1912 the P & O liner *Oceana* was sunk in the English Channel by a collision with another vessel. She settled in fifteen fathoms of water with the tops of her masts showing above the surface, and immediate salvage operations were planned: the ship had carried £771,068 in bullion bound for Bombay in wooden treasure chests.

The salvors could have blasted their way down in the strong room, but they were not sure of the location and knew they might blow the room itself apart, scattering the gold hopelessly. So they decided to do it the hard way.

This meant getting the strong-room keys from the desk in the captain's cabin. There was a very strong tide, however, and a great deal of wreckage lying about. Three times the diver got into the cabin, only to be sucked out again by the current. On his final try, he reached the desk and clung to it with one hand while rummaging for the keys with the other. He found them.

When they finally reached the strong room, the keys fit only three of the five locks on the door; they had to smash off the other two with a hatchet to get in. One diver would descend to the bullion room while his partner would remain on deck. This man would take the ingots handed up from below, pack them into lifting baskets, and send them to the surface. On each dive, the men changed places. They succeeded in bringing up £768,126 worth of gold; less than £3000 remained when the operation ceased.

One of the first iron ships successfully raised intact was the paddle steamer *Wolf*, which around the turn of the century sank some ten miles out in Belfast Lough following a collision. She was a big ship for her time, 243 feet long, twenty-seven in the beam, and weighing 850 tons. She was down in seven fathoms; a mere eight-foot tide precluded tide lifts.

The salvors, Harland and Wolff of Belfast, had six pontoons left over from a previous operation. These furnished a 500-ton buoyancy; two more very large pontoons specially constructed for the *Wolf*, each seventy feet long and twelve wide, gave another 432 tons.

The six small pontoons were attached to a raft above the bow of the sunken vessel, while the two big ones were attached to a second raft over the stern. The rafts were then connected by two huge beams so they formed a floating platform the size and roughly the shape of the *Wolf* below. Since the sunken steamer had twenty-five portholes on each side, twenty-five cross-logs, or joists, were fastened to the platform. On each end of each joist was a wrought-iron box bracket that carried a hexagonal cast-iron sheaf, grooved for ten ½-inch links of 1½-inch-diameter chain. For tightening or letting out each chain, a five-foot-long screw with a ¾-inch pitch was mounted above each box bracket.

Then heavy hooks were sent down to the divers, who fixed one in each of the fifty portholes. The lifting chains were fastened to the hooks; each porthole thus bore a seventeen-ton strain.

On their first lift, the crew cranked the *Wolf* up six feet as the screws drew up the lifting chains. Then two chains tore loose; the pontoons had to be reflooded to take strain off the chains so the divers could recouple them. Then the lift was begun again. Thirty-five days later, the salvaged hulk was towed to Abercorn Basin for repairs.

In the spring of 1913, another sunken vessel, the *Umeqaka Maru*, offered a man named MacFarland, from the British Salvage Association, an interesting problem. She was lying on her portside off Japan in six fathoms shelving to nine; her upper, or starboard, side was just awash at low tide.

MacFarland had to right the vessel before he could raise her. First he had three 40-foot tripods fastened to her starboard side. Tackle connected each tripod to six-inch cables, which in turn were moored to anchor groups some distance from the wreck. The falls from the tackle were picked up by the salvage ship *Arima Maru* and a large rock-crushing ship.

Then hundreds of sandbags were attached to the starboard side to give it more weight, while 200-ton hydraulic jacks were placed by divers between the bottom and the port sheer strake.

The salvage vessels pulled on the tackle to draw down the starboard side, and the hydraulic jacks pushed up against the portside. She righted. MacFarland constructed a 242-foot cofferdam around the *Umeqaka Maru*'s deck, and the ship was pumped out so it would surface and could be hauled in for repairs.

It is significant that this job in Japan was carried out by an Englishman. Even before World War I, Britain had historically led the world in marine salvage techniques and operations. Several factors contributed to this pre-eminence. First, Lloyd's had acted as a prime insurer of ocean-going cargoes and vessels since the seventeenth century. This made British merchantmen more adventuresome than those of other nations. And no matter where ships went down, Lloyd's underwriters naturally wanted to recover what they could—which encouraged the formation of professional salvage associations.

Second, Britain's undisputed naval might in all of the world's great oceans meant that British salvors could follow the fleet and practice their trade in remote corners of the globe.

But perhaps the most decisive factor was the nature of British coastlines and tidal waters. The coasts are the best-lighted in the world, but also are among the most treacherous. Ships or cargoes not salvaged within a short time probably were not to be salvaged at all, for cargoes would rot, and imperishables such as gold or jewels would be scattered by the scouring of the tides. Vessels sunk in all but the least-exposed positions were battered by tremendous storms, broken up by fierce underwater currents, and corroded by sea water.

Though there were a bare half-dozen salvage firms of any real consequence in Great Britain before World War I, there were fewer elsewhere. America had two or three; Sweden, Denmark, and Germany each had one.

FORMING THE SALVAGE SECTION

Then came the war, spurring, as war so often does, new developments, new techniques, new arrangements. All the British firms were taken over by the Admiralty, and in November 1915 Captain C. Greatorex was put in charge of the newly formed Admiralty Salvage Association, with the title Director of Naval Equipment. Captain Christopher Metcalfe was Head, Salvage Section, and Engineer-Captain Teed was Supply Officer, being responsible for pumps and cables and the like, and for the training of men to handle this equipment.

The Salvage Section was designed originally to salvage only military vessels, but the brutally successful German submarine campaign, making no distinction between freighters and warships, altered that. Soon even Lloyd's refused to insure the merchant fleet, so the government had to promise to underwrite all vessels entering or leaving British ports. Metcalfe was instrumental in the creation of the convoy system, with ships traveling together under escort of warships and anti-submarine vessels. He also pushed the idea of arming the merchantmen for their own protection.

The main work of the Salvage Section soon became the repairing of torpedo-damaged merchant vessels. If a stricken ship was still afloat, tugs would bring it to port. If it sank in a feasible recovery area, the Salvage Section prided itself on not losing even one tide before starting operations. Their effective network covered not only British ports and the Channel, but also the Mediterranean.

One of the Section's most potent tools was the so-called *standard patch*, made of grooved timbers that fit into one another so that the square or oblong patch looked very much like the top of an old-fashioned roll-top desk. This simple construction made the patch flexible enough to be fitted to the curvature of almost any damaged hull.

Another advantage was that the patch could be fabricated right on the deck of the stricken vessel, often by the ship's carpenter. It then would be lowered from the deck to the divers waiting below, the bottom edge weighted so it would sink in the proper position. They would bolt it to the hull and make the edges watertight with cement.

The effectiveness of the standard patch can be seen in the case of one merchantman, which was torpedoed but somehow remained afloat. The ship was beached, a standard patch was fitted, she was pumped out, and the tow for port began.

As soon as she reached open sea, another German torpedo struck her. They got her beached before she sank, and fitted a second patch over the hole. Watertight and pumped out again, she was taken in tow by the tugs.

When she was an hour under way, a third German torpedo struck her. She was *again* patched up and, after being beached on the Isle of Wight while the salvors attended to other vessels, was gotten into dry dock for repairs.

This peacetime-style salvage work brought a remarkable man, Captain Frederick W. Young, to the fore. He had been Chief Salvage Officer with the Liverpool Salvage Association, and at war's start had been given responsibility for the safeguarding of harbors with mines and nets. When Metcalfe resigned in the spring of 1918, Young, then a commodore, took over.

EXPLOITS OF FREDERICK W. YOUNG

His fame actually had begun a few years before the war with the extremely complex operation on the 6000-ton HMS *Gladiator*. This warship had been struck by the American Lines steamer *St. Paul*[5] in the Solent, near the Isle of Wight, during a blinding snowstorm on April 25, 1908. She went down with a fifty-foot hole ripped in her starboard side. The damaged side was down and the decks were toward shore; at high tide only her portside showed above the water.

Because she was on a hard and steeply shelving beach, Young's first concern was to get her closer to shore so she would not slide off into deeper water during bad weather. The task was complicated by an eight-knot tide, which formed heavily swirling eddies severely limiting the divers' bottom time.

First the ship's 15-ton guns were removed; funnels, ventilators, and other top hamper were cut off with pneumatic chisels; then all openings were made watertight with wooden patches (set in with bolt hooks). Finally, the jagged steel around the wound in the hull had to be smoothed down.

At this point they realized that all the portholes were still open on the lower, starboard side, and would have to be closed from inside by divers working their way down through the wreck in pitch darkness. The famous Christopher Lambert and another diver, named Binnie, drew the task of closing the watertight door of the boiler room. The engine room had to be got through—a room filled with pipes, machinery, dynamos, pumps, ladders, and steel gratings, all dumped over at a 93-degree angle with the list of the ship—and their only entry was through a ventilator amidships. Lambert waited at the ventilator to tend Binnie's air and life lines as he crawled from there down toward the guts of the ship.

Before going through the shaft, Binnie paused. Trapped in the broken plating nearby was the corpse of one of the *Gladiator*'s drowned sailors. The diver solemnly shook hands with the dead man, then went down and spent an hour dogging down the door.

Was his gesture with the corpse just cheap bravado, thumbing his nose at death? No. Few divers have that sort of temperament. The dead man was not an object of fear; rather, in a certain way, they were kindred things. Both, after all, were beneath the sea. And both, if things went wrong, would remain there.

"Just for luck," Binnie confirmed when asked about the handshake.

Once the vessel was tight, five river gunboats were moored to it bows on, so their centrifugal pumps could be used. Young secured two 100-ton-buoyancy pontoons to the *Gladiator* with nine-inch cables passed under the wreck from steel bollards bolted to the upper, port, side. Thus their buoyancy would be exerted for turning rather than lifting.

The actual drag into shallower water was accomplished by steam capstans on shore, which had eight-inch wire cables passed through a 100-ton pulley aboard the *Gladiator*. By this means the ship was brought twelve yards farther inshore and was lined up parallel to the beach.

Then seven more pontoons were fixed, five on the starboard side, and two on the port to prevent her rolling over that way if they accidentally brought her through the vertical during the operation to roll her over. Two huge iron tripods were secured to the portside, one abreast of each mast. Six-inch wire cables were run from the masthead over the heavy casting at the end of each triangle, and then to a salvage steamer moored a hundred yards seaward by a seven-ton stern anchor. Other six-inch cables led from the masthead to the capstan-operated shore purchases.

When Young was ready, everything was begun at once. The capstans turned, the seaward salvage steamer pulled, the gunboat pumps splashed six thousand tons of water an hour from the ship's compartments. It was enough. The list was reduced to a negligible seven degrees.

Because the starboard side was still several feet under water, Young could not just pump out the ship to raise her. He first had to enclose the entire upper deck of the vessel in an enormous cofferdam, which extended above the surface and below the deck casing on the starboard side. The water was first brought down below the upper-deck level, then portable pumps were brought in there and on the boat deck to work on the lower compartments.

The operation took five months.

During the war but before Young became Head of the Salvage Section, he carried out one operation which perhaps sums him up better than any other. Like any great salvor he was constantly fascinated by engineering problems. He would try anything if he thought it would work, whether it was the prescribed way of doing it or not.

The Salvage Section was faced with two operations: the huge hospital ship *Asturias*,[6] which had been torpedoed in the English Channel and beached at Salcombe; and a torpedoed Q-ship that had sunk in Cawsand Bay. The recommendation was to not salvage the Q-ship, since the other vessel was much more important.

Young, however, noted two things. First, it was Monday and the operation on the hospital ship could not properly begin for a week; and second, the report of the diver who had surveyed the Q-ship noted that there was hard rock under her nose and hard rock under her stern, but that the center part of her keel was free due to a gap in the reef at that point. He thought about that for a while, then went to Metcalfe.

"If the diver's report is correct," he said, "I will guarantee to be back in London by Friday with the ship beached."

Young traveled down to Plymouth by train that afternoon. There he got hold of two hopper barges that had been previously converted to crude lifting craft by dividing their hulls into sections with steel bulkheads. These were in effect a series of tanks that could be flooded or blown to sink or raise the craft's position in the water by four and a half feet. Each barge was capable of exerting twelve hundred tons of buoyancy.

Tugs got the barges into Plymouth Sound, but a whole night was lost in chasing them about after they tore loose in a sudden, fierce blizzard.

As soon as he got them back, however, Young had them secured to the Q-ship with nine-inch steel cables run under the free part of the sunken ship's hull by divers. The lifting craft were watered, pinned down to the wreck, then unwatered as the tide came in. Up came the Q-ship from the reef. In successive tide lifts, she was towed shoreward and on Friday beached, ready to be pumped out on Saturday.

By Friday night, Young was back in London, ready for the *Asturias*.

During the war, the Salvage Section raised some five hundred ships, worth, conservatively, £50 million. Most of these operations were affected in one way or another by Young's genius. And in February and March 1917 he carried out the salvage operation that was to revolutionize the profession and point the way for Ernest Cox at Scapa Flow. This was the recovery *with compressed air* of the British submarine *K-13*[7] at Gareloch.

Pumping a sunken vessel full of compressed air to raise it was first considered by the London Wrecking Company as far back as 1880, when they planned to raise the *Grosser Kurfurst*[8] by this unheard-of method. But they went broke before they could try.

Frederick Young, therefore, was the first man to raise a vessel by this method, which he later repeated with the dreadnought *Britannia*.[9]

COMPRESSED AIR FOR THE *LEONARDO*

He did not remain alone in the field for long, however. On the night of August 2, 1916, the 24,000-ton Italian battleship *Leonardo da Vinci* was blown up by a German time bomb in her powder magazine. The £4-million behemoth, which carried thirteen 12-inch guns, turned turtle in thirty-six feet of water and carried 249 men and officers down with her in the roads outside Taranto Harbor.

Divers reported two tremendous gaps, one on either side of the keel, where the explosion had blown away most of the decking above the after magazines. The Italian naval engineers, faced with a salvage job for whose execution they had no ideas, first suggested building a floating dry dock *completely around the ship!* Then, they argued, one had only to pump out the dry dock, and it would automatically raise the wreck.

Indeed? *Buona fortuna!*

While they were kicking around that and other ideas of similar merit, the *Leonardo*'s gun turrets and funnels were gradually being pushed, by her own great weight, down into the sediment beneath the ship. They kept burrowing until they reached the clay under thirty feet of mud.

At this point General Ferrati, Chief of Italian Naval Construction and a brilliant engineer, decided that compressed air was the only way to raise the vessel. He and his associate, Major Gianelli (who completed the salvage operation after Ferrati's death), used scale models to determine that the ship should be floated upside down, and then taken into the Taranto dry dock for righting. So their first job was to make the hull airtight; not a difficult job, actually, since the hull itself had suffered little damage in the blast except for the holes aft.

Once these were repaired, hundreds of tons of ammunition were removed to lighten the vessel. One by one its interior compartments were made watertight and then pumped full of compressed air. Soon the water inside the vessel was twenty-six feet below the level outside, held down only by compressed air. Air locks were constructed on the overturned hull so workmen could remove additional cargo to lighten her, and could pack in scores of tons of cork to help in the lift.

The operation to make the *Leonardo* tight had begun in the spring of 1917. By November, her bows were showing a tendency toward buoyancy. But Gianelli now faced another problem. The dry dock in which they proposed to put her could take a vessel drawing a maximum of forty feet; in her current condition, the *Leonardo* drew fifty feet. This meant that the gun turrets, funnels, and other top hamper buried so deep in the mud would have to be removed. But it was this top hamper, down on the hard clay, that was supporting the vessel. Therefore all the preliminary work on removal was done from *inside* the ship. In one of the turrets they lowered the water level to fifty-six feet below sea level—twenty feet below the surface of the surrounding mud.

While the waterproof patches were being set on the inside of the turrets and funnels prior to their removal, Gianelli had eight 350-ton-capacity pontoons brought up, watered, and sunk parallel to the wreck, four on a side. The slide rule showed that the compressed air to be forced into her hull would give sufficient buoyancy to raise her, but he wanted to be sure.

Other workmen with dredgers were digging a channel, one and a half miles long, from the *Leonardo* to the Taranto dry dock. The dry dock itself was prepared for its giant tenant with massive timber supports arranged to be a mirror image of what the top-turned-bottom of the *Leonardo* would look like once she came up out of the mud.

The lift began on September 17, 1919. The ship came alive with remarkable ease in only a few hours, and the next day was maneuvered into the flooded-down dry dock. Then the dock was pumped out to rise under her and bring her out of the water for the first time in over three years.

They still had the problem of righting the massive warship. Since there was no adjacent area of the Taranto Harbor deep enough for the maneuver, the Italians dredged a deep basin in the middle of the harbor, and in January 1921 the *Leonardo* was removed from the dry dock and towed over there. She was carrying four hundred tons of solid ballast, and Gianelli ordered the gradual infusion of seventy-five hundred tons of water into her starboard compartments. She began listing with eight hundred tons of water aboard, gradually speeding up as more was added, until with a rush she flipped right side up and came to rest with only a slight starboard list.

The last act of the salvage drama was recovery of the 12-inch-gun turrets from the mud in which the *Leonardo* had lain. Gianelli did this with a very large, 1000-ton-lift annular pontoon. It was watered and sunk over each turret in turn, pinned (that is, fastened tight to the turret with cables), and then blown, carrying gun and turret to the surface. The entire operation cost £150,000.

Even more than Young's pioneering work with compressed air, the *Leonardo* foreshadowed the world's greatest salvage operation. This was an operation that, in view of the individual courage, initiative, and ability to improvise shown by professional salvors, is singularly satisfying. Nothing else ever carried out, anywhere, can even remotely equal it in scope, attainment, and breath-taking gall.

For it was, from the beginning to end, the work of *one man*. He conceived it after governments had dismissed it as impossible; he financed it; he engineered it; he oversaw it; and for nearly a decade of his life, he lived it.

The man: Ernest Frank Guelph Cox.

The operation: to raise the German Imperial Fleet, which had been scuttled at Scapa Flow, Orkney Islands, in 1919.

---

[1] See pages 127, 147.
[2] See page 63.
[3] See pages 68–69.
[4] See pages 382–83.
[5] See pages 255–58 for a subsequent operation on the *St. Paul*.
[6] See pages 325–26.
[7] See pages 111–12.
[8] See pages 31–32.
[9] See pages 326–27.

CHAPTER FIFTEEN

Cox of Scapa Flow

Ernest Cox, when he determined to raise the fleet at Scapa Flow, had never raised a sunken anything in his life. Not even a rowboat. He was not a salvor of any sort, nor even a qualified mechanical engineer. Instead, he was a scrap-iron monger called, among other things, the "Super Junkman."

He was born in 1883 and quit school at the age of thirteen; but without any formal qualification he had advanced through a number of engineering jobs by his enormous drive and singular aptitude. In 1907 he married Jenny Jack Miller, went to work at her father's Overton Steel Works, and by 1912 was ready to found his own forge. His wife's playboy cousin, Tommy Danks, financed the scheme on the proviso that Cox would never ask him to set foot in the place. During World War I, Cox and Danks, Ltd., took government munitions contracts; after the war, Cox bought his partner out and with uncanny timing went into the scrap-metal business.

He didn't know it yet, but he was almost ready for Scapa Flow.

A FLEET IS SCUTTLED

Under the terms of the Armistice, seventy-four German warships (eleven battleships, five battle cruisers, eight scout destroyers, and fifty regular destroyers) had been interned at the immense natural bay of Scapa Flow in the Orkney Islands. They were to be held there until noon on June 21, 1919, when Germany would formally surrender. British warships patrolled the fleet, but the skeleton crews aboard were Germans under nominal command of Rear Admiral Ludwig von Reuter; no British officer or crewman was permitted aboard.

On the evening of June 20, Vice-Admiral Sir Sydney Fremantle, Commander of the British watchdog fleet, was notified that the Armistice had been extended to noon of the twenty-third as a convenience for the German leaders. He decided to fill the time with a bit of torpedo practice, so his entire fleet steamed away on the morning of the twenty-first except for three destroyers awaiting repairs (only one could even get steam up), a depot ship, and a few drifters and armed trawlers.

At high noon on the twenty-first a prearranged signal went up from Von Reuter's flagship. Pennants immediately were hoisted on all German vessels, red Communist flags appeared at the mastheads, whistles blew, bells rang, and the several thousand German sailors began cheering lustily. Meanwhile, the officers and petty officers were below, opening sea cocks and smashing intake pipes from the salt-water strainers in the hulls. They bent sea-cock spindles so they could not be closed; they threw the actuating wrenches overboard. On the destroyers, which were moored two and three to a buoy, mooring cables were wired down to bollards, while shackle-pin ends on anchor chains were hammered over so they could not be unscrewed.

While the pitifully small complement of British sailors watched in consternation, the entire German fleet began reeling about drunkenly, careening, bumping, smashing, sinking—by the head, by the stern, on their sides, turned completely turtle. The British drifters and trawlers tried with gunfire to drive the Germans back aboard to close the valves; equipped with life jackets, the Germans had jumped overboard or used lifeboats to head for the nearest shore. Only eight of them were killed and five wounded.

The British tried to save what they could, but it wasn't much; a few of the destroyers, three cruisers, and a battleship were dragged into shallow water. Fifty of the German ships went down in eleven to thirty fathoms—ships ranging in size from 750-ton torpedo boats to the 28,000-ton *Hindenburg*.

Not until fifty-one ships of the Japanese Combined Fleet would be sunk in the lagoon at Truk by American carrier Task Force 58 on February 17, 1944, would there be a similar concentration of sunken warships; certainly there never had been one before. Fremantle, steaming in from Duncansby Head that evening, was coldly furious with Von Reuter.

"The honor-loving seamen of all nations," he said, "will be unable to comprehend this act—with the exception, perhaps, of yours."

Meanwhile, there was an enormous shortage of metal for railways, ships, industrial and agricultural machinery, autos, girders, typewriters —even razor blades. Shells, guns, and tanks were broken up and melted down. In 1921 Ernest Cox went his competitors one better by buying old Admiralty battleships and breaking them up at his Queensborough scrap-metal yards on the Isle of Sheppey. And then, in 1924, he bought a German dry dock from the British Government for £20,000.

Cox really had no use for the tremendous U-shaped structure; he wanted the 400-foot, 40-foot-diameter steel pressure cylinder it carried (once used for testing German U-boats), to cut loose and sell for scrap. He did, which left him the bemused possessor of a dry dock.

AN OBSESSION IS BORN

Then, on a trip to Copenhagen to sell non-ferrous metals to the Danish firm of Peterson and Allbeck, Cox got talking about the shortage of scrap metal. Peterson remarked, offhandedly and almost as a joke, that Cox ought to use his dry dock to raise some of the fleet at Scapa Flow.

"I don't say you can lift up the battleships, but I know there are thirty or forty destroyers lying there, none of them over a thousand tons. And that dock will lift three thousand tons at a time."

Indeed? Why *couldn't* Cox lift up battleships? The *Hindenburg*, for instance. There was twenty-eight thousand tons of scrap metal waiting to be salvaged. Nobody had ever done anything like that before, had they?

And an obsession was born . . .

When Cox moved, he moved fast. He spent *one day* in a technical library, studying and thinking; then he went to the Admiralty and offered to buy a few of the smaller destroyers "as is" on the bottom of Scapa Flow. The Admiralty, however, was nothing if not fair. They suggested that Cox check the site before making such an offer; more importantly, they also suggested that he check the report issued after an official Admiralty survey made at Scapa Flow five years before.

"There can be no question of salving the ships," the report had stated. "And, as they offer no hindrance to navigation, they need not be blown up. Where they were sunk, there they will rest and rust."

The destroyers were lying in such jumbles about their mooring buoys that they would be prohibitively costly to raise, the experts concluded.

As for the larger ships, there was no known method of raising any of them anyway.

Cox, however, was not an expert. He was a working engineer. His life was solving engineering problems, and Scapa Flow was one of massive proportions. The experts' opinions had little chance of affecting his decision anyway, since he never bothered to read the report.

ERNEST COX BUYS A NAVY—ON THE BOTTOM

He did, however, go up to Scapa Flow as suggested, to see firsthand what an incredible, impossible job it would be to raise *any* of the ships. Then he returned to the Admiralty and offered them £24,000 for twenty-six destroyers and two battleships. Dazed, they took his money. Ernest Cox had bought a navy.

Incredible as it may seem, his day in the library and his day in Scapa Flow had been enough to give him a scheme. His giant floating dry dock had a 3000-ton lifting capacity; the destroyers weighed only 750 to thirteen hundred tons each; therefore, he thought, his dock could bring up two or even three of them together in a clot if they could not be disentangled. In his mind, that took care of the destroyers. A few weeks and they would be out of the way. Their scrap-metal value would pay for burning off the forward gun turrets of the giant battle cruiser *Hindenburg*, which lay on a nearly dead-even keel in ten fathoms on a shingle bottom. The turrets were clear of the water at low tide, so his men could get at them with oxyacetylene torches.

The turrets would finance raising the 28,000-ton *Hindenburg*. He would strip her once she was up—thus making her in effect a giant pontoon—and would use her to raise the other vessels. It was a beautiful scheme, a grand procession of orderly events, and it had only one drawback (resulting from Cox's massive ignorance of professional salvage methods).

It wouldn't work.

But that was all in the future. Right now he had a fleet on the bottom of Scapa Flow, a floating German dry dock, and a great deal of salvaged battleship anchor chain he planned to use in place of lifting cables. He had no salvage crew. No salvage equipment. On the Island of Hoy, where he planned to center his operations, there were no workshops, no sheds, no living accommodations, nothing. Not even electricity.

The day after Cox bought his fleet, he began hiring. Two of the best were Thomas McKenzie and Ernest McKeown, who became known as "the two Macs" and were his joint Chief Salvage Officers. Then, over their objections (much of what he did, down the years, would be over their objections), he cut one upright wall of his U-shaped dry dock right off, and sealed up the hull end where it had been. His dock was now L-shaped. Then he cut it halfway through athwartships and had it towed the seven hundred miles of open sea to the Orkneys. He beached it in Mill Bay, near Lyness, on Hoy, and there finished the cut. He now had two L-shaped sections of dry dock, each two hundred feet long and eighty feet wide, each equipped with pumps, air compressors, dynamos, and engine and boiler rooms in the upright section, and with twelve sets of hand-operated winches on the flat deck area.

These twenty-four pulleys each had a 100-ton pulley block with triple-geared hand winches. The pulley block, in turn, was secured to 100-ton tackles, and these were bolted to the dock's upright wall by massive steel plates. The lifting chains ran from the tackles through the grooved pulleys, with the gypsy (or free) end dangling off the lip of the deck into the water. Two men were required to work each winch handle.

McKeown and Cox had their first nose-to-nose: McKeown wanted nine-inch wire cables, Cox wanted the old anchor chains because the cables would cost £2000 each. Cox won. For the moment.

THE FIRST DESTROYER

The lift of the first destroyer, V-70, began in March 1924. It was a 750-ton vessel lying in ten fathoms of water about two miles from the Mill Bay beach—upright, thus giving the divers an easy shot at getting a bight of lifting chain around the stern propeller bosses. At low tide the ends of the chain were winched in aboard the two dock sections anchored over the destroyer on either side until they were taut. The rising tide raised V-70's stern, and another of the lifting chains was gotten under the hull a bit forward of the stern. In this way, all twelve were placed, with divers pushing the messenger wires for the chains under the vessel athwartships with a long metal rod (pricker).

On a chilly March morning, twenty-four 2-man gangs manned the winch handles in unison, at low tide, and got the V-70 up six turns of the screw. The tide helped as it rose, and they got another six.

With an explosive, shot-like sound, the No. 10 chain rose with miraculous speed from the water, shooting a broken link across the face of the dock like a shell. Cox bellowed at everyone to hit the deck: as the suddenly uneven strain was transferred from chain to chain, they all broke. Broken links, purchases, cables, huge shackles, blocks—they all went flying in every direction.

V-70, released, dropped like a stone.

By some incredible luck, no one was hurt beyond bruises. They stood up gingerly, awaiting the inevitable profane explosion from Cox.

He merely said: "I'll get wire as soon as I can, but it'll take a week or so. Still, there's plenty to do ashore, so get busy." When they still waited, he finally bellowed, "*Come on, now, what are you waiting for?*"

The two Macs, willy-nilly, had won the round after all.

As one of the workmen put it, "If he hadn't been a mixture of a genius and a mule, he'd never have *started* a job that size, let alone have finished it. Apart from McKeown and McKenzie, there wasn't one of us who knew the first thing about salvage, and *they* didn't know that much . . ."

The lifting cables arrived in April, complete with flattened centers to give a better rest for the vessel to be salvaged. Essentially the same procedure as with the chain was used for reeving the 250-ton, nine-inch wire cables under the submerged hull of the V-70. All tackles were in place so the lift could begin with low tide at 4:00 A.M. on August 1, 1924.

Ten turns were taken; all cables were taut but none was "necking"— the rapid vibrating movement of lifting cables that usually presages a break. Ten more, and V-70 was one and one-half inches off the sea bottom. Cox kept them going at twenty turns and a rest, twenty turns and a rest, until V-70's top hamper cleared. Cox saw for the first time that the torpedo tubes were missing, and flew into a dancing, screaming rage.

"McKenzie! What the devil . . . have your damned divers snarled up the cables and wrenched the tubes off?"

"Ask the fish," said diver Bill Peterson. "Or ask some of the quiet boys ashore!"

"They've been pinched?" shrieked Cox. "I'll get the police. I'll . . . I'll . . ."

He did nothing: there was nothing to do. Everything reachable and removable and small enough to be portable had long since disappeared with the Orkney Islanders in the wee hours of dark nights.

V-70, in successive tide lifts, was brought into the breaking-dock. She was worth as scrap some £1500, despite an effluvium from the rotting sea animals and vegetation that, as one workman put it, "would have blinded a dock rat." Cox never did break up V-70, his first prize at Scapa Flow, despite his need of operating capital. Instead he sealed her, fitted her out as a workshop for his carpenter, and called her *Salvage Unit No. 3*.

V-70 came up on August 1; and in bringing her up Cox had found his method for the small destroyers. S-53 came up on the twelfth, S-55 on the twenty-ninth, G-91 on September 12, G-38 on the twenty-seventh, S-52 on October 13, last for the year because the shore plant needed repairs so it would be usable during the icy winter months.

As they were working on G-91, a diver down between two of the jumbled destroyers was trapped when a funnel from one of the ships collapsed on top of him, pinning his air and life lines. Two divers worked in desperate haste to free him, while McKenzie got on his phone to try to "talk him through" the horror of being trapped on the sea floor.

But when Mac picked up, he found he was listening to a very poorly rendered "Home, Sweet Home." "Hello!" exclaimed McKenzie. "I . . . er . . . how are you, now?"

"Fine, sir. What do you think of my voice?"

"Pretty awful, but we can stand another verse."

Divers, by nature, habit, training, and instinct, are not animals that panic easily.

In all, Cox and his men raised twenty-five of the small German destroyers between August 1924 and May 1926. The ones lying upside down, which the experts had pronounced unsalvageable, had free water underneath, which made the reeving of the lifting wires easy. Each cable drawn under carried with it the pilot line for the cable from the next winch in line, so they sometimes set an entire string of cables in the incredible time of forty minutes.

For the mooring cables on the heaps of jumbled destroyers, which again were supposed to give so much trouble, Cox used gelignite. McKenzie's men became so expert with the explosives that no one could tell a cable that had been blasted in half from one that had been hand sawed.

By 1925 the destroyers were so routine that they could bring one up in four days; at one point, six were raised in a two-week period. If they were upside down when they surfaced, Cox would flip them. It usually took an hour. The two docks would move into deep water, then one would pay out cable while the other took it up. This acted as a parbuckle, and the destroyer merely rolled over in its lifting cradle.

By summer of that year, ten destroyers had been sold to Alloa Shipbreakers for £23,000—more than half of Cox's original £45,000 outlay.

He felt it was time for grander things: the 1300-ton scout destroyers. Fearing that his two sections of dry dock would not be able to lift this dead weight, he spent a good deal of his £23,000 on another of the huge German floating dry docks. It was U-shaped, of course; he planned to sink it hard on the bottom, lift up the scout destroyers enough with his L-shaped docks to drop them onto the sunken dock's flat deck, then unwater the dock to bring it and the destroyer to the surface. Presto! A salvaged destroyer.

It didn't work.

They were unable to maneuver the destroyers between the sunken dock's uprights. Cox floated it and cut off one of the uprights to make it L-shaped; the destroyers then could just be sort of sidled onto it from the open side of the L.

It didn't work.

The dock, big as it was, tipped so much that it threatened to slide the first destroyer right off into the mud. He relowered her quickly with the destroyer still aboard: too quickly. She drove one corner deep into the bottom, buckled plates, started rivets, and filled completely. Now he had a *really* sunken dry dock. Eventually they got it up, but it was one of the worst jobs they tackled.

And all for naught. Forced to fall back on his two smaller docks as pontoons for the big destroyers, he found to his chagrin that they handled thirteen hundred tons as easily as they did seven hundred and fifty.

The last of the destroyers that Cox raised came up on May 1, 1926; and the salvor was thinking grand thoughts again. Time for one of the big babies, and why not start at the top? The *Hindenburg*, battle cruiser, twenty-eight thousand tons. Larger, by four thousand tons, than any vessel ever raised in the history of salvage. A fine ship upon which to work out one's aggressions.

Unfortunately, the General Strike was called just then, the greatest labor stoppage Britain had ever seen.

Not one single man struck Cox, so great was his influence on them; but the General Strike pushed up the price of coal £2 a ton. Cox needed coal, hundreds of tons of it; coal he couldn't afford at the higher price. Not even loyal workmen could help with that.

Oh no?

Workmen could work. Work they did. The 25,000-ton *Seydlitz* had her bunkers loaded to the gunnels with coal. Cox stripped away enough of her armored hide to get at it, brought up his mechanical grabs, and fed the hungry fireboxes on his salvage tugs, *Lyness* and *Ferrodanks*, and on his other ships and shops.

FIRST ATTEMPT ON THE *HINDENBURG*

Back to the *Hindenburg*. Ah yes, the *Hindenburg*. She was seven hundred feet at the waterline, ninety-six feet in beam, and drew twenty-seven feet. Down in twelve fathoms, she had thirty feet of water over her quarterdeck and ten over her foredeck. Even at low tide, everything but the boat deck and the navigating bridge was submerged.

Cox surveyed the nearly upright vessel, and decided finally to make a pumping job of her. That meant closing every opening in the vessel—including the sea cocks, ports, ventilators, and hatches that the Germans had opened. Over *eight hundred separate patches* had to be placed by the divers, ranging in size from one and one half feet to an incredible forty-foot by twenty-one-foot funnel patch of doubled three-inch timber and a dozen 6-inch iron H-beams that weighed eleven tons. The patches were made tight with "puddings"—oakum-stuffed canvas fitted around the edges and compressed as the patch was tightened down until they were watertight.

The work was made easier by the lucky find of a metal plate with the *Hindenburg*'s entire pipe-and-valve system etched on it—indispensable, as so many openings had to be patched by divers working inside the ship by a sense of feel alone. It took six 2-man crews from May until August 1926 to complete the patching and tallow all joints against minor leaks.

Meanwhile, Cox's four L-shaped dry-dock sections (the second dock had been raised and cut in half) were moored over the wreck, two on a side; sixteen anchors, some laid half a mile away, were needed to hold them in place. Footbridges led from the docks to the wreck and between the docks. To windward were moored two of the salvaged destroyers as weatherbreakers against the Orkneys' terrible storms.

On August 6, eight 12-inch centrifugal and twelve 6-inch submersible pumps were started. The water level began lowering—but not enough. Major leakage somewhere. The divers soon discovered that the abundant little fish that hung around the wreck, a variety known as saithe, had eaten all the tallow from the patches. Cox was livid; McKenzie was practical.

He mixed 10 per cent Portland cement with the tallow.

Even the saithe found this indigestible; and McKenzie discovered that this mixture had better sealing properties than tallow alone. The pumps were started again but there was still too much leakage. Diver Bill Peterson went down inside the hull to search for the trouble. He found it, but his lines got terribly fouled, and his backup diver, Nobby Hall, had to free him; their lines were so mixed up that they had to be brought up together.

"You two been havin' a dance down there?" groused the tender who untangled them.

More air. Still no noticeable drop in the water level. Divers were sent down outside the hull to look for leaks that had been missed, and one of them sent up a signal that he needed help—fast.

They found him with as much of his backside as would fit sucked up into an 8-inch sea cock on the vessel's side. The suction was so strong that the only way he could be freed was to reflood the entire vessel to ease the pressure. They did, at a cost of several hundred pounds.

"You were a very expensive bit of plugging," McKenzie remarked.

"I was sent down to stop the leak, and I stopped it," he said.

Finally, pumping began in earnest. Submersibles were lowered from the forward gun turret, down the turret trunk, right into the bilges. To the pumps already working were added eighteen 6-inch centrifugals. After five days, the bow came alive; thirty-six hundred tons of water an hour were gushing from her. The stink of decaying vegetation, one man remarked, "would have played 'The Death of Nelson' if it could have been piped through a trombone."

The bow came up listing, and the higher she came the more she listed. Fifteen degrees' port list. Thirty. Forty. Fearing the boat would capsize and drown his men, a bitter Cox let her down. Then he tried the stern. The same thing.

"The damned ship is heavier on the portside," Cox said, "and that's all there is to it."

Nobody argued; they had realized that in trying to raise the ship one end at a time, they were in effect balancing twenty-eight thousand tons on a three-foot-wide keel. It wouldn't work as long as she was overbalanced.

Cox brought up one of the destroyers, grappled her to the *Hindenburg*'s starboard side, and filled her with water. From the battle cruiser's steel foremast he ran a doubled wire cable to another destroyer beached on Cava Island three-quarters of a mile away.

On September 2, Cox tried again, bringing her up level this time. When the upper deck was just awash, the cable from the beached destroyer let go. No one, incredibly, was cut in half by the whipping steel snake; but the ship heeled over to 25 degrees port. It was twilight, and a full gale—55-knot winds—had blown up, but Cox and his men, bitterly stubborn, refused to quit. Through the night they toiled, in waves so high that all the diving boats sank. The *Hindenburg*, just off the bottom as she was, wallowed like a pig.

At dawn the starboard dock's main boiler failed. It supplied at least half their pumps; the *Hindenburg* would sink again if power could not be maintained. Desperate, Cox had the *Ferrodanks* brought up and tried to make enough steam with her boilers. He couldn't.

Six months and £30,000 had been wasted.

The men stared at Cox, some of them with tears in their eyes. He had thrown his entire being into the attempt; with fixed labor, wage, and supply costs of £1000 a week, he was down to £10,000 and was faced with possible ruin.

Cox turned to McKeown and said briskly, "We'll fetch her up next spring. I've been thinking it out, and I see the idea now. Meanwhile, we can get the *Moltke* worked over."

He made not another mention of the *Hindenburg* until he was ready to try her again in 1930.

VON MOLTKE

The *Von Moltke* was 23,000 tons, five thousand less than the *Hindenburg*, and at 610 feet, nearly a hundred feet shorter. She was just as beamy, however, ninety-six feet, drew nearly as much water, and lay in thirteen fathoms, with a 17-degree starboard list.

The *Moltke* had one other little peculiarity: she was upside down.

In theory, that actually made her easier to raise. The hull, undamaged except for the opened sea cocks (which, because she was upside down, were easily accessible), could be made tight, and then she could be pumped full of compressed air to raise her. It had worked on the *Leonardo da Vinci*, a vessel of comparable size. But the *Leonardo* had been down in less than half the water that the *Moltke* was. Still . . .

The first problem was to cut away the growth of sea plants from the hull, which was done by men in hip boots, first with billhooks, then with razor-sharp axes. Some of the plants were taller than a man and as big around as a forearm. Once the divers could see the bottom valves, these were sealed—wooden plugs individually carved for the small ones, a mixture of underwater cement and sand for the larger.

Pumping began in mid-October with the salvors' battery of air compressors putting in three hundred thousand cubic feet of air every twenty-four hours. They needed 15 to 22 psi, certainly not a high pressure, but the tremendous volume of water to be pressed meant ten days before the bow came up.

And up. Eight feet out of the water—and the stern still hard down. A 33-degree port list developed, which meant that the ship's interior was "common"; the air could pass freely from chamber to leaking chamber and, since the bow was a bit higher to begin with, it all rushed forward.

This meant that they had to seal all bulkheads; it also meant air locks had to be fitted into the hull so that workmen could pass into it once pressure began to rise inside. The air locks, twelve-foot steel boilers six feet in diameter, were bolted to the bottom over the No. 2 stokehold and the forward engine room. Then oxyacetylene torches were used to cut through the ship's hull inside the lock and to cut manholes between all compartments for freedom of movement by the workers. Electric lights were strung for illumination and as a means of signaling an emergency order to evacuate the ship.

During the sealing of bulkheads, a control valve was installed in the bow section to bleed air from the vessel. The man on the release valve, misinterpreting some orders, shut down this bleeder valve. The bow began to go up as more air gathered there, increasing the pitch. McKenzie, aft, realized something was wrong when he saw the air around him and his crew turn milky—the result of rapid expansion and partial vaporizing from the drastic drop in air pressure.

Thinking the forward air lock had let go, McKenzie led his men in a mad scramble through four successive bulkhead manholes as the air whipping through tore off their hats and jackets and smashed clumps of coal and big flakes of rust against them. No one was hurt, and later they all thought it had been a very funny incident.

Lifting began again in May 1927. Began was all. They could raise either end at will, but the 33-degree port list remained; Cox's efforts to remedy this took on the flavor of high comedy. On the *Moltke*'s starboard side he hung a three-hundred-ton section of a raised destroyer, filled with two hundred tons of water. He sealed side tanks and bunkers, then blew those on the portside and watered those on the starboard. Next he pinned two sections of dry dock to the starboard side with a series of twenty 9-inch cables, and filled *them* with water.

On May 20, another lift was attempted. Interior pressure was brought up to twenty-two pounds; finally the nose came up. There was a slight list, but not bad.

Then one of the 9-inch lifting cables parted. A second went, then a third. Fourth. Fifth. Cox bellowed to slack all of them off, easing the pressure; fifteen of the twenty held. Examination by divers showed they had not broken with the strain, but had been cut through on the sharp deck edges by the *Moltke*'s enormous weight.

Smooth metal pads were placed between each cable and the cutting edge, and the lift was begun again. As the bow came up, the list decreased to a negligible 3 degrees. At 1:15 P.M. the stern came up and the whole huge vessel broke water like a surfacing whale, great waterspouts twenty feet high leaping and spurting around her as the 22 psi of air bled down to the 10 psi needed to maintain buoyancy.

On June 16, the tow for Lyness began. The intervening time, sixteen hours a day, had been spent in blasting away the superstructure, funnels, masts, and other top hamper. A gale was blowing up, and the two Macs were worried about the midships gun turret, which they had wanted to remove and which Cox had refused to bother with. The gun turret dug into the bottom, and *Moltke* lurched to a stop. They had to cut away the gun—unfortunately, the toughest metal known at that time—and then sling the huge battle cruiser just as they had the destroyers. The docks could not have begun to support her dead weight, but with the ship already buoyant, they furnished enough extra lift to get her beached on Cava Island.

They then had to lighten her further for the 280-mile tow to the Rosyth Shipbreaking Yard on the Scottish mainland. This entailed running a standard-gauge railroad line out across the bottom of the overturned vessel's hull for a three-ton railroad crane truck. Six-foot openings replaced the air locks, and 10-ton floating cranes were brought alongside to remove the ship's machinery. In all, they took off two thousand tons of steel and iron, and another one thousand tons of non-ferrous metals and armor plate. They also set a world's record for oxyacetylene torches by cutting a foot of 12-inch steel plate every three minutes.

THE VON MOLTKE TOW—UPSIDE DOWN

Cox decided to tow her upside down and stern first, which meant bolting heavy steel towing bollards to the propeller bosses, and setting up a kitchen, a bunkhouse, a messroom, and a powerhouse full of compressors on the bottom of the ship.

It also meant finding a place to put the vessel at Rosyth in the Firth of Forth so it could be cut up for the purchasers, Alloa Shipbreaking Company. Cox finally talked the Admiralty into letting him use one of their empty dry docks to hold the vessel once it arrived. He thought. He desperately needed money to keep operating, and the *Moltke* was worth £60,000; but his bankers refused to lend anything on a vessel still at Scapa Flow that was valuable only at Rosyth.

The trip began on May 18, 1928, with three tugs (*Seefalke*, *Simson*, *Pontos*) from Bugsier, Reederei and Bergungs, Hamburg, doing the towing. Cox was aboard, as was McKenzie; as soon as they got into the Pentland Firth, an unseasonable gale blew up, which made the overturned hulk begin rolling and spilling her air. They could not run for shelter, because if the *Moltke* was allowed to broach to, she would tip, fill, and sink. Their twenty feet of freeboard soon were reduced to six.

When the gale finally cleared and the rolling stopped, Cox had himself let off at Wick, muttering, "I myself am damned glad to get off her"—but it was characteristic that he refused to leave until the danger to his men had passed.

Cox went on to Rosyth, where he was met by a bland-faced official who announced he would have to refuse entry when the ship arrived.

"I'm sorry, but those are the Admiralty's orders."

Cox rushed furiously to London, there to learn that the experts were afraid the capsized ship would smash their dock. They wanted security against damage; he had nothing but the *Moltke*, so he signed her over as security. This was serious, as he could not begin breaking up the ship until any possible Admiralty damage claim might be settled, but he had no other choice.

Back in Rosyth, he engaged the Admiralty pilot to meet the *Moltke*; by an incredible mix-up, the captain of the tug *Seefalke* had engaged the Firth of Forth pilot.

The two pilots got into a screaming match over jurisdiction and precedence, while the *Moltke* was proceeding with monstrous upside-down dignity directly at the big central pier of the Firth Bridge. It was obvious that the tugs would pass to one side of the pier, the *Moltke* to the other—if it cleared at all.

Only one thing to do. They immediately had to cast off all towlines, thus giving the *Moltke* another historic first: it was the first capital ship in recorded naval lore to pass under a major bridge out of control, upside down, and unattended. River traffic was in a terrible snarl, with ships and boats scooting off in all directions amid black and bitter curses, before they brought their unruly charge under control.

Cox's divers had worked in the empty dock, setting up shoring which would, they hoped, be an accurate template of the ship's truncated top hamper, so the dock would not be injured. The ship was eased in, the water gingerly pumped out.

Cox waited; sure enough, one morning to Scapa Flow came an official Admiralty envelope that contained a bill for damages to His Majesty's dry dock at Rosyth, and a letter ordering him to pay those damages forthwith against seizure of the *Moltke* as security.

He sat with the folded bill in his hand for several minutes, afraid to open it and look at it. Then, with an act as much mental as physical, Cox unfolded the paper to look at the figure.

The bill was for £8.

THE UNSTABLE *SEYDLITZ*

Meanwhile, work already was well along on the 26,000-ton *Seydlitz*. She was 656 feet long, 104 feet in the beam, lying on her starboard side in eleven fathoms. Even at high water, some twenty-five feet of her portside were above the surface. Cox, after looking her over, came to the incredible decision that he was going to raise her *sideways*. The two Macs gave loud, raucous cries of doom, but he was adamant. They would seal all openings on the portside of her midline, pump her full of air, and pop her out of the mud.

Because he was short of money, he removed eighteen hundred tons of 12-inch steel plate from the portside to be sold for scrap in America. This was to come back to haunt him; eventually, for balance, he had to replace it with eighteen hundred tons of gravel shoveled in by hand. Then he had her divided into eight watertight compartments that could be blown independently of each other. Eight air locks were placed: converted boilers six feet high with six-foot diameters.

Sealing and strengthening the bulkheads took until Christmas 1926. Some of the patches were larger even than on the *Hindenburg*: more than a thousand square feet. The stern was tight and dry by February, with the rest of the vessel ready by June 1927.

When they started the lift, both stern and bow had been raised and lowered separately and experimentally, and all seemed well. On June 20, it began. She came alive, keeping dead level. Cox had done it: for the first time in history, a vessel had been raised on her side!

When *Seydlitz* had three inches of freeboard, there was a sudden muffled thud deep within the vessel's bow. Cox immediately ordered air released from all compartments, but it was too late: another dull thud.

Bulkheads were collapsing under the heavy pressure, and the whole forward part of the ship was common. The bows came rearing up like a growth-encrusted sea monster, paused, quivered . . .

The *Seydlitz* rolled upside down and sank.

The ship ended up in fairly deep water at a 48-degree angle, kept from rolling completely over by her top hamper's being jammed in the mud. She had carried all their air compressors over with her, had thrust underwater over half their air locks. It took until the end of September, while crews inside were sealing the starboard half of the hull, for the divers to cut away the bridge and other superstructure, which had prevented her from ending up on an even, if upside down, keel.

A lift was attempted in the first week of October; she came up, reducing her list from 48 degrees to twenty—when she flopped the other way for a 50-degree list. They tried again and again, but the ship just was not stable. By November 1, they had brought the *Seydlitz* up a staggering *forty times* without ever getting trim.

Cox was furious now. He cut the ends off a bunch of big steel boilers so he could fill them with quick-hardening cement once they had been placed on the bottom under the low side of the listing *Seydlitz*. This time, when she was lowered again, the edge of the hull jammed against the steel cylinders. That put her on an even keel, and they began rebalancing her. On the October 25 lift she came up listing 25 degrees—but stable. To correct the list, Cox pinned one of his indispensable drydock sections, flooded, to the high side with twenty-two 9-inch wire cables.

On November 1, they brought her up with the bow a bit raised, but with the vessel essentially stable. Then ten of the twenty-two cables holding the dock to her side snapped, one after another, with heavy explosions like cannon shots. No one could figure out why they didn't all go, as is usual in a series breakage of that sort; but then they saw that the *Seydlitz* had begun rolling, breaking ten of them, then had stopped rolling, saving the other twelve.

She had stopped with a list of only 8 degrees.

At Lyness, in preparation for the tow to Rosyth, they got seven more feet of freeboard by the removal of inner machinery and by blasting off her forward gun turret. This was a mixed blessing: it removed, in her topsy-turvy position, a good deal of her stabilizing weight.

The tow started in May 1928, with McKenzie in charge. The weather reports were good, and they had a fourteen-foot freeboard. As usual, an enormous gale blew up as soon as they hit the open water. She was very unstable, with huge seas sweeping her from end to end, soaking everything, including the food. They spilled so much air from under her sides that freeboard was down to five feet.

Four sleepless days later the storm eased off a bit. Every air compressor had been banging away at full speed just to keep up with the spillage of air; if even one had failed, they would have foundered. In the midst of this came a classic query from the tug master.

"Can you raise the ship a little, Mac?"

Mac's reply has been lost to history. They made the Rosyth dry dock on the sixth day with only the whaleback-like bottom of the giant cruiser not awash, and dry-docked it upside down as the *Von Moltke* had been.

NEW TRICKS TO RAISE THE *KAISER*

In December 1927, a month after the *Seydlitz* had been raised successfully, Cox put his crews to work on the 24,500-ton *Kaiser*, which was lying bottom up with an 8-degree list in thirteen fathoms of water. The same methods were used: concrete patches, wood plugs, bulkheads strengthened and made watertight, air locks fixed on the hull leading into each separate section. To keep her on an even keel, the longitudinal bulkheads between port and starboard stokeholds were made tight so different pressures could be maintained in the two sides.

Ships are very unstable at the point in a lift at which they hover between positive and negative buoyancy, so Cox used his concrete-filled cylinders again on the seabed below the *Kaiser*'s port keel. He knew that a few tons of displacement too much on one side or the other would tilt her the degree or two necessary to send thousands of tons of water rushing athwartship, destroying months of work.

He also came up with a new idea, which he would explain to no one. First, a boiler full of concrete was sunk a ship's length aft while they were still sealing her. In March 1928, just before they made the lift attempt, he had the solid steel propeller shafts from the *Seydlitz* and *Moltke* brought out on barges and moored nearby, along with several sets of two-hundred-ton crane tackles.

The lift started on March 20; almost immediately, Cox was sent into one of his towering rages. A lad named Sandy Thomson had forgotten to remove the light bulbs from their jerry-built interior wiring, had ducked back aboard, and had been caught by the lift. Cox had an inflexible rule, as a safety thing, that no one should be aboard at those times.

"Sorry, sir," said Thomson with a straight face, "but you said she had to be raised by tonight. So I went down to give her a push up."

It broke Cox up, abruptly terminating the tongue-lashing.

And the *Kaiser* was up that evening. By the thirtieth, the men were ready to start towing to Lyness. Cox stopped them. First he had cuts made in the form of a great rough square through all the decks directly around the vessel's heavy conning-tower section. Further cuts were made through the *Kaiser*'s hull, fore and aft, above the conning tower. Into

these, so that they lay on the old double bottom, were inserted the
steel propeller shafts from the *Seydlitz* and the *Moltke*, parallel, with
the two-hundred-ton crane tackles hung from them. Then everything
was made solid with cement.

The *Kaiser* was towed directly over the heavy cement-filled boiler
on the bottom, and Cox calmly released all of the air in the ship. Down
she went, smashing the conning tower onto the boiler with her entire
25,000 tons.

The conning tower was rammed right up inside the vessel, through
the holes in the decks above it. The two-hundred-ton tackle chains were
fastened to keep the huge mass of metal hanging up inside the ship,
and the air vents were shut and compressed air was fed back in. He thus
had made a neat shallow-draft package of the ship.

By mid-June the *Kaiser* was ready for the trip to Rosyth, which was
made with such ease that the compressors had to be run only two hours
in every twenty-four.

In May and June 1929, almost as a grace note, Cox salvaged the
4200-ton fast mine-laying cruiser *Bremse* from the north side of Scapa
Flow. The British sailors back in 1919 had tried to beach her and almost
had made it: she was lying capsized with a heavy list, her bows aground
but her stern in eleven fathoms of water. He divided her up into five
sections, made each watertight, and in July blasted away her bridge
superstructure and top hamper. Oil was encountered for the first time
in the *Bremse*; one flash explosion knocked the men about and singed
one of them.

Once she was tight, he parbuckled her to correct her 8-degree list,
using his L-shaped docks and 9-inch cables. She came up after two days
of blowing. Since she was a cranky ship, Cox broke her up at his Lyness
facilities.

SECOND *HINDENBURG* ATTEMPT

His heart wasn't in it, however. Cox was ready once more for the
Hindenburg. She had touched his pride, and he was determined to conquer her.

Work was begun in January 1930, with an overhaul and reoutfitting
of their four L-shaped floating dry-dock sections. By the end of April,
all four were in place over the wreck. Only three hundred patches had
to be replaced out of the original eight hundred, and a new one made to
cover the place where the ship's last remaining funnel had broken off
during the intervening years.

The greatest worry, of course, was instability. In pumping her out,
Cox knew there would be thousands of tons of water just waiting to

roll her again. So in January he cut out a slice thirty feet wide and forty feet long—the engine room—from one of the salvaged destroyers. He sank this vast wedge beside the *Hindenburg*, rammed it under her port quarter, and filled the wedge with six hundred tons of cement. The cement covered the battle cruiser's propeller and shaft housing on the portside.

In April, twenty-foot-high boiler shells, seven feet wide, flanged, were bolted over the main hatches to reach above the surface and serve as cofferdams. The entire bridge structure also was sealed to become a giant cofferdam. From a central control panel installed there, the six main pumping stations throughout the vessel could be centrally coordinated. Cranes were set up on floating docks alongside for the lowering of submersible pumps once the water level began falling. They began pumping on July 15, and the bow came up in just two hours. Ten feet of it were up without any list, three more than he had ever gotten in 1926. Nothing could go wrong—

Something did. She took a sudden heavy list . . . to *starboard*. She never had tipped that way before. Wearily, Cox had her set back down on the bottom, ordered the men to put a second forty-foot wedge under her starboard quarter, and then went off on a three-week vacation —his first since the operation had begun at Scapa Flow in March 1924.

When he returned, the lift was again begun and they quickly raised the bow to sixteen feet. Some of the plates near the stern, which was taking all of the vessel's vast weight, began buckling. Cox ignored them, gambling that the ship wouldn't break her back with 90 per cent of her in the water. With the bow still dead level, they brought up the stern successfully.

This was the only lift to which Cox brought his wife and daughter. This is partly due, perhaps, to the fact that if he tore a coat or got grease on a sleeve, his wife invariably would wail, "Oh, Father, *look* what you've done!" Whenever he walked across a slanting deck, she would cry, "Father, you'll *fall!*"

To which Father's only reply was a single word, muttered ferociously under his breath: "Women!"

But he was too proud of the *Hindenburg* to leave his ladies at home. The men expected a show, and they got it. When the deck was awash, Cox, wearing hip boots, went aboard to take possession. One of the men, overcome by the moment, leaped after him—and landed, not on the deck, but in a hole in the water-covered deck. He disappeared from view, reappearing in a few seconds crying piteously that he could not swim.

Cox dragged him out and then, in an excess of high spirits, hoisted him up for a piggyback ride to safety. Only Cox stepped in another hole and they both went down full length. The men froze, waiting for Cox's usual profane explosion of wrath as he reappeared. But his wife, Jenny, got in the first words.

"Oh, Father," wailed her clear feminine voice, "look at your *clothes!*"

The *Hindenburg* was towed to Rosyth on August 23, 1930, arriving there only three days later after an extremely easy passage.

Work went on, but Cox was doing it only out of his fierce pride. He was £20,000 out of pocket over all and wanted to break even. Work began on the 20,000-ton battle cruiser *Von der Tann*, even before the *Hindenburg* was ready for the tow to Rosyth. It was bottom up in fifteen fathoms, with a 17-degree starboard list, and they determined on the same procedure as with the *Kaiser:* clean the bottom, concrete the bottom valves, and fix air locks.

FOUL AIR ON THE VON DER TANN

There were two major differences, however. The air locks had to be much longer to reach the surface, for there were four fathoms of water over the portside and seven over the starboard. Second, foul air was encountered from the decaying animal and vegetable matter aboard.

Cox was most concerned for the safety of the men, flushing her twice with fresh air as soon as the first air lock was in place. When minor fires and small explosions from oxyacetylene burning continued, he had the ship sprayed with a chemical antidote that smelled as putrid as the bad air, but was supposed to remove the danger of fire.

It didn't. As they were sealing the vessel's final bulkhead, they cut through a pipe filled with foul air. It exploded. McKenzie was blown right up a ladder to smack his head against the bottom of a hatch coaming. He was found floating face down in the water and spent several days in the hospital. The three men with the torch were blown backward into the compartment, which immediately began flooding through the shattered bulkhead. They scrambled for the highest corner, where what air there was would be trapped, and there they stayed with water to their necks until, three hours later, rescuers cut through the hull with torches.

Von der Tann was refloated at the end of November, and on February 5, 1931, was towed to Lyness Pier. Scrap-metal prices had fallen so disastrously with the depression that Cox did not even bother to break her up, but instead started immediate work on the *Prinz-Regent Luitpold*, a 25,000-ton twin of the *Kaiser*, lying capsized and with an 18-degree port list in a discouraging eighteen fathoms of water.

FIRST FATALITY: *PRINZ-REGENT LUITPOLD*

Much higher air pressure would be needed to refloat her because of this, along with a remarkable length of air lock in order to reach the surface. They needed forty-four feet just to clear the water on the starboard side, and sixty feet on the port. They decided on twelve sections, with an air lock for each. Work began in May; almost immediately they encountered foul air. They flushed the ship several times with compressed air, and again used chemicals. The ship also contained so much coal dust and burnt oil that the men often worked in smoke helmets.

Despite all the precautions, there was an explosion in the extreme foresection of the hull on May 27. Apparently, when they had exhausted the air in a compartment to bring the water level up, the water had brought with it a gas bubble that was expelled into the section and somehow ignited. Two men were badly burned; a carpenter named William Tait was knocked unconscious. Water rushed in through started rivet holes and the sprung air lock, so the men had to climb to the surface through a cascade of water to escape.

McKenzie, Peterson, and Sandy Thomson made repeated attempts to get down to Tait, but he drowned before they reached him. This death signaled the end at Scapa Flow for Ernest Cox. He finished the *Von der Tann*—lifting commenced on July 8, and she was up three days later with ten feet of freeboard—but he quickly sold the *Bayern*, the final vessel he owned on the bottom, along with his entire Lyness plant, to McCrone and Hardy of the Alloa Shipbreaking Company. After this firm was absorbed by Metal Industries Group, an immense British consortium, work went forward at Scapa Flow along the lines Cox had established. Most of his crew, including the two Macs, remained on.

Ernest Cox showed a net loss of £10,000 on his eight years at Scapa Flow; but while he had been pouring his tremendous drive and curious creativity into the raising of those shadowy monsters from the ocean floor, his neglected scrap-metal business had made him a millionaire.

Cox lived until 1959, traveling, organizing, throwing his immense drive into the defense of Britain during World War II. But none of it had the savor and salt for him that Scapa Flow had had. He, and the sunken German fleet, were a strange marriage of man and purpose that together form an epic accomplishment unequaled in the history of salvage, and indeed seldom equaled in the history of individual human endeavor.

BOX SCORE FOR ERNEST J. COX

1924

Destroyer	V-70	750 tons	August 1
Destroyer	S-53	750 tons	August 13
Destroyer	S-55	750 tons	August 29
Destroyer	G-91	750 tons	September 12
Destroyer	G-38	750 tons	September 27
Destroyer	S-52	750 tons	October 13

1925

Destroyer	H-145	750 tons	March 14
Destroyer	S-136	750 tons	April 3
Destroyer	S-36	750 tons	April 18
Destroyer	S-138	750 tons	May 1
Destroyer	S-65	750 tons	May 16
Destroyer	S-56	750 tons	June 5
Destroyer	S-32	750 tons	June 19
Destroyer	G-39	750 tons	July 3
Destroyer	G-86	750 tons	July 14
Destroyer	G-40	750 tons	July 29
Destroyer	V-129	750 tons	August 11
Destroyer	V-78	750 tons	September 7
Destroyer	G-103	1300 tons	September 30
Destroyer	B-110	1300 tons	December 11

1926

Destroyer	B-112	1300 tons	February 11
Destroyer	B-111	1300 tons	March 8
Destroyer	B-109	1300 tons	March 27
Destroyer	G-101	1300 tons	April 13
Destroyer	G-104	1300 tons	April 30

1927

Battle cruiser	*Moltke*	23,000 tons	June 10

1928

Battle cruiser	*Seydlitz*	25,000 tons	November 2

1929

Battleship	*Kaiser*	24,500 tons	March 20
Light cruiser	*Bremse*	4000 tons	November 27

1930

Battle cruiser *Hindenburg*   28,000 tons   July 22
Battle cruiser *Von der Tann*   20,000 tons   December 7

1931

Battleship *Prinz-Regent Luitpold*   25,000 tons   July 9

Total ships raised: 32   Total tonnage raised: 172,000

CHAPTER SIXTEEN

Seal and Blow

The impact of Cox at Scapa on the art of marine salvage has been incalculable; but it was slow in becoming apparent. Mechanical lifts remained the order of the day for many years, with some salvors suspicious of the idea of compressed air to raise vessels. And meanwhile, divers, being a highly individualistic bunch, went their idiosyncratic ways. Many of those early hard-hat boys liked to tip a glass or two, and a few of them indulged that particular appetite even when on the job—once, at least, with deadly results.

DIVERS' TALES

It was at Lough Swilly during World War I. A torpedoed ship had been beached there for repairing, and one of the divers down in the hold found a case of whiskey several fathoms below the surface. Cork is compressible, but this diver didn't mind a bit of seawater mixed with his whiskey,[1] so he smuggled a bottle to the surface.

He and two other divers broached it that night, with him taking the first healthy swig. Within a few moments he collapsed, and before they could even bring a medic, he was dead. On his breath was the odor of bitter almonds.

In the cargo had been a quantity of cyanide, which had dissolved into the sea water trapped in the hold and thus had entered the whiskey bottle past the loosened cork.

Another case occurred following the war. Divers were breaking the cargo out of a sunken ship and sending it up to the surface in slings; but one man sent up virtually nothing despite having been down in one of the holds for a number of hours.

When he finally emerged and climbed the ladder, he seemed to be a bit unsteady.

"Are you all right?" asked his tender anxiously after he had unscrewed the helmet.

"I'm all right, qui' all right," mumbled the diver.

The man obviously was drunk; most odd, since he had gone down sober. The Chief Salvage Officer checked the diver's breath the next morning, pronounced him "sober as a horse at a funeral," and sent him below.

He came up reeling drunk.

The Salvage Officer checked the cargo manifest; sure enough, there had been several cases of whiskey in the hold in which this particular diver was working. But how was it getting inside the diver?

The ship, in heeling over and sinking, had trapped air in the angle between the bulkhead and the top of the hold. Soon after discovering the whiskey, the diver discovered this air bubble—where the pressure was, of course, the same as that in his diving suit. He took a bottle up with him, sat on top of a crate with his helmet above water, unscrewed his faceplate, knocked the head off the bottle, and got quietly drunk sixty feet below the surface.

Any shift in the vessel's attitude sufficient to move the air bubble away from his corner would have drowned him; but, as Robert H. Davis once remarked, "Divers cannot afford to suffer from nerves."

Another diver without nerves was one engaged in the mundane job of cleaning a ship's bottom with a couch-grass brush and other tools of the trade. His tender, happening to glance over the side, saw the man's cleaning tools floating on the surface.

He immediately signaled the diver by telephone, demanding anxiously if anything was wrong. No answer. Repeated calls produced no reaction. Alarmed now, the tender tried the old hand signals that every diver knows. These finally elicited a telephone response.

"What the hell do you want?" demanded the diver.

"What are you doing now?" asked the Salvage Officer, who had observed the tender's efforts.

"Doing? Why, scrubbing my guts out on this blinking hull. What d'ye think I'm doing?"

"Indeed?" purred the Salvage Officer. "What are you scrubbing it with? Your knuckles?"

There was a long and pregnant pause as the diver searched frantically about him for the cleaning tools that were floating at the surface.

He had been asleep.

Another British salvage diver, James Citrine, had such a great reputation that the Liverpool Salvage Association once sent him to the Cape Verde Islands just to search out the leak in the hull of a wooden ship. Citrine said grumpily that he'd never known a diver to find a leak in a wooden ship yet, but he went.

Several divers had searched and quit, and aboard was a Spanish diver who had been equally unsuccessful. The diving stage, rigged fore and aft beneath the ship's bottom, was still in place. Citrine got on his gear and went below.

The harbor lay open to the Atlantic, so there was a good swell, which of course made Citrine's footing rather hazardous. He had been down less than two minutes when an unexpected surge made him lose his balance and thrust out his hand to steady himself.

He stuck his arm right into the hole they sought.

He had no telephone in the antiquated diving suit he was wearing, so he merely gave the *I am fouled; send diver* signal. The Spaniard was jammed into a suit and sent to the rescue. Citrine grabbed his arm, guided it into the hole, pulled his own arm out, and surfaced. He unsuited, told them the Spaniard was guarding their hole, and left for England again.

The ship was repaired, and Citrine's reputation soared.

Although Britain's dominance of marine salvage actually had been increased by World War I, salvage operations *did* go on elsewhere in the world. On the Dvina River in Russia, not far from the Arctic Circle, Russian divers continued operations on one sunken vessel straight through the winter.

They were working in a river, which was frozen to a depth of three or four feet. They merely chopped holes in the ice, set up compressors beside them, and sent the divers down. Their tenders kept skim ice from forming on the holes, in addition to tending the lines.

One of the few confirmed attacks by a squid on a diver occurred in December 1923, when French diver Jean Negrey was working on the sunken battleship *Liberté* in Toulon Harbor. The animal dropped on his back, entwining its tentacles with his air and life lines so he had to be brought to the surface. Even then it would not let go until it was hacked to pieces—with the diver in much greater danger from the axe than he was from the obviously terrified squid.

American divers also got involved in some odd affairs shortly after the war. In 1921 a small motor barge that ran cargo across a corner of the Gulf of Mexico between Galveston, Texas, and Tampico, Mexico, struck floating debris off the Mexican coast, flooded, and went down in shoal water.

The crew got off in a twenty-foot lifeboat, sent word to the owner, and waited until diver Glen Blake arrived from Corpus Christi, Texas. Blake had come in a hurry, with just his suit and compressor, so he had to use the lifeboat as a diving boat. They lashed the hand pump down amidships and rigged a diving ladder aft, and Blake went over the side.

While he was down, a dozen sharks showed up. One of the two men on the hand pump, between stints, whacked one of them on the head with a crowbar.

The result was spectacular: the big fish came clear of the water with a leap that would have shamed a marlin—and landed right smack amidships in the small, crowded boat. His lashing tail snapped the ¾-inch steel pump handle right off, and soon opened a score of seams, so the boat began shipping water badly.

Everyone was aft, keeping the pump between himself and the shark, when somebody remembered that no air had been going below to Blake since the fish had come aboard. The pumpers distracted the shark while the tenders dragged the diver up. He was blue in the face but still breathing; as they yanked off his belt and iron shoes, somebody else grabbed his heavy diver's knife from his belt and used it on the shark.

Blake survived; the shark didn't.

Somewhere around the same time, two New York divers, Billy Burke and Al Blumberg, were dispatched to Florida to patch the bottom of a good-sized schooner that had stove in her hull on an Everglades river.

The two men found the job conventional except for one thing—alligators. The river teemed with them. And on the boat was a single, small-caliber rifle with only a few rounds of ammunition. The site was very isolated, the owners were in a hurry, and sending downriver for additional weapons would delay the operation.

It finally was decided that the schooner's first mate would be on deck with the gun while they were below; two crewmen with pike poles would ward off close attacks; and a piece of "heavy artillery" would be rigged up for pre-emptive strikes.

This heavy artillery was a grindstone slung from the end of a movable boom. The job of repairing the thirty-foot hole in the hull took Burke and Blumberg several months; during that time the grindstone man became so expert that few of the alligators even survived—let alone attacked the divers.

During World War I, all of the Allies' ship-salvage work in European waters was carried out by the Royal Navy. The United States had a diving force, to be sure, but it was scattered from service to service throughout the Navy, with the heaviest concentration in the submarine service. When the hostilities ended, there was a sizable American cutback in both equipment and training for diving or salvage work until the twin sinkings, in the 1920s, of the submarines S-51 and S-4.[2]

U. S. NAVY'S WEAKNESS IN SALVAGE

It was only following these disasters that the U. S. Navy's Deep Sea Diving School was begun (1926). Apart from this school, the Navy maintained virtually no independent facilities for salvage work between the wars, depending instead on annual salvage contracts on a no-cure, no-pay basis with Merritt, Chapman and Scott Corporation. This firm operated stations at New York; New London, Connecticut; Key West, Florida; and Kingston, Jamaica.

War, of course, is one of the spurs that cause salvors to work out new methods; it also creates the greatest number of salvage jobs. Then ships are more important than lives or money, and the work goes forward at any cost and under any conditions. A quick look at the localized Spanish Civil War between July 18, 1936, and March 29, 1939, when the Loyalist government surrendered to Franco's Falangists, shows what this can mean. During that time, 148 ships were sunk along the Spanish coasts, which in normal times would see a dozen sinkings a year at most. Between 1939 and the end of 1941, 107 of these ships were salvaged.

The Spanish guns were barely still when Hitler invaded Poland on September 1, 1939. Between the time the United States entered the war, in December 1941, and July 1942, four hundred ocean-going Allied vessels were sunk by enemy submarines, mines, and surface craft—*along the Atlantic Coast, and in the Caribbean and the Gulf of Mexico!*

The U. S. Navy, with no salvage savvy or equipment of its own, just could not cope with such hideous attrition. There was a wondrous flap as everyone began trying to do everything at once. Commander W. A. Sullivan was rushed over to survey British ship-salvage operations; he recommended the establishment by the Navy of the Atlantic and Pacific Salvage Services.

But all it resulted in, between 1939 and 1947, was a new contract with Merritt, Chapman and Scott. This one was a cost-plus, fixed-fee contract for work on Navy ships, for which the salvage firm received $19 million. Not that the civilian salvors did a poor job; they didn't. That

$19 million resulted in the salving of $675 million worth of shipping under the direction of the Navy's superintendent of salvage.

Following the burning and capsizing of the *Lafayette* (really the French liner *Normandie*) at New York's Pier 88,[3] the Navy hurriedly established the Naval Training School (Salvage). Shipyards began designing and building special salvage vessels to Navy specifications (such as deepwater rescue tugs like the *Foundation Josephine*); and these two factors resulted in a highly organized Navy salvage group by 1945.

For this group the Navy likes to claim the staggering harbor clearance projects in North Africa, Sicily, Europe, and the Far East, which resulted in the reclamation of ships and equipment worth more than $2 billion by war's end. But as we shall see in the next section, in places such as North Africa the incredible results were wrought by a pitiful handful of brilliant and dedicated men, working against almost insane odds and usually without the support (and sometimes with the active hostility) of ranking American and British brass in the area, who could not understand the importance of the Navy's salvage efforts.

A decision finally was made, and the Navy decommissioned the salvage school in 1957; Navy salvage personnel are now trained at the Deep Sea Diving School, situated in the U. S. Naval Weapons Plant, Washington, D.C.

In the European theater there was relatively little shallow-water salvage as such; there just wasn't time. Most of the work was done in harbor clearance, or on stranded ships driven up on Allied-held beaches. Often, those in shallow water that were not actually blocking harbors were left where they were until the war's end, when work could be done on them under less-mad conditions.

Typical of these was HMS *Breconshire*, which was sunk near Marsaxlokk, Malta, by a German air raid in March 1942. As far as practicable, the cargo of oil and heavy war matériel was removed from the 9600-ton ship then, but the 475-foot-long carcass, sixty-six feet wide and thirty-eight feet deep, was left where it was: on its portside with an 81-degree list in sixty feet of water.

Seven years later, in May 1949, the Admiralty's Boom Defense Department was ordered to remove the hulk. Salvage masters O. T. Harrison, C. Jones, and A. T. Brown determined that the superstructure should be completely removed, and that the vessel should then be divided into working sections, much as Cox had done at Scapa, with spill holes and air connections in each compartment.

Eight divers with cutting torches soon removed the superstructure, as well as the oil and the rest of the cargo—including bombs. They found that five steel plates were missing from her hull; the reason, of course, why she had sunk. Then they moved inside, working often in total darkness as they sealed oil tanks, put in vent holes and air connections, and removed loose steel work and plating.

Eventually they found the five missing plates on the sea floor and brought them up so that forge workers ashore could roll them out flat. Then the divers took them down and replaced them on the *Breconshire* so that the ship could be made tight all around for blowing.

In August, three salvage vessels (*Dispenser, Retrieve, Sea Salvor*) moored around the sunken craft and banged compressed air into her. On the ninth the bow lifted and the ship immediately heeled over to 120 degrees, as Harrison and his assistants had foreseen. Pressing went on.

Suddenly, in a mere six seconds, the *Breconshire*'s bow rolled through 35 degrees to end up at the surface in a slather of foam, bottom up, 25 degrees off vertical. By August 14, the stern had been brought up and she had been trimmed with a 10-degree port list. On August 31, she was towed to the ship breakers.

UNCONVENTIONAL METHODS AT MASSAWA

Although not strictly a shallow-water operation, the repair job done on HMS *Dido* perhaps belongs here as an illustration of the way salvors had to improvise in the war's early years—and of why they didn't have time to search out shallow-water wrecks. In 1942 the light cruiser *Dido* was one of *only four* operative Allied warships in the entire Mediterranean. All were light cruisers, and enough of their armor had been removed in an attempt to meet the League of Nations' size-and-weight limitations that *Dido, Euryalus,* and *Cleopatra* all had been damaged by the concussion from near misses by German bombs.

Dido could limp along, but she was in no condition to fight, for her stern beneath the engine room was flooded. She needed repairs fast; but the Alexandria facilities were tied up with the damaged *Valiant* and *Elizabeth*[4] and the facilities that Commander Edward Ellsberg was just getting pieced together at Massawa[5] in the Red Sea could not handle a ship of the *Dido*'s size. That meant South Africa, five thousand miles away—reducing by one fourth the Allies' effective naval fighting force in the area for several weeks.

Ellsberg went to Alexandria and there convinced the higher brass that he could take *Dido* at Massawa. She was of 7500 tons displacement, 530 feet long; and Ellsberg's only operable dry dock was 410 feet long, with a lifting capacity of only six thousand tons. But he convinced them.

His proposed method was simple if unconventional. Since only the *Dido*'s stern was damaged, he planned to run the stern up on the too-short dry dock and leave the bow floating at nearly its normal

draught. The craft would be secured fore and aft with steel hawsers to prevent her sliding down the slanting deck; to prevent strain on the ship's hull, he would not unwater the dry dock's forward compartments as much as the after ones, thus fitting it to the angle of the cruiser's keel.

Dido arrived on August 18, 1942, and was successfully placed in the dry dock. There was a good deal more damage than the ship's captain had expected: steel stringers would have to be installed in the stern; cracked steel plates would have to be replaced; by the starboard propeller was an enormous crack through a double thickness of plate as large as a garage door; on the portside was a similar, smaller crack. There were cracked girders inside.

All that the Royal Navy could give him was twelve days for the job. Ellsberg, before he saw the extent of the damage, said they would do it in eight. After the damage had been surveyed, the British foremen (four of them) and thirty shipyard mechanics who had been sent along with the ship said that even twelve days would not be enough; Ellsberg countered by signaling the fleet to send him the second of the cruisers at the end of *six* days.

Then he told the civilian mechanics that at Massawa in wartime every man did every job of which he was capable. No union hours, he told them; no tea breaks. It was three 8-hour shifts of ten men each day, and if they didn't want that, they should pack up and leave.

"We'll have a go at it, anyway, Captain," said the head foreman.

The damaged steel was removed in three days; the repairs, most of them, were completed in five. But the doubler, or outer-course plate, was not in place by the morning of the sixth day. Six inches from the top of this plate was a sharp knuckle in the ship's counter. The existing plates had to be matched by a sharp fold, or knuckle, in the replacement plate if it were to be riveted and welded for the correct watertight seal.

Ellsberg told them to knuckle it into place with sledge hammers.

The foreman objected, saying it was impossible, that it should have been done ashore in their keel bender with five hundred tons of pressure. Ellsberg informed him that in their jerry-built plate shop there was no keel bender, and then sent for his two best steel men, Bill Cunningham and Horace Armstrong. They were great brawlers and heavy drinkers—in Ellsberg's odd collection of salvors only because he had rescued them from the clutches of the Military Police. Ellsberg showed them the knuckling job.

"Now, boys, you see those Englishmen over there? It is their job to do this, only they say they can't. And what's more, Bill, and you, too, Horace, they say you can't either!"

The two men looked at one another, then at the steel—red hot now, at the li__ __e bent, from an acetylene torch directed by Lloyd

Williams. Then they started swinging their hammers, a blow from one man alternating with a blow from the other. Their only pauses were for Williams to heat up a new section of steel.

The fifteen feet of knuckling took them an hour and a half.

When they were finished, Cunningham asked Ellsberg if he needed any other little thing done aboard the *Dido*. When Ellsberg said he didn't, the massive steelworker turned to his companion: "C'mon then, Horace, we'd better get going back to that Eyetie dry dock an' *get some work in* this morning."

The *Dido* was afloat on August 25, the sixth day, when the next cruiser came in through the mouth of Massawa Harbor.

WARTIME SALVAGE IN THE PACIFIC

Over in the Pacific it was sometimes a different story. American salvage divers there often were sent down on ships sunk in shallow water. Not to raise them; there were no salvage facilities as such any closer than Pearl Harbor; but for a variety of other reasons. With the Japanese hospital ship *Moro Maru*, it was to determine what had sunk her.

The *Moro Maru* was very plainly marked: prescribed white mast with red cross near its tip; large red crosses on the deck; special lighting fixtures to illuminate the crosses when the ship was in darkness. Yet she had been sunk some fifteen miles seaward from Manila Bay in shallow water late in the war (1944) during the Battle of the Philippine Sea. The Japanese had issued a formal complaint to Geneva against the United States.

It was possible that in battle a hospital ship could sustain damage from a few direct hits that had gone wild, but to actually sink it would require sustained and carefully planned action. So the *Chanticleer*, a submarine rescue vessel doing duty as a general salvage ship, was anchored over the *Moro Maru*, and divers were sent down for a visual inspection of the ship.

They found all the hospital-ship markings, lights, and fixtures plainly visible in the clear water; they also found machine-gun-bullet holes across her decks, which showed that the vessel had been strafed. But then master diver Joseph Karneke began to find discrepancies. All the charts were missing. All the books were gone from the shelves. Yet on the captain's bunk was the Japanese skipper's full-dress uniform carefully laid out.

He reported this topside, where two experts from the official investigating board ashore (the salvors dubbed all such officials "the SOBs from out of town") were waiting impatiently. Before they could react to this odd piece of news, a fantail comedian called down through

Karneke's phone in an official voice: "They want to know if the captain is in the uniform."

Part of Karneke's assignment was to find military reasons why American ships or aircraft might have sunk the ship. These would include such violations of a hospital ship's neutral status as armaments or contraband (materials not useful in running a hospital ship). In his investigation he found no such contraband or armaments, but also found no mortal damage to the ship and, oddest of all, no bodies. If the *Moro Maru* had been sunk by American action, how had the Japanese been able to evacuate all the wounded from the wards? Why had not one crewman been killed?

On the third day, the divers discovered a detonator fuse—but nothing to detonate. Not even a pistol. One diver cut himself on a bayonet; it turned out to be a medical scalpel. A diver named Pitman was sent into the engine room to look for a reason for the sinking, but he fell off a ladder and knocked his air valve wide open. This rammed him up against the top of the compartment in a blow-up, so his air had to be cut down from the *Chanticleer*. In descending, he got hopelessly hung up on the engine-room valves.

As they were trying to get him loose, air raid warnings were sounded, so they had to take a terrible chance and jerk him to the surface—hoping they wouldn't rupture his lines, which somehow they didn't—and then the *Chanticleer* had to cut and run for it.

They never got back to the ship. When the brass demanded to know why it had sunk, the only reason they could adduce was that the Japanese had opened the sea cocks and deliberately scuttled her.

Shortly after the unsatisfactory operation of the *Moro Maru*, the divers of the *Chanticleer* got involved in the examination of a Japanese ship whose papers may have had a marked influence on the ending of the war. During the Second Battle of the Philippine Sea, in November 1944, scores of ships were sent to the bottom by bombs, mines, torpedoes, and gunfire. Many of these were in reasonably shallow water, and the divers were instructed to examine these for secret papers or other information concerning the Japanese war effort.

JAPAN'S "UNSINKABLE" *NACHI*

Karneke descended to a heavy cruiser lying with a 20-degree starboard list in less than a hundred feet of water. He did not know what ship it was, so he began searching for papers. First he came across a gun tub still manned by its drowned crew. All of them were frozen in their positions of the moment at which the blast had killed them and ruptured their stomachs. The gases that normally would have floated them thus escaped, and they remained there at their posts. He found that their faces had been eaten away down to the bone by crabs.

In the charthouse he found an unusual number of charts and papers lying about, so he gathered them all up. These greatly excited their resident Naval Intelligence officer; the divers were ordered to search minutely for all papers—personal and otherwise.

Karneke's papers identified her as the fabled *Nachi*, flagship of Vice Admiral Kiyoshide Shima, which the Japanese Navy had boasted was indestructible. In the past, she had shaken off five-hundred-pound bombs, torpedoes, rockets, and direct hits by shellfire. But she had been caught trying to escape from Manila Bay on November 5, 1944, and had absorbed a dose of nine torpedoes, thirteen 1000-pound bombs, six 250-pound bombs, and sixteen rockets. She had finally gone down.

Karneke found that each compartment of the vessel was a watertight shell without doors or hatches, so that damage was localized totally to the compartment hit. The decks, also, had been as heavily armored as the hull, with thick layers of steel plate.

The divers worked in teams, with one man tending the other's lines as he entered unknown compartments. While the working diver of one team was ramming books and documents into a mailbag, his partner left his lines to wander down a corridor and into a compartment in search of souvenirs.

But the list of the *Nachi* made the door swing shut behind him, cutting off his light. He panicked, forgetting that he could just follow his own lines back out, and started screaming. His partner had to rescue him; there was no more souvenir hunting aboard the *Nachi*.

"Few things are as good for discipline," Karneke remarked, "as to hear a man scream on the bottom."

While cutting through a compartment wall with oxyacetylene, Karneke ignited some of his own torch's unburned gas and was knocked out when his telephone, blown from its well, struck him in the temple. He came around, still dazed, stuck his leg through the hole he had cut, and felt his iron boot seized in a terrible grip. It took another diver, Krassic, twenty minutes to free him. Karneke was sent up while Krassic carefully reconnoitered the unknown monster that had attacked so viciously.

After a few minutes, Krassic sent up a gleeful report. "Tell Karneke that the thing he had his foot caught in was a Japanese toilet!"

They finally found the ship's safe and blew it open with a putty-like material known as Composition C, which was twice as powerful as TNT. A diver named Posey was sent down to check, and reported that it was full of money.

Posey was ordered to return immediately, but he said that he was fouled. Then he said it would be just a few minutes more. Finally he came up. At his belt, his shoes, his cuffs, any place he could think of, wads of money were visible. When his helmet was removed, he was able to see what a poor job he had done of hiding it.

"Jeez," he marveled, "how'd all this stuff get stuck to me?"

It wouldn't have done him much good, as it was Japanese 10-yen notes: the *Nachi* had been pay ship for the Japanese fleet. Intelligence was delighted with the two million yen ($500,000) they had found, since Japanese currency for use in spy operations was always hard to come by. They were even more delighted, however, with the papers that the divers had found.

They contained, the Naval Intelligence officer told them later, "Japan's entire war plans and orders against the West, along with details of her defenses and preparations for meeting the coming invasion. Not often, if ever, has so much critical military intelligence turned up in one place."

Just after the war, Karneke was involved in another odd shallow-water salvage operation. The Navy, attempting to provide a refueling post for seaplanes, had sunk four immense neoprene balloons filled with aviation gasoline in California's Monterey Bay. They were held in place by a mesh of heavy wire strands that were gathered below the balloon in a point and then jointly anchored to a big clump of concrete with a cable. In the top of the balloon was an opening with a small hose leading to the surface and a fueling nozzle supported by a buoy.

The plane was to land, taxi up to the buoy, and refuel. No pumps were needed, since water pressure would push gasoline out the nozzle as soon as it was opened.

Unfortunately, the idea hadn't worked out. First, the swell in Monterey Bay had walked the anchor clumps about for several hundred feet. Passing boatmen, who had discovered that the aviation gas worked fine in boat motors if it was cut to an acceptable octane with kerosene, had emptied three of the four balloons. These had promptly collapsed.

The salvors' job was to recover the surviving balloon and find the three collapsed ones. Karneke went down to the six-foot-high clump of concrete with a lifting hook, which he was to put through the pad eye on top of the block. But the clump was bucking like a bronco in the swell as he tried to climb aboard. Finally he overinflated his suit enough so he could drift to the top of it and place his hook.

The crew on the diving boat lifted the balloon aboard to swing it in over the side. It hit the rail and split with a large *poof!* Hundreds of gallons of high-test aviation gas were dumped all over their boat.

For two hours they hosed and washed, nobody smoking, nobody wearing shoes, trying to get it washed into the sea. Of course they couldn't start the ship's engines, so they had to wait until the tide turned and dissipated the highly inflammable fuel.

Later they found and recovered the other three balloons.

The end of World War II produced in merchant-marine circles the same result as the end of World War I: an abrupt overabundance of freighters. As a result, a sunken ship's cargo was often much more important than the ship itself, especially if it was a scarce item such as foodstuffs.

SEVEN MILLION CANS OF SALMON

The 5525-ton freighter *Diamond Knot* was en route to Seattle, Washington, from the Bristol Bay ports in August 1947, down to her Plimsoll line with 154,316 cases (7,407,168 cans) of choice Alaska salmon, cannery equipment, herring oil, salted fish, and a small cannery tender. The salmon alone was worth $3.5 million. At 1:15 A.M. on August 14, in the Juan de Fuca Strait between Vancouver Island and the state of Washington during a dense fog, the heavily laden freighter was struck by the 10,681-ton *Fenn Victory* six miles north of Port Angeles.

A full fourteen feet of the *Victory*'s prow was sunk in the *Knot*'s side; the two ships were carried westward by an ebbing tide as two tugs, *Matilda Foss* and *Foss No. 21*, tried to free them with burning-torches. When they finally succeeded, they took the *Knot* in tow stern first toward Crescent Bay's sheltered waters. The Nos. 2 and 3 holds filled with water, however, and she kept riding lower until the crew was evacuated. At 8:45 A.M., in the heavy tidal currents off Tongue Point Reef, *Diamond Knot* rolled onto her starboard side and went down in 135 feet of water.

The insurance companies paid off, then asked Walter Martignoni, San Francisco salvage master, to attempt recovery. He brought in a crew of men headed by master divers Walter McCray and Fred Devine. After a preliminary survey dive, Martignoni decided that the wreck was not salvageable but that the cargo was.

Electromagnets were ruled out because of the depth and the small amount of iron in the salmon tins; extreme currents prevented underwater stevedoring. Martignoni decided, therefore, to attempt sucking the one-pound cans from the vessel with two 12-inch pipelines.

He set his divers to making the *Knot* as watertight as possible while he and salvage expert Loring Hyde figured out how to recover the fish oil. At the deepest part of the tanks, attachments were made to the hull, and suction hoses were secured to them. Above the level of fish oil in the tanks, further openings were made for the tapping in of high-pressure air hoses. As they pumped in compressed air, it drove the oil down and out through the vent hoses and up into waiting barges.

They recovered $22,000 worth of herring oil; then they were ready for the salmon.

A mother barge, to which all their floating equipment could be lashed, was anchored over the wreck. They used fire-fighting jet pumps to furnish enough water pressure to blast the cans from the cardboard cartons, and tremendously powerful air compressors for sufficient suction to draw the cans up to the barge through the pipes. Crane hoists were used to position and control the underwater siphon lines. Shifts of divers were kept on the bottom twenty-four hours a day.

In the No. 2 hold, two million cans waited. The suction hoses were sent down and positioned, and air at 90 psi was forced through the manifold. From the manifold's jet openings, water at 300 pounds pressure was shot out. Cardboard cartons were blasted apart, so the tinned salmon rolled free. The suction hoses slurped up one thousand gallons of water and eight hundred cans a minute, shooting them to the barge above. When No. 2 was cleared, they went on to No. 3.

Wind and rain and heavy seas hampered operations with broken air lines and bent or buckled siphons; and diver after diver had to be popped into the decompression chamber to avoid the bends after strong currents had snatched them from the bottom and swept them right to the surface. Operations went on for seventy-seven days.

But when they stopped, 90 per cent of the ship's port (upper) side had been cut away, plate by plate, to reveal the cargo. They had recovered 5,744,496 out of 7,407,168 cans. Some 480,000 cans were in parts of the ship not accessible; the rest had been scattered across the floor of the bay at the moment of collision. Of those recovered, 27 per cent had been spoiled by sea water; the other 4,179,360 cans were relabeled and sold. Total gross salvage recovery was $2.1 million.

The only sobering note in the affair was the captain of the *Fenn Victory*. The day following a board of inquiry that found him mutually at fault with the *Diamond Knot*'s master for the collision, he hanged himself in his cabin.

---

[1] Due to the compression of the air inside the bottle, water would force its way in around the cork's compressible sides.
[2] See pages 116–24.
[3] See pages 296–98.
[4] See pages 287–89.
[5] See Chapter Eighteen.

V

Safe Harbor

A harbor, even if it is a little harbor,
is a good thing.
SARAH ORNE JEWETT
River Driftwood

CHAPTER SEVENTEEN

Caissons, Compressors, and Pumps

War is imperious. It defines objectives, establishes priorities, demands victories—and cares only for results. Since virtually the beginning of naval warfare, a prime objective has been to deny safe harbor to the enemy's vessels. Sometimes this can be done by blockading the ports you wish to interdict; more often, it is done by blockships.

Here war's wastefulness becomes apparent. Blockships can be perfectly good vessels whose only sin is that they happen to be in a certain place at a time when they become less important than closing off a port. So they are merely run into the proper position to be most annoying to the enemy, and there they are sunk. Sometimes they are the opposition's vessels, but more often they are your own.

Very often, when the smoke has cleared and the harbor is safely back in your hands, your salvors find themselves in the embarrassing position of trying to figure out clever ways to raise or dispose of ships they previously were figuring out clever ways to sink.

Sometimes the only enemy is carelessness, accident, or weather. The result is the same. A ship sunk in the channel of a port or harbor by fire, collision, or storm is just as pesky a problem as one with the sea cocks opened. The *Royal George*, after all, was really just a harbor-clearance project.[1]

HARBOR CLEARANCE IN CRIMEA

The Crimean War (October 1853 to March 1856) caused what was probably the first organized attempt to clear a harbor of blockships. Russia entered the war on the Greek side because Czar Nicholas I saw policy advantages in it; France and England entered on the Turkish side essentially to oppose Russia. Sebastopol fell to them on September 11, but before it did, Russia sank a number of ships in the harbor mouth at a depth of about ten fathoms.

After the war ended, the British were stuck with cleaning up the mess. In the era of wooden ships and iron men, ships would eventually disintegrate from *teredos* or be covered by mud. Iron and steel ships were not so obliging. A British colonel named Gowan won a modicum of fame on one of them, the 5000-ton ironclad *Vladimir*, with a salvage method quite novel for the day.

The *Vladimir*, which was full of mud, lay essentially upright on the harbor floor at a depth of sixty-two feet. For the lift, Gowan planned to use 2½-inch iron chains, and four pontoons he had built specially for the job. Each was one hundred feet long, sixty-five wide, twenty-two deep, rectangular, not cylindrical, and compartmented inside. At each end of each pontoon was a big wheel on an iron pedestal, and fixed to each pontoon was a 15-horsepower portable steam engine.

The lifting chain was run over the wheels on the pontoon, and the after compartment was flooded to act as counterbalance for the *Vladimir's* weight once the lift started.

The steam engines powered both the winches drawing up the chains and the centrifugal pumps that helped lighten the *Vladimir*. Gowan brought her up off the bottom successfully, and had her towed out of the channel for resinking.

It was one of the first successful uses of lifting pontoons, and one of the few times in history they have been motorized.

THE FORGOTTEN *MAINE*

Another early and extremely famous example of harbor clearance was the raising of the U.S. battleship *Maine* in 1911, a vessel of 6682 tons, carrying four 10-inch guns and six 6-inch guns. Her presence in the harbor at Havana, Cuba, in February 1898 was due to a "visit of courtesy" that fooled no one: as the Spanish soldiers and Cuban autonomists clashed more and more openly, the Maine had been sent to oversee American interests.

On the evening of the fifteenth, the Maine changed position so that her guns were squarely trained on the Spanish shore batteries. A few hours later, there was a tremendous explosion in the area of her forward powder magazines. Two officers and 264 seamen were killed; the commander of the vessel, Captain Charles D. Sigsee, reported it as "a bursting, rending and crashing sound or roar of immense volume, largely metallic in character." Other officers called it "an underwater explosion."

This would indicate sinking by a Spanish mine. But the British steamer Deva was the only other vessel in Havana Harbor that felt the shock; and there was no column of spray at the time of the explosion—which would suggest interior ignition. But the tight security around the ship's magazines meant, in such a case, that the Maine had been deliberately scuttled.

Spain sent divers to check whether the Maine's plates had buckled inward or outward; the U. S. Navy did the same. Each government held a formal (and separate) court of inquiry. Predictably, the Spanish court found that the ship had not been destroyed by a mine. Predictably, the U.S. court found that it had.

There the matter might have rested, except that Hearst's war, as the Spanish-American War was called, broke out on April 21. And the American rallying cry was "Remember the Maine!" Commodore George Dewey's six-ship flotilla destroyed the ten-ship Spanish fleet in Manila Harbor on May 1, and Teddy Roosevelt's Rough Riders went pounding up San Juan Hill two months later. Puerto Rico was taken on July 28; armistice was signed on August 12.

The Maine, which was supposed to be remembered, was promptly forgotten. No more thought was given to the hulk, in fact, until 1909. By that time, increased traffic by larger ships in Havana Harbor made her a danger to navigation. It would have been simple to festoon her with explosives and cut her down to a heap of rubble, but those still rankled by the Spanish charge of scuttling demanded that she be raised. This would settle the question once and for all, they said.

Congress voted half a million dollars for the project and told the Army Corps of Engineers to get busy. A certain Major Ferguson was put in charge of things. He considered pontoons first, but the Maine lay in fifty feet of water and mud, and Ferguson was no Colonel Gowan. The state of the art of pontooning, or at least the state of Ferguson's art of pontooning, excluded them from consideration. So a cofferdam was decided upon.

Ah. Reasonable. Such things as divers patching leaks, the warship's sides being built up to reach the surface so she could be pumped out . . .

But no. Not the Engineers. The Engineers decided to build *their* cofferdam *all the way around the ship*. Not *on* the ship; *around* it. That would then be pumped out, and there the *Maine* would lie, in a little dry pocket in the middle of Havana Harbor, like beached Leviathan of which Psalms speaks so divertingly.

Back to the old drawing board, Ferguson decided a year and a million dollars later, with nothing at all accomplished. This time it was decided to cut the ship in half, bulkhead the cut on the front end of the sound after section, float that, and tow it away to be sunk in deep water. This meant a cofferdam only half as large as originally planned.

They went to work on it. The construction was actually quite ingenious, being done with a series of cylinders, fifty feet in diameter, filled with clay dredged from the harbor floor. Interlocking them were thirty-two hundred sheet-steel pilings driven down into the mud on the outer side of the cylinders, so the whole presented a smooth, unbroken wall to the water pressure it would have to withstand once pumping began.

Meanwhile, the *Maine* was cut in half with explosives, the bulkheads were strengthened, and the after section was pumped and towed away. Pumping out of the cofferdam began on June 5, 1911. If a cylinder began shifting, water was pumped back inside the cofferdam to equalize the pressure while the weakened portion of the wall was strengthened; then work would be resumed.

Once the cofferdam was pumped dry, the *Maine* was exposed in all her ugliness. She was covered with a heavy deposit of mud, oyster shells, and coralline cement. The metals were badly corroded, with scabbards, belts, and even cartridge cases fused into solid masses. Ferguson found, on examining the section of the *Maine* where the explosion had occurred, that the plates were buckled inward—which could be caused only by an external explosion.

The section was repaired enough to be floated and towed into deep water to be resunk. It has never been discovered which individual or group set the mine; a real possibility exists that it was merely an accidental floater that drifted into the ship's side and was detonated by rapping against the hull.

Then the First World War started, and the wartime salvage jobs began. On December 21, 1916, a heavy storm had blown the S.S. *Araby* up onto the French coast of the Strait of Dover, from which French tugs brought her off. Her steering gear was damaged, so they began a tow to Boulogne Harbor. Just inside the entrance, the towing hawsers parted, and the *Araby*, caught in a strong tidal flow, was swept across the mouth of the harbor and jammed there.

When the tide went out, the heavily laden ship, down to her

marks with oats, broke her back as the bow and stern settled on the bottom and her midship section was unsupported over the deep channel.

The Admiralty Salvage Section was not yet in full swing at that time, so they called in outside aid in the form of Lieutenant Colonel R. V. Jellicoe of the Royal Engineers. He looked over the *Araby*, then decided to patch her with concrete. He put wooden forms on either side of the midships fracture, and filled them; when it hardened, the concrete formed a bulkhead that shut off the bow and stern sections from the sea while leaving the fracture itself open to the water.

On January 11, 1917, she was unwatered, and towed at high tide out of the entrance and farther up into the harbor. They kept repeating the pumping and towing, getting her farther and farther up harbor, until she finally broke in two completely.

The inventive Jellicoe clustered 800-ton-capacity pontoons around the sunken sections, sank and pinned them, then blew them to raise the sections, separately, and tow them on successive lifts farther up into the harbor.

There the two pieces of the *Araby* stayed until July 1918, when the area where they lay was needed for other things. The Admiralty began emptying and pumping out the sections, but one worker was killed by poisonous gases generated by the rotting oats, and two more were killed trying to save him. But the sections finally were floated and towed into deep water outside the harbor for final disposal.

Meanwhile, back in England, the redoubtable Frederick Young[2] had begun building his reputation as a master innovator. The troop ship *Onward* was lying along the quay at Folkestone when a spy-set thermite bomb exploded in her hold. Within instants she was burning fiercely.

The dockside facilities were much more important than the *Onward* herself, so her captain opened her sea cocks and sank her. It put out the fire; but unfortunately, in going down, the ship turned turtle and ended up on her top hamper and blocking the quay. The Admiralty, desperate for docking space, called in Young and gave him a month to clear the *Onward* away.

He first sent divers down to cut off the masts, funnels, and other top hamper. Then on the quay they constructed five enormous timber tripods. Cables fastened to the deck of the *Onward* were threaded up over the tripods and out onto the quay behind. Two salvage tugs moored close up against the ship; they dropped cables down, which were taken by divers around the hull and attached to the whaleback visible above water.

Finally, Young brought out five locomotives, one for each of the cables strung over the tripods. These began pulling backward on the cables at the same time that the two tugs hauled back on *their* cables.

The *Onward* rolled over so she was right side up. Young pumped her out, and well within the month he had been allowed, had her in dry dock and matériel again moving across the vital quay.

REMOVING THE *VINDICTIVE*

The last operation that the Salvage Section carried out before it was disbanded after the war was also under Young's guidance, and was one of his most brilliant. It began on May 10, 1918, when Commander A. E. Godsal clandestinely took the 5750-ton cruiser *Vindictive* into Ostend Harbor. The Admiralty wished to interdict the harbor to the use of German submarines, and the 320-foot-long cruiser, fifty-seven feet in the beam and drawing thirty-six feet, seemed the way to do it.

Vindictive crept into Ostend Harbor under the cover of dark, then coolly fired flares to find the best position for truly bottling up the harbor. German shore batteries opened fire and killed Godsal and his First Mate, Lieutenant John Alleyne. Lieutenant Crutchley, thrust suddenly into command, got the stem of the ship close to the eastern pier, her stern into the channel, and ordered the firing of explosive charges in her double bottom beneath the boilers, engine rooms, and magazines. She went down instantly, with the crewmen escaping by fast motor launch.

Preparatory to scuttling her, the British thoughtfully had packed her full of sacked cement so the enemy would not be able to raise her. When the Germans abandoned Ostend near the end of the war, they in turn sank many small craft around the British blockship.

The Admiralty pottered about, trying to decide what to do with the *Vindictive* after the war; they were still deciding when, in May 1919, the *Vindictive* settled the question by quietly breaking her back. Not one to let decisions be made for it, the following month the Admiralty, with exquisite timing, Rendered Decision. Raise her. How? Why, Frederick Young, of course. Just the lad for the job.

As it turned out, Young was indeed the lad for the job. Since 180 feet of her bottom was missing entirely, Young decided to get necessary buoyancy by making all the compartments above the destroyed ones watertight, and then pumping them full of compressed air.

Young cleared the harbor around her of the other, smaller sunken craft, then had to remove the concrete, mud, and sand that filled her holds. The mud and sand were removed, where possible, with two 12-inch pumps, one in the water to roil up the silt, the other to pump the resultant mixture overboard. Hand labor by divers cleared the rest. The cement was blown away, bit by bit, with the use of minuscule explosive charges.

Finally Young's men had cleared eighty-two compartments, which would furnish, he estimated, thirty-five hundred tons of lift. Then everything had to be sealed. Since the Germans had stripped all usable metal from the exposed portions of the wreck, this entailed closing hundreds of holes and refitting missing deck plates.

Young also had to make sure she didn't break in half during the lift. Fortunately, the ship's being hard down on the bottom prevented any scissor action at the fracture, so he tied her together with massive girders spanning the crack, somewhat like giant staples. Similar, smaller girders were used on the sides of the hull, as a doctor stitching up a patient after an operation. Timber and concrete bulkheads were used to further strengthen the fracture area.

Then, lifting tunnels were dug under her so that lighters and pontoons could aid the compressed air in the lift. The harbor channel had to be redredged to accommodate the ship's estimated draught. Two lifting lighters, two pontoons, and two salvage ships—the *Reindeer* and the *Mariner*—were used on the lift. The lighters were attached to the stern, the pontoons to the bow, while midships the salvage vessels prepared to pump out water and pump in air with six steam-driven compressors.

The lift began at midnight, August 14, 1920, with the lighters and pontoons flooded and pinned and the tide rising. By 11:00 A.M. the next day, her stern had been brought up with the blown lighters. By 1:00 P.M., she was up and drawing thirty feet. Sand banks on either side held her, but a second lift brought her into the channel for removal upharbor.

There she was beached and, apparently because the British didn't know what else to do with her, was given to the Belgian Government to serve as a monument to the war. In raising her sixty-two hundred tons from the harbor floor, Young set a record for his day.

JOHN IRON'S REMARKABLE EFFORTS

Years after the war, another of the great wartime salvors, John Iron,[3] worked on a number of intriguing harbor-clearance projects for his prewar employers, the Dover Harbor Board. While serving as Harbor Master in 1926, he raised the British monitor *Glatton*.

Glatton had caught fire in Dover Harbor in 1918. Because she threatened the shipping congregated there, Admiral Sir Roger Keyes ordered her torpedoed. The ship promptly turned turtle in some six fathoms of water, coming to rest at a 66-degree angle on her starboard guns, conning tower, and the upper edge of her boat deck.

In all, some nineteen companies made bids on removing her, ranging between £45,000 and £60,000. Finally the Liverpool Salvage Association was brought in, and with Iron directing operations did the job for £12,000.

Before doing anything else, Iron used centrifugal pumps to remove several thousand tons of mud from the *Glatton*. With oxyacetylene underwater torches, his divers cut away the four-foot-thick tripod mast and its supporting struts; with small explosive charges, they blew out the mast's strengthening bars. In time, everything thrust down into the mud below the level of the conning tower was cut away with torches and brought to the surface—including the ship's funnels and bridge.

Then Iron sealed everything on the port (upper) side down to the midship line, including manholes, light ports, hatches, ventilators, even the gun tubs of the 6-inch guns. Finally, pairs of 9-inch wire cables were secured to the guns to keep her from righting herself once the lift was begun. Let into the various compartments were pipes attached to air hoses from Iron's two big compressors. Two lighters were pinned down to the ship with eight pairs of lifting cables as adjuncts to the compressed air.

Iron started his compressors on March 15, 1926, pounding seventy thousand cubic feet of air an hour down into the *Glatton*. Up she came, to be moved during two successive tides some fourteen hundred feet. On the sixteenth, she was placed along the eastern pier of the submarine harbor, well out of the way of commerce.

Another of Iron's remarkable efforts in Dover Harbor came with the twin blockships *Lavonia* and *Spanish Prince*. They were both 5000-ton steamers, some 420 feet long and forty-five feet in the beam, that had been sunk in ten fathoms of water at the harbor's western entrance to keep German submarines from firing torpedoes at moored shipping from outside the harbor.

Iron decided the easiest way to get rid of them was to cut them into sections, drag each section separately to the surface, and dump it on the rocks well away from the harbor channel. Tunneling under the vessels for the passage of the 9-inch lifting cables presented some problems, since the bottom was predominantly chalk and flint. So, using a 12-inch pump, Iron sank 20-foot-square sumps on either side of each section to be raised.

Working from the sumps, divers blasted the 45-foot tunnels under the ship with high-pressure hoses, announcing location and progress to each other with taps on the ship's hull above their heads. They became very accurate at gauging one another's positions. In one tunnel, a diver, feeling his way toward the face of his tunnel through the complete blackness under the ship, encountered, instead of the tunnel's end, the similarly groping hand of the diver coming in from the other side.

Once the sections had been cradled, of course, Iron dead-lifted their 1500-ton weight to the surface for removal.

He completed the lengthy operation in 1932.

Another very inventive British salvor was Captain J. O. Ingram, who was hired by the French city of Havre to remove a sunken British steamer that was a serious danger to navigation. Two French firms had preceded Ingram, trying to clear the ship away and failing because of a nearly impossible rider the harbor authorities had insisted on attaching to the salvage contract.

In future maintenance operations, the Frenchmen had reasoned, they would have to do some dredging. If the salvors missed part of the British steamer, left it on the bottom, the pieces would get caught in the dredger . . .

Zut, alors! The dredger would be finished.

So whoever salvaged that steamer would have to assemble the entire keel right there on the dock, they said, so they could inspect it and certify that none of the ship's metal ribs had been left on the bottom.

Which meant that the salvors could not use explosives to blow the keel to pieces. Ingram brought up barges, which he anchored on either side of the wreck. On the barges were power sources—steam engines, which could be used to manipulate heavy wire cables. The cables were strung between the two barges, with heavy weights attached to them below each barge; with the engines to impart a sawing effect, they became in effect giant saw blades. Ingram wore out a good many cables, but he cut down through the vessel in slices very much like a butcher cutting off pieces of roast. Then he hauled up the ship's keel and ribs, a section at a time, and reassembled them on the dock until the entire ship lay there—in a rather dilapidated condition, to be sure, but all there just the same.

ST. PAUL FORESHADOWS THE NORMANDIE

European ports were not the only ones with harbor-clearance problems during and after the war, although American salvage firms did not have to cope with blockships. One of the most inventive and famous jobs—eerily foreshadowing another ship, the *Normandie*,[4] in another war—was that carried out by Merritt and Chapman Wrecking Company on the converted liner *St. Paul* in 1918.

The 12,000-ton liner had been converted into a Navy transport, and on April 25, 1918,[5] she was being taken from the South Brooklyn Ship Yard to Pier 60, North River, New York Harbor. Two tugs were towing her "dead"—cold boilers, no steam up, no crew, just a few riggers from the navy yard to moor her.

Caught in a strong ebb tide just beyond the Battery, she listed heavily to port when she swung broadside to the current. The riggers thought the list was more pronounced than the push of water might have done, so the tugs poured on all the coal possible. They got her into the slip between Piers 60 and 61 successfully—and there she simply rolled over to port. Her top hamper and smoke stacks smashed down on the south stringpiece of Pier 61. No one was injured.

There she lay, whale-like, on a bottom that would not be easy for the salvors to work with. Underlying the North River, about a hundred feet down, is bedrock. Above this is hardpan—a mixture of boulders, clay, sand, and gravel—and topping this is hard-packed, very sticky mud. On top of everything is twenty to thirty feet of very soupy mud, which rises in great clouds about anything that moves. It was in this thirty feet of soupy mud that the *St. Paul* lay.

The salvage master was R. E. Chapman, but the man making most of the field decisions was Captain "Izzy" Tooker. He first had everything heavy and removable taken off the liner: stacks, anchors, chains, masts, rigging, compressors, and pumps. The guns (which had just been installed) had to be removed from the massive steel plates that underlay the mounts.

Meanwhile, other divers were digging tunnels under the hull for a half-dozen lifting slings. To aid in this process, floating derricks were brought up alongside the ship to dig holes in the mud at measured intervals with clamshell buckets. The divers started from these holes to wash the passages under the hull.

Their 4-inch water hoses for tunneling were great, ponderous affairs, heavily weighted with scrap iron, nozzled down to an inch, and operable only at a very low water pressure because such refinements as back-pressure ducts had not yet been invented. The divers also had the problem of getting rid of the mud they washed away (the holes dug along the hull were to serve as mud receptacles). Worst of all, the mud was jammed with waterlogged lumber, old crates, barrels, barrel hoops, jettisoned rotted burlaps, cans, bottles, trash, sewage, and garbage.

It took about a week for each tunnel, with teams of divers working toward each other from both sides of the hull. When they were close enough to communicate, they used the long prickers Cox's divers were later to use at Scapa Flow.

Once the lifting slings were in place, a dredge and dump scows began digging a huge trench beside the *St. Paul*, as long as the ship's hull and wider than the vessel's beam. While this work went forward, divers were closing off cargo ports, ventilator ports, scuppers, outlets, inlets, and drains on the starboard side of the vessel down to the mid-line.

Ashore, other teams were running heavy steel anchor cables from Pier 60 to enormous steel girders that had been buried deep in the ground behind Pier 59. These were drawn up tight as bowstrings; when the lift began, Pier 60 was going to take most of the weight and had to be firmly anchored so it would not be torn loose.

On the upward side of the vessel, steel A-frames thirty feet high were built, twenty-one of them, with cables running over them from twenty-one steam winches on Pier 60. The other ends of these cables were run down to twenty-one cement blocks that had been sunk under fifteen feet of clay in the next slip.

As the day for righting the liner drew closer, Tooker had his men rig two immense winches on Pier 60. Then six 100-ton concrete blocks were poured on the bulkhead between that pier and Pier 59 in forms prefabricated for this purpose.

On the day of the parbuckling attempt, Tooker hung his six 100-ton blocks on the *St. Paul*'s starboard side and fastened pontoons to the portside. The four biggest floating derricks available were hooked into four of the wire slings previously gotten under the vessel by the divers; the other two slings were run over to those two big husky winches on Pier 60.

Then, all the winches and the four floating derricks took the heaviest strain they could without any of the gear breaking or letting go, and—waited.

And hoped that the mud under the vessel's port bilge would give under the strain before the lifting tackle did. When the mud suddenly collapsed to slide down into the trench that had been dug beyond it, the *St. Paul* also slid: keel first down the sloping mud bank.

Even before she came to rest in a somewhat upright position, Tooker had his men taking up turns on the winches and the floating derricks. This brought her almost completely level, with her decks not far below the surface. She was cofferdammed in preparation for pumping.

Meanwhile, the portside openings were available for the divers to close off; they also found the open ash chute on the portside that had caused the sinking. The divers worked inside in complete darkness, fifty feet below the harbor surface at times, several feet below the surrounding mud. In all, some five hundred separate openings had to be closed up. One hatch had seventeen bolt holes around it, which would have to be matched up perfectly with the bolts in the hatch they were fabricating. A diver took down a thin sheet of lead, which he hammered down over the opening—thus getting an impression not only of the hole but of the bolt holes also. The steel-plate patch was made from this, and it fit perfectly down to the last bolt.

While divers were sealing those holes, others were making other holes in the transverse bulkheads between compartments. Explosives were used on the first two, but these caused extensive damage. They went instead to the slow, clumsy electro-gas burning torches of the day. The divers using these arc torches had to wear clouded masks over their helmets to protect their eyes even in the murky water inside the ship.

For the ship still was full of water, of course—water and a great deal of mud, which had come in while she had been capsized. That was why they wanted the vessel's interior common. Water could be taken from the whole ship by big centrifugal pumps in a central location with suction hoses leading into just a few compartments.

The derricks were paired on either side of the *St. Paul,* using the lifting cradle not for lifting but to keep her from rolling as she came up. Pumping began on September 28, 1918—five months after she had rolled over. With twenty pumps working, it took only two hours for her bows to come alive, and less than that again for the stern to come up. As she rose, divers were down outside looking for bubbles, which would indicate leaks; into these they stuffed straw or oakum. Once she was up she was towed back to the shipyard for renovation.

Almost exactly the same methods were used thirteen years later at Newport News, Virginia, on the *Segovia.* She was a combined passenger/refrigerated-freight steamer that still was in the process of being built when she caught fire on the night of December 19, 1931.

Like the *Normandie,* she was rolled onto her starboard side and sunk by the weight of water that had been pumped into her to extinguish the fire. Like the *St. Paul,* she slapped smokestacks and masts against the pier, crumpling them. And the salvors followed the same general procedure as that used by Chapman and Tooker: reinforcing the pier, installing ten electric winches—each with three drums—from which were run thirty heavy cables to the *Segovia's* upper deck. Eight restraining cables were anchored to the pilings of the next pier to keep her from rolling too far once she started. They also dredged a trough alongside the ship, as Tooker had done, and slid her into the trench so she could right herself. Divers, often working in mud to their armpits, sealed her up, and electric pumps with a 14,000-gallon-per-minute combined capacity soon dried her out.

Divers figured very prominently in all these operations; it becomes quite easy to see generic *Diver*—blasting out lifting tunnels, working in mud to his armpits, sealing holes inside a hull fifty feet down. Which means we forget the human reality of these clumsy, copper-headed creatures, forget that these are men whose lives often depend on individual decisions made either by themselves or other men.

Joseph Karneke, still a student diver in those pre-World War II days, was putting a plate on the bottom of a barge's after well in the Anacostia River, Washington, D.C. He was underneath the vessel on the river bottom, reaching up to put in place each bolt to secure the plate, when he suddenly realized that the barge was no longer at arm's length above his head, but was right in front of his eyes. He was not leaning back, but was flat on his back; he had unconsciously assumed this position as the barge had lowered.

He called up excitedly through the phone, warning them that the barge was sinking. It wasn't; the tide was going out. By this time the 500-ton craft was resting on his helmet and breastplate heavily enough to pin him down. They tried to drag him out with his life line (1500-pound test) but it nearly parted.

Karneke then suggested a tunneling hose with a nozzle pressure of 750 pounds. The drawback there, however, was that the barge was forty feet wide and the tunnel necessary to reach him would have to be twenty feet. That meant an hour. He would be crushed by then.

Next they tried tying the nozzle to his life line in hopes that he could drag it to himself by pulling on the line, which descended through the open middle well. But by then the barge was down so hard on the line that he couldn't even move it.

So they turned on the tunneling hose and directed its jet along the life line. After a few minutes, it had blown away enough sediment for Karneke, flat on his back with the weight creaking down on his helmet, to move the line. Inch by painful inch he pulled it toward him, until there was the sudden beautiful rattle of pebbles against his helmet as the approaching high-pressure jet of water bounced them around. When he got a hand on the nozzle, he directed it down, to blow out a nest around him so he was free of the crushing weight of the barge.

Then he enlarged the passageway along his life line so they could jerk him over under the middle well.

His tenders were able to get hold of his heavy diving boots and pull him up into the barge—feet first. The master diver who was Karneke's instructor saw him emerge unscathed from the depths. Instead of rushing forward with outstretched arms to rejoice in his pupil's narrow escape, he bellowed, with every appearance of livid rage, "Goddam it, Karneke, how many times I gotta tell you I don't want you coming up feet first?"

Diving is just not a recommended profession for highly sensitive people.

---

[1] See pages 22–24.
[2] See pages 203–6.
[3] See pages 158–59. Iron salvaged 240 *vessels* during the war!
[4] See pages 296–98.
[5] This was *ten years to the day* since she had sunk the British warship *Gladiator* (see pages 203–5) in the Solent.

CHAPTER EIGHTEEN

Ellsberg at Massawa

~~~~~~

On October 2, 1935, Italy invaded Ethiopia. During the campaign, which ended on May 5 the following year with Mussolini's annexation of the embryonic African nation, the Italians converted the ancient Arab slave-trading port on the Red Sea, Massawa, into a modern port. They created a complete naval base, with concrete quays, electric cranes, naval shops and warehouses, an airfield, submarine piers, depots for the storage of explosives, coast-defense guns—even an excellent highway leading to the Ethiopian highlands.

When Britain finally decided that she had to enter World War II (September 1939), all the German and Italian ships east of Suez rushed to Massawa to wait out her surrender, which their propaganda pictured as imminent. Inconsiderate Britain not only refused to give up; she even continued to hold the Suez Canal. This made the ships congregated at Massawa extremely vulnerable, for they had no way of receiving supplies from Italy.

Next, British and colonial African troops compounded this effrontery by striking into Ethiopia, taking the heights of Keren in a brilliant nighttime assault, and then Asmara—a mere forty crow-fly miles and seven thousand feet in elevation away.

SABOTAGE AT MASSAWA

That was enough for Massawa. All forty freighters, passenger liners, and warships that lay in the harbor were scuttled; fourteen bombs were detonated in the port's two big steel floating dry docks, which then also were scuttled; the electric cranes were tipped off their tracks into the harbor; the machinery in the naval shops was smashed; and finally, several ships were placed stem to stern right across the harbor mouth and scuttled.

British soldiers took the port in April 1941 mainly because it was there and because a victory, any victory, was sorely needed to offset the dismal war news from elsewhere. But in the fall of that same year, Rommel's Afrika Korps drove from Benghazi toward Alexandria.

Suddenly Massawa, wrecked, blocked, gutted, stinking hot, became the Allies' only safe port in northern Africa.

Edward Ellsberg, fifty years old at this time and long retired from active service, arrived at Massawa early in 1942 after the Japanese attack on Pearl Harbor had brought him back into the U. S. Navy. His orders: make it into a seaport again.

He arrived alone, without equipment of any sort. The temperatures ranged from 120 degrees Fahrenheit in the summer to a chilly 100 degrees in the winter; metal temperatures—and most of the work would of course be done on metal in the open sun—averaged 160 degrees. A report by the Royal Navy board that had surveyed Massawa sums up the position as regards salvage shops and equipment:

"The whole of the machinery of the Depot and the workshops, all cranes, portable plant and tools and equipment were firstly effectively sabotaged by the Italians; secondly, thoroughly looted by the Free French and remaining Italians; thirdly, anything portable of value left had been appropriated by the British army."

The electric driving motors of each machine tool had been smashed with sledge hammers, and driving gears were broken or missing in all the shops: machine, carpenter's, electric, boat, ship-fitter's, pipe, even the foundry. The foundry's indispensable graphite crucibles had been shattered. There was not one chisel, hammer, or saw left.

Ellsberg wangled, temporarily, five civilian supervisors (master machinist, electrician, sheet-metal man, pipefitter, carpenter) from the American contractors in cool, clean, high Asmara—the contractors who were supposed to co-operate with him but who spent most of their time opposing him. Then he hired a few dozen Italian workmen, some POWs, and a mass of Eritrean laborers.

Ellsberg's crew began scavenging. They cannibalized hundreds of smashed motors to get a few that would work. From a scrap heap came three old, thin, cracked graphite crucibles that had been overlooked in the binge of destruction. Within two days, half a dozen 3- and 5-horsepower electric motors had been assembled; these were attached by the driving trains they had reoutfitted to a lathe and a milling machine so they could turn out milled parts for other motors and machines. The crucibles made possible the casting of gears—from brass and aluminum rather than iron or steel, because these metals were more malleable and would be gentler on their crucibles.

By the beginning of May 1942—less than six weeks after Ellsberg's arrival—the naval repair base was once more ready for business.

On the water, however, Ellsberg still had to get a dry dock into operation. Anchored in the open roadstead outside the harbor was a 6000-ton-capacity Persian dry dock, undamaged, which had been passing through when the British had arrived, and had been impounded. But five vessels had been scuttled across the mouth of the harbor.

Ellsberg noticed that one of them, however, the *Oliva*, had swung her stern away from the bow of the next ship in line, the *XXIII Marzo*, to go down on her side. This left an acutely angled, very narrow channel between the two ships. The channel was so narrow that his two tugs had to bring the 400-foot dry dock through with one tug in front, pulling, the other behind, pushing. They did it beautifully, making a smart 90-degree starboard turn to miss the two sunken Italian dry docks.

This was on May 7. The freighters, which for two years had been shuttling men and supplies between Alexandria and Tobruk, needed repairs so urgently that the British Mediterranean Command pumped in the first vessel on May 8.

It was the Greek armed freighter *Koritza*. They docked her and then turned to the several-inch layer of barnacles on her hull and the crop of mosslike grass on her plates. Ellsberg had planned to have the ship scraped and out of dry dock in three days; but the Eritrean workmen, hired through their sheiks, refused to move beyond a certain pace.

So Ellsberg called in the sheiks, and told them that if they did not finish the ship in three days all of their men would be fired. This would entail a great loss of face for the sheiks. Second, they would be paid for three days on each ship, so the faster they cleared the vessels, the more money per day they would make.

By 6:00 P.M. on the second day, the *Koritza* was out of the dry dock; by 7:00 A.M. the next morning, the *Athos* was in. In the next

120 days, they pushed through eighty vessels: a record for a single dry dock never equalled in the history of marine operations.

This was salvage work, but it was not harbor clearance; and cleared is what they wanted Massawa Harbor.

IMPROVISING ON THE ITALIAN DRY DOCK

Ellsberg's first target was Massawa's greatest prize: the larger of the two dry docks scuttled by the Italians. It had seven bomb holes in its cellular horizontal main hull structure, from bombs that had torn out the bottom, the intermediate bulkheads, and the dock floor above. The Royal Navy Board survey had decided, "Upon consideration of all reports received, the Admiralty have abandoned all idea of salvage. The salvage work would be long, difficult, and probably unsuccessful."

They had made the negative recommendation on the basis of a work force including fifty divers, several salvage ships, and four hundred shore mechanics, working a year to patch up the holes and raise the dock. Ellsberg had fifteen men total. Two supervisors, five divers, eight mechanics. He had two diving suits and a compressor, which were the personal property of one of the divers. He had no salvage ship.

But he had guts—and a plan. He started work on the dock.

He first laid in vast amounts of drinking water for his crew and lined up every possible source of ice to keep it cold for them. Then he got several thousand feet of steel pipe and fittings, lumber, a few thousand feet of electric wire, and shore help: twelve Italian pipefitters and electricians; six Arab carpenters; thirty Eritrean laborers; and five Maltese riggers.

The dock was six hundred feet long by one hundred feet wide. Its deck was fifteen feet deep, with eight sections that had been watertight until the bombs had gone off. Its upright walls were thirty-five feet high, fifteen feet thick. Their main purpose was stability; now, with the dock lying in fifty feet of water with a slight upward pitch forward, a few inches of the wing-wall tops were clear at high tide. At the stern, the walls were awash. This gave the salvors two 15-foot-wide platforms from which to work; platforms were a must, since they had no salvage boat.

Work began on May 11, 1942.

Ellsberg made the first survey himself, suiting up and going down to check the condition of the wing walls. Intact! Despite the fact that the *deck* was pocked with seven holes big enough to drive a truck through, the wing walls were intact. He came up from the 95-degree water convinced that his plan would work.

He wasn't going to bother with the holes. Instead, he would seal all openings in the wing walls, blow them with compressed air (the water from the walls would be expelled through the bomb holes), and bring the huge dock up like a diving bell.

The one drawback was that he had no air compressors. He decided to worry about that little problem once the walls were airtight. To do this, all scuppers, drains, and air ports had to be sealed. As his divers started this, his mechanics began laying compressed-air mains: one down the top of each wall, with connections that would lead to each of the watertight sections in each wall. There was a 6-inch mushroom ventilator above each compartment, and blank steel flanges were put on these so the air connections could be tapped in. Further connections were strung across the eighty-foot gap between the walls from the starboard to the port mains. To carry the cross-connection air main, his riggers strung two ½-inch wire cables with a wooden footwalk between.

In the adjacent commercial harbor (separated from the naval harbor by the Abd-el-Kader Peninsula) another salvage operation was going forward: a commercial venture, under contract from the Admiralty, run by a man named McCance. He wore whites, a monocle, and the traditional pith helmet of the British raj; in six months' time he had salvaged nothing. His men were always "working on" a scuttled freighter, the *Gera*, and a large floating crane the Italians had sunk beside Massawa's main wharf.

This man had air compressors, two of them, immense, new, glorious Ingersoll-Rands. Ellsberg lusted after these with a nearly carnal desire. Also, McCance had under charter a Danish salvage ship he never used, complete with crew and equipment. McCance refused to lend any of it. Ellsberg went to Asmara and pleaded, cursed, pounded tables, and pulled strings; finally the commercial salvor was *ordered* to lend the ship and the compressors.

Ellsberg lined up two more compressors, ancient, decrepit Italian jobs, and loaded them all on the Danish ship. The four compressors would give a combined total capacity of seven hundred cubic feet a minute—pitiful, but it would have to do.

At seven on the morning the lift was to start, the Danish vessel boomed the compressors over to the exposed tops of the sunken dock's upright walls. Then the Danes sadly returned to their inactivity, since McCance "couldn't spare them" for anything more than the bare transport job. Ellsberg's men connected the compressors and started them up.

Started up the Ingersoll-Rands, that is.

The antique Fiats were not so co-operative. They were semi-diesels which required hand cranking while a chemical cartridge was slow-burned in a special receptacle on top of the compressor. When they finally did start, Ellsberg found that all four compressors overheated terribly in the intense sunlight, so that four-man crews had to be kept running on a 24-hour-a-day basis just to supply water for the radiators as it boiled away.

As the air started in, the tops of the walls started pouring it back out; not from damage or holes, just from gaps left by poor workmanship when the dock was built. They calked with whatever they could find—generally by battering shut the gaps with sledge hammers and chisels. By one the next morning, the sixteen primitive air gauges he had scrounged (all different types, with different calibrations, intended for measuring different things) suggested that the water might have been pushed down two feet all around. One of his greatest problems in judging progress was that he had no blueprints of the dry dock, no plans, did not even know its size or capacity.

The next morning, one of the Fiat compressors quit entirely. Even without it, however, they had four psi by eight that evening, and some of the plates were beginning to bend outward slightly from the inner pressure, for which they had not been designed.

By 11:00 P.M. on the second day, they had six psi—and the second Fiat began firing erratically. But the dock had come alive. In two and one half days they had started her from the bottom:—the dry dock upon which the Admiralty had abandoned "all idea of salvage."

On the third morning the Fiat quit entirely; one man broke an arm trying to start it. Ellsberg brought out his Eritreans (who, after the confab with the sheiks, had become scraping fools) from the Persian dry dock to scrape the Italian dock's barnacles as it slowly rose.

Now he played his trump: the eighth, farthest aft, compartment of the deck was still sound (except for sea valves open from the Italian scuttling effort), because the bomb set in it had not detonated. Ellsberg pumped air from both Ingersoll-Rands into it, forcing out the water through the opened valves and adding twelve hundred tons of buoyancy. It was enough to lift the stern of the dock completely from the water.

This also brought out the next two compartments forward, and workmen could now get at them without diving. Temporary wood-and-canvas patches were placed so these compartments would hold air well enough to raise the next ones in line, and so on, until the whole deck had been temporarily patched and the dock was up and floating. They were aided in this work by a freak explosive effect: all the bottom plating had been blown up and inward instead of down and outward, so the divers patching the bottom of the deck did not have jagged edges of metal to cut away.

Ellsberg and another man went down into the after, whole compartment, got a manila bridle around the 200-pound TNT bomb, and slung the thing out for the demolition boys. Thus on May 19, only nine days after the salvage attempt had started, the dock was afloat, ready for permanent repairs as soon as they could find the steel plate to fix it.

They had paid a heavy price, however. Four of Ellsberg's fifteen-man salvage crew had been lost permanently because of physical disabilities induced by the incredible Massawa heat. Of the men remaining, 25 per cent were at any given time in the hospital being treated for aggravated prickly heat; all the men 100 per cent of the time had terrible heat rashes. One thing that helped offset the attrition was the arrival of ten South African ironworkers, still in full battle dress, who had been picked from their military units and sent to Massawa by a South African general who had toured the facility and been deeply impressed by the job Ellsberg's men were doing.

In June 1942 their first salvage vessel arrived from the States: the *Intent*, with salvage master Edison Brown, Chief Engineer H. M. Keith, and twelve salvage men aboard.

THE SCUTTLED *LIEBENFELS*

Ellsberg immediately sent the ship out to the scuttled German freighter SS *Liebenfels*, last of seven blockships lined up across the mouth of the South Harbor, which lay a few miles away from the Naval Harbor, with the Commercial Harbor and the Abd-el-Kader Peninsula in between. Ellsberg had access to the Naval Harbor by the lucky shifting of the *Oliva* as it had been scuttled; he wanted to get the South Harbor open also.

Master diver Buck Scougale reported that *Liebenfels* had been sunk by a bomb exploded in the port forward bilges of the No. 2 cargo hold. It had blown a twenty-foot piece from the hull and shattered the bulkhead between No. 2 hold and No. 1. It also had torn some of the hull away from No. 1. Since two-thirds of the damage was in No. 2, Ellsberg decided to seal up No. 1, leave No. 2 open to the water, then pump out No. 1 and the rest of the vessel's compartments for enough buoyancy to raise her.

In sinking the vessel, the saboteurs had smashed the valves of the dozen sea chests between No. 2 and the boiler and engine rooms so they could not be closed. It was impossible, because of wreckage jamming the vessel, to get inside to repair them; so Ellsberg merely had his divers close them off from *outside* the ship. Each had a perforated grating on the hull to cover the connection, and the divers sealed them with canvas-covered wood frames and pudding patches, held down with hook bolts through the gratings. They took only half an hour apiece.

Inside, Scougale closed off drainage manifold valves by driving in tapered wooden plugs. Thirty tons of cement sealed up the hull rupture by No. 1 hold. Finally, heavy rectangular wooden cofferdams (of tongue-and-groove two-inch planks) were built over the cargo hatches, their upper ends ten feet above the surface.

Pumping began on June 30, the day after the Battle of El Alamein began. Working were seven 4- and 6-inch pumps—self-priming American Jaegers and larger, more cumbersome British models, which had a total capacity of six thousand gallons a minute.

When the pump engines began heating, Ellsberg stopped them one by one to remove and throw away the thermostatic control valves from the discharge lines. The water level kept falling, until they had to rig new pump platforms fifteen or twenty feet down in the *Liebenfels*. This meant servicing by squirting oil or grease with one hand while hanging onto an improvised ladder with the other.

By midafternoon the bow came alive, but then their pumps began stopping, one after the other. They found that the magnetos, down there in the damp hold, were grounding out. Even spraying with carbon tetrachloride only dried them temporarily. And the pumps had to be lowered again, carried on the shoulders of men descending narrow, slippery ladders.

They could get and keep no single compartment dried out, so the ship began listing to port, a list that increased until the pumps had to be lashed down to keep them from sliding off their platforms.

As the third day of twenty-four-hour pumping dawned, with Ellsberg and his men exhausted, *Liebenfels* had a 24-foot draught (four feet less than her loaded draught); but their Persian dry dock could only take a 19- or perhaps 20-foot draught—if Ellsberg were willing to sink her to a really frightening depth. He needed the ship up four more feet, therefore, which meant completely drying out the boiler room, engine room, and No. 3 hold. By the third night, they hadn't made it. Pumps kept stopping. And the *Liebenfels* had taken to flopping back and forth between port and starboard lists, which meant they had to pump water back and forth across the shaft alley in the No. 4 and No. 5 holds to counteract it.

Fourth morning. Holding her for the moment at a 10-degree list, Ellsberg ordered the Persian dry dock cleared. Early afternoon. He started to take her in. And the key pump in the engine room stopped; without that, he would lose stability altogether.

List: 20 degrees, adding a degree every seven minutes. At 30 degrees, he estimated, she would roll. That meant thirty-five minutes to replace the magneto of the engine-room pump with their lone spare dry one, and hope it would fire up immediately.

In removing the old magneto, Engineer Keith had to keep from rotating the shaft and thus destroying the firing order of the cylinders. He did the replacement by the light of a flashlight, and the engine fired immediately. In the next few hours the ship began slowly righting herself, and they began removing a magneto at a time, replacing it with the previously removed magneto which had meanwhile been baked in an oven to dry it, and thus getting all pumps working well again.

By morning the list was down to 13 degrees, so Ellsberg took her in—after first sinking the dry dock to an outrageous depth and with a corresponding 13-degree list, over the objections of the tow master. He had to repair the *Liebenfels* immediately, even though it meant using most of their scrounged and hoarded steel, because he could not afford to have the dry dock tied up.

Brown and his salvage ship, the *Intent*, were sent back to the South Harbor to start work on the *Frauenfels*. The *Frauenfels* lay deeper than the other vessel had, and Brown's salvage crew also had been cut down by the weather; but some new 6- and 10-inch pumps had arrived on another salvage ship, the *Chamberlin*. Brown's divers began shoring up the main deck inside, since there was enough water above her to collapse the decks once pumping had begun, unless they were strengthened.

At the same time, HMS *Dido* arrived to have her damaged stern repaired,[1] followed closely by the other cruisers, *Kythera*, *Euryalus*, and *Cleopatra*. Ellsberg was in Alexandria for one day while the vessels were being shifted, and returned to find that *Cleopatra* somehow had dropped off her keel blocks in the Persian dry dock. The ship suffered only a small dent and a minor leak, and the dry dock suffered only four minor leaks. But she had completely crushed their wooden keel blocks. Without keel blocks the dry dock was useless.

Ellsberg was horrified to find that the Dock Master had on his own authority sent word to Alexandria that their docking facilities would be inoperable for six weeks while heavy timbers were sent out for new keel blocks.

Ellsberg immediately sent off word that the dry dock would be shut down for only four days, and then pointed out to the bewildered Dock Master that there were literally hundreds of keel blocks in the salvaged but still unusable Italian dry dock just a few hundred yards away.

THE SECOND DRY DOCK

On August 31, work began on the second, smaller scuttled dry dock. Five of its six deck sections had been blown out, though in this one also the bomb farthest aft had not blown. Similar problems were faced, except that this dock was completely submerged, so they had to place a wooden scaffolding eleven feet high and 330 feet long on top of the walls, giving the workmen a walkway two feet above the water at high tide. Ellsberg had a new Sutorbilt low-pressure salvage air compressor brought by the *Chamberlin* on the job here; its two 200-horsepower engines delivered twelve hundred cubic feet of air a minute.

The dock was ready for blowing on September 10, just ten days after sealing had begun. By the thirteenth, the starboard side was up enough to expose the storage and machinery compartments in the upper chambers, which were pumped out for further buoyancy. Men went in to plug leaks between them and the flooded lower compartments.

Meanwhile, the compressors, especially the Sutorbilt, had begun heating up badly. Their lubricating grease not only melted, but actually fried, so a virtual bucket brigade of the hardest grease they could find was continually fed into the compressor's bearings.

On the evening of the fourteenth, three ironworkers—Armstrong, Jones, and Larsen (we last met Armstrong wielding a sledge hammer aboard the *Dido*)—were in the after compartment of the starboard side to stop a heavy leak, when Ellsberg found that the Sutorbilt was so hot that its bearings were about to seize. He agreed with mechanic Jim Buzbee that they would have to shut it down and let it cool, or lose it completely.

But just then, in one of those inexplicable occurrences that plague all salvage operations, the portside of the dock came up. And came up with the stern higher than the bow.

"For God's sake, Jim, start that compressor up again!" Ellsberg roared at Buzbee. "Never mind if we ruin it now! *Start it up!*"

Too late.

The stern kept coming up, the bow dipping—and water rushed into the forward hatches of the bow compartments. The whole dry dock just sank straightaway, carrying the compressors (except for the Sutorbilt) down with it, leaving the salvors paddling about in the water.

All except Armstrong, Larsen, and Jones. They were still in the after starboard compartment. Ellsberg yelled at his divers to go to the lost salvors' aid, but they just looked at the tremendous welter of white water above the still-settling dock and shook their heads.

Ellsberg, although over fifty years old, dived in from the launch, which had picked them up. The milky, swirling mass of white water rushing into the compartment carried him straight down to the booby hatch. An arm was sticking out of it. Ellsberg yanked back the cover, seized the arm, and pawed for the surface. The man he dragged up was Armstrong.

As others seized him, Ellsberg dove again. He reached into the now-open hatch, caught another arm, dragged a second man clear. Lloyd Larsen.

On the third trip, Ellsberg had to cling with his thighs to the rim of the hatch, thrust his whole upper body inside, and grope blindly. His fingers brushed cloth, he grabbed, had Jones, and was able to drag him out.

Horace Armstrong, the hammer-wielding man, died.

By 5:00 P.M. the same day, a grim Ellsberg was back at the dock, ordering the Sutorbilt (it had been on a barge alongside, not on the dock itself) repacked with grease and fired up. Gasoline-driven compressors were brought in to replace those lost. By 10:00 P.M. the starboard side came up again, and they began drying the upper compartments. At 3:30 the next morning, the portside came up. Then all the air was rammed into the forward tanks on the starboard side until the stern came up. They shifted some three-inch pumps over the walkway to the portside, and Ellsberg redistributed air to keep her up and even, while repairs went forward on her.

It had taken sixteen days and one life.

Meanwhile a third salvage tug, *Resolute*, had arrived on September 3. Despite the lack of divers and diving equipment, Ellsberg put it to work on the *Moncalieri*, one of the Naval Harbor's blockships, the *Chamberlin* on another, the *XXIII Marzo*. The *Intent* already was in the South Harbor on the *Frauenfels*.

AWFUL BOTCH: RAISING THE GERA

Meanwhile, something was almost happening over in the Commercial Harbor, where the commercial salvors were mucking about. McCance had made two apparently bungling attempts to raise the big floating crane that had been scuttled alongside the commercial wharves—it lay in only 40 feet of water, and had merely had its sea cocks opened to flood it. McCance had somehow managed to ruin its previously watertight main deck, then had wired London it was unsalvageable and ought to be blown up. The Admiralty refused.

McCance, also, had for nine months been trying to raise the *Gera*. In September he actually succeeded in getting her sealed up with heavy cement patches on the bomb holes fore and aft, which had sunk the small commercial steamer. He started pumping on the fourth and had her main deck awash by the fifth; by the seventh, *Gera* was afloat. Ellsberg began planning ways of fitting her into the dry-dock schedule.

But for the next ten days she remained in this condition; afloat, but badly heeled. Somehow McCance seemed unable to gain on her.

Captain Colin Lucas of the Royal Navy asked Ellsberg if he could lend McCance four pumps. It seemed that those he had aboard the *Gera* had broken down one by one and had refused to start again. They were afraid the ship would capsize.

Ellsberg took two 6-inch and two 4-inch pumps over on the *Resolute*. Then he learned that the pumps had all quit because McCance had let his men use *salt water in the radiators*—which eventually had frozen the engines by depositing salt in the cylinder jackets.

By September 25, all was once more quiet aboard the *Gera:* Ellsberg's four pumps had also broken down. Colin Lucas, fed up, on his own discretion (and with subsequent Admiralty approval) canceled McCance's entire salvage contract at Massawa. Ellsberg took over. By 7:30 P.M., *Resolute* was alongside with every salvage pump they could find.

Captain Reed of the *Resolute* got pumps going fore and aft in search of stability for the ship, but it was doubtful if he would get it. The commercial salvors had not even known enough to completely dry a few compartments and thus prevent the sickening rolling from side to side of the vessel.

It was an incredible scene. The greatest hazard was pumps; Ellsberg was afraid that the weight of broken-down pumps aboard the ship might actually be enough to capsize her. They kept tripping over pumps: gasoline, steam, reciprocating, centrifugal, diesel, electric, submersible, even huge donkey boilers and diesel-driven generators.

Two days later, *Gera*, stable and upright, was in the Naval Harbor with all her machinery spaces and holds properly dried out, awaiting her turn at the dry dock. But *Gera* had a parting shot in her locker.

On October 29, Reed said he was afraid that the forward patch was about to let go. The upper half of it was only wood and canvas, and *teredos* had gotten into it. Within hours, a 6-inch pump could barely keep ahead of the leakage. Their big trouble was her draught: she rode lower than the Persian dock could go even if flooded down to her lowest safe depth. This was because of the scores of tons of unnecessary cement McCance had poured into the vessel in a clumsy attempt to patch her, and because, in a panicked attempt at stability, he had tossed five hundred tons of rock ballast into her holds.

Ellsberg, knowing he would lose the *Gera* otherwise, ordered the Dock Master to put the Persian dock down two feet lower than she was designed to go: in that position she would have only inches of freeboard, and would have less than three hundred tons of reserve buoyancy between her and her own sinking.

The Dock Master refused.

Ellsberg said that if the dock was not down when *Gera* arrived, he, personally, would board her and throw the Dock Master overboard.

The dock was down when *Gera* arrived.

They still weren't home free, however, since *Gera* was beamy, and the clumsy cement patch on her portside added a full three feet to that. If they caught the patch on the dry dock's wing wall and tore it loose, a thousand tons of water would pour into the *Gera* and sink both her and the dry dock instantly.

The patch caught. For an hour they jockeyed her like a Cadillac being fit into a VW parking place, doing all of it *by hand* with hand lines. Finally she scraped in, they brought up the dock, and the *Gera* was safe.

Ellsberg found that hundreds of tons of useless concrete had been set in her portside double bottoms, nowhere near the blown-open plates they were supposed to be patching. It took them a week to blow out the concrete with minuscule, delicately measured dynamite charges before they could even begin rebuilding the ruptured wing walls. On November 14, sixteen days after she had entered the dry dock, she was out again. Six ships waited to take her place.

Edison Brown on the *Intent*, meanwhile, had run into trouble with the *Frauenfels*. His twelve-man crew had begun cementing up the vessel's two bomb holes, making her hull tight, and building cofferdams around her deck hatches, on July 16. On October 1, with the *Resolute* joining in and a forty-eight-man total crew, pumping began.

The bow would not come up, no matter how hard and long they pumped. So they had to start with the stern, even though they had a bare ten feet clearance there with the next blockship in line. With the stern up, the bow still stuck. Finally, at midnight, she came—like a bucking bronco. Only then did they discover that a large section of her port plating had been blown out vertically by the explosion, and had been buried in six feet of mud. Thus the plates had acted as a sort of huge bow anchor.

A MINE ABOARD THE *BRENTA*

Despite a 55-knot gale, they got *Frauenfels* into the dry dock on October 4. On the twentieth, work began on the *Brenta*, which had lain just behind her in line. But Buck Scougale nearly walked into a large submarine mine in the ship's No. 2 hold, so Ellsberg sent to Alexandria for an explosives officer. While they were waiting for him, Ellsberg sent the *Intent* out after the *Tripolitania* instead. This was one of several ships that had been scuttled at the forty-miles-distant Dahlak Islands by merely opening the sea cocks.

When *Intent* returned successful on November 6, Ellsberg put her back on the *Brenta*. On the eighth, Scougale measured the mine in the hold, recording diameter, height, and the number of lead horns. Ellsberg rigged one of *Brenta*'s forward booms above the hold's entrance, then removed the *Intent* a thousand feet away. From the salvage ship, a line was reeved off a small, portable, gas-driven winch through the block on the *Brenta*'s boom. The bridle on this line had sister hooks to engage the lifting eyes on the mine.

The next day, Scougale fastened the sister hooks to the mine's eyes, then left. The mine was winched out of the hold from the salvage ship a thousand feet away, and was left hanging for an hour to make sure there was no delayed detonation mechanism.

Ellsberg and the British commander, Davy, moved in. They refused the explosives officer's request to accompany them; they needed an expert around to explain what had happened, Ellsberg said, if the mine blew up. They came in under the dangling mine in a twenty-foot punt, had it gently lowered into their boat, and then were towed to a deserted beach where they gave the mine to the explosives officer to play with.

While *Intent* had been off after the *Tripolitania*, Ellsberg had been working on the immense floating crane in the Commercial Harbor, the one McCance had worked on for nine months unsuccessfully. Since the crane, unlike the dry docks, had no wing walls to be sealed for buoyancy to lift it, McCance, in damaging the main deck so it was no longer airtight, had left Ellsberg with only one possible salvage method.

Compressed air could not be kept in the crane; water could not be pumped out; there was no tide for tide lifts: Ellsberg was faced with a dead-weight lift of four hundred to six hundred tons—in Massawa, where his greatest lifting force at hand was fifteen tons.

GASOLINE STORAGE TANKS FOR PONTOONS

What was left? Submersible pontoons to be sunk alongside the wreck, pinned, and pumped out to bring it to the surface. A familiar method, already in use in the late 1800s. Ellsberg himself had used it to great advantage on the S-51 'way back in 1925.

Only, there were no pontoons in Massawa and no way to build or get any.

Ellsberg put his men to sweeping one-inch steel guide wires under the crane, for the heavy lifting hawsers he would need once he found some pontoons. The truth was, he already had his eye on some horizontal, cylindrical gasoline storage tanks near the military airfield. They were forty-five feet long, eleven feet in diameter, held thirty thousand gallons each of aviation gas . . . Each would furnish, Ellsberg estimated, one hundred tons of lift. Wonderful!

Of course, there were a few drawbacks. First, they had no internal bulkheads: their interiors were common. This meant he had to blow or vent all or nothing on each pontoon. There were no hawse pipes and no lifting eyes. The final major drawback was that Shell Oil owned them.

He solved this by filching half a dozen of them (each as big as a

Pullman car) using heavy crawler cranes and low-bodied trucks. He fitted them with ten-inch steel pipes right through the tanks from one side to the other, for hawse pipes; he fitted one-inch air-hose connections in the top and six-inch vent valves in the bottom. He put on lifting and securing eyes.

When all this had been done, he called up Shell's man in Cairo and said he wanted to move six of Shell's big oil tanks down to the quay so they would be there ready for shipping once Shell wanted to move them. Ellsberg said that, to keep his men busy, he would repair the tanks from the damage of the last RAF air raid before Massawa had fallen, so they would be usable again as gasoline storage tanks. Shell was enchanted; of course, Shell never heard anything about pontoons.

Since the crane was only one hundred feet long, Ellsberg could get only two pontoons to a side: he hoped they would be enough, with their combined lift of 420 tons. If not, he would have to add a pontoon at each end of the sixty-foot-wide crane.

Ellsberg tested the first pontoon at the end of October. It acted terribly, as he had expected. It was, after all, as Ellsberg remarked, "as uncomplicated inside as an empty tin can."

It took them several tries to get the fifteen-ton gasoline tank sunk horizontally—with both ends keeping level. When they succeeded, diver Ervin Johnson took the loop of one of the doubled lifting wires already placed under the crane, and threaded it through the pontoon's hawse hole. Through the loop's end he stuck a 2½-foot, five-inch-diameter steel pin. After he repeated this with another loop on the pontoon's second hawse pipe, it was pinned in place.

Then the after one broke loose, and the pontoon popped to the surface, back end first. It took them until 3:00 A.M. to cast it loose, refloat it, unwater it, rewater it, resink it, and repin it.

On November 5, they started on the other pontoons. Those on the other side of the crane did not have a loop of lifting wire to be threaded through their hawse holes, of course, but rather the two ends of the folded wire. Once these were threaded, they were made tight with three sets of wire clamps—steel castings molded to the lay of the lifting wire—tightened down with 1½-inch bolts.

All pontoons were in place by the seventeenth, well lashed so they would not shift when the bows of the crane were lifted first. Air was started into the pontoons on the eighteenth (three hundred cubic feet a minute, expelling six tons of water a minute); he gave a full charge to the forward pontoons, a half charge to the after ones. The bow came up after only an hour of pressing, and the stern ten minutes later.

Resolute towed it to the Persian dry dock; it was repaired, scraped, painted, and refloated a day later. The machinery was disassembled and put into working condition, and by December the crane was in shape for lifting the 1000-ton Italian mine layer *Ostia*, which had been capsized in fifty feet of water beside the Commercial Harbor's most useful quay. The biggest problem with the *Ostia* was her mines: the Italians had planned to blow the ship to pieces with them once she had been scuttled. They had not gone off but they were still armed, their primers fitted.

It took two weeks to remove the detonators, one by one, in the dark. The divers on this were Petty Officer Sinfield and Peter Keeble, who was in Massawa temporarily, helping out. When blowing the lifting tunnels under the ship, Keeble and Sinfield had to work lying flat on their bellies with fire hoses; grit kept continually clogging their exhaust valves. When it did, they would roll over on their backs and keep working, using their spit cocks as temporary exhaust valves.

For buoyancy they used Ellsberg's gasoline-tanks-cum-pontoons, lowering them with the eighty-ton crane Ellsberg had salvaged the month before. When *Ostia* had come smoothly up, Edison Brown of the *Intent* edged her away from the quay with towlines. Ellsberg was standing by, a worried look on his face, and Brown leaned out of the wheelhouse to reassure him.

"Relax, Lootenant—we *got* the sonofabitch."

That is a good comment on Ellsberg's service at Massawa: whatever the job was, he somehow got it done. That same month (December 1942) he received orders to proceed to the North African ports, where there were a good many more harbors that needed clearing.

[1] See pages 237–39.

CHAPTER NINETEEN

In Bomb Alley

When the Allies arrived to take over Oran, Algeria, in late 1942, it was under control of a French naval commandant, Capitaine de Frigate Duprés, who still felt loyalty to the Vichy (collaborationist) government of France. He had therefore scuttled twenty-seven French vessels in the harbor, most in water deep enough so only their masts and smokestacks were visible. Six of them had been anchored bow to stern in two parallel rows across the entrance.

Lieutenant George Ankers, USN, had twelve divers and mechanics and three assistant officers; but he had only a few diving rigs and a few hand tools to work with.

He had arrived while the six blockships across the harbor mouth were still afloat in either the bow or the stern, although the sea cocks were still open and the ships were gradually sinking. He wanted desperately to throw a cable around the floating end of as many ships as possible. They could then be pivoted at right angles so when they sank totally it would be with passageways between them. But he had no ship. Then the British salvage ship *King Salvor* arrived from Gibraltar, under command of Lieutenant Commander White. White had ship and equipment, but no divers or mechanics.

Each man felt he should command the operation; as they squabbled, ships kept sinking. Finally Ankers' men got a cable onto the bow of the *Boudjmel*, in the inner row of blockships, and got it to right angles. They saw a narrow gap between two ships in the outer row, *Spahi* and *Pigeon*. *Pigeon* already was down hard, but *Spahi* . . .

Just as they got to her, she rolled and sank on her starboard side.

Local American naval authorities gave orders that Ankers was to be in command. The Allied Naval Commander-in-Chief, British Admiral Cunningham, hearing this, called in the just-arriving Ellsberg and ordered him to replace Ankers with White. If Ankers went out, Ellsberg discovered, the divers would find ways to keep from accomplishing anything. Divers under water are a law unto themselves.

Ellsberg's solution was to keep Ankers as head of things in Oran, restore White as the *King Salvor*'s Salvage Officer, and then order him to Bône, forty miles distant, which was under nightly Axis air assault and in desperate need of salvage work. Meanwhile, *King Salvor* would remain in Oran until White could get the port organized for salvage work.

Everyone was happy.

Ellsberg looked over his salvage contingent. He had the American salvage officer and divers, he had a British salvage ship and equipment, and he had a contingent of French salvors whose equipment was so ancient that it was dangerous to send anyone down in it. The Frenchmen had been ordered (by the same French officers who had sunk them) to raise some French submarines in the harbor for *la gloire de la France*—then, as now, touchy about her prestige.

TROUBLE WITH THE *SPAHI*

Ellsberg countermanded the order. He wanted the capsized *Spahi* raised before anything else, so that there would be open passage for Allied warships, freighters, and troop carriers into Oran. The French Commandant promptly ordered the French salvors to work on a thirty-year-old French battleship, *La Bretagne*, which was upside down in the French naval harbor of Mers-el-Kebir, some three miles away.

The *Bretagne* was outmoded, undergunned, ill-constructed, and worn out, so Ellsberg again countermanded the order. He wanted all hands turned to the important business at hand, the *Spahi*. It was an ancient freighter full of hogsheads of wine, and had been sunk merely by opened sea valves. The divers sealed these, but blowing could not begin until her bulkheads were strengthened to take the pressure.

He divided her up into five sections, intending to blow her just down to the mid-line, so she would float on her side. She was sealed and ready for blowing within six days.

But the French authorities had not been bested yet. Commandant du Port Duprés (who had neatly switched sides to the Free French and had stayed on) planned to bring a French passenger ship, the *Ardois*, in from the outer harbor through the narrow gap between the *Spahi* and the *Pigeon*. This gap could handle Liberty ships half loaded; Ellsberg was afraid it could *not* handle the *Ardois*.

He was right.

The French harbor pilot, very possibly under orders to do so, rammed her right into the *Spahi*. They finally scraped her through with tugs. Ellsberg sent divers down to look.

There was a two-yard-wide hole in the port (upper) side of the previously sound *Spahi*. This meant several days of lacing the jagged gash with reinforcing rod, building a wooden form, and then pouring a concrete patch—they had neither time nor material for a steel patch.

Just as they prepared to pour cement, the Commandant du Port ordered that the *Ardois* be taken back out of the harbor. By the same pilot. The tow came tearing out at high speed, straight for *Spahi*.

Cupping his hands, Ellsberg shrieked at the pilot, "God damn you! Stop her! STOP HER!"

Crunch!

They had to use the tremendously powerful *King Salvor* to bring her off, that time. Gone were their forms, their reinforcing steel; in their place was a hole twenty feet long and twenty feet wide, large enough to drop a Sherman tank through.

To cheer the disconsolate Ellsberg, Captain Bill Reed arrived from Massawa with seven of his crack salvage team from that port, including master diver Buck Scougale. Since Ankers' men were working on the *Spahi*, Ellsberg sent Reed and his boys over to work on three scuttled French dry docks.

Ankers figured two more weeks to patch the *Spahi*, with a few more days to let the cement harden. But there was a new problem: the hogsheads of wine. They had a neutral buoyancy in the water, so Ellsberg had ignored them in figuring how much lift he needed to get the vessel off the bottom. But as the ship came up—and about one third of her would be raised above the surface—one third of the hogsheads of wine also would come up. They would assume their own weight as soon as they were out of the water, and so would be heavy enough to prevent the ship's floating.

That meant stevedoring, with divers, a third of the wine casks from the *Spahi*. They had tense moments when the first one came from the holds: would it float or sink? If it went down, that meant more time lost in rigging some sort of sling from a dockside derrick.

It floated. Barely. In a thousand-pound hogshead of wine, there was *five pounds* of buoyancy! But it was enough.

Each cask held 140 gallons of wine. The salvage crew, secretly broaching the first one raised, got so drunk that they could not even work the next day. Ellsberg brought in a set of Army guards with loaded rifles and bayonets to keep the salvors out of the salvaged wine, and the work went on.

But not for long. The *Spahi* had to be abandoned for a series of torpedoed vessels that needed help from the *King Salvor*.[1] So it was not until January 4, 1943, that Ankers' divers could begin sealing the *Spahi* with thirty tons of cement. On the seventh, despite six inches of driving rain brought by a terrific wind, the compressors began banging air into the five compartments, all hoses being operated by a single control manifold on the diving float alongside the vessel.

At noon, the bow came up, and stayed up; the cement patch was holding, and leakage was negligible. All the compressors were switched to the after compartments to bring the stern up. But she wouldn't come. As Ellsberg had feared, the bulkheads were leaking so badly that the *Spahi*'s interior was common. With the bow up, the air just moved forward and geysered out the forward cargo hatches. The same thing happened when they tried the stern.

Ellsberg put the ship back on the bottom and sent two French tugs after a hundred-ton floating crane, which by some weird chance had been overlooked in the scuttling operations. He had the crane hook a towing bridle onto the *Spahi*'s nose and lift as he turned all compressors on full. Her prow came up. More lines were tossed around her, like cowboys lassoing a steer; *King Salvor* and the two French tugs grabbed on, and they dragged the vessel around through 110 degrees to open the channel wide.

Then everybody poured on all the steam they had, and dragged *Spahi* upharbor as far as they could before she stuck fast.

Oran Harbor was open to vessels of any size.

THREE SUNKEN DRY DOCKS AT ORAN

Meanwhile, Bill Reed and his men had been at work on the three dry docks: Petit Dock (2000-ton capacity), Moyen Dock (4200), and the enormous Grand Dock (25,000-ton capacity)—the largest dry dock in North Africa. The Petit Dock had been flooded by opened valves in water shallow enough that the tops of all compartments stood free from the water even at high tide. Reed merely connected up the dock's electric cables with shore power sources, closed the valves, and used its own pumps to pump it dry. It was put into service immediately.

Commandant du Port Duprés apparently had seen the error in his ways after sinking that dock, because he had gotten tricky on the other two. The Moyen Dock, though also in shallow water, had been sunk with the submarine *Danae* still aboard. Only one side of the dock had been flooded so she would capsize to port and come to rest with the *Danae* lying up against the inside of the port wing wall.

The Grand Dock had been treated even more cavalierly. In twelve fathoms of water, all the flood valves had been opened, and charges of TNT had been set off in the port wing wall. Instead of capsizing the dock as it sank, the TNT merely blew open the side of the dock.

After the Petit Dock was raised, Reed went after the Grand Dock. Lieutenant Perrin-Trichard and his French salvors worked with Reed's crew: the Frenchmen did the plumbing work—laying lines on the harbor bottom to carry air into the compartments—and the Americans did the sealing. Ellsberg planned to raise it as he had the docks in Massawa: by blowing it with compressed air.

The difference was that this dry dock was 720 feet long, 140 feet wide, and sixty feet high. There were fifty compartments to be made watertight instead of eight, which meant several miles of air hose and a great number of air compressors, which they didn't have.

When work began, they found that each compartment had eight-inch-diameter air-vent outlet pipes that had to be sealed, and that wooden plugs wouldn't work. So forms had to be built and cement poured to seal each one of them. Openings that could be gotten at only from inside the tank were very hazardous, since the divers had to work their way down through the reinforcing ribs with a good chance of getting hung up or jammed between them.

Perrin-Trichard solved the problem of air compressors, oddly enough, with the ancient French battleship *Bretagne*: she had several very old, very cumbersome electric compressors aboard. Ellsberg scrounged up fifty air gauges, but they were all high-pressure ones, virtually worthless.

He planned to raise one end of the dock at a time; if he tried to bring both up together, the free water inside would rush about and capsize it. But raising one end meant there was the danger of putting too much weight on the submerged end and breaking the dock's back.

To avoid this, he first pumped air into the bow to make it a bit light but not nearly enough to bring it up; then he pumped heavily into the stern until, just after dark, the immense stern broke water. They strung temporary lights, closed off flood valves, and unbolted deck manholes. This meant they could put down suction hoses from their water pumps and dry those after compartments completely. By midnight of the day the lift had begun, they were able to start raising the bow.

They kept right on until dawn without results; and when light came they saw why. Above the sunken nose of the dock was a tremendous froth of white water: the air they were pumping in was going right out again.

A diver reported that the bow section had been pushed too hard down into the mud despite Ellsberg's precautions—a result, of course, of their lack of adequate gauges. From starboard to port, the bow had buckled athwartship; a wrinkle of burst rivets and buckled plates formed a line of leakage right across.

Ellsberg, for no reason he could think of, said to Reed, "Keep the compressors going, Lieutenant."

Reed did. All that day. All the next day. The next night. Reed pointed out that the air was just coming back out again, but Ellsberg was adamant. He had a hunch, like Featherstone sending the Foundation tugs out to search for the *Leicester*.

In midmorning of the third day, January 13, 1943, the bow of the dock finally began, slowly, to rise. Once it was up, they were able to temporarily seal the fold across her bow and keep her up.

GENERAL DELIVERY TO THE RESCUE

The Moyen Dock, it developed, presented an unusual salvage problem because of the *Danae*. Ellsberg wanted to ignore the submarine entirely; just patch the portside of the dock and blow it—the starboard side already was watertight—and bring up dock and submarine together. But in going down, the *Danae* had flipped over and had punched her conning tower right through the dock amidships.

The air they pumped in escaped from this hole, of course; but it could not be repaired, since the sub's conning tower was still sticking in it. So the sub had to be raised first. Reed wanted to blow it with compressed air, and Ellsberg let him try, even though he knew they would get only four hundred tons' buoyancy before air would start escaping from the damaged conning tower. They needed six hundred.

Reed tried, and the sub did not rise, so he brought out Oran's only floating crane, which would lift a hundred tons, fastened a heavy wire sling around the sub's stern, and brought that up. But they had only one crane, so they could not get the other end up.

The next morning, Ellsberg looked out toward the salvage site, and rubbed his eyes. There now were two identical cranes over the sub, one preparing to lift each end. When he got out to the salvage boat, he discovered that the Army had brought the crane several hundred miles up the coast to help unload Sherman tanks from some newly arrived Liberty ships. Buck Scougale, seeing the crane come in, had asked the French Captain where he was taking it: *Le général* somebody-or-other, a name he could not remember, the Frenchman explained.

"I'm from General Delivery," said Scougale importantly. "The General wants this crane right away for a hurry-up job alongside that other crane you can see ahead."

The Army was most unhappy with General Delivery, but the submarine and then the dock came up promptly.

Often Ellsberg's harbor-clearance activities in North Africa were not so much concerned with opening a harbor as with keeping it open. The 20,000-ton converted Cunard Line steamer *Scythia* was struck by a German torpedo while bringing troops to Algiers on December 23, 1942. She made port under her own power, flooding badly and down by the head, but still afloat.

The ship was thus immobilized in Algiers, where one of the numerous German bomber raids was bound to tag her with direct hits. There was no dock in North Africa large enough to hold her, except the one that Bill Reed was trying to raise in Oran. Which meant she had to be sent back to England. But the Lloyd's agent in Algiers said she was not seaworthy enough for the trip, and as a result her master—quite rightly—refused to take her out. If he had, the British Board of Trade would have lifted his license.

Ellsberg offered to get the vessel to Oran, where enough repairs could be made for the trip to England. The Lloyd's agent refused permission for Oran also, and took Ellsberg down to show him why. There was no starboard side at all in the cargo hold that had taken the hit; only a hole twenty-five feet high and sixty feet long. Water was up nearly to the lower side of the bottom deck, on which they were standing, and which formed the top of the cargo hold.

No one could put a patch over a hole that size, the Lloyd's man argued. Not with the facilities at hand. Ellsberg agreed. But when he was alone, he began wondering why a ship with only one flooded hold should ride down so far in the head. He went exploring, and found that the No. 3 lower hold, actually a series of deep tanks for liquid cargo, also was flooded.

Why?

Because shrapnel from the torpedo had knocked a few small holes in the tanks (which had a twenty-three-ton combined capacity) and they had gradually filled with water. Ellsberg merely told the local people to seal the high holes in it and heavily shore the tank tops and after bulkhead to make sure they could withstand air pressure. Then they should bring in air compressors and press the water out of it through the holes lower down. With cargo shifting, the bow would rise eight feet and the whole vessel three, up to her normal loaded draught. The compressors would be left aboard, working, for the trip to Oran, where permanent repairs could be done.

The whole operation—including the tow, after enthusiastic agreement by the Lloyd's agent—took five days.

LUBRICATING WITH SEA WATER

Another troop transport, the 16,000-ton *Cameronia*, was immobilized the next night, Christmas Eve, at Bône, where an average of forty German bombs fell a night. A torpedo had struck aft of her engine rooms, damaging neither propellers nor rudder, but instead piercing the shaft-alley bulkheads with shrapnel. The shaft alley had flooded, and the steel propeller shafting bearings could not be oiled.

The people at Bône were trying to figure out a way to get her to Algiers, 250 miles away; without lubrication, the Babbitt metal in the shaft bearings would melt out and the shafts would freeze. Ellsberg, who had spent the previous nine years as chief engineer for Tidewater Oil, told them that the *Cameronia* could make the trip as she was, with no repairs at all.

The sea water that would be forced in continually by the action of the waves would act as lubricant and keep the shafts from heating up. Water-lubricated, the shaft bearings could stand up to even high speed for short distances; at minimum speed she could make Algiers easily.

She did.

The following year, 1943, Allied fortunes changed as the British Eighth Army began winning the desert war. Alexandria was suddenly safe again. Peter Keeble, the South African salvor who, like Ellsberg, had been bouncing all over the Mediterranean and North African ports, found himself in that port early in 1943. There the sins of a certain Australian, "Jumper" Collins, the Port Salvage Officer from Tobruk, were called to account in the form of the "liberated" German tug *Max Barendt*.

A SAGA: THE *MAX BARENDT*

The *Max* was a long-distance tow ship that, in 1942, had been struck by an RAF bomb when Tobruk had been in German hands. Without exploding, the bomb had gone right through the ship from top to bottom, out through her double hull, and buried itself in the mud. The *Max* had gone down by the head. "Jumper" was a good salvage officer—he put a plug of concrete in her bottom, pumped her out, and raised her—but he was no engineer. He knew nothing of such things as brack water, leaky joints, or absent boiler lagging.

After he had dried her out, he made the mistake of firing her up. The results were remarkable. Pouring steam, poor *Max* began roaring like an enraged elephant, leaping and shaking like a man with St. Vitus's dance. Jumper and his valiants fled; somehow *Max* didn't blow herself up, but survived while her fires burned down.

Needless to say, *Jumper's Folly*, as *Max* was quickly dubbed, had to be lugged to Alexandria for refitting.

There, Keeble was put in charge. He renamed poor old *Max* the *Captive*, and since a tug was needed desperately there in Alexandria, hurried through the repairs. When she was ready for her shakedown trials, Keeble invited participation by the dockyard captain, a dignified gentleman named Coppinger, and other assorted high brass.

They cleared the jetty, and the commanding officer gave a smart tug on his whistle lanyard. There was a high, harsh scream overhead as of an enraged eagle; then a crash; then a roar of high-pressure steam. As Keeble watched in horror, the *Captive*'s siren leisurely toppled off its steampipe and smashed down among the dignitaries assembled on the bridge.

The steam valve was shut down smartly. The CO, cool in crisis, jerked the engine-room telegraph handle to STOP ENGINES.

The telegraph chains parted and fell down the pipe in a brisk shower of rust. *Captive* was running with engines at FULL AHEAD, with no whistle, and with no communication with the engine room beyond the old-fashioned speaking tube.

The CO ran to the tube and shouted down it to stop all engines. Unfortunately, the tube was blocked halfway down. A runner was sent from the bridge to apprise the chief engineer that the engines must be stopped. Before the runner got down there, the helm jammed over hard and stayed there.

The *Captive* began running in circles.

A quick-witted officer ran out on deck, and with a shower of blows, kicks, and curses, got the rusted windlass unfrozen. They heaved a sigh of relief as the anchor splashed overboard and the anchor chain rattled out of its locker.

And kept right on rattling out. Nobody had bothered to clench the inboard end. The ultimate link flicked airily from the locker, across the deck, and over the side.

At this point the Admiralty tug *Respond*, did. It circled around them like a collie around an old ram, to eventually shepherd *Captive* back to its slip in disgrace.

Keeble wisely chose to dive for the anchor while other members of the salvage team faced the brass. Diving, at times such as that, does have its compensations.

That same year, Keeble was involved in two harbor-clearance projects that displayed to the fullest the man's remarkable ingenuity. At Benghazi it was a vessel in the outer harbor that was a menace to the troopships and Liberty ships coming in to unload. Keeble's way of handling this craft became the standard for harbor clearance wherever they found a sand, mud, or limestone (as opposed to hard, or bedrock) bottom.

Keeble and another diver laid scores of obsolete depth charges in a ring around the vessel—at some distance from it. Then they detonated them all at once. This did two things. It blew a crater in the harbor floor with the ship in the middle of it, so everything else was farther beneath the surface. And second, since all the charges were detonated simultaneously, thousands of tons of incompressible water were driven down on the ship from all directions.

By the time they had repeated the blasts twice more, each time tightening the ring of explosives, all that was left was a small heap of scrap metal rising a bare half-dozen feet above the harbor floor. The ship's beam had been reduced from seventy feet to ten!

The harbor-clearance operations conducted by Keeble at Tripoli must stand with Ellsberg's at Massawa as a magnificent example of men producing under pressure, careless of themselves, of equipment, and of ships. This is a very different sort of effort than that of a Cox, whose grim determination drove him onward year after year. It is more like men under fire performing feats far beyond their normal capacities.

OPENING TRIPOLI HARBOR

Before retreating from Tripoli, the Nazis had scuttled seven blockships across the narrow mouth of the harbor. They were sunk to their upper works, one almost on top of the other. The largest was the 8000-ton *Giovanni Battista*. It was booby-trapped under water (100-pound canisters of explosives with trip-wire-activated, spring-loaded detonators).

The other six ships had in their holds reinforcing rods, machinery, anything metal the Germans had been able to lay their hands on, with thousands of tons of concrete poured in on top.

Keeble met his superior officer, Commander Wilber Rippon, aboard the *Battista*, and was given the news. The Allies planned to start moving thousands of tons of supplies into Tripoli; supplies needed by the Eighth Army to drive Rommel back from the Mareth line.

The authorities were allowing Keeble ten days to get the harbor open for the convoys.

Keeble worked his men in three teams. Below were the divers, setting explosive charges which had been packed into canvas hoses and fitted with detonators. On the higher, only partially flooded upper decks were artisans working with acetylene torches to cut free whatever metalwork they could. Working parties hauled off the steel that had been removed.

The divers hung strings of explosives about the clumps of concrete like popcorn strings on a Christmas tree. They had to watch constantly for booby traps, and they spent all of their time ashore stealing bottled oxygen, bottled acetylene, tools, and matériel from any service that had what they needed.

The crews worked during air raids, even as German planes dropped bombs and strafed them. Divers were down so much that they did not even unsuit: they merely removed their helmets and slept on the deck still laced up in their cumbersome rubber and twill.

Within four days, small craft and lighters could shoot the gap they had made. Within nine days there was a 130-foot-wide passage.

But it was only eighteen feet deep. The tremendous rubble of cement and twisted reinforcing rods still was there. They somehow had to deepen that channel.

Keeble went aboard an LST (landing ship, tank) in the great convoy anchored outside the harbor. He congratulated the skipper heartily telling him that he had been selected for the honor of bringing into port the very first deep-draught ship to enter Tripoli Harbor. Very soon, the delighted captain would receive a signal to proceed from the SNO (Senior Naval Officer). Keeble advised him to come in smartly—at, say, eight knots—so he would have good steerageway on the ship.

Keeble then went ashore to the SNO and told him that they were ready for ships to start entering the harbor. He had noticed that one of the craft, an LST, already was hove short; the SNO, he suggested respectfully, could give this ship the signal to proceed as the rest of the convoy weighed anchor.

The SNO thought it a delightful idea.

Keeble stood on the still-sunken *Giovanni Battista* as the LST, loaded to the gunnels with nice, heavy tanks and trucks, came snoring in through the harbor mouth. There was a grinding crash, she reared like a stallion, she shuddered, hesitated—then her heavy prow came smashing down in a tremendous welter of water.

And she was through and swinging toward her anchorage. Her broad, flat bottom, smashing down on that concrete and steel conglomerate, had substantially deepened the channel.

German bombers kept coming in and sinking ships at Tripoli, so the salvors were forever starting over again. In March 1943, two flights of Junkers JU-88's slipped in without warning and struck three vessels: the ammunition carrier *Ocean Voyager*, a tanker loaded with 100-octane airplane gas, and the destroyer *Derwent*. The tanker was burning, listing badly, and the *Derwent*, also listing badly, was drifting in a circle.

Keeble's salvage ship, *Gamtoos*, managed to beach the destroyer where a salvage party could begin manning pumps and shoring bulkheads even before the raid was finished. The tanker had sunk, but her gasoline was still there, burning fiercely. In the center of it was the *Ocean Voyager*, loaded with hundreds of tons of bullets and bombs.

Gamtoos was gamely running in, hoping to get a line on her and tow her out of that ring of fire, when she went up. *Gamtoos* found herself deposited six hundred yards up on the beach from the resultant wave; *Ocean Voyager* simply had ceased to exist, although one of her fifty-ton boilers came down some distance away.

They finally patched up the *Battista* enough forward so they could blow the front compartments and raise her nose from the mud. A waiting tug dragged *Battista*'s snout around and up onto the shelving beach, they stopped their battery of pumps, and she sank instantly. They now had a channel five hundred feet wide and deep enough for a vessel of any draught.

THE VALIANT SAGA

In 1944, Keeble was involved, with Petty Officer Nichols, in one of the war's most famous individual salvage operations: the 36,000-ton battleship HMS *Valiant*. *Valiant*'s odyssey really began three years before, when she and the *Queen Elizabeth* were anchored in Alexandria Harbor. On the evening of December 18, 1941, a convoy had come in from Tobruk through "bomb alley," as that particular stretch of the Mediterranean was then called. Through the harbor's boom defenses, behind this convoy, had come three 2-man torpedoes of the Italian Navy's incredible sabotage outfit, the Tenth Light Flotilla.[2]

The Italians were unable to fix their torpedoes to the vessels' hulls, so they put them underneath. All the frogmen were captured, still in rubber suits and SCUBA gear, and were placed under custody in the *Valiant*. Five minutes before the torpedoes were due to blow, the frogmen warned the British of the impending explosions.

Before they could react, torpedoes went off under the *Valiant* and the *Queen Elizabeth*. *Valiant* ended up with a sixty-foot hole in her bows, but the blast missed essential machinery and she was successfully gotten into dry dock for temporary repairs. Eventually she made it through the Suez Canal to Durban, South Africa, and then to the States for permanent repair.

Queen Elizabeth, however, was in a terrible way. Her boilers were blown almost through her funnel, and seven stokers were killed. She laid her belly down hard against the mud alongside Gabarri Pier, keeping a freeboard aft of only two feet. Britain's Mediterranean naval might had been reduced to the four cruisers that were eventually repaired by Ellsberg at Massawa.

There was one factor in Britain's favor, however. *All the frogmen had been captured!* The Axis powers did not know that they had been successful. From the air, both *Elizabeth* and *Valiant* appeared undamaged—their reduced freeboard was not apparent from altitude. So the British ran a bluff.

All normal above deck routine was continued on the sunken ships. Leave boats went ashore with sailors aboard them, bands played, crews mustered at the usual hours—visitors were even allowed aboard.

The vast charade worked. The Italian navy, in reality unopposed between Gibraltar and Suez, refused to venture from port. Seeing her ruse was working, Britain strengthened her hand with another bluff: HMS *Centurion*.

Centurion was so old that she had taken part in the Battle of Jutland against Von Scheer's German Imperial Fleet in May 1916. She had been decommissioned in the 1930s, had her guns, turrets, and armor removed, and had been made into a target ship for British gunners. But her engines and internal machinery were still in place, so she was run down to Alexandria and anchored in the harbor. With a complete array of *wooden guns and wooden armor!*

She was also loaded down, however, with a tremendous firepower of the latest anti-aircraft guns, including the then-new rapid-fire weapon called the Chicago Piano. Whenever Axis planes came in, they were met with a frightful barrage from the *Centurion*; as a result, they kept her in the books as an active Allied superdreadnought—along with the crippled *Valiant* and the sunken *Elizabeth*.

By 1944, *Valiant* had long before been repaired and had entered the war in the Pacific Theater of Operations. In operations against the Japanese in the summer of 1944, she was damaged enough to be put into dry dock at Trincomalee, Ceylon. The dock, built to take the world's largest battleship, 42,000-ton HMS *Hood*, had promptly capsized and sunk in twenty-five fathoms of water[3] beneath the *Valiant*. The battleship remained afloat, but her rudders and screws were struck by the end of the dock. The shafts of the two inner propellers were jammed so solidly against the gland that they would not even turn, and the cast-iron A-frames holding them to the hull were bent and cracked.

Valiant could move with the inner propellers inactive—but even at eight knots she threatened to shake herself to pieces with the vibration. The ship needed a dry dock, and the closest one that could handle her was at Alexandria. So back she went, across the Indian Ocean and the Red Sea, and got as far as Suez Bay.

And there she stopped, three hundred miles short of Alexandria. She could be taken no farther without repair of some sort. Commander-in-Chief Sir John Cunningham called Peter Keeble, who by this time had a reputation as a man with ideas in "make-do" salvage, to Cairo.

Remove the parts and run the ship on one rudder and two propellers, Keeble advised. Fine, said Fleet Engineer Murray; but how could they do it if they couldn't get the ship into a dry dock?

Take them off with a pair of divers working with oxyhydrogen torches, said Keeble. Drop the removed parts to the harbor floor rather than trying to winch them to the surface and probably damaging the precious outer propellers in the process.

Cunningham gave him a week.

Nichols was a cutting-torch genius, and he beefed up the existing torches through modifications to awesome strength. They would need it. The shafts were 18½ inches in diameter, solid tempered steel; the cast-iron A-frames had oval arms that in section were forty-two inches wide by 14½ inches thick. Each propeller, shaft section, and A-frame formed a unit weighing twenty six tons.

Keeble had so many pipes, hoses, tanks of air, oxygen, and hydrogen, that his launch, drawn up under the *Valiant*'s stern, was dubbed "The Gas Works." Nichols went down first, straddled the shaft some five feet from the gland, and began cutting. He did four hours, until one of the hydrogen manifold unions blew; when it was repaired, he insisted, despite a terribly burned thumb, on another two hours. Keeble replaced him, and after six hours was through the shaft.

Nichols took off the one vertical leg of the A-frame in four hours while Keeble slept in his diving suit. Now everything hung from the remaining vertical leg of the A-frame. Nichols cut while Keeble watched. When they were two-thirds through, the two-inch cut began widening, so Keeble fixed a fifteen-pound charge of explosive in a canvas sock around it. They got out of the water and detonated. The entire starboard assemblage fell off. Half through.

Keeble and Nichols switched off in the cutting on this one, also, until it was cut through. The A-frame was cut as the other had been, the charge was set, and a diver from the *Valiant* went down to report that both screws had been removed successfully.

Valiant ran right up to seventeen knots on her first test, without vibration of any sort; she was so successful that she went back into active duty and finished out the war on two screws and only one operable rudder. Keeble and Nichols set an underwater stamina record that has never been approached, let alone equaled; and Robert Davis later characterized their effort as "the most outstanding underwater cutting operation ever undertaken."

CLEARING MINES AT PIRAEUS

Keeble's wartime salvage career ended with the harrowing harbor-clearance projects at Piraeus and Leontas, Greece. Not only was the Greek civil war hotting up, with Communists and non-Communists killing indiscriminately in the streets; the Nazis had done a thorough harbor-sabotage job before they pulled out. SS demolition teams had scuttled ships beside quays and then blown sections of the quays down on top of them. A 100-ton pontoon crane dock had been capsized and sunk upside down in the gap between Leontas and the outer harbor. They had dumped trucks and locomotives into the Corinth Canal, and scuttled a motor launch in its mouth. They had also sowed scores of mines in both harbors.

Keeble's first concern was the mines. Every sort was represented there—pressure, time, contact, magnetic—and sweeping would be time-consuming and too dangerous. So he came up with a plan, which was soon adopted in Normandy as the standard procedure (using special equipment developed as a result of Keeble's Greek experiments).

He put down on the harbor floor every diver he could muster—including himself. They walked the bottom in predetermined patterns, abreast, missing nothing. Mines were disarmed by the removal of primers and detonators. If the diver found an unknown type, or a type he knew could be disarmed only by explosives experts, he marked it with a pellet buoy for conventional mine-sweeping operations.

None of the divers was killed or even injured, although there were a few cases of bad nerves.

The rest of the operation was routine salvage work, except for the constant danger of booby traps. The 100-ton capsized crane dock, down in eleven fathoms of water, proved to be the easiest task of all. The wing walls, unlike the tank construction of dry docks, were made of open steel latticework.

Keeble made up hose charges—explosives packed in a length of rubber hose with a detonator—and wove the hoses in and out through the metal struts. Then they were all detonated at once. The dock collapsed, crushing those struts that were still sound and giving a forty-foot clearance, which opened the harbor to naval traffic.

---

[1] See pages 170–73.
[2] See pages 456–57.
[3] See pages 300–2.

CHAPTER TWENTY

In War and Peace

~~~~~~

Over at the other end of the Mediterranean, meanwhile, another very remarkable man was learning salvage—the hard way. Lieutenant Lionel Crabb had never been under water before he arrived, an indifferently qualified demolitions man, at Gibraltar in 1942. He soon learned by trial and error to use the crude SCUBA equipment then available (a leaky rubber suit and a Davis Submarine Escape Apparatus to breathe through); when the *Willowdale* steamed in from Huelva with twelve hundred tons of wolfram in her holds, Crabb was ready to go down and examine the freighter's hull for limpet mines set by Italian frogmen.

LIONEL CRABB LEARNS ABOUT MINES

And he found one, on the bilge keel near the engine room: a torpedo-shaped object three feet long, painted green, fastened to the hull with three clamps. These had been tightened with clockwise twists, and Crabb, working alone, as is the preference of most explosives men, was not at all sure that a reverse twist might not set the thing off.

It didn't; but what does one do with a mine on which, in all probability, is a hydrostatic switch to blow it up with a change in water pressure? Crabb couldn't surface with it, nor could he merely drop it and flee. He found by experiment that it had a neutral buoyancy, however, so he moored it to a buoy and left it well clear of the ship at the same depth he had found it.

By the next morning, Crabb and his superior officer, Commander Hancock, had decided that the mine was safe but was a new type, which needed examination. And they felt that the edge of the Gibraltar airstrip, which ran across the neck of land joining the Rock with Spain, would be a good place for their experiments. They towed buoy and mine over to their chosen spot with a rowboat, but there found heavy barbed-wire entanglements which prevented bringing it ashore. That left the airstrip itself—congested with stored Spitfires.

Crabb carried the twenty-five-pound mine ashore in his arms like a sleeping baby, and they got it down between two planes without being seen. Best not alert the Royal Air Force to what they were doing, Hancock explained. It might spread unwarranted alarm and even, perhaps, despondency.

They got it apart without setting it off, and Hancock, highly elated, went off to lunch with the Admiral, carrying some of the harmless parts to show him. Crabb, meanwhile, found that two of the three highly volatile and quite deadly detonators had turned up missing. After lunch, Hancock found the live, sensitive detonators loose in his own pocket; he absentmindedly had carried them to the meeting with the Admiral.

The *Willowdale* operation set the tone for Crabb's salvage work at Gibraltar; most of it involved mines and torpedoes and a running duel with the Italian saboteurs of the Tenth Light Flotilla. It was an odd sort of duel, since Crabb was unaware of their existence at Gibraltar[1] to the very end; he knew only that Allied shipping at Gibraltar often had mines fixed to the hulls and that his crew had to deal with them.

Petty Officer Bell found one on a certain vessel, removed it, and moored it off to a buoy. But he made the mistake of telling a Naval Intelligence officer about his find. The Intelligence officer, being an excitable sort, ordered him from the water, then energetically got out a rowboat, threw a line around the buoy, and began towing it toward an isolated rock sticking up from the middle of Rosia Bay. There, he reasoned, the mine would be safe and sound until Crabb got around to destroying it.

But when he was in the middle of the open bay a chop came up. He became alarmed: his frail craft, he feared, soon would sink;

he released his towline. The buoy would support the mine and Crabb could come and get the beastly thing in the morning.

Instead, line, mine, and buoy disappeared swiftly beneath the water. Horrified, our doughty warrior took visual sights on everything in view and rowed hastily ashore. He got word to Crabb (through channels, of course) and Crabb was instructed to "go out and find the mine."

To hell with the bloody thing, Crabb announced. Had his man Bell been allowed to finish checking the ship on which it had been found?

Certainly not, sniffed Intelligence; one mine, after all, was quite enough.

Crabb returned to the ship and found another one on it. It was another new type, with a very good chance that it was booby-trapped. One swift and easy way to find out. He removed the mine. Nope. No booby trap.

He staggered home and to bed—having been diving from dawn until dusk for six straight days—but was rousted at first light with orders to report to Admiral Sir Frederick Edward-Collins. Edward-Collins coldly told Crabb that he should go find that mine. Crabb respectfully pointed out that he had absolutely no way of knowing where it was, that wherever it was, it was in deep water, and that it might be time-set to explode at any moment.

Go out and find that mine, Lieutenant, repeated the Admiral.

"On the face of it, sir," Crabb replied, "the order is a trifle presumptuous." Whether the presumption was in giving the order, or in expecting Crabb to successfully carry it out, has never been explained; but Crabb went.

In the area of the Intelligence officer's visual-sight cross-bearings, Crabb went over the side to test his diving equipment before they began sweeping. He dived to thirty feet to check his mask, saw below him a monstrous, bloated jellyfish, and swam lower to view this wonder. It was the buoy, still attached to the mine.

On June 6, 1944, the Normandy landings made the Mediterranean a backwater of the war. The Germans had had a great deal of time to sow mines and to block the ports of the English Channel, and had made good use of it. Landing craft were damaged by the hundreds, as the Allies poured men and matériel ashore; repairs had to be effected in the shortest possible time.

The British and American salvage services profited greatly from the lessons learned in the Mediterranean. From Peter Keeble, they borrowed the technique of repairing without docking: removing damaged plates, propellers, or other equipment with underwater oxyhydrogen cutting torches and then welding in patches with subsurface arc-welding units.

CHERBOURG, 1944

Two operations at Cherbourg, France, in the summer of 1944, show how well the large and aggressive salvage services had also learned the art of improvisation. First was the 900-ton vessel *Netztender*, 140 feet long and thirty-five feet in the beam, which had been sunk immediately against the quay walls of Bassin Charles X. Until the ship could be shifted, unloading-berths for five Liberty ships were interdicted.

Divers surveying the wreck found that she had been scuttled by an explosive charge that had blown out both port and starboard hull by the engine room and that, because the craft's interior was common, had flooded her from stem to stern. She lay in an upright position on an extremely rocky ocean floor. This made the work of passing ⅝-inch messenger wires under the hull quite easy; they were placed thirty, fifty, eighty, and one hundred feet back from the bow, then stoppered off and left.

Meanwhile a floating crane was brought up, and two more messengers were swept under the *Netztender*'s prow, carrying with them 9-inch lifting wires to be strung to the crane. Since this was moored with heavy beach gear, it was able, using the tide, to raise and swing *Netztender*'s prow some 60 degrees.

A lifting crane was then flooded down and pinned to each side of the wreck by 9-inch wires run through on the messenger wires previously stoppered off. The craft were unwatered with the rising tide; the vessel came off the bottom.

A tug was run in beside each lifting craft to carry *Netztender* shoreward until she grounded. Two more lifts brought her above the low-tide mark, where French salvage crews could get at her and repair her.

Even more ingenious was the operation involving two ships blocking Cherbourg's desperately needed Gare Transatlantique. In fleeing, the Germans had paused long enough to scuttle the 2500-ton *Granlieu* (three hundred feet long, forty feet in the beam, and thirty feet in depth) some five feet out from the end of one of the Gare's piers. She lay on her starboard side in five feet of mud, ten feet of her bow across the front of the pier and the rest of her length blocking the slip itself. A 12,000-ton whaler, which had been sunk on her portside and in line with the *Granlieu*, finished the blockade.

The whaler was much too heavy for the salvage forces to shift; but divers tunneled through the mud under *Granlieu* to pass four evenly spaced messenger wires around her stern.

Three lifting craft were then brought up, one on either side (bows toward the *Granlieu*'s bows), with the third directly over the stern and faced the other way. Nine-inch cables replaced the messenger wires, and the bow-to-stern craft took up both ends of the cable farthest aft. The other two craft took up the other three cables.

Divers then set yet another heavy lifting wire to the *Granlieu*'s stern, which was run out to an ARS (a harbor-clearance lifting craft), which had previously laid out two sets of beach gear. Finally, 80-ton submarine pontoons were pinned to the sunken ship's superstructure to keep her top hamper from dragging in the mud once the lift began.

Compressed air was pumped in to lighten *Granlieu*'s stern; then the lifting craft were flooded down, pinned, and unwatered with the rising spring tide. They brought the stern ten feet off; the ARS brought her around 50 degrees with a strain on the first set of beach gear, dropped that, and took a strain on the second; and brought her around the other 40 degrees for a right angle to her original position. This whole phase of the operation took only three hours.

This gave them a ship lying in line with the side of the pier it originally had been blocking. On the port (upper) side, Army Engineers erected a superstructure that in effect extended the pier by three hundred feet and helped furnish docking area for three Liberty ships. The whaler was left untouched.

Wherever possible, in French, Belgian, and Dutch ports, wrecks were by-passed if they did not actually prevent entrance to a harbor. Many of these bulks lay for twenty years or more, until expanding world commerce made action imperative.

The main fairway at IJmuiden Harbor (leading directly to Holland's Port of Amsterdam) was littered with three large ships (*J. P. Coen, Tjikini,* and *Van Renselaar*) and a host of tugs, trawlers, aircraft, and general debris. The British had sunk ships to keep the Germans from using the port in the war's early years; the Germans had returned the favor in later years.

Supervising Engineer J. van Dixhoorn decided on dredges to achieve the same results that Keeble had attained at Benghazi in 1943 with explosives.

Since there was a sand bottom at IJmuiden, Van Dixhoorn used huge dredges to drag sand from beneath the wrecks, sinking fourteen of them to a depth where even their top hamper was at least ten fathoms below the surface. Work was begun in August 1964 and completed less than a year later. Some 4.5 million cubic yards of sea bottom were shifted, 2.5 million cubic yards of which were used to form an artificial beach beyond the harbor's southern breakwater. The entire cost of the operation was $1.9 million.

Though the continental United States was plagued with few war-created harbor-clearance projects, one very famous one took place in New York Harbor in 1942–43. It has remarkable parallels with the *St. Paul*[2] in 1918 and the *Hanseatic* in 1966.

FIRE ON THE NORMANDIE

The *Normandie*, 1029 feet long, 117 feet in the beam, 79,280 gross tons displacement, was the second largest ship in the world. She had been launched in 1932, had a cruising speed of 30 knots, and five days after Pearl Harbor had been expropriated from the French for conversion into a troopship, as had been done with the *St. Paul*.

Fire started aboard the *Normandie* on February 9, 1942, at 2:30 P.M., when sparks from an oxyacetylene torch ignited one of 1140 bales of kapok life preservers stored in the main salon. The ship had the world's most efficient seagoing fire-prevention system: unfortunately, none of it was operable at the time.

The fire was out of control by 2:49, when the first alarm went out; the second was at 3:01, third at 3:03, fourth at 3:12, fifth at 4:10. No one could claim the alarms were ineffectual. Three fireboats (*Duane*, *John J. Harvey*, *Firefighter*), six hook-and-ladders, and twenty-four engine companies all arrived to pour their hundreds of thousands of tons of water into the furiously burning liner.

By eight o'clock they had brought the fire under control on the three upper decks. But they had also pumped in so much water that the ship was listing dangerously to port. Drainage holes were hurriedly cut in the starboard side as the list increased momentarily. By 12:20 the next morning, orders to abandon were given; two hours later, she rolled over in her berth.

There was a long and acrimonious Senate investigation of the affair, with charges being hurled in every direction—chief among them that the *Normandie* was a notoriously unstable ship, and that just the weight of the fifteen thousand men she was supposed to carry as a troopship would have been enough to capsize her. But on April 20, 1942, Secretary of the Navy Frank Knox announced that the *Normandie* would be raised.

Salvage operations were conducted by Merritt, Chapman and Scott under over-all direction of Captain W. A. Sullivan of the Navy's Bureau of Ships (replaced in mid job by Captain B. E. Manseau. Sullivan had gone to North Africa with a number of skilled Navy divers to complete the work begun by the ailing Edward Ellsberg). Wreckmaster was one John Tooker—son of the Captain "Izzy" Tooker who had served as wreckmaster on the *St. Paul*.

CONTROLLED PUMPING

There the parallel ends. The *Normandie* had rolled away from Pier 88, not toward it; and there was not sufficient room between her hull and the pier for dredging a trench in the mud as had been done with the

St. Paul. Another problem faced by the salvors was the fact that 250 feet from her bows she was resting, not on mud, but on a knob of bedrock.

This meant "controlled pumping": making the hull watertight, strengthening the bulkheads, then removing water from the submerged sections while putting water into the exposed sections. The idea, of course, was a delicate balancing act that eventually would bring the vessel up and back to an even keel. It also meant patching the vast hulk *before* she was righted, rather than after as was done on the *St. Paul,* even though her portside was deeply buried in the ooze of the river bottom. Only thus could they be sure of not crushing the hull at the point where it lay on bedrock.

The portside of the *Normandie* contained 356 portholes (air ports in Navy parlance), many open, none designed to be waterproof under pressure, and all of them lying below an average of seventy feet of water. There were also sixteen "barn doors": cargo ports large enough to handle automobiles, all of which had to be fitted with watertight covers. Ten thousand cubic tons of mud had settled inside the ship (average depth: ten feet) and had to be removed. The pumps were constantly being clogged with detritus such as glass, lumber, metal scraps—one of them tried unsuccessfully to swallow a grand piano. And the mud could not just be squirted over the side in the usual manner; it all had to be laboriously hauled away.

The most invidious problem for the divers was broken glass, mostly from spun-glass insulation on the electric wiring. It pierced hands and gloves; it slashed suits and threatened air hoses. Because of the glass and detritus, divers often had to work in three-man teams: one working, the second tending his air hose, the third tending the second's hose. Some seventy-five divers were down during each work shift.

After the mud and the portholes, came the bulkheads. Each existing compartment in the vessel had to be permanently separated so it could be flooded or blown as needed, but the original bulkheads were neither watertight nor sufficiently strong to withstand the stresses of such sequential pumping. For making them stronger and watertight, three-by-twelve wooden beams were used, set in place by the divers with 1685 tons of concrete.

Everything above the main promenade deck was removed, including the masts, two decks, the funnels, and all the top hamper. The promenade deck also had to be strengthened, as did the hull. Thousands of pipelines had to be closed off between compartments, and forty-five hundred separate patches had to be set. The water was so murky that divers could communicate only through telephone messages relayed by a central switchboard on the diving ship above.

With the seventy-five divers, six hundred to seven hundred shipyard workers labored on each shift (of which there usually were three a day).

These men removed five thousand tons of superstructure as the divers removed the mud and six thousand tons of debris from inside the ship. Work went on for eighteen months; they were ready for final pumping in August 1943.

Divers probed under the ship with high-pressure air hoses to break surface tensions between hull and mud. After that, it took only three days to bring her up with a 45-degree list (total capacity of the ninety-three pumps was forty thousand tons of water an hour, but care had to be taken so she would not come up too suddenly and capsize all over again). Then the remainder of the one hundred thousand tons of water she originally had held was removed, and she was towed away.

The raising of the Normandie cost $3.75 million; the refitting was projected at another $20 million. That would give them the original white elephant: a massive troop transport with a history of instability, already rendered obsolete by the increasing productivity of America's wartime shipyards.

Cooler heads prevailed. The Normandie was sold for scrap; it brought only $166,000, a fraction of the cost of raising her. The economics involved are precisely what has prevented the scores of salvors who claim they are about to raise the Andrea Doria[3] from actually getting down to it. There is no way they could come out financially from such a massive undertaking, even if a workable method of salvage could be found.

The Normandie is almost a textbook case of how *not* to handle a pierside ship fire. The Hanseatic, a German passenger vessel that caught fire on September 7, 1966, is a classic example of correct procedure. The ship was tied up at Pier 84, North River, New York, when fire broke out in the diesel generator room on B Level from a leaking fuel line. The intake ventilator system carried the flames up through seven decks and spread them throughout the ship.

The million-dollar fire started at 7:30 A.M.; it took seven hours to bring it under control. Three fireboats, eleven hook-and-ladder trucks, and thirty engine companies participated.

But water was used only to cool hot bulkheads and to quench small blazes in the woodwork or other combustible material. The main thrust of their work was in smothering the fire with three hundred gallons of foam concentrate and thirty-three hundred pounds of CO_2 gas. As a result, water never rose above the floor plates of the machinery room where the fire had originated, and did not reach the door sills in cabins on the upper decks. There never was the slightest danger of the Hanseatic rolling over; indeed, the greatest list that she took during the operation was less than 2 degrees.

PEARL HARBOR

Mainland harbors remained unscathed during the war, but the surprise attack by the Japanese on the eighty-six-vessel Pacific Fleet at Pearl Harbor on December 7, 1941, was a true military disaster. Although Japan lost forty-eight of its one hundred attacking aircraft, and three midget submarines, the United States lost 3303 men and the battleship *Arizona*, and had severe damage inflicted on four other battleships—*Oklahoma, Nevada, California,* and *West Virginia*. Also permanently crippled were three destroyers, a target ship, and a mine layer.

Though the work of clearing Pearl Harbor went on for years, the battleships *Pennsylvania, Maryland,* and *Tennessee* were soon back in action, as were the cruisers *Helena, Honolulu,* and *Raleigh*. Support facilities such as a seaplane tender, a salvage ship, and a dry dock were also soon repaired.

The dry dock had been partially flooded down beneath the destroyer *Shaw* when the attack came. The Docking Officer tried to flood it down completely to release the destroyer, but a Japanese bomb blew off the forward section of the destroyer and damaged the dock. Once the smoke had cleared, Pearl Harbor Naval Station salvors fitted a blunt wooden prow to the craft, and under her own power she made the two thousand-mile-plus voyage to a West Coast shipyard. She was back in action, fully repaired, within six months.

The salvage operation at Pearl Harbor was a massive job of tough, slogging work under pressure and with great supply shortages; they were big ships with big holes in them, which entailed patching up the holes and pumping out the water.

Joseph Karneke was sent down to assess damage on the 33,000-ton *West Virginia*. Her superstructure was undamaged, and she seemed only to be riding a bit low in the water, though she was resting on the bottom. They had hopes that the hole that had sunk her was a small and readily patched one.

Karneke dived on the portside, because she was listing that way, from a salvage vessel right alongside the ship. He landed on the bottom in deep mud and reached out toward the hull. Nothing. He floundered a few paces in the direction in which it should have been: still nothing. A few more paces. No *West Virginia*.

Feeling rather silly, he called up to his tender on the telephone. "I can't find the ship."

"You're headed all right," said the puzzled tender. "Your bubbles disappeared inside the ship."

Then Karneke caught on: the hole was so big that he had walked right into it without knowing it. He continued walking, and got thirty-five feet *inside* before he even found any wreckage. The next day, he and another diver measured the gaping wound and found it 105 feet long and thirty-five feet from top to bottom. Five torpedoes in sequence had neatly stitched the side of the giant warship. Good detective work by the divers in locating fragments warned the United States that Japanese torpedoes had reciprocating engines, far superior to the American steam turbines.

Obviously, the *West Virginia* was going to be a major shipbuilding operation rather than a hurry-up fitting with standard patches by divers. But the so-called experts (who understood neither salvage nor the limitations of diving) were impatient.

"What are you waiting for? Why haven't you started diving?"

"We're waiting to find out what you want the divers to do," Karneke replied patiently.

"It should be pretty obvious. It's to get these ships up!"

Karneke, the job's master diver, turned to another man already suited up, Tex Rutledge, and told him to get down there on that ship. A few minutes later, Rutledge called up to the surface and asked what he was supposed to do now that he was down there. Karneke deferred to the expert.

"Tell him to go to work," squawked this worthy.

"Doing what?" persisted Rutledge.

"The ship is sitting on the bottom," said Karneke briskly. "We got to get it up. Go to work."

A few minutes later, from the amplified telephone, which could be heard all over the diving ship, came a series of terrible grunts, groans, and moans of great effort.

"What are you doing?" cried Karneke in apparent alarm.

"What do you think I'm doing?" panted Rutledge. "I'm in under this battleship and I'm lifting. Can you see if she's coming up any?"

Many of the repairs at Pearl were carried out by divers using light, compact shallow-water diving helmets instead of the conventional bulky brass ones. This shallow-water gear was useful down to sixty feet and greatly simplified operations in the warm Pacific waters. The main difference between it and the SCUBA gear that has rendered it obsolete since the war, was in the mask and breathing apparatus; the automatic regulators were fixed to the diver's weighted belt, and the air source was at the surface.

THE TRINCOMALEE DRY DOCK

Less than three years after the Japanese attack, Allied victory was inevitable. But though the Japanese were losing, they were not yet defeated. Two oceans away from Pearl Harbor, the decision was made to attempt salvage on a sunken British dry dock at Trincomalee, a port on the northeast coast of Ceylon, in the Bay of Bengal. It was an immense thing, the world's largest—fifty thousand tons, 845 feet long, 173 wide, and seventy-five deep. It was this dry dock that had sunk under HMS V*aliant* in the summer of 1943.[4] There was need for absolute secrecy in the salvage attempt by the Admiralty Salvage Section, since the Japanese did not know that the dock had sunk in the first place.

The loss of the dry dock was not the result of enemy action, but rather of a sticking pressure gauge, which showed one of the forward tanks as flooded when it really was empty. This made her take a 9-degree list as they were flooding her down, and one of the V*aliant*'s screws punctured a watertight section. The dock was quickly filled, but it still smashed the inner propeller shafts of the battleship as it went down.

Salvage master Captain W. A. Doust's forty-six-man diving team, headed by master divers R. P. Brown and H. W. Varney, examined *eight miles* of riveting before Doust decided she would have to be cut into two sections. This meant special design alterations for their underwater oxy-electric torches, since the dock lay at twenty-five fathoms.

Once this was done, Doust pressed four compartments of the damaged section to lift it off the bottom—and discovered for the first time that the supposedly flooded tank had collapsed inward from water pressure as the dock had sunk. This damaged portion was towed forty-five feet away from the rest of the dock, and allowed to settle back to the harbor floor.

The divers then had to build a pontoon over the undamaged section of the dock's well to help with the lift, and feed air from surface compressors through flexible pipes into the twenty-eight sound compartments. Doust made fittings for the pipes with an adaptation of the Cox submerged bolt-driving and punching gun.

This remarkable underwater tool was invented in 1920, but was not developed by the Royal Navy until 1939, under the impetus of the war. It became a sort of secret weapon for the Allies. Activated by a dense, fast-acting explosive, the Cox gun could fire threaded bolts into mild-cured steel plates seven-eighths-inch thick with such gusto—850 feet per second muzzle velocity—that it would take a ten-ton pull to extract the bolt. Doust merely fired hollow bolts (nipples) into the steel hide of the sunken dry dock, to which the air hoses could be attached.

The first lift of the immense dock was attempted on August 27, 1944; participating were the salvage vessels *Ocean Salvor*, *Barclose*, *Barfoam*, and *Bartisan*. They were winching up with 6-inch wire rope to supplement the pontoon and the air compressors, and lifted so hard that on one ship the steel wire actually left an impression of itself in the steel bow apron.

The dock did not budge; examination showed there was a tremendous suction being exerted by the seventeen feet of bottom silt in which she lay. Divers with high-pressure hoses scoured away the mud from the sides, but she still would not budge.

Finally they had to tunnel under the dry dock with their air hoses to break up the suction; then the dock came easily to the surface.

The damaged section, meanwhile, remained where it was; Admiralty salvage experts considered it too badly mauled ever to be raised. A transplanted Iranian named Victor Baroukh, however, refused to accept this judgment. For long years after the war he persisted in attempting to raise the damaged section of dry dock with primitive equipment and only two or three divers.

His persistence paid off; in the 1960s, Baroukh finally brought the dock to the surface. Very large holes had been cut into the pontoon in several places, which Baroukh claims is clear evidence of sabotage. It seems more probable that this was the result of work by Captain Doust's men; but this does not negate the fact that Baroukh performed a truly remarkable salvage feat. When the British Naval Attaché at Trincomalee cabled news of the lift to London, the Admiralty sent back not one, but two cables expressing complete disbelief.

At this writing, Baroukh was considering selling the dock in either Hong Kong or Formosa.

Meanwhile, after the war's end, residual military-oriented jobs kept popping up even though hostilities were finished. One of these was the removal of anti-torpedo nets from many of the world's great harbors. This generally was just a matter of bringing out a net-tending vessel and rolling up the nets; but this was not true in San Francisco Bay.

SAN FRANCISCO'S ANTI-TORPEDO NETS

San Francisco's nets were of steel wire hoops, some eighteen inches in diameter and interwoven by hand, and spanned the mile-wide Golden Gate: at each end of the net was a huge buoy, with a series of smaller buoys strung along the length. Tremendous tides swished back and forth through the relatively narrow channel leading to the 420 square miles of bay; without some sort of anchoring on the bottom of the nets, they would have streamed out almost horizontally.

At each corner of the nets, therefore, a ten-ton pyramidal clump of concrete was partially buried in the bottom silt and further moored with a radial pattern of anchors around the base. A whole fleet of net tenders served the nets, keeping them in proper condition and opening them for the passage of ships.

Yet the tides were so strong that the concrete clumps "walked" about on the sea floor. Sections of the nets were continually being twisted and had to be replaced; and ships often fouled their screws in the nets. All these jumbles were merely cut away and dropped, until heaps of dismembered or interlinked rings were scattered about the floor of the bay inside the Golden Gate. When it came time to remove the nets and clean up the Gate, they were a problem of formidable proportions.

First the salvors tried to hook a line into the mass of twisted netting and raise it. But the ten-ton anchor clumps were all enmeshed, so they always came also. The barges would merely tip up and dump the whole mess back on the bottom.

The clumps had to be cut away first by divers with underwater torches, working only during the one-hour slack between the vicious tides. Diver Joseph Karneke, though he knew that seven times the amount of the Mississippi's volume at New Orleans passed through the Golden Gate at peak tide flow, wondered if perhaps a diver could stay down during the tide rush. They knew there was great turbulence at the surface, but nobody knew whether it persisted to the bottom.

When Karneke got word that the tide was beginning to flow, he checked around him carefully and saw nothing unusual happening on the bottom. He went on working. Then it abruptly got darker. He looked back. A towering black wall was rushing toward him. It was mud and sand being rolled along by the tide. He was slammed flat up against the face of the cement pyramid, spread-eagled, unable to get off, with his line streamed out in a great arc between him and the surface salvage vessel.

Realizing he was unharmed, and having three hours to wait until the tide abated, Karneke gingerly retrieved his torch and began working again. And he discovered to his delight that it was easier to work with the tide than at slack water; not only was he held steady against the clump, but the links to be cut were held perfectly steady in the rush of water. He just had to be careful not to get past the edge of the clump—where he would instantly have been swept away.

The divers' bottom time per dive was expanded from one to four hours, and the job was completed in weeks instead of months.

UNUSUAL SALVAGE ASSIGNMENT: BIKINI ATOLL, 1946

One of the most unusual and little-known postwar harbor-salvage projects was the repair and maintenance work carried out on target vessels in the natural lagoon harbor at Bikini Atoll during the series of nuclear bomb tests in July 1946. Some one hundred target ships were anchored there in convoy formation for the July 1 air shot. The battleship *Nevada*, painted orange and renamed *Scarlet Fever*, was to serve as the bull's-eye for the blast. These dead hulks had a propensity for breaking free of their moorings and drifting about, so salvage vessels had to ride herd on them and keep them from sinking.

Once the radiation level from the explosion had been reduced, the salvage ships had to go back in, put out fires aboard with water or foam, and save as many burning or crippled ships as they could. Those listing badly and shipping water were supplied with pumps to keep them afloat until the twenty-fifth, when the second, underwater blast was detonated. The "convoy" also had to be rearranged into a new pattern, and several submarines had to be moored at various depths with cables from anchors on the bottom.

Following the second blast, the salvors had the job of recovering radiation recorders from the swamped fleet. The Navy had thought that recovering twenty-five hundred of the twenty-five thousand recorders would suffice; but the explosion created unforeseen variables in the blast and contamination patterns, so the salvors were ordered to bring up as many recorders as possible to ensure proper averaging of the results.

Many of the ships were still afloat, and monitors with Geiger counters had to precede the salvors to mark off "hot spots" with chalk. The water itself showed very little contamination, but the sandy bottom was loaded with it from fallout of radioactive particles.

Many of the recorders had been fastened to buoys, and the "hot" sand beneath them made recovery difficult. Divers armed with boltcutters were lowered from the surface only as far as necessary to reach the buoy. The divers soon rebelled: because working suspended in mid-water was very cumbersome, they went right to the bottom and worked from there, trying to fool the radiation monitors aboard the salvage vessels by thoroughly washing the sand from their boots on the way up. But the dosimeters fastened to their suits gave them away: those on the lower legs measured wildly higher than those elsewhere on their bodies.

Not only did instruments have to be recovered from those ships that had sunk; the damage to the ships themselves had to be assessed. The divers were allowed only ten minutes bottom time, so they often had to "sprint" along the length of the sunken vessel. A diver loaded down with suit, weights, belt, and eighteen-pound boots is not going to set any dash records. Some of them brought back roentgen readings a thousand times over estimated safe levels; but none of them suffered any apparent ill effects—possibly because many of the film badges were pressure-sensitive as well as radiation-sensitive.

The Korean "police action" did not produce a great deal of harbor-clearance work, mainly because the U. S. Navy dominated the waters around Korea and the skies overhead. What salvage work there was, generally was the result of mines placed by small, speedy Communist "mosquito" boats, or by junks or sampans. Wonsan Harbor was the main target.

The North Koreans used moored contact mines, which would sink to predetermined depths, arming themselves in the process hydrostatically with the increasing water pressure. Mooring was by a weighted wire; the mine sank to its proper depth, and the wire unreeled so as to hold the mine a fixed distance below the surface.

The mine sweepers merely tried to cut the mooring wire, so the mine would pop to the surface—theoretically disarming itself. On the surface it could be detonated by rifle fire.

These were old-fashioned horned mines left over from previous wars; inside the lead studs were glass vials of acid, broken by a mere pound or two of pressure, which ran the acid into a cup holding a pair of electrodes. The acid touching the electrodes was what detonated the mines. To disarm the Korean mines, the Navy developed a special, fancy pin which could be inserted into any horned mine to neutralize the arming mechanism.

But then the Navy classified the pins; couldn't let this new and deadly counter-weapon fall into enemy hands. No, indeed. The trouble was that the Navy was remarkably successful in keeping it from the hands of the salvage men who were supposed to be using it, too.

They soon found that a carpenter's nail of the proper size would work as well as the classified disarming pin, and the mine-clearing went blithely forward on schedule.

One other war-resultant salvage job that ought to be mentioned here was the operation, of unprecedented magnitude, that was undertaken to clear the Suez Canal of sunken shipping following the 1956–57 mid-East crisis. Smit of Holland and Svitzers Bjergnings Enterprise of Denmark had general management of the clearance job, under the auspices of the UN.

Work was begun in January 1957 by a thirty-three-ship salvage flotilla including vessels from Belgium, Denmark, Germany, Italy, Sweden, Yugoslavia, and thirteen from Smit's fleet. A total of 450 salvors were involved, including 150 from Holland. Before the end of March that same year, the canal was open to vessels up to six thousand tons; by April 8, ships up to twenty thousand tons were once again passing through.

In that short period of time, by strictly conventional means, forty-one wrecks obstructing the channel had been cleared away.

Even though war is the usual effective reason why harbor-clearance projects must be undertaken, natural forces such as cataclysmic storms also do their share.

PONTOONS, WATER BALLAST, AIR, AND BEACH GEAR ON AFDM-2

AFDM-2 was a floating dry dock with a fifteen thousand-ton docking capacity, which was caught in the Mississippi estuary at New Orleans by Hurricane Betsy on the night of September 9, 1965. The steel dry dock of three U-shaped sections bolted together (614 feet long, 116 feet wide) was, at the time the 120-knot winds struck her, holding the freighter *Elizabeth Lykes*.

She was torn loose from her special mooring spuds and driven upriver three miles with her charge, sustaining over one hundred small breaks in her wing walls and deck from runaway ships ramming into her. A huge oval hole also was punched in her starboard wall. *Elizabeth Lykes* apparently had a mind of her own, for she tore loose from her docking blocks, slid out of the dry dock, and floated an extra half mile upstream before grounding.

AFDM-2, meanwhile, was *flipped over* by the wind, so her wing walls were down in the water, one aground in eighty feet of water, the other, farther from shore, afloat in 110 feet.

The dock's replacement value was over $7 million; it was determined to raise her. First, two salvage vessels, the *Cable* and the *Salinan*, towed her across the river to the western shore, and salvage by the Marine Salvage Division of Merritt-Chapman and Scott (under direction of the Naval Ship Systems Command) was begun on November 23. They planned to snug one side of the capsized dock down hard against the bottom and then parbuckle her: roll her 180 degrees into a proper upright position. The salvors planned to use a combination of inflatable rubber pontoons, water ballast, compressed air, and land-based beach gear; the first time this particular mix of methods, to a predetermined plan, had ever been attempted.

They decided to roll all three sections over at once, still bolted together, rather than separately. To their advantage was the fact that only one wing wall, the portside, which would be under water during the parbuckling, had to be made watertight. Once a site was found with the requisite firm and gradually sloping bottom (the foot of New Orleans' Pacific Street), they began rigging sixteen sets of beach gear: land-based engine-powered winches used through nine-part purchase tackles, which, in turn, would be rigged to 1⅝-inch cables from the dry dock.

They started blowing and patching the alternate sides of the dock on November 27, replacing with steel plate the temporary concrete patches the divers had put on the holes under water. But on February 16, 1966, flood-stage waters broke the dock loose and carried it across the river. It was mid-March before she was back in place, and mid-June before work was recommenced. As the patching was completed, sixty-eight pads for the pontoon pendants were welded to the outer face of the starboard, or offshore, wall. From these, the chains and cables necessary for the pontoons were strung over the submerged top of the wall and lashed to the inside face. Ashore, the deadmen for the winches were sunk into place in the solid ground behind the Pacific Street levee.

Water ballast (18,900 tons of it) was added to the port (inner) wall in mid-July. This grounded it in eighty-three feet of water. At the same time, two thousand tons of mud and water were removed from the starboard side to lighten it. Then the parbuckling was begun.

This stage called for a 60-degree position change, but they could not bring the giant dock into this attitude. They found that a tremendous weight of mud, clinging to the horizontal stiffeners inside the hollow walls, made her heavier than they had anticipated. It took until August 8 to remove an additional two thousand tons of mud and water.

By August 10, 3940 tons of water ballast had been added to the midships buoyancy chambers. With the beach gear exerting six hundred tons of pull, the dock came up to 80 degrees. They wanted 90. They added twenty-five hundred tons of extra ballast, trying to compact the mud on the slope beneath the dry dock, which was holding her, but it didn't work. The addition of sixty-eight pontoons (six hundred tons of force) to the starboard wall also didn't work.

A hydraulic dredge came in and dug a trench fifteen feet wide, ten deep, and several hundred long, along the dry dock's chine line. The dock reached 90 degrees by noon of August 17; the next day it reached 109 degrees.

From that point on, the beach gear was worthless. They had to bring her through the other 70 degrees by controlled pumping, as had been used on the *Normandie:* a careful balancing of water ballast with compressed air, each element being fed in predetermined amounts into predetermined compartments. Thus they would add two thousand tons of water ballast to the starboard, outer (and now upper) wall, while displacing 560 tons of water ballast with compressed air in the port wall.

On August 21, the dry dock totally surfaced right side up in a mere eight minutes. This was 161 degrees from her original, inverted position. They bled the air down to atmospheric pressure in the blown compartments, while unwatering the ballasted compartments with two 6-inch and three 4-inch pumps.

On the twenty-fifth, she was towed back downstream to Todd Shipyards, where she had been when the storm had struck nearly a year before. This was the last major operation carried out by the Marine Salvage Division under Merritt-Chapman and Scott control.

THE *SHIGA*: SALVAGED JETLINER FLIES AGAIN

The third effective cause of harbor-clearance projects is the inescapable element of human error. Dry docks one expects in harbors; land-based jetliners, one does not. But on November 22, 1968, at about 10:00 A.M., the Japan Airlines DC-8 *Shiga* belly-flopped with its landing gear down in seven feet of water some three miles short of San Francisco International Airport. Aboard were ninety-six passsengers (including several infants) and eleven crewmen. No one was hurt or even shaken up, and everyone was evacuated safely.

Within minutes, a twenty-five-man salvage crew of U.S. and Japanese experts was assembling at the site, hoping to salvage what they could of the $8.3 million airplane. Salvage master was Art Reinholm of Bigge Drayage Company; his greatest worry was electrolysis between the salt water and the aluminum hull, which might begin permanent corrosion within twenty-four hours of the crash.

Reinholm's first idea was to use flotation saddles under the wings to keep them from sagging and breaking off, and then put massive lifting straps around the *Shiga*'s nose and fuselage just behind the wings. Then, he thought, three floating derricks (barge cranes) could lift the plane enough to float a 150-foot steel-decked barge underneath it. The crew worked against a low-tide deadline, hoping to free the 200-ton jetliner from the 50-degree water by 5:00 P.M. of the crash day; but problems such as first pumping six thousand gallons of jet fuel into a salvage barge kept slowing down the operation.

They worked all night, and by the next morning the cradle lift had been abandoned. Bob Korst, a veteran of seven previous airplane salvage operations, had taken over as director and wanted to put outsized elliptical steel rocker beams under the wings just out from the fuselage, and then use these to hoist the plane from the water. SCUBA divers Chuck Hankins and Bob Mosher had the task of jamming the rocker beams into the mud under the wings.

The operation was successful; on November 24, the plane was lifted from the water at 3:20 P.M. by four fifty- to eighty-ton-capacity barge cranes. Korst had twenty thousand gallons of fresh water ready for sluicing down the plane, which had to be lifted forty feet from the water so the barge could be slid underneath.

The lift itself cost $250,000; total refurbishment cost of the operation, including jet-engine overhaul, was about $2 million. On March 26, 1969, the *Shiga* was flown again, and since has returned to service with JAL. Many passengers ask by name for the aircraft, feeling that it is a lucky plane.

The same sort of feeling, perhaps, as the belief that lightning never strikes the same place twice?

---

[1] See pages 456–57.
[2] See pages 255–58.
[3] See pages 468–69.
[4] See pages 287–89.

VI

On the Beach

. . . to some the sea deep-yawning shows
Bare ground amid the billows, surge with sand
Raving; three ships the south wind's sudden clutch
Hurls upon hidden rocks . . .
                                        . . . three the east
Drives on to banks and shallows from the deep,
A piteous sight, and breaks them on the shoals,
And heaps the sand about them . . .
                                                VIRGIL
                    The Aeneid, Book I, vv. 107–14.

25. A rare photo of the *Maine* lying on the floor of Havana Harbor after the Army Engineers built a huge cofferdam of interlocking cylinders around the vessel and then pumped out the water. Sunk in 1898, the *Maine* was raised in 1911 to prove she had not been secretly scuttled. Note waterline near top of cylinders. PHOTO CREDIT: *U. S. Bureau of Ships*

26. A-frames like those used to right the capsized *St. Paul* in New York Harbor in 1918 are here used on the *Empress of Canada* in Liverpool Harbor in January 1953. With the gear in place, 250 men took only 56 minutes to right the *Empress*. PHOTO CREDIT: Wide World Photos

27. The 79,280-ton *Normandie*, in 1942 the world's second largest ship, lies on her side in New York Harbor after being capsized by water poured into her by 30 fire trucks and 3 fireboats. Later salvaged at a cost of $3.75 million, she brought $166,000 for scrap. PHOTO CREDIT: *Wide World Photos*

28. The USS *Oklahoma*, sunk in the Japanese attack on Pearl Harbor, December 7, 1941, here is seen being righted by 21 sets of winches and cables run from deadmen on Fort Island over wooden A-frames to the ship's hull. PHOTO CREDIT: *Wide World Photos*

29. JAL jetliner *Shiga* "flies" again two days after she came in short of the San Francisco International runway to belly-flop in the Bay (November 1968). As barge cranes lift her from the water, elliptical steel rocker arms under her wings support her 200-ton weight. PHOTO CREDIT: *United Press International*

30. Freighter *Evanger* on a California beach, 1943. Though steam is up, engine will be dead from sand in sea suction intake. Immense wave not only is putting thousands of tons of shock load on the hull; with the quiet water at bow and stern, it means a sand bar is already forming amidships which will break the ship's back. PHOTO CREDIT: *Williamson's Photo Shop, Seattle*

31. The Liberian freighter *Santa Kyriaki*, caught in the surf zone—the "shifting battleground" between waves and beaches. Hurled here by a Christmas Eve storm in 1965, the 2800-ton vessel was completely swept by giant seas. PHOTO CREDIT: *Articapress Fotographie*

32. In refloating the *Santa Kyriaki*, 70,000 cubic yards of sand were excavated to create this "basin" around the ship. Finally swung at right angles to the beach, prow toward shore, she was brought off on March 8, 1966, by tugs and her own reversed engines. PHOTO CREDIT: *Cees van der Meulen*

33. U. S. submarine *H-3* on the beach at Humboldt Bay, California, after going ashore in December 1914. Naïve Navy brass decided to use the 9700-ton heavy cruiser *Milwaukee* to get the power they thought could be used to horse the little sub off the sand. PHOTO CREDIT: *U. S. Bureau of Ships*

34. Inevitable result: the *Milwaukee's* excess power snapped the towlines; she herself went ashore. Two days were spent removing her 438 crewmen, many by breeches buoy, as this old photo shows. Too heavy to move, *Milwaukee* remained as a monument to human stupidity. PHOTO CREDIT: *U. S. Bureau of Ships*

35. Hard on the rocks off St. Abb's Head, Britain, in November 1958, the 4956-ton Swiss motorship *Nyon* is prey to the weather, working freely on the rocks and progressively damaged by successive tides. The salvors knew they could not save the whole vessel. PHOTO CREDIT: *Wide World Photos*

36. Therefore the inventive salvors cut *Nyon* in half, saving the after section with her valuable machinery, leaving the fore section on the rocks, where wave action soon destroyed her. In 1959, fitted with a new fore section, *Nyon* returned to service. PHOTO CREDIT: *Scotsman Photos*

CHAPTER TWENTY-ONE

Early Strandings

Strandings are the oldest form of shipwreck; and the earliest form of marine salvage, apart from life salvage,[1] is the attempt to get a stranded ship back into the water more or less in one piece.

One great factor in this simple equation was the tendency of nearly all early sailors[2] to stay within sight of land as much as possible. But staying close to land means, bluntly, that there are more things to run into. The second factor was technology. Until Siebe's close suit was invented and used on the *Royal George*, there wasn't any. None, at least, that had much chance of raising anything larger than a rowboat.

It was not until the 1930s that divers could cut through anything tougher than timber under water, since it had to be done by hand. The development of reliable underwater metal-cutting tools—torches relying on mixtures of oxygen and acetylene or hydrogen, or oxy-electric torches—made a vast difference to marine salvage. Since World War II, underwater arc welding has been possible, requiring only 15–20 more volts and amperes than open-air jobs. There are now power-operated divers' bolt-drivers, punching guns, drillers, borers, impact wrenches, wire and chain cutters—the list is nearly endless. The principal problem is keeping water from the power source and adequately pressurizing such things as lights and cameras.

THE IRRESISTIBLE GROSVENOR

Thus, even with ships run aground, the early notable salvage attempts were directed at precious cargoes rather than at the vessel itself. Perhaps the most famous of these was the East Indiaman *Grosvenor*, which still is a powerful lodestone to salvors even though she went down in 1782. The ship lies within *one hundred feet* of land, with her top under a mere *three fathoms* of water—but nobody seems able to get at her. Because of where she lies, one of the oddest marine salvage techniques ever devised was attempted on this particular vessel.

The *Grosvenor* left Trincomalee, Ceylon, on June 13, 1782, carrying 150 passengers and crew, and a fortune in jewels and bullion: nineteen boxes of diamonds, rubies, sapphires, and emeralds, worth (then) £517,000; 720 gold bars worth £420,000; specie valued at £717,000; and 1450 unvalued silver bars. On August 4, while Captain Coxon believed his vessel still some one hundred leagues from the African coast, the foretopman reported breakers. He was disbelieved. A few minutes later, the *Grosvenor* struck a submerged reef off the coast of Pondoland, some 750 miles from the settlements at the Cape.

With some loss of life, the crew got ashore. A few of them survived the terrain, and attacks by hostile tribes and wild animals, to bring word of the wreck to South Africa. The first organized attempt to raise the treasure was made in 1787. It was a failure. In 1842 a Captain Bowden, with Malay divers, spent ten months at the site for the British Admiralty. His men actually reached the ship's deck, but could not raise the hatches. He took cross-bearings and reported that the vessel was rapidly settling into the sand.

A private venture called the Grosvenor Recovery Syndicate floated shares in 1905 at Johannesburg, South Africa. A salvage master named Wright spent eleven months fixing the craft's position in a gully between sandbanks by boring through the sand with an auger to get timber samples. He recovered 250 coins and thirteen ship's guns—two of which were presented to Cecil Rhodes.

Encouraged, the Syndicate raised more money to charter a suction dredge. Wright had reported six to ten feet of sand over the *Grosvenor*, which the dredge might have handled; but so much new sand had come in that the dredge could not even get close enough to the wreck to operate. Wright then removed several hundred tons of rock from the gully's landward end in hopes of dragging the hulk ashore. One of his divers was killed, however; that, and the sand, defeated the expedition.

In 1921 the Grosvenor Bullion Syndicate was formed by Mr. M. L. Webster, who planned to profit by others' earlier mistakes. He decided to *come up from underneath rather than down from above*, by tunneling through the sandstone sea bottom to the wreck.

Even in 1921, the wreck lay 130 miles from the railway, twenty-five miles from the nearest village, and fifty miles from the nearest town (Port St. John). It often took three months just to get a needed piece of equipment to the site. But despite the problems, salvage master C. D. Chapman—who had vast experience in digging gold-mine shafts in the Rand—began the inclined tunnel to the *Grosvenor*. The first 127 feet were angled down, to get well below the sea bottom; then it went out horizontally right along the line of the gulley. The work was done by blasting through sandstone; when the tunnel was 690 feet long, they estimated their position as only thirty feet short of the sunken vessel.

Chapman here put in two watertight compartments they planned to use as air locks once they had broken through the sea floor below the ship; and one of the seven cores Chapman took with a diamond drill contained teak and lead—a nearly infallible indicator of success.

Then the money ran out. The Bullion Syndicate was disbanded, and the *Grosvenor*'s exact position was lost. Several later attempts all have ended in failure, including a recent one by a post-World War II syndicate using our old friend Peter Keeble as consulting engineer. All they recovered were a few cannon balls. Future attempts doubtlessly will be made, however: sunken treasure ships die hard.

LA LUTINE AND THE BELL OF DOOM

Another very famous and very recalcitrant vessel stranded with bullion aboard was the 32-gun British frigate *Lutine*. The ship had been French, but in 1799 had been impressed into service with the Royal Navy. In October of that same year, during the war with Holland, British troops on the Channel island of Texel, off the Dutch coast, had £140,000 in back pay due them. When HMS *Lutine* was ordered to carry this money to Texel, some financial men asked permission to send with it some gold and silver to their commercial contacts in Hamburg, Germany.

As a result, the *Lutine* left Yarmouth Roads, England, carrying £1,175,000 in gold, silver, and specie, which was insured at Lloyd's for £900,000. Some eighteen hours after sailing, completely off course, she struck a sand bar in the shifting, treacherous Zuider Zee. The lone survivor never gave a coherent reason for their wild course deviation. The shocked underwriters at Lloyd's paid off and then began trying to salvage what they could.

Not much, it developed: The Dutch claimed the ship and its treasure for themselves. After war's end, the Dutch Government offered local fishermen a split on all money recovered; the fishermen turned over to the Hague some £56,000 of treasure; but how much was recovered and not reported will never be known. The Dutch estimate at least £27,000 was spirited away before their tax collectors arrived.

That still left a very handsome cache of loot beneath the Zuider Zee, and in 1801 a certain Frenchman, Pierre Eschauzier, got Dutch permission to search and salvage the wreck. Eschauzier not only found no money; he could not even find the *Lutine*. And Lloyd's objected so strongly to the operations that the British Government forced the Dutch to accede to Lloyd's sharing in any recovery.

Eschauzier, perhaps in frustration at the long delay, had meanwhile died, and the Zuider Zee's shifting sand bars had completely covered the vessel. It was not until 1857, after an enormous storm had uncovered traces of the ship again, that any solid attempts could be made. First results indicated it wasn't worth the trouble: thirteen silver coins, one gold Louis, and five brass hoops. But the salvage work went on until 1861, with some £44,000 worth of gold and the famous *Lutine* bell being recovered. Lloyd's got half the gold and the bell, which still hangs above the Caller's rostrum in the Underwriting Room.

Meanwhile, the salvors were beaten by creeping quicksands in 1866; between then and 1908 only £1000 worth of treasure was recovered, along with several guns and about two hundredweight of timber that was eventually made into a massive table and carved chair by Lloyd's. In 1908 a huge air-suction pipe was towed out to the site, and much of the wooden hull was exposed. But they found that the treasure room had collapsed beneath the great weight of cannon balls that rested upon it, which had oxidized into a solid mass that could be removed only by small, delicate blasts. One piece of iron thus detached bore on its underside the impression of a gold ingot, and a few grains of the metal actually were clinging to it. But the sands returned with the winter months, and no treasure was recovered.

Today the *Lutine* lies under forty feet of water and twenty feet of sand, apparently inviolable, the vast bulk of its treasure still with it. No remains have ever been found of the 154 men who presumably went down with the ship.

Successful operations on another ship, the iron cargo vessel *Royal Charter*, driven up on the rocks by a vicious storm near Anglesey, Wales, on October 26, 1859, attest to the problems would-be salvors can face when working in and around the surf. The vessel took £350,000 and five hundred men down with her; a vivid account of the salvage operation was written for *The Uncommercial Traveller* by a certain newsman named Charles Dickens. He reported the sovereigns "scattered like seashells" along the beach, among great pieces of iron plate that had been pounded into odd shapes and masses. The scores of recovered dead had not drowned: they had been beaten to death by the surf. Many ingots were twisted lumps; one had been driven right into a piece of the vessel's iron plating. Virtually all of the gold was recovered.

THE U. S. LIFE-SAVING SERVICE

Natural forces such as these, operating on the shipping along her shores, led Britain to begin lighting and patrolling her coastlines in the 1700s. It was not until 1876, however, that the United States Government established the U. S. Life-Saving Service. Until then, American beaches had been guarded only by lifeboat stations maintained by the Humane Society and manned by volunteers working on a part-time basis.

The invention that had the greatest impact on the stranding of vessels was the wireless. Guglielmo Marconi flashed the letter "s" from Cornwall, England, to Newfoundland on December 12, 1901; within a few years, the U. S. Navy had begun setting up direction-finder wireless stations along the coast, which would, upon radio request, furnish bearings to ships' captains so they could plot their positions.

About 1920, the U. S. Coast Guard started operating radio beacons (distance-finding stations), which automatically transmit a 60-second signal in Morse code every three minutes, twenty-four hours a day. Ship captains can pick up two stations, triangulate, and thus accurately get their vessels' positions.

Work in the Life-Saving Service was hard, demanding men of great courage, physical stamina, and mental resources. Take the case of the *Albert Dailey*, a Maine schooner, loaded with coal, that went ashore with a six-man crew on Smith Island, Virginia, on January 7, 1883. At 1:00 A.M. on the eighth, the fog lifted momentarily, and a beach patrolman got a glimpse of the vessel. His flares brought answering flares from the ship, so he ran three miles through the sand, non-stop, to the Smith Island Life-Saving Station.

The surfmen dragged their surfboat back the three miles by hand, then launched it into the darkness and fog. But though the vessel was only 250 yards from shore, it took them until 4:30 A.M. just to find it. They took the crew and their belongings off, and the next day the *Dailey*'s captain came to terms with a salvage ship that had showed up from Norfolk, Virginia. The wreckmaster set heavy anchors offshore with the idea of winching her seaward with ground tackle once the weather had abated.

But the weather didn't; it worsened. By dark, a howling snowstorm had boxed in the *Dailey* completely. The salvors and the five crewmen of the *Dailey* who had returned aboard refused to abandon, feeling themselves secure enough with a surfboat tied alongside.

At 11:00 p.m., however, a shore-station patrolman found part of the surfboat and some hatches from the *Dailey* washed up on the beach; the tremendous northeast gale had begun breaking up the ship. It took the men three hours to drag their Lyle gun to the *Dailey* through the blizzard; by then, only her masts and rigging were still above water, for a continuous series of breakers was sweeping right over the vessel.

They burned six Coston flares in succession without any response, then tried unsuccessfully to get their surfboat launched. At dawn they could see that the men on the *Dailey* had lashed themselves to the rigging but were hanging motionless and covered with ice. The beach crew fired two lines aboard; none of the men even moved to make them fast.

By 11:00 a.m., the lifesavers could not stand it any longer, and rashly tried to launch their boat again. They were driven back the first time; the second, they got close; on the third attempt, they were able to bring off four half-frozen men. They returned for the other four; one had already died of exposure, and one had been washed overboard during the night.

The *Albert Dailey* and her cargo were a complete loss.

TRAGIC OPERATION ON THE CITY OF NEW YORK

Ten years later, the Whitelaw Salvage Company—actually a San Francisco junkman named T. A. Whitelaw who did salvage work—was involved in a long, grueling salvage attempt on the Pacific Mail Steamer *City of New York*. The ship had left San Francisco Bay in dense fog on October 26, 1893, with 104 crewmen and 133 Chinese passengers, but had gone on the rocks a short way outside the Golden Gate, off Point Bonita.

Surfmen from the Fort Point Station went aboard to bring off her passengers and crew successfully, and were then joined by surfmen from the Golden Gate Station in the task of transferring the mail and a quarter million dollars in specie to the salvage steamer *Fearless*.

That left the *New York* herself. For several weeks, the men of the *Fearless* worked to lighten her by removing cargo; but storms continually swept her exposed position until her hull was battered beyond any hope of salvage. She finally was sold for scrap to T. A. Whitelaw. He put the crew of his salvage steamer, *Samson*, aboard her to strip off all her metal fittings and her anchors, chains, davits, doors, ventilator ports, plumbing, and the like. Then they began cutting up the ship herself with dynamite, to sell the iron as scrap.

For two winters the *Samson* toiled, with divers James Dolan and George Baker doing the necessary underwater work. It was chancy just being aboard the 109-foot, 217-ton vessel, for the bottom was rocky, and nearly perpendicular cliffs rose directly behind her. On New Year's Day, 1895, a southeast gale blew up to confirm the risk. By the third, the *Samson*'s captain had to let go his heavy stern anchors so his ship could come about and ride facing into the gale on her bower alone.

By noon the pitching was so bad that a second bow anchor was set; but within half an hour both were dragging, and the salvage vessel, even with her engines on FULL AHEAD, was being driven back on the jagged fangs of rock that awaited her.

The captain flew his distress flags, but the scud was so thick that none of the men at either the Point Lobos or the Fort Point station saw them. By 3:00 P.M. he was blowing his whistle as a distress signal. No one heard it or even, because of the thick weather, saw the puffs of steam as the whistle sounded. And by nightfall the waves were too tumultuous for any of the salvors to leave the vessel in their small boats.

At 3:00 A.M. the Fort Point Station burned a Coston flare to show they finally had seen the distress signals. The tug *Reliance*, under Captain Silovich, came out immediately from San Francisco to try to aid the *Samson*. At 3:30, not knowing aid was coming, the two divers, Dolan and Baker, launched the *Samson*'s yawl. It was swept to leeward, broached, and capsized; they drowned.

At 4:00 A.M. the *Samson* touched bottom for the first time; eight more men left her in the vessel's other boat. At dawn the *Reliance* spotted the men in the lifeboat. Silovich coolly ran his tug almost onto the rocks, came about, and some of his men cast off in a lifeboat to drift down the line to rescue the *Samson*'s boat.

Then they determined to try to save the four men who had remained aboard the *Samson* (because the lifeboat would have swamped with twelve men aboard but had a chance with eight). Silovich ran the *Reliance* to within sixty yards of the *Samson* and dropped anchor, hoping to run down his own cable to the stricken vessel.

But an enormous breaker swept over both boats. The *Reliance*'s cable held; the *Samson*, seized by the towering wave, was smashed against the rocks. The four men aboard her were lost; within minutes, she caught fire and burned to the water.

A CARGO OF RAILS: THE *ABERCORN*

Another early Pacific Coast stranding ended in death and failure, yet had an oddly happy ending. The British bark *Abercorn*, 1262 tons gross weight, was carrying two thousand tons of railway track to Portland, Oregon, on January 10, 1888. When the *Abercorn* picked up the Columbia River bar pilot, the fog was so thick that the tugs that were to bring her in were unable to find her.

The pilot lost his bearings, and wind and current carried the ship far north of her supposed position. On the morning of January 12, she went ashore ten miles north of Gray's Harbor. Her huge cargo rammed her down tight on the sand, and the pounding waves soon swept away her masts, her deck hamper, and then the crewmen, one by one, who were clinging desperately to the rigging. Only three men managed to struggle ashore; twenty-one drowned.

The *Abercorn* rested there, rusting, for six years.

Meanwhile, a struggle for survival of a different sort had begun between the three little sawmill towns on Gray's Harbor. Ocosta, on the bay's southern rim, had gotten a railroad connection and was booming. Aberdeen and Hoquiam were dying.

Dying, but not dead. In 1894 the good citizens of Aberdeen decided to go down fighting. They would build their own railroad spur, they said; all able-bodied men in town were asked to donate ten days of work. These stouthearted lads laid the roadbed and cut the ties. But then came crisis. They had no rails, and they had no money to buy any.

But a certain Captain George Pease had, unbeknownst to the rest of the city, been building a long trestle from the beach out to the rusting *Abercorn*. *Abercorn*, full of iron rails. He hired men to bring off those two thousand tons of track; and then Aberdeen's two leading citizens, Messieurs Weatherwax and Wilson, purchased the rails and donated them to the township.

Stirred to new heights, the Aberdeenians laid rail from their fair city to the railhead, and a new day dawned for Aberdeen and Hoquiam.

With one small drawback. Aberdeen travelers always knew they were approaching their destination; because of the rails' six-year immersion in swirling salt water, the train would rattle, clank and bounce over those last few miles of pitted and corroded rails.

Few in flourishing Aberdeen felt called upon to complain.

In those early, pre-World War I days of salvage, salvage masters sometimes resorted to rather desperate methods in getting a stranded ship off the rocks. One such was Captain C. E. Hughes-White. During a West Indies hurricane in 1908, a 500-ton schooner was driven over two consecutive reefs by wind and wave. Hughes-White was faced with a situation in which he could not blast—he had no explosives; he could not bring in tugs; and he could not dig a channel up which a high tide might come to float off the vessel.

What was left? Manpower. Hughes-White pressed into service a hundred of the local blacks and thirty of his own sailors. He fixed towing lines to the vessel, put men standing in the shallows seaward of the inner reef on the lines, and told them to start pulling. To smarten up their performance, he used an ox whip. Hughes-White could not be called a man of prejudice: he plied the lash on black and white alike.

With considerable alacrity, the men dragged the vessel into the shallows outside the first reef. They rested—sore-backed—while Hughes-White found a break in the outer reef. Then, like the Volga boatmen, they dragged her close enough to the reef pass so she could make it through to the open sea.

Hughes-White was not just a bullying, unfeeling brute; he was a pragmatic man with a job to do. Later, during World War I, he again showed his pragmatism by sinking a German submarine (*UC-16*) in a manner unique to naval archives. His prey had gone to ground, so Hughes-White in his minesweeper, HMS *Melampus*, rigged the paravane gear. This device is like a pair of torpedo-shaped bodies with a wire between them, which are towed behind a mine sweeper to cut the cables of submerged mines. To his paravane, Hughes-White fixed a heavy explosive charge and then began dragging the thing just a few feet off the bottom—a very difficult feat in those days before the invention of sonar.

He hooked the U-boat, the explosive went off, and the sub went up.

Hearing of Hughes-White's unorthodox methods, a senior officer at the Admiralty called for a court of inquiry so he could take the feisty captain to task. The inquisitor sniffed, "You do not appear to have studied or used any form of attack as laid down by My Lords of the Admiralty."

Hughes-White's retort sums up the most necessary quality of a good salvage man. "Good God, no!" he exclaimed. "I used common sense!"

Willard Bascom has perceptively called the surf zone a "shifting battleground," where two antagonists, waves and beaches, struggle for supremacy in a battle that is as eternal as the earth itself. When men and ships get caught between these two incredibly powerful enemies, weird things sometimes happen. Ships that by every criterion should be destroyed are saved without difficulty; others are ground to kindling almost before the first gaping bystanders can arrive.

One victim of the surf-zone battleground was the 2297-ton *Tripolitana*, which was caught in such a gale on Christmas Eve 1912 that even with all engines on FULL AHEAD she was driven up on the rocks and smashed down on Looe Bar near Port Leven, not far from Penzance, Land's End, Cornwall. She ended up 150 feet from the water with her stern buried in twelve feet of sand.

The local Lloyd's agent—and these are generally very knowledgeable gentlemen—said she would be an easy job to drag back to the sea. The captain of the salvage ship *Belos*, from Penzance, agreed and undertook the job.

But the *Tripolitana* wouldn't drag. He set men to digging her out and getting her on an even keel so jacks could be used. But the February

1913 attempt failed. A hundred men plied shovels until April. At high tide a number of tugs heaved on her. Nothing. Back to the shovels. By September, the ship lay in a great man-made channel reaching to the sea. At high tide on the fifth, when she had four feet of water about her, the tugs tried again. Nothing.

That night, the sand washed back around her.

Three more attempts were unsuccessful between then and October 29, when a gale blew up that was so heavy it caused a tide sixteen feet above normal. A giant wave picked up the *Tripolitana* effortlessly and tossed it back into the ocean like a man tossing a stick for his dog to retrieve. Two hundred yards away, another wave contemptuously tossed the ship back up on the beach again—an impossible distance above the high-tide line.

On March 26, 1914, she was sold to a shipbreaker at Falmouth, and was broken up for scrap where she lay.

A FATAL ERROR IN JUDGMENT: THE *MIMI*

Sometimes the salvage men co-operate in their own destruction. The 2400-ton *Mimi* lost her bearings during heavy weather on the night of February 13, 1913, and went aground three miles north of the Nehalem River, Oregon, with twenty-eight crewmen aboard. She ended up three hundred yards from shore, aground on the bar in thirteen feet of water. The crew was in no danger, and stayed aboard until salvors of the Fisher Engineering Company arrived under a contract from the insurance carriers to refloat the ship. They put out heavy anchors seven hundred yards offshore in twenty-four feet of water, with 1⅛-inch steel cables running from the anchors to the *Mimi* to a large engine ashore.

During the next days they worked the ship seaward whenever the seas ran high enough to scour sand from beneath her. By April 15, salvage master Albert Crowe had removed so much ballast that the lifesaving men from the Tillamook Bay Station were afraid the ship might capsize when he took a heavy strain on the ground tackle. Crowe refused to have them stand by with lifesaving equipment, however; he did not even have a salvage tug standing by in case something should go wrong.

As a result, when the ship came off at flood tide just after midnight, no means of rescue were at hand. The ebbing tide swung the *Mimi* broadside to the open sea and immediately capsized her to port— leaving the twenty men aboard in desperate straits. Some were hanging on the starboard rail, others to the rigging. A few tried to swim ashore immediately, before their strength should be sapped by immersion in the icy waters, but they got caught in the wreckage and drowned.

By dawn, another man had died of exposure. The *Mimi*'s master, Captain Westphal, tried to launch a boat, but it was flipped over and swept away. A second was launched and smashed.

That afternoon, the waves abated enough for the lifesaving crew ashore to try launching boats. They could not get closer to the wreck than 150 feet. Lines fired from their Lyle guns could not reach it.

At 5:30 the next morning—the survivors had been clinging to the rigging for twenty-nine hours—a surfboat was able to get close enough to take off one man. It returned three more times to bring off three more.

That's all there were left. Four. The other sixteen had been drowned or had died of exposure. The *Mimi* herself was a total loss, breaking up in the surf shortly thereafter.

One other salvage operation deserves mention here as illuminating how man often co-operates with the warring elements in the surf zone to his own discomfiture. Two days after Christmas 1916, the freighter *Melanie* and the 9000-ton tanker *San Onofre* collided during heavy fog and intense gales off Great Britain. Thinking their ship doomed, the *Melanie*'s captain and crew fled aboard the only slightly damaged *San Onofre*. But the captain of that vessel, smelling salvage awards, persuaded half a dozen of the crewmen to return and work the *Melanie*'s pumps. He would tow her to safety, he proclaimed.

The men returned and the tow began; in keeping with accepted salvage practice, he towed her into shallow waters so that if she did go down, salvage might still be effected. Too shallow, in fact. The *Melanie* grounded, and her weight acted as a giant anchor for the *San Onofre*. This hapless vessel veered in toward shore and soundly grounded herself. The *Urania*, which had been escort vessel for the tanker, came whipping in to aid the stranded vessels and ran herself smartly up beside them.

There all three of them lay, like beached whales, near Breaksea Point. Yet another set of salvors—professionals this time, fortunately—arrived, and, one by one, brought the stranded ships successfully free.

It took eight years of claims, counterclaims, suits, and countersuits before some sort of salvage-award settlement was finally reached.

---

[1] See Appendix II.
[2] The Polynesians seem to have been a rather striking exception, sailing eastward through the open, empty Pacific to populate the Polynesian Triangle with little more to guide them than an almost mystical urge to follow the sunrise.

CHAPTER TWENTY-TWO

The Admiralty Salvage Section

World War I found the British Admiralty totally unprepared for the appalling amount of salvage work it would have to do, but it also found Britain with a great many private salvage firms in operation. No other maritime nation in the world had such a reserve of skilled and trained personnel upon which to draw, and the Admiralty Salvage Section gained a pre-eminence in the field that it has never relinquished.

A COMPLEX OPERATION: *SILURIAS*

One creative civilian salvor was Tom Ensor, who was called in to try to save the *Silurias*, at that time one of the most powerful dredgers ever built. She was anchored in Gareloch just before World War I started, when a heavy storm dragged her anchors and drove her hard ashore—so hard that she capsized on a steeply slanting beach with her funnel, dredging tower, and buckets jammed into the shingle (flat pebble) beach.

Ensor had to turn her over before pumping her out or raising her, so he attached pontoons to the dredging tower and whatever other top hamper he could, and then pumped compressed air into selected compartments that would, he felt, help in the turning process. Ashore, he decided, would be a series of steam engines operated by two batteries of boilers; these would pull with steel cables attached at very short intervals along the vessel.

So far, so good. But how did he keep from merely pulling the *Silurias* to pieces? A strong enough cable, pulled by a strong enough steam engine, could cut right down through the metal hull of any ship. So he first built a heavy log framework all the way around the hull. These logs had steel-lined grooves in them so the cables could not go through and bite into the hull itself. The inside of the *Silurias* was extensively strengthened with braced twelve-by-twelves. Finally, holes were hack-sawed through the hull plates for the passage of lifting cables.

Ensor removed a thousand yards of seabed so the vessel had a more level resting place, and then turned his attention ashore. The dredger was going to exert a dead weight of two thousand tons, so he got four old boilers, filled them full of cement, blasted out pits in the rock for them, and then poured cement around them. Each was good for two hundred tons of pull. He next cut 12-inch-diameter steel propeller shafting into eighteen equal lengths: each of these, also sunk in cement-lined holes, served as a bollard capable of withstanding a hundred-ton pull. Estimated total: twenty-six hundred tons.

From the boilers to the *Silurias* to these improvised bollards were run a total of ten miles of 6- and 8-inch steel cables. When the steam engines were started, elaborate signals were used between the operators of the two batteries of boilers so that neither would pull faster than the other and distribute the strain unevenly.

The first hitch brought the dredger's funnel ten feet out of the mud in which it had been buried; after the next, the pontoons were excess and were cast loose; the final lift brought *Silurias* around to an upright, even keel without any damage beyond that suffered in originally capsizing.

SALVAGE AGAINST THE ODDS: *ULIDIA*

Another extremely resourceful civilian British salvor of the day was Captain E. J. Gray. In 1917, the 6000-ton steamer *Ulidia* was driven ashore by a gale in Saroka Bay, Russia—three hundred miles from Archangel and well within the Arctic Circle. Since the vessel was worth £80,000, her crew made two strenuous but unsuccessful attempts to refloat her. A Russian salvage company tried with the same results; and in the spring, after the ice had gone out, a big Russian icebreaker tore the stranded vessel's sternpost off in an ill-conceived attempt to drag her free.

Gray and another Englishman arrived in July 1919, having hired a Russian tug and crew for a salvage attempt. They patched the holed bottom with quick-setting cement and began pumping her out for the first time; but their 12-inch pump proved insufficient for the job. They brought in a second, and a British engineer to tend them. After winkling the *Ulidia* off the beach, they towed her for fifty-four hours without sleep to a tiny Russian seaport hamlet that had a pier. Here they let the vessel down on a box patch they had placed underneath her keel in hopes of stopping leakage through the ill-patched bottom. Having no other way to hold the patch in place, they ran a chain right around the vessel and pulled it up tight.

Russia's new Communist government decided that since the ship was afloat, it was time to confiscate; but Gray and his partners, getting word of the impending piracy, took *Ulidia* to sea just as she was. They faced incessant gales on a vessel leaking so badly they had to keep their pumps working twenty-four hours a day; they also had to keep shifting the pumps from compartment to compartment just to keep the ship afloat.

In this manner the three men brought the *Ulidia* through twenty-two hundred miles of open northern seas—with that single chain around the box patch between them and sinking—to England.

LIVE TORPEDOES: YOUNG SAVES UC-5

Once he had transferred his talents from the Liverpool Salvage Association to the Salvage Section of the Admiralty, Captain Frederick W. Young[1] engaged in some classically inventive operations on stranded vessels. One of the most harrowing was on the German submarine *UC-5*. On May 1, 1916, the U-boat went ashore on Shipwash Banks off Harwich because of bad navigation or bad luck or both. Unfortunately for the German sailors, they struck the bank at high tide, just after the turn, so there was no slightest chance of breaking loose.

As they lay there, the British destroyer *Firedrake* came thundering down on them under full steam. The Germans feverishly drew lots: one man would stay behind to blow up the *UC-5*—and coincidentally himself—while the others would jump overboard and swim to the destroyer and safety.

All went as planned—almost. Up came the *Firedrake*, bristling with armaments and hostility, over went the Germans, off went the charge. But the poor soul left behind, unable to leave this world in bits and pieces, made it such a small charge that both he and the *UC-5* survived it relatively intact.

Young, aboard the salvage ship *Ranger*, was dispatched to get not only the *UC-5*'s papers for study, but also the sub itself. He found one tiny spot of trouble with that: *UC-5* had been on a mine-laying expedition, and there still were a dozen armed mines in her laying tubes. They could not be disarmed in the tubes, and as long as the submarine lay on the sandbank they could not be gotten at for the removal; but the token charge detonated by the German sailor had damaged the submarine's hull just enough to flood it.

Young decided on a mechanical lift with a 500-ton Admiralty lifting barge, which, he hoped, could bring her off with progressive tide-lifts. Slipping the 9-inch lifting cables under her proved a harrowing business, since the slightest jar might set off mines containing enough aggregate power to wipe out the sub, the lifting barge, the *Ranger*, and a respectable portion of Shipwash Banks besides.

Young hoped to get five feet of lift from the first tide, but the barge canted so far with the sub's weight that the *UC-5* stayed where she was. At low tide the stubborn Young tightened his cables down further, grimly determined to bring home the submarine. So a heavy storm blew up. Since his tugs were fastened to the lifting barge by short, quarter-mile towing hawsers, and the barge was pinned to the sub, their only recourse was to hang on.

But Young's brilliant assistant, Commander Kay, felt differently. With two volunteer engineers, he got aboard the bucking lighter and began filling the tanks on the side away from the sub with sea water. Though this lowered the barge in the water, it also brought it back to an even keel; by dawn, they were able to bring the sub off.

Their problems were not over, however. As they neared the Cork Lightship they found the sea shoaling abruptly and also found that the *UC-5*'s mine-release gear had broken adrift. Two of the mines were nearly out of the tubes. If they had fallen out during the tow . . .

Young made a grid of wire to cover the bottom of the tubes. But then the storm returned and the sub began to bounce up and down. Young quickly jammed several yielding collision mats under the sub, between it and the sea bottom. And they worked. The waves merely banged the *UC-5* against the relatively soft mats; the mines did not go off.

With quieter weather and high tide, they brought the U-boat into Harwich Harbor for beaching and removal of the mines.

In March 1917 Young was faced simultaneously with a sunken Q-ship and the *Asturias*, sunk at separate locations. With the Q-ship successfully raised,[2] Young turned to the *Asturias*, a massive liner converted into a hospital ship. It had been struck by a German torpedo and had gone ashore near Salcombe, Devonshire.

The ship's sternpost and one propeller and shaft had been blown away, and thirty-five crewmen had been killed. And in addition, an after bulkhead had been rent, allowing both the engine and boiler rooms to flood. The water in them rose and fell with the tide. To get his pumps down where he needed them, Young disassembled them on deck, had the parts hauled down ladders to the lower decks, and there reassembled them. In trying to regain stability aboard the vessel, he used more pumps than had ever been assembled on a single ship before.

Next he had a steel cover made for the hole open to the sea that once had been the propeller tunnel, and then had divers put it in place—lined with bags of cement. As the cement got wet, it hardened, forming an effective temporary seal. To clog up the other gashes and holes in the bulkheads, he used anything he could find, including beds, mattresses, oakum, straw, even old clothing.

On April 9, less than a month after the torpedoing, he made his first try at refloating the vessel. Eighteen-degree starboard list. In the next few days, Young flooded and brought her up again a total of eight times. Interspersed with his efforts were a string of fierce spring gales; yet he finally got the ship up, stabilized with compressed air, and into port after a rather harrowing tow.

Like the *Asturias* operation, Young's efforts on the British dreadnought *Britannia* utilized compressed air even though both salvage jobs antedated his epoch-making use of compressed air to raise the sunken submarine *K-13*.[3] This big British battlewagon was returning from duty in the North Sea when a tremendous gale swept her up on the beach at Inchkeith, a rocky island near the entrance of Scotland's Firth of Forth. Both tugs and torpedo boats strove with might and futility to drag the ship off; when Young arrived on the scene, he discovered why. The storm had rammed the *Britannia* down hard on the rocks, and her own great weight had done the rest. Rocks had not only pierced the ship's bottom; the double bottom, or false bottom, had also been fractured.

Young put his men to removing everything portable from the ship, including ammunition and fuel, to lighten her as much as possible. It worked: he was able to patch the upper, or false, bottom, with quick-drying cement. This gave him a tight ship, even if the real hull still was pierced in many places by rocks, and let him pump out the flooded engine and boiler rooms.

He got the engines working again while other crews were fitting air hoses down into the flooded space between the real and the false bottoms. The ship's own engines gave him power to run the compressors and air pumps, and to drive the water out through the rents in the hull of the ship. By maintaining pressure once the between-bottoms space was dry, he had a layer of buoyant air for the ship to ride on while he brought her into dry dock.

Once Frederick Young had been placed in command of the Admiralty's Salvage Section, Commander Kay began to run some rather tricky salvage operations of his own with the salvage vessel *Ranger*. One involved bringing off a ship that did not have quite enough water under her for the tugs to drag her free. Kay calmly called for a destroyer, which he set to running back and forth in front of the stranded vessel under full steam, parallel to the beach and as close as the destroyer skipper could come without grounding his own vessel. This set up such a heavy wash that the ship began rolling and bumping, and the tugs were able to jerk her free.

Probably his most inventive job was raising the freighter *Westmoreland* after she had been struck by a German torpdeo off Saint Bees Head, near Liverpool. The No. 2 hold, forward, had a piece of hull ripped out big enough to drop a tract home through.

The *Westmoreland*'s captain tried valiantly to save his ship by keeping her limping toward Liverpool. Finally, however, she was so far down by the head that her propellers were completely out of the water and her bow was touching bottom. At low tide, she settled down. This meant that at high tide the water poured into the ruptured hold. As if this were not bad enough, the *Westmoreland*'s interior transverse bulkheads had not been built all the way up to the decks, so that the water merely poured over the bulkheads from No. 2 into the adjoining holds.

The *Westmoreland* just plainly sank. At high tide, her upper deck was some thirty feet below the surface.

Kay found that the explosion also had torn a forty-foot hole in the shelter deck above the ruptured No. 2 hold. His first order set his divers to work on a trunkway, or series of watertight walls, from the shelter deck right up to the main deck. When this was finished, it effectively isolated the damaged areas of deck and hold from the rest of the ship.

Then large submersible pumps were put down to lower the water in the other, and still-sound, sections. Soon the *Westmoreland* swung clear of the bottom, up enough so that tugs could tow the still-sunken vessel some two miles closer to shore. Now the cargo hatches were out of water, and the cargo finally could be unloaded—including hundreds of cases of butter, none the worse for their long salt-water immersion.

With the holds clear and dry—apart, of course, from No. 2—Kay had his men build tons of timber props in all directions between bulkheads and decks, so the ship was strengthened against stress from any conceivable direction. Meanwhile they left No. 2 hold and the hole in the shelter deck wide open. Heavy seas could wash right into the hold, could vent through the shelter deck, and then could wash right out again—all without exerting any pressure against the transverse bulkheads isolating this damaged area from the rest of the ship.

Kay's first attempt to bring the ship into dry dock was fourteen weeks after she had been torpedoed. It failed: even pumped out as much as possible, she was still so far down in the head that her screws were out of water. Kay calmly ordered the entire vessel flooded down again, had the bows raised as far as they would go, and *then* had the after sections pumped out—but just enough to bring the stern on an even keel with the head.

She rode very low, but she rode; and thus, using water to trim his ship, as a submarine uses it for ballast in trimming to dive or to surface, Kay brought the *Westmoreland* safely to port.

WHEELER'S FIVE VESSELS IN TEN DAYS

All of which may suggest that Captain Young and Commander Kay were the only two salvage officers operating at fever pitch and with remarkable success for the Salvage Section. Nothing could be less true; one salvor, Lieutenant J. G. Wheeler, set a record for consecutive non-stop salvage jobs that in all probability still stands.

It began in June 1917, when Wheeler and his salvage vessel, HMS *Linton*, were hard at work saving a ship named the *Elford*. They had just gotten it to the point where its safety was assured, when Wheeler received a hot rocket from the Admiralty to abandon the *Elford* and go after the *Oldfield Grange*, which a German U-boat had just torpedoed in the English Channel off Worthing.

Wheeler and the *Linton* arrived to find the *Grange* already beached —with a thirty-six-foot hole in one side, and nine smaller holes in the other. In an incredible sixty-hour burst they stopped up the fractured bulkheads, brought her off the rocks, decided she would stay afloat with the use of two 12-inch pumps, and began towing her to Netley.

But another wireless message arrived. The *Eustace* was aground on Selsey Bill, a point of land in Sussex near Portsmouth, after being torpedoed by another German submarine. Wheeler unceremoniously dumped the *Oldfield Grange* by running her ashore in the safety of Stokes Bay, dismantled and removed his pumps, and rushed off after the *Eustace*.

The *Linton* reached the crippled vessel a bit after midnight; they set up their pumps and got down to it. To drain the lower decks as they raised the ship with the pumps, they punched out rivets so the water could cascade out through the holes. By six o'clock that evening, the *Linton* had the *Eustace* under tow; by four the next morning, she had her in Stokes Bay—where she was run up and beached beside the *Oldfield Grange*. Then they took off again.

This time it was the *Marguerite*, a collier with some fifty-two hundred tons of coal aboard. She was merely disabled, not crippled, so Wheeler threw a towline on her, turned about, and dragged her back to Stokes Bay.

There he ran her up smartly on shore beside the *Grange* and the *Eustace*, whirled the panting old *Linton* around, and swept out again— after the *Mahopac*.

When they had beached *that* disabled freighter beside the other three, they had saved (if one counts the *Elford*) five vessels in ten days—on a grand total of six hours' consecutive sleep.

With the sardonic laughter of the sea-gods ringing in our ears, we turn from the achievements of these brilliant and dedicated professionals to the remarkable botch made by the U. S. Navy in the name of salvage on the West Coast of the United States at about the same time.

A DUBIOUS EXCHANGE: H-3 FOR THE *MILWAUKEE*

H-3 was a three-year-old submarine with a 14-knot top speed and a twenty-seven-man crew, which went ashore some four miles north of the entrance to Humboldt Bay, California, on December 14, 1916. She ended up broadside on Samoa Beach, two hundred yards offshore in a pounding surf. Her crewmen stayed inside, occasionally blasting long mournful signals on her whistle, until beach men from the Humboldt Life-Saving Station trudged out to fire a line aboard with their Lyle gun.

Only nobody came out of the sub to make it fast.

Finally the station keeper sent men for a surfboat. While they were gone, a second line was gotten aboard the sub. This time men issued forth to fasten the tail block and hawser, but managed to thoroughly foul the gear in the process. They then shyly returned below decks and battened down the hatches again.

It took the Coast Guard crew several more attempts to get the rescue gear aboard from their boat, get their breeches-buoy line set up, and then politely knock on the hull so the crew could issue forth to be officially rescued.

By December 20, several ships had attempted to bring the little submarine off. There had been the Coast Guard cutter *McCulloch*, the monitor *Cheyenne*, the Navy tug *Arapahoe*; none had been able to budge her. Finally the Navy called for bids from the private sector, and several were submitted. All, the local Navy brass felt, were exorbitantly high.

After all, these worthy officers who knew nothing of salvage reasoned, the tugs and cutters and monitors had failed because they had not been strong enough to rescue the submarine. Therefore, what was needed was a salvage ship with some *power*. They got one: the 9700-ton heavy cruiser *Milwaukee*, pride of the fleet. It had *power*: 24,504 horses' worth of power. The *Milwaukee* had more power than all the principal tugs on the West Coast combined.

The Navy was going mosquito-hunting with a cannon.

In from the open sea lumbered the *Milwaukee* to put a heavy towing hawser aboard the *H-3*. Then those 24,000-horsepower engines were revved up, and the cruiser went churning away from the beach.

The hawser snapped like laundry twine.

The *Milwaukee*, unexpectedly freed of both hawser and submarine, veered wildly to bury her heavily armored hull in the sand. As her officers rushed about aimlessly, the Coast Guard wearily shot a line aboard and, by breeches buoy, began removing the sailors. It took two days: there were 438 men aboard the cruiser. The most charitable thing to be said of the salvage operation is that no lives were lost.

But the *Milwaukee* was. There was literally nothing available on the West Coast of sufficient power to drag that hulk of iron and steel out of the shallows. She lay there with the waves pecking at her, knocking off a bit here and a chunk there, until she eventually rusted away to nothing.

Meanwhile, as the Navy brass bumbled back to its offices, a contract for commercial salvage on the *H-3* was very quietly let. The professionals cut a long narrow trench through the sand of the Samoa Beach peninsula from Humboldt Bay to the submarine; when it was deep enough, *H-3* was towed into the bay, quickly repaired, and sneaked back into service.

SEVEN DESTROYERS ON THE ROCKS

Another bizarre stranding incident involving the U. S. Navy on the West Coast occurred a few years after World War I. On September 9, 1923, the steamship *Cuba* was wrecked on San Miguel Island, off the California coast. No lives were lost, but a great storm of wireless messages clogged the broadcast bands as the owners, the captain, salvage ships, shore stations, and the Coast Guard all tried to communicate with one another at once.

This had nothing at all to do with the U. S. Navy, except for the seemingly unconnected fact that eighteen vessels of the Navy's Battle Fleet were on war-training maneuvers in a dense fog some seventy-five miles north of Santa Barbara and quite close to San Miguel Island.

An important part of the squadron was seven destroyers, all first-line fighting ships built between 1918 and 1920, each 310 feet long, four-stacked, and fast. The flagship was the destroyer *Delphy*, leading her wolf pack of lean killers at twenty knots in the dense fog and, unfortunately, thirty miles off course. Perhaps this was a result of her communications with her shore stations being badly jumbled by the *Cuba* transmissions; but the fact remains that nobody aboard had the foggiest notion of where they were in relation to where they should have been. They did not even know they were off course.

Just north of Point Arguello, at the Honda Rocks, *Delphy* ran head-on into a rocky promontory jutting some one hundred yards out into the ocean. Perhaps the six following destroyers were already too close to change course; perhaps their commanders had been as youths avid readers of *The Charge of the Light Brigade*. In any event, without a tremor or a wink, the *Lee*, the *Young*, the *Nicholas*, the *Woodbury*, the *Chauncey*, and the *Fuller*, 250 feet apart in perfect and eye-pleasing battle formation, rammed head on into the jumbled rocks flanking the *Delphy*.

It was only through cool work by the crewmen that no more than twenty-two men were lost. Engineers immediately doused their boilers before in-rushing sea water did it for them; some men leaped heroically into the crashing surf to carry life lines ashore from the stranded vessels. Work was done by flashlight, since there was no power on the ships, and this firefly display caught the eye of a woman ashore. She summoned help, beach gear was rigged, and 630 men were brought safely away.

Salvage was discussed and rejected, since the lightly built destroyers had crumpled up like Dixie cups when they hit the rocks. The Court of Inquiry was held behind closed doors, and the findings have never been made public.

Over on the East Coast, however, in the area around New York Harbor, the Navy's salvors were faring better in removing war-precious cargoes from stranded ships.

In January 1918, the British transport *Dara* was outward bound for Europe, loaded with grain in a dense fog, when she ran blindly onto the ram of the anchored battleship *Indiana* near the Ambrose Channel. The *Dara* reeled away to go aground on the mud flats near Fort Wadsworth. At mid-tide, her well deck was five feet above the water, and within a few hours her hatch covers were forced by the water-swollen grain. Each hatch, with grain puffed five or six feet above the coamings, looked like a giant charlotte russe.

Master diver Frank Meier went down to find a fifteen-inch circle, almost perfectly round, punched out of the side of the vessel by the *Indiana*'s ram. Since the ragged, torn steel had been pushed ino the hole, he and his crew merely sealed it with a two-foot-square toggle patch.

The morning after the collision, a wrecker with a clamshell bucket began scooping the swollen cargo into a pair of small grain barges rigged with steam siphons to drain the water off. The barges took the grain to an elevator in Brooklyn, where compressed air was used to suck it into a high hopper. From there it was fed into a hot-air drier, and was air-fed into a storage bin to be checked by government inspectors for mold or rot.

Aboard the *Dara*, meanwhile, a pump was rigged to drain the holds once the clamshell scoop began striking the wooden sealer in the bottom, and electric blowers followed to blow everything bone-dry.

Dara had broken from the mud as she had lightened; when she was empty, she rode with the wooden toggle patch several feet above the water. A welding barge moved in to fit and fabricate a steel patch and slap it on the hull, where it was bolted and welded in place. The next morning, *Dara* steamed under her own power to the elevator in the Erie Basin where her grain had been stored, reloaded, and that night joined a convoy of other low-speed freighters bound for Britain.

The entire operation had taken ten days.

THE *PHILIP'S* DURABLE CARGO

Nine months later, in the same area, another foggy night caused a very similar accident between the 4000-ton British steamer *Port Philip* and the U.S. supply ship *Proteus*. The *Philip*, rammed amidships in the fog, went down so fast that her fifty-five-man crew had to go over the side. She ended up with her decks under a mere thirteen feet of water, her holds jammed with several thousand reels of barbed wire for trench warfare, and hundreds of Model-T Ford touring cars and light trucks intended for troop transport.

The big problem with the wire was how the divers down in the holds could handle it without ripping both their gloves and their very vulnerable diving suits. This was solved by lowering small hooks on short whips of cable from hoists on salvage barges anchored above the *Philip*. The diver would merely shove a hook into the nearest bale of wire, give a haul-away signal, and stand clear.

The rolls often were intermeshed, however, so sometimes twenty or thirty would start up at once; then one or more of them would break free and drop down on the diver below. Many divers were slashed up, but none seriously. The wire would be immediately immersed in light oil, then reloaded on another vessel.

They were just about to start on the cars and trucks when, on November 11, the Armistice was declared. Almost overnight, the *Philip* went in value from several million dollars to zero. It was abandoned by the Navy, its owners, even the British Government. The sole entity concerned with it now was the Army Engineers, since the *Port*

Philip was a danger to a navigable waterway, and the Army wanted it cleared away. Bids were advertised for its removal.

But scrap-metal prices were as rotten as ship values. The firm receiving the contract decided to copper its bets by trying to salvage the crates of disassembled cars and trucks. Huge, open tanks of oil were placed on the deck of the salvors' floating derrick, small flat scows were moored alongside, and auto mechanics stood by on the nearby sea wall at Battery Park.

The divers would send up each crate, and the wood would be knocked away while the water drained off. The section of truck or auto then was immediately submerged in an oil tank for a predetermined period, hoisted clear to drain, swung over to a scow, and transported to the sea wall. The mechanics waiting there cleaned off the oil, assembled the vehicles, tuned up the engines, gassed them up, gave them a trial run, and sold them to waiting auto dealers or private parties for $300 or $400 a car. The only complaint was that blowouts were distressingly frequent: the tires had been weakened by their long immersion.

The *Port Philip* was cut up for scrap with dynamite strings.

---

[1] See pages 111–12, 203–6.
[2] See pages 205–6.
[3] See pages 111–12.

CHAPTER TWENTY-THREE

Mostly Peaceful

~~~~~~

In Britain, the end of the war meant the return of the great wartime salvors to peacetime jobs, and such commercial firms as the Liverpool Salvage Association blossomed anew. Sometimes a talented salvor on peacetime duty had to launch a double operation—one to save the cargo, a second to save the ship.

LIVERPOOL AND GLASGOW SALVAGE ASSOCIATION

The *Bardic* was a White Star freighter that, in heavy fog, struck and held on the rocks near Britain's Lizard Light at 1:00 A.M. on August 31, 1924. The crew got safely away except for the master and a few ship's engineers, who volunteered to stay aboard to keep up steam for the pumps. The *Bardic* was carrying wheat, chilled beef, and baled wool, and they wanted to save that as well as the vessel, if they could.

Commander I. J. Kay and the salvage ship *Ranger* arrived to find the freighter down forward, holed, listing to port, and grinding viciously against the rocks. The engine room was flooded, and most of the holds had water in them up to twenty-two feet. Kay brought up two 600-ton lighters, and for six days of good weather unloaded wool and beef and got the pumps working. When bad weather drove off the lighters, salvors stayed aboard to keep pumps going with an aggregate volume of 1,160,000 gallons of water an hour. They needed it: the *Bardic* had an eleven-foot hole in her bows.

On September 9, the gale worsened so that the salvors had to be removed for their own safety. Kay flooded the *Bardic* down completely before they left, to lessen her grinding on the rocks. When the weather abated on the twenty-fifth, they returned with more pumps and also some air compressors. Some of his telegrams to the London underwriters sounded like sickroom bulletins:

"NO APPARENT CHANGE IN CONDITION. TEMPERATURE 31 DEGREES" (in No. 4 hold).

By the twenty-eighth, four tugs and a salvage vessel, the *Trover*, were able to get her off the rocks and into Falmouth Harbor; she was in dry dock by October 3. It was found that 140 of her hull plates had been totally destroyed by the pounding on the rocks, and that much of her interior framing had been smashed. She was later completely repaired and returned to service.

One of the oddest of the Liverpool and Glasgow Salvage Association's assignments was the work they did on the *Gustave Schindler*, a tanker that stranded on the Baleur Bank, Nigeria, August 17, 1928. She was pulled free by a Nigerian Government tug, but during the night sank in forty-two feet of water.

The owners declared her a total loss and demanded payment by the underwriters; these gentlemen in turn wanted to save as large a portion as was possible of the 2972 tons of bulk palm oil that made up her cargo. Liverpool and Glasgow was chosen for the attempt, and sent a top salvage team out to Nigeria.

Palm oil is lighter than water, which meant they could not just open the hatches and start scooping it out: once loosened, it would float to the surface and be swept away by the river current. The salvage master therefore started with wooden cofferdams built around the hatch covers and up above the surface of the water. Through these, he lowered steam coils to melt the semisolid oil; from the cofferdams it was pumped into surface craft, which took it to Port Harcourt (Okrika). More than a third of the cargo, some 1060 tons, was recovered in this way.

Explosives were used to rupture the bottoms of the bulkheads between holds so that the oil could be drained from hold to hold until it reached one that was cofferdammed. To fix the explosives—and also to periodically readjust the steam hoses—divers often worked thirty feet deep in the liquid palm oil, which they treated, for diving purposes, just as sea water.

The Liverpool and Glasgow seems to have been especially adept, during those postwar years, in salvage operations involving bulk liquid cargoes. This was certainly true on the tank steamer *Oliva*, which went aground near Bennan Head on the Isle of Arran, in the Firth of Clyde off Scotland's southwest coast, just a month (September 17, 1928) after the *Schindler* had done so in Nigeria. The *Oliva* was a 5694-ton vessel carrying fifty-five hundred tons of highly toxic and inflammable bulk benzine.

After the owners had tried unsuccessfully to get the *Oliva* free with tugs, they called in Liverpool and Glasgow. The operation required guts and nice judgment: several tanks had ruptured, so that several thousand gallons of benzine were floating on the water around the wreck. It was necessary to let this half-mile ring of death dissipate before salvage began—which in turn meant clearing the ruptured tanks so pollution would not continue.

Suction pumps were out, because the benzine merely vaporized in the pipes and didn't go anywhere. The salvors decided to force the liquid mixture of hydrocarbons out through the ruptures in the tanks with compressed air. This created a potentially fatal concentration of fumes aboard the *Oliva*, however, so they would set the compressors, fill their fuel tanks with a fixed amount of gasoline, start them, and hurriedly leave the wreck. When the compressors would run out of fuel and stop, the salvors, after waiting until the fumes had dissipated, would return to refuel the compressors. To avoid sparking off an explosion, they fed the compressors' exhaust pipes down into the water.

Once the holed tanks were cleared, they brought the vessel's forepart off the rocks with compressed air only twelve days after the stranding, and by October 21 she was dry-docked at Elderslie. (The intact half of her cargo had first been pumped into another tanker.)

One of Liverpool and Glasgow's most interesting operations was the *Suevic*, for it featured a technique used quite often in strandings and in no other sort of salvage: cutting a ship in half as she lies, and saving one of the sections (usually the after, which holds the ship's valuable machinery) for mating with a new end.

The 450-foot-long White Star liner had been stranded on Britain's rocky western coast. A third of her length was aground and badly pierced; another third was clear at high tide but settled on the rocks at low. Midships were two high, sharp pinnacles, which had holed her, and held her, and on which she worked very badly at low tide.

The salvors decided to cut her in two, but first they had to free her from those pinnacles. This was done with careful blasting. Explosives are used extensively on ships aground, usually to blow away rock spurs that have pierced the hull, or to clear a path back to the water. Holes for the explosives can be hand- or pneumatically-drilled, either from surface vessels or by divers alongside. The blasting of submerged rock is a real art, for the salvor must consider the amount and strength of the tide, water depth at both ebb and flood, depth and area of the rock in relation to the stranded ship, and the nature of the rock itself: whether igneous, sedimentary, or metamorphic. Each type reacts differently to the detonation of a charge.

Forward of the engine room were four holds, three of them flooded, and one, No. 4 hold, closest to the engine room, with twelve feet of water in it. The engine room and everything behind it were tight and dry, so they decided the cut would be made in the No. 3 hold, some one hundred feet aft of the bow.

No. 4 hold was pumped out, but the water was left in the space between the false bottom and the hull; then, fore and aft, above and below each deck, the hold's forward bulkhead was tremendously strengthened with 12-inch pine balks.

The actual cutting was done from outside the ship, since the holds still held so much cargo that work inside was impossible. The plating was between three-fourths inch and one inch; the keel was $12\frac{1}{2}$ inches by $3\frac{1}{4}$ inches, solid bar steel. Cutting was done with explosive gelignite cartridges varying in size from one to ten pounds. An eight-pound charge in a canvas sock, electrically fired, sheared the keel. Above water, the charges were lowered over the side from the deck; below, they were set by divers.

The divers were in constant danger from tides and currents, which threatened to sweep them into the working, partially opened crack. Sheep carcasses came floating out of the cut in a steady parade like an insomniac's nightmare. The final cut was that of the main deck plates, with men crawling to the edges of the cut to set their charges as the ship bounced and rolled. The cutting took six days, with nine to twenty-four inches of steel being cut per charge.

Once the after section was alive, the salvors' greatest consideration was to keep it from being battered against the rock-solid foresection. On the day before the final cut, five anchors were laid in a half circle around the stern and fastened to it with steel hawsers. Steam was gotten up in the boilers, and the *Ranger* and two tugs, *Herculaneum* and *Blazer*, made fast to the stern.

When the cut was made, all three surged back with engines full astern, as the *Suevic*'s engine did the same and steam winches cranked the vessel back against the anchors. She pulled free from the forepart without further damage, and was taken to dry dock for refitting of a new nose.

JOHN IRON, DOVER HARBOR MASTER

Our old friend Captain John Iron[1] was involved in a truly amusing salvage operation based on cutting ships in half during World War I. The *Nubian* and the *Zulu* were British torpedo boats, each of which had been stranded after being damaged. *Nubian* had struck a mine and was beached with her stern blown off; *Zulu* had been struck forward by a torpedo, which holed her, and then had been driven above high-water mark by a heavy gale.

John Iron was sent out to salvage what was left of the *Zulu*. He spotted some Royal Engineers on maneuver, and inveigled their commander into setting them a training exercise of blasting a channel through the rocks from the water to the smashed *Zulu*. The eighty-five sappers were so enthusiastic, they blasted a fifty-foot-wide channel some three hundred feet long.

With this in readiness, Iron cut the *Zulu* in half and dragged the undamaged after section out into open water at high tide. He then collected the undamaged foresection of the *Nubian*—which he had already removed from the ruined section aft—and had both sections towed to a naval shipyard.

Here, since the *Zulu* and the *Nubian* had been sister ships, identical in size and shape, the two sections were fitted neatly together to form a new ship.

Called, of course, the *Zubian*; a name much superior, it should be noted, to, say, the *Nubu*.

Though Captain Iron had gained fame during the war in general salvage, bringing off stranded ships was his forte. In 1929, for instance, as Harbor Master for the Dover Harbor Board, he salvaged, in January, the 6674-ton Dutch steamer *Merauke*, which had collided with another ship near the Varne Lightship. She was towed to Hythe and beached, down by the head so thoroughly that her bows grounded with nine feet of water over decks while her propellers were a full ten feet out of the water astern. Iron towed her to Dover despite the fact that she was "opening and shutting amidships like a concertina."

Just a month later, when the 1940-ton steamer *Dafila* was driven high up and dug into the sand after going ashore near Dungeness on the Newcomb Bank, Iron noticed that at flood tide there was just enough water for shallow-draught tugs to sneak up on either side of her without grounding. He ran them in quickly, lashed them on either side of the *Dafila* with hawsers, and, before the water began to ebb, had them run their engines at FULL AHEAD, their sterns toward shore. As he had hoped, the powerful screws of the tugs scoured away enough sand from beneath the *Dafila* so she could be successfully dragged out into open water and thence to Dover.

The entire operation took three days.

Also in February, Iron saved the Belgian Mail Steamer, *Ville de Liège*, after she had missed Dover Harbor and run aground during her Ostend-Dover run. She hit with such force that a full two-thirds of her length was run up on the rocks and holed in dozens of places; Iron set his men to whittling wooden pegs of applicable sizes and pounding them ino the holes, then at flood tide brought her off and into her usual Dover Harbor slip. Just as he brought her in, one of Iron's eight-inch pumps quit. So closely had he figured his pumping needs that the *Ville de Liège* sank beside the pier with just this slight loss of pumping capacity. In the quiet harbor, pumping her out and raising her again was no real problem.

Iron's final notable stranding of that year was another foreign vessel, the 3872-ton Italian *Nimbo*, which struck a drainage works off the Sussex Coast in November. She settled in very rough rocks with a three-foot-wide gash, thirty feet long, in her side. Iron's divers reported that three of her holds were tight and dry, so at low tide he ordered his men to cut a yard-square hole in the hull of each undamaged hold. When the tide rose, it flooded in and filled the entire ship with water.

Now it was down tight on the bottom, so Iron could get to work.

He fabricated a large timber patch to cover the rent in her side, fitted toggle patches over the three inlet holes his men had previously made in the hull, and pumped the vessel out for the tow to Southampton. His various patches were so well made, and his initial pumping so thorough, that not one pump had to be switched on during the tow.

One of the most famous World War II cartoons by Bill Mauldin shows his two tattered heroes, Willie and Joe, walking past a British tommy. The weary Briton is seated on a tire half-buried in the mud; the earth is littered with shell casings, discarded ammo boxes, neglected barbwire, a German helmet.

"You blokes leave an awfully messy battlefield," he remarks.

In a way, this sums up the position as regards strandings during the greater part of World War II. Once the industrial might of the United States was committed to wartime production, the fate of individual ships often became a matter of little moment. Pausing to drag off the rocks a vessel that had gone ashore was often not considered worth the sort of "sitting duck" exposure to Nazi U-boats the salvage effort might entail. And once the Allies began the invasions of Europe and the steppingstone invasions of the Pacific islands, events were moving too fast. Stranded vessels were often just left where they had struck, to rust into worthless hulks.

USS *THOMAS STONE*

North Africa in the dark days of 1942 and 1943 was a notable exception to this very broad generalization. There the salvors fought like demons to get stranded ships back to work supplying men or matériel for the desert war. The USS *Thomas Stone* was a new type of vessel, newly designed: an Armed Naval Transport. She was carrying fourteen hundred assault troops, their landing craft, and tanks, when, on November 7, 1942, she was struck by a German torpedo.

The *Stone* was 95 per cent undamaged, but the other 5 per cent was vital: her lower hull aft, the rudder post, and the ruddet were wiped out, along with nine seamen. The *Stone* was left completely unable to steer. It happened only 150 miles from the coast and twenty hours from H hour of the North African invasion being engineered by Dwight Eisenhower. Her captain, Olton "Benny" Bennehoff, was outraged. His job, by God, was to put those fourteen hundred men into battle, and he intended to do it.

And he did. He packed them into their landing craft in good weather on a smooth sea, gave them as an escort the British corvette *Spey*, which was supposed to be protecting the *Stone*, and sent them scooting shoreward at eight knots. He estimated this would bring them to their landing zone just on time—and it did.

Meanwhile, there was the *Stone*, the convoy gone and her escort gone. Benny coolly waited until HMS *Velox* and *Wishart* arrived. The two destroyers began towing the erratically yawing *Stone* toward Algiers, later aided by the tug *Saint Day*. Bad weather kept parting their hawsers, so it took four nights and three days.

At Algiers, Benny was given the fast shuffle: he had to anchor in the outer harbor because of the shortage of mooring slips, hence was outside the anti-aircraft defenses and took a tremendous pasting during the almost nightly German air raids. One 1000-pound bomb passed right through her port quarter to explode where her stern once had been, without inflicting any more damage at all.

Then a full gale blew up, which started dragging the *Stone*'s anchors. Benny called for tugs, but the two that arrived were too small: even at FULL AHEAD they could not keep the *Stone* from going up on the rocks. The stern entered the shore breakers, struck, then served as pivot while the bows swung around until she was nose to the shore. The storm grounded her at Cape Matifou, eight miles from Algiers Harbor.

Edward Ellsberg first had his divers blast holes in the rock bottom of the bay, into which he set anchors for ground tackle. Everything portable was removed from the *Stone*, while soundings were made to find the shortest route of level bottom leading to deep water. They had to avoid rock ridges so the *Stone* would not break her back in being dragged seaward.

Ellsberg figured to get a thousand tons of pull from his anchors and steel hawsers, utilizing fourfold sheave blocks rigged luff upon luff to multiply their purchase; but the *Stone* was resting two thousand tons on the bottom. Six inches of sand overlay the bedrock, however; once they had the ship started, this began shifting, supplying, in effect, a thousand tons of lubrication. The *Stone* was brought off and towed to England for permanent repairs.

AN UNCONVENTIONAL ATTEMPT: THE *LEOPARD*

The *Stone* operation had its reasonably unconventional elements; but Peter Keeble's assault on the sands holding the Free French destroyer *Leopard* was so wildly unconventional as to border on farce. It was 1943, and already the outmoded destroyer was of no conceivable use to the Allied war effort; Navy brass wanted salvage only for Free French morale-boosting. The 2000-ton ship had been run right up on to a beach east of Benghazi at a booming twenty knots. She was listing to port nearly to her beam-ends, with a sandbank being built up along her seaward flank by the wind and waves.

To complicate matters, the captain, who spoke no English but was pathetically eager to save his ship, had off-loaded everything portable the day after the stranding, in order to lighten her. It had lightened the *Leopard*, all right—making it that much easier for the waves to drive her even farther up the beach. Keeble immediately flooded whatever compartments weren't already ruptured, then tried to figure out some way to shift those thousands of tons of sand that imprisoned her. The problem, of course, was not repairing the holes—that could be done by pumping cement into her bilges; the problem was getting her off the beach in the first place.

What was needed was a suction dredger to ream out a ten-foot channel from the ship to deep water. No dredge was available. But on his way back to Benghazi, Keeble ran afoul of a company of South African sappers commanded by an old friend named George Cowling. Cowling had come across a deserted salt factory in his wanderings; he proposed filching, for Keeble's use, the salt-pan pumps. These, he argued, had been specifically designed for handling abrasives such as salt; what they would do to sand, he was sure, would be a proper caution.

Keeble pointed out a little feverishly that salt-pan pumps required rigid steel piping, and there was none available in North Africa.

Was he mad? demanded the sappers indignantly. Didn't he know that Benghazi had been badly battered by German bombs? A few more torn-up streets wouldn't matter: they would dig up as much as was needed of the city's drainage system. As they started this task, and set up the sand pumps on a flat-bottomed Z-lighter, Keeble and Cowling went to work designing a cement pump for repairing the vessel. They ended up with a double-barreled affair made of short lengths of former sewer pipe. One barrel would receive the ready-mix cement, the lid would be closed, and a blast of compressed air would be forced in. At the bottom of the barrel was a handmade flap valve, which would open to let the cement be driven out through a three-inch flexible hose.

As this barrel was being emptied, the other would be filled, thus assuring a constant supply of cement. This weird contraption sealed the *Leopard*'s damaged hull within twenty-four hours of its arrival on site.

The barge with the sand pumps had been dragged down the coast to the *Leopard*; meanwhile, divers had gone down with the hose nozzles, and the pumping had started. Day after day it went on, first bringing the destroyer to an even keel, then deepening and widening the channel itself. The salvors began laying buoys to mark the edge of their passage. They modified the pumps so the suction hoses could be positioned by derricks on the deck of the barge rather than by divers. Finally, their launch set out the six anchors to seaward that would hold firm the ground tackle used to drag the *Leopard* off the beach.

The day before they were ready to move the ship, a heavy storm blew up, and the *Leopard* broached to and was smashed up high on the sand beyond any hope of repair.

Sometimes, in dealing with stranded ships, the salvors do all they can, then just wait for nature to help them out.

In January 1958, near Latakia, Syria, a British salvage ship, the *Sea Salvor*, used wind and weather to salvage the 3649-ton freighter *Almerian*. Caught by hurricane-force winds, the 337-foot vessel was driven so far up into the shallows that she was in only eight feet of water. She needed sixteen to float.

Upon arriving from Malta, the *Sea Salvor* first lightened the vessel by removing 580 tons of cargo—which still left her six feet short of floating. After lightening her, the salvors laid out three separate sets of 3-ton anchors (each anchor backed with a second, with the hauling cables then run through a sixfold purchase to a 5-ton winch or capstan), as well as six other anchors and ground tackle in strategic places. Each anchor, thus rigged, could provide the effective pull of three 2000-horsepower tugs.

Several attempts to bring her off were made between February 11 and 20 without result, apart from slewing her about a bit on her bottom. The purchases were kept taut, but the salvors could only pray for a gale.

The barometer began falling on February 21; by evening the *Sea*

Salvor herself was threatened by deteriorating weather. They refused to move, however; that night the *Almerian* came off the rocks safely.

THE ZEELAND FLIES A KITE

One of the cleverest uses of wind in a salvage operation was in 1963 on the stranded Liberty ship *Amazon*. The 7281-ton vessel had gone on the beach at Cape Bon, Tunisia, on Christmas Eve, and had stayed there until the arrival of the Dutch tug *Zeeland*, Captain A. Veen commanding, on the morning of the twenty-eighth.

Several attempts were made to get a pilot line aboard, but all their efforts were foiled by a fierce wind, Force 8, blowing directly from the sea to the land. Once a rocket gun got the messenger briefly aboard, but when they tried hauling across a heavier line, the messenger snapped; the *Zeeland* ran out of rockets before getting a second aboard. Thus, no towing cable could be stretched between the vessels to bring the *Amazon* off.

In one of the *Zeeland*'s lifeboats was a radio and aerial, and to raise that aerial was—a kite. The men on the *Zeeland* got the box kite into the air so they could begin maneuvering it into place.

Once it had passed over the *Amazon*, the sailors aboard the Liberty ship fired *their* rocket gun, carrying a line up and over that of the kite. Its weight dragged the kite low enough so they could seize its sagging line. Then it was just a matter of waiting until the crew of the *Zeeland* bent the messenger wire for the tow cable on the kite's line, and then hauling it in.

By the eighth of January, the *Zeeland* and the *Utrecht*, with the use of ground tackle, were able to bring the ship off the beach.

[1] See pages 158–59, 253–55.

CHAPTER TWENTY-FOUR

Supertankers

~~~~~~~~~~~~~~~~~~~~

Since World War II, some of the most provocative operations on stranded ships have been on that new breed, the supertanker. The wreck of the *Torrey Canyon*, in March 1967, will probably have a greater impact on methods of handling stranded vessels than the loss of any other single modern ship, because it emphasized the immense damage that a ruptured supertanker full of crude oil can inflict on an area's marine ecological balance.

AN EARLY SUPERTANKER

A quick look at an operation early in the war will serve as a good introduction to the complexities of salvaging stranded tankers. The Atlantic Refining Company's *E. H. Blum* was broken right in half by three explosions at fifteen-minute intervals on the night of February 16, 1942. At 11,600 gross tons, the *Blum* was one of the two largest all-welded tankers in the world at that time. Remember that tonnage: 11,600.

The two separate pieces were abandoned by their crew; the salvage steamers that sped to the site off the Virginia capes on the Atlantic seaboard found only the front half of the vessel. This they took in tow to Norfolk, Virginia, spotting the three-hundred-foot stern section up on the beach at the capes *en route*. After dropping the forepart, they returned to look the stern over.

It was lying in thirty feet of water in an exposed area, raked continually by breakers and with its oil tanks open to the pounding. They thought it would soon break up, but with the return of good weather, found the section still firm and whole because it had buried enough of its hull in the sand to keep from working with the wave action.

The salvors laid out ground tackle with heavy anchors to seaward, and fitted a rough concrete bulkhead over the open fractured end. Once it was tight, they blew the oil tanks (which by this time held only water) with compressed air. They were driven away periodically by heavy seas, but in less than three months had also brought this section into Norfolk.

The two pieces were welded together, necessary repairs were made at the fracture point, and the *Blum* was soon once again in service.

THE AFRICAN QUEEN GOES AGROUND

That was in 1942. After the end of the war, tankers began stretching, as peacetime demand for petroleum got heavier and heavier. The *African Queen* was a "supertanker" built in Kiel in 1955. She was 590 feet long, seventy-four in the beam, and drawing thirty-two. And she had a gross tonnage of 21,500. In thirteen years, tanker tonnages had nearly doubled.

The *African Queen* got into trouble trying to find the Delaware River on December 30, 1958: During a heavy storm and with his radar inoperable, Captain Kia Danielsen turned into what he thought was Delaware Bay. He ran his ship hard aground ten miles from the nearest shore, some twenty miles short of his destination and not too far from Ocean City, Maryland.

Danielsen tried backing and filling, but one hundred feet of the tanker's bows broke off, swung to starboard on a hinge of hull plate, and battered the ship for several minutes before breaking completely free. It slid down the length of the vessel's starboard side, paused at the stern to maul the hull beside the engine room, and then drifted casually off into the night.

An SOS brought the Coast Guard as the ship filled and sank; the entire crew was safely gotten off. By the night of the thirty-first, Merritt-Chapman & Scott's salvage ship *Curb* had arrived from New York at the request of the owners, African Enterprises, Ltd. In the next forty-five days the salvage firm used forty-three men and mountains of equipment, and spent $150,000 trying to rescue the ship; then they withdrew, battered by the weather, but beaten by the fact that the owners had decided salvage was not feasible.

Their record of achievement was not impressive: they had anchored what was left of the bow to keep it from drifting; they had made a small wood-and-concrete patch on the tank deck; they had assessed the rest of the damage.

They had also formally returned possession to the owners.

The owners briskly relinquished title to their underwriters at Lloyd's, fearful of being sued for beaches ruined by drifting oil—the point of such paramount importance in the case of the *Torrey Canyon*. The underwriters, fearing the same thing, officially abandoned the *Queen* also. She was up for grabs, and the looters were not slow to start grabbing. Almost everything of value that was portable disappeared. It was not that the *Queen* was unsalvageable; far from it. Despite the Merritt-Chapman & Scott episode, the professionals could easily have gotten the vessel off if it had seemed economically feasible. It didn't. It wasn't.

But then on the scene appeared the most unlikely set of salvors since Ernest Cox. Beldon Little and Lloyd Deir did metalwork, rigging, heavy-equipment operating, scrap cutting, mechanical work—anything and everything for scrap men and junk yards around their home town of Holland, Virginia. They were first intrigued, then obsessed with the *African Queen* sitting out there in the shallows. On March 13 (a Friday, yet!), 1959, after talking an appliance dealer named Paul Brady into bank-rolling them for $5,000, they set out for Atlantic City bearing life jackets, a Coleman stove, and a kerosene lamp. And a paint brush.

They found the awesome *Queen* squatting in thirty feet of water, angled 12 degrees to starboard. On her they painted KEEP OFF with their brush, and posted a "legal notice" that the "Industrial Maintenance Company of Holland, Virginia" had taken over the ship.

On March 23, they began hiring a crew. Since they were used to working with steel, they decided that was what they would patch with. (Merritt-Chapman & Scott had opted against steel, because they feared that welding-sparks would ignite the oil fumes filling the *Queen*.) A measure of Deir's and Little's knowledge concerning salvage techniques: for their entire six months aboard the *Queen* they walked warily around the professional salvors' wood-and-concrete patch—because they never figured out what it was.

Patching with steel meant they needed sheet steel, lots of it, a couple of dozen pumps, a power source, and a diver. They also would need a barge or a scow to bring out their material.

They ended up with two scows—a 36-foot LCVP and a 33-foot Navy airplane-rearming boat—twenty-two surplus Navy electric submersible pumps, and a power source jerry-built from a marine diesel engine to which they coupled a generator whose own engine was burned out. Finally they got a sheet-metal worker who was an amateur SCUBA diver, Maurice Simmons, and another backer, a Suffolk, Virginia, real estate speculator named Alvah E. Sadler.

SALVAGE BY A MOTLEY CREW

Salvage operations started when Simmons, in SCUBA gear, went down inside the flooded vessel to slam and dog down portholes in the food locker. Then they pumped the locker out: a triumph, of sorts.

Simmons began working his way forward along the starboard side, outside the vessel, looking for the damage that had sunk her. He knew it couldn't just be the sprung rivet holes, which he sealed with wooden pegs; he was right. On June 7, when he was within fifty feet of the tank deck, where the truncated hull abruptly ended, he found a vast section of hull that looked, he said, like a relief map of the moon. Holes, rips, gashes, tears, and hanging plates marked where the bow section had hung and pounded for several minutes before scraping its way aft.

The damaged area was twenty feet high and thirty feet long. Somehow they had to patch it if they hoped to raise the *Queen*.

This meant a hard-hat diver, which meant a diving stage—which had to be constructed from scratch. It was completed in three weeks, a masterpiece of improvisation. To the bottom end of a steel latticework boom was welded a thick pipe as a base. Thus the forty-seven-foot boom could stand vertically in the thirty-five feet of water beside the damaged hull. A double track was welded to the latticework, on which could run a steel-pipe framework operated by an electric motor on top of the boom. The diving stage, fastened to this steel-pipe framework, could be raised or lowered at will.

Their work area was the starboard boat deck, directly over the damage. Davit winches could haul up heavy loads of supplies, they figured; directly overhead was the engine-room cargo boom for hauling steel aboard; and the deck was long and wide enough (barely) to handle the patch once it was put together. Its disadvantages included a 12-degree slant toward the water, so waves would sweep its lower edge at high tide.

Beldon Little bought ⅜-inch steel in strips twenty feet long and five feet wide; six of them, he figured, welded together, would serve as a patch of sufficient size.

Meanwhile, master diver Duke Morris and his tender, Woody Crisp, had arrived on June 30. They were the operation's biggest expense, a frightening (to Deir and Little) $115 a day. Morris, faced with thirty feet of water in the engine room, couldn't get down to see what shape it was in because of a thick coating of oil on the surface. By accident, Deir discovered that paste detergent dumped into the water in sufficient quantity would clear it for a few hours at a time. Eight years later this was to be indispensable in cleaning up the *Torrey Canyon* mess.

Morris brought up the bad news that the patch could not be bolted on from outside by bolts through patch and hull, because it was impossible to reach the hull on the inside to tighten down the nuts.

Deir left the others building a template from a gridwork of pipe so they could accurately shape the patch to the hull's curvature, while he returned to his workshop in Holland, Virginia, to brood about the patch. It was an awesome problem. Big as the side of a barn and weighing ten tons, it somehow had to be "molded" to the shape of the *Queen's* battered hull, kept in that shape until it had been fastened in place, then strenthened and made rigid against the battering of the waves. He also had to figure out how he was going to fasten it to the hull if he couldn't bolt it.

He finally came up with tap bolts; they would fit into prethreaded holes in the hull, thus dispensing entirely with nuts. But this meant the holes in the patch and hull would have to be drilled, not burned with an acetylene torch.

Okay. For this, a T-shaped pneumatic drill. And to drive the bolts? An impact wrench. This was an inspired idea, for impact wrenches—air-driven devices used by auto mechanics to tighten down lug nuts on wheels—impart their turning motion by compressed air. To ensure absolute accuracy in drilling, nuts would be welded eight inches apart on either side of the place where the hole would be drilled. Steel rods then would be screwed into the nuts, to stand up from the hull like parallel steel fingers; and the T-shaped pneumatic drill would slide up and down on these rods.

His next problem: how to shape or "mold" the patch to fit the template of the damaged hull's curvature. He decided to weld the strips together to form a patch, then attach a cable to the patch's mid-line at a selected point. Lifted from the deck, the patch would naturally sag of its own weight at the edges. When the correct curve—or sag—had been achieved, 10-inch steel I-beam girders would be welded to the upper (outer) side of the patch to hold it rigidly in that curved position.

The I beams themselves would be bent by cutting small wedge shaped pieces out, then bending the beam until the lips of each wedge were touching, and then welding the cut closed.

This brought Deir to his final problem, that of lashing the patch against the hull until it could be bolted down permanently. He decided to do it with cables threaded through horizontal rows of holes at the top and bottom of the damaged area in the hull, then passing through (at the top) or across the face of the patch (from the bottom) to be lashed to deck shackles.

Then the bolts could be set, and the ship pumped and finally raised. In theory.

On July 18, diver Duke Morris began burning the rows of cable holes in the hull, and the pipe template was lowered over the side. It disclosed that the damaged area was forty feet long, not thirty; a harried search for more sheet steel began.

Work began on shaping the twenty steel I beams that would be used to hold the patch in shape. The patch was slung from the cargo beam by the cargo hook, with its top edge jammed up against the bulkhead of the deckhouse, under a pile of big pipes, and its bottom edge fixed to the deck with three massive bolts. Across its outer surface were lashed a cable and a chain to keep it from bellying up too much at key points.

That weekend, SCUBA-diving steel man Simmons and Deir stayed on the *Queen* while everyone else took off for some shore time. The two men welded four shaped I beams to the patch by midnight, then went to bed. In the small hours, a tremendous gale struck the ship. Huge seas began sweeping the boat deck and the patch, slamming the ten tons of steel on the deck. The three bolts holding the lower edge sheared off; then the cargo hook began straightening out. Within minutes, both patch and I beams had been beaten nearly flat.

Somehow, in the middle of that screaming storm, the two men got another cable secured across the patch to keep it from sliding right off the ship. To do it, Deir, who was an ex-steeplejack, had to run down the sloping patch between waves, drop to his knees at the very edge, reach two feet under the patch to thread the cable through a shackle, and then run back up the patch to safety before the next wave struck.

By the following Wednesday the full crew had the four flattened beams reshaped and back in place—along with the other sixteen. Lengths of railroad track were added to top and bottom of the patch as further strengthening. It was flipped over, the inner seams were welded, and it was lowered into place. The cables worked perfectly to lash it down, so Duke Morris and Maurice Simmons could start getting the bolts in place.

Deir then began preparing the pumps for the massive job they faced once the patch was firmly in place: fourteen cargo tanks and the engine room, holding a total of 13 million gallons. Deir also was rigging electric lines and hoses for two generators, one to run the pumps and a second for a compressor to blow those tanks that still were intact, to increase the vessel's buoyancy. The rest of the salvage crew began the arduous task of sealing the hatches, ventilators, portholes, and doorways. Blades from disk harrows were found to work perfectly in sealing portholes.

In the second week of September, Deir was put into the hospital by the flying metal cover of a standpipe; as he had been trying to weld it down, his torch had ignited oil fumes in the pipe. But he was back to work on the eighteenth when their twenty-two pumps were switched on. One began arcing under water; in the confusion, eight more burned out. Alvah Sadler came up with fifteen more pumps. The stern came alive on the twenty-first, the bow on the twenty-second.

Sadler had a hired tug standing by to start towing the crippled vessel into Norfolk on the twenty-third. Hurricane Gracie was pounding the Carolina coast and moving north; if she caught them in the open sea, they knew they would lose the *Queen*. And their pumps kept fouling, a critical problem since they were just barely keeping ahead of continuous leakage into the battered ship. On Sunday, September 25, however, they brought her into Norfolk Harbor.

After months of effort, they managed to sell the hulk to a New York scrap dealer, Sam Kahn, for $134,000. This was almost exactly what the salvage operation had cost them. Kahn, in turn, eventually lost $75,000 on her in selling her to a European scrap dealer. She was towed to Europe, and in May 1961 was cut up for scrap in an Antwerp shipyard.

It is one of the most amazing examples of individual initiative in the history of a professional based on just that.

MARE NOSTRUM TOWED ON A BUBBLE OF AIR

A bit over five years later, September 19, 1966, the supertanker *Mare Nostrum* ran at full speed onto the rocks off Hallaniya Island, in the Indian Ocean, near Oman. The *African Queen*, built in 1955, had a gross displacement of 21,500 tons. The *Mare Nostrum*, built a few years later, was 34,000 tons. Tanker sizes had kept going up.

Mare Nostrum had rammed into the rocks so hard that most of her bottom had been taken out. Her crew had abandoned her, believing she would break up momentarily. Salvage tugs had rushed for the scene, but reports of her awful condition caused all of them to turn back except the Wijsmuller tug *Friesland*.

When the salvors arrived to begin work on a no-cure, no-pay contract on October 1, they had to use their motor lifeboat just to reach the ship. The vessel was totally surrounded by ugly upthrusting rocks, and a Force 5 southwest wind was blowing. Inspection of the damage caused further misgivings: all but three of the ship's thirty cargo tanks had been ripped open.

The salvors knew that trying to repair the bottom of the ship would be hopeless, so they decided to strengthen her engine room and after tank covers, then blow her tanks so she would float on a "bubble," or cushion of compressed air, even though her bottom was still gaping open.

They trundled aboard scores of compressors and miles of hose. For nine days they pumped in air, moving the ship bit by bit toward deep water as she gained buoyancy. With high tide on October 14, the *Friesland*'s and the *Mare Nostrum*'s own engines, working in concert, hauled her into deep water.

But they still were eight hundred miles from Aden, and thirty-four hundred miles from their ultimate destination, La Spezia, Italy. This was the nearest port that had dry-dock facilities capable of handling the vessel. The eight-hundred-mile tow to Aden took until the twenty-seventh; there, divers went down to burn off all the jagged edges of the ruptured bottom plating. Some of these great shards of steel projected as much as thirty feet from the hull.

When the tanker arrived at Suez on December 7, with only a fourth of her bottom plates intact, and only compressed air inside to keep her from sinking straightaway, there was a ten-day delay to get special permission for the canal. Finally, two Suez tugs towed her through. From Port Said she was towed across the Mediterranean without incident to arrive safely at La Spezia on January 6, 1967.

The *Mare Nostrum* was just one of thirteen hundred ships this century has seen lost to peacetime accident and storm. In modern times, the vast majority of such losses are due to strandings—on rocks, on sandbanks, on sunken wrecks. The development of exceedingly sophisticated radar and sonar gear would seem to preclude such accidents except in the worst possible gale conditions; but electronic instruments still must depend on men for maintenance and interpretation, and are still subject to failure, as is any man-made machine.

Some observers feel that standards of maintenance and crew discipline maintained by some flag-of-convenience countries contribute to the stunning toll of recent years. Japan, Britain, and the United States, for instance, maintain very high standards—and record very low losses.

The year 1967, when the *Mare Nostrum* was saved and the *Torrey Canyon* was lost, was a particularly disastrous one. Lloyd's Register of Shipping showed it the worst peacetime year in history, with 337 ships totaling 832,803 tons being wrecked around the world. Of these, fifteen disappeared totally without trace or assignable cause. Most of the rest were lost to the eternal dangers: foundering, collision, fire aboard, running aground.

The *Torrey Canyon* was one of those run aground. This accident is still reverberating throughout the world, for it involved the governments of Liberia, Britain, France, and the United States; it was instrumental in a new awareness of environmental pollution; and it will eventually result in legislation spurring new salvage techniques to handle the pollution from such giant tankers.

At 974 feet long, *Torrey Canyon* was one of the largest ships in the world. Her entire hull was merely a series of floating crude-oil tanks, with, as sort of an afterthought, a superstructure built over them and two steam-powered turbine engines (generating 25,270 horsepower) buried somewhere within them. Fully loaded, she carried 850,000 barrels of crude: a staggering cargo of 117,000 tons! Her own fuel tanks contained 12,300 tons—*700 tons more than the entire capacity of the* Blum, *in 1942 one of the world's two largest oil tankers!*

The ship was registered in Monrovia, Liberia[1], but was owned by Barracuda Tanker Corporation, Head Office, Hamilton, Bermuda, where its effective and concrete being was to be found in a filing-cabinet drawer at Butterfield, Dill and Company. Barracuda was *not* a subsidiary of Union Oil, even though it was a purely proprietary concern set up to supply ships under lease to Union—a perfectly legitimate tax convenience. But it made things a bit difficult when it came time to sue somebody. The litigants—which were nations, not individuals—didn't really know, at first, upon whom to serve papers.

The *Torrey Canyon* carried a thirty-six-man crew under Captain Pastrengo Rugiati. She had radar effective up to forty miles, loran, a radio direction finder, a ship-to-shore radiotelephone, and a recording fathometer. Insured for $18 million, she carried a Lloyd's Register of Shipping rating of 100A1 for seaworthiness: highest possible.

LOSS OF THE *TORREY CANYON*

On the morning of March 18, the *Torrey Canyon* entered the area of the Scilly Islands, forty-eight barren hunks of rock lying twenty-one to thirty-one miles west of Land's End, Cornwall, Britain, en route from the Persian Gulf to Milford Haven with a full load of crude oil.

At 8:18 A.M., Rugiati decided to take the 200-foot-deep, 6.5-mile-wide passage between the Scillies and a granite reef known as the Seven Stones. The British Admiralty's *Channel Pilot* warns large vessels against this passage; unfortunately, Rugiati did not have a copy of this useful little book.

The Channel was dotted with fishing boats; Rugiati was unable to make a turn when he should have. At 8:48 he realized that his ship was headed right for Pollard Rock, sixteen miles from the Cornish coast. He yelled at his helmsman to come hard left, but for some never-explained reason the steering-system selector switch was in the automatic-control position: the wheel was disengaged.

It took two minutes to throw the switch, engage the helm, and bring her hard left; it took only 1:58 minutes for the tanker to pile up, hard, on Pollard Rock.

Distress signals went out as Rugiati tried unsuccessfully to free his vessel from the rock on which she was impaled. Seven vessels answered his call; but first on the scene was the *Utrecht*, owned by the same Wijsmuller Company of Holland which had saved the *Mare Nostrum*. By the time *Utrecht* arrived, Wijsmuller already was telephoning the *Torrey Canyon*'s operating agents, Pacific Coast Transport in Los Angeles, for a no-cure, no-pay salvage contract.

Such a contract, successfully executed, would be worth a minimum of a million dollars.

Hille Post, captain of the *Utrecht*, had men aboard the stricken tanker by 12:40 P.M. Two Royal Navy helicopters were standing by to remove the crewmen if necessary, since the ship was by this time flooded, rolling, and pounding heavily, and had lost some five thousand tons of oil. The crew was busily pumping out more, so the *Torrey Canyon* was already surrounded by a six-mile oil slick. The mine sweeper *Clarbeston* arrived with one thousand gallons of detergent; the naval tug *Giant* was under way with the rest of the Royal Navy's current supply, thirty-five hundred gallons. By the next morning, the nineteenth, three more Wijsmuller tugs—*Titan, Stentor,* and the leased Portuguese tug *Praia da Adraga*—had arrived.

Six feet of crude and water, mixed, were in the *Torrey Canyon*'s engine room, the boilers were down and the pumps inoperative, the emergency generators were on, and all buoyancy forward had been lost as heavier sea water displaced the crude in the forward tanks. Her starboard foredeck rail was awash with an 8-degree list; gale-force winds were blowing up. Fourteen crewmen asked to be taken off.

That night, after *Utrecht*'s cable had parted in an attempt to haul her off, all but six men—Captain Rugiati, three crewmen, and two salvors—were removed by lifeboat and helicopters in a twelve-foot swell.

Within thirty hours of the stranding, the oil slick was eighteen miles long by four wide: a fine film at the edge, eighteen inches deep around the ship. Prime Minister Harold Wilson put Maurice Foley, Parliamentary Under-Secretary of State for Defense (Royal Navy), in command of operations. Political and legal problems were fierce: the ship, privately owned by non-British nationals, lay in international waters outside Britain's three-mile territorial limit. Whatever the government did—including nothing—would seem wrong to *somebody*.

On March 20, Defense Minister Denis Healey announced that twenty ships were on the clean-up job, using twenty thousand gallons of emulsifier (detergent) and spending £500,000. Critics demanded that the tanker be burned no matter who owned it; or, at the very least, that her remaining cargo be pumped into other tankers. Those so urging were ignorant of the fact that, since the removal would have to be by a vacuum system (*Torrey Canyon* was without power, of course), it would be a job of several months' duration. And this was assuming that effective hose connections between tankers could even be maintained, which was doubtful.

On the same day, Wijsmuller's salvage expert on the scene, Hans Stal, reported that fourteen of the *Torrey Canyon*'s eighteen cargo tanks had been ripped open. Some sixteen to nineteen feet of rock were sticking up into the bottom of the vessel like a giant thumb. Her fuel tank, pump rooms, and bow storage areas also were holed.

By Tuesday, the twenty-first, tensions were growing between Union Oil and the British Government: the slick covered a hundred square miles and was on the move. It was expected to reach the Cornish coast—Britain's main seaside resort area—that same week.

Salvage work went forward despite the tensions; but at noon on Tuesday the engine room exploded. Many were injured; two men, Rodríquez Virgilio and salvage expert Hans Stal, were blown overboard. The thirty-six-year-old Stal, rescued from the water after the uninjured Virgilio, died en route to the hospital at Penzance. A spark had probably ignited the below-decks oil-fumed atmosphere. Wijsmuller already was out $50,000, however, so they refused to abandon this early in the game.

By Wednesday, the twenty-second, the six feet of water in the engine room had become fifty-five; the only practicable plan was to blow the tanks, as had been done on the *Mare Nostrum*, so the ship would float on a bubble of compressed air. Pilots David H. Eastwood and Thomas J. D. Price, flying British European Airways (BEA) Sikorsky 61N Heavy Lift helicopters, moved compressors weighing up to six tons from the salvage ships to the *Torrey Canyon*.

Meanwhile, a fourteen-man science-and-engineering committee had been set up under Britain's chief scientific adviser, Sir Solly Zuckerman, to consider alternatives if Wijsmuller's salvage attempts should fail. That would mean destroying the tanker and the eighty thousand tons of crude she still contained; trying to break up the huge oil slick while it was still at sea; or, failing that, coping with the oil once it reached the coves, beaches, and estuaries of the Cornwall vacation coast. The Army, they decided, should be given responsibility for the beaches and the waters out to three hundred yards; the Navy, clean-up responsibility from three hundred yards on out.

On the weekend of Easter week, March 24, 25, and 26, Wijsmuller made its great effort. In its favor were very high tides, some six feet higher than those running when the *Torrey Canyon* had gone aground. One problem: where did they take her once she was off? She was worth $10 million (off the rocks) even in her battered condition; but no country on earth would want the oil-spewing hulk hauled into its coastal waters.

SALVAGE ATTEMPTS FAIL AS BEACHES ARE POLLUTED

The question proved academic. Several attempts were made with all compressors banging away as the tugs *Utrecht, Stentor, Titan,* and *Praia da Adraga* (combined horsepower; nearly 7000) tugged; but on Easter Sunday afternoon a break in the ship's hull, probably due to eight days of continual pounding, became visible. By midday Monday, the twenty-seventh, the ship had broken in two, and twenty-five feet of open water separated the pieces. They hoped to save the stern section, but it slid farther off the rocks and sank.

Over that same weekend, forty-mile gale winds had driven oil up on fifty miles of Cornish beaches; the first stories about the pitiful condition of seabirds caught in the slick began to appear.

At 9:00 A.M. on Tuesday, the twenty-eighth, Wijsmuller withdrew; since the company had salvaged nothing, it received nothing. That afternoon, Union Oil abandoned the wreck to the underwriters (the American Hull Insurance Syndicate and certain underwriters at Lloyd's). Almost immediately, the Royal Navy started bombing, with the intention of igniting and destroying the oil before it could move ashore and ruin the beaches. This was gross butchery, but was the only thing left once explosive surgery (exact, hand-placed charges) had been dismissed as too risky.

The strike aircraft, Royal Navy Buccaneers, made their runs at 2500 feet and 500 mph, dropping forty-one 1000-pound bombs whose high-incendiary explosives had been specially treated with aluminum for maximum flaming. Fuses were set with .035-second delay for armor-piercing before detonating. Thirty direct hits were scored.

Behind came Royal Air Force Hunter jet fighters, jettisoning fifty-four hundred gallons of aviation gasoline in underwing aluminum fuel tanks to extend the burning. Dense clouds of black smoke billowed up from the tanker as flames raged for two hours after the strike.

March 29 saw assaults with rockets and sixty-two hundred more gallons of aviation fuel. Napalm dropped on the slick would not ignite it. The planes returned on the thirtieth with another fifty tons of bombs.

The bombing cost £200,000.

From June 8 through 13, the Plymouth Command Clearance Diving Team, Lieutenant Cyril Lafferty commanding, dived down to examine the wreckage at eleven fathoms to see how much oil was left within. The only oil remaining was that coating the inside of portions of some tanks, in a semi-solid state.

The *Torrey Canyon* was dead.

But the *Torrey Canyon cause célèbre* was just getting under way. As the bombs fell, the massive cleanup of the Cornish coast began; so did the tragic losing battle to save the oil- and detergent-polluted sea birds. The trouble with cleanup was that beaches once cleaned would be repolluted by high tide; the trouble with the birds was that they kept dying.

A thousand Royal Marines led the cleanup forces, backed up by twelve hundred British soldiers. Men went hand over hand down high cliffs on assault ropes, or were lowered with their detergents from helicopters to remote beaches. Civilian help was spotty, sometimes a hindrance; most effective were the Women's Volunteer Services. The U. S. Third Air Force donated eighty-six men, thirty-four vehicles, and half a million dollars; seventy-eight English and Welsh fire brigades turned out en masse.

The work paid off. The troops could withdraw by mid-May; the beaches were purged by early June. After poor early-season showings, holiday bookings were back to normal by late summer.

The operation confirmed that dispersal by chemical means was probably the best way of handling large slicks; the problem at Cornwall was that there was just too much oil. Some fifty thousand tons of it escaped from the tanker before it was bombed; about fifteen thousand tons evaporated or dispersed by other natural processes, leaving thirty-five thousand tons to be handled by the detergent emulsifier/dispersant. The British used in all about thirty-five hundred tons—enough for fifteen thousand tons of oil. Leaving twenty thousand tons to go ashore.

DESTRUCTIVE RESULTS OF OIL SPILL

Several unpleasant facts also emerged.

A beach that looks clean on the surface might be thoroughly polluted by a thick subsurface layer of oil caused by seepage or tidal action. Plowing and harrowing is the only way to remove or bury such pollution.

Most sobering is the fact that a detergent that will be effective with the oil[2] is very highly toxic to marine plant and animal life in the intertidal zone, on the beaches, and on the shore. Worst hit are shellfish such as bivalve mollusks (clams, mussels, oysters); the oil and detergent combined are much more toxic than either of them alone.

In the open sea, the oil has no effect on marine life whatsoever, since it remains at the surface. Mixed with detergent, however, it sinks and creates havoc down to three fathoms on shallow-water denizens, which can't get out of the way.

Worst hit of the wild life are the birds. Feathers lose their waterproofing, removing their natural insulation, so the birds are thoroughly chilled. Lungs, throats, and intestines, clogged with detergent froth, are seared badly by both detergent and oil. The crude also causes peritonitis, liver and kidney ailments, paralysis, and blindness. A heavy coating means 100 per cent fatalities; a light coating reduces this to 80 per cent.

On the Cornish coast, twenty thousand guillemots and five thousand razorbills were killed. Area breeding was reduced by 25 per cent; of 7849 individual birds rescued, all but 450 died within a few days.

On April 9, a thirty-mile by five-mile slick from the *Torrey Canyon* reached the Brittany coast. France was totally unprepared, as 35-knot gales sent the oil scudding ashore. At sea, sawdust was used to disperse it; ashore, civilians with shovels and rubber boots did the cleanup. It cost France $3 million.

The court of inquiry, ostensibly held by the Liberian Government but composed of a three-man board of American businessmen, opened on April 3 at Genoa, Italy. The board found Captain Rugiati solely to blame for the loss of the *Torrey Canyon*; his ticket was lifted in September 1967. Many observers have made a great thing of the board's prejudice, trying to claim that Barracuda Tanker or Union Oil were the real culprits. This seems rather ridiculous in light of Rugiati's massive and admitted errors in judgment on the morning of the wreck. Since ships have sailed, it has been the rule at sea that the master is responsible for his vessel. Harsh it may seem, but no ship at sea is a democracy; it cannot afford to be. And having the power means taking the responsibility.

On May 4, the British Government issued a formal writ in High Court against Barracuda, naming the *Torrey Canyon's* sister ships, *Lake Palourde* and *San Sinena*, in a proceeding *in rem:* moving against a thing when a person (here, the corporate person, Barracuda Tanker) is out of reach. On July 15, the British caught the *Palourde* when it stopped in Singapore for an hour. The writ was nailed to the mast, "arresting" the tanker until Barracuda put up an $8.4 million bond. The French missed the *Palourde* by five minutes, but later caught up with her in Rotterdam and again made Barracuda post bond.

Union Oil, which leased the *Palourde,* as it had the *Torrey Canyon,* then brought suit in United States District Court to limit liability to her "limitation fund"—which in the United States means the salved value of the ship and cargo. Since one of the *Torrey Canyon's* lifeboats washed ashore some time after the mishap, Union and/or Barracuda would have been liable for $50.

The Appeals Court ruled, however, that such limitation of liability was available to the owner, but not to the charterer. After this decision, Union began talking settlement. On November 11, 1969, Barracuda and Union agreed to pay an aggregate of $7.2 million in damages to the British and French governments jointly for the havoc wreaked on the Cornish and Brittany coasts.

The insurance carriers, which already had paid out $16.5 million for replacement of the ship, had to pony up again. Lloyd's covered about 70 per cent of the damages; the rest was covered by the American consortium.

NEW ANTI-POLLUTION IDEAS

That the *Torrey Canyon* affair will have far-reaching effects on certain aspects of marine salvage seems inevitable. The UN's IMCO (Inter-Governmental Maritime Consultative Organization) has begun looking at some far-reaching international agreement possibilities: giving a nation affected by pollution (1) official status at the board of inquiry into the accident; and (2) the ability, under international law, to take actions to protect its coastlines from vessels outside its territorial waters (even though such action may be adverse to private interests or even the flag government under whose laws the vessel is sailing). IMCO also has been considering compulsory insurance against such damage to be carried by shipowners and operators, and possible liability of owners and operators to nations or individuals not directly involved in the accident (i.e., people owning beaches fouled by oil).

Many of the larger oil companies, reading the signs, have begun voluntary examination of efficient burning by the tanker herself of waste or slop oil remaining in her tanks after discharge; flushing and everyday mishaps aboard tankers dump 284 million gallons of oil a year into the world's oceans.

Ocean Science and Engineering,[3] under contract with the U. S. Coast Guard, is now designing and will fabricate when completed an oil-salvage system that is intended for delivery by aircraft to the site of a stricken oil tanker such as *Torrey Canyon*. This system will remove the oil from the tanker *before* it spills out on the ocean surface. OSE also hopes to develop other equipment for the control of surface pollutants once an oil slick is released.

A West German firm, Badische Anilin und Soda Fabrik, has developed a very promising plastic foam called Hygromull. It is spread by boats and removed by pumps, and absorbs and retains large quantities of oil-saturated surface water.

It is easy to blame or accuse private industry when a genuine tragedy of the *Torrey Canyon's* magnitude occurs. But it must be remembered that the vessel had the highest rating of seaworthiness; her owners and operators were not negligent in her loss, and they had adhered strictly to all the legal directives of international maritime law under which they sailed. If the provisions or interpretations of that law are inadequate to meet the complex needs of modern naval commerce, those engaged in that commerce can scarcely be blamed. It is up to governments to establish adequate guidelines for industry to follow.

But, meanwhile, tankers already are in operation with a 200,000-ton deadweight; 500,000-ton tankers (*over four times* the size of the *Torrey Canyon*) will soon be a reality. It is frightening to consider the consequences of a half-million-ton oil slick; but eventually such an accident will occur, once a sufficient number of such behemoths exist to make it statistically inevitable. In the years 1965–69, ninety-four tankers foundered. Tanker collisions, major and minor, now occur at a rate of two per week.

Already a tanker nearly twice the size of the *Torrey Canyon*, the 207,000-ton Shell Oil's *Marpessa*, has sunk. It went down on December 15, 1969, fifty miles northwest of Dakar, Senegal, after an explosion had ripped her open and flooded her engine room. The $13-million supertanker was on the second leg of her maiden voyage, and was the largest ship in history to sink.

Fortunately, the vessel was *en route* to the Persian Gulf after delivering a load of crude to Rotterdam, so she was empty. If she had been loaded, we would have been no more ready to cope with the resulting pollution than we were with the 118,285-ton *Torrey Canyon* thirty months before.

Will we be ready when it happens to a 500,000-ton vessel?

---

[1] A flag-of-convenience nation with, on paper, the world's greatest merchant fleet at 24 million gross tons.
[2] The detergent breaks the oil down into little droplets and surrounds each drop, making an oil-in-water solution, which makes it easy for the droplets to disperse by natural action.
[3] See pages 95–98, 472–81.

VII

Goodies and Gobblers

> Today, since treasure hunting has become a dirty word, the name has been changed to Marine Archaeology . . . Even though some of the 'marine archaeologists' would have a hard time spelling their title.
>
> ROBERT MARX

CHAPTER TWENTY-FIVE

Mediterranean Beginnings

~~~~~~~~~~~~~~~~~~~~~~~~~~~~~~~~~~~~

Sir Leonard Woolley, British historian and archaeologist, once remarked, "The purpose of archaeology is to illustrate and to discover the course of human civilization." Unfortunately, early archaeologists were given more to destruction than they were to discovery, since their essential *modus* was to stock museums with objects of worth and artistic merit rather than observing, recording, and interpreting the material *in situ*.

Archaeology as an organized science is remarkably recent. Even Egyptology, the "grandfather" of archaeological disciplines, dates itself from September 14, 1822 (deciphering the name *Rameses* on the Rosetta Stone). Until that time, modern man knew about the prehistory of the Middle East only what was found in the Bible. Mesopotamian, next-oldest department of archaeology, began in 1840.

The investigation of prehistory was not even recognized as a science until the work of Boucher de Crève-coeur de Perthes in 1850; Renan started his digs in Phoenicia only in 1860, and Schliemann his at

Hissarlik (ancient Troy) in 1870. Excavations at Crete were started as recently as 1900, by Sir Arthur Evans.

MARINE ARCHAEOLOGY A RECENT SCIENCE

Which brings us to marine archaeology. Just as digging on land for artifacts does not make an archaeologist, so digging under water does not make a marine archaeologist. The early men under the sea did not realize that digging is merely a tool—one of many—of a complex and demanding science.

There are four main types of sites that are valuable to marine archaeologists: ancient shipwrecks, submerged shore areas, sunken cities, and wells used by ancient cultures for sacrifice.

Random finds go back in recorded history as far as A.D. 200, when the Greek traveler and geographer Pausanias remarks upon fishermen at Methymna (Greece) bringing up in their nets a human head carved from the wood of an olive tree.

What happened to the olivewood head is not recorded, but what happened to an incredibly good rendering of the Gorgon Medusa in the form of a bronze figurehead that was brought up off the coast of France in 1877, is. It was sold to a scrap-metal dealer.

An incident earlier in the century is even more illuminating. In 1802 one Thomas Bruce, Earl of Elgin and Ambassador to the Ottoman Empire, decided to make the friezes of Phidias "safe," as the guerrilla conflict began hotting up between the Greeks and their (then) Turkish occupiers. Bruce calmly lifted the friezes from the Parthenon and the Acropolis, packed them into sixteen huge crates, and sent them off toward England on the brig *Mentor*.

A storm ran the ship onto a reef near Kytheria; she sank in ten fathoms of water. Elgin, coldly furious, hired through his secretary, W. R. Hamilton, a series of inept salvors for these treasures he called "of personal, more than intrinsic value." One man, Basilio Menachini, was promised the British Vice-Consulship at Constantinople for his efforts.

Hamilton finally used a group of naked divers from Samos to recover the friezes; they were piled on a lee shore under mounds of seaweed and protected by relays of watchmen for two years while the Graeco-Turkish War raged in earnest. Finally they were brought to England.

The London *Times* of the day summed up contemporary attitudes toward archaeology. "It would have been indeed lamentable if, after escaping for so many years the ignorance and prejudice of the stupid Turks, they should have been lost just as they were on their way to a civilized country."

It should also be noted that the friezes "of personal, more than intrinsic value," cost the Earl £5000, including the loss of the *Mentor*. In 1816 he sold them—by no possible stretch of anyone's imagination could they be called his property—to the British Museum for a cool £35,000.

Then, in 1900, Captain Demetrios Kondos, a Greek master sponge diver who commanded a Greek sailing galley, was blown off course by a heavy Mediterranean storm. He came to anchor in the lee of a headland, marked with a distinctive yellow mineral stain, off the tiny village of Potama on the island of Antikythera, near Crete. Since they had to wait out the storm anyway, his helmet divers went over the side to look for sponges.

EARLY MEDITERRANEAN FINDS

Elias Stadiatis landed on the bottom in 150 feet of water to find himself surrounded by great eerie figures: heavy bronze statues, huge white ornamental horses, human figurines, nude women sunk to their waists in sand. When he seized the salt-blackened arm of one of the bronze statues, it came off. He carried it to the surface with him as proof of his wondrous tale.

Captain Kondos was no fool. He immediately descended to the bottom to measure some of the monstrous statues. When they arrived home in Syme, he showed the bronze arm to the village elders, who sent the two divers to Athens. Archaeologists Panajotis Cavvadias and Velerios Stais at the National Museum were so excited that they organized Greece's first archaeological expedition.

The naval vessel carrying the archaeologists and divers arrived at Antikythera in late November 1900, just the wrong time of the year, since heavy winds, heavy seas, and heavy storms were common. The site was deep, twenty-five fathoms shelving to twenty-eight, giving the divers only five or six minutes' bottom time. The sponge divers hired for the work, having a very hazy notion of the bends, tended to ignore decompression stops; as a result, two were crippled and a third was killed.

The material was brought up in a most haphazard manner, but it was treated with remarkable delicacy and care. Scuptures, pottery, even glass vases were salvaged unbroken. Some of the bronzes, which dated from the Periclean Age (fourth or fifth century B.C.), were superb. The marbles, derivative, hurried, badly eaten away by shellfish, seemed to be from about 100 B.C. From the condition of their bases it was obvious that they had been forcibly torn away from their places. That, and the mixing of ages in the ship's cargo, indicate that it had been bound from Athens to Rome shortly before Christ, and that it had been manned by Roman seacoast raiders. They probably were part of the force that, in 86 B.C., pillaged much of Greece under orders of the Roman dictator/emperor, Sulla.

Oddly enough, the most important find at Antikythera was a weird lump of bronze that Stais could identify only as some sort of mechanism. It had gear wheels, dials, inscribed plates, and a Greek inscription that precisely dated the wreck. It was not until 1955 that scholars Derek Price and Georges Stamires succeeded in fitting the pieces together. It had been a wooden box with hinged doors that had held a bunch of gears. And it had been used to calculate the position of the stars and the planets in any given year. In other words, an astrolabe. An astrolabe . . . in use on an obscure vessel of brigandage some sixteen centuries before astrolabes were supposed to exist.

It is the sole mechanical object extant from ancient Greece.

Antikythera was just the beginning, however. In 1907 another Greek sponge diver, this time three miles offshore near Mahdia, Tunisia, ran across a number of rows of great cylinders that he thought were shellfish- and algae-encrusted cannon. The water was twenty-two fathoms at the site, the rock bottom silted over with a thin layer of mud and sand. As he moved in, he saw that the cylinders were really marble columns. In the mud near them were bronze figures and carvings.

He and his partners began peddling them in the *souk*—the Arab market or bazaar—where French archaeologist Alfred Merlin bought some. Recognizing their value, Merlin persuaded the Tunisian Government to stop the depredations by the Greek divers.

Merlin and Salomon Reinach, the world's most influential classical antiquarian, got the backing of the French and Tunisian governments, as well as several wealthy private individuals, to put together a marine archaeological expedition. They had two vessels, the tug *Cyclope* and the divers' tender *Eugène Resal*; between 1908 and 1911 they made six separate expeditions to Mahdia.

On the sea floor, the archaeologists found, were sixty columns in six rows. When the divers began probing beneath them, eight inches of lead-sheathed, decomposed timber were found and broken through. This revealed many delicate bronze statuettes, capitals, roof friezes, votive vases, and marble statues, which had been protected by the wood. The mud had also acted as a preservative, especially of the marble: it had kept the shellfish from boring in and destroying the fascia of the columns.

"Nothing comparable has come to light since Pompeii and Herculaneum," Reinach exclaimed in awe.

Most of the sculptures were from the late, "decadent" period of Greek art, and there were enough of them to fill six complete rooms of the Alaoui Museum at Bardo, Tunis.

The ship at Mahdia had undoubtedly been another raiders' vessel, like that at Antikythera—perhaps from the same fleet, sunk in the same massive storm. If so, the raiders had been eminently successful: they had carried off an entire temple! Since the site was quite unimpaired when the archaeologists began working, they were able to find cooking utensils, 1500-pound wooden anchors (topped with lead weights to make the flukes dig in), ballast—even a lamp with its charred wick still in place. These things allowed them to date the wreck, and to determine that it had been badly overloaded even though it had been an immense ship for its day: 400 tons gross displacement, 130 feet long, forty feet wide.

The next site discovered beneath the Mediterranean also began with a fisherman and a statue. In 1925, at Cape Artemision on Euboea Island, Greece, a fisherman named Evangelos Leonidas caught in his nets what he thought was the black, swollen body of a drowned swimmer. It was only when he poked the corpse with a finger that he realized his "dead man" was a bronze statue. After eight months of cleaning by Professor George Karo of the German Archaeological Institute, Athens, it was found to be the magnificent *Ephebos of Athens*.

Karo found funds for an expedition, mostly from wealthy Alexander Benakis and led a motley crew of sponge fishermen and Greek Navy divers to the site. Over the three years they labored, the finds were startling. One was a unique bronze of a stable lad riding with tremendous illicit gusto one of his master's horses. About six hundred feet offshore they found the massive arm of a statue, and later the entire body: a bronze of Zeus over six feet tall, considered by many to be the finest Greek bronze in existence. The heroic figure now stands in the New York headquarters of the United Nations.

In the end, Karo was defeated by insufficient funds, the wrong equipment, strong currents, and the fact that his divers could not appreciate the dangers of working at twenty-five fathoms. One man rocketed gaily to the surface from twenty-three fathoms down, sat on his diving stool laughing at their silly worries as they unbolted his helmet, then slumped forward, dead of a massive air embolism.

Fishermen have continued to bring up fragments, and even whole statues, in their nets from the wreck of Cape Artemision; Karo himself admitted that the site had been insufficiently worked.

In the same year that Leonidas brought *Ephebos of Athens* up in his nets off Artemision, another fisherman netted two Roman amphorae in twenty-two fathoms of water off Albenga, Italy. The Italian State Archaeologist from Liguria, Professor Nino Lamboglia, wanted to try a marine archaeological dig at the site, but nothing was actually done until twenty-five years later, when World War II had come and gone.

With peace restored, Lamboglia asked the Italian Government for backing, but was turned down: their archaeological allotments were being spent on land, where the politicians could see the progress. Amateur divers? Too busy searching for Mussolini's reputed hoard of gold and buried treasure. Private enterprise? This time he was successful. Sorima Salvage Company of Genoa offered free aid to the scientist.

Work was begun in February 1950, when the *Artiglio II* of *Egypt* fame arrived over the Albenga wreck. In typical commercial-salvage style, divers surveyed the site. On it they found masses of amphorae—scores of them, hundreds of them. Well, that was easy. Stick a line around the neck of a mess of jugs to send them topside. Soon a gentle rain of amphora shards drifted down on the site, as many of the delicate wine jugs broke in the ascent.

The most obvious amphorae disposed of, the salvors sent their Galeazzi Observation Chamber down with a man in it to direct their Benna. This is the huge clamshell grab that worked such wonders on the *Egypt* and that is nearly a trade-mark of the Sorima operation.

And the Benna worked wonders: in a single day of voracious munching it brought up over a hundred amphorae. The huge bucket also smashed the ship disastrously, shattered hundreds of amphorae it hadn't been able to pick up, and crushed delicate, highly valuable (archaeologically speaking) metal fittings.

When Sorima was through, Lamboglia sadly folded his tent and stole away: the wreck had been virtually ruined for any scientific purpose. The blame is not Sorima's, nor is it really Lamboglia's: it was just a case of the wrong salvage techniques being used by the wrong set of salvors on the wrong wreck.

They should have used SCUBA divers.

SCUBA gear has been the single greatest factor in the development of marine archaeology as a science rather than a hit-and-miss matter of picking up "goodies" (as Bob Marx calls them) off the sea floor and peddling them to well-heeled tourists in the nearest waterfront bar. And the Mediterranean Sea has been the traditional center for the development of skin- and SCUBA-diving techniques, just as it has been for the development of marine archaeology. There are several factors that account for this.

First, the sheer volume of shipping in pre-Christian days in the "cradle of civilization" was much greater than previously believed. And the ships were much, much larger; so large that we now know the great merchant argonauts of Greek, Roman, and Phoenician times were not galleys at all, but sailing ships driven by square pieces of bullhide sewn together. Many of the ships had 1000 tons gross displacement.

Second, tremendous amounts of varied cargo were carried in the terra cotta cargo jugs—amphorae—which, though easily broken, are impervious to sea water. They were the jerry cans of the ancient world: in them might be wine, oil, water, perfume, grain, tiles—indeed anything that would fit through a jar mouth four or five inches across. Amphorae in quantity on the sea floor are irrefutable evidence of a sunken vessel from antiquity.

Third, the Mediterranean is virtually without tides. Generally speaking, it is bounded on all sides by rock, and its underwater circulation, through subsurface currents, is gentle if existing at all. Thus, a ship could sink upright, land on the bottom under its load of amphorae, be gradually covered by plankton and coral polyps as it was also eaten away by shipworms (*teredos*) and submarine animals. But the amphorae, the earthenware dishes, the lead, and the bronze would resist both corrosion and disintegration.

EARLY HISTORY OF SCUBA DIVING

Popular mythology today assigns to Jacques-Yves Cousteau the invention, in the midst of a sort of vacuum, of the self-contained, flippered diver. As Mr. Cousteau has himself been at some pains to point out, nothing could be further from the truth. He has been a singular catalytic agent in the popularization of skin-diving, but in the development of the basic techniques he is a rank newcomer.

As far back as 1650, Italian physiologist and physicist Giovanni Berolli studied the bones and muscle structure of animals and men to determine the most scientifically *usable* sort of swimming aid. He invented a close-fitting swim suit with web or frog feet as a result. The Germans adapted and modified the idea in 1726.

The prototype rubber foot fin as we know it today was invented by Frenchman Louis de Corlieu in 1929 (patented in 1933). He began marketing it in 1935; it spread so rapidly throughout the warm-water world that in 1938 American Owen Churchill saw Tahitians using crude copies of it. Polynesians in the neighboring Marquesas Islands (immortalized by Melville's *Typee*) were using fins made of woven palm or pandanus fronds. Churchill bought De Corlieu's American rights; American, British, and Italian frogmen all used the De Corlieu designs during World War II.

Once men had discovered this means of getting about swiftly under water, they were not slow in putting it to use. Underwater sport spearfishing was begun in the Cap d'Antibes on the Mediterranean shore during the 1920s, and was widely publicized by a fiercely enthusiastic writer and humorist, Guy Gilpatric. As early as 1929, Gilpatric was experimenting with diving goggles crudely fashioned from puttied-up flying goggles, but he was only one in a tradition reaching back to the Mediterranean sponge divers of the 1500s. When a Frenchman named Fernez created a workable pair of goggles in the 1930s, he was repeating a discovery that had been made every ten years or so for at least fifty years. Cousteau used the Fernez goggles near Toulon in 1936.

Nor is the Self-Contained Underwater Breathing Apparatus (SCUBA) just something dashed off in a weekend by Cousteau and Émile Gagnan. W. H. James, using the primitive diving suits of his day, invented a workable SCUBA unit in 1825 by coupling a copper helmet to a cylinder of oxygen. The first effective unit (because it got rid of the diver's exhaled CO_2) was developed by H. A. Fleuss in 1878. It used a chemical removal system that in all essential respects is the same as that used today by the deepwater Sealab experiments.[1] Oxygen rebreathers of this sort reuse the air after the removal of the carbon dioxide. It means smaller tanks can be carried, and it means that on a military mission there are no telltale bubbles to rise to the surface.

Today the rebreather is almost never used by sport divers or by professional divers working at compressed-air depths; the open-circuit units, which exhaust the diver's exhalations directly into the water, are a much easier, safer rig to use. These were made possible by the development of the demand valve (it regulates the inflow of air according to the diver's needs), which was first patented by Benoist Rouquayrol in 1886. Robert H. Davis had a very practical self-contained breathing apparatus in use during World War I, adapting it later to his Davis Submarine Escape Apparatus (DSEA).[2]

French naval officer Yves le Prieur also anticipated Cousteau and Gagnan in the 1930s with a hand-valved lung that gave a diver, depending on his depth, ten to twenty minutes of down time. Soon after, Georges Comheines invented the semi-automatic regulator, which sparked Gagnan and Cousteau in their design.

Their Aqualung was a fully automatic air lung that utilized not only a demand-regulator valve but also a reducing valve for delivering at low pressure the air compressed to very high pressure in the tanks. Gagnan, by trade an inventor, had developed a butane regulator for automotive fuel systems; it was a modification of this regulator that became the Aqualung. Cousteau was a French naval officer who was an adventurer in the classical, exciting sense of the term.

THE AQUALUNG IS TESTED

In June 1943, at Bandol, on the French Riviera, Cousteau and his friends Philippe Taillez and Frédéric Dumas, entered the water with three cylinders of air compressed to 150 atmospheres and the Gagnan regulators—each as large as a bedroom alarm clock.

Skin diving as we know it had been born. As those three men splashed into the Mediterranean and history, marine archaeology as a science suddenly became possible. Suit divers, trudging about on the bottom, kick up so much mud and silt that they cannot work an exposed submarine archaeological site scientifically. SCUBA divers could. And soon would.

But the war was first, with certain farsighted military men in Britain, the United States, and Italy[3] recognizing the tremendous potential of the SCUBA for wartime sabotage assignments. Early in 1943, even before the testing of the Gagnan-Cousteau Aqualung, Lieutenant Commander Bruce Wright of the Royal Navy approached the Admiralty's Experimental Diving Unit with the idea of adapting the whole sport of underwater spearfishing and sport diving to wartime techniques.

As a result, the frogman was born in Britain, with Dunlop Rubber designing, then crash-developing, a close-fitting, streamlined rubber/stockinet suit with a rubber neck yoke and a lightweight, light-fitting latex hood. In 1950, Cresson Kearny, working with Willard Bascom on a new suit to be shown at a Navy "Swimposium," invented a warm underwear SCUBA divers could use in arctic waters. Their foamed neoprene "underwear" was too warm, so they began using it without the outer protective rubber suit—thus creating the prototype "wet suit." The wet suit, of course, depends on preventing the layer of water between suit and skin from circulating after it has been warmed by the diver's own body heat, while the air bubbles in the neoprene insulate him against the cold.

Wartime naval experience on both sides of the conflict also was most useful to peacetime archaeological salvage in the area of diver physiology. A hard-hat diver working all out will consume about two liters of oxygen per minute[4]; a SCUBA diver consumes three to three and a half liters per minute. The difference is critical, pushing up, as it does, the rate of CO_2 evolution proportionally.[5]

Cousteau, Dumas, and Tailliez, meanwhile, were living under the German thumb in occupied France, spending as much time as possible in the water while hiding from the Nazis the frightening possibilities of SCUBA gear. Their "study room" was a 4000-ton freighter called the *Tozeur*, which had been sunk near Marseilles by a mistral just before the war began. The ship had ended up with her prow in the surf and her stern in sixty-five feet of water; it made an ideal place for developing sound techniques of diving, wreck exploration, and underwater motion-picture photography.

Once, in the aftercastle of the sunken vessel, they discovered a giant bubble of brilliant liquid, which had risen to be trapped in the top of the compartment since it was lighter than water. They scooped a small vial full of it and took it to Cousteau's wife, Simone, who after sniffing it pronounced it to be eau de cologne.

On another wreck, the 5000-ton British steamer *Dalton*, which had sailed into Planier Island, near Marseilles, on Christmas Night 1928, Frédéric Dumas had an experience that started one of the standard safety techniques now used by skin divers all over the world. The *Dalton* lay with fifty feet of water above her bow, eighty above her stern. Dumas was picture-taking during a mistral so heavy that none of the other divers was out when, as he entered the engine room, something seized him by his inhalation pipe. This was the air hose leading around the left side of his head from his mouth to his tank.

Dumas could not see what held him, but by feeling behind him discovered it was a broken pipe covered with razor-sharp dog's-teeth clams. The free end of the pipe had passed between his face and his pipe unnoticed as he had swum down into the compartment. He backed up slowly and painfully, his hands slashed by the clams, with the constant fear of slashing his throat on them also, for the ten feet of pipe he had traversed before snagging on it. He got his pictures and fled.

That was the birth of team diving: the "buddy system" recommended and used by skin divers all over the world.

All over the world during the war, hard-hat divers were discovering, willy-nilly, the art of skin diving, just as Cousteau and company were. At Massawa on the Red Sea[6] the water was so stiflingly hot and regulation diving equipment was so scarce that divers began converting captured Italian gas masks into crude diving masks. They removed the filters, canisters, and canister tubes; in their place went a non-return valve and a union for a sixty-foot length of light-gauge hose intended originally to feed oxygen to an oxyacetylene torch.

The divers would often switch masks under water so their surprised tenders would find themselves hauling up different divers from the ones they had let down.

Over in the Pacific, Joseph Karneke pulled a very similar trick on his tenders aboard the *Chanticleer* during the salvage of a sunken Australian PT boat in Exmouth Gulf. He was using a rig exactly like those at Massawa—but developed, independently, for the salvage work at Pearl Harbor.[7] They had found that if the air stopped flowing into the mask for any reason, the diver had to immediately jettison his equipment and swim for the surface; without a non-return valve, all the air would be sucked back from the mask by the vacuum created in the line.

While Karneke was adjusting the lifting straps beneath the boat, his air hose was pinched under the bottom of the vessel so he could not get free. He gave four sharp jerks on his line—standard signal to be brought up—then jettisoned his equipment and swam to the surface. He came up beside the *Chanticleer* just as everyone rushed to the far rail. He went up the ladder and walked across the deck to see his own mask and belt being passed from man to excited man.

"What's the trouble?" he asked his tender.

"Something's happened to Karneke! They just pulled up his outfit and he wasn't in it." Then the seaman froze, wide-eyed. "Hey! You're Karneke!"

At war's end, Cousteau and Gagnan were ready; royalty agreements were reached in 1945, and the first trade-marked Aqualung was manufactured and sold in France in 1946. They got a U.S. patent on the equipment in March 1947. The first customers were the Underwater Demolition Teams (UDT) of the U. S. Navy, which purchased the rigs from their petty-cash funds. Then a U.S. distributor named René Bussoz took ten Aqualungs for attempted sale to American sportsmen. In 1951, on a trip to the States, Cousteau learned that the ten units had been sold but that Bussoz's associates were strongly advising him against reordering.

"They feel that the market is saturated," he explained seriously to Cousteau.

At this writing, somewhere around a million Aqualungs have been sold throughout the world.

Cousteau meanwhile was getting ideas about underwater archaeology and treasure hunting, perhaps, from an amateur skin diver he and his newly formed Underseas Research Group One had run across in the Cape Verde Islands. When they expressed surprise that he was not diving on the Riviera, where Cousteau had known him before, he announced that he was "salving a wreck."

With what contractor was he working? they asked; the hiring of a skin diver by a commercial salvage firm was then almost unheard-of.

None, he replied. He was working alone. "I have the hatch off. I am at work."

An insurance company in Dakar had hired him to raise a sunken treasure of . . . 4000 tons of cocoa beans! After analyzing his task, he had hired a native with a small boat, anchored the boat over the wreck, and had given a butterfly net to the native.

"The jute bags of cocoa beans are floating against the overheads. Holding my breath, I swim in under the hatch and cut open the bags. I push the beans toward the hatch. They float to the surface. The native scoops them up with the butterfly net."

The next time they saw him he was back on the Riviera—retired. On the proceeds of his butterfly net and cocoa beans.

ARCHAEOLOGICAL SCUBA DIVING BEGINS IN THE MED

Cousteau, Dumas, Tailliez, and, following their lead, many amateur divers in the Mediterranean, began actively engaging in archaeological-salvage SCUBA diving. Four main teams soon evolved: Cousteau's Underseas Research Group, Marseilles (Commander Georges Beauchat), Club Alpin Sous-Marin de Cannes (Henri Broussard), and Club de la Mer de Juan-les-Pins (Louis Lehoux).

Except for Cousteau and company, these were all amateur divers;

but their contributions to marine archaeology in the Mediterranean basin cannot be overestimated. In friendly competition they made a great many archaeologically important finds; even more importantly, they virtually stopped the looting or plundering of sunken vessels and other sites of antiquity by weekend or casual skin divers who wanted to take home or sell "souvenirs" from the ocean floor.

A good example is the 1951 find by the Club Alpin Sous-Marin de Cannes near Saint-Tropez. They recovered nine huge sections of Roman columns, each six feet thick and with an architrave five by eighteen feet. With the columns were three Doric capitals made of Carrara marble, which probably had been cut in Italy and had been en route to a Roman temple at Narbonne when the freighter carrying them had sunk.

The French Navy's Underwater Research Group (at that time under the direction of Philippe Tailliez) spent several seasons on the Île du Levant, in the Hyères Islands. Working ninety feet down on a first-century B.C. mound of amphorae, they brought up more than five hundred of them, as well as coins, ship's tools, and hardware. They also uncovered a full fifty feet of the sunken vessel's wooden hull.

In 1948, after reading Alfred Merlin's reports on his 1907 marine digs at Mahdia, Jacques-Yves Cousteau and the Undersea Research Group returned to the site in their vessel, the *Élite Monnier*. It was essentially a training exercise in underwater search-and-locate methods, but they also hoped to recover archaeologically interesting artifacts. The landmarks mentioned by Merlin had changed, however; and at twenty-two fathoms their bottom time was only fifteen minutes a dive, three dives a day.

They developed the Cousteau sled, which could tow a skin diver at a fixed rate of speed and constant depth behind a power launch; but . . . no wreck. Next, they towed six divers in a V-formation with the sled, to cover more sea bottom. No wreck. After narrowing the search to a one-hundred-thousand-square-foot area, they used a wire grid so the divers could swim the line markers. Still no wreck.

With their time on the site almost gone, Philippe Tailliez finally spotted a column while being towed haphazardly. They got only eleven hours of diving time on the wreck, but established that it lay north-south, and brought up four columns (one weighing three tons), fragments of pottery, copper nails and bolts worn to needle points by the abrasive action of the water, and even some of the ship's ribs retaining patches of the varnish it had worn two thousand years before.

COUSTEAU AT GRAND CONGLOUE

Then, in 1952, began for the men of the newly acquired *Calypso* the dig at Grand Congloue Island, a deserted bit of limestone some ten miles east of Marseilles. The job was to last until 1959 and would take the life of one diver.

The ship at Grand Congloue, which was to yield a fantastic wealth of archaeological data and was to be the most exactly identified of all ancient Mediterranean wrecks to date, was discovered by a free-lance SCUBA diver named Christianini. While recovering in a Toulon hospital from the bends which ended his diving career, he told Frédéric Dumas of the site. There were a "lot of old pots sticking out of the mud" there, he said, and they marked a fantastic lobster bed!

Dumas, hoping the "pots" might be amphorae, talked Cousteau and Professor Fernand Benoît of the Marseilles Archaeological Museum into searching for them. Cousteau himself spotted them by accident at twenty-three fathoms during his return from thirty-seven fathoms.

They had fifteen divers aboard, so serious work began immediately. A platform was built ashore from which the divers could work in almost any weather; soon they had brought up hundreds of pieces of the ancient pottery. The mud was hardened to an almost rocklike consistency, so they began working extensively with a suction pipe large enough for the divers to straddle and direct at the bottom. This was hung from an enormous land-based boom at the surface (very much like the boom constructed by Captain Thomas Dickinson to salvage the gold from HMS *Thetis* in 1832); the material sucked from the bottom was fed into a filter basket at the pump's outlet valve, after first being loosened with blasts of compressed air.

All together, they recovered over *eight thousand* amphorae from the site; the magnitude of this discovery can be seen by the fact that the temperature of the water was only fifty-two degrees, limiting dives per man to three a day for only seventeen minutes' bottom time each dive. Almost every amphora had an in-residence octopus; twenty of those without an octopus were *still sealed* with cork set in pitch and covered with an ancient volcanic mortar. This pre-Christian Roman vessel had carried nearly as much wine (each of its ten thousand amphorae held eight gallons of wine concentrate) as a modern, standard California wine tanker. One amphora still contained the wine; forgetting his role as scientist for an unfortunate moment, Cousteau opened it to take a swig. They never found another with its contents intact; perhaps even worse than the scientific loss, the wine was terrible.

As they delved deeper into the mud, they began recovering Italian pottery (they would eventually recover twelve thousand pieces of fine-quality dinnerware) with traces of its varnish still adhering to the clay. Their archaeologists were always dreaming of finding one in the filter basket with its varnish intact, so Dumas accommodatingly created one: he covered a bowl with black shoe polish and sent it aloft.

"Here it is!" yelled the archaeologist, his voice shaking with excitement. Then he saw the shoe polish on his hands.

Eventually they recovered several in the fully-varnished state he had envisioned.

In May 1953, they reached the ship's wooden keel to begin bringing up lead deck sheathing, iron fittings and tools, and lead-coated copper nails.[8] The finds gave us our first clear idea of ancient shipbuilding methods. Standardized bowls, dishes, and pots showed there had been mass production, with wooden molds. Underwater TV, first used at Bikini Atoll in 1947, first used for salvage in 1951 on the submarine *Affray*, was here used for the first time in archaeological salvage. Its use has since become standard.

From the amphorae and other artifacts recovered, and from the wreck itself, the archaeologists were able to form a remarkably complete history of the Grand Congloue vessel. It had belonged to a Roman citizen named Marcus Sestius (he is mentioned several times in the *Annals of the Roman People* by the Augustan Age's greatest prose writer, Titus Livy), who was a resident of the Greek island of Delos. Sestius was an honorary Delian, also a merchant and commercial adventurer, probably a sort of fifth columnist helping to make Delos dependent on the Roman trade.

The ship had sailed from Delos in 230 B.C. with ten thousand amphorae full of wine for the Roman colony at Massalia (modern Marseilles). Each amphora of wine was worth a slave in Massalia. En route it stopped off at the Greek colony on Italy's Gulf of Gaeta, where it picked up more wine—Roman, this time, transported in distinctive slender amphorae—and a good many of the colony's black varnished dishes and pots.

This stop was its downfall; the ship, undoubtedly overloaded, probably foundered in a storm.

Finally, the size of this ship shattered many of our preconceptions about the size of early Mediterranean vessels. The Grand Congloue ship was the size of a nineteenth-century frigate. This is much too large to be worked exclusively by galley slaves, so it obviously carried a hefty spread of "canvas"—probably bullhides sewn together.

Despite the work of Cousteau and the Mediterranean SCUBA clubs, academic archaeologists were remarkably slow in embracing these new and exciting techniques. It was only in 1961 that a major university —Harvard—began offering SCUBA-diving courses to its archaeology students. The First Marine Archaeological Congress, held at Cannes in 1955, was attended not by professionals, but by the amateur divers who had been doing all the work. At that time fewer than five professional archaeologists *in the world* had ever bothered to personally inspect an underwater site.

THE INCOMPARABLE PETER THROCKMORTON

Another most persistent and successful archaeological salvor, this one in the Aegean, was the American wanderer Peter Throckmorton. His most exalted scientific position was as a field archaeological assistant; besides an ability with languages and a license as a ship's engineer, he seemed qualified mostly to be a bum and a loafer.

Peter Throckmorton, all alone, discovered the oldest known ship in the world.

Nor was this vessel, which he discovered in twenty-two fathoms of water off Cape Gelidonya in Turkey, an isolated discovery. It was a culmination. Because Throckmorton wanted to seek out archaeological sites under water, he taught himself Turkish and spent several seasons aboard a Turkish sponge caïque, the *Lufti Gelil*, using SCUBA gear to check sites the Turkish hard-hat sponge divers told him about. All together he discovered thirty ancient vessels; he took position readings of them, made sketches, and took underwater photographs.

One of them, the vessel off Cape Gelidonya, especially intrigued him. He brought up some pottery that classical archaeologists identified as coming from Greece's Bronze Age. No site discovered before could even remotely approach the antiquity of this wreck: the pottery dated from 1400 B.C.! When the vessel had sailed, it would have been a contemporary of the Greek *Argo* used by the legendary Jason in his search for the Golden Fleece.

Now in a frenzy to learn more, Throckmorton sought help from an American yachtsman. They raised some bronzes, which Throckmorton intended to turn over to the Turkish Government; instead, the yachtsman put him ashore empty-handed, keeping the bronzes and then sailing back alone to the site to loot it as best he could.

It was three years before Throckmorton got necessary backing, in 1960, from the University of Pennsylvania Museum, the Littauer Foundation, and a bookseller-cum-diver named Nixon Griffis. With the money, Throckmorton, a research assistant named George Bass, Frédéric Dumas, and a couple of female British archaeologists, chartered the good old *Lufti Gelil*, and its Captain Kemal and crew, for a season of work at the site.

Besides painstakingly charting the wreck, they recovered the world's largest cache of Bronze Age artifacts—more than a ton of them. The way was cleared by Dumas, when a sort of "natural platform" they were using as a work area on the bottom turned out to be a conglomerate mass of copper ingots from the ship's cargo cemented together by up to eight inches of calcified limestone. Their problem was breaking through the mass without destroying its positional relationships (so important to archaeology), to get at the artifacts underneath.

Dumas came up with the idea of using a common automobile jack to break the mass into workable chunks, which could be winched to the surface and there reassembled in their original order. And by noting the traces of hull planking *under* the copper, they were able to draw accurate plans of the ship's construction.

Their ton of artifacts included oxhide-shaped ingots (broken into halves, quarters, eighths, or smaller pieces, they served as units of exchange, a sort of crude coinage); ploughshares, picks, shovels, axes, adzes, knives, arrowheads, spear points, and bowls, all of bronze; the tools, metals, weights, whetstones, religious charms, crockery, and personal seal of a traveling tinker—also all in bronze; bronze shish kebab skewers; and even the spat-out pits of olives eaten by the crewmen.

In 1961 George Bass, who had been at Cape Gelidonya, began submarine excavation of a wreck Throckmorton had discovered near Yassi Ada Island, off Bodrum, Turkey. Bass had the backing of his nominal employers, the University of Pennsylvania Museum; of the American Philosophical Society; and of the institution that has been the world's most persistent backer of marine archaeological projects, the National Geographic Society, of Washington, D.C.

This is the most scientific and modern marine archaeological dig in history, with all the sophisticated paraphernalia usually associated with land digs, and with a great deal else besides. The sixty-foot-long wreck lies on a sea bottom sloping from nineteen to twenty-four fathoms in depth; it was charted with measuring frames, and plane tables were made of the site. Calibrated position poles located objects (each marked with plastic tags) so that drawings and photographs could fix locations within one centimeter of error.

They determined that the wreck had been unexpected (the six anchors were still bunched on deck), and that the ship was thirteen hundred years old. This dating later was confirmed by four gold coins from A.D. 600–650 found in the captain's cabin. Plates, pitchers, cups, a wine dipper for the spouted serving pots—all were in place for the captain's dining service. Along a beam in what had been his cabin were Greek letters spelling out *George the Elder, Sea Captain* . . .

Presbyteros George: the earliest documented ship's master. The find somehow made the wreck very much more real for them.

Since then, nine hundred amphorae have been lifted upward in baskets by air balloons. High-pressure water hoses are used for rough work, but gentle, hand-created currents by divers clear away silt in delicate search operations. Working with the crew for a time was marine archaeology's newest tool, a two-man submarine, the *Asherah*; it took continual series of strobe-light stereophotographs for the architect who had been employed to plot exactly the dimensions and position of the hull.

[1] See pages 68–70.
[2] See pages 115, 124–25.
[3] See pages 287–88, 291–93, and Chapter Thirty.
[4] A liter equals 1.065 U.S. liquid quarts.
[5] "Shallow-water blackout" results from a supersaturation of oxygen in the diver's lungs; his body gives no warning to hyperventilate, even when CO_2 from his own increased exhalations reaches a critical concentration. This is one of the great dangers of closed, or rebreather, systems as opposed to open-circuit Aqualung units.
[6] See Chapter Eighteen.
[7] See footnote 6, page 397.
[8] These show again the disturbingly sophisticated technical knowledge possessed by the ancients: Since the nails were destined to hold lead sheathing to the hull, they had been lead-dipped to prevent sea water touching both metals in conjunction, setting up electrolysis and thus eroding the metals. Knowledge of electrolysis, until this discovery, was considered an exclusive possession of modern times.

CHAPTER TWENTY-SIX

Pieces of Eight

~~~~~~~~~~~~~~~~~~~~~~~~~~~~~~~~

When we turn from the Mediterranean to archaeological salvage in the Caribbean, the mind goes immediately from amphora-laden galleys to gold-laden galleons and all the clichés that accompany them: raging hurricanes; cruel Spanish grandees; buccaneers; Long John Silver's redoubtable parrot, Cap'n Flint, screeching "Pieces of eight!"

The trouble is that the clichés have a basis in fact. Cities such as Port Royal *were* strongholds of the remarkable "Brethren of the Coast"; the "ancient" wrecks one speaks of in the Caribbean *do* date from the sixteenth and seventeenth centuries; and their cargoes *were* usually those "pieces of eight" that Cap'n Flint screamed about.

An amazing number of treasure ships foundered on the Spanish Main. In Florida waters alone are 281 known sunken vessels that were carrying gold, silver, or precious stones when they went down in the period after 1525. Another seventy-five "possibles" sank during that same period. During a single hurricane—for instance, that of October 1844—158 vessels were sunk in Cuban waters alone.

The Spaniards, during their years of looting Central and South America, lost a full 5 per cent of the galleons making the hazardous voyage home with the proceeds. The literature would have us believe that most of these were lost to pirates, but reality is much more prosaic: bad storms or bad navigation.

They carried to the bottom more than $600 million (*that* day's values) in silver and gold bullion, coins, and gems during some 250 years of operation; 99 per cent sank in only a few fathoms of water. Despite this, early salvors were remarkably unsuccessful in recovering treasure.

EFFECTS OF THE SEA ON WOODEN WRECKS

One difficulty, probably the greatest, was in finding the sunken vessel in the first place. A man surviving a shipwreck is apt to be less than precise in fixing positions. Even more obstructive is the fact that most galleons went down on the windward side of reefs, their guts torn out by the coral. In such areas, coral can grow half an inch a year. Only a few years are needed for the ship, cannon, cannon balls, anchors, and the like to lose their distinctive shapes and outlines. Wooden hulls, within a few years (unless protected by mud or sand), will be eaten away by *teredos*.[1]

More destructive than its denizens is the sea itself. Chemical action between iron objects and salt water, for instance, eventually converts such things as cannon balls into virtually pure hematite. Wrought iron merely disintegrates into an unidentifiable mass. Silver, unless protected by large masses of other metals, degenerates into silver sulfide. Copper or brass will become encrusted with a patina; pottery and earthenware will be disguised by a crust of oyster shells. Only pewter, lead, and gold are virtually untouched by the action of the water.

In the Americas, gold was where the action was for early salvors. Lord Elgin filching marbles from the Parthenon was a philanthropist of the first order compared to the Spaniards in their almost ferocious search for their own sunken ships. They started out with Carib divers, but the supply soon died out (the Caribbean's best Indian divers, the Lucayans of the Bahamas, were decimated to extinction). By the mid-sixteenth century the Spaniards had to begin using black Africans, many of whom had never seen the sea before being sold into slavery.

Yet many of them became strikingly good divers. The Spaniards preferred the women to the men—their extra fat tissue helped prevent chilling, so they lasted longer. The blacks were used as both pearl and salvage divers; indeed, large ports such as Havana, Vera Cruz, Cartagena, and Panama City kept salvage ships with black divers aboard in constant readiness for the recovery of treasure or valuables from sunken vessels in the vicinity.

In the 250 years the black divers were used, some 100 million pesos'[1] worth of treasure was successfully recovered. Contrary to popular belief, neither the Indians nor the blacks used diving bells or the simpler diving tubs; they preferred free diving.

The blacks were slaves and the Caribs nearly so, so they never did any treasure hunting on their own; but as early as 1544 the Florida Indians were recovering large amounts of treasure from shallow-water Spanish wrecks along Florida's "Hurricane Coast." They were seldom used by the Spanish despite their excellence as divers, because they were so fiercely independent, treacherous, and rebellious.

The British also got into the act, beginning "wracking" operations out of Bermuda almost as soon as the English colony was established there by members of the Virginia Company in 1612. After 1650, Jamaica's Port Royal became the center for "wracking"; again, black, not Indian, divers were used.

WILLIAM PHIPS: AN EARLY TREASURE HUNTER

Until the perfection of SCUBA gear made possible Kip Wagner's unique operations begun on Florida's east coast in 1955, Sir William Phips was the only officially confirmed treasure hunter to take gold from a Spanish galleon. He was born in Maine in 1651, served his apprenticeship as a shipwright, and migrated to Boston. He learned to read and write at the age of twenty-two, married well, bought a small vessel, and began trading—principally to the West Indies. It was during his voyages to Cuba and Hispaniola that he began to hear tales of the Spanish Plate Fleet, which had been lost some eight years before his birth.

The sixteen galleons that had been in the Plate Fleet had sailed from Spain from Puerto Plata, Hispaniola, but had been driven by a hurricane onto the Ambrox, or Ambrosia, Bank, south of the Bahamas, on November 15, 1643. All were sunk except the *Santíssima Trinidad*, commanded by Captain Francisco Guerres. They had an estimated $21 million aboard in gold, silver, and gems.

Phips heard just enough about the treasure fleet to verify that the wrecks actually had occurred. While asking questions in waterfront bars, he turned up a sailor with a name one would hate to find on his hotel register: John Smith. John claimed to have seen a galleon on a reef between Turks Island in the Bahamas and Cuba, confirmed that Indian divers had been recovering occasional silver ingots and pieces of eight ever since the fleet had gone down, and sold Phips . . . a treasure map!

Up to this point, Phips sounds like every sunken treasure seeker who has ever caught gold fever. But here the tale takes a rather remarkable turn. He took to England his story, John Smith, and his sunken treasure chart, interested the Duke of Albemarle in the venture, and through him King Charles II. The king needed money, and Albemarle was a fast talker; in 1684 Phips found himself master of a British frigate, *The Rose of Algier,* under orders to return to the Ambrox and fetch back the doubloons.

It didn't work out quite that way. In a year of searching, he was strikingly unsuccessful, doing little besides putting down a series of mutinies among his crew. In 1685 he returned to England.

Charles II had shuffled off this mortal coil; James II, obviously not an easy mark for a man trying to sell a gold brick he hadn't even found yet, canceled Phips's commission, took his ship away from him, and levied a £500 charge for repairs to the *Rose.*

But Albemarle had a golden nose. He talked a few friends into financing a second try, subscribing £3200 for the venture. Phips set out in 1696 in the *James and Mary* and a small tender called the *Henry.*

He appears to have hung about Puerto Plata for a time with his nose in his tankard; in any event, he somewhere ran across an old Spanish seaman who said he knew where the ship of the Vice-Admiral himself had foundered. To check the story, Phips sent the *Henry* out to Ambrox Bank under command of Francis Rogers on January 13, 1687.

By the end of January, Rogers had decided it had all been a terrible mistake. At the penultimate moment, however (the day before their scheduled return to Puerto Plata), ship's naturalist Hans Sloane sent a diver down after a biological specimen. The diver brought up, instead, a report of "many cannons" on the sea floor. On the next dive, a silver ingot was found.

Phips rushed to the site, and kept divers down until May 2. The depth was six or eight fathoms; the divers were Indian or Negro; Phips used or did not use a diving bell; the bell, if used, was or was not actually a diving tub. Sources differ on all these points.

There is no doubt about the results, however. Phips returned to England in September 1687 with thirty-four tons of silver, coins, gold ingots, and pearls. The loot was worth £300,000 then; Phips got one sixteenth and a knighthood. He also was made the Governor of Massachusetts. The crew got a salvage reward, the king got £20,000, the backers got rich, England got gold fever, and the investors in scores of subsequent treasure-hunting ventures got taken.

At least fifteen other Spanish treasure ships are known to have been wrecked at various times on the Silver Banks, among them *Nuestra*

Señora de la Concepción, which took a million in gold down with her on November 2, 1641. Lest the reader think that SCUBA has made it a mere matter of picking your wreck, anchoring over it, and scooping up the ingots, he should consider the attempt on the *Nuestra Señora* by Jacques-Yves Cousteau's highly skilled team of divers aboard the *Calypso*.

They first identified the area of the wreck by ballast stones dumped below the crown of the reef as the ship had been gutted by the coral.[2]

Once he had confirmed that they were over a wreck in some six to eight fathoms, Cousteau sent out exploration teams of divers to chart individual finds in hopes of determining which way the vessel was moving when it struck the reef. One heartening discovery was a large black metal cooking cauldron of the same sort that was known to have been carried by the *Nuestra Señora*.

They first cleared the site of loose sand and debris with a water jet attached to a fire pump on the diving launch sent out by the safely off-anchored *Calypso*. Then they searched for fragments of the ship's timbers that would confirm it as the *Nuestra Señora*, while taking soundings of the coral to determine the perimeter of the collapsed galleon. Since her belly would have been ripped out on the reef, they had to know the most likely place the gold would be. They also had to determine if the ship—as was often the case—had split in two when she had gone down. This, of course, would have meant two sites to chart and check instead of just one.

INDISPENSABLE TOOL: THE AIR LIFT

Finally they were ready to begin salvage operations on the remains of the wreck. For this they used a modification of the air lift, which is in reality a sort of giant subsurface vacuum cleaner.

The air lift, by the way, which, along with SCUBA and the prop wash, has been singularly important in the development of marine archaeology, is an extremely simple device: A large open-ended vertical pipe is dangled downward. Around its lower end on the outside is an air chamber supplied with compressed air by a hose from the surface. The inside of the chamber is perforated with hundreds of tiny holes so that small bubbles are released into the vertical pipe. As these move upward, their velocity (and the fact that the density of the column inside the pipe is lower than the column of water outside) causes water to rush up the pipe. Naturally, this creates a suction at the bottom of the pipe. The system is open, simple, cheap, and most satisfactory for bringing up delicate objects.

Cousteau's version was a large-diameter hose, supported by an improvised float, some fifty feet long. Air was supplied by a 200-hp air compressor; the air lift could handle fifty tons of water an hour, along with five tons of sand, silt, and coral debris—any of which might contain gold from the wreck. These wastes were sucked up by the hose into metal baskets on the float, after passing through strainers to trap anything of value. The debris raining down through the sifting screens was fed back into the water through a lateral length of pipe twenty yards long, so it would not fill the excavations on the salvage site beneath.[3]

An air lift such as Cousteau's required a three-man operating team. Care had to be exercised, because it was powerful enough to ingest a man's arm. The divers working the air lift wore flippers with the fins cut off, so they were in effect rubber boots, giving additional traction and mobility. They also wore twenty-pound weight belts, and work lights built into their masks.

Pieces too large for the air-lift pipe were sent to the surface in a gondola beneath a gasoline drum used as a sort of balloon. Inflation of the "balloon" was by a small, hand-carried cylinder of compressed air.[4] Included in the material sent up this way were many of the one-ton, mushroom-shaped, coral outgrowths known as cannon coral. Found only around large deposits of metal such as cannons, they often contain valuable artifacts from wrecks; hence they have to be smashed open with hand tools for retrieval of possible objects embedded within. Coral can be removed from such small metal objects in a hydrochloric acid bath.

The ubiquitous cannon, by the way, is of little use in dating or identifying a vessel. A Spanish ship might have carried French, British, German, or Belgian guns, either purchased from the forge of origin or obtained as booty from a defeated enemy vessel. Cannons forged in the 1500s were still in use two hundred years later; old, cracked, or worthless cannons often were carried as ballast in place of stones.

At the *Nuestra Señora* site, gold fever mounted among Cousteau's men as ton after ton of coral debris was raised and examined. Artifacts by the hundreds were found; but none of the *Nuestra Señora's* fabled treasure. But at any moment . . .

Trenches were cut across the site so cross sections could be obtained. Excitement ran high when a whole cache of cargo seals was found; they were often used to seal gold or silver packets. But still no gold. Was it possible that earlier, unrecorded salvors had stripped the wreck of its precious horde?

No. After several weeks of backbreaking labor it became certain that no one had stripped *Nuestra Señora* of her gold. With the cargo seals had been found a brass weight from the ship's scales, and someone thought to examine it carefully.

In the early days of sailing, every five years the various maritime nations' boards of trade would check on the ships' weights to make sure they were still honest. After so doing, the board of trade would impress upon the brass the inspection date. The brass weight Cousteau's divers had recovered was stamped with the date 1756. The *Nuestra Señora de la Concepción* had sunk in 1641.

They had been trying to recover the *Nuestra*'s gold from the wrong ship. On this note, *Calypso* picked up her air lift and went home.

THE AMERICAS' TOP MARINE ARCHAEOLOGIST

When one considers archaeological salvage in the Americas—as opposed to outright gold hunting—one figure towers above all the others: Robert F. Marx. Few of Bob Marx's associates would recognize him in the milieu of university degrees, museum grants, and foundation backings that surrounds so much of marine archaeology today, now that it is a fashionable, or "in," science in academic circles. For he is a loner, a wanderer, a *doer:* he has done more for marine archaeology on weekend skin-diving expeditions with his wife, a buddy or two, a case of beer, and a gallon of ice cream, than all the learned societies and foundations together.

Not that organized and science-oriented involvement in marine archaeology is not vital; it is. But the Bob Marxes, Teddy Tuckers, and Mike Wilsons are also vital. They are the guys who get under the water to make the finds, who face the day-to-day dangers and discomforts that no man who has never nursed coral cuts, wedged his head into the painful pressure of deep water, or faced that truly heart-stopping moment when a twelve-foot shark turns toward him, can ever fully comprehend.

The difficulty with Marx is that he is hard to take seriously. He has too much fun. Consider the time that he and Teddy Tucker, along with several others, were working a wrecked Spanish galleon near Bermuda. Tucker himself is no mean figure in marine archaeology, having located 150 wrecks in Bermudian waters alone (he carries those sites around in his head, not on paper).[5]

Tucker knew that Marx had uncovered the tar-coated ribs of the galleon they were working together, so before dawn, when Marx would return to the spot, Tucker dived down to embed in the tar an exact replica of an authentic Spanish doubloon.

On his first dive, still early in the morning, Marx spotted that telltale glint of gold. He immediately surfaced with his find, wild with excitement. As he held it above his head, Tucker snatched it from his fingers before Marx had a chance to examine the coin in surface light.

"Marx found a gold coin, hot damn!" Tucker exclaimed.

So saying, he tossed it to another member of the party, carefully briefed, who was standing near the bow of the small yacht. He missed; the coin went overboard and sank.

Tucker and the others leaped in to look for it; but after a few minutes they told Marx that he would have to keep searching alone. They wanted, they said, to find their own coins.

Marx indeed looked alone. He dived for thirteen hours straight, hundreds of snorkle dives, until darkness drove him back aboard the boat. Finally, physically sick with exhaustion and even more sick at heart over his irretrievable loss, he crept to his bunk while the others partied on the deck overhead.

As Marx lay in the dark, exhausted, trying to decide whether to throw up or not, Tucker entered to tell him that the doubloon had been a fake.

What Marx told Tucker has not been recorded.

Tucker is famous for his stamina under water. When working an air-lift tube at an archaeological site, he often stays on the bottom twelve hours straight; the only way to get him up before dark is to turn off the air compressors supplying his hookah breather[6] and the air lift, so he *has* to come up.

Because Marx has fun even on serious archaeological expeditions, because he started out as a despised treasure seeker or "pirate," because he calls all recovered artifacts "the goodies" and all sharks "the gobblers," many of the scientific types who have taken to hanging around the fringes of the tropical water world on their big foundation paychecks have made the mistake of not taking him seriously.

But cheating this major figure in marine archaeology of the scientific standing he deserves is an error, and a bad one. Consider the man's record of achievement since 1955. He discovered the location of the Federal ironclad, the *Monitor*, off the Cape Hatteras (North Carolina) lighthouse. He discovered, off Punta Matancero ("Slaughter Point") on the Yucatán coast, a Spanish vessel called at the time by Mendel L. Peterson of the Smithsonian Institution ". . . the richest merchant ship and most important marine archaeological discovery yet made in the Western Hemisphere." He has carried out, for the Jamaican Government, the archaeological excavation of the "old city" of Port Royal, which was sunk by an earthquake in 1692. And finally, he made the supreme archaeological discovery of the Western Hemisphere: he found the verified remains of two of Christopher Columbus' ships.

He has done these things with only the most haphazard and sporadic backing, always with makeshift equipment, insufficient personnel, and usually with the active hostility of the governments in whose waters he has been operating. In his inventiveness and ability to improvise no matter what goes wrong, Robert Marx stands (or should I say swims?) firmly in the tradition of the great ocean salvors.

MARX'S FIRST FIND: THE MONITOR

The *Monitor*, the "Yankee cheesebox on a raft," defeated the Rebel *Merrimack* at Hampton Roads, Virginia, on March 9, 1862. She had been designed by fiery, imaginative John Ericsson (builder of the world's first screw-propelled vessel) for durability: 172 feet long, forty-one in the beam, with only 1½ feet of freeboard to present a low silhouette to enemy gunners, she had a nine-foot-high revolving gun turret twenty feet in diameter, which housed two 11-inch Dahlgren cannons.

On December 29, while being towed from Fort Monroe, Virginia, to the blockade of Charleston, South Carolina, the *Monitor* began leaking badly in a heavy gale. The towline parted. All but sixteen of her crew were safely brought off after a signal flare showed her tug, the paddle steamship *Rhode Island*, where its charge had got to; but when they returned for the rest, the rescuers could not refind the low-lying ironclad in the storm and dark.

Monitor was never seen again, for the position at which she had gone down could only be guessed.

In 1947, however, a Navy subchaser picked up a sonar trace of something they thought *might* have been the *Monitor*. In 1954, the Monitor Historical Society, under President Raynor T. McMullen, went searching for the lost vessel. Iron wrecks usually disintegrate after about seventy years on the bottom, but there seemed good reason to suppose that the *Monitor* might have survived. She had been constructed of one-inch fine charcoal iron plates; the deck plates were of double thickness, and the turret of *nine*. Even with scaling, flaking, and corrosion, the turret should still have been identifiable. Finally, the vessel in all probability had been deeply buried in the sand—which would have been of material aid in preserving its iron from corrosion.

At the time of the Monitor Historical Society's unsuccessful search, Bob Marx was a Marine stationed at Camp LeJeune, North Carolina, guiding light of a sport-diving club called the LeJeune Sea Urchins. Convinced by his research that the *Monitor* had sunk off the Hatteras Lighthouse, Marx and his club (on weekends) put in two hundred 24-hour diving days to cover five hundred yards out to sea from the lighthouse and two miles to each side. Nothing.

Then he learned that the Hatteras Outer Bank coastline had receded nearly a mile since 1865—which meant the *Monitor* would lie a full mile from shore—and he met an odd recluse and hermit named Ben Dixon MacNeil. MacNeil was a retired journalist—an amateur historian who had devoted most of his life to a study of the *Monitor*.

He claimed to have made seventy-five airplane flights, beginning in 1943, searching for the *Monitor*, and to have spotted her on the seventy-sixth, when the conditions had been perfect: water completely still; plane at eleven hundred to twelve hundred feet; sun behind the plane as it flew toward the shoreline; water clear of sand (only possible following an east or northeast wind, since south or southwest winds stirred up sand from the shoals).

Marx and MacNeill, and pilot Donald "Andy" Anderson, began spotting-flights on June 6, 1955; Marx and Anderson aloft, MacNeill below directing their passes by walkie-talkie. Then Marx's current girl friend unwisely showed up with a reporter; MacNeill, in a terrible rage, withdrew amid threats to shoot Marx if the search went on.

The search went on. At 11:15 A.M. on June 12, during their twenty-ninth flight, Marx saw the dark, oval shape of the *Monitor* in the sand. He dropped a ten-gallon gas can as a marker, then laid out further markers around this from a dory. When he returned to shore, MacNeill was waiting with his shotgun. The locals took it away from him, but refused to lend or rent Marx a boat from which he could dive to the *Monitor*.

A downcast Marx returned to Camp LeJeune to find nationwide press coverage awaiting him. He was ordered by the Marine Corps to report to Washington, D.C.; his feat, after all, reflected glory on the Corps. But a congressman from California got very angry because the news of the find had not been given to him first (Los Angeles was Marx's adopted "home town") so he could gain political capital out of it.

On such petty men do the outcomes of great enterprises often rest. Suddenly a full-scale Congressional investigation into Marx's claim was launched (always from the premise that he was a glory-seeking liar); and suddenly two- and three-star generals were scuttling down Pentagon side halls to avoid the young Marine.

Marx returned bitterly to LeJeune, there to find Clay Blair of *Life Magazine* waiting; Time-Life Corporation would finance an attempt to get conclusive underwater photographs of the *Monitor*. On July 8, at Hatteras, Marx, Blair, and Lieutenant Keith Ingram chartered a 64-foot shrimp boat, the *Sterling*, skippered by Harmon Willis. Marx's buoys had all been blown away by intervening gales, so they began a box search of a square-mile area off Buxton, spacing "buoys" (lard cans attached to concrete building blocks with sixty feet of ¼-inch rope) every 350 yards over the search area.

They soon realized that the *Sterling*'s fathometer was too insensitive to be of any value—although Marx kept getting readings in the southeast corner of their grid. So they borrowed, for one day, the *Stirni*, a 110-foot converted submarine chaser belonging to the Coast and Geodetic

Survey and skippered by Commander C. R. Reed. It not only had the latest electronic detection gear aboard; it specialized in locating wrecks in order to plot them on navigational charts. When the *Stirni*'s fathometer and sonar both got positive contacts in that same southeast corner of the grid, it and its associated vessels, the *Parker* and the *Bowen*, dragged the area with a massive 6000-foot weighted cable. It, too, snagged in that southeast corner. It seemed probable they had found the *Monitor*.

At 8:12 A.M. on July 11, Marx went over the side of the *Sterling* in SCUBA gear at the point plotted on the chart ("Point Z") where the soundings, sonar, and drag had made contact. He found bottom at seven and a half fathoms (forty-five feet), with six-foot visibility. On the bottom was a slightly curved, gutter-like depression—exactly what a strong current will scour away on the lee side of a buried object. Beyond it he found a large metal bulkhead protruding five feet from the sand, and estimated its diameter as twelve to twenty feet. He also found gun ports; they were either closed or clogged with sand.

Marx had found the *Monitor*.

He returned to the surface elated, renewed his air tanks, and returned to the bottom with Ingram. They landed right on top of the turret by following a new buoy line Blair had placed.

Then Marx got dizzy and sick. He had to inflate his life vest to pop to the surface, pouring blood from mouth, nose, and ears. His Aqualung had been contaminated with exhaust fumes from the compressor, and an eardrum had been ruptured in the too-rapid ascent.

Then a squall hit, driving the *Sterling* from the site. When they returned several hours later, their buoys had been blown off the wreck. Ingram was too cold to dive again. Marx, sick as he was, tried to get down to the bottom, but the pain in his ear was too intense. They finally had to leave.

When they pulled up anchor, they snagged on what was in all probability the *Monitor*'s turret: their anchor fluke was bent out 90 degrees.

A second attempt at photographs was financed by *Life* and carried out beginning August 4 by Blair, *Life* photographer Peter Stackpole, and, since Marx still could not dive, a Navy Underwater Demolition Team (UDT) whose members volunteered to spend their leave time diving. After twenty sights to get a perfectly correct fix, they sent the divers down to work circular patterns on a 100-foot line at the end of a shot rope. They found nothing. The sonars of the Coast and Geodetic Survey ships all pinged at the correct site, but neither the fathometer nor the drag found any bottom irregularities.

The mystery was solved when Marx, morosely doing his salving from the bridge of the *Stirni* rather than under water, accidentally turned on the fathometer as they lay over the site. It gave a reading of 6.5 fathoms; but when he had seen the *Monitor*, the reading had been 7.5 shading to 8.

Later, fishermen and officers from the Hatteras Coast Guard station confirmed that it was not at all uncommon for a single storm to scour six or eight feet of sand from one area and dump a like amount somewhere else; this time, on the *Monitor*.

No further attempts have ever been made to locate, photograph, or salve the historic ironclad.

After getting out of the Marines and going broke several times in such ventures as importing tropical reef fish—his fish all got so seasick they died en route to the States—Marx ended up at Cozumel Island, off the east coast of the Yucatán Peninsula. He found a large cannon lying on the coast of the mainland near Punta Matancero and was told that, after a heavy storm, shoe buckles, buttons, and small brass crucifixes sometimes were washed up on the beach. An Indian reputedly had found three gold coins there.

THE WRECK AT PUNTA MATANCERO

It was 1957, two years after the still-rankling *Monitor* fiasco; Marx was interested in treasure, not archaeology. He made a few exploratory dives; two more cannon cemented to the reef proved a ship had been there, not that one had sunk. In 1957, surprisingly little was yet known about wooden shipwrecks; but Marx knew that a cannon without its carriage could have been jettisoned during a storm to lighten a ship in danger of foundering.

Months later, when he found some wrecks elsewhere and noted that iron and other metals from a wreck usually discolored the reef under which the wreck lay, Marx remembered similar discolored blotches on the reef off Punta Matancero. When Clay Blair and a *Time* photographer, Wally Bennet, came down to Cozumel in September 1957, Marx got them interested in diving on the possible wreck at Punta Matancero.

It was so rough on the site that they had to anchor Marx's boat, the *Aguilucho*, two hundred yards off the reef with all three anchors, and swim in. They could work only with snorkeling gear, because his air compressor didn't work. At each comber sweeping over the site, the three divers had to dive for the bottom to grab a knob of coral to keep from being swept away.

But they began to find things. A couple of green wine bottles, a large piece of ship's timber with a teakwood chest cemented to it, a nail, a silver buckle, seven diamonds, and four emeralds. The gems turned out to be paste, and the "treasure chest" contained a black powdery substance that turned out to be silver sulfide: the deteriorated blades of horn-handled silver knives.

Despite the paucity of their "riches," they made a pact over rum to work the wreck together and split the treasure three ways.

Most treasure-hunting expeditions come to grief for two basic reasons: inaccurate maps and inept planning. For the first, they didn't need a map; they knew the site already. For the second, they planned to work the wreck in June, when the heat would be pernicious but the winds at their weakest. In June 1958, Blair and Bennet returned with a mountain of equipment, including two hookah units with a 100-foot air hose on each.

The water was terribly rough at the exposed site, so rough that instead of searching they just broke off as many basketball-sized chunks of coral as they could and threw them into potato sacks. When they broke open the coral that first night, they found dozens of brass crucifixes, twenty silver buckles, two brass maravedis (Spanish pennies), buttons, glass beads, musket balls, bone handles. A one-day bonanza (flat calm) gave them the teakwood chest, three pewter plates, twenty brass holy medals, and two silver spoons so perfectly preserved that the hallmarks were legible.

And they had begun to learn how to work an archaeological salvage site. Any wooden ship over a hundred years old, they found, would be marked only by coral- or sand-covered metal objects. The *teredos* would have had all exposed wood. Even the metal remains would be covered by a natural cement formed by the corrosion products of iron combined with coral sand. They learned to dig the sandy areas around the wreck first, especially on the seaward side of the reef. "Digging" of sand pockets on the wreck site itself was by fanning with hands or ping-pong paddles. Near cannons was a good place to search for treasure; the iron absorbed the chemical "assault" on silver by sea water to leave the core intact, with only an outer layer of silver sulfide. Even if iron, steel, wood, or leather *is* found in good condition, it will begin to flake and disintegrate as soon as it is removed from the water unless preservative measures are taken immediately.

On the wreck at Punta Matancero, the volume of "trade goods" type items they found, and the lack of any ballast stones, suggested a merchantman with an enormous load of goods in her hold. But a ship of what nationality? What date? They were not to find out easily. On their ninth day at the site, they were arrested by the Aduana—the customs officials—for "disturbing an archaeological site"; their boat was searched "for dynamite and gold."

As soon as the rum-bribed officials disappeared, they began working the wreck feverishly, burying in the woods behind the beach all the artifacts they found. These included such things as ten onyx amulets, each shaped like a closed fist, and a sixteen-inch gold chain.

Their precautions were well taken. The Commander of the Mexican Naval Base at Isla Mujeres arrested them again, searched their ship for gold—even using skin divers to search it below the waterline—and finally posted a permanent customs guard over the wreck until they should get a "permit" to work it. They tried every government body they could think of for a permit—the Navy? Bureau of Fisheries? Bureau of National Monuments?—but when Blair and Bennet had to leave, no official answer had been obtained.

As weeks and then months passed, Marx decided his countless requests had been ground up in the machinery of bureaucracy. He knew it was no treasure galleon, but was obsessed with identifying the wreck and learning its history. He was being subverted into marine archaeology.

GENTLE BLACKMAIL BY PABLO BUSH ROMERO

In April 1959, Marx returned to his Cozumel hotel room after a day of diving to find a man closely examining the "goodies" scattered about. He identified himself as the wealthy Mexican businessman Pablo Bush Romero, founder of CEDAM (*Club de Exploraciones y Deportes Acuáticos de Méjico*)—the country's first skin-diving club.

Bush admitted blocking Marx's permit because he wanted to salvage the wreck at Punta Matancero himself, and said he could have Marx deported within twenty-four hours because of the artifacts in the hotel room. If Marx would join the CEDAM expedition, however, no mention of artifacts or deportation would be made. In return, Marx would receive half of all recovered artifacts not declared of "intrinsic archaeological value" by the Mexican Government. Marx agreed to the terms.

The CEDAM expedition was overfinanced and overexposed: a Mexican Navy helicopter; a C-82 Flying Boxcar from PEMEX (Mexico's government-owned petroleum consortium); a private yacht, the *Pinch-Hitter*, from wealthy American banker George Clark; tons of supplies from private donors. Marx's *Aguilucho* was pressed into service, as were the two-masted schooner *Cozumel* and the diving boat *Marlin*. As many as two hundred people might be at the diving camp on a given day, including film stars, government officials, TV and radio personalities, pressmen, friends . . .

Everyone except divers. The rough, monotonous work on the reef devolved on Marx, Carlos "Pete" García-Robles, Alfonso and Reginald Arnold, Torribio Dorantes, Commander Alfonso Argudín (Chief of Mexico's Navy frogmen), and a trio of peripatetic Americans (Bob Allen, John Frizzle, George Clark).

The first week was lunacy; none of their compressors worked, so everyone dived with snorkels. Blair and Marx tried to systematically map the enormous site (an entire reef 250 yards long and sixty yards wide), but their "survey" boat capsized. No formal map of the area ever was made.

A major find became a major setback when one diver recovered six pounds of gold leaf intended originally to gild an altar. The press expanded this into 300 kilos (660 pounds) of gold leaf; a rumor immediately started that they would be raided by a band of Castroite terrorists from a secret base in the Quintana Roo jungle.

This brought instant escalation: everyone was issued pistols, which quickly resulted in dangerous fast-draw contests. Two Mexican Navy corvettes appeared to cruise offshore; a bunch of helicopters came fluttering in for air surveillance; fifty Marine guards were posted around camp and opened fire one night on two divers who had gone into the bushes to relieve themselves.

Yet when weather, dysentery, exhaustion, and malaria stopped diving after three weeks, results were staggering. Excluding pins, needles, beads, and paste jewels, *fifty thousand items* had been recovered. There were five thousand crucifixes (easily cleaned in a mild solution of muriatic acid and fine white sand), six thousand belt and shoe buckles, four thousand buttons, two thousand knife handles, table utensils, costume jewelry, bottles, glasses, musket balls, thimbles . . . and a watch.

This was found by Marx on his last dive before curling up with cramps and becoming delirious from malaria. It was gold, with its outer case, inner case, stem, glass, and face intact. It had been made by William Webster, Exchange Alley, London, 1737 or 1738.

The Mexican Government declared all fifty thousand items (plus every single pin, needle, and bead) of "intrinsic archaeological value," so Marx never got his half of the recovered artifacts. His only souvenirs are a few of the brass crucifixes and some buckles he bought years later from a New York antique dealer. He never found out how they got there.

He did, however, identify the ship through some excellent detective work in old archives. They had tentatively named the vessel, because of the number, variety, and nature of the "goodies" found, HMS *Woolworth*: the goods all dated from 1720 to a possible 1750, with the watch giving them the earliest *definite* date: 1737. So Marx (who had taught himself Spanish over the years) began snooping in old newspapers in the library of Mexico City's Franciscan Institute of Latin-American Studies. *La Gaceta de Méjico* for February 17, 1736, reported the sailing of a Spanish vessel named . . . *El Matancero!* There was further mention of the vessel in 1737 and 1738, and then—nothing.

Clay Blair (who could neither read nor speak Spanish) talked the

Saturday Evening Post into sending him to Seville, Spain, to snoop the Archives of the Indies there with the help of German-born research specialist Enrique Otte. Otte was successful.

El Matancero had been seventy-five feet long, fourteen in the beam, and had carried six anchors and sixteen cannon. She had been owned by a very big man in Spanish grandee circles, Francisco Sánchez, Marqués de Casa Madrid, of Cádiz, and had been maintained for the Indies trade.

By 1740 this trade had died to a trickle, due to the War of Jenkins's Ear[7]; yet on November 30, 1740, *El Matancero* left Cádiz for the West Indies, her cargo manifests corresponding exactly to the artifacts the divers had recovered (with the addition of many bales of contraband English goods, cloth, and clothing). On February 22, 1741, probably while fleeing from the squadrons of English warships that had begun to control the Caribbean, she went ashore at (then) Yalcu Shoals off Yucatán. Her captain and mate were blamed with the smuggling; since they had safely gone down with the ship, they could not incriminate the undoubted real smuggler, ship's owner Don Francisco Sánchez.

CENTRAL ARCHAEOLOGICAL FIND OF THE AMERICAS

In April 1966, Bob Marx and his wife, herself a trained archaeologist, made what probably is the central archaeological discovery of this hemisphere: they located two of Christopher Columbus' ships in St. Ann's Bay, Jamaica. Barring a future discovery of a Viking or a Phoenician vessel, it is the oldest find that can ever be made in the Americas.[8]

Marx first got interested in St. Ann's Bay after reading an account of Columbus' fourth (and final) voyage in Samuel Eliot Morison's 1943 Pulitzer prize winner, *Admiral of the Ocean Sea*. The fourth voyage, begun in April 1502, was not a prosperous one for Columbus. His ships were small, four caravels seventy feet long, twenty-three feet in the beam, and with a nine-foot draught, with thirty- to forty-man crews. He did not really have official favor any more, but he still was obsessed with the idea of a Central American strait that would let him through to the Orient.

Columbus lost one caravel to Indian attack in Panama, and a second to general unseaworthiness at Cape Tiburón on what is now the Panama/Colombia border. He tried to sail across the Caribbean to Hispaniola, but strong winds carried him westward to Cuba's south coast instead. From here, with the pumps working constantly just to keep the two worm-eaten hulks afloat, he made for Santa Gloria (today St. Ann's) Bay, on Jamaica's north coast.

On June 25, 1503, he ran his ships aground "about a bowshot distance from shore" and sent a small boat to Hispaniola for aid. It was 370 days in coming; Columbus died, a broken man, shortly after his arrival back in Spain.

In his book, Morison charted where *he* believed the two wrecks ought to lie. In March 1966, using this chart as a guide, Marx, his wife, and a few volunteer skin divers began their search on a Sunday-outing basis —since the Jamaican Government was not interested in giving him any backing.

The divers swam in a row across the floor of the bay, probing the bottom sediment with ten-foot metal rods for any solid objects. On the fifth weekend, Marx's wife struck something so solid, beneath eight feet of sediment, that she couldn't pull out the rod without help. Six hours of hand excavation with buckets uncovered a segment of wooden beam. They first thought it was just an old wharf piling, but then they unearthed several "tree nails"—the wooden pegs used in Columbus' day when iron spikes were in short supply. They also found obsidian, which is native to Central America but not to Jamaica; ceramic shards; ballast stones; nails, and flint.

In checking their chart, Marx found they were within one hundred feet of the spot Morison had suggested.

Marx removed enough sand and mud to photograph the timbers as they lay; then he filled in the mud again to prevent deterioration of the buried artifacts. Realizing the immense potential importance of the find, he wanted official sanction from the Jamaican Government to explore the site, plus the best science available once the work would commence.

Finally, in January 1968, the Jamaican Government agreed to sponsor a one-week exploration. For this work, they handed out a princely $150! Marx was so short of funds that they had to sleep on the beach in three tents they bummed from the local Boy Scouts. His divers, hearing horrendous tales of sharks, quit—leaving Marx and his wife to do the diving work.

Meanwhile, however, Dr. Harold Edgerton of MIT agreed to examine the site with a specially designed sonar, and Dr. George Bass of the University of Pennsylvania Museum[9] sent down a coring device to help in the search. One of the men accompanying it, Bob Judd, was an experienced diver. He and Marx took thirty-odd core samples from eight to ten feet beneath the sediment. It was a tedious job, for the coring tool had to be driven into the bottom with a fifty-pound hammer. It took half an hour just to draw it back out in such a way that the sample would not be destroyed. Each sample was tagged for location and stratigraphical depth by Mrs. Marx and any other ladies who happened to be about, and transferred to a jar of water. All but one core carried artifact traces.

Finally they removed a fragment of the vessel's oak rib for carbon-14 dating. This showed the oak was twelve hundred years old; in other words, seven hundred years old at the time of being cut for construction of the caravel. Edgerton's sonar furnished further evidence: beneath the sediment of the sea floor were two large objects having the approximate length and beam of the missing caravels.

In July 1968, Marx got his wish—a full scientific exploitation of the site was announced by Mauricio Obregón of Colombia. In charge of the French archaeologists would be Frédéric Dumas, under contract from the Jamaican Ministry of Development. W. H. Bailey and Garry Thompson, British Government artifact-conservation experts, would keep the unearthed remains from deteriorating once they were removed from the sea.

Obregón's preliminary examination also suggested that preserved beneath the mud are the keel, ribbing, and some of the curve lines of the broad-bowed, narrow, high-pooped caravels. Work is now going forward on this most important site in the Americas' brief history of marine archaeology.

---

[1] A peso was not a coin at all, but a unit of value—equal to 8 silver reals—created solely to measure the wealth being returned from the New World. A "peso of eight reals" soon was corrupted to "piece of eight."

[2] The other common way to identify a wreck on coral reefs is to look for symmetrical shapes in the coral: anything perfectly round, perfectly rectangular, perfectly straight. Such shapes appear very rarely in nature, and even more rarely on reefs.

[3] An early air lift was built by Captain Hiram Perkins of the schooner *Fleetwing* during the 1890s operation on the 1500-ton steamer *Orinoco* off the Venezuelan coast (see pages 35–37). Perkins used it not to raise treasure, but merely to clear coffee beans from the *Orinoco*'s hold.

[4] In 1961, in Ceylon, salvage SCUBA diver Mike Wilson raised a sunken Volkswagen in this way. After closing all the doors and windows of the vehicle, he merely vented a spare Aqualung cylinder into the car. It soon surfaced, he pushed it by hand to the edge of the lake where it had gone in, and a winch brought it from the water. In the car was a briefcase containing all the prosecution papers for a current Ceylon murder trial.

[5] In 1955, after finding six Spanish cannons on a Bermudian reef, Tucker began excavating around them with his hands and a ping-pong paddle to fan away loose sand. Starting with a bucketful of silver coins and a 1561 bronze druggist's mortar, he picked up gold ingots, gold buttons inset with pearls, 2,000 silver coins, and a gold bishop's cross (of American Indian origin) set with several emeralds. "I guess we are the only treasure divers in history to fan ourselves into a fortune," he remarked later.

[6] Hookahs are merely SCUBA units attached by a light air hose to a surface compressor so the diver is not cumbered with air tanks and the necessity of refilling them. Their value is in depths of less than 33 feet, where there is no limit to a diver's bottom time apart from his own stamina, and no need for decompression stops no matter how long he is down.

[7] A trade war between England and Spain, which broke out in 1739 after an otherwise obscure Captain Jenkins recounted in dramatic detail how the perfidious Spaniards had attacked his ship, plundered it, and in the battle had hacked off his ear with a cutlass. The war soon merged with that larger and more prosperous conflict, the War of the Austrian Succession.

[8] A group called the Santa María Foundation, headed by Fred Dickson, got permission from the Haitian Government in October 1968 to salvage and authenticate a wreck they claimed was the *Santa María* in Cap-Haïtien Bay. Archaeologist Mauricio Obregón of Colombia points out, however, that even if it is the site of the 130-foot flagship from Columbus' first voyage, all that is under discussion are "a couple of nails and a piece of anchor."

[9] See pages 377-78.

CHAPTER TWENTY-SEVEN

Gold, *Cenotes*, and Sunken Cities

As recently as 1955, G. C. C. Damant, the man who recovered more gold,[1] from the *Laurentic*, than anyone else has ever taken back from the sea, could remark: "The only gold worth going after is in a newly sunk ship, when the government shows you a bill of lading and where the strong room is."

And Damant was perfectly and totally right. In 1955.

That this is no longer true is due to a hurricane in 1715, a Spanish piece of eight washed up on a Florida beach in the same year Damant made his statement, SCUBA gear, and a retired American housebuilder named Kip Wagner.

The hurricane, on July 13, 1715, was by all accounts a beauty. Catching an eleven-vessel Spanish treasure fleet near Cape Canaveral, it smashed all of them on the reefs except one. This ship brought back news of the disaster to Spain. From 1719 to 1723, a Spanish salvage expedition labored to raise perhaps half of the loot; but they seem to have been an inept bunch. When they had recovered some 350,000 pieces of eight, three hundred English rovers under Captain Harry Jennings arrived in five ships from Jamaica, overcame the sixty Spanish soldiers guarding the treasure, and made off with it.[2]

It might be well here to point out the reasons why the Spaniards lost such an embarrassing amount of their gold to reefs and storms:

> June, too soon
> July, stand by
> August, come they must
> September, remember
> October, all over.

This West Indies jingle refers to the hurricanes, which come to the Caribbean during a well-defined time period. At first, the Spaniards tried to avoid this period: the treasure ships originally left for Spain in June. But sailings were delayed by a growing tangle of red tape; the musty little civil servants behind the desks in Seville, after all, did not have to face the treacherous and terrifying Straits of Florida during a September sailing. Other factors also contributed to the staggering losses: winds unfavorable for west-to-east passage made it necessary to brave the dangerous reef-and-shoal areas of the Bahama Channel; the ships were heavily barnacled and mossed from their long time at sea; the hulls were wormeaten; and the crews invariably had been decimated by death, disease, accident, and desertion.

The flotilla sunk by the 1715 hurricane had been a Combined Armada: no Silver Fleet had sailed for two years because of the War of the Spanish Succession.[3] Yet after the single attempt by the Spaniards, no further officially recorded searches seem to have been launched for the treasure. Men soon forgot where it was supposed to have gone down.

WORLD'S LEADING TREASURE SEEKER

Then in 1955 a retired house contractor named Kip Wagner went walking along the beach near Cape Canaveral two days after a hurricane. Near Sebastian Inlet (north of Vero Beach) he found a Spanish piece of eight, the irregularly shaped silver coin (about the size of an American silver dollar) that was originally worth eight reals, and which was called a "cob-lump" by American colonists. Because there were no stamp presses in Mexico, each piece was individually chiseled from a flat silver bar, then hand-stamped with the Spanish Royal Coat of Arms on the obverse and a cross on the reverse.

This was not the first coin Wagner had found along this strip of beach over the years; it was the fortieth. And none of them had been dated later than 1715. This one did it. Wagner went gold hunting.

Like all treasure seekers, he had a map. In 1774 a cartographer named Bernard Romans had made a remarkably accurate chart of the Florida coast, on which he plainly marked the exact spot where the 1715 fleet had gone ashore. The chart, and the coins, made Wagner sure that the wreck must be out there somewhere.

His decision taken, he made his first investment: a fifteen-dollar surplus Army mine detector—one of the old stove-lid-on-a-broom-handle jobs with the crackling, defective earphones, which turn up so often in late-late shows on television. He began using it in the sand dunes *behind* the beach; and he began to get results. Cannon balls. An old ship's spike. Then, one day—silver.

Just an odd coin here or there, but Wagner felt it was the storehouse site from the 1719 Spanish recovery operation. He began putting his "salvage crew" together: his family physician, a couple of Air Force colonels, an ex-Navy demolition diver, a river-and-waterways agent, two expert boat handlers, a banker . . .

They began the search by air, looking for the telltale signs: discoloration of the reef, regular shapes amid the irregularities of nature, dark masses of ballast stones . . . Ballast stones it was; and then a cannon lying on the bottom. This led to the purchase of a boat, a forty-foot Navy shore-leave launch they christened *Sampan*. The group of amateur treasure hunters incorporated as Real Eight Company—a name taken from the Spanish *ocho reales*, value of a piece of eight.

They got a search permit from the Florida Board of Antiquities in Tallahassee, and a pin-point lease on the wreck from the state of Florida,[4] as they have on the site of each subsequent galleon they have discovered. This means they get to keep 75 per cent of any money realized, while Florida takes 25 per cent. It also means that a marine archaeologist will be furnished by the state to help in the evaluation and preservation of recovered artifacts, and that a state trooper will be assigned to guard the wreck against any hijacking attempts.

On that first wreck, they staked out and mapped the site by squares, noting the position of the stones, the ship's guns, and the depth of the sand overburden. Only then did they begin using their air lift. After the ballast stones had been shifted, they found a greenish-black mass, weighing fifty pounds, under some black, rotted, *teredo*-destroyed timbers. The mass turned out to be a clump of silver coins. By treating it with a solution of zinc and caustic soda, they were able to reconvert a good deal of the silver sulfide back into metallic silver (a process known as electrolytic reduction).

Soon they were finding K'ang Hsi porcelain (from 1662 to 1772), still preserved in its packing of petuntse—the same clay (unfired) from which the pottery had been made. This almost priceless porcelain had a fascinating history: by trader's caravan from inland China, to the Philippines by Chinese junk, by the annual Manila galleon to Acapulco, overland by mule to Vera Cruz, thence to the plate galleons—to a sudden end on Florida's Hurricane Coast.

For many months they found no gold; then a SCUBA diver uncovered a cache of a thousand gold doubloons lying in a heap on the sand. Their most valuable discovery was a golden dragon pendant that was actually a whistle (after 250 years in the sea, it still blows clear and sweet!) with a golden toothpick in its belly and its tail formed into a tiny spoon for ear-picking. The dragon was on a two-thousand-link, eleven-foot golden chain, hand carved by Chinese artisans. It is the only extant example of the Spanish captain general's chain of office.[5]

In February 1966, Real Eight held its first public auction. Artifacts worth $1 million were sold; the dragon and chain was valued at $50,000. In 1967 the company and its associates, Treasure Salvors (a California-based group of professional salvage divers headed by Mel Fisher), recovered $472,020 worth of items at a cost of $26,637. As of 1969, they had salvaged over $6 million in treasure and artifacts. The wrecks (they have located eight of the ten) still hold an estimated $50 million worth of treasure.

Over the years, the operation has been greatly refined. They now use two-way radios, beach facilities, light scout planes, powerful dredges, and magnetometers so sensitive that they can differentiate between iron, on the one hand, and gold, silver, and other non-ferrous metals such as copper and brass, on the other. The air lift has been replaced by a one-time "secret weapon": the prop-wash.

REAL EIGHT'S "SECRET WEAPON": THE PROP-WASH

This simple device rivals SCUBA and the magnetometer as a tool for the modern treasure salvor. Originally developed by Chesapeake Bay oystermen to blow away the mud that covers oyster beds, the prop-wash can clear a thirty-foot area of sand and silt to a depth of ten feet in fifteen minutes—the work of a diver during eight hours of bottom time.

The prop-wash is an elbow-shaped aluminum tube, six feet long and two or three feet in diameter, that fits on the transom of a boat. It directs the wash from the vessel's propeller down at the bottom as the craft is held stationary with a four-point anchoring system. It is effective to the usual maximum depth of a sunken Spanish treasure galleon on a reef—seven fathoms.

Because diving on the 1715 fleet is limited by weather to the summer months, Real Eight has gotten salvage rights on portions of the Great Bahama Bank and also from the Colombian Government, so they can carry out year-round operations. They have constructed a Museum of

Sunken Treasure to delight the tourists, and have bought two other companies since going public in 1967.

In this country, Real Eight's unprecedented (and unexpected) success in gold hunting as a profession has opened the gates. Suddenly, finds are being made all over the continent—solid finds of wrecks which have great archaeological or monetary value or potential.

In 1966, an American soldier named Duncan, while waiting in California to be shipped to Vietnam, rented an outboard motor boat to take his wife and three friends SCUBA diving. At eight fathoms in the Outer Santa Barbara Channel, off Seal Cove, a small inlet on the western side of San Clemente Island, Duncan found a number of what he took to be deteriorated ship's timbers. Scrabbling among them with his bare hands, he turned up, some six inches below the surface, a small gold ingot. On later dives that same day, they recovered coins, relics, and another ingot.

The artifacts proved to be worth $60,000. It is probable that they had run across one of the annual Manila galleons from the Philippines that had lost its course and come to grief on the jagged rocks lining San Clemente Island's western side. Duncan was shipped out to the Far East; the others were never able to find the wreck again.

Two years later, off Oceanside, California, another group of amateur divers, headed by Wilfred Takasato and Paul Brown, began searching for the eighty-five-foot *Trinidad*, a sixteenth-century Spanish vessel supposedly commanded by Francisco de Ulloa. Ulloa had been a lieutenant of Hernán Cortés, conqueror of Mexico; and the *Trinidad*, one of history's "lost ships."

But historian and amateur archaeologist Dr. Joseph Markey maintains that forty years ago he uncovered the *Trinidad*'s logbook in the Archives of the Indies at Seville. The vessel, he says, carrying a possible $11 million in Aztec gold artifacts, reached the mouth of the San Luis Rey River in 1540—a full two years before Juan Rodríguez Cabrillo "discovered" California.

In August 1969, Takasato—who obviously believes Markey's claims—began searching with thirteen other divers for the *Trinidad*, after getting exclusive search and salvage rights from the city of Oceanside by posting a two-thousand-dollar performance bond and promising the city twenty-five per cent of the value of the take if anything was recovered. Their chief locating tool was a "secret" device called the Attractometer, an invention of former oil-company consultant and MIT graduate Paul Brown. Its workings are so secret nobody has any information on what it does, but it seems to operate along the same lines as a magnetometer.

On August 21, less than three weeks after the search began, Takasato reported finding with probes what they believe is the *Trinidad* under some six feet of sand, half a mile off the California coast. Initial tests on some of the timbers indicate sufficient age to have been part of a sixteenth-century Spanish vessel.

Only time will tell whether it is the *Trinidad*; and if it is, whether there is any treasure aboard her.

UNFAIR TEXAS CONFISCATION

With the location and salvaging of gold and valuable artifacts from wrecks a solid reality, unforeseen problems are arising. In 1967 a salvage company called Platoro, Inc., began searching off the Texas coast for sunken vessels from which, during storms, silver coins have for many years been washing ashore. The wrecks are believed to be part of the plate fleet of Luis de Velasco, Spanish Viceroy of Mexico, who was shipping back to Charles V the booty seized from the Aztecs. The fleet was sunk by a 1553 hurricane off Padre Island, Texas, in the Gulf of Mexico.

Platoro's divers found the vessels in five fathoms of water and under ten to twenty feet of sand, and spent months clearing the site sufficiently to recover ballast rock, cannons, cannon balls, twelve hundred fifty silver coins, three rare astrolabes, several badly deteriorated mahogany crossbows, and crosses and other religious artifacts.

At this point, the state of Texas stepped in to claim that it owned *all* of the recovered artifacts and silver, seized them, and stopped Platoro from further work. In 1969, while litigation was still going forward (a fifty-fifty split finally was decided upon), some hijackers plundered three of the wrecks, leaving only craters, 450 feet long and 150 feet wide, scooped out in the sand.

With the horse gone, Texas closed the barn door by putting a state boat, radar equipped, over the site to patrol and protect the rest of the treasure. If any is left. Such wrecks are only found after very extensive and highly specialized scholarship on the part of the salvors, followed by costly, difficult, often dangerous on-site work. For a state to *then* claim the recovered treasure or artifacts is patently absurd. One can only look with revulsion at the Texas action which deprived Platoro of its legitimate return, forced it from the site, and then left the wrecks unguarded so that modern brigands could rob them with impunity.

NOTABLE SUCCESSES OF ALEX STORM

Canada, with its cold northern waters in which the Spaniards never sailed, seems a barren spot indeed for SCUBA-wearing treasure hunters. But there are ten thousand shipwrecks along Canada's rugged eastern coast alone, many of them dating back to the eighteenth century, and a highly skilled researcher and SCUBA diver named Alex Storm has been quite successful with them. Like Bob Marx, he is a searcher of old records and reader of old histories. Like Marx, he scorns tales by the locals as inaccurate, and contemporary newspaper accounts as even more inaccurate; archives, logbooks, old charts, shipping registers, and cargo manifests are his hunting grounds.

Storm always researches in absolute secrecy, and always makes sure that the government, private owner, or insurance underwriters to whom the vessel belonged had formally and positively abandoned all claims to it. In 1965 he found a French supply ship, *Le Chameau*, which had foundered while en route to Louisbourg, Nova Scotia, in 1725. It had been carrying supplies for the French colony established there in 1713 to control the entrance to the Gulf of Saint Lawrence; aboard the vessel were monies and goods worth as artifacts, today, half a million dollars.

Several other would-be salvors, however, brought suit against Storm, claiming prior discovery rights to the wreck. The courts found their claims without merit; meanwhile, as they sat back waiting for litigation to drop part of *Le Chameau*'s treasure in their laps, Storm returned to the archives.

In 1968, after months of research and a secret half year of diving in the icy, fourteen-fathom water off Scatari Island, a dab of land twelve miles east of Louisbourg, he and two other SCUBA divers found HMS *Feversham*. The 36-gun galleon, attached to Admiral Sir Hovenden Walker's fleet, had sunk in a tremendous gale in 1733.

When Storm and his partners, Adrian Richard and Harvey MacLeod, broke into the strong room they found barnacle-encrusted coins that are proving to be nearly priceless. They are Dutch daalders, the only ones left in existence. Even more exciting is one of the first American coins ever minted. Its estimated value is $5,000.

If the Mediterranean basin has it all over the New World as far as antiquity goes, Mexico boasts a type of marine archaeology that is unique to this hemisphere: *cenote* diving. *Cenotes* are natural formations in the soft limestone rock of Yucatán, giant wells that were the only source of fresh water for the early inhabitants. At the dawn of Mayan history they assumed deep religious significance as the home of Chac, the rain god, and soon were receiving offerings that included human sacrifice.

THE CENOTE AT CHICHÉN ITZÁ

The most famous *cenote* in Yucatán is the immense one, 190 feet across, that dominates the ancient Mayan ruins at Chichén Itzá. In the mid-1500s, the Spanish bishop of Yucatán, Diego de Lande, gave a vivid description of the well and the religious observances carried out there. It was approached by a broad roadway through groves of trees and past great Mayan sphinxes, much like the Sacred Way at Karnak, Egypt. In times of drought, enormous processions carried to the *cenote* willing human victims, drugged or excited with wine, who were then thrown in to appease the angry god Chac.

In 1885 the U. S. Consul to Yucatán, Edward Herbert Thompson, was led to Chichén Itzá by an Indian guide after becoming obsessed with the *cenote* through repeated readings of De Lande's book. Thompson returned to the States, studied dredging, and raised money from the American Antiquarian Society and the Peabody Museum to buy a hand-windlass derrick, a thirty-foot swinging boom, a steel bucket scoop, and all the mechanical paraphernalia necessary for dredging operations. Somehow, after transporting this material to Yucatán, he and a team of thirty Indians got it through the jungle to Chichén Itzá.

Before setting up his dredge, Thompson hurled life-sized wooden manikins into the *cenote*, hoping to establish the most feasible spot for the sacrificial offerings to have gone in. Then he set the dredge to work; for days it brought up only stones, rotted leaves, an occasional tree. The skeletons they found were animal, not human.

Finally, two cream-colored, egg-shaped objects were recovered. They were copal, (also called *pom*) a resinous Mayan incense that emits its perfume when held over a flame. Artifacts followed in every bucketful: arrowheads, pottery shards, spear points, disks, jade figures, obsidian knives. Then small, crushed golden bells began appearing. Thompson realized that nearly all the articles had been broken in some way—"killed" before being offered to the god.

It was the same with the human sacrifices. The first human remain was the skull of a small girl; this was followed by some ninety skeletons of girls and men, most of them old men.

Thompson's dredge finally began scraping the limestone bottom of the *cenote*, but he felt there were still a great many artifacts yet to be found. He decided that diving was the way to do it, although the *cenote* was a fearsome place for divers in the cumbersome hard-hat suits then available. The eighty-foot walls rose perpendicularly from the surface of the water, which itself was stagnant, thick, and totally without light. All diving, he knew, would be by touch alone.

Thompson returned to the States, found the money for diving gear, and hired a pair of Greek sponge divers from Florida. They were able to bring up small carved objects too delicate for the dredge's clumsy jaws: hieroglyphic stones, many beautifully sculptured with human figures; a big copper disk engraved with pictures of the sun god; three hundred gold objects (some weighing up to a pound), and 250 pieces of finely worked jade.

37. The Dutch trawler *HD79*, stranded in the dunes on the Isle of Texel, January 1960. Ground tackle was laid out while draglines, bulldozers, pumps, and hose pipes scoured away the sand to lower the vessel six feet. A month after stranding, tugs hauled her out. PHOTO CREDIT: *N. V. Bureau Wijsmuller*

38. The 974-foot tanker *Torrey Canyon* breaking up on the rocks off Britain's Cornish coast, March 1967. Her 117,000 tons of crude oil formed a 100-mile-square slick, which polluted 80 miles of British and French coastline, killing 25,000 sea birds and destroying undersea life in the intertidal zone; and cost $7.2 million to remove.
PHOTO CREDIT: *Royal Navy*

39. Bob Marx's homemade air lift spurts water and mud into the sifting screen during his underequipped, understaffed, underfinanced, yet tremendously successful, archaeological excavation of the sunken city of Port Royal. Salvors check carefully for artifacts. PHOTO CREDIT: *Bob Marx*

40. One of the few pictures ever taken under water at Port Royal (due to the thick, turbid mud). A diver works on the sunken 32-gun frigate HMS *Swan*, one of many vessels hurled into the Port Royal harbor by the 1692 earthquake and tsunami that inundated the city. PHOTO CREDIT: *Bob Marx*

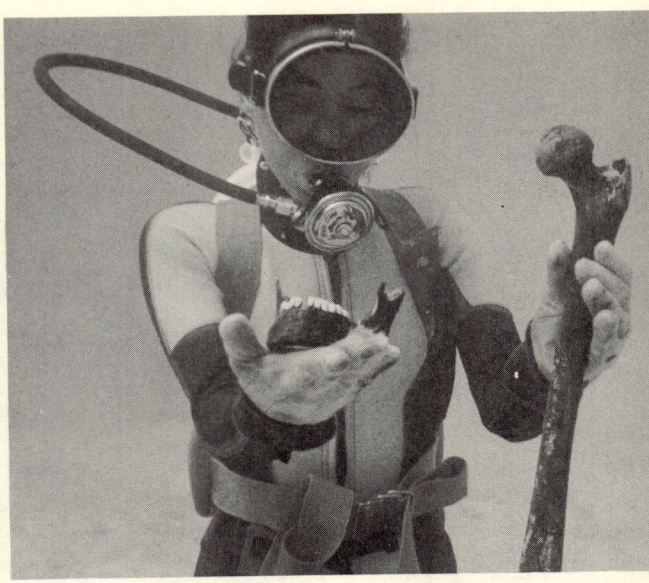

41. Archaeologist Nancy Farriss Marx, Ph.D., Marx's wife, under water at Port Royal. The human jawbone and thighbone she displays, unearthed in the ruins, owe their remarkable state of preservation to the protective mud that coats the sunken city. PHOTO CREDIT: *Bob Marx*

42. Bob Marx displays silver and pewter artifacts recovered from a sunken building, probably a tavern. Marx, this hemisphere's leading marine archaeological diver, spent three years at Port Royal in the longest continual submarine excavation ever undertaken. PHOTO CREDIT: *Jamaica Tourist Board*

43. The royal ship V*asa*, sunk in Stockholm Harbor in 1628 on the day she was launched. In May 1961, after a five-year salvage effort, V*asa* was floating on her own keel in this specially prepared dry dock. Sprinkler system was installed so the vessel would not dry out. PHOTO CREDIT: *Statens Sjohistoriska Museum, Stockholm*

44. To preserve the V*asa*, largest organic object ever rescued from the sea, her timbers were subjected to a continual spray of polyethylene glycol. The natural drying process probably will continue for 20 years. Shown is the 1400-ton vessel's lower gun deck. PHOTO CREDIT: *Statens Sjohistoriska Museum, Stockholm*

45. CURV (Cable-Controlled Undersea Research Vehicle), the unmanned robot submersible (originally designed by Howard Talkington of NOTS for torpedo recovery) that made the actual recovery of the lost nuclear bomb at Palomares, Spain, in 1966. PHOTO CREDIT: *U. S. Navy*

46. *Deepstar 4000*, one of Westinghouse's three experimental deep submersibles (the 4000 refers to her designed maximum depth in feet). The beetle-like sub is testing special Navy instrumentation while its manipulator picks up a bottom sample. PHOTO CREDIT: *Westinghouse Undersea Division*

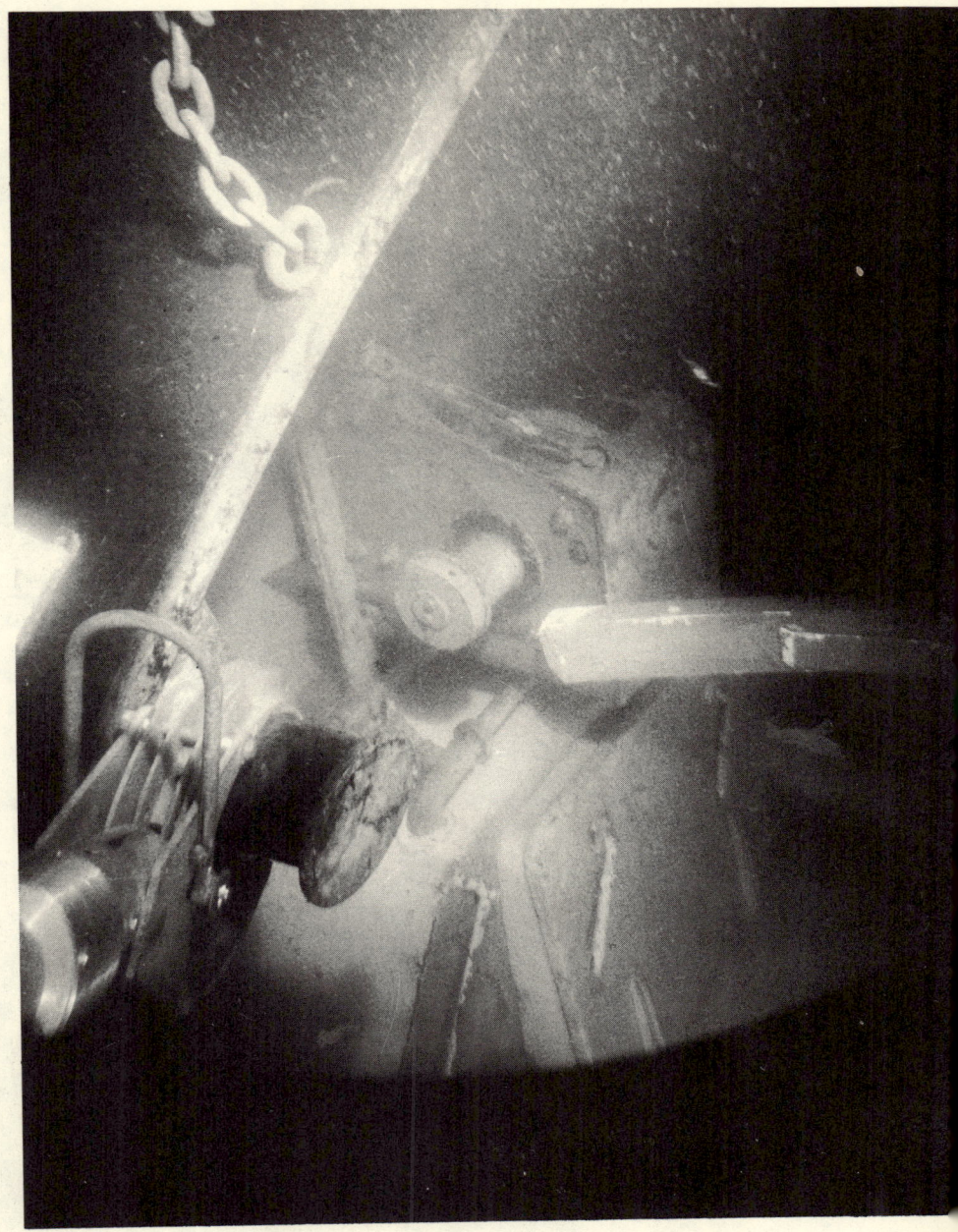

47. Hyco's *Pisces I* engaged in an underwater salvage operation at 670 feet (July 1969). *Pisces'* manipulator (left foreground) thrusts a heavy iron toggle through the hawse pipe of the sunken tug *Emerald Straits*. Lifting cables were then fitted around the toggles. PHOTO CREDIT: *International Hydrodynamics*

48. Salvors from Wijsmuller of Holland show the remarkable weightlessness of the pea-sized granules of polystyrene used in raising the 108-ton trawler *Jaco-Mina* in July 1965. Pellets are 98% air and 2% plastic, and produce only upward thrust. PHOTO CREDIT: *N. V. Bureau Wijsmuller*

49. The *Martin S*, a 4200-ton Danish freighter raised from 100 feet of water at Greenland in May 1967 by Van den Tak of Holland and Karl Krøyer of Denmark. Heavy beams strengthened decks and hatches against the tremendous upward thrust exerted by Krøyer's polystyrene spheres. PHOTO CREDIT: *Karl Krøyer*

In 1960 the Chichén Itzá *cenote* saw another "dig," this one by Pablo Bush Romero's CEDAM[6] with the financial backing of the National Institute of Anthropology and History of Mexico, the Mexican Navy, and the National Geographic Society. An air lift was chosen to raise the many artifacts they were sure Thompson had missed. To lower their equipment into the well (including an eight-by-twelve-foot divers' barge), a heavy derrick was installed on the rim. The divers could be described as a motley crew: one wore a green scaly monster's suit left over from the movie *The Creature from the Black Lagoon*.

Once the air lift was in operation (it stirred up too much muck and mire to be totally successful), they first recovered a number of balls of copal, as Thompson had done forty-six years before. When work ended four months later, they had incense burners, beads, bits of jade, whole or broken pottery, hundreds of little copper bells (Thompson seemed to have gotten all the gold ones), wooden idols of the rain god Chac, and a number of human remains including the skull of a young girl.

Neither the National Institute of Anthropology nor Romero's CEDAM was completely satisfied, so a third attempt on the *cenote* was begun in Sepember 1967, led by the American archaeologist-diver Norman Scott. Scott had two tremendously ambitious schemes, one of which Thompson had dreamed of doing: to drain the entire well. As the thing was two hundred feet across, with an average water depth of forty feet, this meant draining away some eight million gallons of water.

To do the job, Scott used two high-velocity centrifugal pumps—one on a styrofoam-supported raft on the *cenote*'s surface, the other at the rim of the well—each able to handle one hundred thousand gallons an hour. To carry the water away from the site were eight hundred feet of irrigation pipe.

It didn't work, for a very simple reason; in the *cenote* were unsuspected underground streams, which kept feeding water back in.

Scott's second idea was an even wilder one than draining the giant limestone hole. He planned to set up a filtration system. The water would be pumped through the system (and treated chemically in the process) as if the *cenote* were a gigantic swimming pool, and then returned, clear and purified, to the well. They could then remove the many giant trees that cluttered the bottom of the well, and could more easily penetrate the fifteen feet of mud and bottom ooze covering the artifacts.

Divers stayed down working the air lift, meanwhile, discharging the material onto the screening table in the middle of their raft. They soon suspended that part of the operation because it kept the turbidity level too high despite the elaborate filtration setup.

Once the water had cleared, work went forward rapidly. Most of the recovered artifacts were predictable: copal, gold and copper ornaments, jade beads, carved staghorn, the little copper bells with pebble clappers known as the bells of death. Some of the finds were not so predictable: gold leaf, and certain of the sacrificial dolls.

They found these dolls by the score, crude wax-and-wood affairs pierced with pins. This was not voodoo: rather, the pins indicated a pain or ailment that the supplicant hoped Chac would cure. Some of them were less than a year old, suggesting that old religions die hard.

What was totally unexpected was that some of the dolls bore Latin letters. Dating has so far proved impossible, but the stratification suggests that the Latin-lettered dolls went in sometime during the thirteenth century; that is, the dolls *might* be pre-Columbian, pre-Spanish artifacts. If the dating should support this possibility, the whole Quetzalcoatl[7] muddle takes on renewed significance. The legendary Quezalcoatl's journey to the eastern ocean to embark in a skiff of lizard skin, vowing to return, at least suggests a return to their ships by Europeans (in all probability, Latin-writers) who could have reached Yucatán a century before Columbus.

Also recovered were the remains of another one hundred sacrificial victims, mainly children; in the early days, their hearts had been cut out with staghorn knives also found in the *cenote*, but in later times they had been thrown in alive to drown.

Scott's final find in the Chichén Itzá *cenote* was some remarkable thousand-year-old Mayan pottery called Tepeu. Unlike any other Mayan artifacts, this Tepeu pottery depicted, in brilliant blues, greens, blacks, yellows, reds, and whites, everyday Mayan people of the tenth century. There were warriors, women, children, trade caravans, befeathered chieftains—a priceless find. Further expeditions to the Chichén Itzá *cenote* are planned for future years.

The only other *cenote* in which extensive archaeological diving has been conducted is that of Dzibilchaltun, in northern Yucatán. The city itself was not discovered until 1941, when two American archaeologists, E. Wyllys Andrews and George Brainerd, stumbled across it. Following World War II, Andrews returned for a four-year dig (1956–60); the city was found to cover *twenty square miles* and date back to about 2000 B.C. Over four hundred buildings and many *cenotes* were noted.

The main *cenote* approached that of Chichén Itzá in size: one hundred feet across, nearly 150 feet deep. SCUBA divers from the National Geographic Society brought up basketfuls of broken pots, which allowed archaeologists to work out a pottery-dating scheme for the site. Also found were bone awls and bodily ornaments (some of them made of coral), and enough human bones to confirm human sacrifice like that at Chichén Itzá.

Two of the divers, Luis Marden and Bates Littlehales, went all the way to the bottom of the well; both came up with serious cases of the bends. The American Ambassador's plane rushed them to Florida for the nearest available recompression chamber; after two days in it, they emerged unharmed.

Archaeological diving is also going on in at least one Latin American lake. In April 1955, an amateur archaeologist-cum-SCUBA diver brought up an unbroken pottery vessel from Lake Amatitlán, which lies at four thousand feet of elevation some seventeen miles from Guatemala City. This small beginning led to the eventual recovery of some six hundred artifacts (pottery, incense burners, stone sculptures) during the next few years, with Dr. Stephan F. Borhegyi systematically mapping all discovery sites on the lake for Guatemala's San Carlos University.

Only the lower of the lake's two basins contains the pottery, at nine different sites ranging in water depths from ten to 130 feet. Specific types of artifacts came from specific sites, which in turn correspond to known land middens. Borhegyi found that each represented a Mayan highland culture from a different historical period, ranging between 1000 B.C. and A.D. 1524, when the Spaniards arrived.

The nature of the finds proves that the Mayans, in those twenty-five hundred years of continual development, had evolved from a nomadic hunting and fishing people into the highly complex society the Spaniards found and destroyed.

SUNKEN CITIES IN THE MEDITERRANEAN

It is not far from the artifacts that earlier civilizations dropped, threw, or lost in oceans, lakes, or wells, to the remains of whole cities or cultures that might have gotten misplaced under the sea. The Mediterranean basin is the logical center for such inquiry, since ocean-trading civilizations have been there longer than anywhere else.

A helpful fact is that none of the major harbors of the ancient world was placed near the estuary of a river. This is most important from the standpoint of marine archaeologists, since there was no downflow of fresh water to carry away small artifacts or bury them in alluvial silt. The Vieux Port (Old Harbor) of Marseilles, for example, predates the rise of Rome; indeed, many archaeologists believe that if a lock were built across the harbor mouth so it could be pumped dry, a virtually complete history of Greek mercantile affairs would be exposed.

Piraeus, Athens' seaport on the Saronic Gulf, probably hides beneath the waters of its harbor a similar history. During dredging operations in 1931, an entire shipload of second-century-B.C. marble reliefs was turned up. The marbles were commercial copies destined for Rome's *nouveaux riches*, without inherent artistic worth. Their value lay in the fact that they were copies of the relief work on the shield of an immense ivory-and-gold statue that had topped the Acropolis before the Parthenon had even been built. Depicting Athena Promachos and carved by Phidias, it had been dedicated by Pericles in 438 B.C. The statue has long since disappeared into antiquity—the manner of its destruction is not even known—but these humble, cheap reliefs dredged from Piraeus Harbor at least prove concretely that it once existed.

In 279 B.C., a five-hundred-foot lighthouse (one of the Seven Wonders of the Ancient World) called the Pharos was erected at Alexandria, Egypt. Designed by the Greek architect Sostratus, it was topped by an immense statue of Poseidon, the sea-god. Sometime in the seventh century A.D., the immense structure (even then, a functioning lighthouse!) was toppled by an earthquake. In 1480, Qait Bey, an Egyptian sultan, erected a fortress on its stump.

In 1962 an Egyptian skin diver probably found the rest of the lighthouse when he spotted, at a mere four fathoms and only a few yards from shore, fragments of a huge statue, a column, a sphinx, and a smaller, intact human figure. His find was confirmed by UAR Navy divers who were prevented from either raising or photographing the fragments by the rough and very turbid water.

The Mediterranean contains whole cities, however—not just statues. Cities whose former existence is well documented, in areas that now have subsided beneath the waves.

Both Homer (*The Iliad*) and Pausanias[8] mention Helike (in Achaea, southern Greece), an ancient city destroyed in 369 B.C. by earthquake and flood. The ruins were visible beneath the clear waters of the Gulf of Corinth for a full century before being buried under the silt. It lies at a depth of about twenty-one fathoms, overlaid with a good twenty feet of hard-packed mud. The only expedition to Helike, by the French in 1950, ended in a total failure to uncover any of the buildings.

Caesarea, Palestine's seaport to the Mediterranean some fifty-five miles from Jerusalem, was built in 10 B.C. by Herod the Great on the remains of the ancient Phoenician city of Iol. Pontius Pilate lived in this Jewish port of 100,000, which Rome held until A.D. 639. From then until the twelfth century it was a Moslem seaport; unfortunately, when the Crusaders drove out the Arabs, those Christian gentlemen began a thorough destruction of the city, which was completed 150 years later, after the Arabs took it back. They smashed the Roman aqueducts, which flooded Caesarea and turned it into a swamp.

Edwin Link and his *Sea Diver II*, armed with air lift, descended on the ancient site in 1960–61. His shore diggers found Arab artifacts, including a treasure vault with jewelry and pendants of semiprecious stones (agates and carnelians); under the sediment, he found many Roman ruins, including a mosaic floor. Their excavations did not reach down to the more ancient, Jewish structures.

A sunken city in the Bay of Naples, first discovered during dredging operations in 1928, has marine archaeologists currently excited. Baiae was a Roman spa and resort area called Little Rome in the days of the emperors: Julius Caesar, Pompeii, and Nero each maintained an enormous villa there, as did such literary lights as Cicero, Seneca, and Lucullus. Around its sulfur springs were built baths, temples, palaces, and gardens.

Earthquakes began its destruction; looters completed the job after the fall of Rome. Amateurs with SCUBA gear in 1969, however, discovered three strikingly beautiful statues in the section of Baiae that had sunk intact with a subsiding coastline. One of the statues has been raised, and the site is being mapped for future operations.

Also in the Bay of Naples may lie a submarine Pompeii; and off Posillipo, Italy, are extensive ruins believed to be Paleopolis, an early Greek colony on the Italian coast.

Two of Plato's (428–348 B.C.) dialogues, Timaeus and Critias, suggest the Mediterranean as the site of Atlantis, the fabled lost continent. Plato recounts that Solon (died circa 560 B.C.), the great Greek lawgiver and one of the Seven Sages, was told by an Egyptian priest that Atlantis had been overwhelmed by an earthquake some nine thousand years earlier.[9] Its sinking, said the priest, had left an empty socket into which the waters had rushed to form the Mediterranean.

When we pass from the realm of legend, supported only by tantalizing scraps of scientific discovery, to the realm of extensive excavations in sunken cities, we are reduced to Tyre and Sidon in the Mediterranean Levant, and Port Royal in the Caribbean. There just aren't any others.

PÈRE A. POIDEBARD, STRATEGIC ARCHAEOLOGIST

Perhaps the most strategic of all the scientists who have worked under water was the French Jesuit Père A. Poidebard. His thirty-year involvement in marine archaeology really began in 1925, when Poidebard used airplanes in his search of the Syrian desert for ancient caravan routes from the time of Alexander the Great.

Six years of digging in the various ruined villages that had lain along the route led him inexorably to Tyre, Mistress of the Sea in Phoenician times: Tyre of the silken garments and Tyrian purple, founded in the fifteenth century B.C., withstanding repeated assaults by Syria and Babylon (including a thirteen-year siege by Nebuchadnezzar II), finally falling to Alexander in 332 B.C. Ships from Tarshish traded there[10]; Tyre's seamen traded in Israelite honey, Egyptian wine and wool, Greek sponges, and Spanish frankincense, and reputedly carried red coral to the Orient for the use of Chinese mandarins.

Poidebard again used his planes for aerial photos in hopes of spotting

Tyre's submerged ruins (remember, this was in 1935!); he also put naked divers into the shallows and hard-hat divers into deeper areas. Before the dig ended, in 1937, Poidebard was doing underwater photography with Le Prieur's cumbersome brass box; he even had tried underwater motion pictures. Chief among his discoveries were the Phoenicians' enormous breakwaters, beautifully designed to supplement the natural reef formations, which had given a remarkable degree of protection to shipping in the harbor.

From 1946 to 1950, Poidebard carried on similar work at Sidon, second of the great Phoenician ports (present-day Saida, Lebanon); only his death, in 1954, forestalled his attack on the third of the triumvirate, Biblos. He uncovered the ruins of Sidon's port, the ancient jetty, and the wharves, using, in addition to his divers and flyers, geologists, marine engineers, naval experts, seamen, and archaeologists.

When future work is undertaken on sunken cities, without doubt his methods will form the basis for the procedures followed.

Poidebard was a scientist with a great deal of money at his disposal. When we turn to Port Royal in the Caribbean, the only other site where extensive underwater digging has been done on a sunken city, we find a far different situation; for the principal salvor there was perennially impoverished Bob Marx.

The British, capturing Jamaica from the Spaniards in 1655, immediately turned it into a naval base. The town of Port Royal, which sprang up near the fortifications, shortly became a pirate city, actively catering to the droves of buccaneers whose presence was a real force on the Spanish Main.

Port Royal was built on a long sandbank jutting out into the Caribbean; when, on June 7, 1692, a tremendous earthquake struck Jamaica, the city's destruction was inescapable. The quake began breaking up the sand bar on which Port Royal lay, great cracks appeared in the city's streets, houses began tumbling, and then an immense tsunami rolled over it. Less than two minutes (11:43 to 11:45 A.M.) sufficed to destroy two-thirds of the town and kill two thousand of its inhabitants.

Salvage started immediately, with naked divers going into some of the submerged buildings that same afternoon. Most of them were blacks, escaped slaves from the Spanish pearl fisheries at Margarita Island. None of the buildings was deeper than eight fathoms, and makeshift diving bells were available. By 1725, the buildings the divers could reach had all been stripped, as had been the numerous shipwrecks that dotted the bay.

In the 1930s, an adventure-writing hard-hat diver claimed to have explored the sunken city, going down to depths of thirty fathoms and finding, as Coleridge put it, caverns measureless to man. His account of his adventures is so interesting in the light of later explorations that it deserves brief quotation here.

"Rising out of the deeper water ahead of me were great shapes and designs of coral," he wrote. "Through my helmet straight-shafted spires and huge pinnacles were visible, tall columns supporting overhanging roofs, towers, and windows in walls . . . I went inside, and found myself in a chamber space with several passages leading from it . . . Everything was flooded in blue, not an ordinary shade, but an unbelievably alive one that had in it all the conceivable shadings of one color."

Heady stuff, that.

Our adventurer later identifies the building he has entered as "a massive cathedral." There was indeed a cathedral which sank at Port Royal; unfortunately, that portion of the sunken city that held the cathedral has for several decades lain squarely beneath the modern city of Port Royal.

As to the rest of his adventures there in thirty fathoms of "unbelievably alive" blue, the deepest water to be found in Port Royal Harbor is ten fathoms; he would not have found the other twenty without walking a good five miles straight out to sea. Reality is terribly prosaic: the city lies in ten to twenty feet of water under a choking six-foot layer of viscid mud. Sediment is so thick in the water that divers have a normal visibility of six inches.

THE EXPLORATION OF PORT ROYAL

A first minor attempt at exploration was carried out in 1954 by Cornel Lumière, an underwater film producer who had hoped to find something to photograph. In a week on the site, he didn't shoot a foot of film.

Edwin Link was the next excavator, making a first, abortive attempt in 1956 with his vessel *Sea Diver*. All he found was a lone cannon from Fort James: he had been entirely unprepared for the four to six feet of mud covering the site.

In 1959 he returned aboard *Sea Diver II*, the world's first boat created solely for marine archaeology. It was ninety-one feet long, bristling with booms and winches, with glass observation plates, like those in Captain Nemo's *Nautilus*, set in the bow. The ship had radar and sonar, and a diving compartment with an air lock. For work on shallow reefs was *Reef Diver*, an eighteen-foot water-jet launch fitted with portable echo-sounding equipment.

Link started in June 1959, with the launch and echo sounder, on a complete survey of the site. Dredging (with an air lift) and diving began on the possible site of the King's Warehouse. All they found were mud and modern detritus, so they moved to what they hoped was the east wall of Fort James. Here they began finding the expected seventeenth-century artifacts, although the sediment was so thick that during a ten-week operation they could take pictures on only three days.

Their metal detector proved invaluable, finding them a battered copper stew pot with the stew bones still in it, cannon balls, and an inexplicable fifteenth-century Spanish swivel gun. A brass watch (studied with X rays) had its hands at 11:43, thus giving the exact minute of the earthquake 267 years before, which had stopped not only the watch, but the life of an entire city.

Their greatest haul was in bottles from the twentieth, nineteenth, eighteenth, and seventeenth centuries. One onion-shaped rum bottle, still corked, was sealed by a twisted brass wire. Link drew off some of the contents with a hypodermic needle; it tasted, he said, like vinegar.

Norman Scott, who was to carry out the highly successful third operation in the *cenote* at Chichén Itzá, brought a group of American treasure divers to Port Royal for a two-week stint in 1960. Their efforts netted virtually nothing, probably because they limited their dig to the worked-over areas around the old forts.

In 1965, Bob Marx was hired by the Jamaican Government to make "a scientific and serious marine archaeological excavation" at Port Royal. Marx spent three years on the site—the longest continual submarine excavation ever undertaken. The number of artifacts he recovered is staggering; the buildings explored included taverns, private homes, artisans' shops (silversmith, carpenter, cobbler), warehouses, a fish and a meat market, two shipwrecks, and two turtle crawls.[11]

Here any resemblance to any other digs ceases, for this was a typical Marx operation: underequipped, understaffed, underfinanced. Not for him radar, sonar, portable echo sounders, glass-eyed boats, water-jet launches; he couldn't afford them. His sole piece of equipment was a homemade air lift; his "diving boat" was an old scow with an outboard motor tacked to the back end. His "crew" was a professional diver named Kenute Kelly and an amateur named Wayne Roosevelt, with a Jamaican laborer or two to help with the heavy stuff and his wife ashore to preserve and classify the finds.

Marx wanted to produce for the first time an accurate chart of the sunken city, examine the buildings for design and construction details, and recover enough building materials and artifacts for the possible re-creation of some of the more important buildings.

They mapped the site in November 1965, then spent three months clearing up the modern debris—beer cans, a cook stove, and a truck chassis are good examples. On May 1, 1966, excavation began 120 feet west of the old Naval Hospital in fifteen feet of water. Their first day they unearthed a red brick wall 11½ feet high by eight wide, as well as pewter utensils still stacked as they had been in the housewife's cupboard.

The next day, the wall fell on Marx, pinning his head and torso to the bottom and breaking the air lift. The water was so thick that Roosevelt, on the other side of the wall, didn't even know it had fallen. They used the broken air-lift hose as a jet to blow away the sediment around Marx. From then on, they dismantled walls before excavating under them.

Patterns began emerging. Nearly all the artifacts were found in the top eight feet of sediment, though excavation was to fifteen feet. The best caches were under fallen walls, which had saved them from the very thorough and industrious scavengers of the seventeenth and eighteenth centuries. Thousands of spoons, plates, tankards, and bowls were found, the pewter ones quite valuable, as well as rare organic matter preserved by the thick mud. This included rope, cloth swatches, leather objects, and, amazingly, a complete tobacco leaf. In the tavern of one Richard Collins were five hundred clay pipes and two hundred onion-shaped rum bottles.

During July they examined the sunken 32-gun frigate HMS *Swan*, after finding it *under* a fallen brick wall. The vessel, careened for repairs, had been hurled into the ruins by the tidal wave.

August gave them the turtle crawls: pens made of five-foot wooden posts, thirty-two feet long and nineteen wide, where turtles were stored, live, until they were slaughtered. Inside the crawls were a half ton of turtle bones. Since their flippers had been tied together, they had been unable to swim to freedom even when the wave surged up over the pens.

In September, a frisky octopus became very attached to Marx. Literally. It fastened all eight arms to his head and shoulders and wouldn't let go. When it started to pull his face mask off, he turned the air-lift tube up to highest pressure and applied it to the octopus a tentacle at a time, sucking it away piece by piece. But then the tube of the air lift got stuck to the top of his head. They finally had to shut down the air pressure completely to get him free with his noggin reasonably intact.

By November the weather was worsening with the approaching hurricane season. Despite the weather, they uncovered two standing buildings and made careful measurements and drawings of them. In one was a real find: a silver pocket watch made by Aron Gibbs of London sometime before 1666. When they had cleaned it up, the brass inner movements all worked perfectly.

On December 18, for the intriguing reason that Marx's wife had dreamed they would find treasure that day, they abandoned their 250-

by-150-foot dig for a move to a new area. Their hookah units had quit working, and only one of their SCUBA tanks had air in it, so Marx, after digging a six-foot-deep hole without finding anything, turned the equipment over to Kelly.

Kelly promptly found four remarkably preserved pieces of eight. Marx returned with mask and snorkel; within minutes he had brought up fifty more of the coins. By the time Kelly's single tank was exhausted, they had over five hundred. Later, they found the remains of the wooden chest that once had held them—decorated with the coat of arms of Spain's Philip IV (1621–65)! The chest had probably been loot from one of three Spanish galleons that had broken up on nearby Pedro Bank in 1690.

The work went on for two more seasons, resulting in a wealth of artifacts that fit together into an unprecedented mosaic of seventeenth-century everyday life.

[1] See pages 41–47.
[2] Not nearly so inept seem to have been some Spanish salvors who recovered the treasure from a wrecked fleet in the Florida Keys in 1733: they brought up a good deal more gold than had been registered at Havana when the ships had been loaded. Obviously, a number of men had been smuggling in an attempt to evade the Royal Fifth, which, by law, went to the Spanish monarchy. One can only cry *shame!* upon the naughty rascals and limit them to a footnote.
[3] 1702–13. This war put Philip V, Bourbon grandson of France's Louis XIV, on the Spanish throne. Known as Queen Anne's War in the Americas, it marked the beginning of Spain's decline in the New World.
[4] Only five states have laws regarding sunken treasure in coastal waters: Florida, Georgia, South and North Carolina, and Texas. Apart from Internal Revenue, the federal government makes no claim whatsoever on any part of treasure or artifacts recovered. For tax purposes, IRS takes the collectors' or numismatists' value instead of merely that of the gold or silver content in the artifact.
[5] Traditionally a captain general about to be taken or defeated by the enemy would destroy it, so no others have survived.
[6] See pages 393–95.
[7] The great god Quetzalcoatl, according to anthropologist Herbert J. Spinden, had his origin in a living man, a Toltec king, priest, and astronomer who reduced the Mayan calendar to a system of signs and ideographs *which fitted all languages equally well.* Spinden's suggested date of his death, April 5, 1208, becomes suggestive in view of the possible thirteenth-century dating of the dolls. Could the historical Quetzalcoatl have been a foreigner, a Latin-writing European?
[8] See page 364.
[9] Well before recorded history. Indeed, 6000 years before the union of the peoples of the Upper and Lower Nile.
[10] The location of Tarshish still is unknown, although Tartessus, in southern Spain, seems probable. Tin came from Tarshish, and tin was found only in Spain, Portugal, and along Britain's Cornish coast. Of these, Spain is the most likely.
[11] And it was on weekends stolen from Port Royal, by the way, that this remarkable man uncovered Columbus' ships in St. Ann's Bay!

CHAPTER TWENTY-EIGHT

From *Vasa* to the *Association*

~~~~~~

Though the Mediterranean and the Caribbean are the focal points of marine archaeology because of their warm water and concentrations of ocean-oriented civilizations, legends of sunken ships and sunken cities abound in every other ocean on the globe. Some of them are pure fabrication; others have a solid basis in fact; since the advent of SCUBA gear, some have been proved to be one or the other.

EUROPEAN SUNKEN CITIES

In Brittany, for instance, is supposed to be the sunken Roman city of Ys. Ys has proved rich soil for legend, appearing on an A.D. 400 Roman map close to the sea in the Bay of Douarnenez (some twelve miles from modern Quimper, in northwest France). It was flooded permanently in either 395 or 441. Individual divers claim to have found foundations and stone walls, and at least one SCUBA enthusiast says he found a Roman road running straight across the floor of the bay. No serious archaeologists have seen any of these ruins, however.

Many ancient sunken cities are also known to exist around the coast of Britain. Between Land's End and the Scillies was once the walled city of Lyonesse, which, with its towers and castles and the forest that surrounded it, is believed to have been submerged by rising waters. Tradition holds that the Phoenician sailors of Tyre, Sidon, and Biblos were trading for gold, silver, and linen from Lyonesse as early as 1000 B.C.

Modern Ravenspur, in Yorkshire, marks the site of the sunken Roman city of Praetorium. And as late as the fourteenth century the old port of Dunwich, a former Roman trading station in Suffolk, was an important commercial area, with churches, hospitals, nunneries, and a small palace, a bishopric, and a mint. After its harbor was closed off and choked up with detritus washed in by an immense storm, the water continued its encroachment until the town was covered completely.

The holdings of Godwin, Earl of Essex, whose son King Harold of England ("Last of the Saxons") went down to defeat at the hands of William the Conqueror at the Battle of Hastings in 1066, are believed to form a "sunken city" of sorts. The famous Goodwin Sands, a dangerous series of shoals in the northern Straits of Dover, which are a graveyard of dead ships, are also believed to cover the manor house, outbuildings, and several thousand acres of the Earl's former estate.

VIGO BAY'S STUBBORN TREASURE

Virtually every sea can boast scores of old wooden ships of tremendous archaeological—and monetary—value along its coasts. In 1702, a Spanish treasure fleet bound for Cádiz ducked into Vigo Bay, on the Atlantic, in northwest Spain. Don Manuel de Velasco had brought the twenty-galleon treasure armada from the Indies under an escort of twenty-three French warships; but he heard that an Anglo-Dutch fleet (it was during the War of the Spanish Succession) was blockading Cádiz, and sought safety in Vigo Bay. Instead of unloading the treasure for transportation to safety inland, he laid a log boom across the harbor mouth in the vain hope that this would protect their hoard.

It didn't. Admiral Sir George Rooke, the English commander of the blockading fleet, ran his ships right over the boom one night and into the harbor. When some of the galleons were already burning, the Spaniards belatedly began unloading the reputed £20-million treasure.

Twenty-four French and Spanish ships were sunk in the fray; the rest were captured. None escaped. The largest captured galleon was being removed by Sir Cloudsley (or Clowdisley) Shovell, who was a sufficiently indifferent sailor to run it into an island near the mouth of the bay. The vessel reeled away to go down in twenty fathoms of water.

English sailors were diving for treasure so soon after the encounter that they were still being fired upon from shore. They appear to have salvaged about £5 million worth of gold, silver, pearls, and gems.

Since then, thirteen attempts to salvage the treasure of Vigo Bay have been recorded. In 1732 a French expedition managed to find and recover one of the small boats that had been hurriedly transferring treasure to shore. There was nothing in it. The 1784 attempt did not even find a boat. In 1825, a certain Captain Dickson, working from the British brig *Enterprise*, recovered an unknown sum of silver and hastily sailed away into the night. The Spaniards tried unsuccessfully in 1835.

By 1858 Spain had apparently realized that it would be a long time before anyone found very much in the way of treasure in Vigo Bay; but she had also realized that people would keep on looking. She began to sell salvage concessions on the wrecks. One David Langlands, a Briton, got the first ten-year concession.

He immediately resold it—twice. First buyer was Saint-Simon Sicard; backing him was Hippolyte Magen, another Frenchman, who spent a good deal of time in the Spanish Archives confirming that there actually had been treasure ships in Vigo Bay.

It was while this sound and reasonable records-search was going on that Langlands coolly resold the concession to our old friend Colonel Gowan, he who raised the V*ladimir* at Sebastopol following the Crimean War.[1]

Gowan was short on research but long on practical experience; he and the Sicard/Magen forces formed an uneasy alliance. They planned to use a diving bell and the *aérophore* of Benoist (or Benoît) Rouquayrol and Auguste Denayrouze, a primitive SCUBA gear utilizing the demand valve later (November 6, 1886) patented by Rouquayrol.[2]

It was not until January 1870 that, in filthy weather, diving actually began. So well had Magen done his homework, that in a dozen days they had confirmed the existence of ten wrecks, and incidentally had confirmed the complete surprise of the English-Dutch assault. A Spanish cannon they raised still had the tampion in its muzzle. This plug, or stopper, had done its job well: when it was removed, air trapped there for 168 years whooshed out.

They kept finding things of intense archaeological interest (if the science of archaeology had been anything more than a gleam in the eye of Boucher de Perthes at the time): anchors, human bones, cannon balls, a bag of Brazil nuts (*Brazil nuts?*), fifteen cases of indigo . . .

Unfortunately, they weren't interested in archaeology; they were going broke. So broke, in fact, that they finally stopped to examine some flaky black lumps of heavy fused metal they had been throwing back in disgust, and found they were loaves of pure silver with (as we know now) the outer layer reduced to silver sulfide by the chemicals in the water.

Meanwhile the Spanish politicians and customs agents were harassing them unmercifully, accusing them of hiding recovered gold to escape paying Spain its share each time they brought up another worthless clump of corroded iron.

Finally, the desperate salvors talked Auguste Denayrouze himself into taking over the salvage operations; since the invention and successful use of the *aérophore* in Greek sponge beds, he had carried the sort of reputation that Jacques-Yves Cousteau carries in the popular mind today. Alas! The Franco-Prussian War (1870–71) intervened. Denayrouze was in Paris when the siege started, contracted pneumonia, and was unable to go. An engineer named Étienne swore that he would get through the German lines, go to Vigo Bay, and raise the gold.

Étienne hired a balloon named *Le Galilée* and with it sailed over the German lines.

Well, not *quite* over. He came down on the Beauce plains, where the Germans captured him and decided to shoot him as a spy. A ghoulishly cheerful jailer told him to throw a letter in a bottle into the Marne as the Germans marched him along its bank to his execution. The Marne would join the Seine, his message would float to Paris, someone would fish it out, and *voilà!* word of his death would reach his friends and family, assuring that he would be mourned.

Étienne escaped instead, made a perilous foot-crossing of the Pyrenees into Spain, finally arrived at Vigo Bay—and found that the salvage operation had already folded for lack of funds. It was briefly resumed in 1872, but found nothing.

Since then, eight more attempts have taken place, each ending in defeat. Using SCUBA gear, Americans John Potter and Owen Lee spent several years at Vigo Bay without success; and in November of the same year they started, 1955, a British outfit calling itself Ventures Ltd. took a stab at it. Without, predictably, any success.

VASA

Totally successful, however, has been the unique and unprecedented location, recovery, and restoration of the great ship *Vasa*, launched by King Gustavus Adolphus of Sweden in 1628. The *Vasa*, designed by Dutch naval architect Henrik Hybertsson, was 1400 tons displacement, 165 feet long, forty feet in the beam, and carried sixty-four guns—forty-eight of them huge bronze cannon.

The ship was launched amid great fanfare in Stockholm's inner harbor on August 10, 1628, carrying four hundred sailors, soldiers, and their families on a triumphant tour of the harbor. When she got a few hundred yards offshore, a sudden puff of wind heeled her over hard to port, her loose cannons below deck all ran to the lee side, water poured in the open gun ports, and she . . . sank.

She ended up with just the pennants on top of her three masts visible above water. Thirty people drowned. Within three days, English engineer Ian Bulmer had recovered most of the bronze cannon from the high-pooped, highly carved, red vessel. Bulmer also looped hawsers around the masts, hoping to drag the ship ashore with great numbers of horses pulling on the hawsers. Not surprisingly, he failed to budge the massive vessel; but he did bring it to a dead-even keel.

During the next few years, it became a sort of international game to try to salvage the Vasa: Swedish, French, English, Dutch, and German salvors all made unsuccessful attempts on her. In 1663 a Swedish group, using a diving bell, was successful in jerking loose and bringing up some of her deck timbers as well as fifty-three cannons. Until the 1680s, metal was occasionally recovered from the ship by smashing through her top deck with a heavy weight so the salvors could sort of grope about with grapnels.

The game soon paled. By the time the twentieth century rolled around, Vasa's position in Stockholm Harbor—indeed, her *existence* in Stockholm Harbor—had been long forgotten.

But shortly after World War II, Swedish historian Nils Ahnlund ran across the court-of-inquiry minutes, as well as an account of the diving-bell salvage attempt on the Vasa nearly three hundred years before. He published his research findings; they happened to be read by a Swedish lad named Anders Franzen.

A few years later Franzen, now a petroleum engineer, discovered that the cold, black Baltic Sea around Sweden had an average salinity of only 0.7. The fact electrified him. The shipworm *Teredo navalis*[3] requires an average salinity of 0.9 to live. That meant that Stockholm Harbor had to be free of *teredos*, and that wooden ships sank in that harbor probably would survive better than wooden wrecks in any other ocean of the world.

And in that harbor, somewhere, according to historian Ahnlund, lay the Vasa, which had fascinated him so completely as a child.

By 1954, Franzen had made a contour map of the bottom of Stockholm Harbor with a drag, grapnels, drag wires, and any other method he could make work. When a firm of engineers made an echo-sounding contour map of the bottom for a proposed bridge across the harbor, Franzen was looking over their shoulders. A hundred yards south of the harbor island of Beckholmen was a large hump on the harbor floor.

That hump, according to his researches in the Royal Swedish Navy Archives, could well be the Vasa.

In August 1956, Franzen dropped a six-pound, bomb-shaped, steel cylinder down into the hump. In its pointed nose was a sharp hollow punch. This core sampler, when he drew it back up, carried a plug of oak. Black, close-grained oak, like that the *Vasa* had been made of. But the *Vasa*'s oak had not been black.

Back to the laboratory. There he was told that oak submerged for longer than a hundred years in salt water invariably turns coal black.

That was enough for Franzen. Only a hundred yards from his hump was an old dry dock, which housed the Royal Swedish Navy's Diving School. How about, suggested Franzen, shifting the site of their training dives to his hump? The Navy was happy to agree; dives under actual salvage conditions were better than practice dives any time.

Chief diver Per Edvin Fälting, sixty years old but a man used to helmet diving in totally black water, was the first man down. He landed in mud up to his chest, thrashed about, and suddenly fell another twenty feet to a new mud bath. Undaunted, believing he had fallen from the first to the second deck of a multidecked vessel (such as the *Vasa* was known to be), Fälting began the incredible task of "feeling" the entire vessel from stem to stern. In dive after dive he ran his hands carefully over the hulk.

When he was finished, he drew a sketch of what he thought he had felt, with estimated dimensions. In size and shape, his drawing of a three-decked warship not only suggested the *Vasa*, it *was* the *Vasa* in every significant detail.

Commodore Edvard Clason, convinced, enthusiastically threw the support of the Swedish Navy into the wild salvage project conceived by Franzen: raise the ship whole and entire for restoration into a huge museum piece.

Clason was not the only one convinced by Franzen's enthusiasm. Neptun Salvage Company of Stockholm donated a half million dollars worth of free salvage work. Swedish firms and individuals donated money or labor worth the additional $1.5 million that Franzen estimated would be needed for the project.

Franzen saw it as a three-step operation: first, lift the *Vasa* from twenty fathoms to eight fathoms for easier working; second, repair, strengthen, make watertight, and raise her; third, restore and preserve her.

Captain Axel Hedberg, salvage master on loan from the Neptun Company, first dug tunnels under the vessel's hull for his six big lifting cables. This chore alone consumed two thousand hours of bottom time by hard-hat divers, for each tunnel had to be placed with geometric accuracy. Their great worry was that, if the cables were ill-placed, the ballast-stone-loaded ship would break her back with the lift.

To dig the tunnels, they used a special non-recoil hydraulic jet invented by Arne Zetterström, Sweden's great underwater experimenter who had died so tragically in 1945.[4] The ejected material was not just squirted aside, but was carefully collected for surface examination by archaeologists waiting there. In the mud were hundreds of small, elaborately carved lions, gargoyles, knights, biblical heroes, pagan gods, and monsters—the vessel's original decorations—and such personal items as coins, clay pipes, a sundial.

Two summers of work (the winters were too cold for divers to be down) went into the tunnels and the setting of the lifting wires, which were run up to a pair of salvage pontoons flanking the ship. In August 1959, the pontoons were watered, pinned, then carefully blown. A diver brought up the electrifying news that the *Vasa* was one and a half feet off the bottom with her keel holding together. During the next twenty-seven days, fifteen lifts brought her foot by careful foot shoreward to the desired depth of fifty feet.

Then began phase two: clearing away the forty anchors stuck in the tough oak timber by three centuries of careless ships' captains, the debris, the abandoned equipment from earlier salvage attempts, mud, and a dozen skeletons of drowned crewmen.

Once the detritus had been removed, divers swarmed over her to board up gun ports, repair the *Vasa*'s damaged stern, calk sprung seams and leaks in the hull, and replace those missing wooden treenails that had been used on the ship instead of iron spikes. This took two more years.

In April 1961, they were ready to attempt the final lift. SCUBA divers were doing the work this time, flanking *Vasa* with four inflatable rubber pontoons, two to a side, at the surface. They rove 9-inch steel cables under the hull in place of the earlier ones, then ran them up through hydraulic jacks on the flooded pontoons. These were necessary, since Stockholm Harbor has virtually no tides. On the twenty-fourth the jacks began working, as the pontoons were gradually unwatered.

NEW METHODS OF PRESERVATION

By May 4, she was floating on her own keel in the huge dry dock especially prepared to receive her. Holding her upright was a specially designed concrete platform float. In the dry dock was an extensive sprinkler system installed by the archaeologists so the vessel would not dry out, warp, and rot. Since the hull was the largest organic object ever to be preserved after sea-water immersion, new and bold techniques were developed.

While the preservation work went forward ashore, divers meanwhile were busy at the site where *Vasa* had lain. When they suspended underwater operations in 1967, twenty-four thousand articles had been brought up, fourteen thousand of which were the wooden carvings—

the ornamental grace notes—that had made *Vasa* such a beautifully ornate ship. The remains of eighteen people were found, and the vessel's longboat was recovered intact.

Until July 1970, the archaeologists subjected the timbers of the vessel to a continual spray of an impregnating, water-soluble plastic called polyethylene glycol as the mud was gradually removed (and checked for artifacts) from her interior. The polyethylene glycol stabilized the wood as it was; that is, it prevented dimensional change such as would have taken place with drying out. By preventing drying, they prevented rotting as well. Periodic checks were made on the amount of solution penetration into the thick oak timbers; the natural drying process, now that continual spraying has stopped, probably will take twenty years.

Small wooden objects were soaked in either an arsenic/carbon wax solution, or in the waxlike polyethylene glycol; in either case, the preservative agent gradually supplanted the water in the pores of the wood, saturating and preserving. Wrought-iron objects (muskets, swords, carpenters' tools) of course had disintegrated entirely, leaving only their wooden handles. Cast-iron implements (having a much higher carbon content) were restored to somewhere near their original condition by being heated in hydrogen.

Non-ferrous metals, as pointed out earlier, are little affected by salt-water immersion. The three 24-pounder bronze guns recovered (the rest had been removed by earlier salvors) were restored to such perfect condition that they have since been successfully fired! The makers of pewter vessels have been identified by the still perfectly legible hallmarks. One pewter flask contained, uncontaminated except for a bit of nickel leached from the pewter, the quart of rumlike liquor it had carried to the bottom three hundred years before. Ship's stores and gear—including clothes and boots—came through beautifully (the mud would account for that, as Marx found it had at Port Royal); indeed, butter from the ship's stores, although rancid, was still perfectly edible!

Until it can be determined how extensive will be the remains salvaged from the Columbus caravels discovered by Bob Marx in Jamaica, the *Vasa* will stand alone as our only firsthand example of European vessels during those years of emergence from the Middle Ages into the age of exploration and expansion: in the six hundred years between the eleventh-century Viking vessels recently found in Scandinavian dry digs, and the preserved *Victory* (Nelson's 1756 flagship), there is only the *Vasa*.

In fact, two Viking ships, *Fifa* and *Hjalp*, are known to lie somewhere beneath the sediment of Gulberwick Bay, in Britain's Shetland Islands. There is a good deal of historical evidence that the vessels were sunk there in 1151. They are only a very small part of the rich store of marine archaeological treasures that litter the seacoasts of Britain, for so many centuries the most powerful of all seafaring nations. Very little exploration has been done in these waters to date, because Britain's coastal waters are cold, rough, and treacherous; but there, as elsewhere, the advent of SCUBA gear is gradually making itself felt.

Without doubt, the central event in English history, from the viewpoint of marine archaeology, was the destruction of the Spanish Armada in September 1588. Following Elizabeth's execution of the Catholic Mary, Queen of Scots (1587), Philip II, already angered by England's constant aid to Spain's continental enemies and the raids by English freebooters on Spanish ships, decided to teach Britain a sharp lesson with the "Invincible Armada." The greatest fleet ever assembled (until D day, June 6, 1944, when the Allies crossed the English Channel to land at Normandy), the Armada boasted 130 ships, eight thousand sailors, and nineteen thousand soldiers, led by the flower of Spanish chivalry.

Against these were set a motley fleet of small, light, maneuverable vessels captained by such men as Drake and Effingham, relying on their "long toms"—heavy cannon useful at a distance—to offset the Spaniards' vastly superior fire- and manpower. Boarding and fighting the Spaniards hand to hand was definitely *not* the order of the day.

The result was disaster for Spain: less than a third of her ships got home again. The rest were harried along the Scottish and Irish coasts by the British ships; and those that escaped English seapower were destroyed by English wind and storm in a massive, furious gale.

Between thirty and forty of the ships were wrecked along the Scottish coasts alone; to an outside observer, half the lairds of the Hebrides seem to have dined out on this fact for nearly four hundred years.

THE GALLEON OF TOBERMORY BAY: INCREDIBLE BOONDOGGLE

The galleon that lies in Tobermory Bay, a natural harbor on the Isle of Mull, in the Hebrides, sums up better than any other ship the distortions that occur when nobody bothers to consult what records are available. It also points up again the ludicrous lure of sunken treasure.

Legend tells us the following about the ship in Tobermory Bay. She was either the *Florencia,* commanded by Dom Pareija; the *Flórida,* commanded by Captain Don Fareija; the *Duque de Florencia;* or the *San Francisco,* flagship of the Grand Duke of Tuscany. She was of 900 tons gross displacement, carried fifty-two guns, and had a crew of 486. She was the pay ship for the entire Armada, carrying (depending on whose legend we are using this week) either 30 million gold ducats or £30 million in gold. Her tables were "served in silver" for the officers. Pareija-Fareija tried to depart Tobermory Bay without paying for the provisions he had purchased, and then held as hostage one Donald Glas MacLean, who had been sent aboard to request payment.

MacLean (who sounds rather thick between the ears) laid a train of powder to the magazine and blew the vessel and everybody on her to smithereens (including himself) rather than let them duck out on their grocery bill in this scandalous manner.

That is legend. Fact is something else again.

Some unit of the Spanish Armada was blown up in Tobermory Bay in 1588, with a probable large loss of life. So much is indisputable. That it was the pay ship for anyone is nearly impossible.[5] That it was the *Duque de Florencia* is entirely impossible because the Archives of the Indies in Seville affirm that (a) the *Florencia* carried no gold, and (b) she returned safely to Spain. The view of scholars is that the Tobermory Bay ship is the innocuous *San Juan Baptista,* out of Sicily.

Besides, the entire pay for the Armada was only 1.26 million ducats a month so why would *any* ship be carrying 30 million? Were they planning a two-year siege? And finally, if the Tobermory Bay vessel *was* loaded with gold, would she have risked it all over a dozen ducats' worth of salt pork and hardtack?

On the other side of the ledger is the November 6, 1588, letter from the English Ambassador at Edinburgh to Christopher Marlowe's patron, Sir Francis Walsingham, remarking that the ship was "thought to be verie riche." In 1641, King Charles I gave consent through the Lord High Admiral to the Marquis of Argyll for an exclusive, hereditary warrant to search for the vessel. The Crown was to receive one hundredth of any recovered treasure. Two subsequent Dukes of Argyll were executed by later English monarchs (one several days before the warrant for his execution was signed) so the Crown could try to salvage the wreck for itself. Generalísimo Francisco Franco has written the 11th Duke of Argyll asking that the remains of any Spanish sailors found on the wreck be returned to Spain for burial.

It seems significant, however, that the first attempt to raise the treasure did not take place until 1608—twenty years after, just about the time for a tender rumor to become a full-grown, succulent legend. It is also significant that the salvors recovered nothing, even though the vessel at that time could be seen lying relatively intact on the sea floor.

The Marquis who received the royal warrant disappeared into history without a ripple, but in 1665 the then-current Earl of Argyll hired James Mauld, a diving-bell engineer, to raise the treasure. Argyll was to get one fifth. Mauld found three cannons in three months and quit. Argyll made his own bell, with which he raised another half dozen cannon.

A certain St. John Clare was hired (for a third of the take) by the Duke in 1676; he lasted two months. Hans Albricht van Treileben and Captain Adolfo Smith lasted even shorter times.

In 1677 the clan MacLean, who had supposedly blown the ship up in the first place, claimed they owned the remains because of the Spaniards' unpaid grocery bill. The Argylls won the ensuing litigation.

Three years later, the current Duke engaged one Archibald Miller as salvor. Miller found the vessel silted over in nine to twelve fathoms of water (depending on the state of the tide); he recovered several guns, ballast stones, and a silver bell; and hooked a "golden diademe," but his grapnel lost it before he could get it to the surface. Legend immediately identified this as the crown Philip had planned to wear as King of England. Miller also wrote a letter (November 20, 1683), stating, "I did see a number of dishes both great and small of a white bluish color, but whether they are pewter or plate I know not."

In 1730 a beautiful bronze gun, of French manufacture, was raised and put on display at Inverary Castle. Salvage attempts continued for the next 140 years, rewarded with small arms, cannon balls, coins. In 1870 the Marquis of Lorne hired a diver named Gush to search for the wreck (long since silted over, with its position lost) using an old Lorne family chart. Coins and a brass stanchion for the industrious Mr. Gush.

In 1902 it was a cannon, swords, and fifty coins. In 1903, a Glasgow syndicate got permission from Argyll to attempt salvage, raised a large conscription, and hired Captain William Burns as salvage master. Using a steam lighter, divers, and a sand pump, Burns discovered a mound on the bottom of the bay two hundred yards from the end of the Tobermory pier. Under the mound was a wreck, around it a few coins, some skulls, more cannon balls.

The syndicate was hard-nosed, however; it hadn't spent all of the subscribed money yet. In 1905 they were back with the steam sucker-dredger *Braemar*. With the *Braemar* was a water diviner, Mr. Stears, who claimed he could locate metal. *Somebody* could. The syndicate recovered several pieces of plate, as well as a massive silver candlestick of exceedingly fine design. In 1907, the syndicate went broke.

In 1912, a prodigiously tenacious American salvor, Colonel K. M. Foss, appeared on the scene, raising a breech block, some cannon balls, a few pieces of eight, pewter plate, and a gold coin or two. He said the vessel lay under thirty feet of silt and clay, eight fathoms deep at low tide, eighty-four yards from the steamboat pier. In 1919 Foss was still at it, but was struck with the full blast of one of his own water jets and injured so severely he had to quit. In those years, he had searched, dug, and sieved the bottom almost inch by inch.

Around 1920, one Margaret Naylor picked up working rights on the wreck, but apparently soon dropped them again. History tells us nothing of her efforts.

By 1922, *fifty separate expeditions* to recover the non-existent Tobermory treasure had been launched. They must stand as some sort of monument to the perverse support of Barnum's dictum that one is born every minute.

But 1922 does not mark the end of the affair. In that year it was our redoubtable John Iron[6] who was hired for the job. He did a thorough one. After devising an auger to bore through the clay and take samples from the vessel underneath, he "pricked out" the shape of the ship and buoyed the position with underwater buoys. The auger invariably hit wood, a six-foot blank space, wood, then Hungarian stone, which was undoubtedly ballast.

Next, Iron devised a "submarine cutter": a series of fanshaped blades rotated by a motor with a suction pipe for the loosened clay. With this he cleared the entire ship, leaving the ribs protruding about three feet above the mud bottom. He found a sort of "diademe" or crown of gold (perhaps the same one hooked by Miller in 1683), and a cannon with the initials "P" and "I"—quite possibly for Philip and Isabella.

In 1950 the current Duke of Argyll spent £4000 hiring Royal Navy divers to work the site. They found the vessel once again after shifting five thousand tons of sand and silt. This rewarded them with a section of charred timber and two silver medallions.

They kept searching. In 1954 Ian Douglass Campell, the 11th Duke of Argyll, was back once again with a Royal Navy team. This time it was led by SCUBA diver and wartime salvage hero Commander Lionel Crabb.[7] He didn't find anything, either.

In 1955, Underwater Surveys Ltd., a London salvage firm, used an ex-landing ship, tank (LST) for a sonar survey of the harbor. They ended up at that same abused, probed, sieved, and raked mound about a hundred yards from the Tobermory quay. They trenched the site in a professional marine-archaeologist manner, used an automobile crane as a grab, and slurried out the sediment with high-pressure seawater hoses. This netted them some ship's timber (lead-encased) and a cannon ball. They next used divers to outline the perimeter of the wreck with buoys, as had Iron more than thirty years before. Then they trenched all around the vessel with a dredge.

They found nothing more, and small wonder, after nearly four centuries of salvors had mucked about in the wreck. But the Dukes of Argyll apparently intend to keep searching.

Not that the Armada has been a bust for *every* British treasure seeker. Around the turn of the century, a hard-hat diver on a salvage job near Galway, Ireland, got into the habit of stopping off at a local inn for a pipe and a beer after work. One evening an old fisherman came over to him.

"Why don't ye thry for the galleon?" he demanded, coming right to the point.

"What galleon?"

"Why, yon one, wrecked just outside the bar. Ye can walk about the seabed in that suit of yours?"

"I do it every day," the diver assured him.

"Well, why don't ye walk out and get the treasure?"

Why not, indeed? When the job was done, the diver hung about, going out with the fisherman to drag the spot where the old salt claimed a Spanish galleon from the Armada lay. After a few weeks of this, the grapnel indeed hooked some obstruction, so the diver brought out his diving gear and, with the fisherman working the hurdy-gurdy (the hand pump supplying air to his helmet) he went over the side.

The diver found traces of what could have been a galleon, along with several barrels lying on the sea floor. Upon closer examination, these proved to be stacks of silver dollars; the barrels they had been packed in had long since rotted away, but the coins in this sheltered area had retained the shape in which they had been packed.

The loot, many thousands of pounds, was shared by the diver and the fisherman equally. The diver built a row of tract rental houses with his share and lived on the income for the rest of his life.

He called the row of houses Dollar Row.

LOOTING VS. ARCHAEOLOGY: THE SANTA MARÍA

A total of twenty-four ships of the Armada were wrecked by the intense storm along the Irish sea coast in September 1588. One of these, the *Santa María de la Rosa*, was believed to have gone down in Blasket Sound, near the tip of Ireland's Dingle Peninsula. According to the Archives of the Indies, in Seville, and the recorded testimony of the single survivor in London, she had carried 233 soldiers, sixty-three sailors, fifty thousand gold ducats, and fifty thousand silver coins of undetermined value. The existence of the treasure is fairly nebulous, since it rests on the testimony of the surviving sailor.

In the fall of 1968, a Welsh businessman, Sidney Wignall, sponsored an attempt by fifteen divers, led by Commander John Grattan of the Royal Navy, to locate the *Santa María*—claimed by some to have been the Armada flagship. In the area between three barren islands in Blasket Sound, swept by heavy seas and powerful currents, Grattan led his divers over a total of thirty thousand acres of sea floor in a grid search.

They discovered a long heap of ballast stones on a northwest-southeast axis. Delving beneath and around it, they found three sizes of cannon balls and some terra-cotta pottery.

In 1969, Wignall found his £11,000 investment in the site endangered by the appearance of a second set of salvors in the *Grey Dove*, a former Dutch mine sweeper, let by adventurer Ronald Potter.

"Quite frankly," said Potter, "we are after the money—and why not?"

Wignall countered with an injunction, from the Dublin High Court, forbidding the new, ten-man group of divers from "interfering" with the *Santa María*.

"This ship is of tremendous archaeological and historical interest," said Wignall. "It is of the greatest importance to protect it from people intent on plundering it for personal gain."

Since Wignall is backed by the Irish Tourist Board and five English and Irish universities—and holds sole salvage rights on the vessel from the Spanish and Irish governments—it seems likely he will be able to keep Potter's group off the site.

Meanwhile the treasure, if there is any, has eluded everyone.

AN EXCITING FIND: THE *ASSOCIATION*

One fact about early treasure ships has not eluded modern SCUBA-oriented salvors: even if the gold and silver cannot be found, the artifacts salvaged from the wreck often more than pay for the expense of the search. Such is certainly true of the *Association*, which was discovered in 1967 by several teams of divers on the Outer Gilstone Ledge of the Scilly Islands, not very distant in either time or location from the place where the *Torrey Canyon* went down.

The 90-gun man-o'-war *Association* was the flagship of Admiral Sir Clowdisley (or Cloudsley) Shovell, whom we last met in 1702, while he was busily losing the main Spanish prize ship after the raid on Vigo Bay by running it into an island. The intervening five years had not stiffened up Shovell's seamanship to any appreciable degree. On October 22, 1707 he sailed up the English Channel near Brittany, on his way home from a very lucrative harassment of Spanish and French shipping in the Mediterranean: his *Association* was loaded down with £3 million worth of bullion and silver. Accompanying him were the *Romney* and the *Eagle*, ships of the line; the 8-gun *Phoenix*; and a fire ship named *Firebrand*.

At least Shovell *thought* he was off Brittany. Due to a massive navigational error, he actually was just off the Scilly Islands. A hundred-mile error in the 750-odd miles since his last landfall (at Lisbon) might be considered a bit excessive even by the eighteenth century's imprecise standards of seamanship.

Excessive and deadly. The five ships piled into the Scillies at night to go down with a loss of two thousand lives. The Scilly Islanders took everything they could, including, apparently, the life of the Admiral himself. As Roland Morris, one of the eventual salvors, remarked, for the impoverished islanders the wrecks must have been "an act of grace almost too great to contemplate." On her deathbed many years later, an old island woman reported finding Admiral Shovell washed up on the beach, still alive but unconscious. She strangled him for the jewelry he wore. What makes her story believable is that Shovell was very fond of rings, especially one with an emerald set in diamonds, which the dying woman described perfectly.

In any event, the *Association* lay undisturbed by man on the Outer Gilstone Ledge—some seven miles from Land's End, in open, turbulent water—until June 1967, when Royal Navy divers from the Fleet Air Arm SCUBA team, captained by Commander J. Gayton and diving from the mine sweeper *Puttenham*, discovered twenty cannon on the ledge at fifteen fathoms. They also found a Portuguese coin.

They were working from a 1794 chart unearthed from Royal Navy Archives by Wardmaster Lieutenant Terry Montgomery, whose search had suggested the 800-by-50-yard area where the cannon had been found. They used flotation bags and oil drums blown with compressed air to bring the bronze cannon to the surface.

By July 12, they were recovering cannon balls, round shot, and pulley wheels (often found in association with wooden wrecks). Meanwhile, two civilian diving teams were on site also: a group led by Roland Morris, proprietor of the Admiral Benbow Inn, Cornwall, and an amateur salvage expert (the Blue Sea Divers); and Bill Sutton's group aboard a 150-ton survey ship, the *Regency*. Both groups had salvage and recovery contracts from the British Ministry of Defence.

In mid-July one of Morris' divers, Mark Horobin, found a 9½-inch silver plate bearing an elaborate coat of arms thought to be Shovell's. The certification of the arms took over a year, but in September 1968 Morris was notified that it was indeed the Admiral's personal plate.

The most bizarre find came in August. Under two cannon blasted loose from the reef was a thick layer of pitch in which was preserved a human skeleton. Clutched in one hand were five pieces of eight. Around the skull were other silver pieces stuck in the pitch.

"The man may have been filling his pockets with coins," diver Bob Rogers remarked, "after the ship struck the rocks and was sinking."

With the body were remnants of the man's uniform, the stem of his pipe, and his pewter spoon.

In October, the ex-Marine salvage men, lobster divers, and oilrig roughnecks who were doing the diving in their spare time, began issuing warnings to amateur divers on weekend forays to stay away. The work area was just a few feet from the white water and extremely hazardous. As Sutton remarked, "It needs just one young fool in a diving suit to scupper everything by drowning himself."

Work went on for over a year at the exposed site, with all the recovered artifacts going to the Receiver of Wrecks.[8]

The first auction of artifacts from the *Association* was held at Sotheby's of London in mid-1968: two magnificent bronze cannon were sold, as well as British, French, Spanish, and Portuguese gold and silver coins. The cannon were both French, one made in 1648 during the reign of Louis XIII, the other bearing the Royal Arms of Louis XIV. They were the finds of Roland Morris, and were bought by the gunmaking firm Holland & Holland for $14,400. The coins brought a like amount.

Morris claims his divers have now located a second of the 1707 wrecks, the ship of the line *Romney*. Meanwhile, a January 1970 auction at Sotheby's of London, offering further artifacts and coins from the *Association*, brought £10,175. Admiral Shovell's ornate pewter chamber pot went for a cool £270.

---

[1] See page 248.
[2] See page 370.
[3] See footnote 3, page 113.
[4] See page 66.
[5] As James A. Froude (1818–94), English historian, points out in a significant section on the Armada in his 12-volume English history, "Each galleon had its own treasury."
[6] See pages 158–59, 253–55, 338–39.
[7] See pages 133–34, 138–39, 291–93.
[8] As opposed to the United States, where laws regarding treasure or artifacts from wrecks are left to the individual states, Britain has a rigid system of control. After being held a year by the Receiver of Wrecks, the material is auctioned off by the Crown. The Board of Trade then determines how much the salvors will be given as an award. It usually runs ⅓ to ½ of realized value, less expenses.

CHAPTER TWENTY-NINE

Island Treasures

~~~~~~

It was on the night of April 28, 1789, off the Tongan island of Tofua, that Fletcher Christian's mutiny against Lieutenant William Bligh made romantic heroes of HMS *Bounty*'s load of breadfruit. The story has fascinated writers ever since: Bligh and his eighteen faithfuls in the twenty-three-foot longboat with only seven inches of freeboard, sailing 3618 nautical miles to Dutch Timor without the loss of a man; Christian, back to Tahiti, then off again with eight other mutineers (sixteen elected to remain in Tahiti), twelve Polynesian women and eight men, to disappear from the world for eighteen years.

AN ANCHOR FROM THE BOUNTY

In 1808 the *Topaz* of Boston touched at Pitcairn Island, thirteen hundred miles southeast of Tahiti, there to find the survivors, plus offspring, of the scuttled *Bounty*. Only one mutineer was still alive; the others had killed each other off or had been killed by the Tahitians in fights over the women.

Novelists Nordhoff and Hall fictionalized the *Bounty* story so completely (and yet so accurately)[1] that one forgets the *Bounty* was an actual ship, which was run aground and scuttled on January 23, 1790.

Yet as early as 1933 the vessel's rudder was found at six fathoms in Bounty Bay. It ended up in a museum at Suva, Fiji, where photographer-writer-SCUBA diver Luis Marden saw it. If the rudder, he reasoned, why not more? In late fall 1956, Marden arrived on Pitcairn with his diving gear. First he talked with the fisherman who, in 1933, had found the planks, timbers, and pintles (pins or bolts by which the rudder had been fastened to the transom of the vessel) and had the man show him the site of discovery.

In the surf near shore was a pile of iron ballast bars from the *Bounty*; Marden reasoned that they had been used to warp the vessel ashore after a stern anchor had been put out. Then, before she was burned, a bow line would have been fastened to a tree on the edge of the rocky inlet. He spent six fruitless weeks searching between the ballast iron and the place where the pintles and rudder had been found. No sign of the vessel.

Then, in February 1957, Irving Johnson's yacht *Yankee* called at Pitcairn. While skin diving *outside* the bay, *Yankee*'s crewmen ran across the *Bounty*'s stern anchor, which Marden had deduced should be somewhere out there.[2] It was twelve feet long and in the old (straight-V flukes) Admiralty pattern; round-fluked anchors were not adopted by the Royal Navy until 1810. The *Bounty* had carried five anchors—two bowers, a sheet, a stream, and a kedge.

The *Yankee* hooked it with its own anchor; SCUBA divers then wired the flukes together so both could be lifted from the sea floor. The discovery gave Marden the idea that the ship, while burning, might have also been drifting. He shifted his search operation and soon came across a crescent-shaped oarlock, then a long sandy trench marked with little squiggly protuberances. These turned out to be coral-encrusted sheathing nails. Finally, two more trenches.

The three together neatly outlined the sunken vessel's one-hundred-foot hull. The burning *Bounty* had been veered westward by prevailing winds and currents, her bow pivoting toward shore while her stern had swung in an arc. Marden confirmed the find as the *Bounty* when he brought up some intact one-eighth-inch copper sheathing. Each section of it was marked with the three bold strokes—in the form of a broad arrowhead—that marked all Royal Navy fittings of the eighteenth century.

The *Bounty* was the only such vessel to have foundered at Pitcairn.

THE WRECK OF THE *BATAVIA*

Another famous South Seas wreck with a mutiny involved was the *Batavia*, which sailed from Amsterdam as the flagship of a Dutch East India Company fleet bound for her namesake, Batavia, Java (present-day Djakarta, Indonesia), on October 27, 1628. Besides cloth, wine, cheeses, and trade goods, the big (140 feet long, forty feet in the beam, six hundred tons of cargo) vessel carried twelve bound chests of silver coins worth a quarter million guilders, and a casket of jewels. The voyage was scheduled for a possible four years.

Unknown to Commandeur of the Fleet Francisco Pelsaert, the *Batavia*'s two most senior officers, Captain Ariaen Jacobsz and Undermerchant Jeronimus Cornelisz, had subverted eighty of the army cadets aboard and many of the crewmen. A chief cause of Jacobsz' hatred for Pelsaert—apart from envy—was the attention paid to the Commandeur by a married woman among the passengers, Lucretia van der Mylen, after whom Jacobsz lusted. Cornelisz apparently was just a thoroughly corrupt individual.

During a storm south of Africa's Cape of Good Hope, Jacobsz separated the vessel from the rest of the fleet; the mutineers planned to take over when *Batavia* reached Australia, loot her, and then use her for piracy against other V.O.C. (Vereenighde Oost-Indische Compagnie, true name of the Dutch East India Company) merchantmen.

But the best-laid schemes o' mice an' men, as Robbie Burns was fond of remarking, gang aft a-gley. Unbeknownst to the plotters, between them and Australia lay a whole archipelago of low sand islands, the Abrolhos.

Jacobsz sailed blindly into the Easter group of this deathtrap, all reefs, odd currents, and giant surf, and at 4:00 A.M. on June 3, 1629, struck the barrier coral. As some strove to get the panic-stricken passengers ashore, below decks the soldiers and gunners had broached the wine and brandy, and had settled down to serious looting. At 10:00 A.M. real disaster struck: the ship's timbers burst, flooding the fresh-water barrels no one had bothered to remove, and swamping the bread locker no one had bothered to empty.

On June 6, Commandeur Pelsaert and some of the sailors slipped away before dawn (his point of departure was quickly dubbed Traitor's Island) in the ship's only longboat, leaving 250 people behind, including Cornelisz and eighty others still aboard the foundering *Batavia*.

On the twelfth, the ship broke up; Cornelisz (who could not swim) was washed ashore dramatically on the bowsprit, to find the plans for mutiny still festering despite the disaster. He took over; since water and food were scarce, he advocated slaughtering everyone not in the plot, then shanghaiing the rescue vessel that Pelsaert was supposed to fetch from Batavia—assuming that he arrived there at all.

The only group capable of opposing the mutineers was the veteran mercenary force under Weibbe Hayes; while the cadets (of noble families) had fallen in with the murderous plans joyfully, the despised mercenaries had been cold to the plotters' veiled suggestions. Twenty days after the wreck, therefore, Cornelisz sent the soldiers off in a homemade boat to one of the higher islands to the north, on the pretext that they should seek desperately needed water.

His idea was to maroon this score of stout fighters and let them die of thirst. On July 4, as soon as the soldiers were out of sight, the butchering began. Everyone was slaughtered except the few who joined the mutineers, hoping to save their own lives, and the younger, more palatable women who were kept for the mutineers' pleasures. Lucretia van der Mylen became Cornelisz' private mistress. All together, 125 unsuspecting people were murdered.

Meanwhile, Pelsaert reached Batavia safely on July 7. On the fifteenth, the rescue ship *Sardam* left Java for Australia.

In the Abrolhos, the mutineers were being smashed against a rock they had not expected. During the confusion of their nighttime slaughterings, some of their intended victims had escaped and had waded at low tide to the high island (now called Wallabi Island) where Weibbe Hayes and his staunch mercenaries had been marooned to die of thirst. Unfortunately for the mutineers, Hayes actually had found water. The newcomers not only brought news of the barbaric slaughter: they incidentally swelled Hayes's force of totally unarmed souls to forty-seven.

Hayes cheerfully named his group The Defenders, armed them with barrel-hoop pikes and morning stars (driftwood clubs with ship's spikes pounded into them), erected two solid defensive positions, and drilled his men in the use of their makeshift arms.

Despite the mutineers' muskets, Hayes managed to beat off three of their attacks, and on September 2 Cornelisz went ashore on Wallabi under a flag of truce. He was determined to outwit the stupid clod of a soldier who had proved such an unforeseen obstacle. With the Captain-General (as Cornelisz had taken to calling himself) was the "High Command Staff": four self-styled "lieutenants" who had orders to get the French soldiers among Hayes's mercenaries off to one side.

During the mutineers' next attack, the lieutenants explained, the Frenchmen should attack Hayes's rear so his forces would be caught in an unexpected pincers movement. For this, each Frenchman would receive six thousand guilders in blood money.

But it didn't happen that way, because there was a prearranged signal to Hayes, one worked out by that stupid clod of a soldier in advance to forestall any treachery that might be proposed. The lieutenants were stabbed to death by the tough, loyal Frenchmen; Cornelisz was taken alive, chained, and kept in an earthen prison under heavy guard.

The rest of the mutineers, in desperation, launched a frontal assault on September 17. And on the same day, the *Sardam*, which had reached the latitude of the wrecked *Batavia* on August 20, but had spent the intervening month in fruitlessly sailing up and down the western side of Australia, anchored near Wallabi Island to send a boat ashore. Hayes was just beating off the mutineers once again, and both sides saw the *Sardam* at the same time. Both sides made for it, one to warn, the other to seize. Hayes told Pelsaert, who was in the longboat, of the mutiny; Pelsaert refused to believe him. Then, however, he looked about and saw the heavily armed mutineers making for the *Sardam*. He made his decision on whom to believe: when the mutineers arrived, they found the swivel cannon gaping at their scow, as well as sailors lining the rails with cocked and loaded muskets.

They surrendered without firing a shot.

After being "examined"—being subjected to the water torture later brought to such vicious perfection by the Nazis—all of them confessed to their crimes. Cornelisz held out the longest, ten days, but finally broke. Confessions, under then-current Dutch law, were required before sentence could be passed.

Cornelisz and six others had their right hands chopped off, then were hanged at Seal's Island on October 2. The two youngest mutineers were marooned on the Australian mainland, where hunger, thirst, and the aborigines probably made short shrift of them. The rest were returned to Batavia, systematically broken on the wheel, and publicly hanged on January 30, 1630.

THE SEARCH FOR THE *BATAVIA*

Neither the *Batavia* nor the savage fate of its more savage mutineers was soon forgotten: it had been the first and was to be the last mutiny aboard a Dutch East India ship. The actual site of the hulk, however, was soon forgotten. Western Australia was not settled until 1829, two hundred years after the *Batavia* stranding; the Abrolhos were not surveyed until 1837, when HMS *Beagle* undertook the task. On arbitrary grounds, the surveyors decided that the *Batavia* had been lost on the southern, not the northern tip of the chain, and therefore named the largest island Pelsaert's Island. Searching this island for an 8000-rix-dollar chest the mutineers were supposed to have buried, became a favorite pastime of visitors, tourists, and fishing parties—fifty-four miles away from the *Batavia*'s actual location.

In 1948 an Australian novelist, Henrietta Drake-Brockman, while researching a novel about the incident (*The Wicked and the Fair*, published in 1957), got a copy of Pelsaert's original journal from The Hague. After studying it, she announced grandly that the *Batavia* lay in the northern, not the southern, group. A remarkably bitter controversy was stirred up by her assertion; but one man she convinced was SCUBA enthusiast Hugh Edwards, a writer for the West Australian Newspapers Alliance who had been on several marine archaeological digs in the Mediterranean.

Edwards talked his editor into sending him and photographer Maurie Hammond on an underwater search for the wreck. Three weeks in April 1960 netted them only some "human arm bones," which turned out to be the wing bones of a large sea bird.

In 1963 another SCUBA diver, Max Cramer, talked Edwards out of his research notes, then subsequently found the *Batavia* on the outer reef just a few hundred yards from the spot Edwards and Hammond had searched. He returned with a small cannon and a human skull as proof of his discovery.

Six weeks later, on July 28, 1963, Edwards was back with Hammond and Cramer, two 75-foot salvage vessels, diving equipment, enough cash for immediate needs, and Lieutenant "Hec" Donohue of the Australian Navy's SCUBA team to direct recovery operations.

Batavia was lying at three fathoms on a storm-blasted ledge of dead coral off the outer reef near East Wallabi Island. The sea had enlarged the original gully, and her keel had crashed through the coral, so the ship lay in a "grave" two hundred feet long and twelve feet deep. Some twenty feet down, they found bronze cannons, twelve-foot anchors, bits of blackened oak woodwork, pottery, and the colonnades of a building façade that had been shipped on the *Batavia*. Around the vessel was that unnatural piebald coloring that is itself a dead giveaway to a wreck: bright verdigris stains from the brass, white from the lead, iodine from the iron.

Small but heavy items were brought up with gasoline-drum "balloons" in the usual manner (each 44-gallon drum exerts four hundred pounds of lift when blown with compressed air), and the wreck and the guns' positions were mapped: a grid of ropes with fathoms markings was laid across the site, compass bearings were taken, and the figures were transferred to a marking slate.

A torpedo gantry was fastened to a raft of twenty oil drums lashed together; it was with this that Donohue's team of Army and Navy divers planned to lift the cannons: A sling would be fastened to a gun, a chain from the gantry would be hooked to that, and two burly sailors would winch down on the gantry until the coral holding the cannon gave. With the cannon swinging free underneath, the raft would move over to the salvage ship, where a heavy wooden derrick would lift it aboard.

But some of the cannons required small explosive charges to free them; others weighed three tons, too heavy for the salvage ship's boom. Work was delayed while an all-metal boom was installed.

As they brought up one 3-tonner, a twenty-five-foot wave (not at all unusual even during the "calm" part of the year!) swept over the reef. The slings holding the cannon parted. Freed of its weight, raft and sailors went soaring right over the reef, then were tumbled over and over by the wave like wind-blown leaves. The berserk cannon went careening and smashing about among the divers in a welter of foam so tremendous that they did not even know which way was the surface, which the reef.

By some weird chance, no one was hurt—although the back of one man's head actually was brushed with the 250-pound winch as it let go.

They also salvaged a number of loose rix-dollars—merely green "biscuits" until the coral was cleaned off—by prying them off the reef with a screwdriver. Some of the coins had been worn to thin, almost translucent wafers by wave action; a rix-dollar was by definition 94 per cent silver,[3] soft and easily worn.

Beneath the coral they found ribs and even planking of the *Batavia*. Brass canisters still reeked of the gunpowder they once had contained. Stern-faced Bellarmine jugs (pot-bellied earthenware pots for booze) still lampooned Cardinal Robert Bellarmine, the anti-Protestant Inquisition leader when Holland was under the Spanish thumb in the early 1600s.

Other significant artifacts were the calibrated rim from a celestial globe, a navigator's protractor and mapping dividers, a chemist's mortar, and two astrolabes—one a type previously uncatalogued by museums.

The expedition ended in August 1963, just two weeks after it had started.

The *Batavia* is not the only historically or archaeologically interesting wreck on the Abrolhos Archipelago, but it is the only one that has been verified and extensively worked. Another with an intriguing history that might sometime attract SCUBA-wearing marine archaeologists is the *Zeewyk*, a 1727 Dutch wreck that broke up after impaling herself on the reef. Her crew somehow salvaged *seven tons* of treasure from the vessel, then used her timber to build themselves a tiny sloop to transport the booty back to Batavia, where they dutifully turned it back to the officials of the V.O.C.

Another Dutch wreck in Australian waters that has received some amateur diving attention is the 1656 wreck *Vergulde Draeck* (Golden Dragon). The guns and anchors of this vessel had been so fused into the reef that divers went by them for years without seeing anything unusual.

Finally a fifteen-year-old schoolboy named Graeme Henderson dived into a coral cave and found, sticking out of the reef, what he first thought was a section of sewer pipe but what closer examination proved to be an elephant's tusk. He brought back his father, James Henderson, and a number of other divers. Besides more ivory, they found the cannons and anchors, pottery, and Spanish pieces of eight.

Although successful treasure seekers of Spanish loot have mainly worked the Caribbean, there actually were four major treasure routes used at various times by Spain, England, France, Portugal, and Holland. First was the 1500–1820 Caribbean route, with $8 billion in treasure carried, at a conservative estimate, and $600 million lost. The second route was much longer, from Peru around Cape Horn (1534–1810) to Spain, with only about $2 billion carried and $50 million lost. Third was the Acapulco–Philippines run by the Manila galleons from 1570–1850. This was a hard-luck route: an estimated half of the $1 billion carried was lost. Finally was the Spice Route from 1502 to 1870, with the ships operating loaded each way between Europe and the Far East. Of the estimated $2 billion carried, $50 million was lost.

THE GREAT BASSES

One of the most dangerous areas through which the vessels had to pass on the Spice Route were the Great and Little Basses (the name comes from the Portuguese *baixos*, or reefs), two reefs that parallel the southern coast of Ceylon for about ten miles. On the Basses is probably a greater concentration of wrecks than anywhere else in the world except the Caribbean and the Aegean. Not only are the reefs a beautifully designed deathtrap for unwary vessels; they lie across what has been a main shipping route for three thousand years. The first stone lighthouse (still standing) was erected on Great Basses in 1873 to a design by the creator of the Eddystone light.

SCUBA diver Mike Wilson first visited the Great Basses with Rodney Jonklass in 1958, returning the next year with famed scientist and science-fiction writer Arthur C. Clarke. Because diving on the exposed Basses reef must be done in the slack period between the northeast and southwest monsoons, April and May normally are the only months when it is possible. Unusually calm weather, however, enabled Wilson and two young American boys, Bobby Kriegel and Mark Smith (then fourteen and thirteen respectively) to get out on Great Basses in March 1961 to film a fantasy about a little boy who dreams he is exploring underneath the sea, only to find upon awaking that he really is.

On March 22, diving only with masks, flippers, and snorkels, they saw a cannon ball, and then a small cannon, on the outer lip of a section of reef they had never visited before. In a submarine canyon on the inner side was another small swivel cannon with its brass polished a bright gold by wave action over some 250 years.

In the afternoon they returned with cameras and SCUBA gear. A five-foot cannon was found, as well as two huge anchors. Then a dozen cannons all piled together. Near them, Wilson began finding silver coins.

The next day they returned with knives, crowbars, chisels, and a netted inner tube for holding their finds, which included several bags of loose coins and some chunks of oxidized silver coins. The next day yielded four more lumps of coins, weighing twenty-five to thirty pounds each. When the lumps were broken open, the coins inside were found to be in mint condition. Cleaned in battery acid, they displayed Persian script and a date, in Arabic, of 1113. Since Moslems count time from Mohammed's Hegira, and use a lunar calendar with 355 days instead of our solar calendar with 365, this date worked out to A.D. 1702.

Wilson and the boys returned to Colombo to confer with Clarke. For the next year they tried to establish where the coins had come from, and who now legally owned them. The coins proved to be rupees from the year 45 in the reign of the Mogul Aurangzeb, who ruled most of India from 1658 to 1707; they had been minted in the northwest province of Surat. Each "lump" of coins once had been a bag of one thousand rupees in mint condition; the vessel obviously had been carrying a consignment of silver from India, probably direct from the Surat mint. Mendel Peterson of the Smithsonian could state positively only that the swivel guns were of probable oriental design.

Legal problems grew from the fact that the Great Basses lay just outside Ceylon's six-mile limit, and therefore it seemed there was no one to pass definitive legal judgment on Wilson's claim of ownership.

By February 1962, they were equipped for a proper gold-hunting expedition, with an ancient boat called *Ran Muthu* ("Pearls and Gold") and skin-diving equipment that included a powerful Cornelius 380 air compressor capable of filling a standard Aqualung tank in fifteen minutes. Clarke was seriously injured in an accident at the last minute, however, so it was not until March 16, 1963, that *Ran Muthu* left Colombo. Aboard were Wilson, Rodney Jonklass, and two Ceylonese boatmen: Martin and Laza. They were to be met at the fishing village of Tangalle by Clarke and Hector Ekanayake, who were going down by truck.

Bad weather prevented getting out to the reef, and while they were waiting they found that a new legal ruling placed the Great Basses within Ceylon's territorial waters, where they already held a permit to excavate the site from the government. They also received word that Peter Throckmorton[4] was flying out from Greece to join the expedition.

Throckmorton arrived with several underwater cameras and a submarine balloon hoist for lifting heavy objects under water; along with photographer A. P. Pieris, he completed the expedition's personnel. The salvors lived in a service shed maintained by the lighthouse staff, and under Throckmorton's direction worked the wreck as an archaeological rather than a treasure dig.

The site was sixty feet long, with the anchors at one end and the cannons in the middle, lying at six fathoms in a gully some thirty to forty feet wide jumbled with iron, loose silver coins, musket balls, and cannons. Throckmorton took wood samples and some ballast stones in hopes of identifying or at least dating the wreck; at night he would knock apart coral clumps brought up during the day.

On April 14, 1963, Throckmorton returned to *Ran Muthu* from the site (which could be approached only with their dinghies), to tell Clarke, "I've found the mother lode. There's at least a ton there."

He had found a whole pile of the silver cylinders, which of course were of more archaeological and intrinsic value as they were, than broken up into individual coins. Eight more large lumps were found on their last day of diving.

Besides the silver, little else was recovered apart from the anchors and the cannons; the latter they broke from the reef with an auto jack, as Frédéric Dumas had done at Gelidonya.[5] The cannons had no crests or insignia, but a series of numbers stamped into them (2, 3, 23, 8) gave Mendel Peterson back in Washington enough information to identify them as British.[6]

As with the *Vasa*, Clarke, Wilson, and Throckmorton attempted to preserve as many of the artifacts as possible. The silver coins were cleaned either by an electrolytic process or by a two-bath process (sodium sulphite and hydrochloric acid to remove the coral, then thiourea and hydrochloric acid to remove the outer layer of black silver sulfide). It was due to the cannons that the silver had lasted so well during immersion; the corrosion product, mixed with gunpowder, pitch, and 20 per cent sand, had been an excellent preservative.

The wood fragments were preserved with successive alcohol baths to remove the water, followed by two baths of xylene (with a saturation solution of paraffin added to the second). The paraffin filled the pores, preserving the wood indefinitely in its original shape.

The cannons were bathed in sodium hydroxide, then tapped with a hammer to remove the coral crust. Then another sodium hydroxide bath, with, later, zinc metal added to form a white deposit of zinc oxide as the oxygen was drawn from the cannons' corroded surface. Finally, after the zinc oxide was dissolved with mild sulphuric acid, the cannons were dried and coated with a clear synthetic lacquer or plastic solution. Smaller iron objects could be coated with hot paraffin following the treatment, instead of lacquer or plastic. •

The wreck they discovered on Great Basses has never been accurately dated (apart from the date on the coins) or identified. It was a vessel 125 feet long at a minimum, however, and had carried twenty-four guns. This fits the specifics of a common seventeenth- and eighteenth-century type of Dutch vessel known as a *fluyt*.

THE PORT AU PRINCE

Sometimes the salvors of treasure vessels do not have quite such ideal relations with the local government as Wilson and Clarke had in Ceylon. A quite amusing example of this occurred in 1969 in the South Pacific island kingdom of Tonga.

In 1805 a French-built but English-operated 32-gun warship, the 500-ton *Port au Prince*, sailed from London with a crew of ninety-six and a specific assignment. She was to attack Spanish settlements on both the east and west coasts of South America. Attack she did, ransacking seaports, kidnapping haughty Spanish grandees for ransom, looting churches and convents of their gold and silver candelabra, crucifixes, incense holders and chalices, and creating her own little *auto da fé* by burning Ilo, Peru, to the ground.

The *Port au Prince*'s sins caught up with her in November 1806, when she ran head-on into a reef on the western coast of Tonga's Haano Island. Before they could get her off, the hardy, fun-loving Tongans got aboard, massacred seventy of her crew, and relit the fires of faith by putting the ship to the torch.

In 1969 three Australians, running a game-fishing charter business at Tonga, were SCUBA diving around the northern tip of Haano when they ran across the remains of the *Port au Prince*. Colin Prast of Auckland, spokesman for the three, admitted that the find was essentially luck.

"People had been looking for the wreck over the years on the western side of the island. But what had happened was that the burning ship had drifted away and been carried around the northern tip of the island by the strong current there."

Prast and his partners found three big iron strongboxes, which, he said, contained some thirty tons of coins—gold and silver. He estimated the value of the find at $22 million.

"We cut one open," he reported. "There is no doubt it's from the *Port au Prince*."

Meanwhile, a Tongan had reported to the government that the SCUBA divers were using explosives on the reef without government permission. When an argument arose between the divers and the government—which has an annual budget of less than $1 million and was claiming the treasure—the divers' launch was seized, and forty-eight-hour deportation notices were served on Prast's partners. Tonga hired her own divers, spending $22,000 to outfit them and secure metal-detectors.

But they found no treasure.

Prast's lawyer flew up from New Zealand to get the diving launch returned, while Prast delivered to the press a bit of news calculated to explain the government's ill luck.

"We have moved the treasure from its original position. I don't think the Tongan Government will find it, no matter how long they look for it." He went on to explain, "A Queen's Counsel in Auckland told us the treasure was legally the property of King Taufa'ahau Tupou. But if his men can't find it I think we are entitled to at least a reward, if not a substantial share."

At last report, Prast and his partners are sitting tight, prepared to wait out the Tonganese expedition, while unofficial government sources on Haano indicated that they might soon be willing to talk things over.

AN INGENIOUS JAPANESE OPERATION

Perhaps the best way to close this discussion of archaeological salvage is with an 1850s Japanese operation, for it shows better than almost any other story the endless inventiveness of man when coping with the endless inventiveness of the sea.

An open boatload of imperial vases had sunk in the Sea of Japan, and the Emperor, quite naturally, wanted them back. Once the ship had been located, he ordered the only salvors available, naked Japanese divers, to go down for the vases.

The water depth, however, was far beyond the diving capabilities of these unequipped men, for they were without suits, helmets, or breathing apparatus of any sort. However, they did have a vast knowledge of the sea and its inhabitants.

In the shallows, the divers captured large numbers of small octopuses, then returned to the boats anchored over the sunken vases. To each octopus they tied a line and then lowered the writhing, frightened creatures to the wreck.

The octopus, despite his bad press and (to some) threatening or positively loathsome appearance, is the soul of gentleness. He is very shy, very timid, preferring, as do most cephalopods, to live out his life in some safe cranny or cave. If no cave is available, the octopus will hide in any nook he can find.

A nook, say, about the size of an imperial vase.

As expected, the octopi immediately upon reaching the wreck rushed into the jars, dragging their lines with them, and each of them braced himself with the suction cups of his tentacles against the inside curve of his individual vase. But since he was still fastened to his line, octopus and vase were then drawn to the surface without any trouble.

Recovery of the lost vases was total.

---

[1] Charles Nordhoff and James Norman Hall, *The Bounty Trilogy* (Little, Brown & Co., 1932), comprising "Mutiny on the Bounty," "Men Against the Sea," and "Pitcairn's Island."

[2] Another of the *Bounty's* anchors had been found a few years earlier in Matavai Bay, Tahiti, where the ship had anchored before Christian had taken it off into oblivion.

[3] The very term is a misnomer, since the coins could be from any country as long as they were a standard size and weight: Spanish pieces of eight, English crowns, German talers, Dutch ducatons (dollars—itself a corruption of the Dutch "taaler").

[4] See pages 377–78.

[5] See page 378.

[6] The numbers referred to weight. Peterson suggested that the cannon should weigh 331 pounds each. They weighed 332. It was later found that the extra pound came from coral still adhering to the guns.

VIII

Tomorrow...

Tomorrow we again embark
upon the boundless sea.
  HORACE
  Odes, Book I, vii.

CHAPTER THIRTY

Fish-Men and Submersibles

For the individual man beneath the sea, tomorrow belongs to the SCUBA diver and the almost science-fiction fish-man implicit in him. As the hard-hat diver made the iron duke obsolete, so the unencumbered man in a flexible rubber suit is making the cumbersome copper-pated man an anachronism in deep water.

As early as summer 1947, Cousteau's Undersea Research Group did a series of deep SCUBA dives to discover all they could about nitrogen narcosis—the "rapture of the deep" or "depth drunkenness," which could kill a man by making him gay and carefree. Diving master Maurice Fargues, hauled up from a depth-record attempt after he stopped sending periodic signals up the shot rope, was met at 150 feet by backup diver Jean Pinard.

Fargues's mouthpiece was hanging freely out of his mouth; in all probability he had gaily jettisoned it after writing his name on the slate tied off at sixty-six fathoms—396 feet. They tried unsuccessfully for twelve hours to revive him.

This suggested that the limits for SCUBA, at least with compressed air, were the same as for hard-hat divers: fifty fathoms. A SCUBA diver named Hope Root exceeded this 300-foot limit in 1953, equaling the Fargues record with four hundred feet—but he was also killed in the attempt.

WORLD-RECORD SCUBA DIVE ON COMPRESSED AIR

Then, in June 1968, American SCUBA divers Neal Watson and John Gruener began serious training for an attempt at the record. After first researching and calibrating a new set of diving tables for depths in excess of fifty fathoms (where the U. S. Navy decompression tables stop), they made daily practice dives beyond 250 feet for several months, trying to habituate themselves to nitrogen narcosis. Their goal was to make placing a marker clip on the shot line an automatic action.

During the practice dives, Watson reported interesting side effects from the nitrogen, not noted by earlier divers. One was a tremendous hostility: beyond two hundred feet, he often had a great urge to kill Gruener—who was having the same urges about him. Both men suffered unnerving double vision and shattering vertigo, a feeling that they were spinning around and around as they swam down the line—which seemed horizontal instead of vertical.

They made their record attempt on October 14, 1968, with a weighted line 450 feet long in water two thousand feet deep. At 50, 150, 200, and 250 feet were safety divers on compressed air; on the boat was a fifth diver, equipped with heliox, to go down after them if they got into trouble.

Nitrogen narcosis struck both of them at three hundred feet—fifty fathoms—but they kept doggedly going down. On their return, Watson could not remember setting his clip on the line. When it was drawn up, both his and Gruener's clips were at 437 feet, one inch.

Extremely deep *experimental* dives,[1] of course, have been made by frogman-type divers for years. Sealab aquanauts wear this sort of gear, and once Sealab gets back in operation—as it inevitably will—men will soon be using undersea habitats to swim and work at depths of one thousand feet.

As long ago as January 1968, five men in a special pressure tank at Duke University were submitted to three days of pressure equaling thirty atmospheres (165 fathoms, 990 feet). They were breathing a mixture of highly compressed oxygen (1%), nitrogen (3.6%) and helium (95.4%); the helium, obviously, had been substituted for nitrogen as the carrier gas for the oxygen because of its desirable properties: lightness (one-seventh nitrogen's density), chemical inertness, virtual insolubility (thus entering the blood stream much less readily than nitrogen), and low volatility factor. Yet it still took them eleven days to decompress. This experiment was under the guidance and control of the Navy's Experimental Diving Unit (EDU).

Just thirteen months later, on February 16, 1969, experiments in another direction were made in the 160-ton Project Tektite capsule at seven fathoms on the floor of Beehive Cove, St. John, Virgin Islands. Geologist H. Edward Clifton, oceanographers Richard A. Waller and Conrad Mahnken, and marine biologist John Vanderwalker spent two months in an enriched nitrogen atmosphere to see how they would stand up to the prolonged isolation and confinement, and how their bodies would withstand the constant immersions outside the capsule.

One rather amusing feature of the General Electric-designed equipment was the ring of circular, eighteen-foot-high cages (called "phone booths" by the aquanauts) with domed tops in which air was trapped for use by the divers if their SCUBA tanks should fail. These were no more nor less than miniature diving bells, really very similar to those invented by Lorini in 1531 and described by Francis Bacon in 1620.[2] Man's inventiveness is often circular rather than progressive.

Following the tragic end of Sealab III,[3] the Navy's EDU carried out, in the Duke University chamber, extensive retesting of the type of breathing apparatus used in the February 1969 fatality. Six divers spent fourteen days in the tank at pressures equaling the depth at which Cannon had died (one hundred fathoms—six hundred feet), and were periodically plunged into 45-degree water in another chamber to test the body's physiological reactions to abrupt chilling while subjected to that pressure.

Strange things happen in the chambers when pressure is rapidly raised or lowered. Professor J. B. S. Haldane, son of John Scott Haldane, the Scots physiologist who first suggested "stage" decompression for divers,[4] was being rapidly decompressed—and feeling no ill effects from it—when one of his teeth suddenly exploded.

The tooth had recently been filled; below the filling, a minute air pocket had remained. The rapid decompression made the air expand too rapidly to leak away through microscopic fissures around the filling—so it exploded the tooth.

Another fact of life for men undergoing rapid compression or decompression is burst or ruptured eardrums.

"The drum usually heals up," Haldane has remarked. "And if a hole remains in it, although one is somewhat deaf, one can blow tobacco smoke out of the ear in question—which is a social accomplishment."

In recent years, the old term "squeeze" has taken on a new meaning. There are now sinus squeezes and inner-ear squeezes and elbow squeezes— the term covers any air pocket in the body that cannot get equalized with the ambient water pressure during an ascent. Haldane's exploding filling might be referred to as a "tooth squeeze."

Interior squeezes can be deadly as well as painful. The two most common are the air embolism, already briefly discussed in submarine escape techniques, and pneumothorax.

Air embolisms occur when air in the lung ruptures the lining and makes a transfer to the blood stream. It then is carried to the heart and possibly the brain, where it creates a dead spot. In either case, the embolism could be fatal.

Pneumothorax occurs also when the lung ruptures under internal air pressure, but in this case the air escapes to the chest cavity around the lung. The lung promptly collapses. This allows the bubble of still-expanding air to work over to the other lung and collapse that also. Death, in this case, is inevitable.

Air embolism and pneumothorax occur most often during submarine escape, when the escaping crewman panics and holds his breath. Statistical studies of World War II submarine escape attempts led the Navy, in 1956, to scrap the famed Momsen Lung, which was first adopted in 1929. Until 1964, the Navy followed the British practice of free ascent— no breathing device used at all—assisted only by a gradually inflating life jacket. It then adapted the Steinke hood, an invention of Lieutenant Harris E. Steinke that was tested by him and Commander Walter F. Mazzone.

This is merely a hood with a transparent facepiece that is attached to the escapee's life vest. Into the hood go the diver's exhalations and the air bled from his life vest as it expands during the ascent. This keeps his head dry and gives the wearer a tremendous psychological advantage. This in turn aids him in the vital task of continuous exhaling until he reaches the surface.

Current SCUBA suits will be useless at great depth, since the air cells in the sponge-rubber insulation collapse under pressure, dissipating the diver's body heat into the water faster than the body can produce it. U. S. Rubber has developed a material, however, that has the insulating air cells joined together and then sandwiched between thin rubber layers. The suit has its own regulator valve, which keeps the air cells at a pressure equal to that of the ambient water pressure.[5]

Even a suit of this material, however, would not do the job if the depth (i.e., pressure) were great enough and the exposure long enough. To retain body heat under extreme conditions, augmentation by an electrical or chemical heat source is necessary.

Promising steps in this direction have been made by the Atomic Energy Commission, which has developed a radioisotope-powered, heated wet suit. Should feasibility tests confirm laboratory findings, this suit would allow a diver to remain indefinitely in cold water under extreme pressure without loss of body heat—and thus, of course, without undue loss of energy.

New SCUBA suits are not the only innovations, however. In both industry and the military there is a bewildering proliferation of new diving *systems*. They are usually called Mark-something or DDS (Deep Diving System)-something; but all of them feature some mix of the following elements.

The divers usually are SCUBA men, or might work on an umbilical back to the descent capsule. Suits are rubber, often heated in some way. Breathing systems can be open or closed (rebreathers). On the support ship will be one or more Deck Decompression Chambers (DDCs), which are entered through an Entrance Lock (EL) either from the deck or directly from a Personnel Transfer Capsule (PTC), which can be married to the EL. The PTC is necessary, of course, if the divers are to be working at great depths. At least one of the systems is designed to be air-transportable to the scene of salvage or underwater rescue work. The advantage of having two DDCs with a common EL is that two sets of divers can be decompressed at different rates at the same time.

BREATHING LIQUIDS

All these developments and inventions, however, beggar the real question; we are now at a plateau, as we were when we had reached the limit of compressed air in diving. Then, we came up with the exotic inert gases (mixtures of oxygen with helium, essentially), to overcome the problems presented by an essentially oxygen-nitrogen atmosphere.

Man has reached the outer limits of inert gases. We now can, under laboratory conditions, and soon under field conditions, put men a thousand feet down. In this century, surely, that depth will reach two thousand feet. But even with sea-floor habitats, decompression periods will approach a fortnight in length, and that is too heavy a price to pay.

So, what is the answer?

Men of vision, such as Jacques-Yves Cousteau, believe that the future of the individual man beneath the sea depends on adapting him to the environment: making over the diver physiologically, so he can operate at the reduced temperatures of deep water.

Dr. Johannes Kylstra, of Duke University, has successfully induced mice to breathe a liquid without drowning. Immersed in fluorocarbon, they laboriously breathed it, instead of drowning in it as one had every right to suppose they should. Not only that, Doctor Kylstra also demonstrated that liquid-breathing prevents the bends. He decompressed a mouse from 30 atmospheres to normal atmospheric pressure *in three seconds*—without the animal's suffering any ill effects. This would be equivalent to a diver rising from 1000 feet of water to the surface *at seven hundred miles an hour.*

Fluorocarbon is an isotonic solution supercharged with oxygen—thirty times the amount of oxygen, by volume, as is contained in atmospheric air.

The mouse's respiratory system is mammalian, as is ours; so Dr. Kylstra extended his experiments in 1969 with the help of Frank J. Falejczyk, an East Aurora, New York, marine photographer and hard-hat diver who "relaxes" with sky diving. Falejczyk volunteered to be the subject of Dr. Kylstra's further experiments.

"His windpipe was anesthetized and a double-tubed catheter was inserted through it, one tube going to each lung," explained Kylstra. "The air in one lung was replaced by a 0.9 per cent saline solution at normal body temperature. A 'breathing' process consisting of adding more saline solution to the lung and draining an equal amount was then repeated seven times."

In later tests, both of Falejczyk's lungs were flooded simultaneously.

Overcome the problem of carbon-dioxide elimination, and transfer the laboratory experiments to the ocean itself, and incredibly deeper and longer dives would be possible. Decompression would not be necessary, and the bends would not be a factor (due, of course, to the fact that the divers would not have absorbed any molecules of inert gas).

How much deeper? In 1957 the U. S. Navy discovered that the time required to desaturate a man's body once it has become saturated through breathing a gas pressurized to any given depth is the same no matter how long he stays down. Compressed air gave man a three hundred-foot practical limit; saturation diving will eventually give a limit of about three thousand feet. Beyond that depth, *any* gas, no matter how light, would be pressurized to such a density that the lungs would not have enough strength to breathe it.

But what if a man were breathing a liquid? Then he could probably free-dive to depths of more than two miles, according to Dr. George Bond of Sealab fame. Bond believes we have the technical know-how to do this right now.

"We're all liquid breathers," he has pointed out. "If our lungs were to become dry, we would be dead in a minute or two. So, liquid breathing shouldn't carry any great horror."

The divers would probably be carried to the ocean floor in a research submersible, after having had a tracheotomy to open a breathing-hole in the windpipe. Under mild anesthesia they would be outfitted with breathing bags, pumps, and monitor systems. The bags would contain seven liters of Ringer's solution—which is a purified, salty water used extensively in medicine today. A small, high-pressure oxygen source would then be attached, to oxygenate the solution to the required degree.

Then the lungs and sinuses of the divers would be flooded with the solution, and they would be ready to enter the open sea after very rapid compression in the sub's air lock. They could spend about an hour outside the sub before they would have to be returned and as rapidly decompressed in the air lock. Their lungs would then be gravity-drained. No further decompression would be necessary, and no bends would be experienced.

Such a prestigious diver as Jacques-Yves Cousteau agrees with Bond; he sees this sort of thing as a possibility by 1980, a probability by 1995, a certainty by 2020.

Now, what does all this mean to the future of salvage?

Not very much.

When we get all done mucking about, individual men down at two thousand feet—or twenty thousand—will be able to do exactly what men do at twenty or two hundred feet. Observe. Direct the machinery. Manipulate the tools.

Which means that no matter how deep we succeed in sending divers, their effectiveness is strictly limited by the lifting methods or salvage vehicles we create. In future, man-in-the-sea will be of great help in recovering cargoes or very small objects from depths never before possible; but his usefulness in deepwater—and in this section we will mean a thousand fathoms or more when we speak of deepwater—ship-salvage operations will be peripheral and supplemental at best.

The same cannot be said offhand of the new, small, quick submersibles. These little submarines, manned or robot-controlled, were the darlings of the 1960s; for in them, big business found the ocean-oriented prestige after which it lusted. Their achievements in such salvage operations as the location and recovery of the lost nuclear device at Palomares, Spain,[6] seems at first glance most impressive.

Submarines from World War II had a cruising depth of about three hundred feet and a collapse depth between seven hundred and eight hundred feet. Nuclear submarines can cruise at a thousand feet or deeper, with a probable collapse depth of about two thousand feet. Neither of these, however, is of any use for exploration, observation, or meaningful salvage work on the sea floor. Nor are they the ancestors of today's agile research submersibles.

It was in 1875 that American J. P. Holland invented a one-man submarine. Scheer designed another in 1888, and the following year it was Lake's *Argonaut Junior*, fourteen feet long, five high, *mounted on wheels*. Templo's *Aquapede* (1896) was cigar-shaped, with three compartments, one for the diver and the other two for compressed-air reservoirs.

In 1914, Robert H. Davis, as usual far ahead of his time, patented two designs presaging the Italian "pigs" and the British "X-Craft" of

World War II. One was an actual midget submarine with an emergence chamber; though the second also had an interior space for the divers, they rode outside when the vessel submerged. Both ideas were far beyond what was acceptable to the day's tacticians.

THE ITALIAN "CHARIOTS"

World War I also saw the actual building of the Italians' twenty-three-foot vehicle ("the chariot") which cruised at two knots submerged, with a compressed-air engine. Warheads were 350-pound detachable TNT charges, one at each end. The divers rode the vehicle as they would a horse, their heads just out of water.

The chariot was used in October 1918 to sink the superdreadnought *Viribus Unitis;* unfortunately, the ship had already been taken over by Italy's allies, so the chariots received opprobrium, not praise.

The Italians were persistent, however. During Mussolini's attack on Ethiopia in 1935, Lieutenants Teseo Tesei and Elias Toschi began developing an underwater electric torpedo at La Spezia, Italy's submarine base. It was along the lines of the old chariots: two men rode it sitting astride, using oxygen rebreather units. Mussolini disbanded the unit in 1936, when Britain did not interfere in Ethiopia; but it was reactivated in June 1940 as the Tenth Light Flotilla.

Their torpedoes were fourteen feet long, with a 300-kilogram explosive warhead that was to be hand-detached by the two-man crew, stuck to the hull of the target vessel, and detonated by a time clock. Because the torpedoes moved only at a walking pace and were very cumbersome, the men of the Flotilla called them "pigs." Their mother ships were three submarines: *Iride, Gondar, Scire.*

Iride had her snout blown off by an RAF-dropped torpedo during tests in the Mediterranean. She sank in fifty feet of water.

Gondar was forced to the surface from 510 feet by British depth charges, and Toschi himself was captured. The chariots escaped, so the British did not learn of them.

Scire entered Gibraltar Harbor to attack British shipping there in October 1940. Her three chariots all failed, for a variety of reasons, to reach any targets at all. Undaunted, Prince Valerio Borghese, commander of the *Scire,* tried again in May 1941. Again, all three chariots sank. In the third attempt, two tankers and the British motor ship *Denbydale* were sunk, with their loss being put to Axis submarines.

Then, on the night of December 18, 1941, three more of Borghese's pigs entered Alexandria Harbor behind an Allied convoy, to sink a tanker and Britain's only two remaining capital ships in the Mediterranean—the *Valiant* and the *Queen Elizabeth.*[7] Though the ships were sitting on the bottom (in James Dugan's inspired phrase, "embarrassed, with their drawers full"), the British kept the Axis powers from knowing about it by maintaining normal shipboard routine, and because all six divers had been captured. Even so, Winston Churchill was afraid to tell even Parliament of the sinkings until six months later, when he praised the Tenth Light Flotilla for its "extraordinary courage and ingenuity."

He also sent a private scorcher to his Chief of Staff, demanding a report on "what is being done to emulate the exploits of the Italians in Alexandria Harbor. One would have thought we should have been in the lead."

While Britain strove to get in the lead, the Tenth Light Flotilla came up with the dazzlingly audacious idea of setting up shop in a scuttled Italian tanker at Algeciras, Spain, less than four miles from and in full view of the British installations at Gibraltar. They cut an entry port in the tanker, the *Olterra*, below the waterline, so the pigs could come and go at will, and sank 43,000 tons of British shipping at Gibraltar until finally apprehended, in the fall of 1943, by Lionel Crabb and Lieutenant William Bailey.

BRITISH X-CRAFT

The British, meanwhile, had developed a midget submarine called the X-Craft in 1940, with most of the testing and development being carried out at Robert Davis' Siebe, Gorman and Company. Designing the vehicle itself was easy; the difficulty was in designing SCUBA gear that would let the diver avoid oxygen poisoning[8] when he went beyond thirty-three feet (one atmosphere of pressure) with his tank of pure oxygen and his rebreather. Another was keeping the steel SCUBA cylinders from affecting the magnetic compass and steering of the sub. They ended up using aluminum-alloy oxygen-supply cylinders from downed German bombers as air tanks.

The X-Craft were proper submarines, fifty feet long and of 39-ton displacement, carrying four men: two operators, and two divers who could leave and enter the sub at will through an air lock. They were to manually cut through anti-submarine nets while entering harbors after enemy vessels.

Two daring and remarkably successful attacks on Axis shipping were made by X-Craft. The first was the severe damage wrought on the German battleship *Tirpitz*, in the fjord at Kaafjord, Norway, on December 22, 1943. Six X-Craft made the attempt; only three got through the anti-sub nets, all of which were lost after setting their charges, one with all hands.

Tirpitz was so badly damaged, however, that she was unable to leave Kaafjord for seven months. When she did, she was promptly sunk by British air attack.

In July 1945, a lone midget submarine, XE-3, made an attempt on the Japanese cruiser *Takao* in the Jahore Straits. Lieutenant Ian Fraser sneaked the sub so far in under the big cruiser that it took fifty minutes of blowing and venting tanks to jerk it loose once Seaman M'Ginnes had lashed the magnetic mines to the hull with a piece of rope (the barnacles were so thick the magnet wouldn't work).

The bottom was blown right out of the *Takao* several hours after the submarine had slipped back to its open-water rendezvous with its mother ship, conventional submarine *Spark*.[9]

It was from these bothersome military midgets that the experimental submarines for non-military use grew. Popular acceptance began with the 1960 descent by Jacques Piccard and U. S. Navy Lieutenant Don Walsh to 35,800 feet in the Challenger Deep, near Guam, in Piccard's *Trieste*, an underwater metal balloon with virtually no lateral maneuverability.

Trieste II, so instrumental in finding and photographing the *Thresher* remains,[10] was the same vehicle, taken over, spruced up, and modified to Navy specifications.[11]

THE NEW EXPERIMENTAL SUBMERSIBLES

It was under prodding from the Deep Submergence Systems Review Group, established in May 1964,[12] that private industry began creating its spate of submersibles. The DSSRG had five stated undertakings: (1) Submarine location, escape, and rescue. (The Deep Submergence Rescue Vehicle [DSRV] under development under Navy contract by Lockheed is supposed to take care of this.[13]) (2) Deep-sea search and small-object recovery. (This is where the little subs are supposed to come in.) (3) Man-in-the-sea: Sealab (for the moment, dormant). (4) Large-object salvage (low priority now, due to a lack of funds). (5) Development of a nuclear-powered submersible engineering and research vessel, NR-1. (This was launched on January 25, 1969.)

First of the "deep-sea search and small-object recovery" vessels was *Aluminaut*, of Palomares fame, with design specifications for fifteen thousand feet but so far never tested below 6250. Financed by Reynolds Aluminum and built by the Electric Boat Division of General Dynamics in 1964 (with government help), *Aluminaut* cost $3 million and cost the government $80,000 to rent at Palomares. It carries six, cruises eighty miles, is fifty-one feet long, weighs eighty-one tons, and can lift three tons.

Litton Industries, meanwhile, was building *Alvin*, the other Palomares submersible, for the Navy and Woods Hole Oceanographic Institute.

A compact craft (twenty-two feet long, thirteen tons, two-man crew), with a maxium depth of six thousand feet, it was launched in 1965.

Also used at Palomares were Scripps's *Deep Jeep* (ten feet long, two-man crew, with a two-thousand-foot depth capability) and CURV (Cable-Controlled Underwater Research Vehicle), which actually brought the nuclear bomb up. It originally was developed as a robot-controlled torpedo-recovery unit.

Palomares, in turn, spurred the second-generation research submersibles such as Ocean Systems' *Deep Diver*, brain child of Edwin Link and John H. Perry, Jr.

Deep Diver has an operating depth of 1335 feet and gives divers an on-paper capability of entering or leaving through its air lock down to 1250 feet. In 1968, *Deep Diver* set a record, with free-swimming divers leaving and entering the vessel at 700 feet.[14] *Deep Diver* operates like a helicopter; its four propellers (two at the nose, two at the stern) swivel to give it vertical or lateral movement. The vessel is twenty-two feet long with a five-foot beam, weighs eight tons, and can deliver three knots for thirty minutes under water.

Electric Boat produced *Star I*, which participated in Sealab I off Bermuda in 1964. She was ten feet long and four in diameter, with a four-hour endurance, a one-knot speed, and a maximum depth of two hundred feet. Rechristened *Asherah*, she was put to work for several years at George Bass's archaeological digs off Turkey.[15] Electric Boat's *Star II* has a maximum operating depth of six hundred feet at one to four knots, with a seventeen-foot steel hull five feet in diameter.

Star III, Electric Boat's third-generation vessel, is shaped like a shark, can operate two thousand feet down at speeds up to six knots, and is designed for search-and-recovery work as well as underwater mapping. She has cameras, exterior lights, and manipulator arms, and can stay under water for twelve hours.

Westinghouse has *Deepstar 4000* in operation, designed to operate at four thousand feet; and in November 1969, launched the twenty-foot three-man *Deepstar 2000*.

Lockheed's *Deep Quest*, with its four-man crew, has a designed depth capability of eight thousand feet and can lift three and a half tons.

In July 1968, GM's Electronics Defense Research Lab displayed DOWB (Deep Ocean Work Boat), which weighs just under nine tons. Two remarkable features of this vessel are the fact that it can stay below for sixty-five hours, and its lack of viewing ports for its two-man crew. It relies purely on optical and electronic systems, with no visual system at all. It has been tested to 6420 feet.

Sun Shipbuilding and Dry Dock's highly specialized *Guppy*, not yet operational, is a towed subsurface vehicle that features a three-thousand-foot electric cable instead of batteries and weighs less than just the batteries of many other submersibles. Its hull is five and a half feet in diameter; its work time is forty-eight hours. It uses ballast tanks for descent and ascent, and is designed for offshore explorations by oil companies or research groups. Sun also tested, developed and built the pressure hulls for the Navy's DSRV.

Electric Boat's new twenty-five-foot submersibles, *Autec I* and *Autec II*, have a feature in common with *Alvin:* in times of emergency, the sphere containing the three crewmen is ejected, to rise slowly to the surface and safety.

During July and August 1969 the new Grumman Aerospace Corporation research submersible *Ben Franklin* performed probably the most intriguing task any of them has undertaken to date: a thirty-day, sixteen-hundred-mile undersea drift in the Gulf Stream from Florida to Nova Scotia with a crew of six aboard, headed by Jacques Piccard. The *Ben Franklin* is fifty feet long and weighs 130 tons; from a Piccard design, it cost $5 million. Its general cruise depth was 650 feet, but it made nine exploratory dives to the bottom, fifteen hundred to two thousand feet down.

Some of its findings were startling. Blackfish, always believed to be a maximum three feet long, were found to be thirty. The Gulf Stream is faster, more turbulent, than previously believed (one and a half knots off Florida, three knots off Virginia), and the Continental Shelf is more undulant than had been believed. There are few large fish in this supposedly teeming stream, mainly because plankton and other small marine animals are conspicuously missing. The drifting sub had stability problems because it tended to follow unexpected isotherms—cold-water layers—which moved up and down through the stream, probably following the bottom contour.

The prototype of future submersibles was launched at Groton, Connecticut, on January 25, 1969. This is Electric Boat's *NR-1*, for the Navy: a seven-man (five crewmen, two scientists), $100-million, nuclear-powered submarine 140 feet long and twelve in diameter. Sperry Gyroscope developed the instrument-and-control system; the sub is equipped with underwater lights, television and motion-picture cameras, highly sophisticated positioning and sonar gear, and a mechanical lifting arm.

Although its capabilities are still secret, a two thousand-foot operating depth seems likely, with a long bottom time made possible by the nuclear power source.

Subsurface vessels in the future probably will be constructed of titanium (tested down to twenty thousand feet) or glass; indeed, Corning has built for submersibles a glass/ceramic submersible hull and hemisphere viewing windows that can stand pressures equivalent to thirty-five thousand feet. Power sources possible apart from nuclear might be hydrogen peroxide or other chemicals, or battery-like fuel cells such as those used on space craft. Guidance systems will probably continue to use refined sonar, doppler sonar, and possibly inertial guidance systems—although these depend on expensive and highly delicate gyroscopes.

Blue-green lasers could be used in future to pierce the water with light in searching patterns. "Boomers"—instruments that spring two large circular metal plates apart violently every ten seconds—might be used to probe bottom sediments with sound pulses. Harold Edgerton of MIT[16] has developed seismic-profiling and dual-channel side-scan sonar systems for this same purpose. Off Khalkis, Greece, his probe transducer penetrated forty-nine feet below the crust; it also confirmed large objects[17] beneath the sediment of St. Ann's Bay, where Bob Marx claimed Columbus' ships lay.

These subs are all work vehicles in one form or another, and those that are operational are rented out by their developers to government, engineering and oil companies, foundations, and research groups for one thousand dollars and up a day. Most of them have manipulators, mechanical hands, or other external protrusions to lift, turn, fasten, bore, and dig. Much of the rent goes for support ships.

In the midst of all this pomp and circumstance, we find a submersible that must be rather infuriating to the industrial giants with their costly hardware. This is the sixteen-foot, eleven-foot-wide *Pisces*, a white, turtle-shaped sub that carries a two-man crew, has an operational depth of three thousand feet, has an external manipulator, fathometer, camera, and movie camera in its plexiglas ports, and is owned by International Hydrodynamics, of Vancouver, British Columbia.

So far, *Pisces* sounds like any other giant corporation's prestige submersible, right? Wrong. International Hydrodynamics consisted of three young ex-professional divers (Mack Thomson, Allen Trice, and Don Sorte), a single deck hand, a secretary, three poodles, a telephone, and a thirty-five-foot barge, forty-five years old, as a "support vessel." Inside a deck shack, *Pisces* hung from an I-beam like a giant sea turtle drying in the Seychelles sun.

These three young Canadians, none of them engineers or even college graduates, designed and built *Pisces* all by themselves. The guts of their craft is a ¾-inch alloy-steel ball six feet in diameter; ballast, motors, and controls are around the hull, outside this.

Pisces is probably a better basic undersea craft than the majority of those that big business has turned out on research, government, and foundation money. And *Pisces*, and International Hydrodynamics, are doing what most of the other subs don't seem to have much time for: salvage work.

Thomson, Trice, and Sorte salvaged test torpedoes for the U. S. Navy at the Keyport Torpedo Station, Puget Sound. Torpedoes are designed to float in test firings, but many of them don't; and today's torpedo is worth $70,000 a copy. *Pisces* earned $2100 per fish recovered from the sediment on the hundred-fathom sea floor at Keyport.

Torpedo recovery's long and honorable history stretches way back to 1882, when twenty-student diving classes were held at Newport, Rhode Island, firing range. The divers were cleared for ten fathoms, but regularly went to twenty-one in their search for test torpedoes; indeed, such great salvage divers as Tom Eadie[18] learned their trade at Newport.

One Newport diver suffered a messy death when the flowing tide carried a loop of his life and air lines over a torpedo buried in the sand. The lines touched the propellers, which kicked the engine over. The whirling props rolled up the lines, dragging the diver over to the torpedo and then hacking him to pieces.

When the same thing happened at Keyport, two weeks passed before they found the helmet still containing the missing diver's head; they never did find the rest of him. Many torpedoes, buried fifteen to twenty feet in the sediment, have to be probed for with a metal rod and then carefully freed with a high-pressure water hose. Hence, *Pisces*.

One of the better stories of torpedo recovery comes from England, where a diver was sent down at 5:30 P.M. to recover a test torpedo fired by the battleship HMS *Hood*.

Through a series of mishaps, the diver, named Young, got his air and life lines twisted about the shot rope, which in turn was badly fouled to the hawser he had attached to the torpedo; he ended up suspended between bottom and surface, seventy-eight feet down, completely helpless because he had been flipped upside down.

Working in the dark, divers took until 10:00 P.M. just to find him. They could not arouse him, so they reported his death topside. About this time, the torpedo tore free, and Young's body popped to the surface, feet first. They dragged him from the water to find his helmet three-fourths full of water when they removed the front window. Since it hadn't quite reached his mouth, however, they began cutting away the suit in the forlorn hope that life might still be present.

Young immediately opened his eyes. "Don't cut the goddam suit," he said feebly. "It's a new one."

USE OF SUBMERSIBLES FOR SALVAGE LIMITED

Unfortunately, the minisubs don't fare any better on deepwater salvage than divers do; despite all the new submersibles, Ed Link admitted as recently as 1964 that there is no known ship-salvage method that would be practical beyond the depths at which divers can work.

The record of salvage performed by the submersibles bears him out. *Alvin, Aluminaut,* and CURV were instrumental in recovering the hydrogen bomb off Palomares—by current standards, certainly a deepwater recovery operation: 2850 feet—475 fathoms. But look what they were recovering. A ten-foot bomb weighing nineteen hundred pounds.

Well, then, what *ship* salvage jobs have submersibles done?

One of them is rather embarrassing. On October 16, 1968, during a launch operation from mother ship *Lulu* some 120 miles off Cape Cod, tiny, two-man *Alvin* was involved in a bit of a mishap. They . . . dropped him. *Alvin* quickly sank in five thousand feet of water.

The following June, *Mizar* spent several days in locating the tiny craft, even though they had an excellent "fix" on its position. Photographs indicated the vessel was worth saving, so in August 1969 recovery operations on the 22-foot, 13-ton submersible were begun. After much travail, his buddy from Palomares, *Aluminaut*, was able to insert a folded lift toggle bar into *Alvin*'s open entrance hatch. This was at 3:00 A.M. on the twenty-eighth, after eighteen grueling hours on the bottom for *Aluminaut*'s six-man crew. With this, *Alvin* was dragged from the mud.

On September 1, a heavy nylon three-part net was lowered from *Mizar*, and SCUBA divers secured *Alvin* in it. Riding in its sling, the submersible was towed to shallower water near Martha's Vineyard, where he was delicately raised and placed aboard a barge for transport to Woods Hole Oceanographic Institute.

On October 7, 1969, another of the little submersibles, this one Lockheed's *Deep Quest*, showed that the loss of the *Alvin* was no isolated incident when it stranded itself 432 feet down off San Diego, California. *Quest*, which is forty feet long and weighs fifty tons, was on a routine training recovery of an 1875-pound steel cylinder that had been sunk some five miles offshore purely for that purpose. Apparently, a nylon line attached to the cylinder became fouled in *Deep Quest*'s propeller, entangling the little vessel.

Twelve hours later, the tiny two-man minisub *Nekton* dived down to cut the nylon rope and free the submarine so it could surface again. Speed had been essential, since the *Deep Quest*'s four-man crew, captained by Robert Worthington, had only about forty-eight hours of oxygen available in their self-contained rebreathing system.

A Lockheed spokesman could not explain how the line became entangled in the propeller; but, he said, it should not have been left on the cylinder dropped into the ocean for *Deep Quest* to recover. Which sounds very much like the Navy, back in 1928, sinking submarine *S-4* so their boys could salvage it under optimum conditions, and then getting very petulant and hurt when the sub wouldn't come up nice and pretty as it was supposed to.[19]

One would think the director of a training exercise would welcome the unexpected, since no real salvage operation *ever* enjoys optimum conditions.

Deep Quest has the distinction of having planted the American flag at 8310 feet in the Pacific on February 28, 1969—deeper than any other true submarine has ever gone.

Apart from rescuing each other when they are careless enough to sink, only one deepwater research submersible has carried out a genuine deepwater (by current, not future, standards) ship-salvage operation. It proves again what can be done with wit, ingenuity, and the creative mind that salvage operations (if not giant corporations) stimulate.

RAISING THE *EMERALD STRAITS*

The assignment? To salvage from 670 feet of water the 95-ton steel-hulled tug *Emerald Straits*, which went down in Howe Sound, British Columbia, during the spring of 1969—the twenty-third such tug lost in Canadian waters over an eleven-year span.

The offer? A $110,000 no-cure, no-pay salvage contract.

The taker? None other than the rapidly expanding firm of International Hydrodynamics, Inc. (Hyco).

On June 25, 1969, *Pisces* relocated the sunken *Emerald Straits*. This accomplished, Thomson, Trice, and Sorte used a four-point mooring system to firmly fix over the tug a one hundred-ton-capacity scow, one hundred feet long by forty-two wide. *Pisces*, with what was in effect a tremendous, 60,000-pound-bite wire cutter fitted to her manipulator, nipped off the tug's anchor chains so the sunken vessel's hawse pipes could be cleared. Then the submersible fitted three hundred-pound lifting toggles into the pipes. Holding a sixty-pound weight in her manipulator, *Pisces* carefully pounded the tight-fitting toggles through.

To these toggles was fitted a surface load line from the scow moored overhead. This lifted the front end of the *Emerald Straits*, so a sling of 1¾-inch steel-core cable could be swept under. The bottom of the sling was formed into a forty-foot ring by a spreader bar of two-by-twelve planks. When a load was put on the sling, the flimsy wooden beams were crushed and the sling automatically tightened around the *Emerald Straits*. *Pisces* spent one hundred hours on the bottom, in twenty dives.

The scow lifted the tug to carry it in a horizontal position to eighty-foot water, where a derrick barge plucked it to the surface. Oil and fuel pumped out to make it buoyant once more, *Emerald Straits* was towed into Vancouver for delivery to the Canadian Department of Transport on July 24—just a month after the salvage operation had begun. International Hydrodynamics, their $110,000 check fluttering in their work-grimed fingers, returned to work—and to three more sunken vessels on which they felt their expanded fleet of *Pisces I, II,* and *III* could use the same salvage method.

Neatly leaving the giant corporations that run prestige-oriented submersibles scratching their heads and muttering.

---

1 See pages 66–67.
2 See pages 193–94.
3 See pages 68–70.
4 See pages 26–27.
5 This does not entail another air tank; a capsule about the size of a soda-water charger is sufficient to supply the cells.
6 See pages 80–94.
7 See pages 287–88.
8 The Admiralty Experimental Diving Unit invented a mythical monster called Oxygen Pete to humanize oxygen poisoning for the divers. This has passed into the language; even today, "getting a Pete" is synonymous with a dose of oxygen poisoning.
9 The X-Craft were also regularly used to test anti-submarine defenses at Scapa Flow with dummy runs. X-24 was returning from one such foray, two disreputable-looking seamen lounging about topside, when Britain's largest extant battleship, the *Duke of York,* under personal command of Admiral Fraser, passed the tiny craft. The two filthy, bearded seamen on the X-24 suddenly snapped-to for such a rigid military salute that a thousand men aboard the *York* automatically responded. Thus assured of their attention, one of the seamen raised an Aldis lamp and winked a message at the tremendous battleship: WHAT . . . A . . . BIG . . . BAS . . . TARD . . . YOU . . . ARE. . . .
10 See pages 140–44.
11 Piccard also invented the *Auguste Piccard,* named after his father, a 93.5-foot submersible used to lug people around at the 1964 Swiss International Exposition. It has a (never used) 2500-foot cruising depth, and could carry forty passengers and three crewmen.
12 See pages 143–44.
13 See pages 143–44.
14 This is perhaps the most highly praised feature of *Deep Diver;* yet Robert H. Davis, remember, designed and patented a midget submarine with this capability in 1914.
15 See page 378.
16 See pages 141–42.
17 See pages 395–97.
18 See pages 120–21.
19 See pages 123–24.

CHAPTER THIRTY-ONE

Solving the Problems

Once, the mechanical lift was considered the most effective means of raising a sunken vessel: get a bunch of cables around it and somehow grunt it to the surface. Then came tide lifts, using this irresistible natural force by pinning partially flooded surface lifting craft to the sunken ship at low tide and unwatering them as the water rose. After that, pontoons. Flood 'em, sink 'em, pin 'em on either side of the wreck, then blow them with compressed air.

After that came Frederick Young's trick, perfected by Ernest Cox at Scapa Flow, of sealing up every opening, aperture, and hole in the sunken vessel, and blowing it with compressed air so it raised itself. All methods still are used, and a few salvage operations have tried everything at once: pontoons, water ballast, compressed air, tide lifts, and beach gear.

Some now believe that the various polyurethane foams or polystyrene "beads," "bubbles," or pellets will be as big a break-through for our day as compressed air was for Cox's.

POLYURETHANE FOAM

The first use of the rigid polyurethane foam was in 1964, to raise the seagoing barge *Lumberjack*, which had foundered in Humboldt Bay, near Eureka, California. The barge was down in seventy-five feet of water, where it constituted a hazard to navigation; Murphy Pacific Salvage Company, of Emeryville, California, was given the salvage contract. J. P. Murphy, President of the company, decided to use in the attempt a polyurethane foam called Autofroth, developed by the Polytron Company, of Richmond, California.

A vessel with tanks of the two basic urethane components pressurized with low-boiling expansion agents was anchored over the *Lumberjack*. From the salvage ship, 150 feet of hose led to a dispensing unit on the sea floor beside the sunken barge.

When a diver activated the gun that shot the material into the 500-ton barge's superstructure, the two materials were fed from the surface tanks through separate flow controllers into the static mixing chamber on the ocean floor. From this they were violently expelled by pressurized nitrogen. The sudden decrease in pressure during expulsion caused the low-boiling agent to volatilize. This created a "froth" —millions of tiny bubbles of urethane—to fill the cavity into which the diver was directing his nozzle. The foaming urethane would "cure" within a few minutes into a rigid, cellular material.

Each cubic foot of foam, weighing two pounds when rigid, displaces sixty-four pounds of sea water. Another advantage over compressed air is that the foam is self-sealing on small openings, ports, and vents on the sunken vessel, so that these need not be individually found and closed. Some sixty thousand pounds of foam were used in the *Lumberjack* operation. After a month-long attempt in heavy seas and bad weather (water temperature ranging from 35 degrees to 45 degrees Fahrenheit the entire time), the barge came to the surface.

On April 10, 1968, the 8944-ton ocean-going ferry *Wahine*, 490 feet long, 605 passengers, 122 crewmen, was caught in the entrance of the port of Wellington, New Zealand, by the worst storm (107-knot winds) in that nation's history. The ship went down; fifty-one people drowned.

United Salvage, Ltd. of Melbourne, Australia and Murphy Pacific, proposed to raise the half-sunken craft with polyurethane foam, buoy it, drag it out into deep water, and sink it again where it would not be a hazard to navigation. But another heavy gale broke up the partially submerged craft in the spring of 1969, before they got a chance to try the foam on it.

At the same time that the proposed *Wahine* attempt was being bruited about the news media, Murphy also announced that in 1969 he would use foam to raise the *Andrea Doria*, the sunken Italian liner that is fast acquiring the legendary fame of a *Titanic* or a *Lusitania*.

The 29,000-ton passenger liner, seven hundred feet long, insured for $16 million, and carrying 1134 passengers and 575 crewmen, was struck at 11:22 P.M. on July 25, 1956, by the 11,000-ton freighter *Stockholm*. The accident crumpled thirty feet of the *Stockholm's* reinforced bows like tissue paper, killing five crewmen, and ripped a forty-foot gap through seven of the *Doria's* eleven decks, on the starboard side. Shortly after she was cleared of people at 2:25 A.M., the *Doria* went down in fifty-five fathoms of water, landing on her starboard side. It took three years to settle, for $6 million, the 3322 claims for $116 million that were filed. But long before then, the amateurs and professionals alike had begun eying her with thoughts of salvage.

Her cast-bronze propellers alone are worth a minimum of $30,000; just salving the two hundred thousand pieces of mail she carried, since the U. S. Government pays twenty-six cents a letter for lost and recovered mail, would be worth fifty-two thousand dollars. Art objects such as an eight-by-four-foot solid silver plaque worth $250,000 and $1,116,000 in American and Italian currency are further incentives.

But she lies on the Nantucket Shoals forty-five miles south of Nantucket Island, in some of the worst weather in the world. Because of sudden violent storms and immense fog banks, only a few weeks in the summer are even plausible for anchoring over the hulk. The Purser's safe lies at the starboard side; divers would have to traverse the vessel's ninety-foot beam to reach it, a dreadful undertaking at the limit of compressed air in zero visibility.

ABORTIVE SALVAGE ATTEMPTS ON THE ANDREA DORIA

Despite the problems, suggestions for salvage have been many and varied. Fill it full of ping-pong balls (they would implode 15 feet below the surface). Fill it up with deflated plastic balloons, twenty-five feet in diameter, festoon her exterior with more of them, inflate the lot . . . Sure. Seal her and blow her with compressed air. At that depth, it would be easier to build a new Great Pyramid of Giza. Get a lifting sling under her, water and pin huge Great Lakes ore barges to her, unwater the barges . . . Better build another pyramid.

Salvors who have announced, or made, attempts include James Dugan and John Light in 1956, Lloyd Deir in 1957, Armando Conti and Richard Meyer (who bought salvage rights in 1958 to sell them to a Canadian outfit, the Andrea Doria Project, in 1961), Jim Taylor and a company called Aquatopographers in 1963. In 1964 some SCUBA divers actually brought up a 700-pound statue of the fifteenth-century Genoese admiral Andrea Doria, broken off at the knees.

In 1968, Murphy grandly announced he would not just salvage the ship's treasure and art objects, but would raise the entire vessel in 1969 with the polyurethane foam. He would put, he said $4 to $7 million into the operation.

The foam is perhaps the most novel method so far advanced (although it has been tested, in laboratory and not field conditions, to a depth of only 250 feet); but the cost would be vastly greater than Murphy's estimates. Just to raise the *Normandie* when she rolled over in seventy feet of water cost, back in 1942, almost as much ($3.75 million) as his lower estimate for the *Doria*. After being refloated, the *Normandie* was sold for scrap for $116,000; thus, if the *Doria* is ever raised, she very likely will become the most expensive scrap metal in the history of salvage. Murphy presumably was aware of all this in 1968; and how he would get the foam *out* of the ship after it was afloat was never described, either. In any event, nothing further has been heard of the project.

Two of the great Dutch salvage firms, Wijsmuller and W. A. van den Tak, have made experiments with similar, polystyrene, pellets.

On July 24, 1965, the 108-ton trawler *Jaco-Mina* went down six miles northwest of IJmuiden, Holland. The ninety-foot vessel landed on her starboard side in ten fathoms of water. Since she was too large for the bull-nose salvage ship *Octopus* to lift as a dead weight, Wijsmuller decided to try the pea-sized balls of expanded polystyrene, 98 per cent air and 2 per cent plastic, which they had developed. Besides *not* absorbing water, the pellets produce pure upward thrust rather than compressed air's multidirectional thrust.

While twenty-one hundred cubic feet of pellets were being produced for the lift, divers from the salvage ship *Sepiola* were down on the *Jaco-Mina*, sealing her hull and inserting the hoses.

The filling operation was begun during the winter of 1965, with the large bags of granules being fed into the hull through the pipes by a mixture of air and water. By February 20, 1966, they had filled a sufficient number of the trawler's compartments to lighten the ship so that the *Octopus* could lift her to the surface.

POLYSTYRENE GRANULES USED ON MARTIN S

Not to be outdone, Van den Tak undertook the polystyrene-granule salvage of the 4200-ton Danish freighter *Martin S*, thirty-nine times the weight of the *Jaco-Mina*, in mid-1967. The *Martin S* had been torn loose from her moorings in the natural harbor at Sukkertoppen, Greenland, by a heavy gale in May 1966. Smashed against the sheer cliffs surrounding the bay, *Martin S* capsized and sank, sliding down the nearly vertical cliff to land upright in seventeen fathoms of water. She formed a hazard to navigation where she lay, so bids were let on raising her, despite the multiple problems involved.

She had to be taken elsewhere once she was raised—this meant Copenhagen, Denmark; she was a long way from any salvage equipment; and she had to be raised quickly, because that far north, salvage was possible only from mid-May to mid-September. These factors decided Van den Tak to use, as Wijsmuller had done on the *Jaco-Mina*, a mix of methods: the salvage ship *Bever*, 347 tons with a 110-ton derrick; the shear-legs barge *Arend*, with a 210-ton lifting capacity; and the polystyrene-sphere method invented by Karl Krøyer of Denmark.

Krøyer uses glassy sugar-grain-sized polystyrene spheres called Montopore, developed by Monsanto Chemical. Like Wijsmuller's polystyrene peas, the spheres are pumped into the vessel through pipes with water under pressure; like the foam, the spheres are expanded to fifty times their original size through steam-heating. Both polystyrene methods are superior to the foam in one respect: they can easily be removed from the salvaged vessel, while the foam forms such a rigid structure as it cures that it has to be chopped or hacked out.

On May 20, 1967, work got started, under the direction of Chief Salvage Inspector Z. W. S. Moerkerk, by a twenty-six-man crew; water depth and temperature limited bottom time to one-hour work shifts for each of the ten divers. They found the No. 1 Lower Hold pierced, but because the spheres exert only upward thrust, did not have to seal it. They did, however, reinforce the main deck and hatches, with a dozen double T beams running athwartship, against the spheres' thrust.

On June 17, having cut holes for the five-inch polystyrene pipes at calculated places in the hull, the salvors began pumping 1550 tons of spheres into the No. 2, 3, and 4 holds from the twelve hundred drums of styropor, through the steam-heating and mixing equipment. The *Bever* was cabled to the prow and the *Arend* to the stern to assure stability as the *Martin S* rose. Between them a mere 150 tons of lift was necessary.

The ship came up easily at an even keel. A fresh-water/natrium-nitrate solution was used to sluice down the engines for removing the salt and saving them from corrosion; then the engines and the vessel's deck winches were coated with a preserving fluid. The holes in the hull were plugged, with the spheres left in place to furnish buoyancy during the tow to Copenhagen, successfully completed on August 18 by the ocean-going motor tug *Oceaan*.

The operation on the 1295-ton dredger *Cessnock*, owned by the Clyde

Port Authority, Scotland, again demonstrated the flexibility of the Krøyer-developed method. *Cessnock* had sunk off Prince's Pier, Greenock, in fifty feet of water, during January 1968. Salvage Officer Bob van der Molen first brought over from Holland two 90-foot shear legs of two hundred tons capacity each, so he could parbuckle the *Cessnock* upright, once divers working in murky three-foot visibility, with underwater oxyacetylene torches, had removed the dredger's forty-two 2½-ton buckets and cut holes for the polystyrene pipes.

In all, twenty-seven tons of beads were used to bring the dredger afloat. Her engine rooms were pumped out before she was towed twenty miles to a Glasgow dry dock. There, a grain pump shot the polystyrene particles back out of the vessel into two barges for disposal.

Van den Tak is now developing a polystyrene-bead plant so portable that it can be air-lifted by commercial air freight to the scene of a sinking, for swift, efficient salvage anywhere in the world.

The foams and the pellets, it is obvious, are an exciting new development in ship salvage. Shallow-water ship salvage. For the uncomfortable fact is that polyurethane or polystyrene never has been used beyond a hundred feet, and probably never will be used at depths beyond three hundred. The only vessels *ever* raised from beyond fifty fathoms, in fact, were the 260-ton submarine *F-4*, raised by Julius Furer way back in 1915[1], and the 95-ton tug *Emerald Straits*, raised with the help of the submersible *Pisces* from 670 feet in 1969.

And the only vessel ever salvaged in what is today considered deep water, the minisub *Alvin*, brought up from five thousand feet in 1969, was so tiny (13 tons) that it can barely be classified as anything other than small-object recovery.

Two other new ship-salvage methods should be mentioned here. First is PSI (Pressurized Sphere Injector), developed by Cyclo Manufacturing Company. PSI automatic pressure-adjusting spheres are eleven inches in diameter, with a thirty-pound buoyancy, with two-way valves that let internal air pressure rise or drop with the ambient water pressure. The balls are pressurized in a chamber to the pressure necessary at the depth to which they will be delivered; then they are fed down into the sunken ship by a water-pipe delivery system.

So far PSI has only raised a thirty-foot, five-ton, steel-hulled work boat in controlled tests off the Bahamas, and its relevance to deep-water salvage seems slight.

And in October 1969, seven Britons, an Austrian, and two Hungarians announced that in December of that year they would raise the famed White Star ocean liner *Titanic*, the "unsinkable ship" that sank in 1912 with the loss of 1513 lives after colliding with a giant North Atlantic iceberg. The announced method of salvage was a radical one: water would be broken up into its elements, and the hydrogen that resulted would be piped into containers attached to the sunken vessel until sufficient buoyancy was obtained to bring her up.

Nothing further to date has been heard of this plan.

THE PROBLEMS OF DEEPWATER SALVAGE

Thus, despite the tremendous advances in diver equipment and physiology; despite the bewildering proliferation of deep-ranging submersibles; despite such new lifting techniques as foams, pellets, and spheres; we must return to the eternal problems. The problems that have always prevented man from raising anything very much larger than a rowboat or heavier than a bull elephant from truly deep water.

They are simply stated: How do you find it? Once you find it, how do you make sure you can find it again? How do you hold position over it once you know where it is? Finally, how do you break it free from the bottom and get it back up to the surface?

Simple questions. At most ocean-oriented companies, however, the answers seem so complex that the questions are not even discussed. Remember Ed Link admitting, "No method we know of would be practical beyond the depth at which divers can work." And Link went on to mention that the only deepwater ship-salvage methods known are the old ones: lifting cables and pontoons.

"Surface storms or varying currents would play havoc with the complex of cables. Attaching pontoons—either rigid or inflatable—at such depths would present another web of problems. . . . When the sunken hull became buoyant, it might pop to the surface with such speed that the pontoons would smash or spill their air—and the wreck would plunge again."

This, by the way, is one of the oldest problems in salvage: the fact that suction, between a ship's bottom and the mud, often requires a force to break the vessel free that is much greater than the force needed to lift it. We have seen this bring many salvage operations to at least temporary grief, chief among them the submarines S-51 and *Squalus*, as well as the British operation on the sunken dry dock at Trincomalee, Ceylon. Because so much excess lift has to be exerted to break the vessel free, when it does come up it often comes up out of control.

OSE: SOLVING THE PROBLEMS

Ocean Science and Engineering, however, has patented two methods to break the suction between a grounded ship and the mud around it, so that no excess lift is required.

The first is for use with a metal-hulled ship or other metal object, at any depth to which a submersible work vehicle could go; the second would accomplish the same result on vessels or sunken objects with wood or other non-metal hulls.

In the first method, a floating barge or other lifting vessel with a source of electricity aboard is moored above the sunken ship. A cable from the generator's positive polarity is run down to be fixed at several points to the sunken hull by divers or, in deep water, a working submersible. This in effect makes the *entire sunken ship* an immense electrode (cathode). From the opposing (negative) polarity of the generator, another electrode (anode) is run down to be suspended beside the sunken vessel.

Then the power is switched on.

The sea water between the opposing electrodes acts as a conductor, and an electric current flows between the negative electrode and the positive one. Electrolysis then takes place, creating millions of hydrogen bubbles on the surface of the ship. Bubbles form on the side sunk in the sediment between the hull and the mud, thus inevitably breaking the suction or static friction between ship and bottom. Once the grip of the bottom has been broken, the vessel can then be hauled to the surface by whatever conventional lifting method seems most applicable. This scheme works very well for reducing the friction when ships beached on mud flats must be pulled free.

In the second method, a diver descends to the wreck with a high-pressure hose to which is fitted a long, thin nozzle. With this, the diver probes under the hull in dozens of places, each time injecting a stream of water containing tiny pellets between ship and sediment. These pellets are made of iron and magnesium, the two metals being separated by an insulating material. As in the previous case, the salt water in conjunction with the two metals sets up electrolysis. Again, millions of hydrogen bubbles are formed beneath the ship; and once again, as soon as sufficient bubbles have formed to break the static friction, salvage can go forward along normal lines.

Ocean Science and Engineering, however, is moving much more dramatically into the field of modern marine salvage. By now it is obvious that only new kinds of location-and-recovery techniques that are both radical and technically sound can make it possible to salvage large objects from deep water. OSE, led by Willard Bascom, has devised and is now constructing an entirely new system of deepwater (six thousand to eighteen thousand feet deep) salvage.

In its first eight years of operation, OSE managed to get involved in a bewildering number of ocean-oriented projects: oceanographic, geophysical, and hydrographic surveys; offshore oil exploration and deepwater production research; ship repair and conversion; oceanographic equipment design; scallop fishing; submarine dredging of sand to rebuild beaches; and underwater exploration for tin, gold, diamonds, platinum, and titanium. In fact, the company policy (Bascom calls OSE a group of "philosopher-engineers") is "to work anywhere in the ocean on any kind of a problem."

The company's motto, adapted from Kipling's poem *The Mary Gloster*, has to be one of the most brazen ever flaunted by any American commercial venture:

They asked us how we did it, and we gave 'em the scripture text.
"You keep your light so shining a little in front of the next."
They copied all they could follow, but they couldn't copy our minds
And we left 'em sweating and stealing a year and a half behind.

OSE's deepwater search and salvage scheme was invented by Bascom in 1962 while he was pondering the applications of the deepwater drilling technology his group had pioneered on Phase I of the Mohole Project. Having devised dynamic positioning for holding a ship at a fixed point in deep water, and having solved the problem of finding and re-entering a drill hole in deep water, Bascom felt that similar techniques would be useful for inspecting the ocean floor in detail and doing useful work there. Out of this came the deep search system, which he patented a year or two later.

In April 1968 the Aluminum Corporation of America (Alcoa) retained OSE to build the system into an aluminum ship of an entirely new design. Alcoa and OSE will have an operational vessel in 1971 to be called the *Alcoa Seaprobe*: 244 feet long, with a 2000-ton displacement. This all-aluminum, diesel-electric ship will have long range, instant maneuverability, and the best of instrumentation.

Seaprobe looks like, and can be used as, a deep-water drilling ship: that is, it has a drilling rig capable of supporting a million pounds above a moon pool (interior center well) twelve by thirty-six feet. This means it can handle a pipe string (instead of cable), with all the attendant advantages of strength and rigidity. With pipe, one has the ability to exert torque at the bottom and can pump water down from the surface at high pressures to drive turbines, wash off old wrecks, power machinery, and do other tasks in which large horsepower is required.

Alcoa also is getting something even more important: exclusive rights to OSE's ocean search-and-recovery methods, equipment, and techniques. This means that the *Alcoa Seaprobe* will be doing what no other vessel on earth can do: finding and salvaging objects weighing up to two hundred tons from depths of six thousand feet. Eventually, the search/recovery capability will be extended to eighteen thousand feet.

This solution to deepwater work is logical in concept and straightforward in engineering design, and it is based on a philosophical position that differs markedly from that of the other companies engaged in the race for the ocean floor.

The Navy and its giant contractor corporations (Lockheed, North American, Grumman, General Motors, Westinghouse) who are developing deepwater submersibles for search-and-locate missions (we never hear much about that word "recovery") are all concerned with getting men, instruments, and machines deeper and deeper into the oceans and getting them safely back again. The basic problem of sending men down in small submarines is that as soon as people are involved, all work becomes subordinated to their safety. Usually the small deep-diving submarines cannot be recovered in heavy weather; so the *threat* of a storm prevents launching them in the first place. The men cannot stay down too long, because of fatigue or life-support-system limitations; so dives rarely last longer than one day. The mother ship must concentrate all its efforts on keeping track of where its sub is, and in being ready to retrieve it. This means an expensive ship is kept idle; a ship whose costs are often much greater than the submarine itself.[2]

More important, the submarine cannot *do* very much. Precise navigation is virtually impossible. Visibility is restricted to looking through small view ports—or to special optics and television (some subs have no windows). The complex electronics and mechanical devices used have the usual problems—but in a place where they are hard to repair. And men who are cramped, possibly cold, in some danger, and subject to harassing questions from above, cannot think as well as people at the surface.

MEN STAY AT THE SURFACE

Why not keep the men at the surface, where they have all the comforts of home, and let the instruments go to the bottom in the little steel ball? It's safer—and much more efficient—than sending men down. Perhaps it's not quite so glamorous to stay on top, but it's a lot cheaper, because a surface search ship, which does not have to worry about some of its people down in a submersible, can work twenty-four hours a day continuously without much regard for the weather.

So the OSE-Alcoa system keeps the men at the surface and sends to the bottom only the sensors that are required there. This is the most efficient and practical way to do the job; and for five centuries, getting the job done in the most efficient and cheapest way possible has been the name of the game in marine salvage.

It was stated earlier that the first problem is to find the object to be salvaged. The submersibles do it by going down to look, mainly with what is known in the trade as "the Mark I Eyeball"—sometimes aided by various sonars. It is very difficult, however, to navigate a small submarine along parallel overlapping systematic paths so that the operators can be certain they have searched everywhere. Since their search path is narrow anyway, they are likely to leave unsearched areas (called "holidays"). Moreover, when they find the object sought, they have no way of knowing exactly where they are—or where it is. Finally, of course, the small subs cannot lift more than a few hundred pounds, and so must try to attach a cable from a surface ship to anything heavy that must be raised—always difficult, often risky, sometimes impossible.

THE ALCOA-OSE *SEAPROBE* SYSTEM

The OSE-designed system using *Seaprobe* will first establish the center of the search area as precisely as possible by one of the standard navigational techniques (loran, Decca, Transit, etc.), and then will mark this position with a taut-moored buoy system.[3] Around the perimeter of the search area, other, similar taut-moored buoy systems are placed, all equipped with lights and sonar (or radar) transponders. From this point on, all navigation is done relative to these fixed local points. Having at least three transponder points assures that good electronic position-fixes can be obtained.

Seaprobe then makes a detailed map of the bottom topography in the area. While it is doing this, its position is being constantly recorded in relation to the fixed points. With this map, a search plan is formulated that is adjusted to fit the bottom topography and avoid excess pipe handling. Then the actual search begins, using side-looking sonar and underwater TV cameras contained in a pod that is lowered on the pipe until it is relatively near the bottom. In effect, this system reduces the depth of the water by the length of the pipe, and there establishes a plane that is parallel to the sea surface.

With a *cable*-towed fish or pod (which can be used in water less than one thousand feet deep), the shipboard operator has no way of knowing where his towed sensors are at any given moment in relation to his ship. The hydrodynamic "drag" on the cable leading to the fish holding the instruments makes it trail far behind—or sometimes it will "kite" from side to side in random patterns, depending on the subsea currents.

The OSE system, however, used pipe to support the pod that holds the sonar transducers, TV cameras, lights, magnetometer, compass, and other items. Carefully assembled lengths of 4½-inch pipe, very similar to oil-drilling pipe, are lowered from the derrick through the center well in the *Seaprobe*. This pipe is weighted with as much as fifty thousand pounds of "drill collars" (heavy pieces of pipe at the bottom), which act like a sinker on a fishing line and hold the sensor pod directly below the ship. Small variations in the distance the pod lags behind for any given speed and depth are known and can be used to adjust the navigation if necessary. The sixty-foot sections of pipe can be assembled and disassembled at the rate of one a minute, so raising and lowering the pod takes about one second per foot. The power and signal cables that lead to the electronic sensing element in the pod are enclosed in a streamlined fairing attached to the outside (trailing edge) of the pipe.

Watchers seated in the surface control room can watch the bottom go by on large television screens. They can discuss what they see, make notes (in addition to the TV tape record), and stop the ship for a close look if necessary. But much of the searching is done with a high-resolution, side-looking, shadow-type sonar, which projects beams of sound to each side of the pod. Objects rising above the sea floor "shine" on the chart, and the absence of reflected sound in their lee casts heavy shadows, which a skilled interpreter can identify. There is no instantaneous visual presentation of this sonar; instead, it produces a chart record on which a picture is gradually constructed from a sequence of tiny parallel lines, each representing the image of sound reflected on each side of the pod for about a one-second interval. These sound pictures are easily readable with a little practice—but they are always of the area behind the ship.

Seaprobe will have a pair of vertical-axis maneuvering propellers so it can move in any direction, including sideways, backward, or skewed. Both propellers are controlled from a central panel, which can vary their speed and direction of thrust. This enables the ship to stop and hold still in any position against wind or current during identification of any interesting contact—or during the work of recovering an object.

To take a more detailed look at any contact, *Seaprobe* will stop and lower the pod until the television cameras are close to the object in question. Fine adjustments in position are made by pumping water down the pipe and allowing it to escape through variable orifices in the sides of the pipe near the bottom—the adjustment being controlled by the observer at the console, who is watching the effect of his moves on the TV screen. The reaction to this jet effect can be used to move the pod into precise position. If the object seen is the one sought, a special navigation fix is taken and a sonar transponder is jettisoned on the spot to make it easy to find again.

That takes care of locating the object to be recovered, and of refinding it again whenever necessary. It also permits the ship to adjust its position over the object, since *Seaprobe* is designed to hold in one spot indefinitely, without being anchored at all, merely by adjusting the thrusts of the two maneuvering propellers. If anchoring of some accompanying ship or barge should be desired, however, OSE also has developed a deepwater vibrating anchor with very high holding power.[4]

The final problem is the most acute: how do you get the object to be salvaged—be it lost submersible, nuclear device, or downed satellite—back to the surface? For these small objects, the answer is relatively easy; a large steel trapeze trailing a wire bag can be used to scoop the item from a mud bottom (most of the deepwater sea floor is mud). Or a set of supertongs, like a pair of hands, fingers down, which intermesh beneath the object, can be used in other circumstances. Both are, of course, guided by television observation and their positions adjusted by means of the water jets previously described.

Ships and larger objects are something else again, and clearly will require a whole family of new techniques. It is probably feasible to raise objects of a thousand tons from the deep-sea floor with the method about to be described. Anything much larger than that will probably have to be cut into lift-size pieces. The real problem is to find something of sufficient value to make the effort worth while. Perhaps a lost submarine containing valuable information (or nuclear weapons); or a very large aircraft; or an ancient ship. How one could (within economic reason) salvage a really large modern ship from water more than a few hundred feet deep is not known. The problem is, of course, that the ship would be worth only its scrap-metal value, and in today's economy that value is just not great enough to make deep water salvage practicable.

But to return to our valuable submarine or aircraft or ancient ship. First is the question of how to get the lifting capacity; then is the problem of making use of this capacity. The usable lifting capacity of the *Alcoa Seaprobe* is about two hundred tons plus the weight of the pipe and the weight due to acceleration forces—all multiplied by a reasonable safety factor. But lifting large weights requires some means for displacing sea water with something lighter. Many materials have been suggested for deep water, including gasoline, hydrozine gas, ammonia compounds, glass microspheres, and others. OSE's preferred material, however, is time-honored compressed air. The main problem here is: how does one raise the air to sufficient pressure and get it into the lifting chamber at depth? The highest pressure achievable with air compressors large enough to be usable in salvage operations is about 1000 psi—although some small ones (such as are used for pumping up SCUBA bottles) can pump to 3000 psi. The pressures required to equal the water pressure at a depth of six thousand feet is about 3000 psi; and at eighteen thousand feet, about 9000 psi. And the air is needed in *large* quantities.

A method invented by Jack McLelland and Ed Horton can do the job. On *Seaprobe* it will work like this: Up on the ship, at the head of the pipe string, are three items—an air compressor, a water pump, and an air receiver. This last is a chambered mechanism that maintains a supply of air at a predetermined pressure. This is done by means of an automatic air-operated valve, with a pressure regulator, fixed between the receiver and the drill pipe that leads down to the chamber to be pressurized to, say, 3000 psi.

The compressor feeds air into the receiver; the water pump feeds water into the drill pipe. By monitoring the back pressure in this pipe, the regulator controls the air-to-water ratio that is being delivered. That is, each time the water pump shoots a slug of water into the feed pipe, the regulator follows it with a slug of air.

As each slug of water goes down on top of a slug of air, the back pressure is momentarily diminished; and so another slug of air will follow it, and so it goes, turn and turn about. The result is that each slug of *compressible* air forced down the pipe has a slug of *incompressible* water riding it down; not only that, the weight of all the slugs of air and water above it in the pipe continues to compress it, so the pressure in the pipe increases with depth. At the bottom, the mixture of air and water discharges into a chamber, the bottom of which is open to the surrounding sea water. The rising air will displace the water, and soon the chamber will be full of air at ambient water pressure. It is something like blowing air through a straw into a water-filled tumbler that is upside down under water. In a short time the tumbler will be full of air. This unusual two-phase system makes it possible to use commercially available low-pressure pumps and compressors with output pressures of only 100–200 psi to inject air at the bottom at much higher pressures. It is like an air lift in reverse.

APPLICATIONS

Now comes the question of exactly how to make effective use of this lifting capacity. In deepwater work, as in shallow[5], each job must be considered by itself, and a specific salvage plan prepared; there are no all-purpose solutions. If the problem were to raise parts of a large submarine, it would probably be sensible (and possible) to cut it up with diamond saws, torches, or explosives—depending on the circumstances and the object of the salvage.

But consider how one would raise an ancient wooden ship, say sixty cubits (ninety feet) long, from water a mile deep, without disturbing its structure or cargo. This means it will be necessary to bring up a substantial amount of the bottom muds in and around the ship.

For this, a device invented by Ted Mangels of OSE will be used. It is something like an upside-down dry dock with the usual wing walls and pontoons. It will be lowered on the pipe string, centered and aligned with the wrecked ship, and then carefully lowered and jetted down into the mud around the wreck until its lower extremity is beneath the lowest part of the ship. Then a sliding cover something like the top of a roll-top desk will be closed beneath the old ship. Then, this completed, the sealed package will be retrieved. The lift will be started by putting enough air into the pontoons and wing walls to support the greater part of the weight. The last hundred tons will be furnished by the direct lift of the *Seaprobe* pipe. Appropriate means for bleeding off the expanding air will be used so that the wreck package will be kept under control at all times.

Seaprobe will set down its burden in very shallow water, whence it can be floated to the surface and moved to some place where archaeologists can easily work.

Excited in particular by the possibility of raising intact a wooden ship from one of the early Mediterranean civilizations, Bascom has been studying ancient trade routes and considering where best to search for three thousand-year-old ships since 1962—the year he conceived this deep water salvage project. It has long been his ambition to bring back an intact Greek trireme, or a Phoenician trader, or a Roman galley—just as it sank during the golden age of pre-Christian civilizations. Such ships would have been below wave action in deep, dark, cold storage, so he thinks they will look about the way they did on the day they sank. This is especially true because they have been beyond the depth of the most destructive organisms: man, and marine borers. In this project he has enlisted the active support and assistance of the world's real expert on the salvage of ancient ships from shallow water, Peter Throckmorton. But that is the subject of another book.

The entire *Seaprobe* system will be operational in 1971.

Only in the past decade has man really begun to get occasional glimpses of the vast world beneath the sea, and to understand what he is seeing. Marine salvage, particularly deepwater salvage, has played a large role in this understanding; it may very well play a decisive role in the decades to come. Many doubt whether expanding this understanding will be worth its inevitable cost in men, matériel, money, and human intelligence.

But I think it is important in this connection to ponder the words of the distinguished British biologist and entomologist Sir Julian Huxley, on the occasion of the 100th Anniversary of Harvard's Agassiz Museum of Natural Science. It was in 1959, and Russia's triumphant Sputnik had turned man's face toward the moon and the secrets of outer space. Sir Julian duly noted this interest, but then he paused and added a word of personal preference.

"Frankly," he said, "I should much rather see the sea's bottom than the moon's behind."

So, I think, should most of us. The marine salvors of many nations, working in all the great oceans of the world, are helping to make this preference a reality.

[1] See pages 101–4.

[2] At the MTS meeting in Washington, June 1968, a panel on ship costs estimated the average cost of diving any of the small deep submarines at $1000 per hour.

[3] Bascom designed and built the first deepwater taut-moored buoys in 1950 to measure the waves from the first thermonuclear explosion in deep water north of Eniwetok Atoll.

[4] The anchor is a section of pipe some 20 feet long, with a big arrowhead of spade-shaped steel at the lower end. At the upper end of the anchor stem is a small motor with eccentric weights. When the anchor is lowered, this tip touches the bottom and automatically turns on the motor, which vibrates and drives the anchor deep into the sediment. When the anchor line is pulled taut, the arrowhead flops over and locks at right angles to the stem. From this comes the anchor's remarkable holding power (in deep-sea muds, the holding force against a vertical pull is twenty times the anchor's 1000-pound weight).

[5] For making heavy lifts in shallow water where it is possible to attach chains or cables to the object, OSE has patented another of Ed Horton's ideas: the hydraulic chain jack. This would use an anchor-type chain which, after passing over a wildcat to change its direction from vertical to horizontal, is grasped by a claw driven by a hydraulic cylinder. Since great force can be exerted by a large cylinder, a thousand-ton pull is easy to achieve with a stroke of several feet. Then a second claw holds the chain while the one on the cylinder returns for a second bite. A battery of these on a large barge could be rigged to make a ten-thousand-ton lift if that were needed.

APPENDIX I

LLOYD'S STANDARD FORM OF SALVAGE AGREEMENT
NO CURE—NO PAY

On board the
Dated   19

IT IS HEREBY AGREED between Captain[1]   for
and on behalf of the Owners of the "   " her Cargo and Freight
and   for and on behalf of   (hereinafter
called "the Contractor"[2]):—

The Master should sign wherever possible.

1. The Contractor agrees to use his best endeavours to salve the   and her cargo and take them unto   or other place to be hereafter agreed with the Master, providing at his own risk all proper steam and other assistance and labour. The services shall be rendered and accepted as salvage services upon the principle of "no cure—no pay" and the Contractor's remuneration in the event of success shall be[3] £   , unless this sum shall afterwards be objected to as hereinafter mentioned in which case the remuneration for the services rendered shall be fixed by Arbitration in London in the manner hereinafter prescribed: and any other difference arising out of this Agreement or the operations thereunder shall be referred to Arbitration in the same

[1] Insert name of person signing on behalf of owners of property to be salved.

[2] The Contractor's name should always be inserted in line 3 and whenever the Agreement is signed by the Master of the Salving vessel or other person on behalf of the Contractor the name of the Master or other person must also be inserted in line 3 before the words "for and on behalf of." The words "for and on behalf of" should be deleted where a Contractor signs personally.

[3] If at the time of the signing of this Agreement it is not possible to decide upon the figure to be inserted in Clause 1 the space may be left blank as the question of security is dealt with in Clause 4 and the Form provides for the amount of remuneration, if any, to be decided either by agreement or by Arbitration.

way. In the event of the services referred to in this Agreement or any part of such services having been already rendered at the date of this Agreement by the Contractor to the said vessel or her cargo it is agreed that the provisions of this Agreement shall *mutatis mutandis* apply to such services.

2. The Contractor may make reasonable use of the vessel's gear anchors and chains and other appurtenances during and for the purpose of the operations free of costs but shall not unnecessarily damage abandon or sacrifice the same or any other of the property.

3. Notwithstanding anything hereinbefore contained should the operations be only partially successful without any negligence or want of ordinary skill and care on the part of the Contractor or of any person by him employed in the operations, and any portion of the Vessel's Cargo or Stores be salved by the Contractor, he shall be entitled to reasonable remuneration not exceeding a sum equal to   per cent. of the estimated value of the property salved at   or if the property salved shall be sold there then not exceeding the like percentage of the net proceeds of such sale after deducting all expenses and customs duties or other imposts paid or incurred thereon but he shall not be entitled to any further remuneration reimbursement or compensation whatsoever and such reasonable remuneration shall be fixed in case of difference by Arbitration in manner hereinafter prescribed.

4. The Contractor shall immediately after the termination of the services or sooner notify the Committee of Lloyd's of the amount for which he requires security to be given; and failing any such notification by him not later than 48 hours (exclusive of Sundays or other days observed as general holidays at Lloyd's) after the termination of the services he shall be deemed to require security to be given for the sum named in Clause 1, or, if no sum be named in Clause 1, then for such sum as the Committee of Lloyd's in their absolute discretion shall consider sufficient. Such security shall be given in such manner and form as the Committee of Lloyd's in their absolute discretion may consider sufficient but the Committee of Lloyd's shall not be in any way responsible for the sufficiency (whether in amount or otherwise) of any security accepted by them nor for the default or insolvency of any person firm or corporation giving the same.

5. Pending the completion of the security as aforesaid, the Contractor shall have a maritime lien on the property salved for his remuneration. The salved property shall not without the consent in writing of the Contractor be removed from   or the place of safety to which the property is taken by the Contractor on the completion of the salvage services until security has been given to the Committee of Lloyd's as aforesaid. The Contractor agrees not to arrest or detain the property salved unless the security be not given within 14 days (ex-

APPENDIX I 485

clusive of Sundays or other days observed as general holidays at Lloyd's) of the termination of the services (the Committee of Lloyd's not being responsible for the failure of the parties concerned to provide the required security within the said 14 days) or the Contractor has reason to believe that the removal of the property salved is contemplated contrary to the above agreement. In the event of security not being provided as aforesaid or in the event of any attempt being made to remove the property salved contrary to this Agreement the Contractor may take steps to enforce his aforesaid lien. The Arbitrator or Arbitrators or Umpire (including the Committee of Lloyd's if they act in either capacity) appointed under Clause 7 or 8 hereof shall have power in their absolute discretion to include in the amount awarded to the Contractor the whole or such part of the expenses incurred by the Contractor in enforcing his lien as they shall think fit.

6. After the expiry of 42 days from the date of the completion of the security the Committee of Lloyd's shall call upon the party or parties concerned to pay the amount thereof and in the event of non-payment shall realize or enforce the security and pay over the amount thereof to the Contractor unless they shall meanwhile have received written notice of objection and a claim for Arbitration from any of the parties entitled and authorized to make such objection and claim or unless they shall themselves think fit to object and demand Arbitration. The receipt of the Contractor shall be a good discharge to the Committee of Lloyd's for any moneys so paid and they shall incur no responsibility to any of the parties concerned by making such payment and no objection or claim for Arbitration shall be entertained or acted upon unless received by the Committee of Lloyd's within the 42 days above mentioned.

7. In case of objection being made and Arbitration demanded the remuneration for the services shall be fixed by the Committee of Lloyd's as Arbitrators or at their option by an Arbitrator to be appointed by them unless they shall within 30 days from the date of this Agreement receive from the Contractor a written or telegraphic notice appointing an Arbitrator on his own behalf in which case such notice shall be communicated by them to the Owners of the vessel and they shall within 15 days from the receipt thereof give a written notice to the Committee of Lloyd's appointing another Arbitrator on behalf of all the parties interested in the property salved; and if the Owners shall fail to appoint an Arbitrator as aforesaid the Committee of Lloyd's shall appoint an Arbitrator on behalf of all the parties interested in the property salved or they may if they think fit direct that the Contractor's nominee shall act as sole Arbitrator; and thereupon the Arbitration shall be held in London by the Arbitrators or Arbitrator so appointed. If the Arbitrators cannot agree they shall forthwith notify

the Committee of Lloyd's who shall thereupon either themselves act as Umpires or shall appoint some other person as Umpire. Any award of the Arbitrators or Arbitrator or Umpire shall (subject to appeal as provided in this Agreement) be final and binding on all the parties concerned and they or he shall have power to obtain call for receive and act upon any such oral or documentary evidence or information (whether the same be strictly admissible as evidence or not) as they or he may think fit, and to conduct the Arbitration in such manner in all respects as they or he may think fit, and to maintain reduce or increase the sum, if any, named in Clause 1, and shall if in their or his opinion the amount of the security demanded is excessive have power in their or his absolute discretion to condemn the Contractor in the whole or part of the expense of providing such security and to deduct the amount in which the Contractor is so condemned from the salvage remuneration. Unless the Arbitrators or Arbitrator or Umpire shall otherwise direct the parties shall be at liberty to adduce expert evidence on the Arbitration. The Arbitrators or Arbitrator and the Umpire (including the Committee of Lloyd's if they act in either capacity) may charge such fees as they may think reasonable, and the Committee of Lloyd's may in any event charge a reasonable fee for their services in connection with the Arbitration, and all such fees shall be treated as part of the costs of the Arbitration and Award and shall be paid by such of the parties as the Award may direct. Interest at the rate of 5 per cent. per annum from the expiration of 14 days (exclusive of Sundays or other days observed as general holidays at Lloyd's) after the date of the publication of the Award by the Committee of Lloyd's until the date of payment to the Committee of Lloyd's shall (subject to appeal as provided in this Agreement) be payable to the Contractor upon the amount of any sum awarded after deduction of any sums paid on account. Save as aforesaid the statutory provisions as to Arbitration for the time being in force in England shall apply. The said Arbitration is hereinafter in this Agreement referred to as "the original Arbitration" and the Arbitrator or Arbitrators or Umpire thereat as "the original Arbitrator" or "the original Arbitrators" or "the Umpire" and the Award of such Arbitrator or Arbitrators or Umpire as "the original Award."

8. Any of the persons named under Clause 14, except the Committee of Lloyd's, may appeal from the original Award by giving written Notice of Appeal to the Committee of Lloyd's within 14 days (exclusive of Sundays or other days observed as general holidays at Lloyd's) from the publication by the Committee of Lloyd's of the original Award; and any of the other persons named under Clause 14, except the Committee of Lloyd's, may (without prejudice to their right of appeal under the first part of this clause) within 7 days (exclusive of Sundays

or other days observed as general holidays at Lloyd's) after receipt by them from the Committee of Lloyd's of notice of such appeal (such notice if sent by post to be deemed to be received on the day following that on which the said notice was posted) give written Notice of Cross-Appeal to the Committee of Lloyd's. As soon as practicable after receipt of such notice or notices the Committee of Lloyd's shall themselves alone or jointly with another person or other persons appointed by them (unless they be the objectors) hear and determine the Appeal or if they shall see fit to do so or if they be the objectors they shall refer the Appeal to the hearing and determination of a person or persons selected by them. Any Award on Appeal shall be final and binding on all the parties concerned. No evidence other than the documents put in on the original Arbitration and the original Arbitrator's or original Arbitrators' and/or Umpire's notes and/or shorthand notes if any of the proceedings and oral evidence if any at the original Arbitration shall be used on the Appeal unless the Arbitrator or Arbitrators on the Appeal shall in his or their discretion call for other evidence. The Arbitrator or Arbitrators on the Appeal may conduct the Arbitration on Appeal in such manner in all respects as he or they may think fit and may maintain increase or reduce the sum awarded by the original Award with the like power as is conferred by Clause 7 on the original Arbitrator or Arbitrators or Umpire to condemn the Contractor in the whole or part of the expense of providing security and to deduct the amount disallowed from the salvage remuneration. And he or they shall also make such order as he or they may think fit as to the payment of interest (at the rate of 5 per cent. per annum) on the sum awarded to the Contractor. The Arbitrator or Arbitrators on Appeal (including the Committee of Lloyd's if they act in that capacity) may direct in what manner the costs of the original Arbitration and of the Arbitration on Appeal shall be borne and paid and may charge such fees as he or they may think reasonable and the Committee of Lloyd's may in any event charge a reasonable fee for their services in connection with the Arbitration on Appeal and all such fees shall be treated as part of the costs of the Arbitration and Award on Appeal and shall be paid by such of the parties as the Award on Appeal shall direct. Save as aforesaid the statutory provisions as to Arbitration for the time being in force in England shall apply.

  9. (a) In case of Arbitration if no notice of Appeal be received by the Committee of Lloyd's within 14 days after the publication by the Committee of the original Award the Committee shall call upon the party or parties concerned to pay the amount awarded and in the event of non-payment shall realize or enforce the security and pay therefrom to the Contractor (whose receipt shall be a good discharge to them)

the amount awarded to him together with interest as hereinbefore provided.

(b) If notice of Appeal be received by the Committee of Lloyd's in accordance with the provisions of Clause 8 hereof they shall as soon as but not until the Award on Appeal has been published by them, call upon the party or parties concerned to pay the amount awarded and in the event of non-payment shall realize or enforce the security and pay therefrom to the Contractor (whose receipt shall be a good discharge to them) the amount awarded to him together with interest if any in such manner as shall comply with the provisions of the Award on Appeal.

(c) If the Award on Appeal provides that the costs of the original Arbitration or of the Arbitration on Appeal or any part of such costs shall be borne by the Contractor, such costs may be deducted from the amount awarded before payment is made to the Contractor by the Committee of Lloyd's, unless satisfactory security is provided by the Contractor for the payment of such costs.

(d) Without prejudice to the provisions of Clause 4 hereof, the liability of the Committee of Lloyd's shall be limited in any event to the amount of security held by them.

10. The Committee of Lloyd's may in their discretion out of the security (which they may realize or enforce for that purpose) pay to the Contractor on account before the publication of the original Award and/or of the Award on Appeal such sum as they may think reasonable on account of any out-of-pocket expenses incurred by him in connection with the services.

11. The Master or other person signing this Agreement on behalf of the property to be salved is not authorized to make or give and the Contractor shall not demand or take any payment draft or order for or on account of the remuneration.

12. Any dispute between any of the parties interested in the property salved as to the proportions in which they are to provide the security or contribute to the sum awarded or as to any other such matter shall be referred to and determined by the Committee of Lloyd's or by some other person or persons appointed by the Committee whose decision shall be final and is to be complied with forthwith.

13. The Master or other person signing this agreement on behalf of the property to be salved enters into this Agreement as Agent for the vessel her cargo and freight and the respective owners thereof and binds each (but not the one for the other or himself personally) to the due performance thereof.

14. Any of the following parties may object to the sum named

in Clause 1 as excessive or insufficient having regard to the services which proved to be necessary in performing the Agreement or to the value of the property salved at the completion of the operations and may claim Arbitration viz:—(1) The Owners of the ship. (2) Such other persons together interested as Owners and/or Underwriters of any part not being less than one-fourth of the estimated value of the property salved as the Committee of Lloyd's in their absolute discretion may by reason of the substantial character of their interest or otherwise authorize to object. (3) The Contractor. (4) The Committee of Lloyd's —Any such objection and the original Award upon the Arbitration following thereon shall (subject to appeal as provided in this Agreement) be binding not only upon the objectors but upon all concerned, provided always that the Arbitrators or Arbitrator or Umpire may in case of objection by some only of the parties interested order the costs to be paid by the objectors only, provided also that if the Committee of Lloyd's be objectors they shall not themselves act as Arbitrators or Umpires.

15. If the parties to any such Arbitration or any of them desire to be heard or to adduce evidence at the original Arbitration they shall give notice to that effect to the Committee of Lloyd's and shall respectively nominate a person in the United Kingdom to represent them for all the purposes of the Arbitration and failing such notice and nomination being given the Arbitrators or Arbitrator or Umpire may proceed as if the parties failing to give the same had renounced their right to be heard or adduce evidence.

16. Any Award, notice, authority, order, or other document signed by the Chairman of Lloyd's or a Clerk to the Committee of Lloyd's on behalf of the Committee of Lloyd's shall be deemed to have been duly made or given by the Committee of Lloyd's and shall have the same force and effect in all respects as if it had been signed by every member of the committee of Lloyd's.

For and on behalf of the Contractor	For and on behalf of the Owners of property to be salved
(To be signed either by the Contractor personally or by the Master of the salving vessel or other person whose name is inserted in line 3 of this Agreement.)	(To be signed by the Master or other person whose name is inserted in line 1 of this Agreement.)

APPENDIX II

THE LEGALITIES OF SALVAGE

Civil salvage (as opposed to military salvage) can be very simply defined as the preservation of life or property from some of the manifold dangers that may be encountered by shipping and aircraft in times of peace or war. As defined in admiralty court, however, a civil salvage service takes on a very precisely limited character, with certain elements necessarily present if it is to be classified as salvage.

Definition of Civil Salvage Service

"A service which saves or helps to save a recognized subject of salvage when in danger, if the rendering of such service is voluntary in the sense of being solely attributable neither to pre-existing contractual or official duty owed to the owner of the salved property nor to the interest of self-preservation."

As so defined, a service performed must have four elements before it legally qualifies as marine salvage and is therefore eligible for a salvage award. The elements: (1) the object saved must be *"a recognized subject of salvage"*; (2) the salvors must enjoy some *success* ("a service which saves or helps to save . . ."); (3) the object must have been in *danger* (". . . when in danger"); and (4) the salvors must do their work *voluntarily* ("if the rendering of such service is voluntary").

There is a final consideration, of course, which is the assessment of the salvage award itself.

Subjects of Salvage

What are the recognized subjects of salvage? English maritime law has acknowledged the right of the salvor to a reward from quite ancient times,[1] but the only items legally subject to salvage awards are vessels and aircraft, their apparel,[2] cargo, and freight at risk.[3] Second, life from a vessel, aircraft, or wreck.[4] Nationality of salvor, saved, or owner of the property involved is irrelevant.

CARGO: All merchandise aboard the salved vessel, no matter who owns it. Excluded are the personal effects of the ship's master, the crew, and passengers, and the ship's expendable provisions (such as food and fuel).

FREIGHT AT RISK: Freight that would have been lost to the shipowner if the salvage services had not been performed. FREIGHT AT RISK, insofar as it is indeed saved, must contribute proportionally with the ship and the cargo to the payment of the salvage reward. Interestingly enough, this can include the passengers' passage money.

VESSEL: Any SHIP or BOAT or any other description of vessel used in navigation. For salvage-award purposes, the *owner* of a vessel means *everyone* financially interested in it—including mortgagees.

SHIP: Every description of vessel used in navigation that is not propelled by oars. This does not *exclude* a craft that is *sometimes* rowed, or is capable of being rowed; it excludes only those whose *sole* motive power is oars. *Used in navigation*—as opposed to being merely *connected with navigation*—is the important phrase here.[5]

BOAT: A much more elastic term than ship. This includes any vessel of small size intended and adapted for the conveyance of persons or goods upon the water.

An 1836 admiralty court case with the wildly intriguing title of *The King versus Forty-Nine Casks of Brandy* gave legal definition as recognized subjects of salvage to a number of categories so widely misunderstood that they should be itemized here. These definitions still have legal standing today, although most of them are seldom used popularly within these strict limits.

WRECK: Legally, *wreccum maris*—wreck of the sea. This is limited to those portions of ship or cargo that have been stranded ("by the sea cast") upon the land. This includes *anything* that previously was part of the vessel, its apparel, or cargo. The courts have held, for instance, that rigging, gear, nets, buoys, and floats from fishing boats—if they are being used in relation to fishing—are legally WRECK (hence subject to salvage) if cast upon the shore.

FLOTSAM: Goods from a ship that has been sunk ("or otherwise perished") that float upon the sea.

JETSAM: Goods from a ship in danger of being sunk that have been cast overboard to lighten the ship. This applies only to these goods *if the ship subsequently actually sinks*. No definition seems to exist, under admiralty law, for such goods if the ship does *not* sink; but popular usage includes under the term JETSAM all jettisoned goods no matter what the vessel's subsequent fate.

LAGAN: Goods that, like jetsam, are cast into the sea from a ship that subsequently sinks. Since these goods are themselves so heavy that they also will sink, however, the mariners, before throwing them overboard, "to the intent to have them again, tie to them a buoy, or cork, or such other thing that will not sink, so that they may find them again."

DERELICT: An object that has been abandoned and deserted at sea by those who were in charge of it, without hope on their part of recovering it, and without intention of returning to it. Popular usage would limit the term to an abandoned ship, but this is not necessarily so; it also can be used in connection with cargo.

Since the term DERELICT depends in its application upon the *intentions and expectations* of the captain and crew when they desert their vessel, rather than on the objective conditions surrounding the event, a court attempting to determine whether a ship has been legally abandoned often has a very sticky time of it. Obviously a ship does not become derelict because the men were forced to flee her for fear of their lives, or in search of aid, or to turn her over to a salvor.[6] On the other hand, a crew abandoning a vessel with no intention of returning, but who then are blessed with a weather change that permits their return, do not by the act of returning render the ship *not* derelict.

A salvor, therefore, who meets the conditions of success, danger, and voluntariness in carrying out his service on a recognized subject of salvage, is legally entitled to remuneration unless negligence or misconduct on his own part precludes such remuneration. If a legal and binding agreement of the amount to be received has not previously been reached between the salvors and the salved vessel's owners or representatives, the court will also fix and assess the amount to be received. In admiralty court, twenty-six separate classifications of salvage service to a ship in danger are recognized.[7]

Before briefly examining *danger, voluntariness,* and *success,* we should understand that the legal rights of salvors to remuneration are *absolute rights,* independent of any contract—*including* one fixing the salvage reward, if this reward is not in keeping with the service rendered. Lord Wright stated, "The maritime law of salvage is based on principles of equity." Lord Lushington, a jurist who laid down many of the landmark decisions in British civil salvage law, was even more explicit: "Salvage is governed by a due regard to benefit received, combined with a just reward for the general interests of ships and marine commerce."

Danger

Danger to property or lives is the very foundation upon which any claim for salvage rests. If there is no real and sensible danger present, a salvage reward cannot and will not be made; but the courts admit that it need not be an *instant* danger.[8]

Danger is liberally interpreted by the courts. A signed Lloyd's Standard Form of Salvage Agreement usually leads to a legal presupposition of danger, as does the waving of distress signals or similar conduct. The subjective appraisal of the saved usually is given less weight than the professional appraisal of the salvors, since the saved often are so unskilled that they don't even know they have been in danger. Danger is nearly always assumed to be present when a ship is towed, since the very nature of towing makes it a hazardous undertaking.

Voluntariness

Voluntariness on the part of the salvor generally precludes the crew of the salved vessel, a professional pilot, the ship's owner, a tug towing the vessel under prior contract, the ship's agent, or anyone with a predetermined moral, legal, or monetary commitment to help the ship (such as Coast Guardsmen). Passengers usually are unable to claim as salvors, since in saving the vessel they are saving their own lives and property. Exceptions to this rule are based on the idea that self-interest or self-preservation may not be the *sole* motive of the salvors.[9]

Also generally excluded from salvage reward are the captain and crew of a ship that, through its own fault, has struck another and then rendered the assistance that saved the damaged vessel. The courts feel that, since they caused the danger in the first place, their assistance is involuntary.

Success

Success is the final element necessary for the payment of a salvage reward, and it means just what the word implies. The ship, or some part of her cargo or freight, must be saved. Before salvage can be paid, *something other than human life* must be saved. The mere incurring of loss or expense does not necessarily mean that the salvor's reward—if any—will be high enough to cover them. He might have been inept, his service might have contributed only very slightly to the saving of the vessel, or the value of what was salved might have been too low for a substantial award.[10] The salvor does not have to be the sole or even prime author of the recovery; he will still participate if a reward is paid.[11] There will be no participation, of course, if the salvage service left the vessel in a more precarious position than she had been in originally.

Despite success in recovery, salvage rewards can be reduced or even denied entirely by the courts if the salvors, in performing their services, are guilty of gross mistakes, gross negligence, or gross misconduct. The severity of the reduction depends on the flagrance of the error, omission, or indefensible action.

Just as there are several categories of individuals who, under normal circumstances, cannot participate in a salvage reward, there are also categories into which *any* individual, to be legally eligible for reward, must fall. He must (1) own a salving vessel; (2) be a charterer of it; (3) be the master of it, or a member of its crew; or (4) he must have been personally engaged in the salvage service for which reward is claimed.

If there are two sets of salvors involved, there must be a reasonable (apparent if not actual) necessity for the intrusion of the second set; otherwise they will not participate in the reward. And unless the vessel at peril has been legally abandoned (is a legal derelict), the salvors must always accede to the wishes of the ship's master or owner if such wishes do not interfere with the saving of the vessel.

Salvage Awards

The final element that must be considered in a discussion of the legalities of salvage is the assessment of the award itself. The basic principle: there is no absolute rule or fixed scale of payment or reward. The closest thing to a rule that exists is the tradition—often broken—that the salvor will generally not receive more than a moiety (half) of the value of the salved property. The court will determine the award unless it already has been fixed by a valid salvage agreement between the owner (or his representatives) and the salvors,[12] and will consider many factors. These include the state of the vessel (was it derelict or were there still crewmen aboard?), the salvage value realized, the expenses of the salvors relative to the value of the property salved, and whether the salvage services were exceptionally meritorious or rendered under unusually hazardous conditions.

As Queen's Counsel W. R. Kennedy, then the world's leading authority on salvage law, pointed out in 1891, "The court endeavors always to combine the consideration of what is due to the owners, in the protection of property, with the liberality due to the salvors in remunerating meritorious services."

This means there are two main factors in the assessment of salvage rewards: (1) the salved property; (2) the salvors.

Items concerning salved property that weigh heavily in the assessment of reward are the possible degree of danger to human life aboard the ship at peril, the degree of danger to the salved property, and the actual value of the salved property. Thus salvors who save human life *as well as* property will generally get a more generous award than otherwise. Since salving derelicts is more dangerous than salving an occupied ship, awards often run to one half of salved value, and seldom fall below one third.

The Salvors

Items concerning the salvors themselves that weigh heavily in the assessment of reward are the degree of jeopardy in which they put their lives, the degree of danger in which their equipment and property are placed, the time occupied and the work actually done, the loss and unavoidable expense they have incurred, the responsibility they must assume,[13] and whether the salvors are professionals or amateurs.

Professional salvors will almost always receive a higher remuneration than amateurs for two obvious reasons: They must maintain their equipment and skills solely to perform salvage (that is, they have no other profession, such as fishing, to fall back upon during slack times); and, since they are generally more skillful, the service they render is usually more valuable.

The division of the salvage reward between the members of a salvage team is much more standard than the assessment of the award itself. The owner of the salvage vessel usually receives three fourths, the master one twelfth, and the crew divides the remaining one sixth between them according to their ratings. Special effort, gallantry, or bravery by a crewman will result in a disproportionately large award.[14] If more than one salvage team is involved, recompense will be proportionate to the value of the various services rendered, with judicial opinion generally weighted in favor of the original or primary salvors.

All interests that have benefited by the salvage effort will contribute to the award, with the degree of risk to which the property was submitted having a great deal to do with how much is assessed against whom. Generally, the shipowner must bear the whole brunt of salvage payment *only* when the jeopardy that made salvage necessary arose from actionable fault by himself or his employees. Otherwise, the cargo owner is liable primarily and equally with him in the payment.

Remedies for Non-Payment of Salvage Awards

The salvor has many and quite stringent remedies if payment of the salvage reward is not forthcoming. Almost always he has the right to a *maritime lien* (a privileged claim) against the salved property. His claim can be enforced by a proceeding *in rem* against ship, cargo, freight, and apparel, which means the property can be arrested and sold to satisfy the lien. And this claim takes precedence over all others against the *res* (property) except other salvage claims or a subsequent damage claim.

Nor are *in rem* proceedings his only remedy. If the salvor cannot lay hands on the property to arrest it, in many instances he can move *in personam*. This means he can sue not only the owner of the property he has salved, but anyone having an interest in it. With derelict property, he can keep entire and absolute possession of it from the time he salves it until his services have been paid for.[15]

Let us close this dry little Appendix on the Legalities of Salvage with a short look at the most urgent question of Royal Fish. Defined as "whales and sturgeon found on the shore or caught near the coasts of Great Britain and probably also grampuses, porpoises, dolphins, riggs and graspes and generally whatsoever other fish having in themselves great and immense size or fat," Royal Fish should be offered to Her Majesty the Queen. Her Majesty, we are told, will be "graciously pleased to accept such a gift."

It is a vital point that all salvors should keep in mind at all times. One never knows when one will salvage a whale.

---

[1] See pages 16–17.

[2] Apparel in this connection has a special and very broad meaning that probably includes any equipment of the ship or aircraft that is not part of its hull or engines.

[3] Saving a buoy adrift from its moorings, for example, does not give the rescuer any right to a salvage award (although he has a right to payment for time spent in the effort).

[4] Even though awards for life salvage do exist and have been awarded by the courts, saving life without saving property generally does not result in any award to the salvor.

[5] Thus explaining why a buoy that has broken loose is not a proper subject of salvage.

[6] A most interesting case involving judgment whether a ship was derelict was that of the steamship *Jupiter*, attacked off the Scottish coast by a German submarine which forced the captain and crew to abandon under threat of destruction. The sub inexplicably also went off without sinking her; a second ship found and delivered the *Jupiter* to Leith. The salvors did not claim she had been derelict, but the owners of the lumber the *Jupiter* was carrying did. Since their contract had been terminated by the "abandonment" of the *Jupiter*, they said, they did not owe their freight charges. The court held the crew had left at gunpoint, hence not voluntarily; hence it was not legal abandonment. The lumbermen paid.

[7] (1) Towing, piloting, or navigating; (2) standing by; (3) getting a stranded ship afloat; (4) holding a stranded vessel in position; (5) beaching; (6) rescue of cargo or persons; (7) raising a sunken ship or cargo; (8) bringing a derelict or wreck to safety; (9) bringing assistance; (10) helping a vessel clear an ice field; (11) giving advice of a local danger; (12) saving persons fleeing shipboard danger from their lifeboats; (13) protecting ships, persons, or cargo from pirates or plunderers; (14) supplying officers and men to a shorthanded vessel; (15) supplying tackle or gear; (16) helping extinguish a shipboard fire; (17) rescuing life or property from shipboard fire; (18) removing ship or cargo from the danger of fire; (19) removing a ship on fire from proximity to docks or other shipping; (20) extricating a ship from an ice floe; (21) removing a wreck, etc., that has fouled a ship; (22) saving a ship from impending collision; (23) purchasing or otherwise saving a captured ship from the enemy and returning it to the owner; (24) helping a ship rejoin a

convoy; (25) keeping a vessel from the hands of revolutionaries; and (26) ascertaining by aircraft search whether or not a derelict has sunk, and communicating her position if she has not.

[8] In 1864 the *Ella Constance* was towed into port after the steamship *Isis* found her so completely out of fuel that her crew was burning her main topmast and lifeboats to keep the engines running. She might have made port unaided; but a mere change in weather conditions would have meant terrible danger to her passengers and crew, so the *Isis* was awarded salvage even though no *immediate* danger had been present.

[9] Two British and two Belgian officers, along with twenty-two Belgian soldiers, were caught by the 1920 Russian Bolshevik uprising in which the town and port of Murmansk were seized. They had two options: a wild sleigh ride for the Norwegian frontier, or the seizing of the steamship *Lomonosoff*. They chose the latter, helping the ship's skeleton crew cast off under a hail of bullets from the surrounding Bolshevik ships, returning the fire, and fighting off Communist attempts to board the vessel. The *Lomonosoff* was returned to its owners, and the soldiers were given a salvage reward because there had been another avenue of escape open to them. This made them volunteers as regards the *Lomonosoff*, even though in saving her they had saved themselves.

Another interesting example is the sailing ship *Betsey*, which was stranded at Chichester Shoals, England, in 1904 because her pilot was "incapable through drunkenness" of steering her. The captain and half the crew promptly abandoned, leaving the passengers behind; one of the latter was a merchant sailing captain, however, who took command, brought the *Betsey* off the shoal, and navigated her into Ramsgate Harbor. He received a sizable salvage award.

[10] It should be pointed out also that the salvor who fails totally will not *always* lose everything he spent in the attempt. He cannot get a salvage reward, but he often can recover, on a contractual basis decided before salvage begins, expenses, losses, or damage to his equipment incurred during the unsuccessful operation.

[11] In 1804 the *Jonge Bastiaan* lost her rudder and stove in her bottom on a rock near Harwich, England. After the crew had deserted, the smack *William and Mary*, with great peril to her men, managed to warp the deserted vessel off the rocks. But the *Jonge Bastiaan* sank almost as soon as she was anchored. Her master returned with half a dozen other smacks, and was able to bring off the gold bullion that was the ship's most valuable cargo. *William and Mary*, though not participating in this operation, participated in the reward because there would have been no way to effect the bullion salvage if the *Jonge Bastiaan* had not first been brought into an accessible position.

[12] The Lloyd's Standard Form can be voided (declared invalid) on only four grounds, proof of which lies totally upon the party disputing the Form. They are (1) that the Agreement is tainted with fraud; (2) that the salvors were misled by either misstatement or nondisclosure of fact (and this misstatement or nondisclosure must concern the true condition of the ship, its equipment, or damage sustained, not merely be a misstatement about the value of the property in peril); (3) that the terms agreed upon were inequitable to one or the other party; or (4) that both parties had consented to cancellation of the Agreement.

[13] This includes such things as liability to passengers or to those who shipped the freight at peril.

[14] In 1867 the *Grenada* came across the bark *Golondrina*, which had been deserted by her first and second mates while still in port, and the master of which had subsequently "jumped overboard in a drunken frenzy." The *Grenada*'s second mate got aboard the masterless ship and brought her safely into Swansea, England. He received £300 for his action, which equaled the award to the rest of the crew and exceeded that of the *Grenada*'s master by £100.

[15] Because his rights are so rigidly protected, the salvor is expected to surrender physical possession of salved property *except* derelicts to the owner upon demand.

BIBLIOGRAPHY

BOOKS

BARROWS, NATHANIEL A. *Blow All Ballast! The Story of the Squalus.* New York: Dodd, Mead & Co., 1940.
BASCOM, WILLARD. *Waves and Beaches.* New York: Anchor books, Doubleday & Co., Inc., 1964.
BENÉT, WILLIAM ROSE. *The Reader's Encyclopedia.* New York: Thomas Y. Crowell Co., 1948.
BLAIR, CLAY. *Diving for Pleasure and Treasure.* Cleveland: The World Publishing Co., 1960.
BOWMAN, GERALD. *The Man Who Bought a Navy.* London: George G. Harrap & Co. Ltd., 1964.
BRADY, EDWARD M. *Marine Salvage Operations.* Cambridge, Md.: Cornell Maritime Press, 1960.
BRINDZE, RUTH. *All About Sailing the Seven Seas.* New York: Random House, Inc., 1962.
BUCHSBAUM, RALPH, & MILNE, LORUS J. *The Lower Animals: Living Invertebrates of the World.* New York: Doubleday & Co., Inc., 1960.
BUTLER, SAMUEL (translator). *The Iliad of Homer and the Odyssey.* London: Jonathon Cape Ltd.
CAIDIN, MARTIN. *Hydrospace.* New York: E. P. Dutton & Co., 1964.
CAYFORD, JOHN E. *Underwater Work: A Manual of Scuba Commercial, Salvage and Construction Operations.* Cambridge, Md.: Cornell Maritime Press, 1959.
CHURCHILL, WINSTON S. *The Birth of Britain: Volume 1, A History of the English-Speaking Peoples.* New York: Dodd, Mead & Co., 1956.
———. *The New World: Volume 2, A History of the English-Speaking Peoples.* New York: Dodd, Mead & Co., 1956.
———. *The Age of Revolution: Volume 3, A History of the English-Speaking Peoples.* New York: Dodd, Mead & Co., 1956.
———. *The Great Democracies: Volume 4, A History of the English-Speaking Peoples.* New York: Dodd, Mead & Co., 1956.

CLARKE, ARTHUR C. & WILSON, MIKE. *The Treasure of the Great Reef.* New York: Perennial Library, Harper & Row, 1965.
COCHRAN, HAMILTON. *Freebooters of the Red Sea.* New York: Bobbs-Merrill Co., Inc., 1965.
COLLIER, JOHN. *Indians of the Americas.* New York: W. W. Norton & Co., 1947.
COUSTEAU, J.-Y. & DUMAS, FRÉDÉRIC. *The Silent World.* New York: Pocket Books, Inc., 1961.
———. & DUGAN, JAMES. *The Living Sea.* New York: Harper & Row, Inc., 1963.
COWAN, EDWARD. *Oil and Water: The Torrey Canyon Disaster.* Philadelphia & New York: J. B. Lippincott Co., 1968.
CRAIG, JOHN D. *Danger Is My Business.* Garden City, N.Y.: Garden City Publishing Co., Inc., 1941.
CRILE, JANE & BARNEY. *Treasure-Diving Holidays.* London: Collins, 1954.
CULPIN, HOWARD. *The True Book About Underwater Exploration.* London: Frederick Muller Ltd., 1956.
DAVIS, SIR ROBERT H. *Deep Diving and Submarine Operations.* London: The St. Catherine Press, Ltd., 1962 (7th Edition).
DEBENHAM, FRANK (director). *The Reader's Digest Great World Atlas.* London: The Reader's Digest Assoc., 1964.
DEEP SEA DIVING SCHOOL, STAFF. *Ship Salvage Notes.* Washington, D.C.: U. S. Naval Weapons Plant, 1960.
DIOLE, PHILIPPE. *4000 Years Under the Sea.* London: Pan Books, Ltd., 1957.
DUGAN, JAMES. *Man Under the Sea.* New York: Collier Books, 1965.
EDWARDS, HUGH. *Islands of Angry Ghosts.* New York: William Morrow & Co., Inc., 1966.
ELLSBERG, COMMANDER EDWARD. *Men Under the Sea.* New York: Dodd, Mead & Co., 1956.
———. *No Banners, No Bugles.* New York: Dodd, Mead & Co., 1949.
———. *On the Bottom.* New York: The Literary Guild, 1929.
———. *Under the Red Sea Sun.* New York: Dodd, Mead & Co., 1946.
FRASER, IAN. *Frogman V.C.* London: Odhams Press Ltd., 1958.
GIBBS, JAMES A. *Shipwrecks of the Pacific Coast.* Portland, Ore.: Binfords & Mort, 1957.
HARDWICK, RICHARD. *Skin and Scuba Diving.* Derby, Conn.: Monarch Books, 1963.
HAYES, CARLTON J. H. & BALDWIN, MARSHAL WHITED. *History of Europe*, Volumes I and II. New York: Macmillan Co., 1949.
JOWETT, BENJAMIN (translator). *The Dialogues of Plato.* Oxford: Oxford University Press.
KARNEKE, JOSEPH SIDNEY & BOESEN, VICTOR. *Navy Diver.* New York: Ace Books, Inc., 1962.
KEEBLE, PETER. *Ordeal by Water.* London: Longmans, Green & Co., 1957.
KORN, JERRY. *The Raising of the Queen.* New York: Simon & Schuster, Inc., 1961.
LARN, RICHARD & CARTER, CLIVE. *Cornish Shipwrecks.* Newton Abbott, Eng.: David & Charles, Ltd., 1969.

LONG, LUMAN H. (editor). *The World Almanac and Book of Facts* (1970 Edition). New York: Newspaper Enterprise Assoc., Inc., 1970.
MARX, ROBERT F. *Always Another Adventure.* Cleveland & New York: The World Publishing Co., 1967.
―――. *They Dared the Depths.* Cleveland & New York: The World Publishing Co., 1968.
―――. *Shipwrecks in Florida Waters.* Eau Gallie, Fla.: Scott Publishing Co., 1969.
MASTERS, DAVID. *When Ships Go Down: More Wonders of Salvage.* London: Eyre & Spottiswoode, Ltd., 1932.
―――. *The Wonders of Salvage.* London: John Lane, The Bodley Head, Ltd., 1926 (3d Edition).
MCGUFFIE, KENNETH C. *Kennedy's Civil Salvage.* London: Stevens & Sons, Ltd., 1958 (4th Edition, Revised).
MEIER, FRANK. *Fathoms Below: Undersea Salvage from Sailing Ships to the Normandie.* New York: E. P. Dutton & Co., Inc., 1943.
―――. *Men Under the Sea.* New York: Dell Publishing Co., Inc., 1948.
―――. *Up for Air.* New York: E. P. Dutton Co., Inc., 1940.
MORRIS, CHRISTOPHER. *The Day They Lost the H-Bomb.* New York: Coward-McCann, Inc., 1966.
MOWAT, FARLEY. *The Serpent's Tail.* Boston: Little, Brown & Co., 1961.
PUGH, MARSHALL. *Frogman: Commander Crabb's Story.* New York: Charles Scribner's Sons, 1956.
RAWLINSON, GEORGE (translator). *The History of Herodotus.* London: J. M. Dent & Sons, Ltd.
RIESEBERG, LT. HARRY E. *I Dive for Treasure.* New York: Popular Library, 1954.
SILVERBERG, ROBERT. *Sunken History.* New York: Bantam Books, Inc., 1964.
SMITH, WILLIAM. *Smith's Bible Dictionary.* New York: Pyramid Publications, Inc., 1967.
SNOW, EDWARD ROWE. *True Tales of Buried Treasure.* New York: Dodd, Mead & Co., 1957.
TASSOS, JOHN. *The Underwater World.* Englewood Cliffs, N.J.: Prentice-Hall, Inc., 1957.
THOMPSON, FRANK E. JR. *Diving, Cutting and Welding in Underwater Salvage Operations.* New York: Cornell Maritime Press, 1944.
THORNE, JIM. *The Underwater World, A Survey of Oceanography.* New York: Thomas Y. Crowell Company, 1969.
TWAIN, MARK. *Life on the Mississippi.* New York: Harper & Row, Publishers, Inc., 1896.
WAGNER, KIP & TAYLOR, L. G. JR. *Pieces of Eight.* New York: E. P. Dutton & Co., 1966.
WARREN, C. E. T. & BENSON, JAMES. *The Midget Raiders; The Wartime Story of Human Torpedoes and Midget Submarines.* New York: William Sloane Associates, 1954.
WHYTE, A. GOWANS & HADFIELD, ROBERT L. *Deep-Sea Salvage.* London: Sampson Low, Marston & Co., Ltd., 1932.

WRIGHT, WILLIAM ALOIS (editor). *The Complete Works of William Shakespeare*. Garden City, N.Y.: Garden City Publishing Co., Inc., 1936.
Webster's Geographical Dictionary. Springfield, Mass.: G. & C. Merriam and Co., 1960.

PERIODICALS

ANDERSON, DICK. "Cousteau and Diving," *Skin Diver Magazine*, Vol. 17, No. 6 (June 1968), pp. 26-7, 62.
BASS, GEORGE F. "The Ruins Under the Sea," *Holiday Magazine*. Vol. 46, No. 2 (August 1969), pp. 25, 77.
BENCHLEY, PETER. "I Know What I'm Doing Here—I Think," *Holiday Magazine*, Vol. 46, No. 2 (August 1969), pp. 19-20, 70+.
BISHOP, REGINALD WALTER & FLEET, PETER FARQUHAR. "Diving and Salvage," *I. C. E. Proceedings*, Vol. 21 (February 1962), pp. 347-66.
BLIVEN, B. "Science and Technology: How the *Normandie* Was Raised," *New Republic*, August 30, 1943, pp. 284-87.
BLUM, WALTER. "Helium World—Men Who Quack and Water That Won't Boil—That's the Bizarre Life of the Sealab Aquanauts," *California Living*, March 9, 1969, pp. 19-23.
BONGARTZ, ROY. "Scuba-Diving Junkman," *True Magazine*, Vol. 49, No. 380 (January 1969), pp. 58-60, 70+.
BROWN, JOSEPH E. "*Lusitania* Treasure Hunt," *Saga Magazine*, May 1969, pp. 27-31, 53.
COUSTEAU, JACQUES-YVES. "Diving Through an Undersea Avalanche," *National Geographic Magazine*, Vol. 107, No. 4 (April 1955), pp. 538-42.
———. "Exploring Davy Jones's Locker with *Calypso*," *National Geographic Magazine*, Vol. 109, No. 2 (February 1956), pp. 149-61.
———. "Fish Men Discover a 2,200-year-old Greek Ship," *National Geographic Magazine*, Vol. 105, No. 1 (January 1954), pp. 1-36.
———. "Fish Men Explore a New World Undersea," *National Geographic Magazine*, Vol. 102, No. 4 (October 1952), pp. 431-72.
DOAK, WADE. "Elingamite Revisited," *Dive Magazine*, Vol. 1, No. 6 (August 1968), pp. 56-61.
EDGERTON, HAROLD E. "Photographing the Sea's Dark Underworld," *National Geographic Magazine*, Vol. 107, No. 4 (April 1955), pp. 523-37.
EDIGER, DON & SCOTT, NORMAN. "Newest Secret of the Well of Virgins," *Argosy Magazine*, Vol. 366, No. 5 (May 1968), pp. 65-69, 89+.
HORNER, DAVE. "S. S. Central America," *Dive Magazine*, Vol. 1, No. 1 (October 1967), pp. 12-15, 28+.
HULL, E. W. SEABROOK. "DR/V *Pisces I* Has Salvaged a 95-Ton Tug From a Depth of 670 Feet," *Ocean Science News*, Vol. 11, No. 31 (August 1, 1969), p. 3.
HUNT, GEORGE P. "The Art of Shooting Underwater," *Life Magazine*, March 3, 1969, p. 4.

HUTTON, J. BERNARD. "Commander Crabb is Alive," *Argosy Magazine*, Vol. 367, No. 3 (September 1968), pp. 21–27, 60+.
ISELIN, COLUMBUS O'D. & LEAR, JOHN. "What Sank the *Thresher?*" *Saturday Review Magazine*, October 5, 1963, pp. 57–60.
KEACH, LT. COMDR. DONALD L. "Down to *Thresher* by Bathyscaphe," *National Geographic Magazine*, Vol. 125, No. 6 (June 1964), pp. 765–77.
KLEIN, MARTIN. "Side Scan Sonar," *Under Sea Technology*, April 1967.
LEAR, JOHN. Untitled report, *Saturday Review Magazine*, November 7, 1964, p. 62.
LINK, EDWIN A. "Tomorrow on the Deep Frontier," *National Geographic Magazine*, Vol. 125, No. 6 (June 1964), pp. 778–801.
LONG, PATRICK. "Skeleton Clue to Treasure" (publication unknown).
MACHLIN, MILT. "Argosy Giant of Adventure, 1968: Treasure Diver—Sailing Pioneer—Archeologist—Adventurer," *Argosy Magazine*, Vol. 366, No. 5 (May 1968), pp. 23–29, 60+.
———. "The Supersubs are Here," *Argosy Magazine*, Vol. 366, No. 1 (January 1968), pp. 44–46, 76+.
MACLEISH, KENNETH. "A Taxi for the Deep Frontier," *National Geographic Magazine*, Vol. 133, No. 1 (January 1968), pp. 138–50.
MARDEN, LUIS. "Camera Under the Sea," *National Geographic Magazine*, Vol. 109, No. 2 (February 1956), pp. 162–200.
———. "I Found the Bones of the Bounty," *National Geographic Magazine*, Vol. 112, No. 6 (December 1957), pp. 725–89.
MARX, ROBERT & REBIKOFF, DMITRI. "Atlantis at Last?" *Argosy Magazine*, Vol. 369, No. 6 (December 1969), pp. 23–27.
———. "Bermuda," *Dive Magazine*, Vol. 1, No. 5 (June 1968), pp. 39–42.
———. "Columbus's Last Two Ships Found in Jamaica," *Argosy Magazine*, Vol. 367, No. 3 (September 1968), pp. 32–37, 80+.
———. "Mendel L. Peterson's Seminar in Marine Archaeology," *Dive Magazine*, Vol. 1, No. 3 (January 1968), pp. 32–35.
———. "Mud, Bones and Silver—The Excavation of Port Royal in the Year 1966," *Dive Magazine*, Vol. 1, No. 6 (August 1968), pp. 33–39.
———. "Providence Island: Where Treasure Dreams Come True," *Argosy Magazine*, Vol. 336, No. 1 (January 1968), pp. 58–63, 80+.
———. "Secrets of a Professional Treasure Diver," *Argosy Magazine*, Vol. 367, No. 2 (August 1968), pp. 46–51, 70+.
———. "The Sure Thing," *Dive Magazine*, Vol. 1, No. 1 (October 1967), pp. 20–23, 50+.
———. "Under Port Royal," *Dive Magazine*, Vol. 1. No. 3 (January 1968), pp. 36–41.
——— & WATSON, NEAL. "World's Record Scuba Dive," *Argosy Magazine*, Vol. 369, No. 1 (July 1969), pp. 47, 70+.
REMICK, TEDDY. "U-Boat Sunk off Chicago," *Skin Diver Magazine*, Vol. 17, No. 6 (June 1968), pp. 38–39, 62+.
ROY, C. H. "Up Ship! Salvaging the *Normandie*," *Collier's Magazine*, October 3, 1942, pp. 22–23.
SERPAS, PAUL F. "Trinidad, The Treasure of Trinidad Island," *Dive Magazine*, Vol. 1, No. 5 (June 1968), pp. 60–62.

SOLAINI, MULTANI. "Rare Anchor Block Yet to be Deciphered," *Dive Magazine*, Vol. 1, No. 6 (August 1968), pp. 40–41.

TAYLOR, L. B. "Death of a U. S. Navy Aquanaut—Was It Sabotage?" *Man's Magazine*, Vol. 17, No. 8 (August 1969), pp. 44–47, 98+.

THROCKMORTON, PETER. "Oldest Known Shipwreck Yields Bronze Age Cargo," *National Geographic Magazine*, Vol. 121, No. 5 (May 1962), pp. 696–711.

TZIMOULIS, PAUL J. "What's Down There—And Where," *Holiday Magazine*, Vol. 46, No. 2 (August 1969), pp. 24, 61+.

WAGNER, KIP. "Drowned Galleons Yield Spanish Gold," *National Geographic Magazine*, Vol. 127, No. 1 (January 1965), pp. 1–37.

WAKELIN, JAMES H. Jr. "Thresher: Lesson and Challenge," *National Geographic Magazine*, Vol. 125, No. 6 (June 1964), pp. 759–64.

WIRTH, DICK. "The Black Lagoon," *Dive Magazine*, Vol. 1, No. 1 (October 1967), pp. 28–31, 49+.

WOOD, NATHANIEL. "Submarine Rescue," *Machine Design*, June 1968, pp. 20–25.

WUSTEMAN, JOHN. "The Great Ship *Wasa*," *International Nickel Magazine*, undated, pp. 33–36.

ZANELLI, LEO. "Shipwreck," *Yachts and Yachting*, February 28, 1969, pp. 452–53.

Staff Writer. "The Black Tide," *Time Magazine*, December 26, 1969, p. 29.

———. "Bridgewater Disaster, Heroic Deeds by Man and Ship," *Port of Freemantle Quarterly*, June 1962, pp. 14–21.

———. "Foam to be Used in *Wahine* Salvage," *Lloyd's Register*, 1967.

———. "The Longest Dive—Project Tektite's Aquanauts Begin Their 60-Day Mission," *Life Magazine*, March 7, 1969, pp. 28–35.

———. "*Normandie* Floats Again," *Life Magazine*, August 23, 1943, pp. 36–37.

———. "*Normandie* Risen: 18 Month Salvage Job," *Newsweek Magazine*, August 16, 1943, pp. 45–46.

———. "Plastic Bubbles Lift Dredger," *Fairplay Marine Insurance Review*, September 19, 1968.

———. "Poet of the Depths," *Time Magazine*, March 28, 1960, pp. 66–77.

———. "Presumed Lost," *Newsweek Magazine*, June 17, 1968, p. 74.

———. "Raising the *Normandie*," *Popular Mechanics*, September 1943, pp. 14–15.

———. "The Sea: Back to the Hunt," *Newsweek Magazine*, June 10, 1963, p. 31.

———. "The Sea: How the *Thresher* Died," *Newsweek Magazine*, July 1, 1963, p. 26.

———. "The Sea: U. S. S. *Thresher*," *Newsweek Magazine*, April, 22, 1963, pp. 26–28.

———. "The Sea: Search for the *Thresher*," *Newsweek Magazine*, May 27, 1963, p. 34.

———. "Science: Epitaph for *Thresher*," *Newsweek Magazine*, September 16, 1963, p. 59.

———. "Science: The Untested *Thresher*," *Newsweek Magazine*, January 18, 1965, p. 72.
———. "Silence from the Seamounts," *Time Magazine*, June 7, 1968, p. 29.
———. "Submarines: Overdue," *Newsweek Magazine*, June 10, 1968, pp. 34+.
———. "Super Salvage," *Newsweek Magazine*, June 1, 1942, p. 33.
———. "TV in the Deep," *Newsweek Magazine*, September 1, 1952, p. 44.
———. Untitled news report, *Newsweek Magazine*, September 26, 1966, pp. 44+.
———. Untitled news report, *Saturday Review Magazine*, July 17, 1954, p. 15.
———. Untitled news report, *Saturday Review Magazine*, November 14, 1964, p. 44.
———. "*Yuna*'s Salvage of Tanker *Bridgewater*," Newsletter No. 18, The Adelaide Steamship Co., Ltd., March 30, 1962.
Tug—Towage and Salvage Review. No. 6, New Year 1959.
———. No. 7, Spring 1959.
———. No. 8, Summer 1959.
———. No. 9, Autumn 1959.
Tugs: An Annual Survey by Ship & Boat. March 1968.
Wijsmuller Digest, A Publication of N. V. Bureau Wijsmuller, Towage and Salvage Co., Vol. 1, No. 1 (May 1960).
———. Vol. 1, No. 2 (September 1961).
———. Vol. 1, No. 4 (December 1964).
———. Vol. 1, No. 5 (January 1966).
———. Vol. 1, No. 6 (May 1968).

NEWSPAPERS

BERTIN, LEONARD. "Ancient Wreck Find off Elba," London *Daily Telegraph*, February 9, 1954.
———. "Navy's Heavy Task in Search for Comet," London *Daily Telegraph*, February 2, 1954.
———. "New Finds in Comet Search," London *Daily Telegraph*, February 11, 1954.
———. "TV Camera Sights Main Comet Wreck," London *Daily Telegraph*, February 13, 1954.
CARLEY, WILLIAM M. "Sunken *Andrea Doria* Still Lures Some Men Who Dream of Riches," *The Wall Street Journal*, July 19, 1968.
COPE, MICHAEL. "Big Treasure Find in a Sunken Ship," *San Francisco Chronicle*, November 25, 1968.
COTTRELL, PETER. "Ships Recover Six Pieces of Crashed Comet," London *Daily Telegraph*, January 22, 1954.
COWAN, REX. "The Treasure Hunters," *The Guardian*, July 25, 1968.

DE JONGH, NICHOLAS. "£270 for the Admiral's Pot," London *Daily Telegraph*, January 29, 1970.
DRAPER, GEORGE. "Golden Abacos Legend—Enough Treasure for All," San Francisco *Sunday Chronicle*, January 17, 1965.
DUNCAN, JAMES. "Hidden Treasure—A South Sea Mystery," San Francisco *Chronicle*, October 12, 1969.
EGLIN, ROGER. "Raising the Sunken Millions," *The Observer*, June, 30, 1968.
FRIENDLY, ALFRED. "The Admiral's Treasure," San Francisco *Chronicle*, July 8, 1969.
GODWIN, JOHN. "The Mystery of the 'Jinx Ship,'" San Francisco *Sunday Examiner/Chronicle*, February 9, 1969.
———. "What Became of *Mary Celeste?*" San Francisco *Sunday Examiner/Chronicle*, February 16, 1969.
GRIBBIN, AUGUST. "Sealab III Project was Marred From the Beginning by Problems," *National Observer*, March 17, 1969.
HILLINGER, CHARLES. "The Lagoon of the Dead Ships," San Francisco *Chronicle*, June 15, 1968.
KUSSEROW, H. W. "Target: The *Andrea Doria*," San Francisco *Sunday Examiner/Chronicle*, July 28, 1968.
LARSEN, GORDON A. "The Security I Like Best," *The Commercial and Financial Chronicle*, November 21, 1968.
MCMANUS, LARRY. "Is There Gold Under the Golden Gate?" San Francisco *Chronicle*, May 20, 1946.
METCALFE, JACK. "The Treasure of the *Andrea Doria*," the New York *Sunday News*, August 18, 1968.
MORROW, EDWARD A. "Two Exploratory Undersea Craft Stir Interest," the New York *Times*, July 27, 1968.
NOBLE, JOHNNY. "Treasure Ship May Be Found off Gate," Oakland *Tribune*, May 18, 1946.
PEARSON, DREW. "The Swivel-Chair Admirals of the Navy," San Francisco *Chronicle*, February 19, 1969.
PERLMAN, DAVID. "Quest for Oil and Knowledge: Holes Under the Sea," San Francisco *Chronicle*, July 10, 1969.
PUGH, MARSHALL. "Did Whitehall Hush Up the Facts?" London *Daily Mail*, May 8, 1958.
———. "The Riddle of the Snapped Snort," London *Daily Mail*, May 7, 1958.
———. "Underwater TV: Will Crabb's Crazy Plan Find the Missing Submarine?" London *Daily Mail*, May 6, 1958.
RIESEBERG, LT. HARRY E. "Ship of the Rockbound Cavern" (publication unknown).
———. "Underwater Treasures of the West," San Francisco *Sunday Chronicle*, January 16, 1967, p. 23.
ROSS, MARIS. "Despite New Technology, Last Year's Toll: 337 Ships Wrecked," San Francisco *Chronicle*, November 17, 1968.
SMITH, CLIFF. "Man Must Breathe Like Fish at Ultra-Deep Ocean Depths," San Diego *Union*, January 1970 (exact date unknown).

SMULLEN, IVOR. "Treasure of the Armada," San Francisco *Chronicle*, January 5, 1969.
WAITE, ELMONT. "Ditched Plane—Big Jet Hoisted Out of the Bay," San Francisco *Chronicle*, November 25, 1968.
WEEKS, GEORGE. "Our Silent Spy Game Deep in Ocean," San Francisco *Chronicle*, August 11, 1968.
ZANE, MAITLAND. "The Dunked Jet Flies Again," San Francisco *Chronicle*, March 27, 1969.
Staff Writer. "The *Affray*," London *Daily Telegraph*, June 15, 1951.
———. "Ancient Ship May Hold a Gold Fortune," San Francisco *Chronicle*, September 6, 1969.
———. "*Andrea Doria* May Be Raised at Last," Houston *Chronicle*, July 28, 1968.
———. "Another Airliner Crash off L.A.—Down in Sea, 38 on Board," San Francisco *Chronicle*, January 19, 1969.
———. "Another ship Joins £2m Treasure Hunt," London *Daily Telegraph*, August 3, 1967.
———. "Armada Treasure Ship Located," San Francisco *Chronicle*, November 11, 1968.
———. "*Association* Treasure Ship Wreck Identified by Arms on Plate," London *Daily Telegraph*, September 12, 1968.
———. "Big Sale of Sunken Treasure," San Francisco *Chronicle*, July 15, 1969.
———. "A Bit of *Scorpion* Asleep in the Deep," San Francisco *Sunday Examiner/Chronicle*, November 10, 1968.
———. "A Briney Clue to Columbus," San Francisco *Chronicle*, July 16, 1968.
———. "Cannon Find May Lead to £1m Wreck," London *Daily Telegraph*, July 12, 1967.
———. "Coast Guard Pumps Save Holed Freighter," San Francisco *Chronicle*, March 10, 1969.
———. "Columbus's Ships to be Hunted on Sea Floor," the New York *Times*, July 16, 1968.
———. "Comet Wreck Located in Sea," London *Daily Telegraph*, January 14, 1954.
———. "Death Ship Found," San Francisco *Chronicle*, November 28, 1968.
———. "Deep Diving Experiment in Pressure," San Francisco *Chronicle*, December 9, 1968.
———. "Divers Find 1707 Wreck's Guns," London *Daily Telegraph*, July 6, 1967.
———. "Divers Find Signs of *Affray* Damage," London *Daily Telegraph*, June 16, 1951.
———. "Divers Seek Bullion in Man o' War," London *Daily Telegraph*, July 7, 1967.
———. "Faster Flow, Fewer Fish—Inside the Gulf Stream," San Francisco *Chronicle*, August 9, 1969.
———. "Ferry to be Raised and Resunk at Sea" (publication unknown).

———. "Fifty-five Fathoms Down," San Francisco *Chronicle*, January 23, 1969.
———. "Five Trapped in Capsized Tanker—One Survives," San Francisco *Chronicle*, March 28, 1969.
———. "Four Trapped in Submarine—400 Feet Down," San Francisco *Chronicle*, October 8, 1969.
———. "Freighter Fights to Keep Afloat," San Francisco *Chronicle*, March 22, 1969.
———. "Frogmen Diving for Death Ship," San Francisco *Chronicle*, November 27, 1968.
———. "Group Signs to Salvage *Santa Maria*," San Francisco *Chronicle*, October 13, 1968.
———. "Gulf of Mexico Furor: Shipwreck Booty of Modern Pirates," San Francisco *Chronicle*, August 12, 1969.
———. "Is It a Rock—Or a Wrecked Ship? Gate Treasure Divers Get a Nibble," San Francisco *Chronicle*, June 3, 1946.
———. "Jetliner Drops into the Bay Short of Airport, 107 Rescued," San Francisco *Chronicle*, November 23, 1968.
———. "The Little Aircraft Carrier," San Francisco *Chronicle*, November 26, 1968.
———. "Lloyd's of London, a Male Stronghold, to Let Women Join," *The Wall Street Journal*, February 21, 1969.
———. "Lloyd's of London: The Disaster Center," Newark *Evening News*, July 29, 1968.
———. "Lloyd's to Let Members Hold All Deposits in British Equity Shares; Bond Prices Fall," *The Wall Street Journal*, January 27, 1969.
———. "Mare Island Mishap—The Bungling that Sank the A-Sub," San Francisco *Chronicle*, July 5, 1969.
———. "Midget Sub Recovered," San Francisco *Chronicle*, August 30, 1969.
———. "Minister Flies for Comet Inquiries," London *Daily Telegraph*, January 18, 1954.
———. "Minisub to be Raised," San Francisco *Chronicle*, September 1, 1969.
———. "Month Under the Sea Ends," San Francisco *Chronicle*, August 15, 1969.
———. "Navy Readies Sealab III for Tests," San Francisco *Chronicle*, February 13, 1969.
———. "New Theory in Death of Aquanaut," San Francisco *Chronicle*, February 20, 1969.
———. "Nuclear Sub Disaster—Trouble 'Inside' *Scorpion*," San Francisco *Chronicle*, January 3, 1969.
———. "$1 Million in Gold, Silver—The Spanish Treasure Fleet," San Francisco *Chronicle*, December 8, 1966.
———. "Peruvian Ship Finally Sinks," San Francisco *Chronicle*, March 27, 1969.
———. "Plastic Foam Soaks Up Oil," San Francisco *Examiner*, September 22, 1969.

BIBLIOGRAPHY 509

———. "The Quest for Rome's Sunken Pleasureland," San Francisco *Chronicle*, February 20, 1969.
———. "Rear Part of Comet Seen by TV," London *Daily Telegraph*, February 1954.
———. "Research Minisub Recovered," San Francisco *Chronicle*, September 2, 1969.
———. "Salvage Divers Vie for Armada Flagship Haul," London *Daily Telegraph*, December 1969.
———. "Salvage Drama—Japan Jet Salvagers Work Against Tides in S. F. Bay," San Francisco *Chronicle*, November 24, 1968.
———. "Salvage Plan for a Historic Ship," San Francisco *Chronicle*, November 11, 1968.
———. "Scillies Await Gold Rush," London *Daily Telegraph*, July 9, 1967.
———. "A Sealab Death Suspends Test," San Francisco *Chronicle*, February 18, 1969.
———. "Sealab Springs a Leak," San Francisco *Chronicle*, February 17, 1969.
———. "Ship's Identity Proved by Silver Dish," London *Daily Telegraph*, July 17, 1968.
———. "Six Men and Guitar in 600-Foot 'Dive,'" San Francisco *Chronicle*, July 16, 1969.
———. "Skeleton Clutching Silver May Lead to Sunken Treasure," San Francisco *Chronicle*, August 7, 1968.
———. "The Soggy Jetliner Lands at Last," San Francisco *Chronicle*, November 27, 1968.
———. "'Spindrift' Missing; Open Search for Treasure Vessel," Oakland *Tribune*, January 9, 1940.
———. "Sunken Galleon with $30,000,000 in Gold Is Found," Oakland *Tribune*, April 14, 1946.
———. "Submarine is Located at 1.45 a.m.," London *Daily Telegraph*, April 18, 1951.
———. "Sub Spots Giant Fish in Gulf Stream," San Francisco *Chronicle*, July 24, 1969.
———. "Tanker's Belly Gashed—Oil Spills into Ocean," San Francisco *Chronicle*, March 5, 1969.
———. "There Goes a Bargain," San Francisco *Chronicle*, July 25, 1968.
———. "Three Teams Hunt Treasure from Scillies Wreck," London *Daily Telegraph*, August 21, 1967.
———. "*Torrey Canyon* Suit is Settled," San Francisco *Chronicle*, November 12, 1969.
———. "Trapped Sub Rescued," San Francisco *Chronicle*, October 9, 1969.
———. "Treasure Hunt! Nine Sail for Cocos," San Francisco *Examiner*, February 25, 1939.
———. "Treasure Hunt off California Coast," San Francisco *Chronicle*, August 30, 1969.
———. "Treasure-Ship Warning to Amateurs," London *Daily Telegraph*, August 12, 1967.

———. "Treasure Trove," San Francisco *Chronicle*, April 21, 1946.
———. "A Trumpet Fish Moved Right In," San Francisco *Chronicle*, February 17, 1969.
———. "A Try to Raise the *Titanic*," San Francisco *Chronicle*, October 8, 1969.
———. "Underwater TV Found *Affray*," London *Daily Telegraph*, September 13, 1951.
———. "U. S. Launches Secret 7-Man Atomic Miniature Sub," San Francisco *Chronicle*, January 29, 1969.
———. Untitled article, San Francisco *Examiner*, December 16, 1945.

MISCELLANEOUS PUBLICATIONS

ANDERSON, DICK. "Keller 1,000-Foot Dive" (unpublished narrative), January 19, 1970.
CORRIGAN, FRANK W. "Technical Report of Salvaging of AFDM-2," prepared by J. Edward Klein, Assoc., Inc., for Ship Systems Command, Department of the Navy.
DICKINSON, CAPTAIN THOMAS. "A Narrative of the Operations . . . in H.M.S. *Thetis*" (narrative, privately printed), 1836.
GROSE, W. A. P. "The Salvage Association" (speech), presented to the Sessional Meeting of the Greek Maritime Law Association, Athens, Greece, May 15, 1967.
"Autofroth I Used in Marine Salvage," Product Application Bulletin A66-3, May 1, 1966.
"Business Guide" (pamphlet), published by Fukada Salvage Co., Ltd., Osaka, Japan, 1967.
"Constant Tension Chain Jack Assembly" (patent), as registered with U. S. Patent Office by Ocean Science and Engineering, Inc., Washington, D.C.
"Catalog of Publications, 1968," published by U. S. Navy Oceanographic Office for the Department of the Navy.
"Deep Water Aircraft Salvage" (motion picture story treatment), Publicity Department, Ocean Science and Engineering, Inc.
"*Hanseatic* Fire," Proceedings of the Merchant Marine Council, as published by United States Coast Guard, Vol. 24, No. 8 (August 1967), pp. 159–67.
"Hydro-Pneumatic Salvage System" (patent), as registered with U. S. Patent Office by Ocean Science and Engineering, Inc., Washington, D.C.
KELLER, HANNES. "The 1,000-Foot Dive off Catalina Island on December 3, 1962" (unpublished personal account), undated.
"Lloyd's" (pamphlet), published by The Corporation of Lloyd's, London, and presented by A. T. Shead & Co., Ltd., undated.
"Lloyd's of London" (article), New York: *Encyclopaedia Britannica*, (14th Edition, 1938), Vol. 14, pp. 256–57.

"Lloyd's of London" (pamphlet). London: A. T. Shead & Co., Ltd., undated.
"Loss of the U.S.S. *Thresher*." Hearings Held Before the Joint Committee on Atomic Energy, Congress of the United States, 88th Cong., 1st and 2d Sess. (June 26–27, July 23, 1963; July 1, 1964).
"Method for Surveying and Searching the Ocean Bottom and Recovering Objects Therefrom" (patent), as registered with U. S. Patent Office by Ocean Science and Engineering, Inc., Washington, D.C.
"Oceanography 1961—Phase 2," Hearings Held Before the Sub-committee on Oceanography of the Committee on Merchant Marine and Fisheries, House of Representatives, Congress of the United States, 87th Cong. 1st Sess. (May 22, 1961).
"PSI, A New Concept in Underwater Recovery" (pamphlet), published by Cyclo Manufacturing Co., undated.
"Salvage of *Martin S*" (pamphlet), published by W. A. van den Tak and Karl Krøyer, undated.
"Ship Salvaging System and Method" (patent), as registered with U. S. Patent Office by Ocean Science and Engineering, Inc., Washington, D.C.
"Side Scan Sonar: Mark 1 Dual Channel System" (application notes), published by EG&G International Co., Inc.
"Treasure of the Spanish Main" (pamphlet), published by Real Eight Co., Inc.

INDEX

A-1, 108
A-4, 108
Abercorn, 317–18
Ability, 88
Active, 171
Acushnet, 165–66
Adelaide Steamship Company, 187
Admiralty Boom Defense Department, 236
Admiralty Salvage Association, 202–3, 205–6
Admiralty Salvage Section, 251–52, 322–29
AE-2, 104
AFDM-2, 305–7
Affray, 65, 137–40, 376
African Enterprises, Ltd., 346
African Queen, 345–50
Aglantha, 95
Agraz, Mr., 102–3
Aguilucho, 391, 393
Ahnlund, Nils, 421
Air, compressed, 32, 62–63, 111–12, 206–8, 219, 449–50
Air embolism, 452
Air lift, 384–85, 397n
Air-lock bell, 194
Airplane salvage, 73–98, 307–8
Air supply, in diving, 6–7, 62–67, 450–55
Albemarle, Duke of, 383
Albenga, Italy, 367–68
Albert Darley, 315–16
Albertross, 161
Albisola, 182
Alcoa Seaprobe, 474–80

Aldijk, 133
Algerine, 196
Allen, Ben, 35–37
Allen, Bob, 393–94
Alleyne, John, 252
Alloa Shipbreaking Company, 215, 221, 228
Almerian, 342–43
Alphonso XII, 35
Aluminaut, 86–92, 458, 463
Aluminum Corporation of America, 474
Alvin, 86–93, 458–59, 463, 471
Amas, Japan, 6
Amatitlán, Lake, 409
Amazon, 343
America, 108
American Antiquarian Society, 406
American Hull Insurance Syndicate, 355
American Philosophical Society, 378
American Relief, 166
Amherst, 29
Anderson, Dick, 66–67
Anderson, Donald, 389
Anderson, Fred, 97
Andrea Doria, 298, 468–69
Andrews, E. Wyllys, 408
Andrews, Frank, 83
Angerstein, John Julius, 13
Ankers, George, 174–75, 276–77
Antikythera, 365–66
Antilla, 160–61

Applegarth, Sam, 83
Aqualung, 373
Aquapede, 455
Aquatopographers, 469
Arab, 155–57
Araby, 250–51
Arapahoe, 329
Archaeology, marine, 364–69
  Atlantic, 418–32
  Caribbean, 380–88, 391–97, 399–403, 404, 412–15
  cenotes, 405–9
  Indian Ocean, 440–43
  island treasures, 433–40
  Mediterranean, 365–69, 373–78, 409–12
  modern, 479–80
  Pacific, 403–4, 443–45
  preservation methods, 423–24, 442
  SCUBA and, 368–69, 370–371, 373–78, 384–86
  sunken cities, 409–18
Ardois, 278
Arend, 470
Argonaut, Junior, 455
Argudín, Alfonso, 393–94
Argyll, Duke of, 426–28
Arizona, 299
Armstrong, Horace, 238–39, 269–70
Arnhem Land, Australia, 6
Arnold, Alfonso, 393–94
Arnold, Reginald, 393–94
Artiglio, 52, 53–54

514 INDEX

Artiglio II, 54, 55–56, 368
Asherah, 378, 459
Association, 430–32
Astrolabe, 366
Asturias, 205–6, 325–26
Athos, 262
Atlantic Refining Company, 344
Atlantis, 411
Atomic Energy Commission, 452–53
Atsutsan Maru, 135
Attractonometer, 403
Auguste Piccard, 465n
Autec I, 460
Autec II, 460
Autofroth, 467
Aye Ready Salvage Company, 71
Aygaz, 189–90

B-2, 108
Badders, Mr., 127
Badische Anilin und Soda Fabrik, 358
Baiae, 411
Bailey, William, 457
Bailey, W. H., 397
Baker, George, 316–17
Baker, Thomas, 194–95, 196
Barclose, 301
Bardic, 334–35
Barfoam, 301
Bargellini, Alberto, 52, 54
Barhill, 76, 77
Baroukh, Victor, 302
Barracuda Tanker Corporation, 352, 357–58
Barth, Robert, 69
Bartisan, 301
Bascom, Willard, 79n, 96, 319, 371, 473–74, 480, 481n
Bass, George, 377–78, 396
Batavia, 435–39
Bauer, Wilhelm, 106–7
Bayern, 228
Bay of Naples, 411
Beagle, 437

Beauchat, Georges, 373
Beazley, Risdon, 61, 75
Beebe, William, 194
Beebe Bathysphere, 194
Belgian Prince, 110
Bell, Mr., 292
Bellarmine, Robert, 439
Belos, 319
Bembina, Melchiorre, 49–50
Benakis, Alexander, 367
Bends, 26–27, 453–54
Ben Franklin, 460
Bennehoff, Olton, 340
Bennet, Wally, 391–93
Benoît, Fernand, 375
Berolli, Giovanni, 369
Bert, Paul, 26, 62–63
Betsy, 59
Bever, 470
Biblos, 412
Bigge Drayage Company, 307
Binne, Mr., 204
Bismarck, 15
Blachford, Mr., 44, 46
Blair, Clay, 390, 391–95
Blake, Abel, 197
Blake, Glen, 234
Blakeley, 71
Blazer, 337
Bligh, William, 433
Blockships, 247–59, 261, 266–79 *passim*, 285–87, 294–95
Blow-ups, 26
Blum, 352
Blumberg, Al, 234
Bollard, W., 65
Bond, George, 69–70, 454
Borghese, Valerio, 456
Borhegyi, Stephan, 409
Boston, 87
Boudjmel, 277
Bounty, 433–34
Bourne, William, 105
Bowden, Captain, 312
Bowditch, 145
Brady, Paul, 346
Braemar, 427
Brainerd, George, 408

Brandtaucher, 106
Brandywine, 145
Bray, Mr., 76
Breault, Henry, 116
Breconshire, 236–37
Brenta, 272–73
Bretagne, 280
Bridgewater, 187
Britannia, 206, 326–27
Broussard, Henri, 373
Brown, Mr., 109
Brown, A. T., 236–37
Brown, Edison, 266, 268, 272, 275
Brown, Jock, 169, 171
Brown, Lawrence, 116
Brown, Paul, 403
Brown, R. P., 301
Bruce, Thomas, 364
Brumby, Admiral, 120
Buchanan, Chester A., 83
Bugsier, Ruderei, and Bergungs, 221
Bulmer, Ian, 421
Burgomeister Peterson, 157
Burke, Billy, 234
Burns, William, 427
Bushnell, 120
Bushnell, David, 105–6
Bussoz, René, 373
Butler, Charles, 116
Butterfield, Dill and Company, 352
Buzbee, Jim, 269

C-11, 108
Cable, 306
Cable-Controlled Underwater Research Vehicle (CURV), 91–93, 459
Cabrillo, Juan Rodriguez, 403
Caesar, Julius, 411
Caesarea, Palestine, 410
Caisson, 194
California, 299
Calypso, 374–75, 384, 386
Cameronia, 283
Campbell, V., 75–76

INDEX 515

Campell, Ian Douglass, 428
Canadian Pacific Steamship Company, 37
Cannon, Mr., 451
Cannon, Barry L., 69
Cape Artemision, Greece, 367
Cape Gelidonya, Turkey, 377–78
Captive (Max Barendt), 175–76, 283–84
Carbon dioxide, 64–66
Cardium, 162–63
Carew, George, 21–22
Carr, Mr., 121
Catto, A., 24
Cavvadias, Panajotis, 365
Cecil N. Bean, 180
CEDAM, 393, 407
Cenotes, 405–9
Centurion, 288
Cessnock, 470–71
Chamberlain, 268, 269, 270
Channel Pilot, 352
Chanticleer, 74–75, 239–40, 372
Chapman, C. D., 313
Chapman, R. E., 256
Chariot, 456–57
Chauncey, 331
Cherbourg, France, 294–95
Cheyenne, 329
Chichén Itzá, 405–8
China Mail Steamship Company, 160
Christensen, Carl, 97
Christian, Fletcher, 433
Christianini, Mr., 375
Churchill, Owen, 369
Churchill, Winston, 457
Citrine, James, 233
City of New York, 316
City of Rome, 116
Clarbeston, 353
Clare, St. John, 426–27
Clark, George, 393–94
Clarke, Arthur C., 440–42
Clason, Edvard, 422

Claymore, 58, 59–60
Clear, Mr., 44
Cleopatra, 237, 268
Clifton, H. Edward, 451
Club Alpin Sous-Marin de Cannes, 373–74
Club de Exploraciones y Deportes Acuáticos de Méjico (CEDAM), 393, 407
Club de la Mer de Juan-les-Pins, 373–74
Clyde Port Authority, Scotland, 471
Cole, Cyrus, 127
Coleman, Donald, 76
Collins, Edward, 293
Collins, "Jumper," 283–84
Collins, Richard, 415
Collyer, Andrew, 51
Columbus, Christopher, 395–96
Comheines, Georges, 370
Confederate Davids, 106
Congress, 159–60
Conrad, 142
CONTACT, 261
Conti, Armando, 468
Continental Shelf Station, 67
Cook, Mr., 35
Coppinger, Mr., 284
Corlieu, Louis de, 369
Cornelisz, Jeronimus, 435–37
Corning Glass, 460
Cousteau, Jacques-Yves, 67, 73, 369–70, 371–76, 384–86, 449, 453, 455
Cowdray, 133
Cowley, John, 180–82, 185
Cowling, George, 341–42
Cox, Ernest, 206, 208–30, 466
Cox and Danks, Ltd., 209
Coxon, Captain, 312
Cozumel, 393
Crabb, Lionel, 133–34, 138–39, 148n, 291–93, 428, 457
Cramer, Max, 438
Crilly, Frank, 103
Crisp, Woody, 348
Crowe, Albert, 320
Crutchley, Lieutenant, 252
Cuba, 330
Cubmarine, 86–88
Cunningham, Admiral, 277
Cunningham, Bill, 238–39
Cunningham, John, 289
Curb, 346
CURV, 91–93, 459
Cyclo Manufacturing Company, 471
Cycloop, 188
Cyclope, 366

Dafila, 338–39
Dalmas, Louis, 194
Dalton, 371–72
Damant, G. C. C., 24, 41–46, 399
Dampfern, 166
Danae, 280, 281–82
Danielsen, Kia, 345
Danks, Tommy, 209
Dara, 331–32
David of Hunley, 106, 135
Davies, Robert E., 66
Davis, G., 110
Davis, Robert H., 50, 57, 63, 73, 115, 130, 132, 232, 289, 370, 455–56, 465n
Davis Escape Chamber, 131
Davis Observation Chamber, 50, 55, 57, 58–60
Davis Submarine Escape Apparatus (DSEA), 136, 370
Davis Submarine Escape Lung, 115, 125
Davy, Mr., 273
Dawson, James, 18
Day, John, 105

INDEX

Decompression, 26–27, 63, 453–55
Deep Cabin, 67
Deep Diver, 459
Deep Jeep, 86, 459
Deep Ocean Work Boat, (DOWB), 459
Deep Quest, 96, 459, 463–64
Deep Sea Diving School, U. S. Navy, 235, 236
Deepstar 2000, 459
Deep-Submergence Rescue Vehicle (DSRV), 143–44, 147, 458
Deep Submergence Systems Project (DSSP), U. S. Navy, 67–69
Deep Submergence Systems Review Group (DSSRG), 143, 458
Dei Gratia, 151–52
Deir, Lloyd, 346–50, 468
De Koe, Captain, 188
Delphy, 330–31
Demolition, 34–35, 199–200
Denayrouze, Auguste, 419–20
Denbydale, 456
Derwent, 286–87
Desaguliers, Mr., 49
Deva, 249
Devine, Fred, 243
Dewar, Mr., 196
Dewey, George, 249
Diamond Knot, 243–44
Diane, 188–89
Dickinson, Fred, 398n
Dickinson, Thomas, 194–96, 375
Dickson, Captain, 419
Dido, 237–29, 268
Dispenser, 237
Divina, 132–33
Diving, 4–6, 65–67, 78–79, 197–99, 231–35, 449–50
Diving bell, 193–96
Diving helmets, 9
Diving School, Royal Swedish Navy, 422

Diving suits, 6–10, 23, 65, 197
armored, 48–50, 52, 54–55, 57–58
Diving systems, 453
Dixhoorn, J. van, 295
Docherty, Mr., 76
Dolan, James, 316–17
Dolphin, 108
Donohue, "Hec," 438
Dorantes, Torribio, 393–94
Douglas, 90–93
Doust, W. A., 301–2
DOWB, 459
Drake, Francis, 425
Drake-Brockman, Henrietta, 437–38
Drebbel, Cornelius van, 105
Drieberg, Frederic, 7
Dry docks, 263–66, 268–70, 279–82, 300–2
DSEA, 136, 370
DSRV, 143–44, 147, 458
DSSP, 67–69
Duane, 296
Dugan, James, 456–57, 468
Duke, Angier Biddle, 89
Duke of York, 465n
Duke University, 450–51
Dumas, Frédéric, 370, 371–72, 373–75, 377–78, 397, 442
Duncan, Mr., 403
Dunlop Rubber, 371
Dunwich, 418
Duprés, Capitaine de Frégate, 276
Duprés, Commandant du Port, 278, 279
Duque de Florencia, 425–26
Durand, Leone, 49–50
Dutch East India Company, 435
Dutton, 85
Dzibilchaltun, cenote at, 408–9

E-4, 108, 109

E-11, 113
E-41, 108, 109, 125
Eadie, Tom, 120–21, 462
Eagle, 106, 430
Eastwood, David H., 354
Eddystone, 108
Eddystone Lighthouse, 194
Edgerton, Harold, 396–97, 461
Edison, Thomas A., 64
Edward-Collins, Admiral Sir Frederick, 293
Edwards, Hugh, 438
Edwards, R. S., 127–28
Effingham, Mr., 425
Egypt, 16, 50–57, 368
E. H. Blum, 344–45
Eisenhower, D. D., 340
Ekanayake, Hector, 441
Electric Boat Division, 458, 459, 460
Electronic Defense Research Laboratory, 459
Elford, 328
Elgin, Lord, 381
Elios, 187
Elite Monnier, 374
Elizabeth, 237
Elizabeth Lykes, 305–6
Elizabethville, 52, 53
Elk River, 68
Ellis, William E., 83
Ellsberg, Edward, 116–18, 168–75, 176n, 237–39, 261–75, 277–83, 288, 296, 340
Emerald Straits, 464, 471
Emma Alexander, 160
Empire Woodlarks, 160
Empress of Australia, 172–73
Empress of Ireland, 37–38
Ensor, Tom, 322–23
Enterprise, 419
EOD, 84
Ericsson, John, 388
Eristalis tenax, 6
Erostrabe, Angel, 34, 197
Escape trunk, 132
Eschauzier, Pierre, 314

INDEX 517

Estier, brothers, 39–40
Etienne, Mr., 420
Eugène Resal, 366
Eureka, 67
Euryalus, 18, 237, 268
Eustace, 328–29
Evans, Arthur, 364
Experimental Diving Unit, Admiralty, 65
Experimental Diving Unit (EDU), U. S. Navy, 24, 64, 66, 451
Explosive Ordinance Disposal (EOD), 84

F-4, 101–4, 471
Falck, Dr., 105
Falcon, 116–21, 123–24, 126, 128, 188
Falejczyk, Frank J., 454
Fälting, Edvin, 422
Fareija, Don, 425–26
Farfadet, 108
Fargues, Maurice, 449
Favilla, 76
Fearless, 316
Featherstone, Robert, 180, 181–82, 184–86
Fenn Victory, 243–44
Ferguson, Major, 249–50
Fernez, Mr., 369
Ferrati, General, 206
Ferrodanks, 216, 218
Feversham, 405
Fifa, 424
Firebrand, 23, 430
Fire Diver, 106–7
Firedrake, 324
Firefighter, 296
Fires, shipboard, 159–63
Fischer, Mel, 402
Fisher Engineering Company, 320
Fleetwing, 35, 397n
Fleuss, H. A., 115, 370
Flood, Solly, 152–53
Florence, 53–54
Florida, 425
Foley, Maurice, 353
Fontana, Niccolo, 6–7
Forder, William, 8
Forfait, 7

Fort Snelling, 83
Fosberg, C. G., 75
Foss, K. M., 427
Foster-Brown, R. S., 138
Foundation Josephine, 178, 180–86, 236
Foundation Lillian, 178, 181–84
Foundation Maritime of Canada, 178, 180
Francheschi, Aristide, 52, 54
Franco, Francisco, 426
Franzen, Anders, 421–22
Fraser, Admiral, 465n
Fraser, Ian, 458
Frauenfels, 268, 270, 272
Free escape, from submarines, 106–7, 109, 115, 123–25, 131, 133, 452
Fremantle, Sydney, 210–11
Freminet, Le Sieur, 7, 48
French, George, 24
Friesland, 350–51
Fritjof, 51
Frizzle, John, 393–94
Frohman, Charles, 70
Froude, James A., 432n
Fuller, 331
Furer, Julius, 102–3, 471

G-38, 214
G-91, 214–15
Gagnan, Emile, 370, 373
Galpin, Mr., 76
Gamtoos, 287
García-Robles, Carlos, 393–94
Gayton, J., 431
General Goethals, 115
General Grant, 29–30
Gera, 264, 270–72
Geraldine Mary, 166
GEORGE, 77
George, *Presbyteros*, 378
Gianelli, Major, 206–8
Gianni, Alberto, 52, 54
Giant, 352
Gibbs, Aron, 415
Gien, 181

Gilgamesh, 4
Gilpatric, Guy, 369
Giovanni Battista, 285, 286, 287
Girvan, Mr., 23
Gladiator, 203–5, 259n
Glatton, 253–54
Glencona, 9
Godsal, A. E., 252
Godwin, Earl of Essex, 418
Gondar, 456
Goodhart, F. H. M., 111–12
Goodwin Sands, Dover, 418
Gothenburg Towage and Salvage Company, 51
Gowan, Colonel, 419
Gowan, Mrs., 248
Gracie, Mr., 120
Graham, 157
Grand Conglone Island, 374–76
Grand Dock, 279–81
Granges, 156
Granlieu, 294–95
Grattan, John, 429
Great Basses, 440–43
Greatorex, C., 202
Grey, E. J., 323–24
Grey Dove, 430
Griffis, Nixon, 377
Grosser Kurfurst, 31–32, 206
Grosvenor, 312–13
Gruener, John, 450
Grumann Aerospace Corporation, 460
Guerres, Francisco, 382
Guest, William S., 83–93 *passim*
Guppy, 459–60
Gush, Mr., 427
Gustave Schindler, 335–36
Gymnote, 107

H-3, 329–30
H-42, 108
H-47, 108
Haldane, J. B. S., 451

518 INDEX

Haldane, John Scott, 26–27, 63, 451
Hall, James Norman, 434, 445n
Hall, Nobby, 217
Halley, Edmund, 194
Halstead, Oliver, 107
Hamilla Mitchell, 30–31
Hamilton, W. R., 364
Hammond, Maurie, 438
Hancock, Commander, 292
Hankins, Chuck, 308
Hanover, 167
Hanseatic, 295, 298
Harding, Lieutenant, 172
Harland and Wolff, 200
Harrison, D. T., 236–37
Hawke, Lord, 22
Hayes, Weibbe, 436–37
H. C. Akeley, 156–57
Healey, Dennis, 354
Heans, Mr., 196
Heath, Cuthbert, 14
Hedback, Captain, 51
Hedberg, Axel, 422
Helena, 299
Helike, Greece, 410
Helium-oxygen, 64–66
Henderson, Graeme, 440
Henderson, James, 440
Henry, 383
Herbert, Godfrey, 111–12
Herculaneum, 337
Herd, James, 58
H. F. de Bardeleben, 157–58
Hindenburg, 210, 212, 216–18, 225–27
Hindes, Lieutenant, 133
Hjalp, 424
Hodges, Jimmy, 133–34
Hoist, 88, 92
Holland, J. P., 455
"Hollywood," 27–28
Holt, Mr. 125
Homer, 5, 410
Honolulu, 299
Hood, 15, 288, 462
Hookah, 397n
Hoot, Hope, 450
Horlock, Bertrand, 76

Horobin, Mark, 431
Horton, Ed, 478, 481n
Housatonic, 106, 135
Hughes-White, C. E., 318–19
Humane Society, 315
Huxley, Julian, 480
Hyaena, 10
Hybertsson, Henrik, 420
Hyde, Loring, 243
Hygromull, 358

Indiana, 331
Industrial Maintenance Company, 346
Ingram, J. O., 255
Ingram, Keith, 389
Insurance, marine, 11–18
Intelligent Whale, 107
Intent, 266, 268, 270, 272–73, 275
International Hydrodynamics, 461–62, 464–65
Iride, 456
Iron, John, 158–59, 253–55, 338–39, 428

Jacobson Brothers, 96
Jacobsz, Ariaen, 435
Jaco-Mina, 469
James, W. H., 370
James and Mary, 383
James McHenry, 182
Janssen, Jules, 63
Jarrat, Jim, 72
Jellicoe, R. V., 251
Jenkins, Captain, 397n
Jennings, Harry, 400
John J. Harvey, 296
Johnson, Ervin, 274
Johnson, Irving, 434
Johnson, W. S., 199
Johnstone, J., 59–60
Joint Committee on Atomic Energy, 143
Jones, Mr., 269–70
Jones, C., 236–37
Jones, Corporal, 23–24
Jones, W. E., 162–63
Jonklass, Rodney, 440–42
J. P. Coen, 295

J-Star Camera, 97–98
Judd, Bob, 396

K-13, 32, 108, 111–12, 206
Kahn, Sam, 350
Kaiser, 224–25
Karneke, Joseph S., 74–75, 239–42, 258–59, 299–300, 303, 372
Karo, George, 367
Kay, I. J., 112, 325, 327–28, 334–35
Keach, Donald L., 142
Kearney, 168
Kearny, Cresson, 371
Keeble, Peter, 25, 134–35, 175–76, 275, 283–87, 289–90, 313, 341–42
Keith, H. M., 266, 267–68
Keller, Hans, 66–67
Kelly, Kenute, 414–15
Kemal, Captain, 377
Kevin Moran, 186
Keyes, Roger, 253
Killan, Mr., 132
King, Ernest, 116, 120, 123
King Alfred, 71–72
King Salvor, 170–72, 277, 278, 279
Kinsarra, 72
Kiowa, 83
Klaas Wijker, 188
Knox, Frank, 296
König Wilhelm, 31
Konodos, Demetrios, 365
Koritza, 262
Korst, Bob, 308
Korth, Fred, 142–43
Krassic, Mr., 241
Kriegel, Bobby, 440–41
Krøyer, Karl, 470
Kylstra, Johannes, 453–54
Kythera, 268

L-06, 174
L-55, 104
La Bretagne, 277
Lady Laurier, 165–66

Lafayette. See *Normandie*
Lafferty, Cyril, 356
Laforey, 171–72
Lake, Mr., 455
Lake Palourde, 357
Lambert, Alexander, 34–35
Lambert, Christopher, 204
Lamboglia, Nino, 367–68
Lamont Geophysical Laboratory, 142
Lande, Diego de, 405–6
Landi, Charles, 40, 71–72
Landi, James, 40
Langlands, David, 419
Larsen, Mr., 269–70
Lautrentic, 41–47, 399
Lavonia, 254–55
Lawson, Hamish, 178–80
Laza, Mr., 442
Leary, 165
Leavitt, Benjamin Franklin, 70–71
Le Chameau, 405
Le Diable-Marin, 107
Lee, 331
Lee, Ezra, 106
Lee, John, 9
Lehoux, Louis, 373
Leicester, 177–86
LeJeune Sea Urchins, 388
Leonardo da Vinci, 32, 206–8, 219
Leonidas, Evangelos, 367
Leopard, 341–42
Lethbridge, John, 48–49
Leverett, Sydney, 42
Liberté, 233–34
Liebenfels, 266–68
Life, 390
Life-Saving Service, U. S., 315–17, 320–21, 329
Light, Mr., 46
Light, John, 70, 72–73, 468
Lightning, 194–96
Lindbergh, Jon, 84–85
Link, Edwin, 410, 413–14, 459, 462, 472
Linton, 328–29
Lion Cif, 189

Littauer Foundation, 377
Little, Beldon, 346–47
Littlehales, Bates, 408–9
Litton Industries, 458
Liverpool and Glasgow Salvage Association, 16, 334–37
Liverpool Salvage Association, 233, 253–54
Lloyd, Edward, 12
Lloyd's of London, 12–17
Lockheed, 96–97, 458, 459, 463–64
Lockyer, Norman, 63–64
Lodge, Captain, 30–31
Lombardi, Commander, 76
Lôme, Dupuy de, 107
London Commerce, 167
London Wrecking Company, 31–32, 206
Lorini, Bonajuto, 7, 193, 451
Lorne, Marquis of, 427
Loughlin, William, 29
Loutitt, Tom, 9–10
Lovock, Mr., 125
Lucas, Colin, 270–71
Lucayans, Bahamas, 6
Lucullus, 411
Lufti Gelil, 277
Luiseno, 88
Lulu, 463
Lumberjack, 467
Lumière, Cornel, 413
Lusitania, 28–29, 70–73, 109
Lutine, 15, 313–14
Lyness, 216
Lyoness, Britain, 418

M-1, 108
M-2, 108, 109
McCamis, Marvin 90, 92–93
McCance, Mr., 264, 270–71, 273
McCann, Allen R., 125, 127
McCann Rescue Chamber, 126–27, 147, 194
McCray, Walter, 243

McCulloch, 329
MacDonough, 83
MacFarland, Mr., 201
Machine hydrostatergatique, 7, 48
McKenzie, Thomas, 212–28 *passim*
McKeown, Ernest, 212–14, 218, 220, 222, 228
MacLean, Donald Glas, 426–27
MacLeish, Kenneth, 66
McLelland, Jack, 478
MacLeod, Harvey, 405
McMullen, Raynor T., 388
MacNamara, Robert, 86
MacNeil, Ben Dixon, 388–89
Magen, Hippolyte, 419
Maggie, 30
Mahdia, Tunisia, 366–67, 374
Mahnken, Conrad, 451
Maine, 248–50
Manchester Producer, 167
Mangels, Ted, 479
Manseau, B. E., 296
Manuela Orts Simo, 81
Marconi, Guglielmo, 315
Marden, Luis, 408–9, 434
Mardesich, Jack, 96
Mare Nostrum, 350–51
Marguerite, 329
Maria, 105
Mariner, 253
Markey, Joseph, 403
Marlin, 393
Marlowe, Christopher, 426
Marpessa, 359
Marryat, Joseph, 14
Marseilles (SCUBA group), 373–74
Marseilles, Vieux Port of, 409
Martignoni, Walter, 243
Martin, Mr., 441
Martin S, 469–70
Marvin, Jack, 35–36
Marx, Robert F., 386–97, 412, 414–15, 461
Mary Celeste, 151–54

520 INDEX

Maryland, 103, 299
Mary Rose, 21–22
Massaura, Ethiopia, 260–75
Matancero, El, 391–95
Mauld, James, 426
Max Barendt (Captive), 283–84
Mayflower, 113n
Mazzone, Walter F., 452
Meier, Frank, 331
Melampus, 319
Melanie, 321
Memnon, 157
Menachini, Basilo, 364
Menominee, 167
Mentor, 364
Merauke, 338
Merchant Shipping Act of 1894 (England), 17
Merlin, Alfred, 366, 374
Merrimack, 388
Merritt, Chapman and Scott Corporation, 235–36, 296, 306–7, 346
Merritt and Chapman Wrecking Company, 255
Metal Industries Group, 228
Metcalfe, Christopher, 202, 203
M'Ginnes, Mr., 458
Michaels, Fred, 121
Michalowski, Mr., 127
Mikimoto, Japan, 6
Miller, Archibald, 427
Miller, E. C., 43
Miller, Jenny Jack, 209
Milwaukee, 330
Mimi, 320–21
Mines, 58, 59–60, 290, 291–93, 304–5
Mines Experiment Station, 64
Mire, Seaman, 180
Mitchell, Captain, 167
Mizar, 88, 95, 145, 463
Moerkerk, Z. W. S., 470
Moffat, J. K., 34
Mohole Project, 474
Molen, Bob van der, 471

Momsen, Charles B., 126
Momsen Escape Lung, 124, 452
Moncalieri, 270
Mongolian Prince, 167
Monitor, 163n, 387–91
Monsanto Chemical, 470
Montgomery, Terry, 431
Montopore, 470
Montrose, 167
Moody, Mr., 93
Moody, DeWitt, 85
Mooney, J. B., 85
Moore, Mr., 115
Moore, Rear Admiral, 102
Morehouse, Captain, 152–53
Morison, Samuel Eliot, 395–96
Moro Maru, 239–40
Morris, Duke, 348–49
Morris, Roland, 431–32
Morro Castle, 160–61
Mosher, Bob, 308
Mountbatten, Louis, 75
Moyen Dock, 279–82
Multiple, 88
Murphy, J. P., 467–68, 469
Murphy Pacific Salvage Company, 467
Murray, Mr., 289
Museum of Sunken Treasure, 403
Mylen, Lucretia van der, 435–36

Nachi, 240–42
Nanking, 160
Naquin, Oliver, 126
Nasmith, Martin E., 113
National Geographic Society, 378, 407, 408
National Institute of Anthropology and History of Mexico, 407
National Transportation Safety Board, 97
Nautilus, 413
Navy, U. S., 329, 332
Training School, 236
Naylor, Margaret, 427

Negrey, Jean, 233–34
Nelson, Mr., 18
Neptun Salvage Company, 422
Nespelen, 83
Nestor, 188
Netzender, 294
Neufeldt and Kuhnke, 50
Nevada (Scarlet Fever), 303
Niagara, 58–61
Nicholas, 331
Nichols, Mr., 287, 289
Nicholson, W. M., 68, 147
Nimble, 83
Nimbo, 339
Nitrogen, 26, 449–51
Noord-Holland, 188
Nordhoff, Charles, 434, 445n
Normandie, 32, 236, 255, 296–98, 469
Northern Star, 165
North Star Bay, Greenland, 94–95
NR-1, 458, 460
Nubian, 338
Nuclear bombs, 80–95, 303–4
Nuclear submarines, 140–46
Nuestra Señora de la Concepción, 383–86

O-5, 115
O. B. Jennings, 161–62
Obregón, Maurico, 397
Observation Chamber, Davis, 50, 55, 57, 58–60
Oceaan, 470
Oceana, 200
Ocean Bottom Scanning Sonar, (OBSS), 84
Oceaneer, 96–98
Ocean Industries Insurers, 18
Ocean Salvor, 301
Ocean Science and Engineering, Inc., 96, 358, 472–80

INDEX 521

Ocean Systems, Inc., 85, 86, 94, 459
Ocean Voyager, 286–87
Octopus, 469
Oil spills, 352–59,
O'Kane, Richard H., 136–37
Oklahoma, 299
Oldfield Grange, 328
Oliva, 262, 266, 336
Olterra, 457
Onondaga, 160–61
Onward, 251–52
Oran, Algeria, 276–82
Ordzhonikidze, 148n
Orinoco, 35–37, 397n
Orion, 59
Orts, Francisco Simo, 81, 87, 89
Ossipee, 165–66
Ostia, 275
Otte, Enrique, 395
Overton Steel Works, 209
Oxy-electric torch, 311
Oxygen, 62–63
Oxygen-helium, 64–66
Ozen, Mohamed, 190

Pacific Coast Transport, 353
Pacifique, 160–61
Page, Horace C., 85
Paleopolis, 411
Palomares, Spain, 80–94, 458–59, 463
Papin, Denis, 193–94
Pareija, Dom, 425–26
Parker, Gilman, 154
Parry, C. N., 76
Pasley, Mr., 23–24
Paulding, 119–20
Pausanias, 364, 410
Peabody Museum, 406
Pearl Harbor, 299–300
Pearson, Drew, 145–46
Pease, George, 318
Pelsaert, Francisco, 435–37
Penk, W., 30–31
Pennsylvania, 299
Perkins, Hiram, 35–36, 397n

Perrin-Trichard, Lieutenant, 280
Perry, John H., Jr., 459
Perthes, Boucher de Crève-coeur, 363
Peterson, Bill, 211, 214, 217, 228
Peterson, Mendel, 387, 441, 442
Petit Dock, 279–80
Petrel, 83, 93
Pewaubic, 71
Pharos, Egypt, 410
Philips, L. D., 49
Phips, William, 194, 382–83
Phoenix, 430
Piccard, Jacques, 148n, 458, 460
Pieris, A. P., 442
Pigeon, 277, 278
Pinch-Hitter, 393
Pinnacle, 83
Piraeus, Greece, 290, 409–10
Pisces, 461–62, 464–65, 471
Pitcairn Island, 433–34
Pitman, Mr., 240
Pitts, Ray, 84
Plate Fleet, Spanish, 382–83
Platoro, Inc., 404
Plymouth Command Clearance Diving Team, 356
Plymouth Rock, 86
Pneumothorax, 452
Poidebard, Père A., 411–12
Pollard, J. B., 76
Polynesians, 6
Polystyrene, 469–71
Polytron Company, 467
Polyurethane foam, 467–69
Pompeii, 411
Pontoons, 103
Pontos, 221
Porcupine, 168–70
Porpoise, 106
Port au Prince, 443–44

Port Philip, 332–33
Port Royal, Jamaica, 380, 382, 387, 412–15
Poseidon, 108, 125
Posey, Mr., 241–42
Post, Hille, 353
Potter, John, 420
Potter, Ronald, 430
Powhatan, 165–66
Pozarica, 173–75
Praetorium, Yorkshire,
Praetorium, Yorkshire, 418
Praia da Adraga, 353, 355
Prast, Colin, 443–44
Pressure, water, 7–8, 24–25, 62–63, 449–53
Pressurized Sphere Injector (PSI), 471
Price, Derek, 366
Price, Thomas J. D., 354
Prickett, Pete, 24, 66
Prieur, Yves le, 370
Prince Salvor, 134, 137
Prinz-Regent Luitpold, 227–28
Privateer, 88
Project Tektite, 451
Prop-wash, 402
Protection, 155–57
Proteus, 332
PSI, 471
Punta Matancero, 391–95
Puttenham, 431

Qait Bey, 410
Quaglia, Giovanni, 52–56
Queen Elizabeth, 287–88, 456–57
Quetzalcoatl, 408, 416n

Racer, 44
Raffaelli, Mr., 54–55
Raleigh, 299
Ranger, 112, 325, 327, 334–35, 337
Ran Muthu, 441–42
Real Eight Company, 401–3
Reclaim, 65, 138–40
Reclaimer, 40

522   INDEX

Reed, Bill, 278, 279–80, 281, 282
Reed, Captain, 271
Reed, C. R., 390
Reef Diver, 413
Regency, 431
Reinach, Salomon, 366
Reindeer, 166, 253
Reinholm, Art, 307–8
Reliance, 317
Renan, Mr., 263
Resolute, 161, 270–72, 274
Respond, 284
Restive, 171
Restucci, Mr., 49
Retrieve, 237
Reuter, Ludwig von, 210–11
Revenspur, Yorkshire, 418
Reynolds Aluminum Corporation, 86, 88, 458
Rhode Island, 388
Rhodes, Cecil, 312
Richard, Adrian, 405
Richards, Charles S., 71
Rickover, Hyman G., 143
Ridyard, R., 30–31
Rippon, Wilber, 285
Rival, 88, 90
ROBERT, 90–93
Rogers, Francis, 384
Romans, Bernard, 401
Romero, Pablo Bush, 393, 407
Romney, 430, 432
Rooke, George, 418
Roos, J. F. F., 196
Rose of Algier, The, 383
Rosie, 59
Rostro, 52
Rouquayrol, Benoist, 370, 419
Royal Charter, 314–15
Royal George, 8, 22–24, 199, 311
Rugiati, Pastrengo, 352–53, 357
Rutledge, Tex, 300

S-4, 108, 119–24, 235, 463
S-5, 114–15
S-50, 117
S-51, 116–19, 235, 472
S-52, 214
S-53, 214
S-55, 214
Sadler, Alvah E., 347, 350
Sagacity, 83
Sailfish, 129
St. Ann's Bay, Jamaica, 395–97, 416n, 461
Saint Day, 340
St. Paul, 203, 255–58, 295–97
Saint-Tropez, 374
Salinan, 306
Salute, 88
Salvage, problems of, 472–80
Salvage Association of London, 16, 51
Salvage Unit No. 3, 214
Salvestor, 175
SALVOPS MED, 83
Salvor, 159
Sampan, 401
SAMs, 177–78
Samson, 316–17
Sánchez, Francisco, 395
Sandbery, C. P., 51–52, 55, 57
San Francisco, 425
San Juan Baptista, 426
San Onofre, 321
San Sinema, 357
Santa María, 398n
Santa María de la Rosa, 429–30
Santissima Trinidad, 382
Sardam, 436–37
Saunders, Tom, 97, 98, 120
Savadkin, Lawrence, 136
Scapa Flow, 209–28
Scheer, Mr., 455
Schliemann, Mr., 363–64
Scire, 456
Scongale, Buck, 266, 272–73, 278, 281–82
Scorpion, 85, 94, 144–46
Scott, Norman, 407–8, 414

Scripps, Mr., 459
SCUBA, 369–73, 449–53
  marine archaeology and, 368–69, 370–71, 373–78, 384–86
  World War II and, 371–73
Scuplin, 126
Scyllias, 5
Scythia, 282–83
SDC, 63, 194
Sea-Devil, 107
Sea Diver, 413
Sea Diver II, 410, 413
Sealab, 67–70, 194, 451
Searle, Bill, 83, 84, 94–95
Sea Salvor, 76, 77–78, 237, 342–43
Sea Scanner, 84
Seefalke, 221
Segovia, 258
Seine, 51
Semper Paratus, 40
Sepiola, 469
Sestius, Marcus, 376
Seydlity, 216, 222–24
Sharkey, 165
Shaw, 299
Sheddon, Robert, 13
Shelford, William O., 65, 138–39
Shelford's Blue Line, 138
Shell Oil Company, 273–74, 359
Shiga, 307–8
Shima, Kiyoshide, 241
Shovell, Cloudsley, 418–19, 430–31
Sibitsky, Martin, 126–27
Sicard, Saint-Simon, 419
Sidon, 412
Siebe, Augustus, 8–10, 23, 49, 197
Siebe, Gorman and Co., 115, 130, 457
Sigsee, Charles D., 249
Silovich, Captain, 317
Silurias, 322–23
Simmons, Maurice, 347, 349

INDEX 523

Simo, Francisco, 97, 98n
Simson, 221
Sinfield, Mr., 275
Sippe, Mr., 39–40
Skill, 83
Skylark, 141
Skyro, 33–34
Sloane, Hans, 383
Small, Peter, 66–67
Smeaton, Bill, 194
Smeaton, John, 194
Smit and Co., L., 167, 181, 188, 305
Smith, Adolfo, 427
Smith, John, 382–83
Smith, Mark, 440–41
Snyder, Ed, 83
Society for Maritime Recovery (SORIMA), 51–57, 368
Solon, 411
Somerset, 160–61
Sonar, 137
Sonoma, 161
Sorte, Don, 461–62, 464
Sostratus, 410
Spahi, 277–79
Spanish Armada, 425–30
Spanish Prince, 254–55
Spark, 458
Sparks, Mr., 178–79
Spaulding, Charles, 7
Sperry Gyroscope, 460
Spey, 340
Springer, Roy, 85
Squalus, 65, 126–29, 147, 472
Squeeze, 25, 451–52
Squid, 233–34
Stackpole, Peter, 390
Stadiatis, Elias, 365
Stais, Velerios, 365–66
Stal, Hans, 354
Stamires, Georges, 366
Stamp, Rosse, 138–39
Star I, 459
Star II, 459
Star III, 95, 459
Stears, Mr., 427
Steinke, Harris E., 452
Stentor, 353, 355
Sterling, 389–90

Stiklestad, 166–67
Stillson, George, 24, 103
Stirni, 389–90, 391
Stockholm, 468
Stoker, Commander, 104
Storm, Alex, 404–5
Storstad, 37
Strathallan, 170–72
Stubbs, Harold, 78–79, 85, 129
Submarines
  dynamics, 104–5
  early, 455–56
  experimental, 458
  history, 105–7
  free escapes from, 106–7, 109, 115, 123–25, 131, 133, 452
  midget, 457–58
  modern, 107–8
  raising, 101
  rescue chambers and, 126–27
  safety equipment for, 115–16, 119, 123–27, 147
  see also specific entries
Submersible Decompression Chamber (SDC), 63, 194
Submersibles, 475–76
  early, 455–56
  experimental, 458–62
  history, 105–7
  at Palomares, 86–93
  salvage and, 462–64
  in World War II, 456–58
  see also specific entries
SUBSMASH, 137–40
Suevic, 336–37
Suez Canal, 305
Suffolk, Duke of, 22
Sullivan, W. A., 235, 296
Sunken cities, 409–18
Sun Shipbuilding and Dry Dock, 459–60
Supertankers, 344–59
Sussex, 158–59
Sutton, Bill, 431

Svitzers Bjergnings Enterprise, 305
Swan, 415
Swanson, Roy, 83–84
Swinburne, James, 51–52, 55, 57
Swordfish, 135

TAG, 83
Taillez, Philippe, 370, 371, 373–74
Tait, William, 228
Takao, 458
Talkington, Howard, 91
Tang, 136–37
Tarshish, 416n
Taskasato, Wilfred, 403–4
Task Force 65, 83
Taylor, Buck, 197
Taylor, Jim, 468
Taylor, W. H., 49
Technical Advisory Group (TAG), 83
Teed, Captain, 202
Television, underwater, 138–40
Tempête, 39–40
Templo, Mr., 455
Tender, diving, 9–10
Tennessee, 299
Tenth Light Flotilla (Italy), 287–88, 292, 456–57
Teredos, 113n, 421
Terror, 158
Tesei, Teseo, 456
Tester, Mr., 35
Thetis, 130–31, 194–96, 375
Thomas Masaryk, 175–76
Thomas Stone, 340–41
Thompson, Edward Herbert, 406
Thompson, Garry, 397
Thomson, Elihu, 64
Thomson, Mack, 461–62, 464
Thomson, Sandy, 224, 228

524 INDEX

Thresher, 67, 68, 85, 101, 140–44, 458
Throckmorton, Peter 377–78, 441–42, 480
Thrush, 112
Tirpitz, 457–58
Titan, 353, 355
Titanic, 471–72
Tjikini, 295
Tobermory Bay, Hebrides, 425–28
Tonga, South Pacific, 443–44
Tooker, John, 256–57, 296
Topay, 433
Torpedo Boat 99, 42
Torpedoes, 456–57, 461–62
Torrey Canyon, 344, 346, 348, 351–58
Toschi, Elias, 456
164–76
Towing, 155, 157–59,
Tozeur, 371
Tracey, Mr., 22
Trapnell, Walter, 42
Treasure
  Atlantic, 418–32
  Canada, 404–5
  Caribbean, 380–86, 391–95, 397n, 399–403, 412–15
  cenotes, 405–9
  Dutch, 435–40
  early salvage attempts, 381–83
  English, 430–32
  Guatemala, 409
  Indian Ocean, 440–43
  Island, 433–40
  laws covering, 416n, 432n
  Mexico, 405–9
  Pacific, 403–4, 443–45
  recovering, 33–47
  routes, 440
  Spanish ships, 380–87, 391–95, 397n, 399–404, 418–20, 425–30

  sunken cities, 409–16
  Swedish, 420–24
Treasure Salvors, 402
Treileben, Hans Albricht, 427
Trice, Allen, 461–62, 464
Trieste, 85, 141–42, 148n, 458
Trieste II, 86, 458
Trincomalee, Ceylon, 300–2
Trinidad, 403–4
Tripoli Harbor, 285–87
Tripolitania, 272, 273, 319–20
Tropero, 180
Trover, 335
Truculent, 132–34
Tubantia, 38–41
Tucker, Teddy, 386–87, 397n
Turtle, 106
Tyre, 411–12

U-44, 110
U-307, 134–35, 137
UC-5, 324–25
UC-16, 319
Ulidia, 323–24
Ulloa, Francisco de, 403
Umeqada Maru, 201
Umpire, 131–32
Undersea Research Group, 373–76, 449
Underwater Demolition Team (UDT), U. S. Navy, 373, 390
Underwater Research Group, French Navy, 374
Underwater Surveys Ltd., 428
Underwriter, 155
Underwriters, 12–15
Union Oil, 352, 354, 355, 357–58
United Salvage, Ltd., 467
United States Navy, 24, 235–36
United States Rubber, 452

University of Pennsylvania Museum, 377, 378
Urania, 321
Utricht, 189, 353, 355

V-70, 213–14
Valiant, 237, 287–88, 301, 456–57
Van den Tak, W. A., 469–70, 471
Vanderbilt, Alfred, 70
Vanderwalker, John, 451
Van Renselaar, 295
Varney, H. W., 301
Vasa, 420–24
Veen, A., 343
Vegetius, Flavius, 6
Velasco, Don Manuel de, 418
Velasco, Luis de, 404
Velox, 340
Ventures, Ltd., 420
Vergulde Draeck, 439–40
Victory, 424
Vidar, 108
Vigo Bay, Spain, 418–20
Ville de Liège, 339
Vindictive, 252–53
Virgilio, Rodríquez, 354
Viribus Unitis, 456
Vittoria, 166
Vladimir, 248, 419
Volunteer, 42
Von der Tann, 227
Von Moltke, 218–22
Vulcan, 168

Waddington, J. F., 106
Wagenfur, Paul, 110
Wagner, Kip, 382, 399–400
Wahine, 467
Waitemata, 59
Wakeful, 76, 77
Walker, Hovenden, 405
Waller, Richard A., 451
Walsh, Don, 148, 458
Walsingham, Francis, 426
Walters, Mr., 134–35
Wandank, 129
Wardwell, Ed, 83
War Knight, 161–62

INDEX 525

Warspite, 195
Washington, 52
Watson, Neal, 450
Weatherwax, Mr., 318
Webster, M. L., 313
Webster, William, 394
Wesley M. Oler, 154–55
Westmoreland, 327–28
Westphal, Captain, 321
West Virginia, 299–300
Wheeler, J. G., 328–29
White, Lieutenant Commander, 277
Whitelaw, T. A., 316
Whitelaw Salvage Company, 316
Whittaker, Christopher, 66–67
Wignall, Sidney, 429–30
Wijsmuller Company, 187–88, 353–55, 469
Wilkins, John, 67
Williams, J. P., 58, 59–60
Willis, Harmon, 389
Willis, Patrick, 125
Willowdale, 291–92
Wilson, Mr., 318
Wilson, Harold, 353
Wilson, Mike, 386, 397n, 440–42

Wilson, Valentine, 90, 92–93
Winchester, James, 153
Winston, Alec, 96, 97
Wishart, 340
Witherspoon, William Wallace, 38
Wolf, 200–1
Women's Volunteer Services, 356
Woodbury, 331
Woods Hole Oceanographic Institute, 86, 458
Wookey, George, 24, 66
Wooley, Leonard, 363
Woollcombe, Edward, 184
World War I, 110–13, 250–53
World War II
  blockships in, 260–90 passim
  salvage and, 235–43
  SCUBA and, 371–73
  submarines in, 135–37
  submersibles in, 456–58
Worthington, Robert, 463
Wrangler, 76
Wright, 120
Wright, Mr., 312–13

Wright, Bruce, 371
Wright, Lord, 17

X-24, 465n
X-Craft, 457–58
XE-3, 458
XXIII Marzo, 262, 270

Yankee, 434
Yassi Ada Island, Turkey, 378
Yellow Submarine, 68, 69
Yoke Peter, 75–78
Yoke Yoke, 77
Young, 331
Young, Mr., 462
Young, Frederick, 111–12, 203–6, 251–53, 324–28, 466
Ys, Brittany, 417–18
Yuna, 187
Yuta, 108, 125

Zeeland, 343
Zeewyk, 439
Zetterström, Arne, 66, 422
Zubian, 338
Zuckerman, Solly, 354
Zulu, 338
Zwart Zee, 167, 181–83